T0328779

People Before Markets

This innovative volume presents twenty comparative case studies of important global questions such as: "Where should our food come from?" "What should we do about climate change?" and "Where should innovation come from?" A variety of solutions are proposed and compared, including market-based, economic, and neoliberal approaches, as well as those determined by humane values and ethical and socially responsible perspectives. Drawing on original research, its chapters show that more responsible solutions are very often both more effective and better aligned with human values. Providing an important counterpoint to the standard capitalist thinking propounded in business-school education, *People Before Markets* reveals the problematic assumptions of incumbent frameworks for solving global problems and inspires the next generation of business and social science students to pursue more effective and human-centered solutions.

DANIEL SOULELES is an Anthropologist and Associate Professor in the Department of Management, Politics, and Philosophy, Copenhagen Business School.

JOHAN GERSEL is an External Lecturer in the Department of Management, Politics, and Philosophy, Copenhagen Business School.

MORTEN SØRENSEN THANING is an Associate Professor in the Department of Management, Politics, and Philosophy, Copenhagen Business School.

People Before Markets

An Alternative Casebook

Edited by

DANIEL SCOTT SOULELES
Copenhagen Business School

JOHAN GERSEL
Copenhagen Business School

MORTEN SØRENSEN THANING
Copenhagen Business School

CAMBRIDGE
UNIVERSITY PRESS

CAMBRIDGE
UNIVERSITY PRESS

University Printing House, Cambridge CB2 8BS, United Kingdom

One Liberty Plaza, 20th Floor, New York, NY 10006, USA

477 Williamstown Road, Port Melbourne, VIC 3207, Australia

314–321, 3rd Floor, Plot 3, Splendor Forum, Jasola District Centre, New Delhi – 110025, India

103 Penang Road, #05–06/07, Visioncrest Commercial, Singapore 238467

Cambridge University Press is part of the University of Cambridge.

It furthers the University's mission by disseminating knowledge in the pursuit of education, learning, and research at the highest international levels of excellence.

www.cambridge.org
Information on this title: www.cambridge.org/9781009165860
DOI: 10.1017/9781009165846

© Cambridge University Press 2022

First published 2022

A catalogue record for this publication is available from the British Library.

ISBN 978-1-009-16586-0 Hardback
ISBN 978-1-009-16585-3 Paperback

We dedicate this book to the fact that another world is possible.

Contents

Contents by Topic

Authors

Matthew Archer is a lecturer in sustainability in the Department of Environment and Geography at the University of York. He has a PhD in forestry and environmental studies from Yale University, as well as postdoctoral research and teaching experience from Copenhagen Business School and the Geneva Graduate Institute.

Douglas Bafford is a cultural anthropologist whose work centers on the spread of conservative religious movements in southern Africa. Drawing on ethnographic fieldwork conducted in Johannesburg from 2017 to 2019, he has written about tensions and debates within evangelical Christian approaches to racism and post-apartheid inequality in South Africa. This research addresses the question of what transformations are happening within ostensibly conservative spaces that complicate understandings of religious and political mobilization around the globe. An extension of this work to be undertaken over the years ahead will consider the transnational dimensions of evangelical thought across southern Africa. His earlier project examined how young-earth creationists and other conservative Christians in the United States mediate competing epistemological and social demands, including the intersection of religious and scientific authority in knowledge production. He received his master's degree in anthropology from Brandeis University in Waltham, MA, USA, where he is currently finishing his doctoral thesis. While not writing or conducting fieldwork, he teaches courses in anthropology and social science at Babson College in Wellesley, MA, USA, and plies the art of long-distance running.

Melissa Beresford is an assistant professor in the Department of Anthropology at San José State University. She received her PhD in anthropology at Arizona State University, her MA in social science from the University of Chicago, and her BA in urban studies and planning from the University of California, San Diego. As an economic anthropologist, Dr. Beresford's research investigates how people respond to economic inequality and resource insecurity. Her work has examined the cultural politics of entrepreneurship and economic development initiatives, informal and diverse urban economies, and urban water insecurity. She is also an anthropological methodologist, focused on researching and innovating methods for qualitative data analysis. She conducts fieldwork in the USA and South Africa, and collaborates on fieldwork based in Latin America and other cross-cultural contexts.

Amy Clotworthy is an assistant professor at the Center for Healthy Aging (CEHA) and the Department of Public Health at the University of Copenhagen (UCPH). With a PhD in ethnology and a master's degree (*cand.mag.*) in applied cultural analysis, both from UCPH, she specializes in studying health systems, public-health policies, medical education and training, and the sociocultural implications of health practices. In particular, her research focuses on studying people's experiences of ageing and health in relation to national and municipal social, health, and eldercare policies, particularly home-based health initiatives. Her work elucidates the relationship between citizens, health professionals, and politicians in everyday life and suggests how governments, the healthcare sector, and municipal authorities can design and implement services and programs that integrate a person-centered, autonomy-compatible approach. Originally from California and Connecticut in the USA, she received a bachelor's degree from George Washington University in Washington, DC, and worked for a lobbying organization for many years before embarking on a career in editing, publishing, and corporate communications. Clotworthy decided to chuck it all to pursue the idealistic life of an academic in Denmark, where she has lived since 2008.

Hannah Elliott is an anthropologist and postdoc at the Copenhagen Business School. She holds a PhD in African studies from the University of Copenhagen and master's and bachelor's degrees in anthropology from the School of Oriental and African Studies (SOAS, University of London) and the University of Manchester. Her research uses ethnographic and historical approaches to examine economic and political transformations on the peripheries of contemporary capitalism. Her latest research has examined the upstream production of certified sustainable Kenyan tea.

Scott Freeman holds a PhD in Anthropology and is a faculty member at the School of International Service at American University in Washington DC. Through a lens of critical political ecology, he has conducted ethnographic fieldwork on aid projects, soil conservation, essential oil production, agricultural labor, and coffee cooperatives in Haiti and the Dominican Republic. He has examined the political economy and imaginary of the vetiver essential oil industry in Haiti, arguing for a critical understanding of the production of ignorance as a facet of extractive global industries. He is also interested in aid projects and the regimes of labor that support aid projects. His work has been featured in *World Development*, the *Journal of Latin American and Caribbean Anthropology*, and he is the co-editor of *Who Owns Haiti: People, Power, and Sovereignty* (University Press of Florida). His book manuscript is an analysis of how aid projects have come to organize and orient aid practice, and the ways that it affects agricultural and environmental aid in particular. He teaches courses on international development, the politics of conservation, and theorizing bureaucracy.

Johan Gersel is a philosopher, educated at Copenhagen University, University College London, and Warwick University. He is currently an external lecturer at Copenhagen Business School. His research centers around normative questions concerning reasons and rationality. He has published several academic articles on how we must conceive of perception, action, and reasoning if truth is to function as an objective guide in human thought and action. He has recently begun applying this research to management questions as well, focusing on questions such as: "How can we ensure that organizational structures facilitate rational decision-making?" and "How do we develop a normatively adequate conception of strategy?" His research takes its central inspiration from the works of Plato, Kant, and Frege, as well as their modern interpreters.

Ina Goel is a doctoral candidate at the Department of Anthropology, The Chinese University of Hong Kong, and the founder of The Hijra

Project, a digital archive to spread awareness about hijras, a third-gender minority community of South Asia. A former INLAKS and DAAD scholar, Ina is a qualified social worker who gained their MPhil in Social Medicine and Community Health from Jawaharlal Nehru University, India. Ina has also worked in various capacities with FHI 360 (a non-profit human development organization), UNICEF, the National AIDS Control Organization in India, the Indian Institute of Mass Communication, and the humanitarian organization Plan International. A list of publications can be found here: https://orcid.org/0000-0003-1991-1675.

Jeppe Groot holds an MSc degree in Philosophy and Business Administration from Copenhagen Business School, Denmark. He has worked with innovation, professional judgment, and value creation in the public sector, in particular with the clinical side of value-based healthcare in collaboration with general practitioners in the primary health sector. From 2015 to 2016 he was the managing editor of *Foucault Studies*. From 2016–2020 he worked with public procurement policy in the Agency for Public Finance and Management in the Danish Ministry of Finance, and is currently working at the Secretariat for the Methodology for Assessing Procurement Systems (MAPS) housed at the OECD.

Hilary B. King is an applied cultural anthropologist and sustainable food systems advocate. She is assistant director of Emory University's Master's in Development Practice (MDP) and Director of Special Projects at Community Farmers Markets (CFM), a farmers market umbrella organization in Atlanta, Georgia, USA. King combines work teaching at Emory with applied work on evaluation and program development at CFM. She teaches courses on international development, anthropology, and food systems. For the past fifteen years she has worked with farmers and food businesses across Latin America, East Africa, and the US, testing out ways for farmers to earn more money and eaters to learn about what they eat and how it got to them. In addition to academic publications, Dr. King's research has helped to identify and build connections leading to innovative new food system initiatives. Examples include the development of weekly fresh produce markets at public transit stations in Atlanta and direct trade relationships between farmers in the Dominican Republic and consumers in the United States. Her work has been supported by a Thomas J. Watson and a Fulbright Fellowship. She is a native Oregonian who makes a darn good latte and handmade tortillas.

Dr Johannes Lenhard is an ethnographer of homelessness and technology venture capital investors. He has since 2011 focused on understanding people sleeping rough and begging in London, Paris and Cambridge. His monograph Making Better Lives was published in 2022. For his second research project, Johannes has since becoming the Centre Coordinator of the Max Planck Cambridge Centre for Ethics, Economy and Social Change in Cambridge in 2017, focused on venture capital investors. Based on intermittent fieldwork between Silicon Valley, New York, London and Berlin, he is currently writing his second monograph explaining VCs' investment ethics. He writes regularly for journalistic outlets such as Sifted, Prospect and Techcrunch and is the co-author of Better Venture, a trade book on diversity and inclusion in tech and VC. Johannes is committed to translating his research findings into direct policy application and has recently co-founded CHIRN (Cambridge Homelessness Impact and Research Network) to facilitate impacting homeless policy and VentureESG to support the integration of Environment, Social and Governance principles in the VC ecosystem. Find him on Twitter or email him directly at jfl37@cam.ac.uk.

Eana Meng is a historian of medicine and a physician in training. She is currently a researcher at the Department of Social Anthropology at Cambridge University, and is a MD-PhD candidate at Harvard Medical School and the Department of History of Science. Her research has traced the lesser-known histories of the use of acupuncture by American activists (including those in the Black revolutionary movement) since the 1970s and the legacies that have emerged from them, which include a five-point ear acupuncture protocol currently used around the world for substance use and behavior health conditions. She is interested in the histories that sit at the intersection of radical politics of health, integrative/alternative healing modalities, community healthcare, the opioid crisis and pain, and crucial dimensions of race, gender, and class. She runs a blog at ofpartandparcel.com. Find her Twitter @Eanam38.

Elisha Oliver is a biocultural anthropologist and visual ethnographer. Her research explores the intersections of space and place, health, and gendered language in rural and urban communities with a focus on women's biopsychosocial health. Currently, she is exploring the following: Graffiti as Political Resistance and Social Justice Activism, Archaeological Memoryscapes of All Black Towns in Northwest Oklahoma, and Infant Mortality in Urban African American Communities. Elisha is an advocate for anthropology as art with the purpose of reaching broad audiences outside academia. Elisha is an adjunct professor at OSUOKC and OCCC. She is a STEM mentor for a national organization and is a founding partner at Paideia Research and Consulting. Elisha earned her PhD in Biocultural Anthropology from the University of Oklahoma. Currently she splits her time between rural Oklahoma and Dallas, Texas.

Lenore Palladino is assistant professor of economics and public policy at the University of Massachusetts, Amherst. She holds a PhD in economics from the New School for Social Research, and a JD from Fordham Law School. Lenore's research centers on corporate power, stakeholder corporations, shareholder primacy, and the relationship between corporate governance and the labor market. She has also written on financial transaction taxes, employee ownership, and the rise of fintech. She has published in the *Yale Journal of Regulation* and *Fordham Journal of Corporate and Financial Law*, as well as the *Financial Times* and *State Tax Notes*. Lenore frequently works with policymakers, media, and advocates on corporate and financial policy.

Jennifer Patico is a sociocultural anthropologist and Chair of Anthropology at Georgia State University. She holds a PhD in sociocultural anthropology from New York University and has conducted ethnographic research in both Russia and the United States. She is the author of *Consumption and Social Change in a Post-Soviet Middle Class* (Stanford University Press and Woodrow Wilson Center Press 2008) and *The Trouble with Snack Time: Children's Food and the Politics of Parenting* (NYU Press 2020). Her work has been published in journals including *Slavic Review, American Ethnologist, Ethnos, Critique of Anthropology,* and *Gastronomica*. Her research interests center around the themes of middle classness, consumption, and conceptions of selfhood and care, with special attention to (implicit or explicit) comparisons of neoliberal capitalist and socialist/postsocialist settings.

Sayd Randle is a S.V. Ciriacy-Wantrup postdoctoral fellow at the University of California Berkeley. Her research focuses on urban climate adaptation and resource conflicts in the US West. She holds a PhD from Yale University's combined degree program in Anthropology and Forestry & Environmental Studies.

Michelle A. Rensel is an assistant adjunct professor in the Institute for Society and Genetics at the University of California, Los Angeles. She received a PhD in Biology from the University of Memphis, where she conducted field and laboratory research on the behavioral endocrinology of cooperatively breeding Florida scrub-jays. As a postdoctoral scholar at the University of California, Los Angeles, she explored estrogen-mediated regulation of spatial memory in songbirds and the molecular basis of stress hormone metabolism in the avian brain. Her more recent research interests include the history of endocrine science, particularly understandings of estrogen as an endogenous hormone *and* as pharmaceutical intervention, as well as the ways in which the science of hormones is used to reinforce or disrupt sex and gender stereotypes. While dedicated to these research aims, her primary interest and passion is for teaching undergraduates about the intersections between science and society.

Andrea Rissing is a cultural anthropologist whose scholarship seeks to understand the social, political, and economic contexts in which agroecological livelihoods can thrive. Her research and teaching interests include sustainable food systems, alternative economies, critical agrarian studies, and political ecology. She is currently a President's Postdoctoral Scholar in the School of Environment and Natural Resources (SENR) at The Ohio State University. Rissing has also worked on dozens of vegetable and livestock farms in Iowa and New Zealand and as a farm-to-school local food coordinator at the University of Northern Iowa.

Michael Scroggins is a postdoctoral researcher at the Center for Knowledge Infrastructures at the University of California, Los Angeles. He holds a PhD in Anthropology and Education from Teachers College, Columbia University. His scholarly interests include: labor, public education and the education of the public, governance, and the productive side of ignorance and failure. At the Center for Knowledge Infrastructures he works on issues of the maintenance and repair of digital infrastructure, invisible labor in data-intensive science, and the political economy of science. Currently, he is conducting fieldwork with astronomers, investigating the role data quality (as opposed to data quantity) plays in establishing, forming, and continuing long-term scientific collaborations. His next project will interrogate how Agtech and data-intensive farm management are refiguring agricultural labor, taking the evolution of the farm tractor as physical, and now, digital infrastructure as the point of departure.

Amanda Shapiro is a PhD candidate at the University of Copenhagen Faculty of Law. Her research focuses on the implications of emerging technologies in health for the rights of women and marginalized communities. Before beginning her doctorate, she earned her JD from Brooklyn Law School. As an attorney, she clerked for a judge and worked in the general counsel's office of a large labor union. She has specialized in civil rights, reproductive rights, the rights of women, the rights of working people, and the rights of people in poverty. Before becoming an attorney, she was a public school teacher in New York City.

Daniel Souleles is an Anthropologist and Associate Professor at the Copenhagen Business School. He holds a PhD in Applied Anthropology from Columbia University. He has performed field research on Catholic hermit monks, private equity investors, employee-owned companies, and computerized stock trading. He writes academic articles on finance, wealth, inequality, and research methods. He has also written a book, *Songs of Profit, Songs of Loss: Private Equity, Wealth, and Inequality* (Nebraska 2019). Sometimes, Daniel plays the banjo.

Morten Sørensen Thaning is a philosopher. He holds a PhD from Aarhus university and a dual Masters in Philosophy and Classical Greek from Roskilde and Copenhagen University. He is currently associate professor of philosophy at the Copenhagen Business School. Sørensen Thaning builds upon the work of neo-Hegelian, contemporary philosophers, the tradition of phenomenology and hermeneutics, as well as upon ancient philosophy in order to understand the connection between freedom, rationality, and human existence. Thaning's current research within organization studies uses concepts and arguments from these philosophical traditions to clarify the nature of decision-making, learning, work, and power.

Aneil Tripathy is an economic anthropologist and climate finance practitioner. His research examines the worldview of climate finance practitioners and the projects they assess and finance. He has published in *Economic Anthropology, Anthropology News*, and the *Journal of Environmental Investing*. He is currently a postdoctoral researcher at the University of Bologna on the ERC consolidator grant no. 772544 funded Impact Hau project. He has been a visiting researcher at Bayes Business School and Lancaster University, as well as an associate of the Centre for the Anthropology of Sustainability at University College London.

Rachel A. Vaughn is lecturer in the UCLA Cluster Program, and formerly served as the 2018–2019 Oral Historian in Residence at the UCLA Center for the Study of Women. Vaughn's research engages the intersections of food politics, discard studies, and feminist science & technology studies. She is the author of multiple articles about food, waste, and sanitation politics; and is co-editor of *Edible Feminisms: On Discard, Waste & Metabolism (Food, Culture & Society)*. Her monographs on the politics of food and waste are both under contract with the University of Nebraska Press and the Ohio State University.

David Wood is an adjunct lecturer in public policy and the director of the Initiative for Responsible Investment (IRI) at the Hauser Center for Nonprofit Organizations. Current projects range from work with pension fund trustees on responsible investment policies, mission investment by foundation endowments, research on the changing nature of the supply for and capacity to receive capital for community investment in the US, and a global survey of the relationship between public policy and impact investment. Recent work has included publication of the *Handbook on Responsible Investment Across Asset Classes* (Boston College 2007); the development of a Responsible Property Investing Center; field definition in sustainable emerging market SME investment; and research into the investor use of corporate reporting on non-financial information. He was elected in 2008 to the Board of the Social Investment Forum. Before he came to the IRI, he taught the history of ethics, including the history of economic thought at Boston University. He received his PhDin History from the Johns Hopkins University.

1 | *Introduction: Why Are You Here?*

DANIEL SOULELES AND JOHAN GERSEL

This chapter introduces the reader to the volume. It presents our conviction that there is a bias toward pro-market, pro-capitalist (which we call "neoliberal") solutions in how people solve problems nowadays, and how people learn to solve problems in universities. We explain what these default neoliberal biases are, and why they are often harmful. We also explain how the case chapters in this book comparatively lay out a series of alternatives to these neoliberal ways of solving problems.

If you are reading this, then you probably came to school to make the world a bit better and are interested in solving problems. As professors we've noticed that in fact the reason a lot of people get an education is so that they can get a job that will then let them help people and solve problems out in the world somewhere. While we think this desire to be practical and effective and helpful out there in the great world beyond is admirable, there are some serious issues with how practical education currently works in the university. As it is, many of the tools and ideas that people learn in their education start with the assumptions that people should be taken as individuals and are often greedy. Because of this greedy individualism, the best sort of society we can (and should) hope for is one that approximates a market in which people are individually free to buy and sell things, as well as themselves, as much as they are able. We feel, as do many of the people we work with, that this market-forward approach to life often hurts far more people than it helps. This book is meant to illustrate why this is and provide you with some alternatives ways to change the world.

We're going to take our shared interest in problem-solving as a starting point. You should be aware, though, that we aren't going to engage with every type of problem-solving. We won't talk about chemical titrations, or stress-testing a railroad bridge. Rather we will focus on what we call "social," or "human problems," or maybe, more precisely, problems that emerge from how people choose to govern themselves and arrange their lives. The interesting thing about these social problems is that they inherently require some form of coordination of human effort. Sometimes coordination happens in mundane interactions and in everyday life such as when we have to find parking, think about workplace management, or find jobs for people who are unemployed. Other times, social problems take on a grander scale as when a whole city faces a water shortage or when a needed innovation requires the pooling of knowledge and capital beyond the scope of any single individual. What all this suggests to us, is that to solve a social problem, we need ways to influence, motivate, or coordinate the efforts of many people.

Given all that, this book has two goals: First, we want to challenge the prevalent idea that whenever you face a social problem, the best way to solve it is always by assuming that people are exclusively selfish and can only be motivated through promises of some form of satisfaction of their self-interest in a market setting. This view of humans is one that is prevalent in many economics, psychology, law, and management classes. What we've found is that when people solve problems this way, they end up creating markets and consumers and reducing the role of government or solidarity in organizing people's lives. Over the course of this book, we will call the ideas that influence this approach to problem-solving "neoliberalism." We will also point out the ways that embracing these neoliberal ideas about humans and their lives blinds many people, companies, governments, and NGOs to other, less individual, and less selfish ways to think about life.

The term "neoliberalism" has seen wide usage, particularly among academics; and some even deem it too amorphous to be of any analytic use. We disagree, though we are not dogmatic on this point. To us, "neoliberal" seems to be a useful way to describe the sort of pro-individual, pro-market, anti-government beliefs that animate a lot of bad problem-solving that we see out in the world. The next chapter of this book will more precisely define the way we use the term "neoliberalism", as well as explain the historical background and reasoning which has led to the acceptance of neoliberalism in contemporary problem-solving. For now, though, it might be helpful for us to use an example of prison labor and clothing production to illustrate the sort of thing that keeps us up at night – the neoliberalism-in-the-wild that haunts us.

Carcel is (or perhaps was, by the time you read this) a Denmark-based fashion company that was started in 2016 by a pair of Copenhagen Business School graduates. Their business model is simple: they employ women's prison labor in Peru and Thailand to cheaply make fashionable clothing which they then sell at a significant mark-up in Europe and North America. According to their own website, they are doing good by paying prisoners to make clothes, and claiming to teach them skills in the context of a meaningful job so that upon release the women might be able to better themselves. Their website notes that the main cause of incarceration for women in these countries is "drug-trafficking committed by single mothers who need to provide for their families." Setting aside whether or not prisoners can even consent to labor, what's remarkable here is that these entrepreneurs notice women who are unjustly incarcerated and the best they can come up with to fix the situation is to exploit their cheap labor via a fashion start-up. There is no political advocacy. There is no advocacy for their families. There is no imagining how to keep women from going to prison in the first place. The state is never addressed, much less considered. Abolition is certainly off the table. These women who had no other options when trying to feed their families remain in prison, only now they get to sew clothes for rich Europeans while passing their time.

This approach to problem-solving that Carcel embodies is emblematic of the idea that social change should occur through industrious entrepreneurship and the individual discipline of the wage-earning employee. For Carcel's founders, prison and incarceration are simply natural facts. By becoming disciplined employees and earning a wage we can imagine that the incarcerated women are choosing to rationally better themselves. Plus, Carcel can then brand a product with this fable. All told, this typifies much of the worst of neoliberal approaches to problem-solving that this book intends to challenge.

The second and more positive aim of this book is to inspire you, the reader, to look beyond neoliberal solutions to the problems that face us. Maybe you are already critical of neoliberal solutions; maybe you wish for something different but doubt that better ways of solving our problems are available. We know, too, that many of our academic colleagues have worked on "neoliberal problems" in their own research for many years now and are often a bit burned out. They are at something of a loss as to what it would take to fix the problems they study; problems which neoliberalism seems to repetitively create. In any case, we hope to inspire our readers by presenting a series of actual cases where problems have been solved by methods going beyond the neoliberal conception of human interaction. By introducing a series of alternative approaches to social problems, approaches that put people before markets, we hope to display the many other ways we can make human life better. To this end, we will present a series of normal human problems such as "Where should our water come from?", "What should a job look like?", or "How should we treat people who do drugs?" For each question, we will present two different approaches to solving the problem: a neoliberal approach and an alternative one that puts people before markets.

What will emerge across our cases is the simple point that the neoliberal approach to problem-solving is *never* the only way to rearrange the human condition, and, more often than not, it seems to make things worse. By reading the individual cases of this book, we hope readers might see similarities to the social problems that they themselves are trying to solve which could lead them to invent novel solutions. Or maybe the great variety of these cases can simply inspire the reader to look beyond the typical conception of the problems facing our society, such that novel ways to practically organize people become newly imaginable.

Throughout the book, we aim for the two contrasting cases to be as empirically similar as possible, but of course some differences will be present as we are dealing with real-life examples. That said, our goal isn't to prove that one solution fits all problems. Rather, we only wish to argue, based on empirical evidence, that before we decide how to approach a social problem, we should critically evaluate options beyond those that treat people solely as egotistical consumers who demand to be kept away from the government. And that point gets proven simply by the success of the alternative approach in its own right. The contrasted neoliberal solution is there to imply that not only did the alternative approach work; it also surpassed what could be expected from a neoliberal solution in the first place. Instead, what really deserves consideration is whether the neoliberal problem-solvers involved in the failed attempt ever seriously evaluated, let alone searched for, a nonmarket-based solution to their problems. If they didn't, then we feel they were unjustifiably narrow in their approach to problem-solving. Such a blinkered approach to governing people clearly impedes our ability to solve the problems we face, but just as importantly it also distorts and demeans our self-conception of who we are as human beings.

Let us return to the case of the incarcerated women who were trying to feed their families. If we choose not to view every human tragedy as a potential for installing a marketlike service, then other solutions seem much more appealing than exploiting prison labor. One could attempt to improve their conditions by lobbying or putting political pressure on the respective governments to increase child support and free the women in question. One could set up a charity to support Peruvian and Thai families on the assumption that if the rich European clothes shoppers hear about the plight of these women, then they might provide assistance without expecting the quid pro quo of a piece of clothing in return. One could even imagine an asylum regime in Europe or the United States in which legal-immigration status would be granted to mothers and their families facing incarceration in their own country for trying to feed themselves. The real travesty of the proliferation of the neoliberal way of thinking is not only that better solutions to our problems might be overlooked, but that we have come to believe that it is both acceptable and even commendable to buy clothes made by prison labor, and that we have come to assume that no one can be convinced to assist other people in need unless they get something in return.

The above alternatives of relying on charity or government intervention are just some of the alternative approaches one might consider, and not even very creative ones at that. With an open mind and a bit of ingenuity you, our readers, can probably come up with even better nonmarket-based ideas – ideas that directly help the people we're worried about. The important point is that, once the neoliberal blinders are off, there is no end to creative avenues from which we can approach problem-solving. No single assumption about how to coordinate human action and motivation unites the alternative solutions we investigate. What we find inspiring in the variety of alternative approaches in the following chapters is precisely the empirical insight that there are many other ways of organizing, of getting people to coordinate and collaborate, than simply by promising individual rewards for compliance. We can be altruistic, show solidarity, and be motivated by obligation, respect, duty, or even love. And sometimes we don't even act as individuals at all. Some of our best behavior is much better understood and influenced through the shared identities we get from belonging to families, cultures, or religions, from going to schools, working at specific places, or even cheering for certain football teams. This book aims to show that there is no reason to assume that we all suddenly become atomized, selfish individuals whenever there is a need to solve some problem or come up with government policy. And not only does that insight make one a better problem solver; it also serves to dignify who we are as humans.

Though we think this book may be helpful to all social problem-solvers, we know that our main audience will be university students, as well as universities themselves and the professors that teach there. As we noted above, many young people who enter universities around the globe are drawn by the promise that a university degree will enable them to become better social problem-solvers. In turn, their time at university or in college might let them become activists, managers, politicians, entrepreneurs, social workers, executives, teachers, government workers, lawyers, doctors, and many, many more vital social roles and jobs. Common to these sorts of aspirations is that the people who do them need to know how to motivate and coordinate people around them, such that they can solve a concrete practical problem. The explicit promise of contemporary universities is that they will teach students how to think about and solve such social problems. This is most explicit in the promises of business universities and professional degree programs when they claim to teach students how to best manage people. In such explicitly practical education, it's not terribly difficult to identify the influence of neoliberal thinking. Yet, we suggest that similar sorts of limitations are also present in more academic courses of studies, such as when political science, anthropology, or sociology claim to teach about how government, cultures, and societies function. It is, for example, within such more traditionally academic departments that we often find the institutes or research groups focused on solving social problems related to immigration, unemployment, racial injustice, or city development. However, even in these more traditionally academic contexts, we feel there are problems with the practical education that students receive.

Our diagnosis is that one substantial reason for these widespread limitations in imagining a world beyond neoliberalism is the fact that even in a critical context, neoliberalism can suck all the air out of a room and make it difficult to imagine other worlds. Many more traditional academic programs and institutions take great, deserved pride in critiquing neoliberalism and exposing its problems. Many of the contributors to this book teach in precisely such places. However, such a wholesale criticism of neoliberalism has left many academics and researchers exhausted. This sort of burnout can leave one feeling paralyzed in the sense that one doesn't know how to actually translate one's skepticism and critical work on neoliberalism into practical action. Often in the best case, the academic approach to diagnosing and describing a situation can practically preclude imagining an alternative world – doubly so if the world under description is exhausting, repetitive, and painful to describe, as neoliberal politics often are. What we suggest is lacking on the contemporary scene, is an education in how one practically develops and implements a nonneoliberal solution to a problem. A solution that, if you are living in a Western democracy, probably needs to be nested and justified within a society that largely operates on neoliberal principles. Put another way, you think you're getting educated in solving social problems, but, by using the tools you are taught to employ, you end up either paralyzed or causing more harm than good. In this way, we see this book both building on a rich tradition of critical scholarship on how the world currently works as well as providing the next step in making good on all this criticism – that is, imagining a better world.

Naturally, universities aren't the sole cultivators of this market-first approach to contemporary society's conception of social problem-solving. However, we still want to focus our attention on how problem-solving is taught at universities for two reasons. First, we do not think that the neoliberal conception of human motivation is *natural*, nor should it be seen as such. That is, the idea that the *best* way of coordinating people's efforts should *always* be to speak solely to their self-interest is so outlandish that no one would accept it on their own. People must be taught to see the world this way and feel that this kind of assumption is natural. We want to intervene where this teaching happens.

The second reason for writing this book with universities in mind is that, often in today's society, it is practically a requirement that one has a university degree if one wishes to tackle social problems on a large scale. This means that, on average, the detrimental effects of market-first problem-solving skills are much greater among those with university degrees. The negative effects of their myopic conception of social problem-solving hurts not only themselves but the entire society around them. Hence, universities, their professors, and their students have a much greater responsibility to ensure that their education does in fact make people better at solving social problems, rather than the opposite. We take our cases to provide empirical proof that if you solely teach students to conceive of humans as economic creatures, pursuers of self-interest, and insatiable maximizers of stable personal preferences, then you have failed in the task of educating skilled solvers of social problems. You've made bad citizens and bad humans. Likewise, if you solely teach students the evils of markets, but do not assist them in how to conceive of and practically organize the world differently, you may have saved them from committing the mistakes of neoliberals, but at the expense of paralyzing them. It may at times be the most effective solution to coordinate people by speaking solely to their self-interest, but it is assuredly not always the case, and the contrast cases you are about to read show examples of how one can actually and successfully approach problem-solving differently. Hence, universities should take care to ensure that students are taught to critically evaluate, in each specific instance, whether this is one of those cases where market forces provide the best approach to social coordination, or whether they are indeed faced with a problem that is better solved by coordinating people through other means than self-interest.

While this book challenges the adequacy of contemporary university education, especially at business and other professional schools, we also hope to assist in remedying the problem. For while we think education may be part of the problem, we also think that it is a cornerstone of the solution. We hope that this book can be used not only as a challenge to existing curricula, but also as an inspiration for alternative forms of teaching. One can then either use this book as a whole as a starting point for teaching alternative forms of problem-solving or, alternatively, focus on content areas or even a single case and delve into the suggested literature on that issue. Alternatively, if you are a student or staff intent on challenging the current teaching at your university, then this book can be read as an argument to which the defenders of the status quo must respond. You can use our argument and the chapters presented here to make your case for change in your education.

The relative success of all the alternative solutions we present here demonstrates that better ways to solve our social problems both exist, and can be found by those equipped with an open mind and a broad array of practical problem-solving skills. In light of the cases presented here, in order to justify the status quo market-first neoliberal curriculum, someone must explain away the apparent success of the alternative approaches we present. This could either be done on theoretical grounds or by questioning the soundness of the empirical argumentation itself. If the defense of status quo is theoretical, our bet is that the arguments in defense of neoliberalism will be some version of the traditional fallacious arguments discussed and dissected in detail in the next chapter of this book. If, on the other hand, the defense of neoliberalism is empirical, then the task of the critic of this book is to come to terms with why, in each contrast case that we present, the alternative solution worked as well as it did.

It seems to us, taking in the sweep of all the chapters in this book, that there is indeed empirical proof that we should solve our social problems by treating the people wrapped up in them as whole humans. We can solve social problems in many ways, many more human ways, and this ought to be reflected in the curriculum of a university education which promises to teach problem-solving. Just as importantly it ought to be reflected in the impulses and assumptions of the organizers, politicians, and leaders of our societies.

We hope the coming chapters will show the possibilities for a better world that we all could build.

2 | Some Philosophical Help with "Neoliberalism"

JOHAN GERSEL AND MORTEN SØRENSEN
THANING

This chapter is unusually long and might be best thought of as being made of three subchapters, all of which help explain the ideas that animate this book. In considering how you might use this chapter, it might be worth thinking about how the sections of this chapter answer different sorts of questions, and they may be of greater or lesser use depending on what you're hoping to get out of the cases. The first section of this chapter ("What Is Neoliberalism") explains what the authors and editors mean by "neoliberalism" and develops the specific idea of "market imperialism" to explain what exasperates the authors and editors. The second section ("The Problematic Theoretical Underpinning of Market Imperialism") presents and critiques the arguments that undergird advocates of market imperialism. The final section ("Conclusion: Network of Thinkers and Art of Government") explains how neoliberalism and market imperialism can operate even though individual people may not explicitly see themselves as advocates of neoliberalism and market imperialism. This last section also summarizes some common attributes of market imperialism and neoliberal thinking.

You may have noticed that in our Introduction we used the word "neoliberalism" to describe a particular way that people and governments think about problem-solving as well as a particular kind of capitalist economy that seems to come along with that thinking and that problem-solving. Our hope in using this term is to draw attention to a kind of thinking that we take to be central to the motivation and justification for the type of market-based problem-solving that we aim to criticize. Once again, we don't claim that market-based solutions are *always wrong*. We merely claim that they aren't *always right* and, moreover, that they shouldn't even be assumed to be the default optimal solution for a given problem. Rather, we suggest that when facing a specific problem, fair consideration should be given to whether neoliberal or nonmarket approaches to problem-solving should be employed. In actuality, as our Introduction suggested, this sort of consideration is often not even reached, because no one even dreams of exploring solutions that fall outside the perspective of markets, individualism, or capitalism.

Given its centrality in our sense of how the world currently works, the goal of this chapter is to clearly define what we mean by neoliberalism. We do this for two reasons. First, it will be easier for the reader to identify what common line of thinking lies behind all the neoliberal solutions that are challenged in the following chapters and cases. Second, we can better present the arguments that have traditionally been employed in the favor of neoliberalism and explain why, for each argument, their persuasiveness evaporates upon closer scrutiny. Neoliberalism is, as a default approach to problem-solving, completely unjustified – or so we will argue. This chapter provides theoretical arguments, perhaps even philosophical ones, as to why we ought to look beyond neoliberalism when we solve problems. This philosophical approach, then, provides an intellectual grounding for the following chapters, which use empirical cases to provide proof that we can imagine nonmarket, non-individual ways to solves problems.

2.1 What Is Neoliberalism?

2.1.1 Our Point of Departure: Two Innocuous Ideas

Centering our volume on the term *neoliberalism* is certainly a controversial choice. Indeed, the term is notoriously amorphous and contested by scholars. For more than a generation, neoliberalism has been explored as much more than a synonym for the economic deregulation and free-market ideology propounded by Margaret Thatcher and Ronald Reagan in the 1980s. Moreover, neoliberalism seems to have few if any self-acknowledged proponents. Therefore, a critical discussion risks targeting a straw man rather than a real position. However, as in the case of other messy, contested global concepts such as Christianity, Islam, socialism, or fascism, neoliberalism is a crucial topic of discussion because it refers to what many thinkers agree, and many people feel, is an influential phenomenon (Brown, 2019: 17; see Slobodian and Plewhe, 2020: 3–5). Furthermore, even if hardly anyone explicitly defends neoliberalism today, and even if it has in some contexts become little more than an intellectual swear word (see Williamson, 2004; Plewhe, 2009: 8), this only challenges us to clarify its distinguishing features, as the influence of neoliberalism has become hidden rather than removed. In fact, the peculiar, "invisible" character of the influence of neoliberalism in contemporary society might itself be one of its most significant accomplishments.

Importantly, we won't provide a historical account of how the neoliberal way of thinking acquired the widespread, if invisible, influence it now has in contemporary society. There is no single global historical trajectory. Rather, the paths that have led to neoliberalism's influence differ from country to country: from actual coups and constitutions partly written by economics professors from the University of Chicago, to well-intentioned socialist governments unwittingly taking the importance of fiscal responsibility to imply the need for neoliberal governance. The present chapter describes a way of thinking, the neoliberal way of thinking, as well as the most prominent arguments that have been used for its justification. Whenever one wishes to challenge a particular neoliberal attempt at problem-solving and the type of thinking used in justifying it, the hope is that the present chapter will provide a terminology that will both assist in clarifying the underlying neoliberal assumptions and show why those assumptions are, in most cases, unjustified.

To get a precise sense of neoliberalism, then, we'll begin our discussion from two well-known ideas that most of us accept:

1. The value of individual liberty; and
2. The fact of the efficiency of a free marketplace – a place where people can engage in voluntary transactions and where the relationship between supply and demand is allowed to determine prices.

We take these ideas to be innocuous and widely accepted, at least among readers coming from a liberal democracy. Let's now take a closer look at these ideas, as neoliberalism really is just a particular combination of market and liberty thinking.

First, we have the core thought of liberalism. This is the idea that there is a fundamental value in the freedom of individuals to choose their own trajectory through life; they are "liberated." This means that justification is needed whenever we want to introduce a societal structure that limits individual freedom (Mill, 1963, vol. 21: 262; Gaus, 1996: 162–166; Rawls, 2001: 44, 112). Or, when structures that limit freedom are retained, justification for this must be given. Typically, liberalists will defend some degree of restriction upon the freedom of individuals. They will claim that it is acceptable to restrict a single individual's pursuit of his own goals whenever such behavior conflicts with the possibility fellow citizens have for being similarly free. For example, I am not free to push you around, no matter how much I may want to, as this interferes with your freedom to not be shoved. Precisely where those lines are to be drawn is one of the fundamental political tensions in "liberal" democracies – how much should we restrain people – and according to which freedoms or values? When might shoving in self-defense be allowed?

Along with this valuation of individual freedom goes the assumption that such freedom is only possible when people have the resources required to pursue meaningful choices. To some, this means that the right to possess private property is an inherent part of what it is to be free (Locke, 1960: chapter V). To other people freedom doesn't consist in the right to privately own stuff, but that right is deemed a necessary means for sustaining the more substantial liberties that are sought after, such as the freedom to pursue one's own interests without substantial interference (Hayek, 1960: 17–18). Notably, these values are compatible with forms of socialist liberalism (social democracy), where the state provides substantial social services through high taxation and/or ownership and control of significant portions of the economy such as healthcare or energy production. They are also, however, consistent with important strands of conservatism, notably the emphasis on social cohesion, as well as with libertarian conceptions of a minimal state that should only provide the most basic services such as policing, courts of law, and an army against external challengers. It's because so many political perspectives embrace some form of liberal rights and constraint of government that we regard this *minimal liberalism* as relatively uncontroversial.

The other idea that most of us take for granted is that free markets can be effective for two important purposes: they can be a useful means of assigning capital to the production of goods, and they can be a helpful way to determine what goods should cost. We've gotten to a place in our societies where most of us specialize in our work. Despite the fact that we eat food, wear clothes, use computers, and so on, it would be really odd to find someone who grows all their own food, makes all their own clothing, and manufactures and programs their own computer. Once we allow for this kind of specialization in production, then everyone needs to acquire a variety of goods, from food and clothes to phones and computers, from other people in order to live their lives, Many also need to supply their surplus of produced goods of a particular type to others. The idea of the efficiency of the free market is that when we need to determine how many of us should produce, say, shoes, as well as settle how much each shoe should cost, then a good way of determining this such that society produces the goods that are needed for human flourishing is to allow free market forces to reign. Forces external to the willingness to engage in trade by exclusively self-interested buyers and sellers, typically the government, thus shouldn't determine the size of shoe production, nor should they determine the price of each shoe.

As a recap, here are the two innocuous ideas we've been talking about from the liberal tradition:

1. Justification is needed whenever we want to introduce or retain a societal structure that limits individual freedom (*minimal liberalism*).
2. The willingness of self-interested producers and consumers to engage in exchange can in some contexts be the most effective means of assigning capital to the production of goods and for determining what goods should cost (*limited marketization*).

2.1.2 Market Imperialism

Starting from these seemingly basic and innocuous claims in the liberal philosophical tradition, neoliberal thinking makes a quite significant leap. A central, unique, and highly contentious claim of neoliberalist thought is that in order to best conserve and develop a liberal (a "free") society, we should aim to align every social practice such that it becomes an actual or virtual free marketplace where goods or services are freely bought and sold by individuals. Everything should be organized as a market and the primary responsibility of the state or the government is to ensure these markets function efficiently while not interfering directly in their mechanisms. This liberal justification of expanding marketization is evident in the work of central neoliberal thinkers such as Milton Friedman (1962), Gary Becker (1978; 1996), and Friedrich Hayek (1988).

We dub this universal pretension, whether it is implicitly or explicitly at stake, *market imperialism*. By imperialism we mean the hostile invasion, seizure, and occupation of other's people's space by foreign invaders. The term *economic imperialism* has been used to describe the aspirations of neoliberal economic theory to become *the* unifying theory of the social sciences (Gray, 1987: 33; Radnitzky and Bernholz, 1987). Analogously, we employ the notion of market imperialism to describe neoliberalism's universal pretention as a problem-solving approach. Market imperialism is the idea that whenever we face a societal challenge, say treating the sick, educating the next generation, or combating poverty, we should approach that challenge by creating a form of marketplace structure and then allow the forces of a free market to govern the interactions of those involved. The uninhibited willingness of self-interested individuals to engage in trade was seen by traditional market thinkers (Smith, 1976: chapter VII) as a good norm for how one should solve the challenge of determining price and production in a limited set of contexts. This approach is also seen, much more expansively, by the neoliberalist as the best way to solve *every* type of social problem that a society may face.

We might summarize the market imperialism of neoliberal thinking as follows:

- We should respond to every social problem by organizing an actual or virtual free marketplace where goods or services are exchanged between self-interested individuals (*market imperialism*).

Our interpretation of neoliberalism focuses on the problematic idea of market imperialism[1]. In Section 2 we criticize the attempts to provide principled arguments to defend market imperialism found in the works of Hayek, Friedman, and Becker. In this first section, however,

---

[1] There are strands of neoliberal thought that do not support the idea of market imperialism, or that even argue in defence of the status quo of nonmarket spheres. The work by Wilhelm Röpke or Alexander Rüstow within the so-called ordoliberal school of neoliberalism might figure as an example in this regard. However, even the market-limiting arguments of the work of Röpke or Rüstow stand side by side with an emphasis on "liberal interventionism" which is meant to "facilitate structural adjustments" in order to secure "the competitive order." In other words, the ordoliberal defense of nonmarket spheres seems ambiguous and half-hearted, to say the least, especially when assessed in retrospective, where one can discern its history of effect; for example in the Scandinavian competition states. Thanks to Thomas Biebricher for bringing this point to our attention.

we concentrate on describing the neoliberal conceptions of the state, civil society, international governance, inequality, and citizenship in which market imperialism is embedded. Note that by making neoliberal market imperialism the core target of our book, our theoretical contribution is therefore actually quite small; all we claim is that market structures are not *always* the best solution to a social problem. However, this small point can be of real political and social importance. It means that whenever we face a social problem, decision-makers cannot immediately assume that we should adopt a market approach and then place the burden of proof squarely on those who champion a different way of thinking about and solving the problem. Those who champion the solving of a problem by relying on market-like structures do not begin from a superior position. The burden of proof is equally on them to provide us with good reasons to think that in this empirical case we should create some sort of market. However, as the empirical cases you are about to read in the following chapters will show, such good reasons are in many cases impossible to find, and the decision-makers often did not even bother to try to find any such reasons before opting for market solutions. In light of these diverse cases, and in light of the more general consequences of forty years of market imperialism, we hope that our small theoretical point can be leveraged to have a large and desperately needed impact on the way we teach and practice societal problem-solving in the future.

Again, our critical focus is on *market imperialism* as opposed to the two basic, innocuous ideas from the liberal tradition, *minimal liberalism* and *limited marketization*. We merely want to empirically disprove the idea that it is *always* the best approach to problem-solving to introduce market structures and rely on the forces of the free market. We simply seek to debunk the myopic dogmatism that, no matter what type of societal challenge you face, marketization is the proper response.

The limited focus of our critique has other significant consequences. First, our focus is compatible with the suggestion that the neoliberal tradition may contain genuine theoretical insights, apart from its problematic market imperialism. For example, neoliberal theory is often distinguished from classical liberal economic theory by emphasizing its rejection of a laissez-faire approach to markets. Neoliberalism actually wants a state and government, but only one whose main function is to maintain markets. Put another way, what distinguishes neoliberalism is "the problem of how to identify the factors indispensable to the maintenance of functioning markets, since the option of simply leaving them to themselves is no longer on the table" (Biebriecher, 2018: 26; see also Slobodaian, 2018). This definition emphasizes the interventionist, actively political nature of neoliberalism, and it gives lie to the prejudice that neoliberals necessarily aim to shrink the state. Our limited critical ambition is also an analytically useful starting point; in that it allows for the wide variety of conceptions of what kind of institutions best ensure the functioning of markets that we find in the neoliberal theoretical tradition (Biebriecher, 2018: 26). Hence, our precise rejection of market imperialism allows problem-solvers to take seriously the neoliberal theoretical tradition's insight about the proper maintenance of markets. In other words, our critique does not extend to the neoliberal idea that markets are constructed rather than a "natural" self-sustaining phenomena. When the application of the market form is a recommendable response to a societal problem, the contributions from neoliberal theories concerning how a competitive market should be institutionally maintained by the national state or by international regulation are relevant to consider. We might recapitulate this useful insight from the neoliberal tradition as follows:

- Markets are not inherently self-sustaining phenomena, but must be actively developed and maintained by government (*market constructivism*).

Second, our sole focus on rejecting market imperialism also leaves important theoretical debates about neoliberalism aside. Most fundamentally, we do not provide theoretical assistance for determining when marketization is justified, and when it is problematic. This task is obviously crucial, but our aim is to help effect a preliminary step; namely, to snap us all out of the tunnel vision of market imperialism and to begin to reassess problems and possible solutions in all their complexity. How we should be guided in this more open-minded reassessment leads into an extensive theoretical discussion about the *legitimate domain of marketization* that goes far beyond the scope of our book. This more expansive question might be spelled out as follows:

- When is it justified to respond to a societal problem by installing, maintaining or advancing markets (*legitimate domain of marketization*)?

2.1.3 The Neoliberal Conception of the State

As we emphasized in the Introduction, we think that this open-minded approach to problem-solving is both urgent and long overdue. The devastating consequences of more than a generation of dominance by market imperialism is becoming ever more obvious. The attempt to subject all spheres of society to market solutions has accelerated to a point where we need to be actively reminded that traditionally, many forms of social interaction were neither understood as, nor structured by, markets. The Hippocratic oath, the oath that doctors have taken at the start of their career since antiquity, commits medical professionals to assist those in need, regardless of wealth. This means that doctors have long conceived of a realm of obligation and human interaction that is not modelled on the paid exchange of services between solely self-interested producers and consumers. Likewise, education, marriage, poverty alleviation, friendship, employee motivation, punishment, burial, the election of leaders, and many other things that make up the normal fabric of our lives, have typically been very distinct in their conception and operation from that of the marketplace, with its individual selfish actors and its focus on profit. The neoliberals have argued that the job of the government is to marketize these aspects of societal life. Even practices initially foreign to market forces should be molded to become a market for competition among free self-interested consumers and producers.

According to neoliberals, in furthering the cause of the marketization of new societal domains the state plays a decisive role. In fact, according to one account, the prefix "neo" was added by some of the founders of neoliberalism to signal the need for reconceiving the state and its role "differently, and more clearly" than had been the case with liberalism (Willgerodt, 2006: 54–55; see Slobodaian, 2018: 6). Their attempt to redefine the role of the state rather than to do away with it puts neoliberalists at odds with libertarians (Mirowski, 2009: 436). Libertarians argue that the state, understood as the societal institutions that are government-owned and funded by taxes, should be reduced to the military, police, and courts whose job is to protect the citizens from theft, breach of contract, and fraud (Nozick, 1974). In this tradition the state is conceived in a minimal way as a "night watchman." The neoliberal state, however, must be able to do more than this; its purpose is to govern decisively and to regulate in detail to allow for market competition and, thereby, produce and guarantee a stable market society with comprehensive marketization (Olsen, 2019: 7). Since the state is conceived as responsible for creating, maintaining, and nurturing the so-called *competitive order*, the neoliberal state can be understood as a *competition state* (Cerny, 1997) rather than merely a minimal, night-watchman state. Indeed, the common theoretical point of departure for most neoliberals is that the state has "positive functions to perform, and they are neither confined to guaranteeing private contracts, or, more generally, enforcing the law" (Biebricher, 2018: 34).

When advocating interventionist politics, neoliberals typically do so in order to further strengthen and sustain the popular acceptance of the competition state. A paradigmatic example is the so-called interventions for adjustment proposed by Wilhelm Röpke and Alexander Rüstow. Röpke and Rüstow advocate interventions by the state if they acceptably combine security with flexibility. Interventions should on this view be designed to "ameliorate the hardship of prolonged unemployment at the individual level, but assume the ability and willingness of individuals to retrain their entire career in order to replace devalued human capital through a more profitable stock" (Biebricher, 2018: 41, cf. 36). In this view, people become a sort of human capital traded on a labor market. Moreover, people-as-human capital are expected to completely change their life course and re-train for different careers and professions should the labor market demand it. What distinguishes neoliberal social policy is thus its individualist character and that it is indeed employed in order to "responsibilize" citizens to become economically self-sufficient.

This approach to unemployment has been influential in Western Europe, not least in the "flexicurity" models developed in the Nordic countries (Pedersen, 2006). They can be termed *competitive interventions* in so far as they help to reproduce the necessary conditions for sustaining and intensifying market competition in society. On a general level, neoliberals have agreed that the superior social policy is economic growth, and that inequality is "not only the natural state of market economies, but it is actually one of its strongest motor forces for progress" (Mirowski, 2009: 438; see also Piketty 2020: 705–716). Put another way, material inequality (some

quantum of human misery) between citizens is an important, necessary feature of social life because it motivates people to compete in
market settings.

As for the state institutions and public organizations themselves,
neoliberals have with considerable success argued that they should be
subjected to practices and principles drawn from the market sphere
"so that even core functions of the state are either subcontracted out
to private providers or run (as the saying has it) "like a business""
(Ferguson, 2009: 172). The subcontracting or outsourcing of public
services to for-profit organizations is often euphemistically labeled
public–private partnerships. In a typical case, this simply means that
a private company is contracted by the state for a number of years to
design, build, finance, and operate a public service that would otherwise have been provided by public sector institutions. Finally, in
order to ensure "accountability" within the reformed state institutions, the neoliberals have sought to restructure them with "techno-
managerial governance", such as numerous audit devices and market
metrics (Mirowski, 2009: 436). In this way, governing for the market
tends to create a lot of state action and often demands extensive
bureaucratization.

One example of this phenomenon from the academic world is the
application of the so-called Research Excellence Framework to public
universities in England. This framework judges "every academic
endeavor by its uptake in non-academic venues (commerce, state agencies, NGOs)" (Brown, 2015: 196). Subordinating academic work to
instrumental demands inevitably draws the focus of universities away
from their traditional core tasks of cultivating humanistic and critical
values and pursuing basic research.

The differences between the libertarian and neoliberal conception of
the liberal state can be summarized as follows:

Different starting premises:

- The state should be reduced to the military, police and courts whose
  role is to protect the citizens from theft, breach of contract and
  fraud, as well as secure property rights (*the libertarian night watchman state*); and
- The role of the state also and most importantly includes governing
  decisively and in detail to create, sustain and protect market competition (*the neoliberal competition state*):

Implications of the neoliberal starting premise:

1) Interventions in the market should be made only in so far as they help to reproduce the necessary conditions for sustaining and intensifying market competition in society (*competitive interventions*); and that

2) State institutions and public organizations should be subjected to outsourcing, subcontracting and market metrics (*market governance*).

2.1.4 The Neoliberal Conception of Civil Society

The notion of civil society is inherited by neoliberalism from the larger liberal tradition. At its most basic, "civil society" refers to social relations between groups and individuals in so far as they have historically developed to take a different form than the relations within state institutions or markets. As members of for example NGO's, social movements, religions, or families, individuals or groups are not directly acting within the framework of state institutions or governing bodies, but also are not merely agents involved in the exchange of goods or services. Rather, they are part of, the "third sphere," of civil society. For neoliberals, civil society is full of promises, possibilities, and dangers. It is first and foremost an inexhaustible reservoir for further colonization by market forces. In this sense, the neoliberals do not accept that civil society should be fenced off, as it were, from the sphere of the market: "Everything is fair game for marketization" (Mirowski, 2009: 437). It is the responsibility of state government to facilitate this process. The role of the competition state is to govern the social relations within civil society so as to cultivate groups and individuals for participation in the market, thereby expanding and intensifying the sphere of market competition within society. At the same time, civil society is assumed to be the domain from where forms of resistance to the state can grow that can be potentially useful for neoliberal aims. Social movements, for example, can mobilize pressure on the state "from below" in order to intensify the competition state, discipline its politicians and help protect the interest of corporations.

Yet, civil society is also a potentially dangerous breeding ground for social movements that seek to disrupt and change the neoliberal form of state government, or who turn their political energy directly against corporations and market activity. Groups within civil society must therefore be constantly monitored, contained, and modulated by an often subtle and indirect government. Despite attempts to change and colonize it, civil society is never completely subsumed. Fundamentally, civil society is a continuously present *horizon* for neoliberal political interventions, partly due to the constantly changing nature of the forms of non-marketized social interactions we engage in as human beings. In this sense, the fundamental neoliberal task of governing for market competition is never fully realized. There are always more social relations and processes to be domesticated by market forces, but also an ever-present potential for challenges and set-backs from recalcitrant groups and social movements. The social bonds in civil society both provide potential support for economic processes and economic bonds between people, while at the same time "overflowing them and being irreducible to them" (Foucault, 2008: 301).[2]

The ambiguous nature of civil society to neoliberal thinkers can be summed as follows:

- Civil society is an inexhaustible social resource for expanding, and a social precondition for sustaining a competitive market society (*civil society as a promise*).
- Civil society is a dangerous reservoir for resistance and potential disruption of market structures and corporate power (*civil society as a threat*).

2.1.5 The Role of International Institutions and Governance in Safeguarding the Market Order

As recent scholarship has investigated, the adherence to a strong competition state is in neoliberalism combined with the idea that nation-states themselves have to be disciplined "from above" (Biebriecher 2018; Slobodian 2018). The international dimension of neoliberalism has been most forcefully expressed as a *philosophy of global ordering*, developed in particular at the University of Geneva by Ludvig von Mises, Friedrich Hayek and Lionel Robbins and many

---

[2] Foucault is here interpreting the eighteenth-century philosopher Adam Ferguson. We use the ambiguous description of civil society he claims to excavate from this philosophy to characterize the phenomenon as it appears from the point of view of neoliberalism.

others throughout the twentieth century. This group of neoliberals not only coined ideas, but also helped to translate them "into policy or institutional design through partnerships with politicians, bureaucrats, or businesspeople" (Slobodian, 2018: 24). The neoliberal philosophy of global ordering has been extremely influential, not primarily because of its contributions to economic theory, but in particular as an inspiration for statecraft and institution-building. Its most significant achievement has perhaps been the establishment of the World Trade Organization (WTO) in 1995, but the ideas of the Geneva "globalist" school have also shaped the institutional development of the European Economic Community (EEC) and the European Union (EU) to a significant extent (Sloboidian, 2018: 182–262; see also Streeck, 2017: 154).

The first neoliberal argument for international governance should be understood in light of their understanding of the nature of competition. For Hayek, and other neoliberals following his line of thought, competition is an endless process of discovery and learning where the outcome cannot be determined in advance (Hayek 1968; Slobodian, 2018: 206, 213). When states compete against each other in order to provide the most favorable policies for investment and enterprise it facilitates such open-ended competition (Biebricher, 2018: 63; Slobodian, 2018: 267). However, in order to ensure that states compete to provide ever better frameworks for competition, they must be committed to secure the free flow of goods, services, capital, and labor. In this perspective, nation states appear in an ambiguous light: The creative and open-ended game of market competition is facilitated by nation states that compete for international investments, but at the same time capital must be able to follow opportunities across borders. Therefore, the neoliberal form of globalism does not envision a world without borders but attempts to erect a "worldwide institutional grid that offers transnational capital multiple exit options" (Brenner, Peck and Theodore, 2014: 129; see Slobodian, 2018: 266–267).

The removal of capital controls, that is, allowing wealth to roam a borderless world, plays a significant role in the worldview of the neoliberals because it induces countries that have successfully drawn investors to establish conditions sufficiently favorable for foreign capital to remain. The neoliberal endeavor hence includes the formulation and enforcement of "international investment law designed to protect foreign investors from diverse forms of expropriation" (Slobodian,

2018: 4). In a sustained effort the neoliberals have sought to build institutions that could force state governments to limit their own sovereign prerogatives (say to tax) in order to protect capital. In simple terms, the principle they seek to enforce is that governing a territory does not entail owning the property within it (Slobodian, 2018: 139). Thinkers in this globalist strain of neoliberalism have even attempted to appropriate the language of human rights to make this argument. By focusing less on the condition of the stateless person, but rather on the rights of the investor, they effectively proposed the right to capital flight already in the mid-twentieth century, and more recently neoliberals have criticized the UN human rights covenants for failing to offer effective protection for property rights and economic freedoms (Slobodian, 2018: 135, 279).

The guiding and immensely influential idea of the Geneva School of neoliberalism is thus to encase market structures and property rights in a framework of codified norms and rules that supersede national laws. The competition laws developed in the European Economic Community and European Union are an example. In fact, in their attempt to shape the transformation from the General Agreement on Tariffs and Trade (GATT) to the World Trade Organization (again, WTO), the economic market order as it was realized in the EEC played a guiding role for the neoliberals (Slobodian, 2018: 256). The principle that common European law overrides the national law of member states, and the fact that individual citizens as well as corporations could appeal to European law in their domestic courts, made the EEC a useful paradigm of an appropriate market order on a global level (ibid.).

Finally, many neoliberals are convinced that the world market needs the institutional support of international law and political norms to be maintained and, not least, protected from misconceived perceptions of popular sovereignty. Democracy is a threat to the functioning of the market order, because democratic majorities inevitably will demand redistribution of wealth (Slobodian, 2018: 272). In 1978, the economist and president of the neoliberal Mount Pelerin Society, George Stigler reflected on the nature of neoliberalism as a "minority view", and asked the following rhetorical question: "If in fact we seek what many do not wish, will we not be more successful if we take this into account and seek political institutions and policies that allow us to pursue our own goals?" (Stigler, 1979; quoted in Slobodian 2018: 237).

The second neoliberal argument for international institution-building is therefore that the will of people must be put on a leash by insulating markets from their potentially harmful interventions. Whereas the first argument emphasized how international law and multi-level governance can function to intensify competition, the second argument focuses on how rules formulated, maintained, and enforced by international institutions may serve to constrain what the neoliberals consider the dangerous egalitarian tendencies of democracy. With imagery that invokes a famous scene from Homer's *Odyssey*, the aim of international institutions and governance is to tie, with hands bound and wax in his ears, the Ulysses of the democratic state to the mast of the world economy (Slobodian, 2018: 273). Thus bound, the state is unable to listen to or follow to the democratic majorities that presumably legitimate it.

The first neoliberal argument for international institutions and governance can be summarized as follows:

- Market competition can be stimulated by the competition between states. Therefore, states must be committed and incentivized by international institutions and governance to offer the most attractive climate for the conduct of enterprise and for investment of capital (*stimulating competition*).

The second neoliberal argument for international institutions and governance can be summarized as follows:

- Democracy is constantly liable to result in government failures where special interests or popular majorities pursue egalitarian policies to the detriment of property rights and the market order. Therefore, democracy must be constrained by international institutions and governance in order to safeguard the market order and property rights (*constraining popular sovereignty*).

The two lines of argument require the same response: International institutions and governance must provide and enforce rules, norms, and laws that strengthen and protect the market order and commit nations to full participation in the world economy. The international rules must be able to override national laws or even be integrated in the national constitution and, thereby, commit the states to secure the free flow of goods, services, capital, and (to some extent) labor. International rules must provide individual capital owners and corporations with exits, and in case they perceive their property rights or right to trade to be infringed upon by the government of the nation state, they should be able to appeal to international courts whose rulings take priority over the courts of the nation states.

2.1.6 Neoliberalism and the Problem of Inequality

The primary challenge which neoliberalism faces from a democratic government is the inherent tendency of the majority to favor some form of wealth distribution in the face of sufficient inequality. It is a common neoliberal idea that pursuing egalitarian policies beyond equality before the law is dangerous to the social order and human wellfare. Inequality is not a phenomenon to be combatted, let alone overcome, but a force of progress that works to the benefit of all members of society (no matter how wretched some may be). To many neoliberals the protection of private property rights is seen as *the* primary political priority at any level of governance. While we initially presented neoliberalism as the marriage of minimal liberalism and the idea of the expansion of the market, it is well-established that for central neoliberal thinkers the idea of liberalism gradually narrowed into the mere idea of property rights with little respect for the further liberal values and freedoms that modern democracies are typically built to ensure. Friedman and in particular Hayek's justification of (semi)authoritarian forms of government, and in particular their will-ingness to admit the suspension of democratic rule and accept a transitional dictatorship under certain circumstances is well documented (Mirowsky, 2009: 446; Biebriecher, 2018: 103–106; 142–149).

While Friedman and Hayek are no doubt extreme compared to the many more moderate neoliberals in contemporary governments, who do respect the typical broader notions of liberties, it should be kept in mind that this inherent tension remains embedded in neoliberalism. Whenever the markets created by neoliberal policies are challenged by democratic demands for equality or obstructed by the respect for further non-property related civil liberties, then the neoliberal needs to evaluate what takes priority, marketization and property rights or minimal liberalism. Despite how this internal discussion pans out within the specific neoliberal debate, one thing is certain: neoliberal thought idealizes a form of inequality typically created by market structures and politically defends this by the questionable claim that even the poor are better off by allowing such rampant inequality (For an extensive empirical criticism of this claim, see Piketty 2014).

The Neoliberal view on inequality can be summarized as follows:

- Everyone will be better off by accepting inequality of outcomes, even if inequality levels remain significant or grow larger (*positive effects of inequality*)

2.1.7 The Neoliberal Conception of the Citizen

After more than three decades of dominance, neoliberalism has according to some of its critics shown its potential to change how democratic citizens understand who they are (e.g. Brown, 2015; 2019). When competition is installed as the fundamental principle of social dynamics, inequality, rather than equality, gradually becomes more legitimate, if not idealized, in every sphere of society (Brown, 2015: 64). Perpetually involved in the game of competition, all actors are conceived as capital and the human capital theory propounded by neoliberal economists (Becker, 1993) increasingly expresses the implicit anthropology of society. The consequence is that the self-conceptions of members of society are increasingly shaped according to the ideal of the individual entrepreneur: "As capital, every subject is entrepreneurial, no matter how small, impoverished, or without resources, and every aspect of human existence is produced as an entrepreneurial one" (Brown, 2015: 63). Each individual subject is cultivated to govern himself as "an entrepreneur of himself", "being for himself his own capital, being for himself his own producer, being for himself the source of [his] earnings" (Foucault, 2008: 226; Slobodian and Plewhe, 2020: 14). Individual decisions are evaluated in terms of market metrics that focus on the return of investment, and state institutions and policies seek to multiply and differentiate the enterprise form throughout the social body.

Think about this idea once more. How many of our choices in life should be thought of as entrepreneurial investments? Often it would probably be better if we decided to do something because it was kind, created something of lasting importance or, simply, because it was the right thing to do. The more our ways of thinking are dominated by an entrepreneurial self-conception, the more such reasons for action are forgotten and exchanged with a concern about what one personally profits from a course of action. Rather than lamenting this narrowing of our reasons for action, neoliberals either applaud the change, or even more sinisterly claim that no change has occurred because deep down, despite the pretty words, we were always already only looking out for our own profits.

As market, competition, and entrepreneurship become the formative powers of society, education in general, and higher education specifically, is prioritized for purposes of capital enhancement and maximizing competitiveness, rather than for "developing the capacities of citizens, sustaining culture, knowing the world, or envisioning and crafting different ways of life in common" (Brown, 2015: 177–178). This conquest of education by economic concerns threatens democracy. When public secondary and higher education in Western countries focus on developing human capital, rather than on providing citizens with the capacity to understand the powers and problems that surround them, their ability to take part in self-government is steadily undermined. What is eroding in this process is ultimately our self-conception as equal citizens, and our ideas of "society" and "the social" as a space where "citizens of vastly unequal backgrounds and resources are potentially brought together in common action. It is where we are politically enfranchised and gathered (not merely cared for) through provision of public goods and where historically produced inequalities are made manifest as differentiated political access, voice, and treatment, as well as where these inequalities may be partially redressed" (Brown, 2019: 27). As this idea of the social increasingly vanishes from our thoughts, speech, and experience, it also threatens to disappear from our visions of the future, our political imagination (Brown, 2019: 52).

The neoliberal view of the individual can be summarized as follows:

- The self-conception of the citizen should be that of an entrepreneur in a double sense:
  1) The ideal form of work and citizenship is supplying a good or service to the market for profit, i.e. to start one's own business (*idealization of entrepreneurship*); and
  2) Each individual should commit to being an "entrepreneur of oneself", perpetually attempting to maximize the returns on investments in his or her human capital (*entrepreneurial anthropology*).

Although our book does not deal with how neoliberalism challenges our conceptions of democracy and a flourishing society, the cases you are about to read depict alternative political responses and non-market based social practices, which go beyond neoliberal dogmas in a variety of different directions. Our hope is that an exploration of these existing alternatives to the current neoliberal market orthodoxy may critically complement the bleak picture painted by some of neoliberalism's critics. Thereby, we in this anthology hope to not only criticize neoliberalism's market imperialism, but also hope to contribute to a refueling of our political imagination, as well as inspire future theories that seeks to limit and restrict the times and places where the applications of market solutions are justified.

2.2 The Problematic Theoretical Underpinning of Market Imperialism

When reading the first part of this chapter, you may have wondered: Given that the problems that face societies are of so many different kinds, why would anyone *ever* have come to accept that a single approach to problem-solving is the default correct option. In other words, how can market imperialism ever appear convincing? In this section, we want to present a series of assumptions about human motivation, political organization, and knowledge, which the major developers of neoliberalist thought have used to justify their myopic praise of market forces as the solution to all human problems. We think that the contemporary prevalence of market imperialism is underpinned by the implicit or explicit adoption of these assumptions, or due to a blindness toward what alternative solutions may exist. Part of the process of removing the blinders, so that we can appreciate other approaches to problem-solving, consists in dismantling the arguments that were instrumental in blinding us in the first place.

Importantly, our critical discussion below assumes the good faith of neoliberal arguments. In other words, we grant that the neoliberals advance a default application of the market form to every kind of societal problem, that they propagate an economization of all social relations, *because they actually think this is the best, or perhaps only way*, to solve such problems. It is important to emphasize that this charitable approach to neoliberalism is not at all shared by all of its critics, nor even all of our authors. One of the largest, longest running traditions in the study of capitalism, Marxism and Marxist thought, would not extend this sort of courtesy to neoliberal thinking. For example, one recent Marxist interpretation views neoliberalism as a movement that grew out of the attempt of the ruling class in capitalist society to undermine the power of labor in light of the falling rate of profit in the early 1970s (Harvey, 2007). In line with Marx original interpretation of bourgeois liberalism (Marx and Engels 1993), this contemporary Marxist interpretation sees the neoliberal appeal to defending and expanding individual liberty as a dishonest or at least self-delusional pretense to class-based exploitation. It identifies the real motivation behind neoliberal arguments for marketization as the attempt to secure the interests and resources of private property owners, businesses, multinational corporations, and financial capital (Harvey, 2007: 7). This may well be true. And, again, it's likely that many of our contributors are persuaded of this line of reasoning. A summary of the different levels of charity one could have to neoliberal theorizing follows:

- Arguments for market imperialism should be interpreted as part of an attempt of the ruling class in capitalist society to undermine the power of labor, or more generally as an attempt to secure, maintain or increase the power of the ruling class (*uncharitable interpretation*);
- Arguments for market imperialism are motivated by the conviction of neoliberals that this approach is the best or only way to address societal problems (*charitable interpretation*).

If you are already committed to an uncharitable interpretation, you have no reason to take market imperialism seriously in the first place. You should therefore not be under the influence of default market boosterism. To you, the cases we provide, should provide for further empirical evidence for your extant suspicion of neoliberal thinking.

That said, the premise of our book is that even if you are personally persuaded of the shortcomings of neoliberalism, you or your colleagues may be propounding market imperialism in your teaching, or you may be subject to this approach as a student, based on the tacit or explicit assumption that market solutions are truly the best or even only to way to address certain societal problems. If this is the case, you will be encountering market imperialism in an academic environment in which reason and evidence are supposed to carry the day. Based on this charitable interpretation, that is, based on the possibility of deliberation and persuasion as a form of political action, we aim to provide two means to break free from market-first neoliberal thinking. First, what remains of this chapter aims to show that there is no viable theoretical underpinning for market imperialism. Secondly, our cases aim to counter the last-ditch defense of neoliberalism, the idea, first made infamous by Margaret Thatcher, that "there is no alternative." The range of cases in our book shows that this idea is, at best, a cynical product of empirical laziness. Alternatives exist, and the way problem-solving is taught in higher education should therefore be more open-minded than is currently the case.

In the following we will evaluate three lines of argument that have all flourished in the major theoretical defenses of market imperialism. They can be called:

1) The "Human nature is self-interested" argument;
2) The "Tyranny is the only alternative" argument, and;
3) The "The market knows best" argument.

To put some philosophical terms on the arguments: the first is **metaphysical** (it concerns what we *are* as humans), the second is **moral** (it concerns what we *ought* to do as humans), the third is **epistemic** (it concerns what we can *know* as humans). All the arguments are typically employed to great polemic effect. Yet, when scrutinized more closely, they all fall apart. In the following we will discuss each argument in turn and present their faults. To assist in this, we will present the premises and conclusions of the arguments explicitly. Though these arguments naturally surface in many slightly different variations throughout the literature, we take our renderings to be faithful to the major line of thought in the various versions.

The three principled arguments for market imperialism can be summarized as follows:

1. The subject is assumed to act as a *Homo Economicus* in all societal contexts: a rational utility maximizer with stable preferences. Explicitly setting up market structures only acknowledges this reality (*The "human nature is self-interested" argument*);
2. The only ways of coordinating human cooperative problem-solving are through coercion or market mechanisms, and coercion is wrong (*The "tyranny is the only alternative" argument*);

3.A. Humans can never grasp the complexities of a social problem and
will thus only solve it by pure luck. The market will at least
produce a viable solution to a problem, if not always the best
(*The "humans are dumb" argument*); and

3.B. Whereas humans will only sometimes find the best solution to a
social problem, markets will always do so (*The "markets are
incredibly smart" argument*).

2.2.1 The "Human Nature is Self-interested" Argument

The first argument runs as follows:

Premise 1: The use of free market forces is the best way of organizing cooperation among exclusively self-interested, well-
informed, rational individuals with stable preferences.

Premise 2: Humans are inherently, and exclusively, self-interested,
well-informed, rational individuals with stable preferences.

Conclusion: All cooperative problems solving is best organized by
the use of free market forces.

Famously, Adam Smith (1776, bk 1, chap. 2) pointed out that when
people go to the market to acquire groceries, we do not expect them to
act out of altruism when they chose which goods to buy. Rather, he
identified that the efficient solution to the cooperation problem of how
much to produce of each retail good in a society, and at what quality,
could be adequately solved by relying on the self-interested behavior of
those freely buying at a market. When it came to buying day to day
household provisions, people were primarily motivated by self-interest
and, in light of that, a free market was an efficient way of handling the
issues of social cooperation related to the production and consumption
of household goods. For other social organization issues, such as care
for the family and societal governance, Smith (1759) thought we
needed to rely on other forms of human motivation, such as our sense
of justice and piety.

The key to the "Human nature is self-interested" argument is the
claim that Smith and likeminded theorists were naïve in thinking that
humans are ever motivated by anything beyond the rational self-
interested pursuit of a set of stable personal preferences. The form of
human motivation that Smith identified at the marketplace is in fact the

only form of human motivation there is. It is simply a harsh anthropological fact that beneath our veneers of morality and loyalty, we are really only acting based on the enlightened pursuit of self-interest. We are essentially and always maximizers of our own personal utility. Hence, in a sense, every social interaction is already a form of a marketplace. Only what we trade isn't solely provisions and dry-goods, but also the satisfaction of more subtle needs, such as our craving for recognition or safety, our intellectual curiosity, the proliferation of a religion we prefer, and many other of our more abstract personal preferences. And if, as the argument goes, we are always and only motivated by self-interest, then the quid pro quo of the marketplace is the best way of getting everyone to cooperate.

The pressing question is why anyone would ever dream of acknowledging that the second premise is true. Scrutiny of the human activities around us seems to immediately display its obvious falsity. Altruistic action abounds, from the care families give to needy children and elderly, to volunteer work, or the loyalty shown to friends, social groups, and even to places of work or the environment as such – even when, and perhaps especially so, these people, places or things don't love you back. Indeed, many of the successful alternative solutions to real empirical problems that you will read in the following chapters function precisely by relying upon the fact that people can be motivated by other factors than self-interest. This is where the neo-liberal argumentation turns insidious. The first step taken in convincing people of our essentially self-interested nature is to move from the idea of the marketplace, where we are interested in money and physical goods, to the idea that we are also self-interestedly maximizing our acquisition of further more ethereal goods, such as confirmations of our self-conceptions, the implementation of our personal sense of justice, and our pursuit of public recognition.

This expansion of our egotistical goals from solely pecuniary and material to include anything one can conceivably strive for is perfected in the work of economist Gary Becker. Smith (1759) famously excluded family life from the arena of human cooperation governed by self-interest. In his major work *A treatise on the family*, Becker's (1981) aim is precisely to expand Smith's conception of our self-interested market motivation beyond those confines. He writes: "This volume uses the assumptions of maximizing behavior, stable preferences, and equilibrium in implicit or explicit markets to provide a systematic analysis of the family" (Becker 1981: x). Becker accomplishes this expansion precisely by assuming that, whatever goals you may have, what you strive for can be understood as some relatively stable preference that you rationally maximize your personal utility by satisfying.

Thus, by a stroke of definition, you are now a maximizing self-interested individual, even when you donate to charities and do volunteer work. For what you are really doing is not motivated by the needs of others. Deep down you are simply pursuing your self-interest by maximizing the utility you get from supporting your self-conception as someone who donates or helps those in need. Moreover, and this is important, according to the neoliberal theory such seemingly altruistic behavior is ultimately substitutable by a sufficient increase in the satisfaction of *any* of your other preferences. There is no amount of commitment to altruism or loyalty that cannot be trumped by enough cookies, fast cars, or money. Every noble goal you pursue, every principle you adhere to, will according to economic maxims be trumped by the promise of sufficient satisfaction of your other desires (Becker 1981; Jensen 1994: 7). Put another way, everyone has their price.

Once we have expanded the notion of self-interested maximizers from the pursuit of pecuniary and material interests to the pursuit of personal utility, then there is obviously no behavior that cannot be analyzed as motivated by the maximization of self-interest. If someone explains that they do something because they owe it to their neighbor, or because they think it is right, then it can be explained as their unacknowledged pursuit of the personal utility they derive from living according to those ideals. And if someone consistently upholds a given principle in their actions, seemingly unwilling to compromise for any substitute, then the answer will always be that this is simply because they haven't been lured with sufficient amounts of alternative utility. None of us are actually ever motivated by ideals or principles, only by self-interest. We may think we are, but we are at best insufficiently rewarded for abandoning our previous higher ground, and that explains seeming cases of moral fortitude against personal temptation.

When the idea that we are self-interested maximizers of wealth and goods is expanded into the idea that we are self-interested maximizers of personal utility, and when enough alternative explanations and theoretical bells and whistles are added to the theory, this theory of human nature becomes impossible to empirically falsify. It becomes axiomatic. However, what is overlooked in the neoliberal argument is that it also becomes impossible to employ in the defense of market imperialism. Consider the following: if we are indeed self-interested maximizers of personal utility, but sufficiently many of us acquire great personal utility by, say, being loyal toward our group and acting in its best interest, or acquire personal utility by behaving altruistically and doing our duties, then why do we need market forces to best organize our cooperation? It seems that our personal preference for loyalty, duty, compassion, and the like, should be sufficient and possibly even superior in the organization of our cooperation than the quid pro quo approach of the market transaction.

In effect the neo-liberal argument above acquires its seeming effectiveness through equivocation. Let us grant that it is true that *if* we were indeed self-interested in the narrow sense of pursuing only wealth and material goods, *then* market forces would be the best way of organizing cooperation. However, as we have emphasized, it flies in the face of all common sense and experience that we are essentially only motivated by the personal pursuit of wealth and material goods. People pursue all kinds of aims, not only wealth and material goods. In other words, a narrow reading of premise 2 is obviously false.

Alternatively, lets follow Becker's flight forward and expand the notion of maximization to the goal of personal utility, such that premise 2 becomes even remotely defensible[3]. That is, let us expand the notion of our self-interested pursuits, such that we are maximizers of personal utility in the sense that we sometimes also pursue further values, such as altruism and loyalty and duty, though only as a means for self-gratification and never as an end in itself. *In that case, premise 1 is false.* Because then it will no longer be the case that the quid pro quo of the marketplace is always the best way to organize our collaborative problem-solving. Sometimes it may be more efficient and preferable to rely on our natural preferences for social cohesion and

---

[3] We still take this theory of human motivation to be false due to its accompanying assumptions about the substitutability of ends, the rationality of agents, and its self-focused conception of all practical deliberation. Though these points are important, we must for simplicity's sake leave them aside for now. Our chapter on healthcare (Chapter 17 in this volume) challenges the neoliberal conception that agents are rational and well-informed in their pursuit of self-interest, and shows how better problem-solving can be performed by rejecting this assumption. Our chapter on water supply (Chapter 4), challenges the idea that our preferences should be conceived as stable.

feelings of obligation. In fact, a series of the cases in the rest of the book present real empirical examples, where relying on non-economic motivation was more efficient in our problem-solving. Hence, there is no reading of the "human nature is self-interested" argument where both its premises are true. It relies on subtle equivocation in its claims to justify the market imperialism championed by neoliberalism.

2.2.2 The "Tyranny is the Only Alternative" Argument

The next argument is probably best introduced in the voice of the economist Milton Friedman, who was both its most famous defender and a major formative influence at the Chicago School of Economics which was, and continues to be, one the main centers of neoliberal thought:

Fundamentally, there are only two ways of coordinating the economic activities of millions. One is central direction involving the use of coercion, the technique of the army and of the modern totalitarian state. The other is voluntary co-operation of individuals, the technique of the marketplace. The possibility of co-ordination through voluntary co-operation rests on the elementary yet frequently denied proposition that both parties to an economic transaction benefit from it, provided the transaction is bi-laterally voluntary and informed (Friedman 1982: 19).

Friedman here provides an argument from exhaustion, which is echoed in the writings of Hayek (1944).

Premise 1: The only ways of coordinating human cooperative problem-solving are through coercion or market mechanisms.

Premise 2: Coercion is wrong.

Conclusion: All cooperative problem-solving is best organized by the use of free market forces.

The problem with the argument is so obvious that it almost merits no explanation. Clearly the first exhaustive premise that we can only coordinate human cooperation through coercion or market mechanisms is false. As just established in the discussion of the former argument, humans can be motivated by many different factors. Each of these motivations can form the basis for human coordination, not just our economic interests or the brute force of tyranny. Maybe I value the social cohesion in our group and so does the rest of the people in our group. This motivational factor can then be used to coordinate our efforts, and this amounts to neither the economic quid pro quo of the marketplace, nor to the coercive techniques of tyranny.

Friedman also employs an individualistic conception of humans which overlooks that in many cases we might need no motivation to coordinate. We might already be adequately coordinated by shared cultural features, such as shared language, shared traditions, or other shared systems of meaning. The typical failure of exhaustive arguments is to overlook viable alternative options, and this argument is no different.

Despite its simplistic nature, this argument is well-known from politics, especially in the USA, where it seems that any mention of democratic socialist reforms, such as universal healthcare and free education, are immediately associated with the repressive tyranny of some vaguely-conceived communist dictatorship. That democratic socialist policy, which relies not on market transactions but on a communal feeling of responsibility for each other, cannot be separated from coercive and oppressive tyranny shows that despite its obvious flaws, the "Tyranny is the only alternative" argument still has widespread political influence.

But wait, you might think, aren't you misreading Freidman? After all, he merely writes that our *economic* activities can only be coordinated by coercion or the free market. Whereas you interpret him as saying that *all human cooperative problem-solving* can only be coordinated by coercion or the free market. It is true that we extend his argument beyond the quote, but there are reasons for doing so. First of all, Friedman himself typically interprets his own statement as having practically universal scope, such that for example the provision of healthcare, the building of societal infrastructure, and education are also trivially and without argument included as activities that are economic in some sense. Secondly, unless the argument is read as including all cooperative activities, it cannot support the market imperialism that neoliberals use it to justify.

If we acknowledge that only our problem-solving concerning specific *economic issues* is limited to either coercion or the market, then one might agree that we should prefer free market solutions to our *economic problems*, which is indeed what we, the authors of this chapter, think. However, the pressing question then becomes which types of problems should be construed as economic, and which problems should be construed as, say, political, educational, moral, or ethical. The essence of market imperialism is precisely the claim that all problems should be solved with market solutions; and the universality of that claim cannot be supported if we acknowledge both that non-economic problems may have other alternative forms of coordination that are viable and accept that not all problems are economic. Hence, on the strong reading of Friedman's argument we presented first, its first exhaustive premise is obviously false. On the second weaker reading, where it only concerns economic coordination, it cannot support the universal application of market solutions that is the very essence of the neoliberal approach to problem-solving.

2.2.3 The "The Market Knows Best" Argument

The final argumentation in favor of neo-liberalism's market imperialism that we want to consider is humbler than the two arguments we've already evaluated. It neither claims that we are inherently and implicitly engaged in self-interested market calculations whenever we interact. Nor does it argue that every non-market approach to cooperative problem-solving is morally reprehensible. It simply claims that though there may be many commendable ways of approaching coordinated problem-solving, as a matter of fact, better solutions are *always* found by employing free market mechanisms. The argument is epistemic; we *always* discover the best solutions by letting decisions of what to do be determined by market forces. This type of argument comes in two forms, one that underestimates our human capabilities for discovering solutions and one that overestimates the ability of free market outcomes to find the optimal solution to our practical problems. We can call them the "humans are too dumb, and the "the market is incredibly smart" arguments.

2.2.4 The "Humans Are Too Dumb" Argument

The argument runs as follows:

> **Premise 1:** To adequately solve the problems we face, our solutions need to be responsive to the relevant complexities of the problems they address.

Premise 2: The societal problems we face are too complex for human cognition to adequately grasp.

Minor Conclusion 1: We cannot through active human reasoning and planning provide adequate solutions to our societal problems.

Premise 3: Market mechanisms are automatically responsive to the relevant complexities of the societal systems we marketize.

Minor Conclusion 2: Market mechanisms can provide adequate solutions to our societal problems.

Conclusion: All cooperative problem-solving is best organized by the use of free market forces.

Argumentation along these lines is famously championed by Hayek (1945), when he argues that the automatic price regulation of the market functions is our only available option for handling problems that are too complex for individual human cognition to grasp. Notice though, that the core of neo-liberalism is its market imperialism, which claims that all problem-solving should be left to market forces. In order to defend that conclusion, the critical issues are 1) if *all* our problems are too complex for human conscious cognition to adequately evaluate, and 2) whether it really is true that the market *always* adequately responds to the relevant features of those problems. The contentious premises of the argument are thus premise 2 and premise 3. However, those premises are both obviously false in the strong universal reading required to justify market imperialism.

Clearly, there are certain problems which humans can easily grasp the complexities of and thus consciously plan an effective solution to. Mundane problems such as who should take the kids to school or where to buy milk spring to mind. More importantly, as many of the coming papers will show, even for quite complex problems such as handling water supplies (Randle, Chapter 5) and organizing parking in major cities (Souleles, Chapter 10), conscious human prediction and problem-solving can outperform market-based mechanisms. Hence, the scope of problems for which premise 2 is true is certainly less than the universal scope required to support the conclusion of market imperialism.

Likewise, there are obviously societal problems where free markets are irresponsive to features we know to be relevant to adequate problem-solving. In particular, problems with easily foreseeable long-term effects are poorly reflected in market prices despite being well-known to human deliberators. This is because the long-term consequences of various market decisions are screened off from immediate economic relevance by the interim fluctuations of the market. In economic terminology, the "externalities," the things outside a market aren't properly internalized in the market. We certainly know that undermining the education system or destroying our ecosystems have long term detrimental effects, both economically, but even more so socially and morally. However, these negative effects aren't, and often cannot be, reflected in contemporary price mechanisms as there is often adequate profit to be made until the widespread negative consequences set in and destroy a given market's larger societal context. Hence, the universality of premise 3 is also obviously false in the strong reading required by the neoliberal argument.

Once again, the remaining question is why anyone would ever believe this argument. It seems to get its motivation from a form of slippery slope fallacy. In their writings, both Friedman (1982) and Hayek (1944) primarily compare the attempts to centrally plan production and consumption of material goods in the Soviet Union with the alternative of letting the gradual rise and fall of prices on a free-market signal which resources are in scarcity and abundance, relevant to human needs. They are both certainly right that when we consider the production and consumption of fairly ordinary goods, then this is surely both too complex a system to grasp in human cognition and also a system fairly adequately reflected in the price mechanism of the market. However, the fallacy in play is when we start to think that because a free market is the most effective method available for solving the problem of national or global production and consumption of ordinary goods, then it must also be the best approach to solving either issues of less complexity or issues of equal or greater complexity which do not deal exclusively with ordinary goods. It is suddenly assumed without argument that the comparatively more complex issue of motivating a specific group of employees, or the organization of consumption of esoteric "goods" such as CO_2, crime, and education, are also problems best solved by relying on market mechanisms. However, this issue requires empirical investigation of the specific problem one faces. It may be that human conscious deliberation can indeed grasp the complexities of the relevant issue and find a better solution than that orchestrated by blind market forces. Or it may be that the market is in this specific case insensitive to the features relevant to adequate problem-solving, features which human deliberation would immediately take into account.

In other words, the tacit presumption that a market solution must be the way forward can only be justified if we accept premise 2 and premise 3 above in their universal interpretations, and those are obviously and undeniably false. What we should accept are the weaker reasonable premises that *sometimes* we cannot grasp the complexities of a problem, and *sometimes* a market of some sort is indeed responsive the relevant complexities that we cannot grasp. But these premises only allow us to conclude that for any problem we face, we need independent argumentation and justification that shows why this case is indeed one of those where blind and passive market forces provide better solutions than conscious human deliberation and orchestration.

2.2.5 The "The Market is Incredibly Smart" Argument

This argument in favor of market imperialism doesn't take its grounding in the deficiencies of human cognition, but rather in the presumed perfections of the market. It goes as follows:

Premise 1: Conscious human deliberation sometimes discovers the optimal solution to a problem.

Premise 2: The market always selects the optimal solution to a problem.

Conclusion: All cooperative problem-solving is best organized by the use of free market forces.

This argument typically relies on drawing analogies between market forces and evolutionary forces, yet, in doing so, fundamentally misunderstands both. The comparison of market forces to evolution has a long tradition. It is exemplified in influential work by Alchian (1950) and Hayek (1988). The rough idea is that a free market will allow for myriad potential solutions to our problems to emerge. Blind market forces will then function by passively selecting the optimal solution, whereas the rest will automatically dissipate. The slogan is captured in Herbert Spencer's (1865) misunderstanding of evolution as a process of natural selection that ensures the survival of the *fittest* – a slogan he used to justify an early form of racist, social Darwinism of precisely the type that underwrites this second epistemic argument in favor of neo-liberalist problem-solving. However, the slogan is false, evolution isn't a directional process of survival of the *fittest*. It is process of survival of those who *accidentally happen to survive*.

The fittest finch ever to exist probably died due to a lucky predator, a random lighting strike, or an uncommon draught. However, the odds of dying are slightly lower among animals better fitted to their environments, which means that if we repeat the process of survival of those who happened to survive an incredible number of times, then we will have a population which is on-average better suited to its environment compared to what random variation alone would have resulted in. Survival in this evolutionary sense is thus 1) due to random, non-directed variation, 2) context-specific, and 3) essentially a group or population-level phenomenon. Some elements of markets work sort of like this: There is great uncertainty as to what firms or solutions will prosper on the market; that is why it is fraught with risk. A lot of bad ideas get funding, and a lot of good ideas fail to prosper. Perhaps, on average, if we look at the companies that persist decade after decade, then they cannot be half bad. Yet very often, better companies have in fact been out there, but perished due to random accidents, such as a single bad CEO, a bankruptcy among subcontractors whose effects spilled over, starting up just prior to the outbreak of a pandemic, etc. Notably, deliberate human intervention can sometimes beat the blind selection of the evolution-like process of the market. Just like selective human breeding have created specialized farm animals at a faster pace and with different results than those that would have occurred by natural selection. For example, instead of blindly allowing market prices to determine which companies survive and how they alter after we internalize the cost of CO_2 by introducing tariffs, we could probably just target specifically harmful industries by deliberate regulation and prohibition, just like we deliberately singled out certain high-volume milk-cows for further breeding.

A second issue of equal importance is the slow speed of development and the high casualty rate inherent to both evolution and market forces. Free-market forces function by allowing everyone to go on in their own way. Just like random mutation in the evolutionary analogy, this creates the required variety for the process to function. Without variety even evolution fails to provide well-fitted creatures, as cases of inbreeding attest to. Of this variety, those companies that are most ill-fitted to their surrounding environment have the greatest odds of perishing. However, just like in nature, where a poorly fitted type of finch may survive for several generations before perishing; likewise, a bad way of solving our problems may persist for a long time before some market mechanism actually kills it. This despite the fact that the most cursory deliberate evaluation would allow us to see that, from a societal perspective, this form of problem-solving was nowhere near optimal, and may in fact be harming lots of people, as in the case of, say, fossil fuel exploration or asbestos manufacturing.

The market isn't infinitely fast, nor infinitely well-informed, despite what economists, corporate strategists, and other market-thinkers like to presume for simplicities sake. Moreover, the problems that face us are sometimes too urgent, or the consequence of failure to great, to allow the market to naturally weed out the bad solutions and adequately increase the chances that good solutions flourish (Beresford's Chapter 20 on South African entrepreneurs deals with precisely this issue).

Think of a case where we let companies compete freely for the distribution of emergency care. Some of these companies are good players; they deliver on their promises and will be rehired. Some will be bad or inefficient players and ought to perish once we see how they perform. However, if we solely use market feedback to determine whom to trust and how to organize, then we also accept that in order to weed out the bad players, we need to allow all those served by them to die when their first aid fails to arrive.

Markets do indeed work somewhat like evolution. Only evolution doesn't work the way market thinkers suppose; it doesn't actively and directly select the fittest, rather it simply selects those who accidentally happened to survive in some given context. This means that after repeated cycles those species or solutions which are better aligned with the environment (which is always changing) or problem at hand have greater odds of still being around. However, neither the market nor evolution provides any guarantee that the best species or solutions haven't perished due to a random incident, a fate that active intervention might have saved them from. Nor is there any guarantee, nor even reason to think, that the market or evolution kills off excruciatingly ill-fitted specimens with any great haste.

Hence, very often we can by deliberate and active intervention pursue solutions that are better than those which accidentally happen to survive at the free market. We can also often sort out the poor solutions right from the get-go, rather than waiting for an extended series of failures to make the market sort this out. We are often in an epistemically superior position, where human deliberation can more quickly identify a better solution to our problems than what the free play of market forces would have provided. Sometimes, it is indeed tough to figure out how to approach a problem, and in those cases reliance on market forces might be of assistance, but that is an empirical question, different for every individual problem we face. Moreover, the burden of proof is surely on those who claim that a repeated game of odds for survival on the blind market is epistemically a better approach than conscious human deliberation about how to proceed. The market imperialism of neo-liberalism cannot be defended on the grounds that it is always epistemically superior compared to deliberate and targeted intervention. For it is quite clear that we are neither as dumb, nor the market as smart, as that would require.

2.2.6 A Final Neoliberal Rejoinder

After such a battering of philosophical argumentation against the universalist pretensions of market imperialism, a typical retreat strategy might seem tempting to the staunch neoliberalist; at least it has been the recourse of all those neoliberals with whom we have discussed these things. The defense goes something like this:

Well, you philosophers speak of ontological assumptions and universal pretentions. I, however, am a practical guy who has had considerable success with modelling and implementing market behavior and solutions. People seem to find *my* approach useful both for discussing topics in the academy and for governing in real life. I would never claim that the economic approach is a universal solution or make ahistorical assumptions about human nature - isn't that game also abandoned in philosophy, by the way? I do make some assumptions, useful for predicting behavior and thinking about policy solutions. But I would never assume that they fit in every case or that they reflect "reality," whatever that might mean. Interestingly, however, in all the cases you mention here in our discussion, I think it would be very interesting and useful to apply the economic approach. So let us take the issues, case by case, and see how the economic approach might usefully illuminate them. In short, when you say, "How would people ever have come to believe that market solutions are universally valid?", I advise you: Get out of the ivory tower and away from the principled arguments of your unhelpful philosophy. Get into the real discussions about actual problem-solving. Then you will see that when real problems are encountered and discussed, theoretically and practically, the economic approach is actually often very useful.

To that reply we say two things: First, the rest of this book does nothing but get into real life, examine real cases, and these cases display how a neoliberal market solution often does more damage than good and is by no means the best way of problem-solving. Second, if that really is your position then recall that when you go into the world to solve problems and analyze situations *then you can never justify a market approach until you have seriously considered what other options are available.* This eagerness to proclaim the down-to-earth practical and case-by-case nature of one's neoliberalism comes with the cost that, in order to justify a market solution, one must just as eagerly have scouted far and wide to see if there were better solutions available. The alternative is to claim that one, on principled grounds, know that market solutions will be the best way to approach a given problem, but such principled grounds required a theoretical defense of market imperialism. And as we have just shown, the theoretical arguments that are traditionally used in favor of market imperialism do not hold up to critical scrutiny.

2.3 Conclusion: Network of Thinkers and Art of Government

Contributions in philosophy, political theory, intellectual history and anthropology – among a number of other disciplines – have used a variety of methods to investigate neoliberalism. One of the most fruitful and cogent is the attempt by intellectual historians to describe how the development of neoliberal ideas as well as their societal influence has been furthered by a network of thinkers, "an organized group of individuals exchanging ideas within a common intellectual framework" (Dean, 2014: 151). Paradigmatic here are the historical accounts of the Mount Pelerin Society (MPS), the influential and still existing network of neoliberal intellectuals founded by Hayek in 1947 (Mirowski and Plewhe, 2009; Burgin, 2012; Slobodian, Plewhe and

Mirowski, 2020). By focusing on specific thinkers and the organizations and networks in which they collaborated, the intellectual historians are able to track ruptures, tensions and diversity of views, rather than assume that neoliberalism is a homogenous ideology (Dean, 2014: 151). This approach is in other words able to acknowledge both internal disagreements as well as continuous development within the neoliberal tradition.

In our sketch of neoliberalism in the first part of this chapter, we have drawn on the work of political theorists, but we have also made use of some of the contributions from intellectual historians. From the picture provided in the first part, together with our discussions of neoliberal arguments of Gary Becker, Milton Friedman and Friedrich Hayek for market imperialism in the second part, we have distilled a list of characteristics of the kind of neoliberal thought that we see showing up again and again.

Nine characteristics of neoliberalism

1. The subject should be assumed to act as a *Homo Economicus*: a rational personal utility maximizer with stable preferences.
2. The problem-solving capacity generated by the market should be assumed to exceed the problem-solving capacity of intentional political action.
3. The primary self-conception of the citizen should be that of an entrepreneur
4. The primary role of the state should be to govern for market competitiveness
5. The state should be run like a business, and/or its functions subcontracted to market actors
6. Market structures should be preserved by state and international regulatory frameworks that are protected from popular influence. Democracy should be constrained (or even eliminated) in this sense.
7. Economic inequality is inevitable, legitimate, and desirable.
8. Civil society is both an infinite resource for marketization and a perpetual threat to market structures and corporate power.
9. Change and variation is preferable to stability

Now, the analyses in the following case chapters will not, as in the approach of intellectual historians, focus on the historical connection between the academic development of neoliberal theory and the application of theory in political problem-solving. Rather the analytical approaches employed in the case chapters take an approach that is found in Foucault's investigation of neoliberalism. The key term of relevance to us is Foucault's description of neoliberalism as an "art of government" (Foucault, 2008: 1–2). The term *art of government* is to be understood broadly as a set of skills in governing or managing the lives of others. When analyzed empirically, an art of government appears as a set of interconnected and goal-oriented, reflective practices.

The Foucauldian approach to neoliberalism as an art of government "contains" three analytic dimensions or axes that are interconnected, but may not all be explicitly treated in a specific analysis. The neoliberal art of government can be analyzed as *normative framework of behavior* (Foucault, 2010: 3). These may be encapsulated in policies or codes of governance that intervene in the environment of a population and attempt to guide behavior and decision-making. All of our contrast cases contain examples of how problem-solving expresses neoliberal normative frameworks of behavior. Characteristic of neoliberal normative frameworks of behavior is that they seek to achieve their aim by relying on and taking into account the initiative, independent agency, and egotistic interests of the subjects governed. Rather than directly ordering or forcing individuals to take specific actions, these frameworks set up conditions for an "economic game" within which individuals are urged and cultivated to be creative, resourceful, and dynamic in their courses of actions.

An art of government can also be investigated as a set of theoretical practices that make neoliberal initiatives and solutions likely, if not certain. They are *forms of knowledge* (Foucault, 2010: 3) that decision-makers and policy developers assume in their reflections and which they refer to when justifying their proposed solutions. An example of a form of knowledge is rational choice theory with its particular assumptions about human motivation and rationality, as well as its methodological prioritization of individual decision-making processes. Although rational choice theory has many shapes and is not necessarily neoliberal, the assumptions of mainstream versions of this theory are eminently compatible with important strands of neoliberal thought. It is thus no coincidence that prominent neoliberal thinkers, among them Becker, articulate their ideas in the form of rational choice theory. Several of our contrast cases show how the assumptions of neoliberal rational choice theory guides problem-solving, although it is far from certain that the decision-makers think of themselves as neo-liberals or have been explicitly persuaded by theories propounded by the likes of Becker.

This brings us to the third analytic dimension of the neoliberal art of government, the *practices of the self*, through which individuals develop their implicit and explicit self-conception (Foucault, 2003; cf. Raffnsøe, Gudmand-Høyer and Thaning, 2016: 369–425). Political theorist Wendy Brown illustrates this level of analysis in her portrait of a current generation of young scholars, who are trained, not to become "teachers and thinkers, but treat themselves as human capitals who learn to attract investors by networking long before they "go on the market", who "workshop" their papers, "shop" their book manu-scripts, game their Google Scholar counts and "impact factors," and above all, follow the money and the rankings. "Good investment" is the way departments speak of new hires, and "entrepreneurial" has become a favored term for describing exceptionally promising young researchers; it is deployed to capture both a researcher's capacity to parlay existing accomplishments into new ones and the more quotidian business of grant getting" (Brown, 2015: 195). Some of our cases focus on how neoliberal problem-solving involves this"micro"-dimension (Clotworthy Chapter 15; Elliot Chapter 18) by conceiving of and turning people into personal entrepreneurs of their own future.

An important consequence of Foucault's analytical approach is that it deliberately ignores whether a concrete influence from neoliberal theories to political practice can be traced. From this perspective, the "problem-solvers" who perpetrate neoliberalism need not be admirers of the ideas of neoliberal thinkers. They may not even conceive of themselves and their actions as having anything to do with neoliberal-ism, and a concrete influence from the intellectual network of thinkers on their way of reflecting may not be discernable. Still, analysis may convincingly show that the practices of government involved are recognizably neoliberal in the sense that they rely on, and express, neoliberal arguments and assumptions for their justification. The neoliberal art of government may in short be "anonymous" in a Foucauldian mode of analysis in the sense that none of the involved problem-solvers acknowledge themselves as neoliberals. It is this ano-nymity which constitutes the main difference to the analysis of the influences of neoliberalism made by intellectual historians.

By accepting the unacknowledged and sometimes highly elusive influence of neoliberalism, the Foucauldian analysis is able to take seriously that neoliberalism at times has political influence despite governments and decision-makers conceiving of their choices as apolitical and devoid of ideology. The decision-makers analyzed may well think of their governmental practice as simply a question of pursuing the most responsible, the most competent, or even the only possible course of action. In these cases, political decision-making is pictured as a matter of technical, often calculative, competence that can remain neutral regarding specific political aims and values, or at least avoids an explicit commitment to neoliberalism that is likely to be controversial.

It is important to add that we are not claiming that neoliberalism as an art of government is universally bad. Just as market solutions work in some areas in order to address a range of problems, the use of the neoliberal art of government can in some cases be the best, or least bad way forward. In relation to his work on social policy and anti-poverty politics in southern Africa, anthropologist James Ferguson has vividly illustrated this point (Ferguson 2009: 172–183). Ferguson shows that in contexts such as Southern Africa where full employment may be an implausible aim, and where the state lacks capacity, policies that directly target citizens such as direct cash transfers and basic income, which have been propounded by prominent neoliberals (Friedman and Friedman, 1980: 119–124), are responses that merit serious consideration.

His general point, however, is not to argue that these policies are unequivocally good measures for combatting poverty. Rather, he suggests that in societal problem-solving we can use or repurpose neoliberal techniques, ideas, and practices. Thereby, we can put them to work "in the service of political projects very different from those usually associated with [neoliberalism]" (Ferguson, 2009: 183). Both Ferguson's specific point about the possible use of basic income and cash transfers, as well as his general point about the possibilities in repurposing neoliberal practices, are valid and thought-provoking. The focus of our anthology, however, is neither to find cases where the pursuit of neoliberal practices may be worth considering, nor is it to assemble new arts of government by repurposing neoliberal practices to progressive political aims. The premise of our contribution is that neoliberalism, in the sense of "market imperialism" that we have described above, is still *the* orthodox or *the* default approach to societal problem-solving, and that this orthodoxy often creates solutions that hurt people and our environment. We want to contrast cases where market imperialism has led to problematic consequences with alternative solutions that address the underlying problem more adequately.

All of our contrast cases analyze neoliberal normative frameworks of behavior created or sustained by the kind of problem-solving that we criticize. Our alternative cases, however, are chosen and analyzed because they in different ways and to various degrees challenge the idea of market imperialism. Over and beyond these two uniting features, some of the contrast cases involve other specific characteristics or arguments of neoliberalism as treated in this chapter. Likewise, some of the analyses focus more on neoliberal forms of knowledge or practices of the self. In order to emphasize these more specific connections with our portrait of neoliberalism in this chapter each of the case chapters will start with a brief framing remark. This remark will connect the contrast case in question back to relevant aspects of neoliberalism as portrayed in this chapter. Thereby we hope to show precisely what features of neoliberalism are at stake in each contrast case.

References

Alchian, A. A. 1950. "Uncertainty, evolution, and economic theory." *The Journal of Political Economy* 58 (3): 211–221.

Becker, Gary. 1978. "The economic approach to human behavior." In *The Economic Approach to Human Behavior*, edited by Gary Becker, 3–14. Chicago: University of Chicago Press.

    1981. *A Treatise on the Family*. Cambridge, Mass.: Harvard University Press.

    1993. *Human Capital: A Theoretical and Empirical Analysis with Special Reference to Education*. Third edition. Chicago: University of Chicago Press.

    1996. "The economic way of looking at life." In *Accounting for Tastes,* edited by Gary Becker, 139–156. Cambridge, Mass.: Harvard University Press.

Biebricher, Thomas. 2018. *The Political Theory of Neoliberalism*. Stanford: Stanford University Press.

Brenner, Neil, Jamie Peck and Nik Theodore. 2014. "New constitutionalism and variegated neo-liberalization." In *New Constitutionalism and World Order*, edited by Stephen Gill and A. Claire Cutler, 126–142. New York: Cambridge University Press.

Brown, Wendy. 2015. *Undoing the Demos: Neoliberalism's Stealth Revolution*. New York: Zone Books.

2019. *In the Ruins of Neoliberalism: The Rise of Antidemocratic Politics in the West*. New York: Columbia University Press.

Burgin, Angus. 2012. *The Great Persuasion: Reinventing Free Markets since the Depression*. Cambridge, Mass.: Harvard University Press.

Cerny, Philip G. 1997. "Paradoxes of the competition state: The dynamics of political globalization." *Government and Opposition* 32 (2): 251–274.

Dean, Mitchell. 2014. "Rethinking neoliberalism." *Journal of Sociology* 50 (2): 150–163.

Ferguson, James. 2009. "The uses of neoliberalism." *Antipode* 41: 166–184.

Friedman, Milton. 1962. *Capitalism and Freedom*. Chicago: University of Chicago Press.

Friedman, Milton, and Rose Friedman. 1982. *Free to Choose: A Personal Statement*. New York: Harcourt.

Foucault, Michel. 2003. *The Hermeneutics of the Self: Lectures at the collège de France 1981–1982*. New York: Palgrave Macmillan.

2007. *Security, Territory and Population. Lectures at the collège de France 1977–1978*. New York: Palgrave Macmillan.

2008. *The Birth of Biopolitics: Lectures at the collège de France 1978–1979*. New York: Palgrave Macmillan.

2010. *The Government of Self and Others: Lectures at the collège de France 1982–1983*. New York: Palgrave Macmillan.

Gauss, Gerald. 1996. *Justificatory Liberalism: An Essay on Epistemology and Political Theory*. New York: Oxford University Press.

Gray, John. 1987. "The economic approach to human behavior: its prospects and limitations." In *Economic Imperialism: The Economic Approach Applied Outside the Field of Economics*, edited by Gerhard Radnitzky and Peter Bernholz, 33–49. New York: Paragon House Publishers.

Harvey, David. 2007. *A Brief History of Neoliberalism*. Oxford: Oxford University Press.

Hayek, F. A. 1944. *The Road to Serfdom*. Chicago: University of Chicago Press.

1945. "The use of knowledge in society." *American Economic Review* 35 (4): 519–530.

1960. *The Constitution of Liberty*. Chicago: University of Chicago Press

1988. *The Fatal Conceit*. Chicago: University of Chicago Press.

Jensen, Michael C., and Willam H. Meckling. 1994. "The nature of man." *Journal of Applied Corporate Finance* 7 (2): 4–19.

Locke, John 1960 [1689]. *The Second Treatise of Government in Two Treatises of Government.* Edited by Peter Laslett. Cambridge: Cambridge University Press, 283–446.

Marx, Karl, and Frederich Engels. 1993. *The Communist Manifesto.* New York: International Publishers.

Mill, John Stuart. 1963 [1869]. "The subjection of women." In *Collected Works of John Stuart Mill,* edited by J. M. Robson. Toronto: University of Toronto Press.

Mirowski, Philip. 2009. "Postface: Defining neoliberalism." In *The Road From Mount Pelerin: The Making of the Neoliberal Thought Collective,* edited by Philip Mirowski and Dieter Plehwe, 1–42. Cambridge, Mass.: Harvard University Press.

Mirowski, Philip, and Dieter Plewhe, eds. 2009. *The Road from Mount Pelerin: The Making of the Neoliberal Thought Collective.* Cambridge, Mass.: Harvard University Press.

Nozick, Robert. 1974. *Anarchy, State, and Utopia.* Cambridge, Mass.: Blackwell.

Olsen, Niklas. 2019. *The Sovereign Consumer: A New Intellectual History of Neoliberalism.* New York: Palgrave Macmillan.

Piketty, Thomas. 2014. *Capital in the 21st Century.* Cambridge, Mass.: Harvard University Press

2020. *Capital and Ideology.* Cambridge, Mass.: Harvard University Press

Plewhe, Dieter. 2009. "Introduction." In *The Road from Mount Pelerin: The Making of the Neoliberal Thought Collective,* edited by Philip Mirowski and Dieter Plehwe, 1–42. Cambridge Mass.: Harvard University Press.

Radnitzky, Gerhard, and Peter Bernholz. 1987. *Economic Imperialism: The Economic Approach Applied Outside the Field of Economics.* New York: Paragon House Publishers.

Raffnsøe, Sverre, Marius Gudmand-Høyer, and Morten S. Thaning. 2016. *Michel Foucault: A Research Companion.* New York: Palgrave Macmillan.

Rawls, John. 2001. *Justice as Fairness: A Restatement.* Edited by Erin Kelly. New York: Columbia University Press

Slobodian, Quinn. 2018. *Globalists: The End of Empire and the Birth of Neoliberalism.* Cambridge, Mass.: Harvard University Press.

Slobodian, Quinn, and Dieter Plewhe. 2020. "Introduction." In *Nine Lives of Neoliberalism,* edited by Quinn Slobodian, Dieter Plewhe and Philip Mirowski, 1–17. London: Verso.

Slobodian, Quinn, Dieter Plewhe, and Philip Mirowski, eds. 2020. *Nine Lives of Neoliberalism*. London: Verso.

Smith, Adam. 1976 [1759]. *The Theory of Moral Sentiments*. Oxford: Clarendon Press.

  1976 [1776]. *An Inquiry into the Nature and Causes of the Wealth of Nations*. Oxford: Clarendon Press.

Spencer, Herbert. 1865. *Principles of Biology*. New York: D. Appleton and Company

Stigler, George. 1979. "Why have the socialists been winning?" *In Ordo* 30: 61–88.

Streeck, Wolfgang. 2017. *Buying Time: The Delayed Crisis of Democratic Capitalism*. London: Verso.

Willgerodt, Hans. 2006. "Der Neoliberalismus – Entstehung, Kampfbegriff und Meinungsstreit." *In Ordo* 57: 47–88.

Williamson, John. 2004. "A short history of the Washington Consensus." Paper commissioned by Fundación CIDOB for the conference, "From the Washington Consensus towards a New Global Governance." Barcelona, September 24–25, 2004. www.iie.com/publications/papers/williamson0904-2.pdf

PART I

Our World

3 | *Where Should Food Come From?*

HILARY B. KING AND ANDREA RISSING

Most people who eat aren't able to see much of our contemporary food system. This is deliberate. As world population has grown, so too has the food system become increasingly elaborate, specialized, and industrialized, all to the point that even those who live near fields or farms can likely only see a part of where our food comes from. This chapter explains a bit of how this system works, and what values it prioritizes. King and Rissing suggest that much of the food system is guided by a sort of market imperialism that values growth in yields and profit over other values that we might associate with food, values such as nutrition, variety, and environmental sustainability. It also demonstrates how neoliberal marketization does not function independently of public government but is sustained and developed by government interventions. By contrast, King and Rissing look at nonindustrial contemporary food systems to show what alternatives might look like, and to illustrate just how well they can address many of the values and aspirations we have for food systems. The alternative approach with its emphasis on food sovereignty, challenges the international frameworks of neoliberal governance that prioritizes the stimulation of market competition.

3.1 Introduction

When we teach classes about sustainable food systems, our students often arrive knowledgeable and anxious. They've seen UN graphs of predicted population growth and they worry about our collective ability to ensure an adequate global food supply. Many bring informed questions about food security and personal commitments to food justice. Their concern often exists in uneasy tension with personal experiences of alimentary abundance. They've shopped at supermarkets carrying mangoes from Mexico, quinoa from Peru, and beef from Japan for their entire lives. Those invested in food justice and sustainability may feel compelled to eschew such global luxuries. They may favor more local and seasonal fare, shopping at farmers markets, or asking their universities' dining halls to buy from nearby farms. For many, figuring out where their food should come from is of paramount concern.

In this chapter, we explore two different paradigms – ways of thinking about – the question, "where should food come from?" Starting in the twentieth century, many US scientists and other agricultural experts answered the question, "where should food come from?" by saying, "from the most productive farms possible." This belief led to a nationwide focus on industrializing agriculture which meant using machinery and chemicals to increase yields to unprecedented levels. At its heart, agricultural industrialization is a process of simplifying farm operations and maximizing their outputs. In the US, industrialization predates the country's movement toward neoliberal capitalism, and it makes certain elements of neoliberal food systems possible. Today, the neoliberal view that markets are the best way to determine value is the *dominant paradigm*[1] for thinking about food systems. During the same period, other scientists and farmers maintained or re-adopted strategies centered on different principles: smaller-scale farms and diversified, environmentally sustainable production systems working under the *food sovereignty paradigm*. These folks answered the question of where food should come from by saying, "from many people growing many species in environmentally beneficial and culturally appropriate ways."

We ground our exploration by looking at how these two paradigms approach the most widely produced crop in the world: corn. More than 164 countries produced a total of more than 1 billion metric tons of it in 2013.[2] Some 4.5 billion people in almost one hundred developing countries rely on maize for 30 percent of their food calories.[3] Corn is a *staple crop*. Looking at how different people grow it gives insight into how different paradigms operate on the ground. The first location, the Corn Belt in the United States, is heralded as the world's breadbasket. Working primarily under the dominant paradigm, it is home to some of the most productive farmers on the planet. We compare that system with corn production in Mexico, where people

---

[1] We adapt this terminology and framing from Martinez-Torres and Rosset, 2010.
[2] CropTrust, 2021.   [3] Shiferaw et al., 2011.

first domesticated corn from wild grasses more than 9,000 years ago, and where many farmers work within the food sovereignty paradigm today.

We begin this piece with the conviction that people working within both paradigms do share goals. They want to build agricultural systems that provide healthy food to everyone, do not deplete the environment, and support the people who work within them. The differences between the paradigms become clear when we look at the strategies people use to meet these shared goals and their reasons for adopting those strategies. The dominant and food sovereignty paradigms approach the question of food production with different baseline assumptions about what is important.

As the Introduction to this volume demonstrates, neoliberalism is not just one thing. In this chapter, we focus on the tendency of neoliberal capitalism to intensify and expand market relations.[4] This "market imperialism" applies market logics to areas of life where they had previously not been as present. In this model, nearly everything becomes fair game for buying and selling, which is assumed to be inherently desirable. In food systems, the current dominant paradigm was made possible by industrialization, which resulted in tremendous surpluses in many agricultural commodities, the most spectacular being corn. Early efforts to industrialize agricultural production predated the golden age of neoliberalism by nearly a century. The two processes are linked because neoliberal perspectives in agriculture could only become dominant as a result of the previous successes of industrialization. Neoliberalism and industrialization are related, but they are not the same.

Industrialization laid the foundation for a food system based on the buying and selling of agricultural commodities as opposed to the growing and eating of food. The dominant paradigm assumes that applying market logics to food production will lead to the best food systems because the best farms are those that grow and sell the most. The food sovereignty paradigm assumes the best farms are multifaceted operations that pursue environmental and community goals in addition to economic ones. These different logics shape the strategies used by proponents of each paradigm. In assuming that the best food systems would result from building an agricultural system that

---

[4] Akram-Lodhi, 2018: 274.

maximizes exchange of agricultural goods for money, the dominant paradigm ignores crucial nonmarket values. The food sovereignty paradigm includes these lost values because it answers the question of "where should food come from" from a different starting place.

3.2 A Dominant Model: Iowa's Ever-Expanding Grain

Corn has been the top crop in Iowa for more than 150 years running! And that's not because Iowa farmers just can't think of anything better to grow. It's because Iowa is the best place on the planet to grow corn.

("Corn FAQs," Iowa Corn Website)

If you know anything about Iowa, it is probably that Iowa grows a lot of corn. And if you take Interstate 80, from Des Moines east to Iowa City, or Interstate 35, from Mason City south to Ames, or any highway in any part of Iowa, that this is an understatement is obvious. Rolling out of town, Iowa's sheer productivity surrounds you. If you drive in late summer, you'll see dizzyingly precise rows of straight corn stalks whizzing by with golden husks drying and silken tassels waving. For miles at a time, glinting silos storing last year's harvest are the only shapes breaking up these unending corn fields. Its vastness can make this landscape feel inevitable.

In 2020, the average corn farmer in Iowa grew 184 bushels of corn per acre. That means that Iowa's 86,000 farms produced 2.3 billion bushels of corn.[5] For some, so few people producing so much grain proves the system's efficiency. It seems incontrovertible that, as Iowa Corn boasts on its website, "Iowa is the best place on the planet to grow corn." Iowa Corn is an amalgamation of the Iowa Corn Growers Association and the Iowa Corn Promotion Board. These organizations and many others exist to support industrial grain production and to "create opportunities for long-term Iowa corn grower profitability," as their website explains. According to these groups and many others, Iowa is *exactly* where this global staple should be coming from.

This was the shape of the landscape that Amanda was hoping to disrupt with her new farm. Having grown up among these grain fields, she envisioned a different kind of agricultural abundance. Rather than a commodity farm, she wanted to establish a food farm. Where her

[5] USDA NASS, 2020.

family and neighbors prized their ability to grow tens of thousands of bushels of corn, Amanda's sights were set on growing smaller amounts of many different types of grain – wheat, oats, rye, barley – and raising sheep, turkeys, hogs, and chickens alongside these crops. If things went well her first few years, she planned to expand into annual vegetable production.

Many things did go well for her in the first few years. She accomplished numerous goals; transitioning some of her family's longstanding conventional grain fields into organic production, adding new grain enterprises to extend rotations and reintroduce diversity on a monocultural landscape, raising livestock whose lifecycles educated her daughter about biology and whose meat nourished her community. Amanda was eating better, seeing more earthworms in her soil, and feeling more connected with her work than she ever had before. By many metrics, her farm had exceeded the goals she had hoped to achieve in her anticipated time frame.

One way in which the farm was performing differently than she had hoped, however, was its bottom line. Amanda priced her products high enough to cover her input expenses and net some profit to boot, but she still wasn't making as much money as she had hoped. She brought this concern to her trusted mentors, older farmers who knew her family and wanted her to succeed. They advised her to focus on corn production again. This advice broke Amanda's heart; she wanted to feed people, but people can't eat the corn grown in commodity systems. Its value lies in being a raw input, not a nourishing food. But as her mentors explained, corn was where the reliable money was, and if she wanted to achieve any of her other ecological goals, she first needed to make sure she was maximizing her farm's profits. Pursuing ecological benefits and community resilience through her farm was well and good, they said, but these ideas could only flow from a profitable farm business, so she needed to focus on selling corn for now. Everything else would follow.

Amanda's original motivating vision and her mentors' perspective represent two different approaches to thinking about how farms should operate – are they holistic vehicles powering beneficial socio-environmental processes, or are they primarily businesses? The second of these perspectives represents the dominant view of agriculture across Iowa. Although it seems obvious to say, "farming is a business," this viewpoint took some time and no little effort to establish. It came about through a structural and cultural remaking of American agriculture during the twentieth century, a necessary precursor to processes of neoliberalization. The people who shaped Iowa's agriculture wanted to create a thriving agricultural system. By many measures, they succeeded tremendously. Iowa is, after all, the United States' leading producer of corn. Iowa grows more corn than most countries, including Mexico. The trouble comes when the idea of a "thriving agricultural system" is uncoupled from the goal of growing food for people to eat and taken instead to mean "growing as much as possible."

The full economics of Iowa's corn production is complex and confusing even to many people who work within it. Neoliberal capitalist threads weave with other types of economic values to create this system, and it would not be accurate to reduce all commodity agriculture to neoliberalism. Nonetheless, we can see three key dynamics lying at its heart. First, most people who work in agriculture understand their primary goal to be *maximizing* and *increasing* the amount of grain grown. Second, federal and state level governments alike have supported this goal through targeted economic incentives and safety nets, funded research programs, and educational programming. Finally, private agribusiness corporations, not the family farmers planting and harvesting the grain, reap the most profit from agriculture. These dynamics reveal an underlying belief that beneficial outcomes can best be achieved through private market relations, indicating the extent to which neoliberal capitalist values have influenced the sector.

To fully understand how Iowa's current corn systems came to be, we really need to start with the notoriously exploitative land treaties that the United States government made in the 1830s with the Ioway, Sauk, Meskwaki, and other indigenous tribes. As these groups of people were forcibly displaced, white settlers with steel plows moved onto their lands. Settler colonialism set in motion all of the agricultural changes that followed, starting with plowing the prairies whose roots had anchored the region's fertile soils for centuries. The eminently standardizable farm grid system all but eliminated the wild carpet of native tallgrass species in a few short decades, as well as the bison populations that were integral to that system.

In the early twentieth century, this gridded landscape itself came to be seen as "wild" by newly minted agricultural professionals who set out to improve US agriculture by transferring business logics onto farm realities. In 1905, Iowa State College in Story County, IA launched the country's first agricultural engineering department. In her book, *Every Farm a Factory,* historian Deborah Fitzgerald tells the story of how the young men who graduated from this program (and similar programs across the Midwest) joined with the country's first agricultural economists to modernize the countryside. These young men were products of one of the federal government's most important educational investments: the land-grant university system. They were also the first generation of professional agricultural experts, and they believed strongly that in order to stay relevant and competitive, farmers needed to start treating their farms like businesses, like "factories for producing things like pork and wheat."[6] They thought that most problems in agriculture were because farmers weren't sufficiently attentive to tracking their receipts or keeping formal financial records; they saw their job as educating farmers to think of their farms primarily as businesses as opposed to places of both life and work.

Taking lessons learned from newly industrialized urban manufac-turing, they spread out across county fairs and field days to teach farmers to calculate enterprise budgets and labor income, to embrace the "quantitative spirit"[7] that they saw as powering the success of factories in cities. These experts of modernist economics worked hard to lay the groundwork from which Amanda's mentors' advice would spring a hundred years later. By explicitly redefining farming as predominately a business venture, their early twentieth-century efforts to map business sector logic onto the farm sector set the stage for the winnowing of scope and expansion of scale that characterized agricultural industrialization for the next century. When Amanda's mentors honed in on her bottom line instead of her earthworm count, they were exhibiting the lasting impact of these early agricultural experts.

Farming in the United States changed rapidly again in the years following World War II due to the coupled roles of agricultural tech-nologies and national agricultural policy. After the war, nitrate factories originally built to make bombs began manufacturing synthetic nitrogen fertilizer instead. And later in the twentieth century, genetic technologies created corn that could withstand applications of herbicides like

[6] Fitzgerald, 2003: 50.   [7] ibid., 35.

glyphosate.[8] These technological developments did not take place in a vacuum, but rather targeted specific crops like corn, because those were what the federal government incentivized for development via geopolitically motivated subsidies.[9] The vast majority of American farmers, the actual people who grow this grain, have seen vanishingly little of the value generated by their labor. Rather, wealth has accrued to the supply-side agribusinesses who sell seeds, chemicals, and fertilizers to farmers, and the processing-side agribusinesses who buy corn as a raw commodity to turn it into finished commodities like livestock feed or ethanol.[10] By growing things that Archer-Daniels-Midland or Cargill couldn't turn into something new to sell, Amanda was reintroducing diverse economic values onto an agricultural landscape that typically only values commodification. When she ran into challenges, the people who cared about her urged her to focus on growing more corn in order to make more money. In the context of her situation, this advice makes sense and reflects her mentors' experience, concern, and knowledge. We live in a world, then, where telling someone who lives in a sea of corn that they should grow more corn is sound advice. This advice is sound because of the success of neoliberal capitalism in determining the shape of agricultural systems in Iowa – there was little room for the alternative vision and logic employed by Amanda.

Unlike some of the other cases in this book, the consequences envisioned by the historical and contemporary architects of Iowa's agricultural systems played out, in certain ways, exactly as they had hoped. The Corn Belt was designed to be a modern marvel of productivity, and it achieved this goal with flying colors. In 1900, Iowa farmers averaged 45 bushels of corn per acre; in 2000, they averaged 144 bushels per acre. In 2016, for the first time ever, Iowa's statewide corn average exceeded 200 bushels per acre.[11] In the words of the Iowa Farm Bureau, the state is now "a farm and agriculture powerhouse."[12]

---

[8] The story of mid-century American agricultural development has been well documented; for an incomplete list, see Winders, 2009; Conkin, 2008; Cochrane, 1993; Kloppenburg, 2004; Olmstead and Rhode, 2008; Weis, 2007. For the international effects of US agricultural technologies and farm and food policy, see Cullather, 2013; Patel, 2012; Latham, 2011; Friedmann and McMichael, 1989.

[9] During the Cold War, the US was particularly interested in exporting food aid to countries considered at risk of "falling" to communism (Patel, 2012).

[10] See Magdoff, Foster, and Buttel, 2000, as well as other essays in this volume.

[11] All statistics publicly available at: https://quickstats.nass.usda.gov.

[12] Iowa Farm Bureau, 2021.

What this way of framing Iowa's agricultural successes leaves out is everything other than grain yields. When success is determined by harvest size, other indicators – such as water quality, human health, topsoil levels, pollinator numbers, or rural communities – might all be in distress, but the system can still be deemed successful as long as yields are increasing and money is being made.

Environmental consequences of large-scale, monocultural production get a lot of attention elsewhere, but they are significant enough to warrant mentioning here as well. For example, maximizing grain yields depends upon regular applications of synthetic nitrogen fertilizer and pesticides, which can wreak havoc on soil microbial communities below ground and pollinator and wildlife communities above ground. An intertwined issue of annual crop production is the fact that fields more often than not lay bare over winter. Without roots in the ground to take them up, soil-bacteria-produced nitrate joins with leftover chemicals during wet springs to flow into waterways. These pollutants flow south from Iowa through the Mississippi River to the Gulf of Mexico, where they contribute to a roughly 6,000 square mile hypoxic sea, one of the world's largest "dead zones."

In addition to environmental consequences, agricultural industrialization is also associated with detrimental impacts on rural communities, such as poorer school quality, higher rates of poverty, and lower wages. One of the first studies to document this phenomenon was conducted in California in the 1940s by an anthropologist named Walter Goldschmidt.[13] Building on his studies, social scientists have confirmed the association between large scale, industrial agriculture and nationwide declines in rural community quality of life.[14] While the first generation of professional agricultural economists fully anticipated that there would be fewer farmers once agriculture modernized – indeed, they saw this as desirable since they considered small farms inefficient – they likely did not anticipate the effects of this decline. Communities saw a drop in the number of churches, poorer quality of schools, and lower civic participation once large farms became the norm. Industrializing agriculture affects communities by impacting the number and quality of jobs available, by changing where inputs and products are bought and sold, by straining nearby ecosystems, and

[13] Goldschmidt, 1947.   [14] Lobao and Stofferahn, 2008.

by harming human health.[15] This hollowing out of rural economies is a result of a view of development that wanted to move people off of farms and into factories.

Growing this much corn outstrips actual human demand. However, this doesn't matter in a system designed to turn corn into profits. The self-proclaimed breadbasket of the world produces more ethanol than food and feeds more livestock than people. The companies that benefit by buying corn as a raw commodity from farmers and processing it into more saleable forms found new ways to make people pay to consume corn. After harvest, some corn is turned into familiar forms like cornmeal. Far more of it, however, is turned into livestock feed, ethanol to power cars, bioplastics for consumer products, and processed food additives like syrups and starches. Where minimally processed corn is an important source of carbohydrates, vitamins, and minerals, these processed corn products are more likely to make you sick if consumed frequently.[16]

So should food be coming from the most productive systems? As an example of the dominant paradigm, Iowa's astounding production exists not in spite of its negative effects on the environment, human health, and rural communities; rather, it is made possible through these externalities. The idea that large scale, mechanized grain production pollutes waterways, harms pollinator populations, and contributes to climate change may be familiar. What can be harder to see is the threads tying these negative consequences to the economic logic that underpins them. When Amanda's mentors encouraged her to put aside her goals of a diverse farm and grow corn instead, they were encouraging her to act more like a business person. Their advice not only explicitly communicated that the primary goal of a farm should be to make money, not food, it also implicitly communicated a belief that positive ecological and community effects will follow in the footsteps of a successful agricultural business once it is established. Their conversation epitomized the forces that have shaped Iowa agriculture over the past century. "In neoliberal capitalism," as development scholar Haroon Akram-Lodhi states, "commodification can be presented as a near moral imperative."[17] Iowa's agricultural dominance, as well as its negative externalities, have both arisen out of a single-minded pursuit

---

[15] Lobao and Stofferahn, 2008: 223, 225–226.   [16] Goran et al., 2013.
[17] Akram-Lodhi, 2018: 281.

of ever-increasing grain yields. This orientation makes sense when viewed through neoliberal economic logics focused on profitability, growth, and trust that businesses serve as vectors for social good. It has driven Iowa to produce unprecedented amounts of corn which has, in turn, made some agribusinesses unprecedentedly wealthy. This orientation, however, has not succeeded in the goals we believe its practitioners hold: food systems that provide food for everyone, benefit the environment, and support the people who work within it.

3.3 Food Sovereignty in Action: Symbiotic Production of Mexican Maize

People started thinking about where corn should come from long before the first kernels were planted in the land that is now Iowa. About 9,000 years ago, indigenous people in what is now Mexico bred and crossbred teosinte, a wild grass with tiny, barely-edible kernels, into something much more like the contemporary yellow kernels we know today.[18] Corn continues to be central to life in this part of the world. In the Mayan creation story, the *Popul Vuh*, the first humans are made of maize. It is common to hear Mexicans self-identify as "people of the corn."[19] This saying demonstrates both corn consumption and the role of maize as an important social, cultural, and political symbol. The average Mexican consumes about 267 grams of corn per day, the highest per capita consumption in the world.[20] Corn is what many people think of when they think of food.

In Mexico, the centrality of maize has profoundly shaped the systems that people have evolved to grow, distribute, and eat it. Unlike the US focus on growing inedible field corn for sale, in many parts of Mexico small-scale farmers have continued to grow corn, beans, and other crops for sale *and* for their own consumption. However, pressures of neoliberal economic reforms have made their choice to continue along this path challenging. The implementation of NAFTA (North American Free Trade Agreement) in 1994 is one example. Guided by the belief that more trade is always better, NAFTA began the process of opening Mexican markets to corn imports from the United States. Many Mexicans saw this as a threat to both farmer livelihoods and the maize that they cultivate, a view

[18] Doebley, 2004.   [19] Pilcher, 1998.   [20] Ranum et al., 2014.

espoused by members of the EZLN, the Zapatista Army of National Liberation, which launched a peasant uprising on January 1, 1994, the same day that NAFTA went into effect. Small-scale farmers and their supporters have fought against neoliberal food policies with the call, *"Sin maíz, no hay país!"* (Without corn, there is no country!). They argue that "food is different" than other commodities,[21] so it cannot and should not be evaluated by the same logics that govern trade of other goods. In this way, many resist market imperialism when it comes to foodstuffs.

Many Mexican farmers, activists, and other citizens have coalesced around *food sovereignty* as an organizing principle for an alternative food system. This term, coined by the international peasant group, La Vía Campesina, refers to "the right of peoples to healthy and culturally appropriate food produced through sustainable methods and their right to define their own food and agriculture systems" grounded in small-scale production.[22] As of 2021, 182 local and national organizations in 81 countries from Africa, Asia, Europe, and the Americas, represent approximately 200 million farmers through this organization founded in 1993.[23]

The logics of the food sovereignty paradigm lead to different food system practices and outcomes than the neoliberal market logics that we just examined. Rather than seeing corn (and other food) as something solely to be bought or sold, a food sovereignty paradigm positions corn as food to be eaten, a carrier of cultural heritage to be protected, and part of a connected human and environmental system. Because of the different way they understand what corn *is*, people working within the food sovereignty paradigm advocate for community-controlled land, prioritize diversified production for local markets, decry seed patents, and champion farmers as stewards of productive resources that can lead to inclusive economic development.[24] Within food sovereignty, the power to shape how food is produced becomes a human right; food itself is no longer a simple commodity.

In order to see what food production can look like under a food sovereignty model, we look at maize production in Chiapas, Mexico. Margarita, a renowned maize grower in Chiapas, is a diminutive

---

[21] Rosset, 2006.   [22] Via Campesina, 2021.   [23] ibid., 2021.
[24] Martinez-Torres and Rosset, 2010.

woman in her mid-60s. Margarita's farm outside of Teopisca changes throughout the year, but each winter, rows of tall, crispy, brown maize stalks hold up bean plants. She walks along plucking the sun-baked pods; some pop open to spill out purplish-black beans in the basket. In a couple of weeks, she will return to harvest the maize cobs currently drying in their husks. Insects chirp, birds fly overhead, dozens of trees and grasses wave in the wind.

Margarita's farming knowledge comes from a long legacy of self-sufficient farmers; it remains an important way of life for many Mexicans, particularly indigenous people. Chiapas is home to 14 percent of Mexico's indigenous population;[25] almost 28 percent of the state's population speaks an indigenous language.[26] The state's land ranges from coast to jungle to highland mountain ranges, a diversity that is not universally amenable to large-scale agricultural industrialization. In this context, elements of "traditional" agricultural systems have remained in place, operating alongside and in opposition to the logics of the dominant paradigm. Though Mexico imports a lot of yellow corn from the United States for animal feed, Mexico's maize farmers produce 90 percent of the white corn used for the staple-food tortillas consumed in the country.[27] Much of this corn is still grown on farms like Margarita's. More than 83 percent of Mexico's 2.8 million maize producers have less than 5 hectares of land but cultivate more than half of the planted area and grow more than a third of the country's maize.[28]

Despite this level of production, many Mexican farmers like Margarita face intense pressure to "modernize" their production systems. Calls to "modernize" these farms are often based on increasing economic efficiency as measured by marketable output like bushels of corn per acre. This call may appear reasonable when examining differences in production levels: in Chiapas, farmers averaged 1.8 metric tons of maize per hectare between 2014 and 2017; in Iowa, farmers averaged 12.5 metric tons per hectare between 2015 and 2017.[29] Within this context, arguments for the benefits of the dominant paradigm – to produce more – can seem self-evident. However, a food sovereignty lens encourages us to look beyond yield for additional criteria that can shape how we evaluate food production systems.

[25] INEGI, 2015a.   [26] ibid., 2015b.   [27] Zahniser et al., 2019.
[28] Eakin et al., 2014.   [29] Zahniser et al., 2019.

Though not developed to meet a twenty-first-century definition of sustainable farming, Margarita's farm is a living vision of productive and environmentally regenerative agricultural systems. Small-scale, diversified farms like Margarita's can outperform monocultures in the amount of *food* that they produce. Margarita grows corn, beans, squash, and other plants together in a complex polyculture, a crop system commonly referred to as a *milpa*. Sustainable farming techniques like this have been practiced for 8,000 years in Mexico, are highly adaptable, and produce large amounts of food.[30] In Mexico, one hectare planted with maize, beans, and squash produces as much food as 1.73 hectares planted only in maize.[31] An acre of corn will produce more corn than an acre planted with multiple food plants, but acres that produce *food* to eat rather than *crops* to be sold can produce more total food.

Looking at Margarita's farm as an example of food sovereignty in action helps us think with a wider understanding of human economic motivations than neoliberal market imperialism assumes to exist. Margarita and other farmers practicing food sovereignty can be seen as a puzzle for the neoliberal market economists who assume everyone's goal is to make the most profit. This assumption imagines a particular kind of economic actor. However, Margarita regularly pursues goals other than making money. Margarita's farm was part of the 75 percent of Mexico's farms that grew a portion of crops for home consumption in 2018.[32] Farmers use *milpa* systems to grow food for themselves, which is an example of subsistence production. Formal market measures such as the Gross Domestic Product entirely miss much of the value of subsistence *milpa* production because farmers do not sell all of what they produce.

The logic behind subsistence production is hard for neoliberal economists to make sense of, but it makes a lot of sense for small-scale farmers. *Milpa* production helps farmers like Margarita meet many different kinds of needs. Upon harvest, they have options with what to do with the fruits of their labor: if prices are attractive, they can sell crops and earn money; if not, they can eat the food itself; and in either case, they can save some of the seeds to plant again in the spring. These crops hold multiple kinds of value. If we evaluate food systems solely through yields of corn that markets convert into money, these

---

[30] Ford and Nigh, 2015.   [31] Altieri, 2012.   [32] INEGI, 2019.

other values and logics are hidden and entirely unvalued. Moreover, the rationales that lead people to practice activities such as *milpa* production also become invisible. The food sovereignty paradigm contends that producing for subsistence is as valid as choosing to produce for a market. Market imperialism, however, disregards subsistence production. Under neoliberal thinking, food grown and eaten but not sold literally does not count as part of the economy even though billions of people around the world eat in this way.

Milpa systems not only produce a lot of food, they also provide symbiotic ecosystem services. The crops complement each other environmentally and nutritionally. Corn, for instance, takes a lot of nitrogen out of the soil, while bean plants return nitrogen to the soil. At the same time, bean plants, which seek sun by sending out tendrils, climb up the hearty maize stalks. Nutritionally, beans contain certain nutrients, like lysine and tryptophan, which combine with nutrients in maize to form complete proteins when eaten together. Other common crops in a *milpa* include squash, full of vitamins, avocados, which provide important fats, as well as chilis and tomatoes. Planting different crops together can also do some of the work that pesticides and herbicides do in places like Iowa. Rather than rely on purchased fertilizers that supply nitrogen, *milpa* production systems typically have on-farm composting to maintain soil fertility and also rely on plants' own abilities to supply appropriate nutrients when grown in concert. Farmers use traditional knowledge to control pest populations rather than apply expensive and harmful pesticides,[33] that are common and basically compulsory in the kind of large-scale monocultures common under the dominant paradigm. These smaller-scale, more diversified systems are less likely to create large-scale environmental externalities, disasters that we collectively deal with but that are not easily included in most economic calculations.

The food sovereignty paradigm includes values other than profits which benefit human communities. One of these is plant genetic diversity. Over thousands of years, humans have developed countless plant varieties that thrive in specific contexts – for maize, these include varieties that better withstand drought, are less vulnerable to certain pests, have stronger stalks, amazing colors, or tastier consistencies preferred for certain dishes. Each of these qualities is unique to certain

---

[33] Morales and Perfecto, 2000.

seeds, and the knowledge of what is special about each of them is held
in the minds of people who grow them. This diversity is immense;
scientists estimate that in 2010, Mexico's *campesino* farmers grew all
fifty-nine varieties of native maize, and more than 1.38 billion genetically distinct corn plants.[34] A major critique of monoculture is that it
decreases the varieties of plants that we grow. This leaves us, as a
species, more vulnerable to shocks. If people like Margarita cease being
farmers, both the seeds that they cultivate and the knowledge that they
have disappear. We end up with fewer varieties of seeds and fewer
people who know the conditions in which they do well. Though
technologically incredible seedbanks like the Svalbard Global Seed
Vault keep seeds alive, it is often not the seeds themselves but the
pairing of them with people's experiential cultivation knowledge that
makes these varieties so valuable.[35] Considering climate change, the
present seems like a bad time to allow 9,000 years of human–maize
innovation to disappear just so that we can grow more of a single,
high-yielding variety of corn.

In many ways, Margarita's beautiful farm, tucked into the moun-
tains outside of Teopisca, Chiapas, is a potent symbol of resistance to a
dominant, neoliberal food paradigm. The social and cultural value of
food systems are inherent in a food sovereignty paradigm which insists
on integrating values such as communal knowledge, cultural history,
and ecosystem resilience. Farmers and eaters show commitments to
these goals in myriad ways, challenging visions of food systems based
on neoliberal privatization, growth, and technological "progress."
They also do so through the creation of and participation in alternative
market spaces. Margarita is an active member of a network in and
around San Cristobal de las Casas, Chiapas that puts on a thrice-
weekly agroecological market, *Tianguis Comida Sana y Cercana*
(Local, Healthy Food Market). This network brings together a diverse
group of small-scale farmers and eaters who want to build more
transparent, diversified, localized, and regenerative food systems. In
spaces like this one, consumers and producers support rural livelihoods
and sustainable agriculture through purchases, expanding access to
fresh fruits, vegetables and other processed goods. They host educational activities that highlight regenerative agricultural production,
explore Mexico's agricultural history, celebrate indigenous farmers

[34] Bellon et al., 2018.   [35] Nazarea, 2005.

and their lifeways, and examine ways in which neoliberal globalization can threaten their existence. Through these practices, proponents of food sovereignty re-embed food systems.

The logics of food sovereignty, explored through this example of small-scale *milpa* production, present us with alternative answers to the question of where food should come from. Under a food sovereignty paradigm, the environmental benefits of *milpa* systems, the subsistence value of crops, the maintenance of lifeways like Margarita's, and the production of food for eating, are fundamental metrics for evaluating food systems. The paradigm of food sovereignty allows us to account for and to take into account a diversity of economic, environmental, and social aspects of food systems as we work to envision where food can and should come from. Margarita, equipped with varied metrics that span economic, social, and environmental criteria, would offer Amanda different advice than her mentors in Iowa because of the paradigm in which she works.

3.4 Conclusion

In this chapter we have seen that growing the same crop under different paradigms produces different results. We began with the conviction that people working within both the dominant and food sovereignty paradigms share goals, including creating food systems that provide enough food for everyone, that do not deplete the environment, and that benefit the people working within them. We have argued that these paradigms have different baseline assumptions that shape their strategies for meeting these goals. The paradigms' assumptions diverge starkly regarding the appropriate roles that business logics can and should play within food production. These differences also extend to ideas about what *else* we should consider as we answer where we want food to come from.

The dominant paradigm assumes that market exchange will reliably ensure that the above goals are met. Shaped by neoliberal logics, market imperialism has led the dominant model to valorize food systems based on their ability to produce, buy, and sell ever-increasing amounts of corn from an ever-decreasing number of ever-larger farms. Within these systems, fewer people farm, but they set new records for corn production. In turn, the buying and selling of these greater yields is taken as an obvious marker of the system's success. In this context,

Amanda's diverse assortment of grains and livestock are seen not as food sources, but as insufficiently profitable enterprises. Commodity crops result from a food system focused on profit rather than on feeding people, which results in disastrous effects on the environment and human health (including for the farmers). This focus derives from the market imperialism thread of neoliberal approaches.

In contrast, the food sovereignty paradigm expands the criteria that we can include in answering a question like where food should come from. Within it, a wide variety of metrics, including economic, social, and environmental ones, are necessary for determining success and evaluating what makes a desirable food system. Under a food sovereignty paradigm, measures like the total amount of food produced, the utilization of ecosystem services between plants, the lack of environmental externalities, and the value of maintaining farmer knowledge and livelihoods can all be included as legitimate metrics of success. When farmers focus on producing food, rather than on selling crops, their relationship to farming systems and the rewards contained therein changes. Diversified production can both produce more food and do so in ways that make use of ecological relationships and ecosystem services. Many of these farmers see the food that they produce as both for their own consumption *and* as part of maintaining natural environments and lifeways. Under a food sovereignty paradigm, these farmers seek protection from the corporate practices and trade agreements that threaten their ability to maintain farms and food systems based on the aforementioned principles. The food sovereignty paradigm advocates policies that enable that prioritization. This requires rejecting the logics of neoliberal market imperialism that boil down many different criteria to marketization.

Ultimately, to answer the question of where food should come from, we need a more expansive conceptual vocabulary to help us evaluate the kinds of food systems we want to build. Food sovereignty is a starting point of where to find inspiration for these broader ideas. More varied ideas can help us evaluate the thousands of food system models that people are currently experimenting with and building. As we see in Mexico, Margarita's version of food sovereignty is one. Even in the heart of the dominant paradigm in Iowa, what Amanda is building is another.

Where you live, there are likely many more. People all over are searching for ways to expand the values that we consider when evaluating where our food should come from. Agricultural cooperatives, both for farmers and for consumers, bring people together to pool resources like skills, money, and property to produce diverse and flourishing food systems that focus on food to eat. Community-supported agriculture programs let people sign up for a weekly food box subscription and help farmers access capital during different points in a growing season. Many of us increasingly plant our own tomatoes. Like us, you are probably glad you don't have to produce everything that you eat, but these practices still reshape what we understand food production to entail. Engaging with our food systems in these kinds of ways can help us all to see the diverse possibilities and permutations that are possible beyond simple calculations of profit and loss. Rather than use the same dominant, market-oriented thinking that produced some of our culinary mess, using the food sovereignty paradigm helps us grow toward more prosperous, and delicious, food futures.

References

Akram-Lodhi, H. A. 2018. "Old wine in new bottles: Enclosure, neoliberal capitalism and postcolonial politics." *Routledge Handbook of Postcolonial Politics* 614: 274–288. https://doi.org/10.4324/9781315671192

Altieri, M. A., F. R. Funes-Monzote, and P. Petersen. 2012. "Agroecologically efficient agricultural systems for smallholder farmers: contributions to food sovereignty." *Agronomy for Sustainable Development* 32: 1–13.

Baker, L. 2013. *Corn Meets Maize: Food Movements and Markets in Mexico*. Lanham, MD: Rowman and Littlefield Publishers.

Bellon, M. R., A., Mastretta-Yanes, A., Ponce-Mendoza, D., Ortiz-Santamaría, O., Oliveros-Galindo, H., Perales, F., Acevedo, F., and Sarukhán, J. 2018. "Evolutionary and food supply implications of ongoing maize domestication by Mexican campesinos." *Proceedings of the Royal Society B*, 285 (1885): 1–10. https://doi.org/10.1098/rspb.2018.1049

Cochrane, W. W. 1993. *The Development of American Agriculture: A Historical Analysis* (2nd ed.). Minneapolis: University of Minnesota Press.

Conkin, P. 2008. *A Revolution Down on the Farm: The Transformation of American Agriculture Since 1929*. Minneapolis: University Press of Kentucky.

Crop Trust. 2021. "Maize". Accessed June 9, 2021. www.croptrust.org/
    crop/maize/.
Cullather, N. 2010. *The Hungry World: America's Cold War Battle against
    Poverty in Asia*. Cambridge: Harvard University Press.
Dimitri, C., A., Effland, and N. Conklin, 2005. "The 20th Century
    Transformation of US Agriculture and Farm Policy." www.ers.usda
    .gov/media/259572/eib3_1_.pdf
Doebley J. 2004. "The genetics of maize evolution." *Annual Review of
    Genetics* 38: 37–59. doi:10.1146/annurev.genet.38.072902.092425
Eakin, H., K. Appendini, H. Perales, and S. Sweeney. 2015. "Correlates of
    maize land and livelihood change among maize farming households in
    Mexico." *World Development* 70: 78–91.
Fitzgerald, D. K. 2003. *Every Farm a Factory: The Industrial Ideal in
    American Agriculture*. New Haven: Yale University Press.
Friedmann, H., and P. McMichael, 1989. "Agriculture and the state system:
    The rise and decline of national agriculture, 1870 to the present."
    Sociologia Ruralis 29: 93–117.
Ford, A., and R. Nigh, 2015. *Maya Forest Garden: Eight Millennia of
    Sustainable Cultivation of the Tropical Woodlands*. Walnut Creek,
    CA: Left Coast Press.
Goldschmidt, W. 1947. *As You Sow: Three Studies in the Social
    Consequences of Agribusiness*. Montclair, NJ: Allanheld, Osmun and
    Co. Publishers, Inc.
Goran, M. I., S. J., Ulijaszek, and E. E. Ventura, 2013. "High fructose corn
    syrup and diabetes prevalence: a global perspective." *Global Public
    Health* 8 (1): 55–64.
INEGI. 2015a. CDI. "Sistema de indicadores sobre la población indígena
    de México con base en: Encuesta Intercensal 2015." Accessed March
    15, 2021. www.gob.mx/cms/uploads/attachment/file/239923/04-estima
    ciones-nacionales-por-entidad-federativa.pdf.
    2015b. CDI. "Sistema de indicadores sobre la población indígena de
    México con base en: Encuesta Intercensal 2015." Accessed March 15,
    2021. www.gob.mx/cms/uploads/attachment/file/239926/06-cuadro-02
    .pdf.
    2019. "Resultados Encuesta Nacional Agropecuaria 2019". Accessed
    March 15, 2021. www.inegi.org.mx/contenidos/programas/ena/2019/
    doc/rrdp_ena2019.pdf.
Iowa Farm Bureau. 2021. "About." Accessed May 21, 2021. www
    .iowafarmbureau.com/About.
Kloppenburg, J. R. 2004. *First the Seed: The Political Economy of Plant
    Biotechnology, 1492–2000* (2nd ed.). Madison: University of Wisconsin
    Press.

Latham, M. E. 2011. *The Right Kind of Revolution: Modernization, Development, and US Foreign Policy from the Cold War to the Present*. New York: Cornell University Press.

Lobao, L., and C. W. Stofferahn, 2008. "The community effects of industrialized farming: Social science research and challenges to corporate farming laws." *Agriculture and Human Values* 25 (2): 219–240. https://doi.org/10.1007/s10460-007-9107-8

Magdoff, F., J. B., Foster, and F. H. Buttel, 2000. "An overview." In *Hungry for Profit: The Agribusiness Threat to Farmers, Food, and the Environment*, edited by F. Magdoff, J. B. Foster, and F. H. Buttel, 7–21. New York: Monthly Review.

Martinez-Torres, M. E., and P. M. Rosset, 2010. "La Vía Campesina: the birth and evolution of a transnational social movement." *The Journal of Peasant Studies* 37 (1): 149–175.

McAfee, K. 2008. "Beyond techno-science: Transgenic maize in the fight over Mexico's future." *Geoforum* 39 (1): 148–160.

Morales, H., and I. Perfecto, 2000. "Traditional knowledge and pest management in the Guatemalan highlands." *Agriculture and Human Values* 17 (1): 49–63.

Nazarea, V. D. 2005. *Heirloom Seeds and Their Keepers: Marginality and Memory in the Conservation of Biological Diversity*. Tucson: University of Arizona Press.

Olmstead, A. L., and P. W. Rhode, 2008. *Creating Abundance: Biological Innovation and American Agricultural Development*. Cambridge: Cambridge University Press.

Patel, R. 2012. *Stuffed and Starved: The Hidden Battle for the World Food System*. New York: Melville House Pub.

Pilcher, J. M. 1998. *Que vivan los tamales!: Food and the Making of Mexican Identity*. Albuquerque: University of New Mexico Press.

Ranum, P., J. P., Peña-Rosas, and M. N. Garcia-Casal. 2014. "Global maize production, utilization, and consumption." *Annals of the New York Academy of Sciences* 1312 (1): 105–112.

Rosset, P. 2006. *Food Is Different: Why the WTO Should Get Out of Agriculture*. London; New York: Zed Books.

Shiferaw, B., B. M., Prasanna, J., Hellin, and M. Bänziger, 2011. "Crops that feed the world 6. Past successes and future challenges to the role played by maize in global food security." *Food Security* 3 (3): 307–327.

USDA National Agricultural Statistics Service. 2020. "Iowa Ag News – Crop Production." www.nass.usda.gov/Statistics_by_State/Iowa/Publications/Crop_Report/2020/IA-Crop-Production-11-20.pdf

Via Campesina. 2021. "The international peasants voice." Accessed May 10, 2021. https://viacampesina.org/en/international-peasants-voice/.

Weis, T. 2007. *The Global Food Economy: The Battle for the Future of Farming.* New York: Zed Books.

Winders, B. 2009. *The Politics of Food Supply: U.S. Agricultural Policy in the World Economy.* New Haven, CT: Yale University Press.

Zahniser, S., N. F. L., López, M., Motamed, Z. Y. S., Vargas, and T. Capehart, 2019. "The growing corn economies of Mexico and the United States." *US Department of Agriculture, Economic Research Service,* FDS-19f-01.

4 | *Where Should Water Come From?*

SAYD RANDLE

This chapter looks at the provision of water by two different Southern California water agencies. One jurisdiction seeks to meet its water needs by financing and buying water from an expensive, energy-intensive desalination plant; the other jurisdiction successfully persuades its residents to reduce and change their consumption patterns of water and saves a huge amount of money as compared to the agency that bought into the desalination plant. What's interesting from our book's critical point of view is that the water agencies had different ideas about how people behave as water consumers. The jurisdiction that bought the expensive and wasteful desalination plant spent far more money and ended up wasting a huge amount of water because they didn't even entertain the idea that people's water consumption habits could change. Like good neoliberals they assumed that people were selfish, that they are attempting to maximize their individual utility, and that they had relatively stable preferences, which it would be foolish to attempt to change substantially. They paid dearly for those assumptions. In addition, the case demonstrates, how even in relation to complex problems such as handling water supplies, conscious human prediction and problem-solving can outperform market-based mechanisms. The case shows, in opposition to neoliberal orthodoxy, that it is possible to plan.

From 2012 till the end of 2016, the US state of California weathered a record-breaking drought. In response to exhortations to conserve the state's reduced supply of water, agricultural fields were fallowed and suburban lawns left to crisp. Given the rhetoric of an ongoing water emergency from the state's governor on down, a few readers likely choked on their coffee upon encountering this February 2, 2016 headline in the *Voice of San Diego*: "San Diego's Oversupply of Water Reaches a New, Absurd Level" (Rivard, 2016). Reading further, residents of the state's second most populous county would learn that, at the height of the historic dry spell, the San Diego county Water

Authority (SDCWA) had such an excess of supply that they would be dumping half a billion gallons of desalinated ocean water into a local lake. Given the money and carbon emissions required to turn seawater into potable water, one could imagine some readers' surprise shifting quickly to anger, and perhaps even despair at this development.

Public water agencies like the SDCWA are tasked with providing safe, reliable, reasonably priced water to their customers. Yet while few would dispute these goals, approaches to achieving them will vary, often driven by conflicting assumptions about the nature of the resource, the local environment, and the public being served. This case study compares two public water agencies in coastal California – serving San Diego county and the City of Santa Monica – to illustrate how neoliberal assumptions can shape water supply arrangements, as well as the environmental and socioeconomic conditions that can result.

In this context, San Diego serves as a cautionary tale of where the neoliberal paradigm can lead government agencies. Roughly 3.3 million residents of San Diego county are served by the SDCWA, a public water wholesaler. Established in 1944, SDCWA provides water to twenty-four member agencies within the county, including cities, water districts, and a military base, all entities that sell water directly to residents. For its first four decades of existence, SDCWA facilitated sprawling suburban expansion across its service area by providing an ever-growing volume of water sourced from hundreds of miles away and bought from a larger regional wholesaling entity. A severe, years-long drought that began in the late 1980s highlighted the risks of relying so heavily on these water sources, spurring a reevaluation of this arrangement. Following years of controversy, a "solution" emerged: the agency would partner with a private firm to develop an ocean desalination facility, and commit to buying a set volume of its outflow for thirty years. This is the arrangement that led to the drought-time water dumping referenced above. Turning to such an inflexible, costly, carbon-intensive arrangement to address their water supply challenges, San Diego's water managers clearly signaled that constraining resource consumption was less thinkable than pursuing this expensive partnership with a for-profit company.

A contrasting case roughly one hundred miles north of San Diego's desalination plant underscores how a different set of assumptions about the public's ability to conserve resources can lead to a radically different water provision arrangement. The city of Santa Monica, located at the ocean's edge in Los Angeles County, has long relied on a mix of local groundwater and imported water for its water supply. In 2011, the city announced that, like San Diego, it recognized the risks inherent in its dependence on faraway sources and would pursue greater water "self-reliance." But rather than partner with a private company or pursue any sort of desalination project, Santa Monica committed to cutting its water demand through an investment in dramatic conservation measures and an exploration of publicly owned and managed wastewater recycling infrastructure. Effective messaging campaigns and financial assistance for home landscape transformations have helped the city cut its per capita water consumption in the years since, highlighting the mutable nature of consumption, in contrast to neoliberal narratives that suggest the inevitable selfishness of individuals. Planning documents indicate that Santa Monica is on track to be completely water self-sufficient by 2023. While a neoliberal mindset might suggest that a public agency has no meaningful chance of reshaping individual or household consumption and that supply expansion is the only reasonable option, this case highlights how other infrastructural pathways and demand patterns are entirely plausible.

4.1 Southern California Water Context

Though this chapter focuses on the differences between the approaches to water management in San Diego county and the city of Santa Monica, the similarities between and shared regional context of the two jurisdictions should be noted. Both are located within populous, largely urbanized Southern California, a prosperous area of a rich country. While the region is marked by dramatic socioeconomic inequality, its water provision infrastructure is well developed, ensuring that virtually all urban customers have water connections and access to as much of the resource as they desire (and can pay for). In contrast to contexts where substantial swathes of the population struggle to procure adequate water for daily use, residents of both Santa Monica and San Diego enjoy steady flows from their taps, provided by public agencies.[1]

---

[1] These conditions are not universally shared across California. In unincorporated communities within the state's agriculture-dominated Central Valley, for

While private water companies are a small part of the Southern California waterscape, public agencies procure and distribute the vast majority of the region's supply. In the early twentieth century, this arrangement was driven by the need to raise funds for growing cities' water infrastructure through public bond measures. However, due to the region's characteristic aridity and boosters' dreams of rapid expansion, these bonds were funding projects far more ambitious than water mains and sewer lines. In 1913, the city of Los Angeles inaugurated a city-owned, 233-mile long aqueduct, a pipeline delivering water to the metropolis from the Owens Valley in northeastern California. But just a few years later, explosive population growth stoked new fears across the region about adequate water supply. In response, in 1928 Los Angeles banded together with eleven other jurisdictions to form the Metropolitan Water District (Metropolitan), a regional water wholesaling entity. Metropolitan's first order of business was to finance and construct the Colorado River aqueduct, a pipeline transporting water from the inland river to the coastal region, completed in 1941. In the decades that followed, Metropolitan expanded its portfolio to include the waters of California's State Water Project, piped to the state's populous southern half from its northern rivers.

Developing enormous dams and rerouting rivers to enable growth in arid regions is clearly an approach to natural resource management that predates the rise of neoliberalism. In the context of the US West, scholars have argued that the practice is best understood as a state-driven mode of capitalist development (Reisner, 1986; Wehr, 2004), albeit one subject to capture and manipulation by local elites (Worster, 1985). This high-modernist approach to water management marked development efforts across the globe in the middle of the twentieth century in countries across the political spectrum, often with assistance from the US Bureau of Reclamation (Sneddon, 2015; Swyngedouw, 2015). In settler-colonial contexts, including the US West and Australia, these efforts to "tame" unruly waterways in the service of transforming deserts into cotton fields were frequently articulated as part of a broader narrative of charmed territorial conquest (Allon and

instance, intensive groundwater pumping has led the household wells relied on by residents to run dry (Cagle, 2015). While this chapter focuses on urbanized contexts where residents enjoy easy access to safe, reliable water provided by public agencies, residents of communities within a few hours drive of these cities do not.

Sofoulis, 2006; Morgan, 2017; Vine, 2018). For much of the twentieth century, large-scale water infrastructure works were wholly public undertakings and largely served to legitimate the state's role in economic development and resource management.

This is not, however, to say that the public sector's robust role in this realm has ever been uncontested in the US West or elsewhere. Water politics in dry California have long been notoriously fraught and complicated. Critics, neoliberal and otherwise, have found fault with the local, state, and federal agencies that have managed the majority of the resource since their inception (see Hundley, 2001 for a detailed accounting). During the 2012–2016 drought for instance, many criticized the institutions and laws that reserve 80 percent of the state's water supply for agricultural uses, which are dominated by enormous, industrialized farming operations (Arax, 2019). Metropolitan has also taken heat, being characterized by critics as inefficient and secretive, enabling development in areas better left unbuilt through ill-conceived water provision guarantees (Gottlieb, 1988; Gottlieb and Fitzsimmons, 1991; Zetland, 2009). Both the San Diego and Santa Monica cases explored below are driven by a desire to depend less on water provided by Metropolitan – but as the next sections will show, the jurisdictions' approach to that shared aim diverge dramatically.

4.2 San Diego

San Diego county sits at the southwestern corner of California. Anchored by the eponymous coastal city, the county's residents are also distributed across a diverse patchwork of suburbs, towns, Native reservations, farms, and deserts. Though the county's geographic area stretches nearly one hundred miles inland, the words "San Diego" are stably associated with its Pacific shoreline in the popular imagination. Beaches, surfers, and temperate, unchanging weather mark most representations of the area in popular culture.

Perhaps, given San Diego's reputation for ever-blue skies and soft breezes, the county's protracted history of water supply drama will come as no surprise. Though varied across its 4526 square miles, much of the county's local climate is semi-arid, with its coastal areas receiving an average of approximately ten inches of rain per year. Home to few large rivers and modest volumes of groundwater, the limits of the county's water supply became a source of intensifying concern among politicians and water managers alike during the population and industrial boom of the World War II years. To assuage those fears, SDCWA joined Metropolitan in 1946 to gain access to its water. This arrangement fueled dramatic growth in the agency's service area for four decades, a period marked by relatively few frictions. But when a lengthy drought struck California in the late 1980s, calls for reassessing San Diego's dependence on the regional agency grew suddenly heated – a shift that continues to shape water management decisions within the county.

By that point, due to sustained increases in both population and per capita water consumption, SDCWA relied on Metropolitan for fully 90 percent of its water supply. As such, in early 1991, when drought conditions led Metropolitan to announce 31 percent across-the-board cutbacks in water deliveries, San Diego water managers felt the squeeze acutely (Erie, 2006). In the end, the reduced deliveries were short-lived, as Metropolitan revoked the order after an unanticipated spring deluge filled reservoirs. But the threat of losing nearly a third of their expected water deliveries led SDCWA to declare a new, more intense need for independence from the regional agency. Notably, in this context, San Diego sought not necessarily to reduce reliance on faraway water sources, but on Metropolitan, the water agency that had managed and delivered such water for the county since the 1940s. The enemy here wasn't just an uncooperative nature, but also a fellow public agency that didn't properly prioritize the county's water deliveries.

Turning to the private sector for assistance in the name of "independence" from Metropolitan and a variable climate was not San Diego's first move. In the 1990s, SDCWA pursuit a range of water sources, some far and some near. A hard-fought farm-to-city transfer brought redirected Colorado River water from the vegetable fields of the Imperial Valley to San Diego's taps, delivering some new water to the agency from 2006 onward (Erie, 2006; Polk, 2015). An urban wastewater recycling project was seriously considered, shelved for years due to local opposition, and now mired in new controversy (Meehan et al., 2013; Rivard, 2019). And a publicly funded and managed desalination plant was considered, building on research by the county's "Water Independence Project" of the early 1980s (Morgan, 2017). But the enormous cost of desalination and one crucial tactical move by Poseidon Water, the private venture capital firm that eventually partnered with SDCWA to develop the plant, finally led the agency to bring market actors directly into the equation.

Poseidon made itself a key player in the San Diego desalination game by short-circuiting the public agency's stated plans for developing their own plant. Since the early 1990s, the SDCWA had in its annual reports identified a parcel of land adjacent to an active power station as its target site to develop a desalination facility, based on the ease of connecting the plant to the energy infrastructure. In 2004, Poseidon obtained a long-term lease on the site, scrambling the SDCWA's plans. However, the company could raise only $167 million toward the construction of its desalination plant, far less than its anticipated cost (Williams, 2018). Poseidon needed a public partner to help with the financing, and the SDCWA still believed it needed a desalination plant. In 2012 the company and the agency inked their Water Purchase Agreement and successfully applied for $734 million in low-interest state bonds to fund the plant's construction (Williams, 2018). Such immense price tags are not uncommon in desalination projects, which have led some theorists to suggest that these infrastructures represent an emergent spatial "fix" for capital (Swyngedouw, 2013; Loftus and Hug, 2016; Swyngedouw and Williams, 2016). Local environmental groups filed lawsuit after lawsuit against the project, emphasizing the anticipated impacts on local marine life. The Pacific Institute, an Oakland-based water think tank, published worrying projections of the plant's anticipated carbon emissions (Cooley and Heberger, 2013) But the project cleared all of the necessary the legal and public relations hurdles, and in December 2015 the Claude "Bud" Lewis Carlsbad Desalination Plant began producing potable water for distribution to SDCWA's member agencies.

Of course, as noted at this chapter's outset, the stringent terms of that 2012 purchase agreement mandated that the SDCWA purchase a set volume of the plant's water. Given that this water was priced around $2000 per acre-foot, a rate more than double that charged by Metropolitan, one would be hard-pressed to characterize this arrangement as economically efficient for the public. Further, observers anticipated the oversupply issue before the plant came online. "Desal Deal Leaves San Diego with Extra Water in Drought," announced a May 27, 2015, headline in the *Voice of San Diego*, atop an article full of criticism of the arrangement from a range of policy experts (Rivard, 2015). Bob Yamada, a SDCWA representative, was quoted defending the project, touting the long-term value of access to a theoretically limitless, "drought-proof" supply of water – even if that pricey supply would, in the near-term, likely be stored in lakes with high rates of evaporation.

One does not envy Yamada, holding a job that requires him to cheerlead for an emissions-intensive project that has contributed to the rise of water rates across San Diego county. His awkward position raises questions about an alternative scenario: what if, instead of pursuing the potentially "infinite" water of the ocean, the SDCWA had sought to cut water consumption rates with similar gusto, negating the need for such supply? The record suggests that the notion that San Diego's residents might reduce the county's need to import Metropolitan water by dramatically reducing their consumption of the resource was not seriously considered, and received far less funding than the desalination plant. Sustained growth in both population and water demand were the baseline assumptions driving the SDCWA's projections and proposed projects (SDCWA, 2005; 2010; 2015). The idea that a significant swathe of San Diego residents might be convinced to abandon the thirsty landscaping that consumes around 60 percent of domestic water in Southern California, or meaningfully reduce consumption with adapted washing and bathing practices, was not central to any planning or projections. While voluntary conservation was encouraged by SDCWA, programs to subsidize replacing turf with native plants or high-volume clothes washing machines with more efficient models never received comparable investment to water-transfer, water recycling, or desalination projects.

For our purposes, it's worth teasing apart a distinction here. Assumptions about sustained population growth are not at all new, or particular to the neoliberal paradigm (as the ghost of Thomas Malthus would certainly confirm). But assumptions that treat individual resource consumption as immutable, unable to be meaningfully cut in the name of collective socioecological benefit, echo neoliberal notions of personhood that deserve some scrutiny. As noted in the Introduction and second chapter of this volume, neoliberalism posits that people make decisions solely as selfish, atomized individuals. This figure of the wholly self-interested, ever-maximizing individual, the type who would never rip out his home's green lawn in the name of collective sustainability, is a familiar one in both popular and some scholarly discourse, frequently framed as the "realist" account of human behavior. Yet, as the late anthropologist David Graeber notes in his review of the disciplinary literature on the subject:

There is no area of human life, anywhere, where one cannot find self-interested calculation. But neither is there anywhere one cannot find kindness or adherence to idealistic principles: the point is why one, and not the other, is posed as "objective" reality. (Graeber, 2001: 29)

Here, Graeber is critiquing social theorists who suggest that beneath seemingly altruistic actions one can always find an ulterior motive, challenging the notion that assuming competition all the way down is the only sensible approach. While few would term the water managers at the SDCWA social theorists, their reports indicate that they were operating with similar notions about what behaviors might be expected. Questioning such an account of human actions could help reframe the tactics for addressing the region's water supply challenges, opening the door to serious investment in and promotion of water-saving measures for residents across the county.

Notably, several of SDCWA's member agencies demonstrated that their customers were capable of dramatic cuts in water use during California's 2012–2016 drought. In April 2015, then-governor Jerry Brown announced a mandatory statewide 25 percent cut in urban water consumption to address the shortage in supply. To avoid putting an undue burden on jurisdictions with already low water use rates, the state developed nine tiers of required reductions, ranging from 8 percent to 36 percent, based on agencies' current rates of per capita per day consumption. The Santa Fe Irrigation District, a SDCWA member agency, was placed in the 36 percent tier based on its eye-popping 2014–2015 water use average of 604.6 gallons per capita per day. Some residents complained about the dramatic cuts at public meetings and to reporters, a few in cartoonishly selfish terms. "We pay significant property taxes based on where we live ... and no, we're not all equal when it comes to water," Rancho Santa Fe resident Steve Yuhas told the *Washington Post*, following up on a social media post in which he declared that people "should not be forced to live on property with brown lawns, golf on brown courses, or apologize for wanting their gardens to be beautiful" (Kuznia, 2015). But district records show that the Santa Fe Irrigation District actually exceeded the state target in its very first month, reducing use from the benchmark month by a full 42 percent.

The careful reader will notice that such conservation rates exceed the proposed 31 percent reduction in Metropolitan water deliveries from back in 1991, the event that triggered SDCWA's intense pursuit of alternative water sources. The agency's trenchant focus on (and investment in) increasing supply rather than reducing demand underlines how assumptions of self-interested individual behavior shaped the approach to solving the region's water issues. Planning based on the notion of stable consumption habits, SDCWA was reproducing economistic ideas about human nature – at the literal expense of San Diego residents.

4.3 Santa Monica

The city of Santa Monica sits at the western edge of Los Angeles county. Compared to San Diego, the city is tiny in both land area and population, measuring only sixteen square miles and home to about 90,000 residents. The water that flows to those residents is managed by the Water Resources Division of the city's Public Works Office. Despite these differences in scale and administrative structure, however, Santa Monica and the SDCWA share some key characteristics. Like the SDCWA, Santa Monica became a member agency of the Metropolitan Water District early, way back in 1941.[2] And for years, the city depended heavily on water purchased from Metropolitan to augment local groundwater production for the city's water supply. Like the SDCWA, Santa Monica has been publicly declaring its desire for increased water "independence" or "self-sufficiency" for some time. But in contrast to the other agency, Santa Monica has bypassed the prospect of desalination and partnerships with private firms in favor of a focus on publicly managed wastewater recycling and demand-reduction programs.

In Santa Monica's case, it was local pollution rather than drought that led to anxiety about an almost 100 percent reliance on flows from Metropolitan. In the mid-1990s, routine water quality tests revealed the presence of the gasoline additive methyl tertiary butyl ether (MTBE) in the Santa Monica groundwater basin, the city's primary

---

[2] Though longstanding, this relationship has not always been comfortable. Robert Gottlieb, the author of two critical books about Metropolitan, served as Santa Monica's representative on the agency's Board of Directors in the 1980s and was vocal about his unfavorable assessment of the institution throughout.

nonMetropolitan water source. Further investigation revealed that gas had been leaking from underground storage tanks and pipelines into soil, leaching from there into the aquifer. The MTBE levels far exceeded the legal standards, leading Santa Monica to shut down most of its groundwater wells in 1995 through 2010. Throughout this period, during which the city hashed out a legal agreement with the polluters and developed new groundwater treatment infrastructure, Santa Monica bought the lion's share of its supply from the regional wholesaler. While Metropolitan never proposed the cuts in water deliveries that San Diego faced in 1991 during this period, the perceived precarity of the arrangement created anxiety nonetheless. In response, in January 2011 the Santa Monica City Council directed staff to develop a plan that would enable their jurisdiction to rely entirely on local water resources by 2020.

Adopted by the city in 2014 and updated in 2018, Santa Monica's Sustainable Water Master Plan features three components, designed to achieve water self-sufficiency by 2023. The second and third of these expand water supply: "developing sustainable and drought resilient alternative water supplies" (in this case, treated wastewater and urban runoff) and "expanding local groundwater production within sustainable yield limits" (City of Santa Monica, 2018: ES-7). In a notable break with San Diego, however, the very first component addresses consumption: "increasing water conservation efforts to permanently reduce water demand" (City of Santa Monica, 2018: ES-7). In this formulation of an "independent" water future, the self-maximizing individual is nowhere to be found. In fact, the more altruistic resident, capable of cutting water use and guided in that direction by public agency rebates and subsidies, is a bedrock of the plan.

Santa Monica water managers had invested both money and effort into understanding local conservation possibilities well before the 2014 plan was adopted. In 2004, the city undertook a project titled "garden\garden," in which a pair of adjacent front yards were designed as a "traditional garden" and a "native garden." The former featured wide expanses of turf and a few clusters of flowers, while the latter was planted with California native plants that required far less irrigation. The city collected data on the two landscapes between 2004 and 2013, eventually finding that the "native garden" used 83 percent less water than its "traditional" neighbor (City of Santa Monica, 2013: 1). This dramatic contrast featured prominently in city publicity materials advertising a range of conservation programs, including one (augmented for a period by funds from Metropolitan), that offered residents a rebate of $3.50 per square foot for replacing grass with lower-water consuming plants, mulches, or gravels. Between April 2015 and July 2017, the city spent a little over $2.2 million to subsidize the removal of 823,399 square feet of turf (City of Santa Monica, 2018: 2–11). The city also funded retrofits of water infrastructures in public facilities (including schools) and offered steep rebates on water-efficient devices for commercial customers. This combination of targeted conservation messaging and substantial investment proved effective in changing consumption patterns: in 2018, Santa Monica reported an 18 percent permanent water demand reduction from its 2014 levels, and anticipated further savings by 2023 (City of Santa Monica, 2018: ES-3).

Notably, the Sustainable Water Master Plan does not contain the word "desalination." Though that document uses many phrases familiar from the San Diego water story, emphasizing "self-sufficiency" and a "drought-proof" supply of water, purifying ocean water is not part of the city's vision for its water future. One could reasonably argue that this exclusion is not unrelated to Santa Monica's key hydrological advantage: a large groundwater basin, which modeling suggests to be capable of bearing increased extraction in the years to come. Yet while this local resource undoubtedly shapes the city's approach to water management, its prioritization of conservation – grounded in the assumption that residents can, in fact, be advertised, rebated, and otherwise cajoled into abandoning long-held landscapes aesthetics, household devices, and daily practices to help shore up the shared pool of available water – is also fundamental to the divergent trajectory illustrated by this plan. While it would be silly to say that Santa Monica residents are not understood as consumers in this context, it seems fair to suggest that their preferences are framed as mutable and subject to change based on an interest in the collective good.

There is, of course, a danger in arguing too forcefully that altruistic-minded consumption represents a break from neoliberal paradigms. As many scholars have noted, pushing responsibility for ills produced by corporations or nation-states onto individuals is often a hallmark of this discourse. In the realm of public water agencies, however, the policy stories told in the name of the figure of the greedy water user – *be realistic, he'll never rip out his grass, and so we need this billion-dollar desalination plant and water purchase agreement with a venture capital firm!* – suggest the importance of highlighting how consumers are also residents and community members. In this context, a desire to use less of a limited resource is directly connected to the reality that such behavior leaves more for neighbors and nearby jurisdictions. That such priorities can, in fact, move the needle bears noting, in the face of conflicting "commonsense" assumptions about water demand and supply.

4.4 Conclusion

Concluding that meaningful reductions in per capita water consumption are indeed possible, particularly in a dry region known for its emerald lawns and swimming pools, may seem like stating the obvious to some readers. But the very fact that water planners in jurisdictions like San Diego do not treat such reductions as a centerpiece of their projections reveals some of the assumptions that can quietly underpin discourses of water "independence." Rather than simply pursuing independence *from* an unpredictable climate or bureaucracy, in some cases they are seeking to enable consumers independence *to* use as much water as they want, regardless of the broader socioecological impacts of these practices.

San Diego, pursuing desalination via a private-sector partnership, has doubled down on a supply-expansion approach to managing the vagaries of resource availability in the twenty-first century. Making this infusion of ocean water central to its projections for the county's future, the SDCWA is following the view termed the "infinity of water" by anthropologist Gokce Gunel, in which "[t]he 'man-made' quality of water – where more can be generated through desalination whenever necessary – allows the actors in the area to envision and embrace its infinity, regardless of existing water scarcity" (Gunel, 2016: 292). In other words, the agency sidesteps thorny questions of how people should live in an arid region, preferring to produce the imaginary of an uninterrupted future via limitless infusions of this vital resource. Disadvantages of this approach are already evident, in the form of increased water rates and mandatory purchase of water when it is not needed. But beyond the expense and the waste, one might also raise the concerning evacuation of public discussions regarding the best local uses of a vital resource like water.

In contrast, Santa Monica's approach refuses such dreams of "infinity." By treating residents as active participants within the waterscape, capable of changing their consumption patterns (particularly given financial support from the agency), the city frames water as a limited resource and the region's water future as a collective creation. It is easy to roll one's eyes at the notion that trading a lawn for a mulchy patch planted with sage might represent a meaningful political horizon. But the assumptions underpinning Santa Monica's water-independence-via-conservation approach represent a notable divergence from the neoliberal paradigm. Demand can be mutable, even in the name of socioecological solidarity. Coastlines of carbon-spewing desalination facilities are far from inevitable.

References

Allon, Fiona, and Zoe Sofoulis. 2006. "Everyday water: Cultures in transition." *Australian Geographer* 37 (1): 55–65.

Arax, Mark. 2019. *The Dreamt Land: Chasing Water and Dust in California*. New York: Knopf.

Cagle, Susie. 2015. "After water." *Longreads*, June 2, 2015. https://longreads.com/2015/06/02/after-water

City of Santa Monica. 2013. "Sustainable landscape: The numbers speak for themselves." www.smgov.net/uploadedFiles/Departments/OSE/Categories/Landscape/garden-garden-2013.pdf

　　2018. "Sustainable water master plan update." www.smgov.net/uploadedFiles/Departments/Public_Works/Water/SWMP_Update%20Dec%202018_FINAL_wAttachments.pdf

Cooley, Heather and Matthew Heberger. 2013. Key issues in Seawater Desalination: Energy and Greenhouse Gas Emissions. Pacific Institute.

Erie, Steven. 2006. *Beyond Chinatown: The Metropolitan Water District, Growth, and the Environment in Southern California*. Stanford, CA: Stanford University Press.

Gottlieb, Robert. 1988. *A Life of Its Own: The Politics and Power of Water*. San Diego, CA: Harcourt Brace.

Gottlieb, Robert, and Margaret Fitzsimmons. 1988. *Thirst for Growth: Water Agencies as Hidden Government in Southern California*. Tucson: University of Arizona Press.

Graeber, David. 2001. *Toward an Anthropological Theory of Value: The False Coin of Our Own Dreams*. New York: Palgrave.

Gunel, Gokce. 2016. "The infinity of water: Climate change adaptation in the Arabian peninsula." *Public Culture* 28 (2): 291–315.

Hundley, Norris. 2001. *The Great Thirst: Californians and Water: A History* (revised ed.). Berkeley; Los Angeles: University of California Press.

Kuznia, Rob. 2015. "Rich Californians balk at limits: 'We're not all equal when it comes to water'." *The Washington Post*, June 13, 2015. www .washingtonpost.com/national/rich-californians-youll-have-to-pry-the-hoses-from-our-cold-dead-hands/2015/06/13/fac6f998-0e39-11e5-9726-49d6fa26a8c6_story.html

Loftus, Alex, and Hug March. 2016. "Financializing desalination: Rethinking the returns of big infrastructure." *International Journal of Urban and Regional Research* 40 (1): 46–61.

Morgan, Ruth. 2017. "The allure of climate and water independence: Desalination projects in Perth and San Diego." *Journal of Urban History* 46 (1): 113–128.

Polk, Daniel. 2015. "The politics and ecology of water: Notes on the drought in California." *Anthropology Now* 7 (3): 61–66.

Rivard, Ry. 2015. "Desal deal leaves San Diego with extra water in drought." *Voice of San Diego*, May 27, 2015. www.voiceofsandiego.org/topics/ science-environment/desal-deal-leaves-san-diego-with-extra-water-in-drought

2016. "San Diego's oversupply of water reaches a new, absurd level." *Voice of San Diego*, February 2, 2016. www.voiceofsandiego.org/ topics/government/san-diegos-oversupply-of-water-reaches-a-new-absurd-level

2019. "Contractors see pure water case as a test for big projects across the region." *Voice of San Diego*, July 1, 2019. www.voiceofsandiego.org/ topics/government/contractors-see-pure-water-case-as-a-test-for-big-pro jects-across-the-region

San Diego County Water Authority. 2005. *Urban Water Management Plan.* San Diego: San Diego County Water Authority

2010. *Urban Water Management Plan.* San Diego: San Diego County Water Authority

2015. *Urban Water Management Plan.* San Diego: San Diego County Water Authority

Sneddon, Christopher. 2015. *Concrete Revolution: Large Dams, Cold War Geopolitics, and the U.S. Bureau of Reclamation.* Chicago: University of Chicago Press.

Swyngedouw, Erik. 2013. "Into the sea: Desalination as hydro-social fix in Spain." *Annals of the Association of American Geographers* 103 (2): 261–270.

2015. *Liquid Power: Contested Hydro-Modernities in Twentieth Century Spain.* Cambridge, MA: MIT Press.

Swyngedouw, Erik, and Joe Williams. 2016. "From Spain's hydro-deadlock to the desalination fix." *Water International* 41 (1): 54–73.

Vine, Michael. 2018. "Learning to feel at home in the Anthropocene: From state of emergency to everyday experiments in California's historic drought." *American Ethnologist* 45 (3): 405–416.

Williams, Joe. 2018a. "Assembling the water factory: Seawater desalination and the techno-politics of water privatization in the San Diego–Tijuana metropolitan region." *Geoforum* 93: 32–39.

   2018b. "Diversification or loading order? Divergent water-energy politics and the contradictions of desalination in Southern California." *Water Alternatives* 11 (3): 847–865.

Zetland, David. 2009. "The end of abundance: How water bureaucrats created and destroyed the Southern California oasis." *Water Alternatives* 2 (3): 350–369.

5 | *Who Gets to Own Land?*

DOUGLAS BAFFORD

The control and ownership of land is one of the surest ways to generate wealth. Moreover, if you own land or treat it as property, you can accumulate it and bequeath it to whomever you like, creating large inter-generational holdings of wealth. This is often why, when revolutions happen, one of the first questions that come up is about land, its ownership, and its potential redistribution. In this chapter, Bafford looks at what happened to land ownership across a number of revolutions in Zimbabwe and South Africa. Bafford identifies how predominantly white landowners in South Africa were able to keep their wealth. They did so with the help of property-protecting neoliberal statecraft that prioritized the protection of the existing regime of property rights rather than challenging inequality of land ownership. In Zimbabwe white landowners lost many of their holdings. Still, Bafford goes on to show the way that international, neoliberal governing organizations punished Zimbabwe's attempt at racial restorative justice with reference to the protection of property rights and the free flow of investement capital.

5.1 Introduction

When I first moved to Johannesburg, the commercial center and largest city in South Africa, I had no intention of studying land or agriculture. My primary objective was to learn about the spread of Christianity and religious responses to racial division, and the sites of my research were urban churches, seemingly far removed from farmland. However, over the course of everyday conversations and even in Christian sermons, it became impossible to ignore anxieties over what people commonly referred to as the "land question." White South Africans, in particular, would express worry over contemporary political calls for land holdings to be redistributed, often with the presumption that to shift ownership would constitute an unjust affront to white farmers. Why continue to look at demographics – who is black vs. who is white – at a time when South Africa ought to be transcending race? They suggested that efforts to take land away from white owners needlessly racialized the issue, all of which served as a further complication of the pressures that farmers were facing on multiple fronts. As a cornerstone of the nation's twenty-first-century political discourse, this question elicited widely divergent responses from each of the major political parties, with candidates and activists alike placing their answers to the question at the forefront of their appeals to South Africa's electorate. Underlying these partisan maneuvers, however, lay a deceptively simple question: How should land be distributed?

The prevailing strategy of the South African government, if not its outward political rhetoric, resonates with the theory described in this casebook as "neoliberal." Practically speaking, this strategy involves careful cultivation of an economy in which social needs are met through free-market processes, disfavoring direct state provision or redistribution of resources. While in many cases this approach involves a "laissez-faire" governing philosophy, we must also consider the proactive interventions the state must enact to make a neoliberal economy work. As it relates to land, the South African state defends a model of ownership in which individual deeds are in force in perpetuity, even if those landed resources were acquired through past injustices and passed down to descendants. This approach has received institutional and international backing, yet it has not gone without protest. A new generation of political activists is challenging the implicit assumptions underlying the status quo that emerged in the years following the end of the apartheid regime. Many of these voices calling for more equitable distribution of land to South Africa's poorer citizens adopt land reform as a symbol of sweeping changes they seek for a reformed post-apartheid future. With such conflicting and raucous voices emerging from multiple directions, South Africa lies at a crossroads.

To help address this problem, it is instructive to turn to a case study in contrast to the complicated landscape in South Africa, whose future is in many ways still uncertain. The land question has attracted just as much, if not more, controversy in Zimbabwe, the country to its immediate north. Emerging from a protracted war for independence in the late 1970s, Zimbabwe under the autocratic postcolonial leader

Robert Mugabe took a much stronger attitude toward its white minority, which like the white community in neighboring South Africa was heavily invested in agricultural production and ownership. Tense relations between whites who remained in postcolonial Zimbabwe and Mugabe's government characterized much of the 1980s and 1990s. In the early 2000s, a policy known as the Fast Track Land Reform Programme (FTLRP) attempted to expropriate land held by whites to be redistributed to black Zimbabweans. This program excited an outcry from white farmers across southern Africa as an unjust state seizure of properly held lands, and it took place amid rising fears of nonstate and para-state violence directed toward whites (Howard-Hassmann, 2010). In some ways, Zimbabwe offers a glimpse at what it might look like to take seriously a political campaign for radical land reform as has historically been discussed, yet only recently gained ground, in South Africa. Mugabe's vision for land reform approaches the postcolonial land question from a decidedly anti-neoliberal standpoint, in contrast with the largely capitalist status quo that has emerged in South Africa.

In what follows, I present an overview of the shared problem, a variety of which is faced not only in southern African countries but in postcolonial and highly stratified societies around the globe. After giving some of the key historical and anthropological context unique to this setting – after all, we cannot understand the solutions to a problem without a clear conceptualization of the problem itself – I turn to each case in depth, first to the relatively neoliberal example of South Africa's decision to rely more heavily on free-market initiatives to address the economic legacies of apartheid, and second to the alternative offered by Zimbabwe's FTLRP of the early twenty-first century. In a final section, I consider these cases in comparative perspective, highlighting the distinctions in their approach to the land question yet reminding us of the challenges inherent in deploying an alternative approach in the midst of a global economic system dominated by neoliberal thinking. African land tenure systems are often overlapping rather than mutually exclusive, and it is important to keep this reality in mind when imagining innovative solutions to problems. It is my hope that considering these two cases together might inspire you to question taken-for-granted ideas about land ownership and what it takes to ensure equitable access to one of humanity's greatest, if sometimes overlooked, resources.

5.2 The Problem

Today's inequitable distribution to land tenure in southern Africa stems from the logic of settler colonialism that took root earlier in the region than almost anywhere else on the continent. As Dutch and later British immigrants arrived at the southern tip of Africa for diverse purposes – some to escape persecution in Europe, others to reap the fruits of bountiful resources they believed were awaiting them in an "untapped" land – they embarked on a project of settlement and interaction (sometimes peaceful, sometimes violent) with multiple existing peoples and groups that would shape the region's trajectory for centuries. With a succession of emergent states divided along ethnic and linguistic boundaries, white settlers eventually took political control of a majority of the land that now forms South Africa, Namibia, Botswana, and Zimbabwe, among others in the so-called scramble for Africa. Southern Africa's colonial heyday was marked by a reliance on land accumulation and transformation to fuel a new agricultural and later industrial economy of extraction. To this end, colonial administrators, and later white leaders of the independent Union of South Africa, sought to seize the rights to land ownership through a combination of negotiated sale, military conquest, and the cordoning of African peoples onto limited and more marginal lands.

The confluence of people from multiple "racial" groups and cultures living in close proximity to one another led whites to pose various iterations of what they called the "native question," which emerged as "the problem of stabilizing alien rule" (cf. Mamdani, 1996: 3ff.).[1] Whites were caught between advocating for "separate development," according to which Africans and Europeans would live in separate societies with distinct trajectories, and the reality that white settler colonialism in southern Africa had long rested on a political economy of labor provided by black workers (agricultural or otherwise) for the enrichment of white communities. Under the formal policy of apartheid, brought about in 1948 with the ascent of the Afrikaner-based National Party, the pathway of separate development was enforced to a greater degree in social and residential domains, yet it did nothing to

[1] Keep in mind that race, as a social construct, was not always self-evident, and racial categories that have historically been used in South Africa (like "Coloured" as a separate group from "African") do not always apply well universally, nor were they necessarily applied consistently even for the same persons.

challenge the reliance of whites on black labor. Indeed, apartheid laws, particularly the 1950 Group Areas Act, both alienated African people from lands on which they had resided for generations and fueled the construction of peri-urban "townships" on the outskirts of all major urban centers, which were classified for whites only, so that black workers could still be brought into cities as workers, without the benefits of residence or state protection. The infamous "pass laws" policed where blacks (and, to an extent, other racial groups) could be at any moment. It is this context of colonial and postcolonial *extraction* – both of resources from the land but also labor from the bodies of the people who inhabit it – that set in motion the material inequities represented most vocally in twenty-first-century land disputes.

In addition to this political and economic context, though, it is equally important to broaden our understanding of land beyond the Eurocentric (and, in many of its iterations, largely neoliberal) perspective characterized by the region's white settlers. From the perspective of indigenous African people, land is organized and used in ways often quite distinct from European models, an observation that colonial interlopers frequently overlooked. Comaroff and Comaroff (1997: 119ff.) describe the efforts of both colonial forces and British missionaries to remake the Tswana land tenure system in a European model, replacing local understandings of ecology with the peasant farming communities with which they were familiar. Tswana reliance on herding was grounded in the ecological conditions of the region, as was their use of small-scale, yet not entirely sedentary, cultivation. As a result of this external pressure, pastoralism gave way to a less efficient agricultural plan in which Tswana people were placed into a dependency relationship with the colonial state, creating a new and exploited working class. Similar land grabs took place elsewhere in Africa, as Jomo Kenyatta (1938), who trained as an anthropologist and later became the first president of independent Kenya, indicates in East Africa. Kenyatta argues that white settlers misunderstood the nature of African land transactions, taking a negotiation to provide a limited-time "entrustment" of the land (cf. Shipton, 2007) for a perpetual transference of inalienable ownership. Like the southern African example, such a history reflects not only the political economy of African colonialism but divergent cultural understandings of the nature of land tenure itself. Is land the kind of thing that can be owned in perpetuity by individuals? Or are there other idioms in which to express land use, whether in terms of collective (or communal or even state-based) ownership or the processes of transferring and distributing land across time?

The anthropologist Sally Falk Moore (1998) writes about these conflicting ideologies of land tenure in Africa, while pointing to the ways in which existing models of land holding do not merely go away when a state attempts to impart top-down changes. For example, in the early years of Tanzania's independence as a socialist state, President Nyerere sought to do away with all privately held land, including the traditional oversight thereof afforded to chiefs, who he thought did not well represent his vision for an egalitarian society. As a result of the abolition of private land titles, small-property holders were caught in the middle of the practical (if now technically illegal) transfer system and the state's claims to be the owner of all the land, with ongoing consequences for titleholders even after Tanzania was forced under international pressure to allow privatization once more (Moore, 1998: 35–36). Such historical processes and iterative changes highlight the need to appreciate the ways relationships between the land, African people, and others cannot be fixed in simple categories. As Parker Shipton (1994: 349) suggests, "African tenures (the plural indicates different understandings of human attachments to land) are neither communalistic nor individualistic in essence. Overlapping and inter-locking rights in land are part of whatever a people deem their social fabric, whether woven around kinship, bureaucratic hierarchy, age grading, or other principles – this fact has long been considered the essence of African tenures." The historical and contemporary relation-ships people have established with the land are just as pluralistic as Africa's cultural diversity. To understand the symbolic and economic orders that have emerged, we now turn our attention to two case studies of land tenure in southern Africa: a neoliberal model of private ownership in South Africa and a more redistributive model erected in Zimbabwe.

5.3 A Neoliberal Solution: Post-Apartheid South Africa

Despite its simplicity, the land question has remained unresolved since the era of Nelson Mandela, the country's first black president elected in 1994 with the dismantling of the white-minority apartheid govern-ment. Concerns over how to address the ownership, use, and allotment of landed property have been among the most divisive facing the young democracy for over a decade (Mariri, 2019). In the weeks leading up to South Africa's 2019 parliamentary elections – only the sixth such national election since the transition to democratic rule in 1994 – I witnessed the bold colors of party banners and advertisements lining the streets of Johannesburg. Despite the dominance of the African National Congress (ANC) party since Mandela's election, a vibrant and rigorously contested multiparty political landscape was signaled by competing color schemes: the ANC's green, black, and yellow; the Democratic Alliance's (DA) bold blue; the Economic Freedom Fighters' (EFF) red and black; and the Freedom Front Plus's (FF+) green and orange. Each of these banners expressed generic appeals to a brighter future, echoing political rhetoric in most other parts of the world, with a revolving repertoire of pat slogans written in some of South Africa's eleven official languages. They also signaled each party's approach to the land question.

The dilemma facing political leaders today is how best to answer the question of how land ought to be managed, owned, and potentially redistributed (and what it should mean to "own" land in the first place). While they recognize a common problem, their answers diverge wildly. The EFF, a Marxist-inspired party formed from leader Julius Malema's break from the mainline ANC in 2013, gained notoriety for its call to take state control of all land so as to redistribute it to the black masses who have been dispossessed through centuries of white domination. Their vision for a socialist state that disrupts the prevailing capitalist status quo has been met with a range of reactions, from the FF+ who mobilized white (especially Afrikaans-speaking) farmers who feared losing family-owned land at the heart of their livelihood to the ANC and DA (the two parties with the strongest representation in parliament) who offered an ambiguous and at times contradictory position on the land question. Indeed, it was perhaps as a result of their clear-cut, albeit diametrically opposed, platforms on land that two more radical parties, the EFF and FF+, saw gains in the election at the expense of the stalwart ANC (Mariri, 2019). Although the ANC won a slim majority of parliamentary seats, it has a more tenuous control over the country's political agenda than at any other point in the democratic era. The ANC fashions itself as the legacy-bearer of the anti-apartheid struggle, and for this reason its rhetoric is characterized by populism and the celebration of nonracialism, tactics it developed during the struggle against apartheid. However, more recently it has weathered criticism for a relatively conservative and hands-off approach to serious land reform (e.g., Žižek, 2013).

According to a 2017 government land audit report, white South Africans own 72 percent of private arable land, despite accounting for just under 10 percent of the total population (Department of Rural Development and Land Reform, 2017). This disproportionate control of land in white hands is in many ways a microcosm of broader economic patterns that make South Africa one of the most unequal countries on earth, with almost unimaginable divides between the "haves" and the "have-nots," still determined largely along racial lines (Murray, 2011). All of the country's political parties locate the origins of this inequity in the colonial and apartheid eras, during which a white minority monopolized not only political control but access to the most productive agricultural and mining lands that have helped to make South Africa one of the strongest overall economies on the continent. At the same time, however, this wealth has been concentrated in frustratingly few hands. A visitor need not look further than the human geography of urban centers like Johannesburg to appreciate how these material divides remain so powerful even in the twenty-first century. Despite boasting one of the highest GDPs in Africa, the country is home to countless people – many of whom are squatters and own no substantial property – living in impoverished conditions, often on the outskirts of high-tech, industrialized cities with rising skyscrapers, luxury car dealerships, immaculate shopping malls, and gated communities that erect literal, physical barriers between social classes. These residues of wealth accumulation and economic dejection symbolize in a blatant medium the ongoing challenge of how to create a truly "free" and multiracial democracy following apartheid (see Makhulu, 2010), and nowhere are these symbols more hotly contested than in conversations and protests over land, and not only in urban centers like Johannesburg.

How did South Africa navigate the transition from white minority governance into this radically different, albeit far from perfect, condition? The late 1980s and early 1990s were a tenuous and uncertain period for South Africa, which moved toward fully democratic elections as a result of a decades-long insurgent resistance, international sanctions and ostracism, and the apartheid government's growing recognition of the intractability of white-minority rule. Adding to the difficulty of dismantling a legal and economic system based on tight segregation, some observers both within and outside the country feared the specter of widespread retaliation against whites still living in South Africa (Crapanzano, 1985). These fears were among the considerations facing the negotiators who would in the 1990s broker a peace arrangement between President F. W. de Klerk's government and resistance leaders. Following the election of Mandela's ANC in 1994, the decision to build a "new South Africa" on nonracialism and inclusivity kept at bay fears of violent uprisings against whites. At the same time, though, the call not to alienate white South Africans transformed into a relative economic conservatism, in which not only whites' presence but capital interests in the new South Africa would be guaranteed. Later progressive figures would see this "compromise" as a failure to radically reform the country's economic foundation (Žižek, 2013; Mangcu, 2014). While political suffrage now extended to all South African adults, many of the existing patterns of land ownership and historical wealth accumulation in white hands persisted.

The introduction of increasingly neoliberal state policies in the mid-to-late 1990s brought with it even more precarious forms of urban life at a time when hopes ran high. Just as under apartheid, workers were attracted to cities, yet when they arrived, relatively few opportunities for secure, reliable housing were available, forcing many into crowded shantytown settlements in the neighboring townships. State promises to support urban, black South Africans dried up, and programs to alleviate poverty were quietly terminated, as a result of which many of the same migration patterns formed under apartheid – especially the regular movement between cities and rural homesteads – continued unabated (Makhulu, 2010). Although no longer constrained by pass laws or apartheid restrictions on where one could reside, the system of migrant wage labor previously established in South Africa continued full-strength under post-apartheid neoliberal governance. Families adapted the best they could, such as through participation in the informal economy and women's organizations dedicated to supporting one another outside of state purview, but such efforts could not efface the daunting material conditions in which they were enmeshed (Makhulu, 2010). Thus, neoliberal reforms had a measurable effect on the rhythms of daily life, whether on rural farmland, where black laborers took low-paying jobs working the land owned by white managers and companies, or in the urban settings where I lived during my first visits to South Africa.

It is true that the new South African Constitution ratified in 1996 was not a blueprint for a wholly neoliberal economy. Most notably, Section 25 laid out the groundwork for the expropriation of land, permitting the state the right to facilitate the purchase of land, presuming the owner is willing to sell at a negotiated price. However, this last requirement, controversial even at the time of its passing, would become a point of special contention in the 2010s, when the emergent leftist EFF revived calls to amend the constitution to permit "expropriation without compensation." Brought to the foreground of (still ongoing) political debates is the following question: Under what conditions can or should the state intervene in private land ownership to effect social equity? While "expropriation" in the abstract had been legalized by the post-apartheid constitution, as a practical matter it did not become used to challenge structures of wealth and traditional labor patterns, just as the abolition of slavery in the United States left in its wake a racialized plantation economy.[2] These mechanisms highlight the difficulty of producing meaningful social change, especially when historic patterns of inequality masquerade under new headings, at times making well-intentioned efforts like the Constitution's expropriation clauses relatively toothless. The ANC, for instance, maintains an image of support for working-class and poor South Africans, yet the impact of its policies tilts in a more neoliberal direction that provides considerably less practical assistance.

Within this context, the state was in no position to make radical changes to land tenure on a nation-wide basis. Section 25 called for the implementation of efforts to increase equitable access to land, which from 1995 onward was realized through grants and subsidies offered to poor South Africans to buy land on their own. However, the existing model – based on "inherited large-scale, capital-intensive forms of production" characteristic of neoliberal agribusiness – remained

---

[2] Even today, the legacies of US slavery remain in place via multiple processes: at the interpersonal level through the production of a "habitus," or a socially imposed way of being and moving through the world that is nonetheless taken to be natural and not critically examined (Hargrove, 2009), and at the structural level through institutional policies that, although *de jure* segregation has been abolished, keep wealth concentrated in white communities and produce a de facto "American apartheid" (Massey and Denton, 1998).

unchanged, such that since the 1990s, "there has been an intentional preservation of the capital-intensive production patterns of the former landowners in the land reform projects" (Rusenga, 2019: 442). Even for the few black farmers who managed to receive land, the transfer was not the panacea that many had hoped. The state failed to follow up with the provision of capital and support to ensure the farms' success, a key criterion given that historical dispossession had deprived them of these tools and skills that had been accumulated within white-owned farms. As reported in an article written on the eve of the most recent parliamentary elections, "New farmers installed on expropriated land have received scant financial, operational, or infrastructural support, despite promises from the state. Others are never installed: Because of woefully slow processing, as many as 4,000 farms bought by the government have yet to be distributed to new owners" (Clark, 2019). The story that emerges is of a struggle to project a certain image of South Africa's economic future. An idealized post-apartheid scenario of shared access to land, open to small-scale black farmers, is hampered by property laws allowing land to remain in privileged hands with impunity, as well as inefficient mechanisms of distribution and support for poor farmers.

Not only does this setup fail to implement the ostensible opportunities presented for land reform, but the ANC government has enacted regulations to increase the attractiveness of South Africa to large corporations. As early as 1996, with the passing of the Growth Employment and Redistribution program, the state introduced "investor-friendly neoliberal prescriptions" that, in addition to the privatization of major industries, led to widespread austerity measures and reduced protections for workers, allowing labor to be exploited in corporations' favor (Jacobs, 2012: 173). Although this program achieved little of the economic success it promised, the regulatory structures it imposed endured. Likewise, it is important to examine more closely the statistics on who (or rather what) owns land and how much. The land audit cited earlier showing 72 percent of agricultural land under white control does not depict the full picture, as there are consequential differences between land owned by individuals and by corporate entities. Regardless of race, individual ownership accounts for only 39 percent of all private land ownership, compared to 25 percent held by companies and 31 percent by trusts, such as the Ingonyama Trust, a politically powerful organization which holds land reserved for the Zulu people. Given the number of unique owners (95 percent of whom are individual persons, while only 3 percent are companies), the landholding power of corporations becomes clear, with a relatively small number of companies holding an outsized proportion of agricultural land. While corporate interests are not necessarily opposed to those of working people, the disproportionate share of fewer organizations controlling a larger proportion of the country's territory raises concerns about how the interests of the majority of South Africa's citizens will be protected. Multinational companies, too, pose a threat to local ownership, although less so, with 92 percent of land owned fully by South African entities (Department of Rural Development and Land Reform, 2017).[3] Still, companies do not have to be owned outright by foreigners to be susceptible to the forces imposed from outside the nation's borders.

In a similar vein, complicating this neoliberal status quo is the international attention given to land reform in South Africa, often as a political pawn. Most notably, US President Donald Trump amplified the concerns of American conservatives that whites in South Africa were facing not only the loss of their property but a simultaneous rise of violence (Williams, 2018). Through this politicization (and distortion) of the land question, redistribution efforts come to be perceived as threats not only to land but to life and liberty. South African President Cyril Ramaphosa responded to these concerns with the reassurance that the fundamental rights of landowners were not being violated (Cocks and Rumney, 2020), but the international dimension of this political program illustrates how it is not merely a South African concern. As of 2021, Ramaphosa's ANC, which barely retains a majority control of the government, faces an uncertain future. It can maintain the trajectory along which it has relied largely on free-market principles to determine access to land, or it can consider implementing

---

[3] An exception to these trends is found in sectional title property, or that which has been subdivided with some restrictions on use. Companies own 75 percent of this land, with the vast majority concentrated in Gauteng (Department of Rural Development and Land Reform, 2017), a relatively small province containing Johannesburg and the executive capital, Pretoria. This arrangement contrasts with freehold property, in which an owner theoretically has rights over the land indefinitely. Alternative forms of leasehold ownership have been proposed in contrast to both models, such as in the EFF's call for the state to own all land and to offer leases for up to twenty-five years to private entities (Economic Freedom Fighters, 2013).

more radical solutions. It is to its neighbor to the north, where a real-life, if uneven, alternative to neoliberalism was launched two decades ago, that we now turn.

5.4 An Alternative Solution: Zimbabwe's Fast Track Land Reform Programme of the 2000s

Even before South Africa transitioned from apartheid rule, the movement for African liberation won a hard-fought victory in the British colony of Southern Rhodesia, eventually renamed Zimbabwe upon the transition to majority rule in 1980. Robert Mugabe, one of the central figures in the protracted military struggle against whites who sought to establish their own independent republic, was elected prime minister and later president of the country, which he oversaw with an increasingly autocratic rule well into the twenty-first century. Like Mandela in South Africa, Mugabe faced the challenge of sizable land holdings concentrated in the commercial farms owned and managed by an even smaller minority of white settlers than in South Africa, most of whom had been born and raised in the region, often for multiple generations. Zimbabwe, often known as the "breadbasket of Africa," produced significant agricultural exports for the region at large, which were a primary source of its economic base. Similar to South Africa in yet another way, the initial Zimbabwean constitution called for land reform and redistribution – the problem was undoubtedly widely recognized – yet Mugabe's initial impulse was to "let sleeping dogs lie," and whites remained in control of much of the country's agricultural base in exchange for relative peace and productivity (Suzuki, 2017).

In 2000 this status quo was disrupted with the launch of the FTLRP, which promised to provide for landless black agricultural workers by redistributing land from white owners. Over a period of several years, large-scale farms, still dominated since the 1980s by whites engaged in commercial farming, were reformed by the state. Sam Moyo, a well-known agrarian scholar of Zimbabwe, describes the structure of the program this way:

The land tenure system was reformed by extinguishing most private property rights in agricultural land and broadening the effective occupation and use or ownership of the redistributed land through socially differentiated forms of land tenure provided to the A1 [smaller plots] and A2 [larger-scale] land beneficiaries. The latter get 99-year lease contracts providing land use rights to individual landholders. The A1 beneficiaries, on the other hand, receive statutory permits to occupy and use land in perpetuity as a family land right, which includes sub-plots to establish a homestead and for cropping and access to grazing woodlands used communally by a number of families. (Moyo, 2013: 45)

As this redistributive program was slowly taking shape, much attention was given to the threats of spectacular violence facing white landowners. Some whites were indeed pushed off their land, whether by governmental order or nonstate actors, such as the organizations of war veterans from the independence movement who had mobilized to reclaim land outside of formal state purview. It was these stories that captivated the international media's narrative of the FTLRP: emphasizing the human rights violations, in some cases including physical violence, impacting white settlers. Nonetheless, this narrative occludes a more nuanced understanding of the structural factors leading to Zimbabwe's land concerns, including colonial and capitalist influences and even ecological factors like drought (Chari, 2013). The immediate effects of the program were, indeed, a markedly more proportional division of land ownership along racial lines (Moyo, 2013: 50–51).

In response, white farmers defended their right to the land using the language of environmental responsibility and belonging. They cited the landscape engineering they had invested into the lands they owned or controlled – such as the construction of dams both to beautify the land for potential touristic uses and to ensure agricultural productivity – as a justification for the value they brought to Zimbabwe's lands, a competency they saw black Africans as lacking (Hughes, 2006). They contrasted their own "conservation ethic" with what they considered to be a more "instrumentalist approach to reservoirs and fish," expressing "outrage at what they saw as a pervasive black tendency to overfish and even to vacuum reservoirs with nets." One ex-farmer, who moved to the capital, Harare, in the early 2000s after the FTLRP, went as far as to describe this behavior toward Zimbabwe's natural resources as "the total destruction of animals" (Hughes, 2006: 282). In her ethnographic work with a similar class of white Zimbabwean farmers and self-styled conservationists, Yuka Suzuki (2017) offers further evidence of whites' emotional ties to nature through proper management of landscapes and wildlife. They treat their knowledge of domesticated and wild animals – the creatures with which all rural

Zimbabweans must learn to coexist – as partly constitutive of their sense of belonging, not only to the nation (a connection that remains tenuous and ambiguous at best) but especially to Africa as a whole. Under pressure from an increasingly strained political situation, white farmers argue that their claims to Zimbabwean land rest on the superior knowledge and entrepreneurial productivity they have wrought.

If white Zimbabweans claim a privileged status due to their agricultural knowledge, what expertise do black farmers bring to the land? The most prevalent ethnolinguistic groups in the country, which are collectively clustered under the label "Shona," have for centuries exhibited a rich cultural connection with the land as a socially and cosmologically orienting principle. Musicologist and folklorist Mickias Musiyiwa (2016: 54) describes the central mythological image of the *mwana wevhu* (literally, "child of the soil," with *ivhu* the root for soil/land) as a recurrent cultural pattern that "embodies the central belief of the Shona concerning what land is, who owns it and how it should be managed." Shona people are figured as children of the land, with their identity tied to an autochthonous sense of rootedness in the ground, both metonymically and mythologically, with the ancestors embodied in the soil itself. Shona religion is so entwined with the rhythms and symbolic significance of agricultural cycles that some have referred to it as "agro-ecological" in its own right (Sadomba, 2011: 13). Ceremonies have historically been arranged to petition for rain during drought periods frequent in this part of southern Africa, yet these ritualistic practices were typically conjoined with other forms of indigenous technology to mitigate drought, such as labor redistributions, drought-resistant crops, and intercropping (Mawere and Mubaya, 2015). In the wake of colonial seizures of land, this imagery was taken up by revolutionaries during and following the independence movement, producing well-known struggle songs announcing "*Zimbabwe iyoyi yanga yanditora mwoyo; hatinete kusvika tatora ivhu redu*" (This Zimbabwe had taken my heart; we will not rest until we take back our land) and recognizing that "the ancestors are the owners of the land" (Musiyiwa, 2016: 53, 57). Given how deeply reliant Shona society was on agriculture, it is little surprise that the soil became a politically and symbolically potent medium through which to express kinship not only with local community but the postcolonial nation of Zimbabwe. These rich cultural connections between Shona society and the land – not to mention the myriad techniques they developed to mitigate environmental disruptions – dispel any notion that whites enjoy a privileged connection with or responsibility to the land.

Nonetheless, this direct experiential knowledge of the land has faced challenges in recent years. From the early British colonization period in 1904 to a survey conducted in 2002, subsistence agriculture fell from 90 percent to 35 percent of the work undertaken by Africans in what is today Zimbabwe (Pilossof, 2014: 360). Fewer Zimbabweans may be as closely tied to the land as in previous generations, as a result of which everyday people's familiarity with agricultural techniques may be weaker than before, especially among urban dwellers in cities like Harare and Bulawayo who are now several generations removed from subsistence agriculture. Thus, despite a plentiful tradition of indigenous knowledge about southern African lands, something that recent land reform efforts have sought to reclaim, Shona and other Zimbabwean peoples now face considerable structural barriers in their efforts to regain autonomy in their ownership of the land. Perhaps most significantly, the FTLRP has not brought about a total paradigm shift as it had promised, in part because it remains enmeshed in a larger neoliberal global system, thus limiting the feasibility of any change. As argued elsewhere in this volume, neoliberalism is a set of philosophical and economic principles driving policy shifts around the globe, even as these forces can have uneven local effects. Since the early twentieth century, the proponents of neoliberalism have constructed global institutions, such as the World Trade Organization, the European Union, and other seemingly apolitical federations, that have sought not necessarily the elimination of government regulation but the active *imposition* of an international order in which markets would not be impacted by political calls for equity and economic change (Slobodian, 2018). Indeed, states themselves have been empowered not to recede from the market but to intercede actively to promote "an economic model based on private profit accumulation, labour exploitation and privileging corporate interests in land and agriculture" (Jacobs, 2012: 172). With international markets, whether agricultural or otherwise, now operating more independently from local influence and decision-making than ever before, it is difficult to effect nonneoliberal pathways like the reforms enacted in Zimbabwe without facing steep consequences.

Moyo (2011: 80) acknowledges that "the expropriatory land reforms in Zimbabwe have led to extensive land distribution and deep structural change in agrarian relations"; despite this promise, the effort remains "tied into the neoliberal policy framework, in which dominant monopoly finance capital drives supplies of agricultural seeds, technologies and credit, at the expense of auto-centric development." Like other "recent agrarian reforms [that] have broken with Bretton Woods' advice to promote market-based agricultural productivity growth and land reform," such as subsidy programs in Malawi, these efforts are still predicated on a transnational "agribusiness" model that demands large-scale production that shuts out poor farmers (Moyo, 2011: 79–80). Economists have noted a drop in the investment capital available to the country's commercial farms, which have in turn affected the viability of large-scale, contract-based production for certain export crops (Scoones et al., 2017). Furthermore, "Once established, some new black agrarian capitalists are forging alliances with white farmers and agro-industry and financial capital in business partnerships and these increasingly demand the re-introduction of private property in agricultural land and advocate for neoliberal economic and agricultural policies" (Moyo, 2013: 51). These black farmers who aspire to large-scale production have found it in their best interests to partner with experienced white farm managers, especially when the latter have knowledge of the cash-crop export markets they are seeking to enter, which extend beyond Zimbabwe's borders. Thus, a new class of landowner based less exclusively on race and more on an emergent capitalist class may be emerging.

This is not to suggest that the FTLRP was a complete failure or that its prognosis is pessimistic. Moyo adds that while "some politically influential and wealthier classes use administrative fiat, ethno-regional sentiments and sometimes force, to expand their landholdings," such inequalities are not going without challenge. "A few civil society organisations call for more land to be redistributed to farm workers, women and youths. As a result, the government is working on a land audit framework which, among other things, seeks to broaden the inclusion of these groups and of other politically excluded persons" (Moyo, 2013: 69). With the assistance of activist movements, Zimbabweans are calling for a grassroots assessment of the successes and limitations of land reform, and they are invested in expanding access to land and capital, especially for those who have been unable to access either, even under ambitious land tenure laws.

5.5 Synthesis: What Kinds of Postcolonial Futures Can We Imagine?

We have seen two distinct approaches to a familiar postcolonial problem: Who gets to own land in a setting marked by generations of historical inequalities? As is often the case with the messy world of social science, the results are mixed. In South Africa, land remains not only a dividing point between haves and have-nots – broken down frequently along racial lines – but a symbol of widespread material alienation. In Zimbabwe, more blacks have gained access to land holdings since the implementation of the FTLRP, yet broader structural problems remain, and many Zimbabweans have not tasted the fruits of these labors. At an abstract philosophical level, these two cases offer tradeoffs between the inalienable, unquestionable rights of individual property owners and the rights of various collectivities – whether parsed as classes, races, ethno-nations, etc. – to a shared well-being and economically prosperous future.

While such philosophical choices are important to bear in mind, we must not lose sight of the practical, lived consequences of each approach. The neoliberal model adopted in post-apartheid South Africa protects the sanctity of individual deeds to lands, including those inherited from previous generations of settlers in the region, but it also complicates the prospects for ensuring widespread access to land resources. On the other hand, the postcolonial alternative enacted in Zimbabwe proceeded from an ethic of righting historical injustices and prioritizing the interests of black farmers to till their ancestral homeland, connecting peoplehood to the land itself (cf. Shipton, 2007), yet this program faces the two-fold difficulty of implementing its ideals in a way that is even-handed and of making a lasting change despite the ongoing specter of global neoliberal agribusiness models. Zimbabwe offers a cautionary tale of the intractability of economic conditions that structure people's material realities and incentives, despite the impact of politically mandated reform.

So what is a viable pathway forward? Despite their calls for recognizing the large-scale structural components that have complicated land reform in both Zimbabwe and South Africa, activist-minded historians and sociologists like the late Sam Moyo are not resigned to the futility of making alternatives work. New political movements, including those aligned with the EFF's push to nationalize land ownership, are proposing alternatives to a state logic that prioritizes market action above *all other* claims and interests. Even in less Marxian formulations, organizations and scholars across southern Africa are increasingly open to models that can bring about incremental change by addressing at a local level the satellite of issues that orbit the land question: not just land title itself but access to capital, the operation and subsidies of large-scale corporate farms, and the administrative infrastructure that has slowed change in both countries. Given how deeply essential land use is to human life and how access to this resource continues to be structured according to historical injustices, these land reform efforts can be seen as one component of a larger global conversation around reparations for past harms of colonialism and racialized violence.[4] As we consider a more expansive purview for what intergenerational harm looks like – and how we can ameliorate it in the present – access to space and resources, especially but not exclusively agricultural ones, and reform of industrialized agribusiness models that now dominate world markets ought to be central points of attention. Land provides a tangible model for how postcolonial redistributions of wealth might be undertaken, but they are only one element of an intertwined system, including such diverse institutions as law, education, and even language policies.

Finally, we must look to the practical realities – "on-the-ground," as it were – that shape whatever land tenure systems will be pursued. The Eurocentric assumption that individual titles would produce secure tenure can be "treacherously misleading. Untitled lands are by no means necessarily insecure, and such titling more often than not seems to heighten insecurity of tenure" (Shipton, 1994: 364). Whatever solutions are proposed, we ought to be imaginative and capacious in our scope for what possible solutions might look like. It is critical to move beyond simplistic, one-sided solutions frequently offered in response to questions of land ownership. As Moore (1998) reminds us, the lines dividing indigenous and colonial (or, in our case, neoliberal and alternative) models of land tenure are not always so clear. Rather than essentializing the differences between European and African, individualistic and communal approaches to land, we can observe what happens when people partake in the elements of multiple,

---

[4] For a fuller discussion of the politics of reparations in the United States, see Coates 2014.

overlapping systems. By questioning some of the deep-seated presumptions built into neoliberal models, though, we discover that a single, market-centric approach is not inevitable, and the more alternatives that can be envisioned, the greater the likelihood of conjuring practical solutions that do not fall neatly into existing proposals.

References

Chari, Tendai. 2013. "Media framing of land reform in Zimbabwe." In *Land and Agrarian Reform in Zimbabwe: Beyond White-Settler Capitalism*, edited by Sam Moyo and Walter Chambati, 291–329. Dakar: Council for the Development of Social Science Research in Africa.

Clark, Christopher. 2019. "South Africa confronts a legacy of apartheid." *The Atlantic*, May 3, 2019. www.theatlantic.com/international/archive/2019/05/land-reform-south-africa-election/586900

Coates, Ta-Nehisi. 2014. "The case for reparations." *The Atlantic*, June, 2014. www.theatlantic.com/magazine/archive/2014/06/the-case-for-reparations/361631

Cocks, Tim, and Emma Rumney. 2020. "South Africa's Ramaphosa warns against using farm murders to stoke racial hatred." *Reuters*, October 12, 2020. www.reuters.com/article/uk-safrica-farm-murder/south-africas-ramaphosa-warns-against-using-farm-murders-to-stoke-racial-hatred-idUKKBN26X0ZT

Comaroff, Jean, and John Comaroff. 1997. *Of Revelation and Revolution, Volume 2: The Dialectics of Modernity on a South African Frontier.* Chicago: University of Chicago Press.

Crapanzano, Vincent. 1985. *Waiting: The Whites of South Africa.* New York: Random House.

Department of Rural Development and Land Reform. 2017. *Land Audit Report: Phase II: Private Land Ownership by Race, Gender and Nationality.* Version 2. Pretoria: Republic of South Africa.

Economic Freedom Fighters. 2013. "Economic freedom fighters founding manifesto: Radical movement towards economic freedom in our lifetime." *Economic Freedom Fighters National Assembly*, July 27, 2013. https://effonline.org/wp-content/uploads/2019/07/Founding-Manifesto.pdf

Hargrove, Melissa D. 2009. "Mapping the 'social field of whiteness': White racism as habitus in the city where history lives." *Transforming Anthropology* 17 (2): 93–104.

Howard-Hassmann, Rhoda E. 2010. "Mugabe's Zimbabwe, 2000–2009: Massive human rights violations and the failure to protect." *Human Rights Quarterly* 32 (4): 898–920.

Hughes, David McDermott. 2006. "Hydrology of hope: Farm dams, conservation, and whiteness in Zimbabwe." *American Ethnologist* 33 (2): 269–287.

Jacobs, Peter. 2012. "Whither agrarian reform in South Africa?" *Review of African Political Economy* 39 (131): 171–180.

Kenyatta, Jomo. 1938. *Facing Mount Kenya: The Tribal Life of the Gikuyu.* London: Harvill Secker.

Makhulu, Anne-Maria. 2010. "The question of freedom: Post-emancipation South Africa in a neoliberal age." In *Ethnographies of Neoliberalism,* edited by Carol J. Greenhouse, 131–145. Philadelphia: University of Pennsylvania Press.

Mamdani, Mahmood. 1996. *Citizen and Subject: Contemporary Africa and the Legacy of Late Colonialism.* Princeton, NJ: Princeton University Press.

Mangcu, Xolela. 2014. *Biko: A Life.* London: I.B. Tauris.

Mariri, Dimo. 2019. "Land at the heart of EFF, FF+ ideological victories in election 2019." *News24,* May 14, 2019. www.news24.com/news24/Elections/Voices/land-at-the-heart-of-eff-ff-ideological-victories-in-election-2019-20190514

Massey, Douglas S., and Nancy A. Denton. 1998. *American Apartheid: Segregation and the Making of the Underclass.* Cambridge, MA: Harvard University Press.

Mawere, Munyaradzi, and Tapuwa R. Mubaya. 2015. "Indigenous mechanisms for disaster risk reduction: How the Shona of Zimbabwe managed drought and famine." In *Harnessing Cultural Capital for Sustainability: A Pan Africanist Perspective,* edited by Munyaradzi Mawere and Samuel Awuah-Nyamekye, 1–31. Bamenda: Langaa Research & Publishing CIG.

Moore, Sally Falk. 1998. "Changing African land tenure: Reflections on the incapacities of the state." *The European Journal of Development Research* 10 (2): 33–49.

Moyo, Sam. 2011. "Alternatives during the neoliberal crisis." In *The Agrarian Question in the Neoliberal Era: Primitive Accumulation and the Peasantry,* edited by Utsa Patnaik and Sam Moyo, 79–80. Cape Town: Pambazuka Press.

2013. "Land reform and redistribution in Zimbabwe since 1980." In *Land and Agrarian Reform in Zimbabwe: Beyond White-Settler Capitalism,* edited by Sam Moyo and Walter Chambati, 29–77. Dakar: Council for the Development of Social Science Research in Africa.

Murray, Martin J. 2011. *City of Extremes: The Spatial Politics of Johannesburg*. Durham, NC: Duke University Press.

Musiyiwa, Mickias. 2016. "Shona as a land-based nature-culture: A study of the (re)construction of Shona land mythology in popular songs." In *Natures of Africa: Ecocriticism and Animal Studies in Contemporary Cultural Forms*, edited by F. Fiona Moolla, 49–76. Johannesburg: Wits University Press.

Pilossof, Rory. 2014. "Labor relations in Zimbabwe from 1900 to 2000: Sources, interpretations, and understandings." *History in Africa* 41: 337–362.

Rusenga, Clemence. 2019. "The agribusiness model in South African land reform? Land use implications for the land reform beneficiaries." *Agrarian South: Journal of Political Economy* 8 (3): 440–461.

Sadomba, Zvakanyorwa W. 2011. *War Veterans in Zimbabwe's Revolution: Challenging Neo-Colonialism and Settler and International Capital*. London: James Currey.

Scoones, Ian, Blasio Mavedzenge, Felix Murimbarimba, and Chrispen Sukume. 2017. "Tobacco, contract farming, and agrarian change in Zimbabwe." *Journal of Agrarian Change* 18 (1): 22–42.

Shipton, Parker. 1994. "Land and culture in tropical Africa: Soils, symbols, and the metaphysics of the mundane." *Annual Review of Anthropology* 23: 347–377.

2007. *The Nature of Entrustment: Intimacy, Exchange, and the Sacred in Africa*. New Haven, CT: Yale University Press.

Slobodian, Quinn. 2018. *Globalists: The End of Empire and the Birth of Neoliberalism*. Cambridge, MA: Harvard University Press.

Suzuki, Yuka. 2017. "The nature of whiteness: Race, animals, and nation in Zimbabwe." Seattle: University of Washington Press.

Williams, Jennifer. 2018. "Trump's tweet echoing white nationalist propaganda about South African farmers, explained." *Vox*, August 23, 2018. www.vox.com/policy-and-politics/2018/8/23/17772056/south-africa-trump-tweet-afriforum-white-farmers-violence

Žižek, Slavoj. 2013. "If Nelson Mandela really had won, he wouldn't be seen as a universal hero." *Guardian*, December 9, 2013. www.theguardian.com/commentisfree/2013/dec/09/if-nelson-mandela-really-had-won

6 | *How Should Food be Produced?*

SCOTT FREEMAN

After the end of formal colonialism, numerous neoliberal international organizations stepped in to manage the international affairs of newly independent nations. The presumption of governments was that the best way to create national welfare was to let markets steer production by integrating the nation into an international capitalist order premised on market specialization and debt relationships. Here Freeman looks at the sort of industrial agricultural production that this kind of geopolitical arrangement engenders, focusing on pineapple plantations in Costa Rica. Cost Rican pineapple planatations are monocrops that exhaust the fertility of the land, provide poorly paid dangerous work, and spread toxic pesticides. International neoliberal governance structures with the overriding priority of stimulating market competion have enabled a system where production for the global is the objective. By contrast, Freeman shows what a food-growing setup can look like if it is oriented toward local production and away from international markets by examining "agroecology" in Haiti.

I want to say something about the decline, the virtual ruin, of rural life, and about the influence and effect of agricultural surpluses, which I believe are accountable for more destruction of land and people than any other economic "factor."

(Wendell Berry)

The question of how to grow economies is often placed at the heart of debates on development and economics. Bringing so-called developing countries to the material status of so-called developed countries has over the years meant an economic transformation and the production of agricultural commodities for export. Producing agricultural surplus, as Wendell Berry refers to, is part of the economic model whereby food is grown not for consumption in the region of production but produced in a very large quantity and exported. The goals of such programs are to increase profits for a company, and to improve national economies of so-called developing countries by growing the export industry that, planners and governments hope, will provide some degree of employment and well-being.

During the late 1970s and beyond, planners from international financial institutions and even within governments used the logic of neoliberalism to fuel an embrace of global economies in order to decrease debt and increase GDP. As a result, exports increased and trade boomed. For agriculture, this meant that large swaths of land were increasingly dedicated to producing food for faraway countries. This, according the economic recommendations of international financial institutions, could improve the economic growth that occurs in a country and provide jobs for citizens of the country. This model of growth relies on the idea that by exporting agricultural products, a given country will increase its measures of economic production, reduce foreign debt, correct trade imbalances, and provide employment. The model appears to create economic possibilities in a large, interconnected, and globalized world. But what has happened to the lives of people who are most intimately involved in producing agricultural products for export? If we look past broad statistics, are the lives, economies, and environments affected by such industries thriving? What are the uncalculated costs – the "externalities" – of such policies?

This chapter looks at two countries to understand the impacts of neoliberal approaches to agriculture and potential alternatives to those approaches. The first case is that of Costa Rica and the rise of the pineapple industry. This example follows Costa Rica's embrace of an agricultural strategy based on the export of food products into the global economy. Costa Rica has rapidly become the top global producer of fresh pineapple. Yet even as Costa Rica's pineapples are more visible in international markets, this strategy has not provided corresponding improvements in the lives for those who work on pineapple plantations or who are close to the very negative environmental impacts of pineapple production.

In contrast, the chapter looks to strategies of agroecology as practiced in Costa Rica and Haiti. Agroecology is a set of heterogeneous practices that rely on environmentally conscious methods long practiced by smallholding farmers, all while producing food for localized consumption. The scale here is far smaller; agroecology is not often the blanket agricultural or economic policy in a given country but rather exists in regional practices that starkly contrast the dominant models. As a result, while the first part of the chapter on Costa Rica focuses on the national priorities and economic plans of Costa Rica, the second half of the chapter presents the experiences of a Haitian grassroots organization, one that supports farmers using agroecology in their own plots. Even though the heterogeneous practices of agroecology may not always be reflected in national policies, they are widespread across the globe. In the first case, the goals are improving indices like GDP and profit margins, while creating economies and environments that are resilient and localized is the goal of the second.

Both cases then, are ultimately about understanding the relationship of food production to the well-being of the country. The first of these cases highlights the neoliberal approach to agriculture: the production of agriculture not as food, but as a commodity that is traded globally in order to produce economic value. What makes this a particularly neoliberal strategy in the case of Costa Rica is that the move toward export crops is the result of reforms that removed price controls, government supports, and protection of domestic food production. Economic advisors and politicians have favored these policies in hopes of increasing agricultural export that would in turn increase economic growth. This is quite different than the approach of the second case, that of agroecology. Here, food production is not based on the production of surplus in order to spur economic growth. Food is not exported into a globalized market in order to generate money for the exporting country. Instead, food is produced for regional and domestic consumption. Food is produced on a smaller scale and in ways that do not require the damaging pesticides and chemical inputs of export agriculture. Labor conditions are far improved as people work their own land rather than work for hourly pay from a large company. Ultimately, the chapter will argue that the search for wealth through the export of food commodities has not provided well-being for people working in and close to these industries. These practices have produced a series of negative social and environmental impacts often not calculated in analyzing globalized trade and production. Thinking outside of that model of agricultural production might mean examining strategies like agroecology, which explicitly link the welfare of human beings and the environment through the production of food.

6.1 Costa Rican Pineapple

Costa Rica is often portrayed as a remarkably sustainable and green country, one with no standing army, and one that has experienced economic stability in part because of its peaceful and environmentally conscious policies. Parks and protected areas in Costa Rica are praised as both economically beneficial but also environmentally sound policy.

With a GDP that is higher than other countries in the region, this combination of economy and environmental policy appears at least on the surface to have placed Costa Rica ahead of its neighbors; Costa Rica has consistently outperformed economies in Latin America up through 2014.[1] This growth was bolstered by an economic strategy that relied upon embracing an economic model based on export economies and attracting foreign direct investment. In short, quickly after the Latin American debt crisis of the 1980s, Costa Rica began a new economic strategy that has relied principally on export. Now, food and agriculture are the major exports of Costa Rica and some of the major contributors to economic production. The export of food products drives economic indicators like GDP and has given Costa Rica a large trade surplus; these indicators reflect growth, which ostensibly means that the economy is strong. The biggest agricultural exports coming out of Costa Rica are bananas and pineapples.

Costa Rica's embrace of an export-based economy occurred following the Latin American debt crisis of the 1980s, but fruit export had long been present. In the late 1800s, foreign investors built railroads that became the infrastructural component that would give rise to the banana plantations of the United Fruit Company, now known as Chiquita. Through deals with the government to incentivize the construction of railroads, American investors received land from the Costa Rican government.[2] Ninety-nine-year leases of both railway and associated land meant that in some areas of Central America, Guatemala for example, the United Fruit Company was the largest landowner in the country. Agricultural exports have since been at the heart of foreign interests in Costa Rica and a key component of the economy.

---

[1] Ferreira et al., "The successes and shortcoming of Costa Rica exports diversification policies," 10.
[2] Edelman and León, "Cycles of land grabbing in Central America."

Costa Rica's agricultural exports have long been dominated by bananas and, to a lesser extent, coffee. The export of food and agricultural products was an entrenched part of the national economic strategy. These exports were facilitated and (in the case of bananas in particular) directed by the hand of foreign actors. This export model in Costa Rica was, till the latter part of the twentieth century, balanced by a state that spent money on social programming.[3] Costa Rica had implemented many reforms that involved a generous social security program and included taxes on imported goods that protected the production of Costa Rican products.[4]

This all changed in the 1980s when new types of economic logics were introduced. Those years were marked by the high price of oil and the increase of US interest rates, which meant that Latin American countries' debt became nearly unpayable. In previous decades, foreign debt had financed farm subsidies and support in Costa Rica. A global recession and high oil prices meant that the debt was a liability and Costa Rica could not rely on trade to cover the expense. Into the 1980s, a series of broader economic recessions and multinational actors encouraged new approaches to state economic reform.

Large international lenders, like the World Bank and IMF offered loans in the 1980s to help the economy in Costa Rica and many other countries. Each of these loans, however, had conditions that were intended to increase growth, but also ensured that the debt to private lenders would be repaid. Costa Rica took structural adjustment loans from the World Bank in 1985 and 1989.[5] These loans were part of a larger set of plans that were to remove Costa Rica's protectionist economic policies seen to be limiting international trade. The hypothesis of these structural reforms was that high government spending should be lowered as a way to thin the budget of the country and direct money toward paying off debt. This was paired with moving the economy from one that was based around producing for internal and regional markets to a strategy based around international trade. The structural adjustment loans required moving investment away from food crops for domestic consumption within Costa Rica, and toward "nontraditional" export crops; those that would move away from the country's reliance

---

[3] Edelman, *Peasants Against Globalization.*
[4] Cattaneo, Ojeda, and Robinson, "Costa Rica trade liberalization, fiscal imbalances, and macroeconomic policy."
[5] Ibid.

on banana, coffee, and sugar.[6] The idea was that these new export crops would generate money that would pay off the private loans.

Despite these policies, Costa Rica's national debt was about the same in the mid 1990s as it was in the early years of debt crisis in 1982.[7] The country has maintained a cycle of taking out new loans to service old ones and providing only fragile economic recovery. In this context, Costa Rica had developed attractive terms for private sector investment. That, in combination with large plots of fertile land and available labor, meant that pineapple cultivation fitted the bill to provide the economic relief that planners envisioned. Ultimately, the conditions for the rise of pineapple were not so different from those of the banana. External investors and corporations entered into an economic landscape that encouraged foreign investment in order to create markets that would generate national economic growth as well as profit for large foreign companies.

Pineapple seemed to fit the bill as a new economic motor for the country. It was a fruit that would grow well in Costa Rica, would rely upon the infrastructure laid down by banana producers, was a "nontraditional" export, and the industry could therefore receive many of the new government incentives. It seemed like pineapple would be a fruit that would bring the type of economic growth to Costa Rica that economic planners of the 1980s and 1990s had hoped for. Pineapple production in Costa Rica skyrocketed almost from the moment of its inception. From 1985 to 1989, pineapple production increased by 55 percent each year.[8] Following that early period, the growth has continued to be shocking: export of pineapple saw 133 percent growth from 1998 to 2003 and 220 percent growth in the area cultivated from 2000 to 2019.[9] Costa Rica is now the largest supplier of fresh pineapple to the US, and pineapple now represents more than one-third (34 percent) of Costa Rican agricultural exports, second only to the export of bananas.[10]

---

[6] Ibid.   [7] Edelman, *Peasants Against Globalization*.

[8] Maglianesi-Sandoz, "Desarrollo de las piñeras en Costa Rica y sus impactos sobre ecosistemas naturales y agro-urbanos."

[9] Paniagua-Molina and Solís-Rivera, "Effect of 'golden pineapple innovation' on Costa Rica's pineapple exports to US market: An econometric approach"; Gonzalez, "Diagnostic and conditions of the pineapple industry in Costa Rica"; SEPSA, "Boletin Estadistico Agropecuario 30."

[10] Paniagua-Molina and Solís-Rivera, "Effect of 'golden pineapple innovation' on Costa Rica's pineapple exports to US market: An econometric approach"; PROCOMER, "Anuario Estadístico."

The growth of pineapple was in part due to the very favorable export climate in Costa Rica that began in the 1980s and 1990s. Costa Rica provided tax exoneration for foreign investment, and an export subsidy for those nontraditional products. Consequently, the government programs and spending that once were targeted at small Costa Rican farmers shifted to encourage private companies to develop export commodities. Between March of 1988 and September of 1989, PINDECO (Pineapple Development Corporation – a part of Del Monte) received the most tax credits of any company in Costa Rica.[11] The subsidies for small farmers and social programming had been drastically reduced because of the economic model offered by international financial institutions (World Bank and IMF in particular) and facilitated by the Costa Rican government. Incentives were provided to foreign companies to produce commodities that would boost exports and therefore, hopefully, economic growth.

Pineapple quickly went from being farmed at the margins of existing crops to the focus of large plantations. Pineapple in Costa Rica became a monoculture plantation crop, the only crop planted in a large, labor intensive swath of land. The existing investments that Del Monte had made in banana cultivation meant that Del Monte was building upon pre-existing infrastructure. The plantations of pineapple require a great deal of labor, water, and pesticides to ensure that the crops grow appropriately and are exported quickly. The crop grows only one fruit per bush, so a great deal of space is necessary to produce quantities of pineapple that satisfy both the demands of export-oriented economic growth and the growing demands of consumers abroad. Pineapple also requires a lot of water. Heavy rains in Costa Rica are heavily supplemented by intensive irrigation drawn from rivers nearby. Additionally, pesticide application is necessary to meet the standards of export and because, like any other crop or plant that is monocropped, pests and disease are a constant issue. The work of watering, spraying, picking, packaging, and transporting pineapple is done by wage workers on contract. As pineapple is tied more and more closely to the economic fate of the country, it deeply affects the people and land that are required to grow it.

---

[11] Vagneron, Faure, and Loeillet, "Is there a pilot in the chain?"; Barham et al., "Nontraditional agricultural exports in Latin America."

Unfortunately, pineapple production has brought about a number of issues in the regions where it is grown and harvested. Principally these can be understood in terms of economic impact and environmental impacts. The growth of the pineapple industry has occurred in tandem with the increase in pesticides in the country. In spite of marketing itself as a green and sustainable destination for tourism and investment, Costa Rica is one of the highest per-capita users of pesticides globally.[12] The increase of pesticides correlates with the rise of pineapples. The sanitary demands and standards of international export markets mean that significant amounts of pesticides and herbicides are used in pineapple production.[13]

Bromacil in particular was a very popular pesticide used by producers because of its ability to eliminate weeds that competed for water and space with pineapples, which have very shallow root systems and slow growth. Before being banned in 2017, Bromacil was widely applied to limit weed growth because in part, it could be applied only four days before planting pineapple. Leading up to its banning was the realization, through a number of studies, that Bromacil, which is highly water soluble, was leaching into groundwater supplies and contaminating well water.[14] In regions devoted to pineapple production, Bromacil was detected in groundwater at levels higher than safe for the protection of wildlife.[15]

But pesticide use also has impacts on human populations. The water used for irrigation spreads pesticides and herbicides across downhill land, seeping further into underground water sources. The water affects human and animal populations by contaminating waterways and also affects the workers that are in direct contact with the chemicals, applying them by spraying the plants. Fruit workers have been affected by the application of pesticides, citing everything from headache and nausea to neurobehavioral effects and cancers.[16]

---

[12] FAOSTAT www.fao.org/faostat/en/#data/EP/visualize; accessed April 12, 2021.
[13] Ferreira et al., "The successes and shortcoming of Costa Rica exports diversification policies."
[14] Valverde and Chaves, "The banning of bromacil in Costa Rica."
[15] Echevarría Saenz et al. "Environmental hazards of pesticides from pineapple crop production in the Río Jiménez watershed (Caribbean Coast, Costa Rica)"; Castillo, Martínez, and Ugalde, "Ecotoxicology and pesticides in Central America."
[16] Barraza, "Pesticide use in banana and plantain production."

Pesticide use and abuse has drawn the attention of international media, but labor conditions have also grabbed public attention. As plantations occupy large swaths of land, individuals who now have no land or little land rely upon them for low wage labor. Unionization attempts have been stifled by pineapple producers and have lead to repression and mass layoffs.[17] Fear of being blacklisted from employment keeps many families from speaking out on these issues. Further, companies like PINDECO employ a very elaborate set of strategies to ensure that the concerns of workers are muffled. The company provides healthcare for its own employees, which, while seemingly a thoughtful benefit, has kept health concerns from reaching public health experts. Labor is discretely contracted, such that any issues while working are not to be addressed to PINDECO but to a labor subsidiary at arm's reach from issues of legal liability. Because of the challenging and high cost of smallholder agriculture, and the rate at which fertile land has been bought and dedicated to pineapple, turning to wage labor in pineapple plantations is a choice that many in pineapple-growing areas make in order to provide a minimum income for their families.

Ultimately, pineapple has not led to regional or local economic gains. The province of Buenos Aires in Costa Rica has an overwhelming presence of pineapple plantations and cultivation, yet the municipality is one of the poorest in the country.[18] The Costa Rican state provides multiple incentives to the pineapple industry, but these favorable policies have not translated into an industry that provides well-being for the regions it works in. The theory that the wealth will eventually "trickle down" has not happened. Pineapple plantations do not produce wealth around them; instead, there is a record of environmental contamination and poorly compensated and dangerous wage labor.

6.2 Agroecology in Haiti and Beyond

As structural adjustment policies increased the focus on export agriculture in Costa Rica, they simultaneously decreased the support for

---

[17] *Guardian.* "Bitter fruit: The truth about supermarket pineapple"

[18] Brown et al. "The politics of pineapple: Examining the inequitable impacts of southern Costa Rica's pineapple industry"; Instituto Nacional de Estadística y Censos (INEC). Encuesta Nacional de Hogares Julio 2018: Resultados Generales. http://inec.cr/sites/default/files/documetos-biblioteca-virtual/enaho-2018.pdf

domestically oriented agriculture.[19] This means that small landowners in Costa Rica, struggling to make a living off small plots, had to look elsewhere for income. In part, this spurred urbanization, and further contributed to the need to diversify incomes. Even when support for small-scale agriculture was pulled, many farmers still had access to land and continue to practice agriculture as one of many income strategies. Family farming in Costa Rica accounts for approximately 73,000 families that rely on family farms for income.[20] Small-scale farming often exists side by side with the labor required by plantations. Landowners may own very small plots of land and may also engage in plantation labor as well as on-farm work.[21]

In contrast to the intensely monocropped pineapple there is a quieter agricultural practice, one that is not often sponsored by country governments nor corporate interests. Accordingly, it appears rarely as a blanket state policy, but more commonly as a patchwork of efforts. Agroecology is the title for a collection of agricultural practices that takes into account not only the production of agriculture, but simultaneously, as its name suggests, concerns for the environment. This approach, in many of its iterations, is far less concerned with agriculture as a means for export production; it considers agriculture as a way to produce food for far more local consumption. Agroecology encompasses a variety of practices that move away from chemical inputs like fertilizers and herbicides or pesticides, relying instead on how more organic cultivation practices oriented to environmental well-being can produce results that are both healthy and economically beneficial for farmers.

This section will look at smaller examples of where and how agroecology is successfully practiced in contexts where national policies may not align. In Costa Rica, as we have already seen, the national focus on export-oriented agriculture has helped Costa Rica become one of the top users of pesticides in the world. Still, even in this context, agroecological approaches are used and embraced by farmers throughout the country and form an important contrast to the broader plantation models that are more visible. Whereas the goals of export-based agricultural production see economic growth and profit as eventually

[19] Galt, *Food Systems in an Unequal World.*
[20] Schneider, *Family Farming in Latin America.*
[21] Lansing et al., "Placing the plantation in smallholder agriculture."

leading to positive change, agroecology aims to provide that well-being as an integrated part of cultivating food.

In Haiti, where I have done the majority of my anthropological fieldwork, the agricultural landscape is quite different from Costa Rica. Agricultural investment by the Haitian state has long been lagging, and aid agencies too have dedicated relatively few of their resources to supporting agriculture.[22] In contrast to Costa Rica's large landowners, Haiti's landscape is marked by many smallholders. Individuals might have multiple small plots and often farm on hillsides. Despite the presence of many smallholders, Haiti has a long history of extractive agriculture and economies. US occupations seized land for the benefit of the United States and foreign extractive agriculture has long been a force that has displaced and disenfranchised residents of the countryside. More recently, in the north of the country, a garment manufacturing factory was funded by international financial institutions such as the InterAmerican Development Bank and displaced Haitian farmers, removing them from fertile land in order to build an export-oriented factory. Haiti's history has been marked by these foreign interventions that have benefitted elites and outside powers at the expense of farmers in the countryside.

While smallholder agriculture is a common practice in Haiti, farming is challenging for multiple reasons. Because many Haitian farmers often do not have access to fertilizers and chemical inputs, many of their practices might fit into the framework of agroecology. But living in a precarious economic context, some farmers apply what fertilizer and pesticide they can access in the hopes of increasing yields. Further, Haitian agricultural markets are extremely challenging for small farmers. Haiti imports a great deal of food staples at discounted prices – a result of neoliberal reforms that slashed tariffs in the 1990s – which puts smallholders at a disadvantage when bringing their food to Haiti's domestic market. With a dire need to produce economically viable crops, farmers may see fertilizers and other chemical inputs as an attractive route to economic productivity. In many ways, moving toward these inputs seems remarkably reasonable; wanting to provide reliable food and income for one's family is what each farmer is striving toward.

---

[22] Shamsie, Yasmin. "Haiti's post-earthquake transformation: What of agriculture and rural development?"

Even in this challenging context, there are groups of farmers and peasant movements that reject the notion that chemical additions are required to produce crops, embracing instead agroecology as a principle that orients both economic and environmental practice. This is in stark contrast to some of the recommendations that come financed by aid organizations. In Haiti, research and practice funded by USAID (the United States Agency for International Development), supports pesticide training and fertilizer training, reinforcing and fostering farmer use of agrochemicals and externally purchased fertilizers.[23] Such programs sell subsidized fertilizers, herbicides, and pesticides to farmers. In this context, while Haitian farmers have long used cultivation strategies that embrace polycropping and organic materials, advice from aid agencies does not always draw on that knowledge.

Agroecology in many ways is a direct contrast to the forms of production and consumption exhibited by industrial agriculture and export models.[24] Intensive, export-led agriculture requires intensive monocropped spaces to produce profitable quantities of food to be exported. A key component of the model is that food is exported from the country and consumed elsewhere. That consumption abroad is what provides the profit for large corporations that are able to set up and maintain these commodity chains. The neoliberal aspect of this approach is the movement of state funding away from social supports of small farmers, and toward policies that open markets to foreign agribusiness and the elimination of export and import taxes in order to encourage participation in global economies. The broad export agricultural model is aligned with the interests of foreign corporations and large-scale measures of economic growth. Agroecological practice directly challenges this model of food production and economy.

Agroecology differs both in how it is practiced and the destination of food. It has been referred to as a science, a practice, and a movement.[25] As a science, it is the study that attempts to explain functioning agricultural systems and their relationship to the environment. As a practice, it is the principals that allow the production of food without

[23] Molnar et al., "Agricultural development in northern Haiti."

[24] Rosset and Martínez-Torres, "Rural social movements and agroecology."

[25] Rosset and Martínez-Torres; Wezel et al., "Agroecology as a science, a movement and a practice"; Sosa et al., *Revolución agroecológica: el movimiento de Campesino a Campesino de la ANAP en Cuba.*

agrichemicals, relying on agricultural practice that has often been handed down through generations. As a movement, it is the groups across national borders that incorporate even broader social concepts like food sovereignty and equality into the production and consumption of food. One such group, *La Via Campesina*, works with various peasant organizations and associations globally. That broader movement is geared at more than eliminating pesticide use and includes farmers who might call their practices organic, natural farming, indigenous, or sustainable agriculture. But key in all of this, at least for *La Via Campesina*, is that agriculture relies on farming systems that rely on farmers themselves, small farms run by families and that integrate crops, trees, and livestock.[26]

One of the principal issues that agroecology (and its associated practices) responds to is the interrelated ecological impacts of industrial agriculture. Monocropping, planting one crop over a large swath of land, is a practice that makes crops susceptible to disease and exhausts soils. Instead, agroecology insists upon relying on a diverse set of practices that welcome and support biodiversity in farming. This may mean integrating various crops that support each other's growth, and do not compete for the same resources.[27] Planting multiple crops in the same plot can also be more economically productive for farmers and diversifies sources of income, which means that these strategies are more resilient in the face of a changing climate.[28] It may involve integrating agroforestry and the use of trees in farming or introducing livestock that works symbiotically with a particular crop.

Movements like *La Via Campesina* respond directly to the monocropped agricultural model that corresponds to industrial agriculture. The problems of monocropped agriculture are both ecological and economic. Ecologically, planting one crop alone increases profit margins but weakens that crop's ability to bounce back from disease and is an invitation to pests and soil degradation. As a result, the monocropped model often requires the application of chemical pesticides, herbicides, and fertilizers in order to facilitate production. The monocropping strategy also depletes soil nutrients. Using this model then requires fertilizer to improve the nutrients in the soil. The

---

[26] Rosset and Martínez-Torres, "Rural social movements and agroecology."
[27] Sylvester, *The Difficult Task of Peace.*
[28] Rosset and Martínez-Torres, "Rural social movements and agroecology."

necessary reliance then on fertilizer (to improve soil quality) and chemical pesticides/herbicides (to eliminate pests) then produces ecological effects: chemical runoff and associated issues with water contamination.

Agroecological movements like *La Via Campesina* are also concerned with the interrelated issues of on farm economics and dependence upon external inputs.[29] Using chemical inputs like pesticides and fertilizers and even foreign seeds means that larger corporations have a sustained presence on small farms. That increases the costs that small farmers bear. Agroecology sees these external inputs not only as ecologically damaging, but also as a way that small farmer's independence is jeopardized by reliance on the models and products of foreign corporations. By relying on strategies like poly-cropping, developing organic compost, using livestock, and adding in different types of trees and plants, the hope is not only to improve the environment around the agricultural plot, but to reduce farmer expenses. Additionally, this increases the independence of farmers to produce their own food on their own terms.

In Haiti, agroecological practices have been incorporated into farming practices supported by the *Mouvman Peyizan Akildinò* (MPA), a grassroots organization in the North of Haiti that has approximately 7000 members. The organization was formed in 1984, in a political climate in which using the word "organization" was dangerous because the dictatorial Duvalier regime considered it to be associated with communism. Their goals are those of peasant solidarity, and to create a space in which people are not fleeing Haiti, but creating a society where peasants are valued, flourish, and are at the heart of a movement to "re-green" Haiti. The organization is member of *La Via Campesina*, and shares their larger vision about agroecology and the self-determination of those who work the land. MPA has agronomists that accompany Haitian farmers in implementing agroecological practices, and committees in each of the various political subdivisions of the region where they work.

The leader of MPA emphasized to me how walking into a garden practicing agroecology is an entirely different experience from walking into a space where pesticides and fertilizers are used. Agroecological

---

[29] Rosset and Martínez-Torres, "Rural social movements and agroecology."

gardens necessarily have multiple types of vegetation, he said. They are not designed to support agroindustry but rather support food grown for subsistence: the products of that garden go to consumption of the family, the community, and the region. Only rarely do some of the crops go to the capital, but the majority of food production is for the region. Such spaces are dappled with shade coming from mango trees, sour sop trees, and avocado trees. In between these larger fruit trees, farmers plant the shorter trees of plantains and various species of bananas, along with the shorter plants that mark manioc buried underground. Spread around the various contours of the garden are beans, important because of their nitrogen-fixing properties that revitalize the soil. All of the crop placement, the president of MPA emphasized, is quite intentional, as crops exist as "families" in which one crop supports the growth of another. In addition to the polycropped gardens, in the flat plains of the north rice cultivation integrates other plants but also uses animals the process of production in order to improve soil and eliminate the need for chemical fertilizers. After harvesting rice, farmers bring cattle onto the rice fields to eat the leftover rice stalks and defecate, providing a natural fertilizer to the land. This, he said, is how we protect the environment, how we cool the environment, and how we protect humanity.

MPA's focus on encouraging polycropping and the use of organic material is not an isolated set of ideas: throughout Haiti, organizations draw on the farming practices that have long flourished on the island. These practices embrace gardens (*jaden*, or *conuco* in the Dominican Republic) that rely on polycropping. These are in large part the strategies of smallholding farmers passed down from generations. Accompanying farmers in garden walks in the southwest of the country is an experience of stepping over vines of sweet potatoes, ducking under banana trees, and walking around the long thin stems of pigeon peas. The practice of planting pigeon peas alongside corn and squash is both an economic and ecological practice: the crops result in a diversified income at harvest, but the crops complement each other, notably via the legumes that repopulate the soil with the necessary nitrogen for the other crops to grow. These practices are the dominant ones practiced smallholding farmers, but organizations like MPA work to reinforce and celebrate them and further work to highlight the ways that external chemical products disturb and negatively affect both the land and the people that work the land.

In this approach to agroecology, agriculture is seen as a key compo-nenet of food sovereignty. One of MPA's goals is to increase food sovereignty by increasing the food that Haitians consume that comes from Haiti. The hope is that each family can eat food that comes from the farms around them and thereby supports farmers and more local food production. As of yet, they've not been able to reach that goal given the import of food from outside of Haiti. During the 1990s, the US arranged a reduction of Haiti's tariffs on imported rice, moving the tariffs from approximately 30 percent to approximately 3 percent.[30] These tariff reductions were part of neoliberal economic reforms and have meant that US rice, subsidized by the US government, is sold in Haiti. This presents a challenge for Haitian farmers: their products must be less expensive than those that arrive from foreign imports.

In order to reduce the inputs from chemical pesticides and fertilizers, MPA works with farmers on the development of organic compost and sprays developed from plants found in the region. In order to deal with pests in agricultural cultivation, farmers use products that are made from leaves found in the region that repel insects. The concern with chemical fertilizer is that the use of fertilizer degrades the soil on which it is applied. The natural alternatives provide improved soil fertility without copious amounts of particular nutrients that not only leave the soil in poorer quality but add to chemical runoff which can lead to other negative issues like algae blooms.

These ecologically oriented methods also are implemented with a farmer's income in mind. Without the cost of buying externally manu-factured chemical products like fertilizer and herbicide or pesticide, farmers have fewer external expenditures. Further, these methods have allowed members to see improved production. The head of the organ-ization said that they keep 85–90 percent of their sweet potato without losses by using nonchemical measures. That means that through using a series of plant-based substances, farmers can not only decrease their expenses on external inputs; the practices also allow for sustained production.

MPA's work is aligned with the work of the Peasant's Movement of Papaye (MPP), a larger and well-known peasant's movement in Haiti. MPP uses agroecological principals and a co-learning methodology that draws on the work of Paulo Freire. Accordingly, their approach

---

[30] Cohen, "Diri Nasyonal ou Diri Miami?"

to education is that of an emancipatory social process that works with farmer-to-farmer co-learning rather than denigrating the knowledge that farmers already have.[31] This approach, and that of MPA, is that agroecology is a political practice that focuses on understanding and altering political and economic marginalization through a recognition of historic agricultural disempowerment.[32] The approach, also championed by *La Via Campesina*, is distinct in that it challenges the power imbalance between foreign experts that come to advise the "unknowing" Haitian farmer.[33] Instead, farmers draw on the practices they have taught each other, and themselves are in the position of knowledgeable teachers and experts. The structure of both MPP and MPA is decentralized, involving local meeting-groups across the areas they work in. Both groups champion a type of learning that moves away from the expertise of others and relies upon reflection and action that centers the experiences and knowledge of farmers themselves.

Though agroecological practices are widespread, they are very much in contrast to the dominant economic practices that draw on one intensively farmed cash crop. In Haiti, such extractive economies date back to Haiti's status as a plantation colony intended to export sugar, indigo, coffee, and other commodities to European powers. From the perspective of foreign powers, Haiti's role was to house plantations, producing commodities for Europe and America. In a sense then, there has always been the presence of a macro-economic policy of extraction alongside the existence of other farming practices that work in the shadows of these regimes.

In moving toward agroecological methods, farmers in both Haiti and Costa Rica work to both maintain incomes and also move toward environmentally conscious cultivation. But this hasn't meant a clear triumph of agroecology. As I write in 2021, Haiti is in the midst of a political and economic crisis, and Haitian government support for smallholding farmers is almost nonexistent. In Costa Rica, farmers using organic and agroecological models are able to produce food that competes in local markets, but in regions dominated by pineapple production, these farmers are often the exception to the rule. Talking to farmers using these practices in southwest Costa Rica, it was clear that though

---

[31] Moore, "Organize or die." [32] Ibid.
[33] McCune, Reardon, and Rosset, "Agroecological Formación in Rural Social Movements."

these practices are used, there is reticence by many in leaving wage labor jobs to engage in what is perceived as more risky organic farming.

Another challenge for agroecological practice is confronting established gender-based roles. In their research on women working in agroecology in Costa Rica, Sylvester and Little found that women who came into the practice of agroecology did so for reasons of health and the environment.[34] One farmer changed her cultivation practices after observing the negative effects of chemicals on allergies and skin conditions. Others the authors spoke to were using indigenous farming practices not because of reasons of health but because of their indigenous identity. The women they spoke to also saw agroecology as a way to improve their own incomes without relying on their partners. More broadly in this case and in research, women find the support of agriculture associations as important, but too often dominated by men.[35] Machismo and microaggressions were common. Women also found the triple burden of labor in productive, reproductive, and community spheres as particularly challenging for their entrance into agroecological practices.

There are moves by governments, including the Costa Rican government, to adapt agroecological principals on a broader scale. This may mean using agroecological principals even in commodities produced for export. For example, agroecological principals have been used in coffee production in Costa Rica. By reducing chemical inputs, pruning coffee plants, intercropping coffee with other annual crops for household consumption, and planting additional shade trees, farmers used strategies without external chemical inputs to practice agriculture.[36] This helped to improve the quality of the soil and also diminish the cost of external outputs. While this does not embrace the critical elements of food sovereignty, proponents argue that the strategy improves the negative environmental impacts of industrial agriculture and improves farm incomes.

6.3 Conclusion

Understanding the impacts of export-based agribusiness means necessarily acknowledging the costs of such practices on the people who

[34] Sylvester and Little, "I came all this way to receive training, am I really going to be taught by a woman?"
[35] Ibid.
[36] Babin, "The coffee crisis, fair trade, and agroecological transformation."

work the land and on the environment. These "environmental externalities" are not calculated when we see rising GDP and other broad
economic indicators. Examining alternatives to export-based agribusiness requires a recognition of smaller movements that do not necessarily take center stage in national economic policy. For that reason, this
chapter compared economic practices at the national level with practices that occur within more regional groups of farmers. The policies
that support export- and plantation-based agriculture align business
and government to ensure that the export of pineapple continues to be
one of Costa Rica's top products. The practices of agroecology in Haiti
and Costa Rica on the other hand are far less publicly visible.
International movements like *La Via Campesina* champion these
approaches. In many ways, agroecological practice is an insistence that
agriculture and food production needs to be locally driven, and few
national policies aim at such a decentralized approach. This comparison between what occurs as national policy and what occurs in smaller
movements highlights the need to pay attention to a wide variety of
food systems that are already being used.

The heterogenous movements and approaches included in agroecology are slowly making an impact on national-level policies. As
country governments start to link agricultural practices with environmental degradation and food sovereignty, laws have been passed in
Latin America (Nicaragua, Brazil, Uruguay) that support agroecology, and still others have laws that protect the environment and the
right to food.[37] In other cases, like Costa Rica and Brazil, despite
policies that support agroecology, the practice exists often in niches.
Political in nature, policies that support aspects of agroecological
practice may be targeted by politicians looking to support larger
commercial growth, seeing the support of smallholders as threatening
to a larger project of agroindustry-based national income. Some of the
advances of agroecology on the national level equate agroecology
with organic agriculture alone, and accordingly the strategy is interpreted as the substitution of inputs while not reconsidering issues of
land, foodways, and export priorities.[38] Varying definitions of agroecology may not then prioritize farmer knowledge and practices as

[37] Giraldo and McCune, "Can the state take agroecology to scale?"
[38] Rosset and Altieri, "Agroecology versus input substitution"; Giraldo and
McCune, "Can the state take agroecology to scale?"

much as they lean toward organic practices that have a favorable environmental impact. Perhaps such practices move the needle of national policy slowly away from toxic chemicals, but they may not challenge the dominant economic models that have proven deleterious for smallholding farmers.

Moving national level policies away from export industries like pineapple may not sustain the same sort of economic growth indicators. But the well-being provided by agroecological practices challenges the notion that producing food for external markets and growth is policy beneficial to all citizens. To return to the Wendell Berry quote at the beginning of this chapter, moving away from agricultural surplus and producing crops for export and profit will move away from practices that have caused a great deal of destruction across the globe. Finding alternative practices will likely mean a large shift in how food is produced. It will most certainly mean paying close attention to farmers' organizations and movements that are already mobilized across the globe.

References

Babin, Nicholas. 2015. "The coffee crisis, fair trade, and agroecological transformation: Impacts on land-use change in Costa Rica." *Agroecology and Sustainable Food Systems* 39 (1): 99–129.

Barraza, Douglas, Kees Jansen, Berna van Wendel de Joode, and Catharina Wesseling. 2011. "Pesticide use in banana and plantain production and risk perception among local actors in Talamanca, Costa Rica." *Environmental Research* 111 (5): 708–717. https://doi.org/10.1016/j.envres.2011.02.009.

Castillo, L. E., C. Ruepert, and R. Ugalde. 2009. "Ecotoxicology and pesticides in Central America." In *Fundamentals of Ecotoxicology*, edited by Michael Newman, 47–54. Boca Raton, FL: CRC Press.

Cattaneo, Andrea, Raúl A.Hinojosa-Ojeda, and Sherman Robinson. 1999. "Costa Rica trade liberalization, fiscal imbalances, and macroeconomic policy: A computable general equilibrium model." *The North American Journal of Economics and Finance* 10 (1): 39–67. https://doi.org/10.1016/S1062–9408(99)00018-2.

Cohen, Marc J. 2013 "Diri Nasyonal Ou Diri Miami? Food, agriculture and US–Haiti relations." *Food Security* 5 (4): 597–606. https://doi.org/10.1007/s12571–013-0283-7.

Echeverría-Sáenz, S., F. Mena, M. Pinnock, C. Ruepert, K. Solano, E. de la Cruz, B. Campos, J. Sánchez-Avila, S. Lacorte, and C. Barata. 2012. "Environmental hazards of pesticides from pineapple crop production in the Río Jiménez watershed (Caribbean coast, Costa Rica)." *Science of The Total Environment* 440: 106–114. https://doi.org/10.1016/j.scitotenv.2012.07.092.

Edelman, Marc. 1999. *Peasants against Globalization: Rural Social Movements in Costa Rica.* Stanford University Press.

Edelman, Marc, and Andrés León. 2013. "Cycles of land grabbing in Central America: An argument for history and a case study in the Bajo Aguán, Honduras." *Third World Quarterly* 34 (9): 1697–1722. https://doi.org/10.1080/01436597.2013.843848.

FAOSTAT. n.d. "Pesticides indicators". Accessed April 16, 2021. www.fao.org/faostat/en/#data/EP/visualize.

Ferreira, Gustavo Filipe Canle, Pablo Antonio Garcia Fuentes, and Juan Pablo Canle Ferreira. 2018. *The Successes and Shortcoming of Costa Rica Exports Diversification Policies: Background paper to the UNCTAD-FAO Commodities and Development Report 2017 Commodity Markets, Economic Growth and Development.* New York: Food and Agriculture Organization of the United States.

Galt, Ryan E. 2014. *Food Systems in an Unequal World: Pesticides, Vegetables, and Agrarian Capitalism in Costa Rica.* Tucson: University of Arizona Press.

Giraldo, Omar Felipe, and Nils McCune. 2019. "Can the state take agroecology to scale? Public policy experiences in agroecological territorialization from Latin America." *Agroecology and Sustainable Food Systems* 43 (7–8): 785–809.

González, Guillermo. 2004. "Diagnostic situation and conditions of the pineapple industry in Costa Rica,". https://laborrights.org/sites/default/files/publications-and-resources/CRPineappleEnglish%20ASEPROLA.pdf.

Instituto Nacional de Estadistica y Censos. 2018. "Encuesta Nacional de Hogares Julio 2018: Resultados Generales." www.inec.cr/sites/default/files/documetos-biblioteca-virtual/enaho-2018.pdf.

Lansing, David, Pedro Bidegaray, David O. Hansen, and Kendra McSweeney. 2008. "Placing the plantation in smallholder agriculture: Evidence from Costa Rica." *Ecological Engineering* 34 (4): 358–372. https://doi.org/10.1016/j.ecoleng.2007.08.009.

Lawrence, Felicity. 2010. "Bitter fruit: The truth about supermarket pineapple." *Guardian*, October 1, 2010. www.theguardian.com/business/2010/oct/02/truth-about-pineapple-production.

Maglianesi-Sandoz, María Alejandra. 2013. "Desarrollo de Las Piñeras En Costa Rica y Sus Impactos Sobre Ecosistemas Naturales y Agro-Urbanos." *Biocenosis* 27 (1–2): 62–70.

McCune, Nils, Juan Reardon, and Peter Rosset. 2014. "Agroecological Formación in rural social movements." *Radical Teacher* 98: 31–37. https://doi.org/10.5195/rt.2014.71.

Molnar, Joseph J., Senakpon Kokoye, Curtis Jolly, Dennis A. Shannon, and Gobena Huluka. 2015. "Agricultural development in Northern Haiti: Mechanisms and means for moving key crops forward in a changing climate." *Journal of Agriculture and Environmental Sciences* 4 (2): 25–41.

Moore, Sophie Sapp. 2017) "Organize or die: Farm school pedagogy and the political ecology of the agroecological transition in rural Haiti." *The Journal of Environmental Education* 48 (4): 248–259. https://doi.org/10.1080/00958964.2017.1336977.

Paniagua-Molina, Javier, and Luis Ricardo Solís-Rivera. 2020. "Effect of 'golden pineapple innovation' on Costa Rica's pineapple exports to US market: An econometric approach." *International Journal of Food and Agricultural Economics (IJFAEC)* 8 (3): 219–231.

Rosset, Peter M., and Miguel A. Altieri. 1997. "Agroecology versus input substitution: A fundamental contradiction of sustainable agriculture." *Society & Natural Resources* 10 (3): 283–295. https://doi.org/10.1080/08941929709381027.

Rosset, Peter M., and Maria Elena Martínez-Torres. 2012. "Rural social movements and agroecology: Context, theory, and process." *Ecology and Society* 17 (3): 17.

Schneider, Sergio. 2016. *Family farming in Latin America and the Caribbean: Looking for new paths of rural development and food security.* Working paper: International Policy Centre for inclusive Growth. www.ipc-undp.org/publication/28051.

Shamsie, Yasmine. 2012. "Haiti's post-earthquake transformation: What of agriculture and rural development?" *Latin American Politics and Society* 54 (2): 133–152.

Sylvester, Olivia. 2020. "Achieving food security in the face of inequity, climate change, and conflict." In *The Difficult Task of Peace*, edited by Francisco Rojas Aravena, 277–295. Cham: Palgrave Macmillan

Sylvester, Olivia, and Mary Little. 2020. "'I came all this way to receive training, am I really going to be taught by a woman?' Factors that support and hinder women's participation in agroecology in Costa Rica." *Agroecology and Sustainable Food Systems* 45 (7): 957–980.

Vagneron, Isabelle, Guy Faure, and Denis Loeillet. 2009. "Is there a pilot in the chain? Identifying the key drivers of change in the fresh pineapple sector." *Food Policy* 34 (5): 437–446. https://doi.org/10.1016/j.foodpol .2009.05.001.

Valverde, Bernal E., and Lilliana Chaves. 2020. "The banning of bromacil in Costa Rica." *Weed Science* 68 (3): 240–245. https://doi.org/10.1017/ wsc.2020.13.

Wezel, Alexander, Stéphane Bellon, Thierry Doré, Charles Francis, Dominique Vallod, and Christophe David. 2009. "Agroecology as a science, a movement and a practice: A review." *Agronomy for Sustainable Development* 29 (4): 503–515.

7 | *Who Decides Where They Live?*

ELISHA OLIVER

One characteristic of the United States has been overlapping waves of dispossession, settlement, and dispossession again. These waves of dispossession and settlement often come with big changes in economic and political systems, and with no small amount of violence. Here, Oliver writes about historically black communities who, in the wake of slavery, established townships on Indian land in what is now the state of Oklahoma. In Oklahoma, too, "Indian Land" was in part established when white settlers forced Indians out of other parts what is now the United States and into Oklahoma. A more recent wave of dispossession has come about due to the oil-fracking boom that has swept the great plains of the United States. With this boom has come oil speculation and speculators seeking to move black communities out of their homes and off their land. Often this sort of dispossession comes in the language of the home as an investment, and the home owner as an investor seeking to make profit. This logic of marketization challenges the idea of the houseowner as a cornerstone of the community and instead implies a self-understanding as a *Homo economicus* seeking to maximize personal utility. Oliver shows how the communities weigh these arguments as people decide what sort of community they want to live in and what money, if any, they should make from their homes.

7.1 Introduction

I learned an eye-opening lesson when I spent time with the folks I write about in this chapter. It is possible to view and understand housing not as a dollar and cents forms of currency, but as a currency of community. This case study isn't a commentary on neoliberal policies, practices, and procedures. It is a collection of community vignettes about people in a small community; what remains of people's land and homes when inevitable change happens, and people's attitudes toward

housing change. I talk about people's attitudes toward housing and community, and specifically contrast people who see housing as a market transaction with people who see housing as a way to build community.

The people whose stories are shared here do not use the descriptive language I've used above to describe themselves or the ways in which

their views and experiences shape their attitudes toward housing. In this chapter we meet Alice, Marie-Louise, Anna, Ms. Maxine, Carl, and Mr. and Mrs. Jackson. Alice, Marie-Louise, and Anna share a very different view of housing than that of Carl and the Jacksons. Alice is a community elder who represents four generations of women who view housing as a mechanism to maintain community; Mary-Louise, a biracial woman with descendant ties to tribal-owned land and housing shares her constructions of home and housing; and Anna, a resident with advanced degrees in political science and sociology advocates for a recentering of housing and who determines where people live. In contrast, Carl and the Jacksons view housing and the determination of where people live as a form of economic advancement. The vignettes shared are not meant to be entertaining anecdotal narratives of life in rural Oklahoma. They are commentaries on modes and nuances of understanding community.

In this chapter I place neoliberalism and neoliberalist thinking in conversation with market imperialism. How do I do this? The vignettes illustrate the ways in which structural forces impact the lived experiences and opportunities of people in the community. In contrast, the vignettes also illustrate the ways in which greed and economistic ways of thinking have crept into the community; today, people think about housing differently from how they used to.

I discuss a rural Oklahoma homestead case study. This case study examines a township in Oklahoma, the past and present inhabitants, and the ways in which they decide where they live. The township was located within an American Indian tribal district.

Very little of the township remains, making it almost impossible to believe a town ever existed, much less held the constructed structures – homes, spaces – that shaped and informed individual and family identities and histories. The homestead spaces in these once-inhabited townships served as identity markers as opposed to economic markers. Remnants of the past are barely visible in the current landscape of wind-energy turbines, oil machinery, untended gravesites, and bovine-trampled spaces. The exploration of family, intratribal, and community relationships, built structures, and pathways of economic systems lends itself to creative problem-solving. The exploration of these components as economic decisions, specifically decisions regarding *"who decides where people live"* and their interrelatedness to nonmarket ways to solve problems expands and diversifies understandings of neoliberal frameworks in relation to individual and collective wealth.

The exploration of these homesteads provides an understanding of the ways in which townships and homestead spaces within the Midwest functioned in the past and function in the present. The presentation of these spaces and the narrative snapshots shared in this chapter create spaces for problem-solving by centering the community collective while being cognizant of the wants of the individual. Each stakeholder with the authority to decide where to live – where to construct their homes – categorizes the home and homestead in diverse ways. These categories often shift and change over time and under unique circumstances.

"Homestead" is a term that represents the home(s), remnants of homes, and land owned by community residents. The homestead sites discussed herein are representations that merge the past and present through supply and demand of homesites and mineral rights. For this case study homesites are components of the land where market value is assigned by those who occupy it. These are sites for mobilizing economic and "social movement" (Frank, 2010: 2). It is a site where the bourgeoisie would lead Black and Indigenous peoples to believe capital controls were nonexistent – where they would have economic freedom beyond oppressive control.

This case study, in many ways, primarily presents the perspectives of women. The reason for this is one of basic biology. Women tend to live longer than men. This is the case in the neighborhood discussed in this case study. Women are the primary descendant stakeholders.

The neighborhood is comprised of diverse stakeholders with diverse ideas of entrepreneurship and economic empowerment. Much of this empowerment and entrepreneurship rests in the ability to maintain ownership of homes. For others entrepreneurship means taking the "buy-out" options offered by the new oil and energy companies that have moved into the area. And, for a select few oilfield workers, entrepreneurship is seeing a lucrative opportunity in the form of a reasonably priced home and buying it with the intent of making a substantial profit.

7.2 A Brief Historical Overview

Eudora was an all-Black town in western Oklahoma. In many conversations with present landowners, some of which are affiliated with energy companies, it is discussed as a township "that never was." It was, however, a thriving township that held a great deal of promise for those who settled there. In the last quarter of the nineteenth century through the very early twentieth, Eudora was promoted as a place for safety and prosperity for Blacks escaping the oppressive South.

In the late 1800s advertisements promised racial solidarity, economic freedom, and freedom from persecution. Many of the families that were living in this new land had been lured to this region with the promise of "a better life." They hoped for a chance to achieve prosperity in joining the land run in April of 1889 (see Oklahoma Historic Society Archival Review, 2019). In the early 1900s the township known as Eudora began to grow as more and more people began to arrive in search of life, liberty, and prosperity. They were following the promises made in Black newspapers – promises to escape the literal and figurative scars of slavery.

Families quickly settled in unclaimed areas nestled between the White communities and American Indian posts. These settlements eventually formed small communities of Black pioneers, yearning to breathe freedom. Community relationships were important to the residents. They established networks that would meet their economic needs. A system of trade was established among residents and between communities. Common items of exchange were garden seeds, vegetables and fruit, and wild game (quail, turkey, prairie chickens, rabbits, opossums, raccoons, and squirrels) (see Crockett, 1979; Franklin, 1980; Shepard, 1988; Wickett, 2000; Saunt, 2005; Oliver, 2018). These items were exchanged for goods and services that the family needed, and often took place between other community members, American Indians, and "outsiders."

Daily life for people in Eudora and the neighboring townships did not greatly differ from their American Indian neighbors and the neighbors in White townships who lived off the land through farming and the production of artisan crafts. During this time, many women used foods and home-crafts in bartering for other needed items for the family, or as an income-generating avenue. Items such as flour, sugar, cloth, livestock, and gypsum became components of economic stability for women.

The townships and the homesteads were sites of cohesion and community strength. The *Dust Bowl* dirt storms, droughts, famines, and economic despair due to the Great Depression resulted in the end of railway economies in these communities (see Crockett, 1979; Franklin, 1980; Shepard, 1988; Wickett, 2000; Saunt, 2005). Many all-Black town settlements in the western quadrant of Oklahoma began to disperse to neighboring towns, states to the north, and to Canada. Could the Eudora residents have remained in this crumbling community? Were they powerless in the decision-making process to leave their homes?

7.3 Where Would They Live?

After much coercion, many residents in Eudora felt they had no choice but to leave their homes. They moved to three surrounding towns. Watonga, El Reno, and Clinton, Oklahoma would become sites for new homesteads and neighborhoods. The Clark Edition neighborhood was an economically thriving neighborhood that offered opportunities for home ownership. This neighborhood was a carryover from the prosperous beginnings of Eudora. It was economically beneficial for all residents. The neighborhood was comprised of a post office, medical offices, restaurants, lodging, entertainment spots, and a variety of stores. Everything needed for community sustainability could be found within a three-block radius.

The neighborhood, in many ways, was more sustainable and economically viable than the township of Eudora. American Indians displaced from their landholdings and poor Whites now lived side-by-side with folks with Eudora origins. The trade-offs of the loss of land and the decimation of family homesteads appeared to take the shape of a prosperous neighborhood with *"freedoms"* to own homes and businesses within growing environments. The experiment in dispersion and displacement gave the appearance of progress – of a successful society in the guise of a wealthy neighborhood. Over time the neighborhood would drastically change and residents would begin to experience life-altering economic impacts.

Beginning in the 1960s the once prosperous community began to decline. By the mid-1970s the economic environment had changed significantly bringing about a closure of local businesses. Members of the Clark Edition community continued to operate collectively; however, by the late 1990s the neighborhood climate was more individualistic, and all local businesses were gone.

Currently, the neighborhood is predominantly comprised of African American women between 25 and 101 years of age, many are descendants of Eudora. The homes are old and in need of repair. Companies with an oil and energy interest solicit residents with calls and in-person visits propositioning the sale of oil and mineral rights. In-state and out-of-state real estate investors approach residents with cash offers for their homes. Consider the following narrative:

Alice (87-year-old elder): "Girl (speaking to Oliver), folks that live in these old places took pride in ownin' sumthin', working to own sumthin', bein' able to decide where we was gone live. My family come from Eudora. We didn't come of our own choosin', but we came nonetheless. When we got here, we looked for a place to create a home life like we had back before. We got pretty close. We worked hard – day and night – worked just as hard as the men folk, maybe harder. You know why they call this neighborhood The Bottoms? It's on account of it being an area that floods. It's a rich fertile area. Folks rich in their own yards because of oil and other stuff. But times got hard, death and taxes done caught up with many of us, and all we have left is to try and figure out a way to keep our homes. That's why many of us sold our mineral rights for $500 . . . to keep our homes, pay our taxes before the city takes them. What choice did we have? I think our choices were limited."

In the snapshot above Alice speaks of movement and migration and provides a glimpse at the ways in which corporate entities and outside agencies attempt to decide where and how current residents live by offering a paltry sum of $500 for mineral rights. A review and comparison of current court documents, solicitation flyers, and phone messages illustrates the drastic changes in the "right to own property" and the ways in which this has altered the decision-making process associated with home ownership. The home ownership decision is often situated within a broader context to include opportunities to live safely and economically. Collective and individual narratives of the past and present illustrate changing socioeconomic networks that open up *"where they live"* decisions to multiple voices and decision-makers.

7.4 Decisions: Response and Responsibility

Life, liberty, and the pursuit of happiness often translates to owning a piece of the "dream." I avoid the use of the concept of "The American Dream," because it is often a "dream" that exists across geography. Examining sites of meaning-making related to this "dream" as a system that encodes sociocultural and economic meanings and values has been necessary when detailing the history and current discussions of homestead spaces within the township of Eudora, and later, the neighborhood of *The Bottoms*. A closer investigation of the spatial orientation among the residents in this community revealed that such an approach would obscure and minimalize the importance of the roles in which individuals would assume in an attempt to ensure the survivability of their communities while simultaneously attempting to limit control by organizations with no familial or historic ties. Keeping this in mind, responses and responsibility regarding decisions about neighborhood survivability and sustainability is explored intimately, intentionally, and intrinsically. Consider the following interview excerpt:

I often wonder how we really got here in this place that is home but not really home? I sit in a unique crossroads of culture. My daddy is Arapaho, and my momma is Black. They each have rightful ties to the land. Forced removals took my people away from a sacred place, and forced removals brought my people to a sacred place. And now, the only land that hasn't been stripped away is the resting places of my ancestors. The small plots that hold hollow and hallowed bones. Who is responsible for this? Who will take responsibility for returning some of, if not all of the land that was ours? The homes are gone but I would like to build there again, but for what . . . To wake up to the sound of pumping oil, the ground shaking, not from the pounding of the sacred buffalo but from these man-made fracking earthquakes . . . This place (with tears coursing down her cheeks) . . . this house I live in may be lost too. Local leaders have introduced programs, like the "Good Neighbor Program"for us [El Reno residents] to learn civic responsibility, and how to be "a good neighbor" but what have these programs really done? Do you know? (I shook my head no in response to her question). Not a damn thing! This is home and not home and if I can't keep my home because of a tragedy, a job loss, or whatever . . . who decides where I'll live then? Where will I go? (Marie-Louise, descendant interview excerpt)

As scholars of the human and economic condition, we strive to explore and explain the ways in which the past and the present influence individual and collective decisions. The interview excerpt intimately illustrates a resident's response to the changing dynamics of family land and the loss of the ability to construct a home. The following snapshot presents the ways in which descendants of Eudora formed a grassroots movement to reclaim land with the intent of (re)building homes.

7.5 Anna

At an October meeting held at a local church, Anna shared her concerns about the sale of homesteads belonging to community members. The church was once one of the original homes in *The Bottoms*. Now it is used for meetings and church services. These meetings cover everything from women's health issues, incarceration, neighborhood improvement, how to reclaim lost land, and how to maintain home ownership.

A lively conversation about a recent visit to the Eudora cemetery was taking place. On a recent visit to the cemetery, several residents discovered that a farmer owning adjacent property allowed his cattle to "use" the cemetery. In addition to the cattle, vandals had knocked over several original headstones. Anna cleared her throat, moved closer to the microphone located at the front of the room, placed a folder filled with documents and maps on the ground, and called those gathered to select a packet from the folder. The women selected their packets and returned to their seats.

Anna, a woman who is usually reserved, had become displeased with new oil company arrivals. The arrivals were preceded by less than equitable home purchase offers. Attorneys for the oil companies, representatives from the wind energy companies, local town government policymakers, and tribal officials were encouraging residents to agree to drilling that was scheduled to take place in areas that encompassed their neighborhood. Each resident in attendance provided detailed accounts of feeling pressured to do their "civic duty" for the betterment of their families, and the local, state, and national economy. They respected Anna as an "educated woman," and looked to her for leadership, advice, and answers. Most of the women in this group expressed that they started the process of piecemeal selling their property which included the remaining homesteads. Many had already sold their mineral rights because they believed there was no point in fighting "Big Business," especially if Big Business was willing to pay each member of the community $500 for their mineral rights. Anna, having listened to each of the concerns from the women, shared the following:

ANNA: You know, I really don't have the answers to your questions, nor do I know how to answer them in a way that will provide any comfort and put you at ease. What I do know is, we don't have to accept the small cash-pay out the companies are offering. Yes, it can help with bills or put groceries on the table, and yes, it may even help you open your own businesses as the company representatives have shared but it's temporary . . . the money is not enough for lasting change.

Anna was asked if she believed it was the place of a small group of neighborhood residents to make decisions for the entire neighborhood. This was her response:

ANNA: From the stories you've shared, the court documents I've read, and the hearings I've attended, I believe it is up to the neighborhood to make a stand in deciding where and how we live. What programs are best in helping us achieve this ... I don't know. It is going to take a group effort to determine what will work best for the remaining property owners ... our remaining neighbors. Our community is aging community but we're still strong, and we have a political voice that must be used.

After Anna finished answering questions, she instructed the women to open their packet to review potential solutions for the issues many of the women faced. One woman shared owing past-due property taxes because of a work-related injury. She was told by a friend that non-payment of taxes would result in local government seizing her property. She contemplated taking a cash-offer for her home with the hope of having enough to pay medical bills and rent another home in the area. Another attendee lost her home owners insurance due to the inability to make needed outside repairs, and was dreading tornado season, a common event in Oklahoma. If a natural disaster occurred, the lack of insurance would leave her with the inability to make a profit on her home. A few attendees owned small parcels of land near the Eudora cemetery but could not afford to "hold-out" when the rest of their family sold their shares.

A list of established programs and services were included in the packet; however, many of the services had gatekeeping mechanisms in place that provided more harm than benefit to participants. Consider the following statement from Ms. Maxine, one of the women at the meeting with Anna:

MS. MAXINE: Now y'all know I don't have time to take these classes. Yeah, I want to take advantage of these grants and things, but I don't have time to classes. I'll be 70 this spring and I still run my home daycare. Keeping up with the childcare classes is a lot ... and did you read the section that you won't qualify if you operate a licensed or unlicensed business out of your home?

That's me, I don't qualify. I'm not sure many of us would with the list of requirements just to receive moneys for home improvement. They (referring to local governing bodies and organizations offering neighborhood improvement programs) want us to live a certain way but make it hard for us to do it. The other side of town is beautiful ... they sink the money there, but we have to jump through hoops and climb ladders just to be turned down. I can't afford to move into a new neighborhood. I'm not sure I would want to live someplace else, but my kids and grandkids are ready for me to sell ... to take one of those offers that come on those postcards from those investors. They say they pay closing costs and all. I could sure use that money but where would I move to and, well (after a long pause) ... what about my daycare?

The narrative snapshots that I present above are homestead issues and disputes that appear to have a repetitive history lacking a viable solution. Many residents don't want to leave their homes; however, they don't want to take a chance of losing their home without the opportunity to gain a financial benefit. The corporate entities and local governments have a different perspective regarding these issues. Their solution to the home owners is: "just sell your property." The following narrative snapshots position an alternate solution alongside the question: "who decides where they live?"

CARL: Look, I purchased this house at a steal, and was able to get the Eudora land at a bargain basement price. You ask me if this is unfair (referring to my question of ethics in the acquisition of properties in the neighborhood) ... Hell yeah!!! It is fair. This is America, the land of Milk and Honey ... a free-market society. I just happen to work for the oil company. I need a place to live too. If my company sends me to a place to start drilling, you bet your ass I am going to look for the area of town with the cheapest homes, buy a home with little need for repairs, do some minor updates, and increase my profits when I move. If the folks in these towns had a money-making spirit about them, they would take the cash. Cash always solves the problem. I see myself as

| | decreasing the wealth gap among these folks. When my contract is up, I will sell this house and make a profit. The folks should take what's offered, buy another property, sell it, and grow their bank accounts. Everybody wins. You throw around these new fancy terms (referring to my use of gentrification in our conversation), I say this is business! |
| Mr. and Mrs. Jackson: | We've lived here our entire lives. Our parents grew up here. Our grandparents moved here after being displaced. If we receive one of the cash offers (referring to offers to purchase neighborhood homes), we're selling. It will break the heart of some of my family members to sell grandma's home, but we're out! We want a chance to provide a better opportunity to our kids ... to maybe set them up with a better financial start. At the end of the day, it's our decision, even if it's unpopular with the family. That's just the way it is. |

The conversations with Carl and the Jacksons was eye-opening and shed light on a different meaning to homesteading. This meaning is one that is popular among businessmen and also select residents desiring to leave the neighborhood for a chance at economic advancement and freedom. To this group, the meaning of homestead sites and homesteading means having a sellable item to increase individual wealth.

7.6 Conclusion

My approach to homesteading rights in this case study refocuses the discussion on "who" gets to decide where they live, rather than how homesteading is decided. In this case study, we become aware of the complexities of homesteading, or *"who decides where they live."* The struggle for collective permanence and homesteading rights is ongoing. Displacement from ancestral lands and the destruction of homesteads required relocation. Land expulsion placed all-Black township residents in neighboring towns. Decades later their descendants encountered neoliberal programs, policies, and practices that polarized their connections to home.

Competing viewpoints and perspectives offer a useful lens in which to view the ways in which property rights transpose and transform land ownership. A selection of the narratives above hints at answering the question of *"who decides where they live"* by focusing on the descendants and their connection to place and the meanings they have ascribed to the home and the land where it is constructed. This moves the descendant community from the periphery of the conversation to the center. In these center spaces history collectively unifies the descendants; however individual desires, selling pressures from oil and energy companies, convoluted government programs aimed at neighborhood improvement, and uncertainty in navigating an everchanging economic climate, particularly one recently impacted by COVID-19, has the power to divide community and family. When the overwhelming selling pressures by oil and energy companies, and convoluted government programs aimed at neighborhood improvement are added to the homestead decision-making process individuals feel their "best bet" is to "take the money" offered for their homes.

Like most people in rural communities, residents often have long family histories that tie them to their homes and the land. They revere the land as a natural resource that supplies provisions for the family and honor the homestead as the constructed resource that keeps them safe.

While this case study has primarily discussed the struggles of descendants in a rural township, these same struggles are experienced in diverse geographies across the globe. We find property rights issues among Canadian women facing neoliberal policies (Bako, 2011), the gentrification of Chinese villages (Kan, 2021), and depopulation in Ecuador, New Zealand, and Papua New Guinea (de Koning et al., 2021). New presences in the community do not have the same familial connections. Often these new presences, such as Carl in the snapshot above, have no intention of long-term residence, and only see the homes in the neighborhood as economic opportunities. So, *"who decides where they live?"*

The intention of this chapter was to present people's contrasting conceptions of housing. Vignettes like those from Alice and the Jacksons reframe the "haves" and "have-nots" in the language of housing and housing decisions. Where one person views home ownership as a cornerstone of community, another person views it as a source of prosperity. Maybe the real problem of this chapter is not *"who decides where they live"* but how long people are able to live outside the reach of economistic encapsulation.

7.7 A Moment of Reflection

In *Open Veins of Latin America,* Eduardo Galeano writes: "This world of inequality is also a world of solitude in which vast numbers confuse being with having." When pondering the question, *"who decides where they live,"* I realized I don't know how to answer the question. In this chapter, housing is a currency for literal and figurative survival. It is the struggle between being part of a community holding onto tradition and culture and liquidating property for economic gain: the not-so simple act of being and having.

On one side of the coin, we see a community comprised of folks hanging onto connectedness through housing. Maintaining home ownership is a form of community sustainability and viability for this group. The attachment to place supersedes and replaces the bourgeois desire for economic gain, and interrupts and disrupts economistic Big Business hierarchies present in the community. These attachments and community adhesions draw attention to differences in understandings of housing and culture, tradition and family, and to moments of community bonds between community insiders/outsiders, rich/poor, being/having.

On the flipside of the coin, we see a potentially nouveau riche community who are willing to leverage connectedness for a new "American Dream – a dream shrouded in a cloak of cognitive dissonance. The members of this part of the community are caught up in their own uncertain trajectory of prosperity and economic gain. They have become mesmerized with the promise of lucrative returns from the sale of property, waiting and watching to see what happens when others sell their family homes. They encounter objections from the half of the community who hold onto their homes with purpose. They take these objections, pile them up plank-by-plank and brick-by-brick, and without much thought, like the Jacksons who are mentioned above, "take the money." They claim a new place for themselves through a constant renegotiation of understanding – the understanding of housing and community, and in this renegotiation, they find themselves, like many of their forefathers and mothers, vulnerably (dis)placed, yet again, and still trying to determine *"who decides where they live."*

References

Abu-Lughod, Lila. 1993. *Writing Women's Worlds: Bedouin Stories*. Berkeley: University of California Press.

Bako, Olivia. 2011. "Neoliberalism and its effect on Canadian women in poverty." *The Lyceum* 1 (1): 1–9.

Baptiste, Edward E. 2014. *The Half Has Never Been Told: Slavery and the Making of American Capitalism*. New York: Basic Books.

Basso, Keith H. 1979. *Portraits of "The Whiteman": Linguistic Play and Cultural Symbols Among the Western Apache*. New York: Cambridge University Press.

1996. *Wisdom Sits in Places: Landscape and Language among the Western Apache*. Albuquerque: University of New Mexico Press.

Boccagni, P., and Loretta Baldassar. 2015. "Emotions on the move: mapping the emergent field of emotion and migration". *Emotion, Space, and Society* 16: 73–80.

Crockett, Norman. 1979. *The Black Towns*. Lawrence: University of Kansas Press.

de Konning, Jessica et al. 2021. "Vacating place, vacated space? A research agenda for places where people leave." *Journal of Rural Studies* 82: 271–278.

Franklin, Jimmie Lewis. 1980. *The Blacks in Oklahoma*. Oklahoma: University of Oklahoma Press.

Giridharadas, Anand. 2018. *Winner Take All: The Elite Charade of Changing The World*. New York: Alfred A. Knopf.

Hanks, William F. 2010. *Converting Words. Maya in the Age of the Cross*. Berkeley, Los Angeles, London: University of California Press.

Kan, Karita. 2021. "Creating land markets for rural revitalization: Land transfer, property rights and gentrification in China." *Journal of Rural Studies* 81: 68–77.

Kennemore, A., and Nancy Postero. 2021. "Collaborative ethnographic methods: dismantling the 'anthropological broom closet'?" *Latin American and Caribbean Ethnic Studies* 16 (1): 1–24.

Lee, Nedra K. 2019, "Boarding: Black women in Nantucket generating income and building community." *Transforming Anthropology* 27 (2): 91–104.

Lee, Nedra K., and Jannie Nicole Scott. 2019. "Introduction: New directions in African diaspora archaeology." *Transforming Anthropology* 27 (2): 85–90.

Oklahoma Historic Society. 2019. "Oklahoma Historic Society website, archival review October 10." Accessed October 10, 2019. www.okhistory.org/publications/enc/entry.php?entry=AL009.

Oliver, Elisha. 2012. "Perceptions of Women's Health Care in Oklahoma: An Ethnography of Lived Experiences." *MA thesis, Department of Anthropology*, University of Oklahoma.

 2018. "At home in The Lows: An ethnography of meaning-making in intimate spaces." Dissertation, Department of Anthropology, University of Oklahoma.

Ra-McDuie, Duncan, et al. 2020. "Collaborative ethnographies: Reading space to build an affective inventory". *Emotion, Space, and Society* 35: 1–10.

Saunt, Claudio. 2005. *Black, White, and Indian: Race and the Unmaking of an American Family*. Oxford: Oxford University Press

Shepard, Bruce. 1988. *North to the Promised Land: Black Migration to the Canadian Plains*. Oklahoma: The Chronicles of Oklahoma 66.

Stack, Carol. 1974. *All Our Kin*. New York. Harper and Row.

Stewart, Kathleen. 1996. *A Space on the Side of the Road: Cultural Poetics in Another America*. Princeton: Princeton University Press.

Tolston, Arthur. 1972 [1966]. *The Black Oklahomans*. Louisiana: New Orleans Printing Company.

Waterston, A., and Barbara Rylko-Bauer. 2006. "Out of the shadows of history and memory: Personal family narratives in ethnographies of rediscovery." *American Ethnologist* 33 (3): 397–412.

Wickett, Murray R. 2000. *Contested Territory: Whites, Native Americans, and African Americans in Oklahoma 1865–1907*. Baton Rouge: Louisiana State University Press.

Worsley, Shawan M. 2010. *Audience, Agency and Identity in Black Popular Culture*. New York: Routledge.

8 | *How Much Land Do We Need?*

INA GOEL

One thoroughgoing assumption of both classical liberal and neoliberal thinking has to do with the supreme importance of property rights. Accompanying most liberal notions of property ownership is the ability to exclude all others from using your property should you wish to. This has led to a curious phenomenon – the absentee landlord. The absentee landlord owns property, controls its use, and profits from it despite not being physically present or practically using the property. In this chapter, Goel looks at how a group of holy, third-gender people in India, hijras, think about property ownership and use. Due to a century or two of colonial degradation, hijras have been stripped of many of their rights to property and its use, and occupy a marginal place in Indian society today. As a result, they maintain an elaborate system of communally maintained use-rights in the cities they live in, apportioning the ability to walk mendicant rounds and grant blessings. This chapter, more than just offering a strict dichotomous set of cases, invites the reader to think about what possession of land or space looks like when we abandon contractual exclusive ownership and instead embrace rights that come from use. The chapter thereby moves beyond the neoliberal tradition and takes the reader right to the edge of the classical liberal tradition of thought, with its emphasis on property rights as an intrinsic component of individual liberty.

Hum logon ke baare mein kaun sochata hai, sabko bas apni fikr hai.
(Who thinks about us, everyone only cares about themselves.)
(Interview with a hijra chief from Seelampur, a working-class area in north-east Delhi, India)

The poor complain, they always do,
But that's just idle chatter.
Our system brings rewards to all,
At least to all who matter.
(Poem by Canadian economist, Gerald Helleiner)

8.1 Introduction

A fundamental aim of classical liberal theories, such as the one propounded by John Locke (1632–1704), is to justify property rights. For Locke the most fundamental property is self-ownership: "every man has a property in his own person. This no Body has any Right to but himself" (Locke, 1988: §6; see Angebauer, 2020). The foundation for the right to self-ownership is for Locke religious. Because human beings are created by God, they "are his Property ... made to last during his, not one anothers pleasure" (Locke, 1988: §6). In fact, were they to "harm another in his Life, Health, Liberty, or Possessions" they would deprive God of this pleasure and thus violate natural law (Locke, 1988: §27; Angebauer, 2020). It is thus our status as God's property, created to serve his purposes, that ultimately justifies why we must respect the property of others. Now, apart from self-ownership, *land* is the most important form of property for Locke: "[T]he chief matter of Property," he says, is not "the Fruits of the Earth and the Beasts that subsist on it, but the *Earth itself*; as that which takes in and carries with it all the rest" (Locke, 1988: §32). Based on his conception of natural law, Locke insists that we are only entitled to own as much land as we need to sustain our life (Locke, 1988: §36). Property right is dependent on actual use.[1] Locke draws this conclusion from how he thinks we should understand our relation to nature's goods, paradigmatically food: We have the right to claim as much food as we need to survive but not more. It is the same principle that applies to the property of land.

In contemporary capitalist societies, the foundation of property rights in actual use, which Locke advocated, has been dissolved. Absentee landlords, for example, are not only a pervasive phenomenon, but also accepted by most of us as a completely natural, self-evident fact of life. The dissolution of property right and actual use is not complete. In some countries, Denmark for example, there are still some use restrictions on property rights: if you own a house as a

---

[1] For Locke our right to own a piece of land is dependent on whether we work to cultivate this land. He thus connects self-ownership and ownership of land through the activity of agricultural work, where we use our body to cultivate the land.

private person, you may be required to live in it – unless it is a vacation house, which is again subject to extensive regulation. But in many countries, such a regulatory framework is virtually absent. One need only walk around mid-town Manhattan at night, and see block after block of luxury apartments with no lights or activity inside, a testament to absenteeism and speculation. Whether you actually use the land, house, or apartment that is your legal property is left entirely unregulated. The neoliberal principles support this latter approach: Owning property should not commit you to use it, because this would infringe on right to maximize your utility as you see fit. In addition, legislation demanding that you, or even someone else, must use the land, house, or apartment that you own, makes the fault of all planning, assuming that human cognition can figure out better solutions than the spontaneous forces of the market.

In the following, I will explore an example of a group of people who in the process of oppression, discrimination, and persecution have responded by developing an exclusively use-based claim to land. This use-based system has made it possible for them to "go on" as a culture (Lear, 2008), i.e. to maintain and develop their way of life under circumstances of extreme adversity. I will describe some patterns in property ownership and alienation in India, specifically among a group of third-gender people called "hijras." Hijras continue to remain outliers in India despite being legally recognized as a protected "third" gender in April 2014 by the Supreme Court of India. To be clear, the point of the chapter is not to describe the hijra's way of life as such, nor is it to suggest that their conception of land ownership is unproblematic. The intention is rather to sketch this extraordinary conception of land ownership that they have been forced to maintain and develop in the face of marginalization and oppression. Sometimes being faced with the extraordinary is the best way of questioning the value of the taken-for-granted; in this case, the right to own more than you can reasonably use of some central human resource, say, intercity housing.

More specifically, my focus on India's hijra's illustrate two points. First, in neoliberal contexts I want to suggest that people who fall outside of property systems due to history, design, or neglect, become forgotten subjects and dispensable citizens. They are structurally made to disappear from the policy process and are often outside the ambit of law. Since the end of the colonial era, India has seen its cities grow dramatically and quickly, adding hundreds of millions of residents over several decades. One feature of this rapid development has been the shortage of affordable or even available land for new residents leading to large areas of unplanned urbanization in many cities, often accommodating those with the fewest resources. Most of the time, informal settlements are distanced and isolated from more planned parts of cities and their cores. As time goes on, what tends to happen to these informal settlements, as the richer, more planned, and more legal parts of cities meet them, is that these informal settlements are snatched away from residents by the government for conversion into alienable, sellable property. When this happens, those who originally settled the land are generally forgotten and abandoned.

Second, thinking about where hijras live and why they have to live the way that they do will help us think through basic liberal assumptions of property ownership and the commodification of land, and their foundation in particular religious convictions. hijras generally don't, and often can't, own where they live, yet they still make a life. This chapter will introduce the clandestine world of Hijras through their working-class queer ways of land sharing and distribution and its connection with religious practices. Using the hijras as an opportunity to revisit what it means to own land and how one gets disowned from land ownership and inheriting property rights would help us reflect anew upon a basic question that all humans face: How much land do we need?

8.2 Understanding Hijras

There are approximately half a million hijras and other "third gender" individuals in India, plus smaller numbers in Pakistan, Bangladesh, and Nepal. The hijra identity is a unique blend of biological, gendered, and sexual identities underpinned by religion and bound by a tight-knit social structure. Hijras include people assigned male at birth who may or may not undergo castration and modifications such as breast implants, as well as some (but not all) intersex people and transgender women.

Distinct from transgender and intersex identities in other countries, hijras occupy a unique and contradictory place in Indian society. They are revered by many as demigoddesses capable of bestowing blessings and reviled by others as deviant victims of bad karma (Goel 2019). Hindu mythology deifies them, and British colonists demonized them. During the Muslim Mughal dynasty, which ruled much of India from the sixteenth to eighteenth centuries, hijras were often compulsorily castrated and became trusted guardians of the harems. In this time period, some hijras also enjoyed prominent positions as political and legal advisers, administrators, and generals.

When the British conquered India, as part of their governance they imposed Victorian sexual mores in India. British colonists accused the "eunuchs" of sodomy, prostitution, and kidnapping and castrating young boys. They saw the third gender as a threat to morality and political authority. The British criminalized being a hijra under the Criminal Tribes Act of 1871, stripped hijras of their inheritance rights, and launched a campaign to erase them from public consciousness. Bereft of inheritance and their property, the hijra community was forced underground. Since then, hijras have lived on the fringes of society. They typically earn money by asking for voluntary donations in exchange for their blessings, performing at weddings and stag parties, begging, and engaging in sex work. Most people who become hijras come from working-class or lower socioeconomic backgrounds. It was only in April 2014 that people who identify as hijras were recognized under a "third gender" category by the Supreme Court of India and are now given reservation under the category of OBC (Other Backward Class).[2] Today, to become and identify as hijra, a person must be initiated through a lengthy adoption process based on hijra ideas of belonging that are not formally recognised by Indian law and that involves a social hierarchy as well as the patronage of a hijra guru.

This chapter will provide two perspectives on hijra ownership of land. First, I focus upon colonial attempts to erase hijras as gender trouble to Victorian sensibilities of morality. This part will explain

---

[2] According to the Constitution of India, "socially and educationally backward classes" are represented as OBCs.

how hijras were branded as a "criminal tribe," stripped of inheritance rights, banned from public spaces, and eventually forced to go underground. This will illustrate how liberal legal systems can alienate people based on the basic terms of participation that they create. Second, I focus on how hijras reclaim their ownership to land and land distribution via use-rights and through their kinship system by forming clandestine networks in modern India. Taken together, these two episodes will help this chapter understand what sort of approach to land ownership is possible despite a criminalized past identity, and ongoing marginalization.

8.3 Colonial Land Usage By Hijras

Historically, hijras didn't so much own property or land, but rather had rights to access it in order to both be regular presences in their community and solicit alms for their livelihood through begging. In their work on the hijras in (what was then called) Bombay, Preston (1987: 377–382) pointed out that hijras on their "regular beats" demanded that the traditional state recognize their right to beg as they held a "hereditary right (*vatan*) to collect a *hak*, 'perquisite,' from the villagers." The hijras

apparently had once held documents to prove their vatan; and the king settled the matter on these facts alone. Hence, the district officers were enjoined not to let "their" hijedas [hijras] trespass on the domain of Kondan and Sankvar. It was the king's duty to ensure that the ancient rights of his subjects were protected from whatever encroachments. In 1853 the Bombay government was forced to decide whether, as the successor to indigenous states, it should uphold its predecessors' grants of the right to beg ...

... The Commissioner of Satara declared he could give no assistance to the petitioners because almsgiving was surely voluntary. But still, his Indian subordinates had "been informed that no persons should be allowed to molest [the petitioners] so long as they conduct themselves properly ..."[3]

---

[3] PA: XIV; 8/94, fol. 2, V. Ogilvy, Commissioner of Satara to Government, July 28, 1853 cited in Lawrence, 1987: 382

... At least for the records the legal issues had been disposed of: "[t]he right of begging or extorting money, whether authorized by former governments or not, has been discontinued. And in the collected wisdom of the revenue history of British India, the right of hijdas [hijras] to beg became a notion of course wholly erroneous."[4]

Under the British colonial regime moral authority was seen as a threat, and hijras' hereditary right to collect alms on their "regular beats" came under question. The results of this colonial era crackdown linger: begging is still not decriminalized universally in India and there are ambiguities and confusion over laws failing to protect those who engage in such activities, particularly those who inherit such a right like those in the hijra community. All this was codified when hijras were banned from public spaces under the Criminal Tribes Act of 1871. According to district records maintained during the colonial administration, hijras were forcefully registered under the category of "eunuchs" which were defined as impotent men and were registered in their male pronouns so that they could be seen as a masculine failure of identity (Hinchy, 2017). Although the Criminal Tribes Act was rescinded in 1952, a collective memory still renders hijras as historical gender deviants with a criminalized sexual variance. Testimony to this fact is that the first colonial anti-sodomy law introduced by the British in 1861 through Section 377 of the Indian Penal Code enabled homosexuality to be considered as an unnatural offense in the post-colonised Indian nation-state until 2018.

At this point, hijra's are no longer allowed to beg, much less bequeath their mendicant rounds to those who follow them in their guru networks. What passes for ownership and property in their lives has been abolished. Their gender and sexuality are even degraded, codified, and criminalized. And yet, despite exclusion from systems of ownership, property, and inheritance, they endure. How can we account for this? One way to start thinking about this, is to think about what happens when people are stigmatized and othered; and

---

[4] H. H. Wilson, "A Glossary of Judicial and Revenue Terms ... relating to the Administration of the Government of British India" (London: Wm. H. Allen, i855), p. 208. cited in Lawrence 987: 382

how do people so marginalized interact with property from which they are excluded?

We can bring out the complexity of exclusionary experiences by understanding the ways of resistance toward it. Resistance can be understood as "weapons of the weak" that are manifested through everyday small acts of material dissent, as theorized by James C. Scott (1989). For "powerless" groups, according to Scott (1989: 29), these acts often fall short of collective defiance and may be prosaic, but are also a constant struggle between the oppressed and the oppressors. They include:

foot dragging, dissimulation, false compliance, pilfering, feigned ignorance, slander, arson, sabotage, and so forth.

Scott argues that when such acts become a "consistent pattern" even if they are uncoordinated, they mean resistance because minority communities lack the institutional means for acting collectively (Scott, 1989: 296). Situating the distribution of land in Scott's framework of everyday resistance then opens up the possibility of understanding how exactly it is that hijras make a life and use land despite their political and legal circumstances. It also lets us see a way of living in a specific space that is different than one that relies on enclosure, property rights, and profit.

8.4 Contemporary Land Usage By Hijras

As a community that continues to thrive on donations and gifts from people, the hijra community developed a system of sharing land within themselves by marking a territorial boundary called an *ilaka* (literally means a turf or locality). The hijras mark *ilakas* for themselves for the purpose of patrolling while on their beat for collecting their earnings collected from ritual blessings, begging, and sex work. During my own fieldwork, I did mapping exercises with members from the hijra community to see how they understood and divided the space they lived in, despite those hijras having no formal title to it. This mapping revealed many aspects of their geographic exclusion, mostly through their vernacular spatial knowledge. What emerges from the maps is that hijra identity and territorial

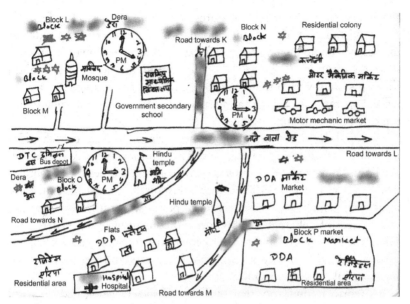

Figure 8.1 Annotated hijra map.
Map by Ina Goel.

belonging go hand in hand with each other. Let's start with one map (Figure 8.1).

The stars on the map mean that that area has a presence of the hijra population (one star being the lowest and three stars being the most dense hijra population based on local knowledge), either working or residing there. The clock on the map indicates a suggestive time of their availability based on their daily schedules. The *dera* on the map represents hijra communal households that are headed by a hijra chief.

What became clear was that actually walking rounds and maintaining a presence in space was what allowed these *ilakas* to keep up the hijra kinship systems of a hierarchical, guru-anchored society. Put another way, much of hijra family life is tied up in being physically present and active in a place. In a liberal and neoliberal perspective, we can imagine an absentee landlord, whereas hijra society requires regular active presence in space to maintain a claim to some specific geography. Reciprocally, maintaining a claim to a particular part of the city is one of the defining features of a group of hijras. To illustrate the importance of all this, the boundaries of these territorial patches are respected and memorized by all the hijras who are lower in rank as land distribution determines the power and harmony of the hijra kinship system within their subgroups. Much of this boundary maintenance is ratified via internal hijra councils responsible for maintaining discipline and punishment.

Given all this, hijras and people who live around them can identify, associate, and distinguish between different hijra subgroups by way of the *ilakas* they work on. In this way, their land becomes their identity. These *ilakas* are always alive with constant movement and negotiations happening over these territorial patches. In turn, *ilaka* activity is a subject of debate in weekly internal council meetings. There, the relation between land and the hijra chiefs are negotiated and renegotiated based on everyday inputs from informers and performance of hijra disciples on the ground.

It's worth noting, too, that this idea of society being tied up with living in a certain place is by no means specific to hijra life. In a study on the Rai coast of Papua New Guinea, James Leach notes that:

The land is very much alive, and enters directly into the constitution (generation) of persons. The relation between land and person is not one of containment, with the land outside and the essence of the person inside, but one of integration ... [T]he constitution of persons and of places are mutually entailed aspects of the same process. In this sense kinship is geography, or landscape. (2003: 30–31 cited in Sahlins 2003)

Given this alternative understanding of land, *ilakas* become a manifestation of the hijra kinship systems in India. Such lifestyles contribute toward producing a culture in India that is often in opposition to the liberal, property-protecting state. In turn, sometimes the state itself has to accommodate the *ilakas*. I found in my fieldwork that the respective *ilakas* of various hijra *gharanas* in Delhi, despite there being no official recognition of such territorial division between different groups of people by the Indian Penal Code, are registered with the local police stations on handwritten sheets of paper and are also available with the senior *gurus* and hijra chiefs of a particular area. They are even registered off the record by the police to avoid any inter-clan disputes and fights that emerge from trespassing, theft, harassment, fisticuffs, and other related issues (Goel, 2016).

The hijra approach contrasts starkly with how most religious communities in contemporary societies, including India, practice land ownership. The standard model is that a religious community, like any other property owner, owns the temple or church and the land it is placed upon. It is through their status as property owners that they lay claim to this land and this mere status makes them present as a religious community in the wider community. The temple or church stands there; whether it is actually used is another question. The hijras in contrast are only present as a religious group to the extent that that they are actively using the land.

The hijras patrol their respective *ilaka*s in the mornings during a fixed time period, after which all the earnings from a particular *ilaka* are combined, divided, and distributed amid their own subgroups based upon the guru's discretion. Through the *ilakas*, their system of land usage functions as an empowering space for hijras to economically sustain themselves despite the hostile relationship between avenues for hijra employment and the Indian Penal Code. Such communal territorialization is passed down generations maintaining order within the hijra community. It is crucial in determining hijra livelihoods and their public spaces of work – be it work done as ritual workers, beggars, or sex workers. All told, this constant living in a specific space starts to give a sense not so much that it is necessary to own land, but rather that space is necessarily open. Commenting on a related philosophical dimension of space in the context of land usage, one hijra guru spoke to me about how much land they *really* need:

At the end of the day, we all need *do gaz zameen* [two yards of land] to be buried in the ground after death.

8.5 Conclusion

This last reflection brings us back to where we began. According to the liberal tradition of Locke, it is the human being's status as the property of God that naturalizes the category of property as an integral aspect of our world and commits us to respect it as such. On this view, our life

properly expresses our status as the property of God when we dili-
gently use what we all own, our body, to work the land, enclose it,
pronounce it as ours, and demand that other people respect it as such,
just as we do theirs. The contrast with a culture like the hijra's is
thought provoking: Here, where the borders between person, community, and land are fluid, the only instance where it is necessary to
conceive of the person as a discrete entity that is tied to a specific piece
of owned land, is in death.

In the seventeenth century when Locke contributed to the formulation of the liberal conception of property, much of the earth was not
claimed as property; it "belonged" to no one and for Locke it was
therefore ripe for the picking. On his view, formed by Protestantism,
God had given the world "to the use of the Industrious and Rational
(and *Labor* was to be *his Title* to it)" (Locke, 1988: §34). The emphasis
on the activity of culturally specific forms of labor as the decisive
criteria for granting property of land led Locke to infamously deny
property to America's Indians who "merely" used the land for hunting
and gathering (never mind spiritual or kinship connections to land).
Locke could only imagine a world where there was enough land for
everyone – as long as people were willing to engage in (agricultural)
labor and would not take more land than what they needed to sustain
themselves. In our contemporary world all land has been claimed as
property, by governments, corporations, or individuals, and in the
process many groups of people like the hijras, who have informally
settled and made use of land have been marginalized. As we have seen
the hijras have been able to develop their way of life in ways that resist
and challenge the idea that ownership of land is determined by property rights. The way of life of the hijras is far from utopian. Yet, its
ability to insist on preserving and cultivating a culture of informal
settlement and use rights can serve to extend the political imaginary
of liberal societies. It is one thing to discuss whether ownership can be
justified without use, i.e. whether we can own a house without actually
living in it. The example of the hijras allow us to go further and raise
questions that challenge even the liberal conception of property. What
would it mean to grant land ownership to religious communities based
on their actual use of the area that the community is serving, rather
than to understand religious communities as just another property
holder? Or more generally, what would it imply to actively create
and support ways of life based exclusively on use rights, rather than

to regard them as backward remainders that ought to be included in the world of property rights? David Harvey (2019), the Marxist geographer, has suggested that in the context of gentrification and urban redevelopment it's often the people who live in and "use" a city, often as renters, who make cities exciting, varied, desirable places to live, often to the benefit of real estate speculators and absentee landlords. Thinking about ownership, title, and rights coming from use breaks up this sort of lopsided benefit and imagines a world where those who live in and use a city are its rightful owners.

What the hijra show us, from a historically difficult location, is how other ways of relating to property are possible once we exchange liberalism's obsession with alienable exclusive ownership with more fluid ideas of use in space. Boundaries still remain. Politics live on in intra-guru counsels. But hijras show a way of life that does not rely on ownership. The history of their othering has pushed them to a position where they have invented, developed, and maintained a land system that also becomes their legacy – and a new pattern of communal land inheritance. In this way, and with a light touch, hijras turn the tables on a few hundred years of structural and systematic marginalization by empowering themselves through a palimpsest system of land ownership that allows us to peer over the edges of the liberal horizon of thought.

References

Angebauer, Niklas. 2020. "Property and capital in the person: Lockean and neoliberal self-ownership." *Constellations: An International Journal of Critical and Democratic Theory* 27: 50–62. DOI: 10.1111/1467-8675.12424

Goel, I. 2016. "Hijra communities of Delhi." *Sexualities* 19 (5–6): 535–546.
2019. "India"s third gender rises again." *SAPIENS*, September 26, 2019. https://www.sapiens.org/biology/hijra-india-third-gender

Harvey, David. 2019. *Rebel Cities: From the Right to the City to the Urban Revolution*. London: Verso.

Hinchy, J. 2017. "The eunuch archive: Colonial records of non-normative gender and sexuality in India." *Culture, Theory and Critique*. 58 (2): 127–146.

Leach, James. 2003. *Creative Land: Place and Procreation on the Rai Coast of Papua New Guinea*. New York: Berghahn Books.

Locke, John. 1988 [1690]. "Second treatise on government." In *Two Treatises of Government*, edited by Peter Leasley. Cambridge: Cambridge University Press.

Preston, L. 1987. "A right to exist: Eunuchs and the state in nineteenth-century India." *Modern Asian Studies* 21 (2): 371–387.

Sahlins, Marshall. 2013. *What Kinship Is – And Is Not*. Chicago: University of Chicago Press.

Scott, J. C. 1989. "Everyday forms of resistance." *The Copenhagen Journal of Asian Studies* 4: 33–62.

9 | *Where Should We Park?*

DANIEL SOULELES

This chapter compares the ways that two similarly sized cities, Chicago and Amsterdam, have chosen to govern their streets. Chicago sold a seventy-five-year concession to manage street parking to a consortium of private investors, whereas Amsterdam's government maintains the ability to directly govern its streets. In turn, Chicago is an illustration of how privatization of a common good according to money-lending logics, far from allowing for flexibility and efficient governance, completely prevents a city from changing with the times. Chicago has lost control over its own streets and can no longer decide what their best use is without paying an extortionate price. Any governing of a shared communal space that has a broader concern than generating profit for a private corporation is here effectively undermined by allowing marketized parking. For the purposes of this book, the Chicago/Amsterdam comparison illustrates the limitations of using privatized business actors to efficiently govern shared city space. It also serves as a counterexample to the neoliberal dogma that government should abstain from planning, because their attempts at doing so cannot outperform the market.

9.1 Cities and Sharing

When you get down to it, cities are all about negotiated sharing. How on earth will tens or hundreds of thousands, or even millions of people live together in a bounded area? According to what priorities will we divide up land, find places to live, allocate children to schools and schools to children, or even decide where and when folks can walk their dogs? Each of these questions has a history behind it. In each dilemma there is an intersection between different people, ways of exercising power, laws and rules, traditions, priorities, and, perhaps most importantly, aspirations for different sorts of cities and different sorts of lives. Take one example: should children go to school in their

171

neighborhoods near their homes, and grow up and learn in and around their family and neighbors, or should children go away to a specialized school, appropriate to their aspirations and affording them the opportunity to meet new people from different places? Both options have benefits and drawbacks (say, meeting new people versus commute times). Both have interested constituencies (educating humans for their communities or the broader society or even the labor market). And either option would radically reshape the social and physical world, the very feel and cosmic vibrations of a city.

In thinking about the grand compromise and negotiation that is living with other people in a city, I'd like to suggest that parking, the placement of cars on streets – one of the most humble, mundane, everyday features of a city – offers a window into just how much can be at stake in these negotiations. As we'll see, parking is really about who has access to a city's streets – which people will find space for their lives, and who will be shut out?

I suspect, though, given how much of an afterthought parking can be, you might need a bit of persuasion to follow me through a chapter on where to stash cars in a given municipality. Take New York City: New York, with around 8.5 million inhabitants spread across 783.3 square kilometers is the densest city in the United States. Moreover, this density is not evenly distributed: Manhattan has around 1.6 million people on 59.1 square kilometers of land. Given that density, even free street parking is difficult to reliably come by as indicated by the fact that a private parking space in Manhattan cost around US$5000 per year in 2018 (Grabar, 2018). Taken together, New York's density and scarcity of street parking is a perfect recipe for, how shall we put it, contradictory municipal priorities.

In the spring of 2016, a series of corruption, conspiracy, and bribery prosecutions ensnared people at the highest level of the city's government, reaching all the way into the mayor's office (Feuer, 2018). The sordid details of the scheme defy simple explanation. However, one of the key players in the corruption investigation was named Jeremy Reichberg who worked as an official police liaison to Borough Park's Orthodox Jewish community. Part of what got Reichberg his start in graft was helping people get out of parking tickets, and helping people get counterfeit "park anywhere" license plates. Reichberg's impulse is understandable too. This is how elected officials routinely bribe their constituents. In 2017, the Mayor of New York himself, issued 50,000 new "park anywhere" placards to teachers and other school workers, bringing the city's total to 160,000 cars that can legally flout all parking regulations. This last instance is particularly wild as most of those teachers will likely, at some point or another, feel the need to park on the sidewalk outside of their schools. However, those sidewalks are generally kept clear of parked cars so that drivers can see children walking to and from the school. With a park anywhere plate, though, people can block drivers' lines of sight with impunity (Grabar, 2019). Pity the children.

Now, most of us can agree, even our neoliberal friends, that a corrupt police liaison, bribed for privileges is likely not the best way to decide who can park where in a city. Moreover, after a bit of thought, we might come around to the idea that mayoral executive fiat is also a pretty terrible way to allocate scarce street space. But the problem remains: who should get to take up street space and why? What is a fair and reasonable way to let cars into a city? What system could we devise? What should we charge? And what sort of life should we allow?

In answering these questions, we'll see that Chicago and Amsterdam offer two diametrically opposed solutions to the problem of parking. And Chicago's case makes a particularly strong argument against a version of market imperialism that would see street parking turned into a commodity and concession.

9.2 The Deal That Haunts the City Still

In 2019, eleven years after it happened, Samuel Kling in the *Chicago Tribune* called it the deal that is still haunting Chicago (2019). You see, in 2008, partially as a consequence of a drop in tax revenue, the city of Chicago was facing a shortfall in its budget. To solve this shortfall, the mayor of Chicago, Richard Daley, proposed selling the right to collect money from Chicago's parking meters for the next seventy-five years. As we'll see over the next few pages, there is a good argument as to the fact that everything about this deal was suspect (more colorfully, Matt Taibbi called it a "blitzkrieg rip-off" and a "hideous betrayal" [2010: 165]). But first, a bit of back ground is necessary to understand how and why a city could even sell parking in the first place. To understand this, we'll have to hear a bit about "finance" and "financialization."

Wherever people generate surplus wealth, they find themselves with the task of managing that wealth and planning for the future. Many of the personal and household budgets of wage laborers (people who work for a living) are focused on this sort of "finance." Someone may work a job and collect a paycheck, and with that paycheck they spend money to buy clothing, shelter, food, and so on. So, in a basic way, there is a kind of financial planning – the check comes once every two weeks, every month, every quarter, and so on. One then needs to manage one's money smoothly through this period so that one doesn't spend too much and is able to meet all future expenses – the known and the unknown.

That is all well and good. But again, anyone who works for a living knows that there are things that are both necessary for life and immediately unaffordable. After all, we all need a place to live, but many of us are unable to afford to buy housing outright. The same is true of getting around and owning a car, as well as paying for an education or for medical care in some places. All of these are essential. Yet, paying for many of these outright would outstrip most working people's budgets. So, we borrow. At interest.

Take a fairly basic example, say, buying a car: Generally people don't have the money right now to just buy a car. After all, not many of us have US$20,000 in the bank. Given that, people will put down a portion of the cost as a down payment and then borrow the rest. That remaining amount which they've borrowed, they pay back at interest over a fixed period of time. This is a "future-oriented" way of managing money, or of "financing" a purchase and, thereby, a life.

To put some real numbers on this scenario, let's imagine a hypothetical person buying a specific car. At the time of writing this chapter in August of 2020, on autotrader.com, one could buy a Blue 2017 Honda accord for just shy of US$20,000. A four-door Honda accord is a nice, reasonable family car. Not too flashy. Not too big. Perfectly reliable. As good an "investment" as a car ever is. Let's imagine, too, that our hypothetical buyer had squirreled away US$5000 to make a partial or "down" payment. Given that, our buyer would need to borrow the remaining US$15,000. At 5 percent interest, and paying this back over five years, this would amount to sixty monthly payments of US$283.07 totaling US$16,984.11 (US$15,000 plus US$1984.11 in interest, paying for the privilege of using someone else's money, and doubling as a monetary penalty for poverty). Those sixty monthly payments of US$283.07 is where things get interesting. What's basically happening is that we're creating a way for someone to pay far less than the cost of a car every month, in order to eventually pay back more than the amount that they borrowed. Our buyer doesn't have US$15,000, but they do have US$283.07 per month, recurring for the next five years. Put yet another way, selling a car to someone relies on some evaluation of their future. How likely is that person to pay back the loan amount at interest? And what makes that interest payment fair to begin with?

Start with the likelihood of repayment. This might be a place where we would like to know more about the person borrowing. Is their job stable and secure? Do they work in an industry that we think will be around in five years? Do they work in a hospital or at a school? Or do they work as an event planner or as a caterer? We might think that hospitals and schools are more stable than catering and conferences. After all, in recessions and pandemics we still have schools and hospitals, but eating out and expensive gatherings tend to fade away. Another thing we might consider is whether or not this hypothetical car buyer is in a salaried job, or a gig job. Do they have reliable paychecks, or do they have to hustle for contracts? If they're hustling, how stable is their hustle? All this adds up to an evaluation of the creditworthiness of the individual. In other words, all this adds up to an evaluation of how likely someone is to make all sixty of those loan payments of principle and interest.

The second piece of this is that interest. Why would anyone think it's fair to charge an extra US$1984.11 to someone who can't afford to buy a car outright already? It's worth noting that most world religions at one point or another have found lending at interest to be a sin. Nevertheless, in the mind of a banker or a capitalist, this "interest" is the cost someone is charging for the use of their money. They see it as compensating them for the opportunity that they have lost when you have their money and they don't. The owner of that money feels that their ability to spend and invest money is valuable and in borrowing, the person receiving their money denies them this opportunity and needs to pay for it. Even more basically, there is an assumption that money in the hands of a capitalist will grow because they will invest it. The 5 percent interest rate is a capitalist/banker/loan shark making an estimate of the foregone profit that they might have made with their money. Hypothetically, they do this in a quasi-market way by competing with other lenders for your payments. In practice, though, lending is a highly regulated industry filled with state-sponsored quasi-monopolies operating according to state control and with state back-stopping and support.

Now that we have a bit of a grasp on how borrowing money with interest tends to work, we can return to Chicago. What Mayor Daley was basically doing, was saying, OK, we are the city of Chicago. We're not planning on going anywhere. We have the ability to tax people, and have an army (the police) to enforce our laws. So, any kind of financial promise we make, people can trust. In addition to an army and a tax base, we also have a lot of money coming in in various ways. One of these ways is parking. We charge a sort of rent to people leaving their cars in the city. Plenty of people live far away from where they work, or where they shop, or where they hang out with friends, and need to leave their cars somewhere when they visit. Also, lots of people live in apartments or places without car storage, so city streets can function as an extra bit of private car storage. All of these activities can generate money. And, from Mayor Daley's perspective, these activities should also generate money on into the future. So, why not lend this revenue stream to someone for the next seventy-five years in exchange for a lot of money now?

As we'll see, there were reasons both specific and general that would suggest this is not the most prudent way to manage a city's finances or the city's streets. First, the specifics.

As Taibbi notes, the process by which Chicago leased its parking meters left something to be desired:

Finance Committee chairman Ed Burke had the job of informing the other aldermen about the timetable of the deal. Early that morning he called for a special meeting of the Finance Committee that Wednesday, to discuss the deal. That afternoon the mayor's office submitted paperwork calling for a meeting of the whole City Council the day after the Finance Committee meeting, on December 4, "for the sole purpose" of approving the agreement.

"I mean they told us about this on a Monday, and it's like we had to vote on a Wednesday or a Thursday," says Colon.

"We basically had three days to consider the deal," says fellow alderman Leslie Hairston.

On that Tuesday, December 2, Daley held a press conference and said the deal was happening "just at the right time" because the city was in a budget crunch and needed to pay for social services (2010: 165).

The next day the Finance Committee met to review the deal, and ten minutes into the meeting some aldermen began to protest that they hadn't even seen copies of the agreement. Copies were hastily made of a very short document giving almost nothing in the way of detail.

"It was like an eight-page paper," says Colon (2010: 165–166).

[T]he measure ended up passing 40 : 5, with Hairston and Colon being among the votes against. I contacted virtually all of the aldermen who voted yes on the deal, and none of them would speak with me (2010: 166–167).

Procedurally, the whole thing was rushed. The aldermen seemed incompetent to evaluate the nature of the deal, compliant in the face of the mayor and his administration, and unwilling or unable to offer any significant critique or analysis of what was happening.

This lack of any meaningful oversight is all the more troubling as Chicago seems to have gotten a terrible deal:

The bigger problem was that Chicago sold out way too cheap. Daley and Co. got roughly $1.2 billion for seventy-five years' worth of revenue from 36,000 parking meters. But by hook or crook various aldermen began to find out that Daley had vastly undervalued the meter revenue.

When [one alderman] did the math ... he discovered that the company valued the meters at about 39 cents an hour, which for 36,000 meters works out to $66 million a year, or about $5 billion over the life of the contract (2010: 169).

The city inspector at the time, David Hoffman, subsequently did a study of the meter deal and concluded that Daley sold the meters for at least $974 million too little. "The city failed to make a calculation of what the value of the parking meter system was to the city," Hoffman said.

"What's even worse is this – if they really needed the up-front cash, why sell the meters at all? Why not just issue a bond to borrow money against future revenue collection, so that the city can maintain possession of the rights to park on its own streets?" (2010: 170).

So, from a specific deal point of view, Chicago messed this up about as badly as they could – they left, at a minimum, a bit under half of the money they might have received on the table if we believe future projections. Moreover, they demonstrated that the machinery of their city government was completely incompetent to structure and evaluate this manner of financial arrangement. Perhaps we can explain this away as local incompetence and inadequate governance. Better leaders and people better at markets and pricing concessions would have made a difference. Though, even this I'm not persuaded of – generally, politicians and bankers have different aptitudes and skills. That said, there is a larger issue that the city inspector alluded to at the end of that last block quote: control of the streets.

The length of the parking-meter deal was seventy-five years. This means that the city of Chicago was promising parking-meter revenue for seventy-five years. This means that the city of Chicago was guaranteeing that revenue over that time, guaranteeing that parking spaces would remain commodified and allocated for private car storage. Insofar as Chicago removes meters or changes its street grid, this deal obligated Chicago to compensate, in full, the parking meter investment consortium for lost revenue. Put as simply as possible, the city of Chicago gave up some of its ability to control its own streets. This manifests in all sorts of ways.

It can happen simply in the case of a special event like a parade or a street festival:

To start with something simple, it changed some basic traditions of local Chicago politics. Alderman who used to have the power to close streets for fairs and festivals or change meter schedules now cannot – or if they do, they have to compensate Chicago Parking Meters LLC for its loss of revenue ...

So, for example, when the new ownership told Alderman Scott Waguespack that it wanted to change the meter schedule from 9 a.m. to 6 p.m. Monday through Saturday to 8 a.m. to 9 p.m. seven days a week the alderman balked and said he'd rather keep the old schedule at least for 270 of his meters. Chicago Parking Meters then informed him that if he wanted to do that, he would have to pay the company $608,000 over three years. (Taibbi, 2010: 169)

It's not just one-offs, aldermen, and their prerogative. This affects basic city planning as well. Anytime a new express bus lane goes in; anytime a bike lane gets added; any time someone removes a parking meter simply to get rid of cars in an area, the city has to pay out the seventy-five-year maximum revenue of the removed space. Seemingly, every time Chicago seeks to make its city less car dependent, friendlier to buses and bikes and people walking around, the parking meter deal looms as a limit on what is possible (e.g. Wisniewski, 2019; CITYLAB, n.d).

Faced with a revenue shortfall around 2007/2008, Chicago chose to give up control over its ability to control its own streets in exchange for an extortionate concession to allow private entities to collect revenue on Chicago's parking meters. The city of Chicago turned a municipal resource – the city's streets, into a source of private control and profit. The seventy-five years of the agreement ensures too, that cars will have a place or at least a cost in the city of Chicago for a long time to come.

9.3 Amsterdam's Disappearing Parking Spaces: It's Not a Big Deal Here

The real sin for the city of Chicago wasn't necessarily commodifying parking (though, we can find plenty of arguable fault there), but rather giving up control over its own streets. We can imagine situations where we might want to have an auction mechanism for allocating some portion of a city's grid. But we can just as easily imagine lots of situations where it's better for the city as a whole to embrace other values in the use of it's streets. In making a contract with a private parking management company, Chicago built a bunch of assumptions about how life should and will continue to work into its agreement. Far from any sort of efficiency and nimbleness, this sort of privatization locked the city into one mode of transit for the better part of a century. The agreement assumed that cars would continue to be a part of the city and generate revenue. The agreement assumed that the sort of city that accommodates and allows cars would continue to exist (or be extremely costly to remove). The agreement assumed that Chicago and Chicago's residents and Chicago's government would not need the freedom to modestly or radically rethink how life in the city works. And this is a problem with financial governance – there is an assumption on the part of people lending money that conditions need to be such that people will be able to consistently and reliably make payments over the life of the arrangement. Financing in this way forces a sort of stability. Even if Chicago government were more competent, financing would still lock the city into the passenger seat of its own future.

Chicago simply magnified this stability, extended it over seventy-five years, and made it punishing to change how cars are stored in the city. It wouldn't really matter to the agreement if citizens wanted a more pedestrian-friendly city, or if they wanted to repurpose streets for mass transit. All of this would be foregone and subordinated to the need to pay seventy-five-years worth of parking meter fees. All this, too, is in dramatic contrast to Amsterdam in the Netherlands.

Amsterdam, with around 2.5 million people living in its metro area, and a population density of around 4500 people per km squared is roughly comparable to Chicago, which has a population of around 2.7 million people and a population density of around 4500 people per km squared. That, though, is where we might say that the similarities stop. Amsterdam, particularly its center, is a preindustrial city, shaped by centuries of mercantile and imperial accumulation around narrow streets and canals. Much of the city was laid out prior to the advent of the automobile. Perhaps more to the point, the city of Amsterdam maintains control of its own streets and has prioritized a sort of noncar livability in diametric opposition to Chicago's outsourced contract binding to parking meters. It's important to note that one need not feel that "noncar livability" is the highest virtue for a city, but rather one should appreciate that Amsterdam has *the ability* to make this choice should they want to. Chicago does not, or at least not cheaply.

The city spokesperson for the city of Amsterdam has explained it simply, "The city is booming, and we want to make space for bikers, pedestrians and public transport ... to stay in control of the livability of the city, that means less space for cars" (iamssterdam.com n.d.). In this vein the city plans on removing 7000–10,000 parking spaces by the year 2025. A similar action on the part of the city of Chicago would cost millions of dollars. Even more than bare numbers, what's interesting is what the city will do with that new space.

More than any grand shift, it seems that streets are being reclaimed in a block-by-block fashion. Bliss (2019) notes that in the city's Frans Halsbuurt neighborhood, rosebushes, benches, and slides are taking the space once occupied by cars. That means that people are gardening in their public streets, children are playing on playgrounds, and there are more places for sitting in public than there once were. Standing behind this sort of micro-urbanism is a pretty savvy politics. O'Sullivan (n.d.) explains:

How can the city get away with it? Put simply, Amsterdam's government has been given a mandate to. The city is currently being run by a coalition of left and centrist parties in which the Green Left party (GroenLinks) has the largest share. A promise to reduce parking space formed part of the initial coalition agreement. It also helps that no driver will actually be stripped of the right to park. Rather than revoking permits, the city will simply not replace any that are given up when drivers leave the city, give up their cars, or die. In this way, the city reckons it can naturally do away with about 1,100 permits a year.

To get rid of yet more spaces, the city has other tricks up its sleeve. Many of the waterside streets and harbor quaysides in inner Amsterdam are in need of repair and renovation. Thanks to the delicate nature of Amsterdam's subsoil, some of them actually need it pretty badly after groaning and buckling under the weight of cars for years. It's a common and eminently fixable problem, but also one that provides an opportunity to winnow yet more motor vehicles off the roads of the city's historic center. Meanwhile, some other major streets are due for remodeling, and their spaces are also on the chopping block.

Much like Chicago's Faustian parking meter deal was amenable to several layers of analysis, so too is Amsterdam's amazing disappearing parking.

First, unlike the city of Chicago, Amsterdam's government has not given away it's right to govern its own streets. Financial arrangements demand payment and can seem to operate according to their own contractual logic, and Amsterdam seems to have avoided this. Second, more positively, Amsterdam's government actually acknowledges the politics of managing city streets and ties this to a larger center-left, green political platform. This gives legitimacy to removing parking spaces. Third, it should be noted, that Amsterdam has not gotten rid of parking meters and parking. Rather they have become fewer and more expensive. Across all of this it's fairly easy to recognize, too, a political prioritization in the life of a city toward pedestrians, children playing, people gardening, friends sitting on benches, in other words, a prioritization of the microsocial life of the city at the expense of private car storage.

9.4 Possible Cities

The point of this chapter was to get you to think about how space on a city street can and should be allocated and managed. I presented a seventy-five-year private financialized concession to run parking in the city of Chicago on the one hand, and on the other a center-left government in Amsterdam systematically removing street parking. One was privatized, designed to maximize profit, and minimize active government management. The other was the outgrowth of a specific governing coalition's broader plan to make a city more livable. One was designed to maximize revenue in the moment, the other is part of a larger governmental plan. Both plans exposed the abilities and limitations of their given local governments. Both plans also shaped life in the city far differently. One prioritized cars, commuting, and personal car storage, and, *crucially* locked the city into this vision for seventy-five years to come. The other prioritized, well, just about any other use you could imagine for a street, and, *crucially again*, kept the freedom to change the streets should politics change.

The larger point in all this, too, is the way that financialization, governing one's city according to the logic of a loan agreement, locks in a certain form of reality, and freezes things at the moment of contract. Often when people argue for running government as a business or like a market, one form of market imperialism, people say that doing so allows a government to be quicker moving, more efficient, and more effective. Chicago demonstrates the contrary. Privatizing parking via a long-term concession essentially froze Chicago's city streets at the moment of contract in order to preserve the terms that made the concession profitable. Most basically, if Chicago wants to regain control over its streets to move away from cars or make any other way of life, it will be expensive to do so.

References

Bliss, Laura. 2019. "Amsterdam's amazing disappearing parking spaces." *Bloomberg CityLab,* June 5, 2019. Accessed December 3, 2019. www .citylab.com/transportation/2019/06/amsterdam-parking-spots-removal-cars-bikes-parks-playground/591067.

Feuer, Alan. 2018. "Tracking graft, from the bootlegger to the mayor." *New York Times,* April 27, 2018. Accessed 14 August 2020. www.nytimes .com/2018/04/27/nyregion/tracking-graft-from-the-bootlegger-to-the-mayor-new-york.html.

Grabar, Henry. 2018. "New York City street parking is preposterously corrupt." *Slate,* May 3, 2018. Accessed December 3, 2019. https://slate .com/business/2018/05/new-york-citys-corrupt-street-parking.html.

iamsterdam.com. n.d. "Smart parking solutions in Amsterdam." Accessed 28 August 2020. www.iamsterdam.com/en/business/key-sectors/smart-mobility/insights/amsterdam-smart-parking-solutions.

Jaffe, Eric. 2015. "There may be trouble ahead for Chicago's big bus rapid transit plan." *Bloomberg CityLab,* Feburary 26, 2015. Accessed

3 December 2019. www.citylab.com/transportation/2015/02/the-cracks-in-chicagos-grand-plans-for-the-bus/386027.

Kling, Samuel. 2019. "That parking meter deal is still haunting Chicago." *Chicago Tribune,* April 5, 2019: 15.

O'Sullivan, Feargus. 2019. "Amsterdam plans to systematically strip its center of parking spaces in the coming years, making way for bike lanes, sidewalks, and more trees." *Bloomberg CityLab,* March 29, 2019. Accessed 13 August 2020. www.citylab.com/transportation/2019/03/amsterdam-cars-parking-spaces-bike-lanes-trees-green-left/586108.

Taibbi, Matt. 2010. "The outsourced highway." In *Griftopia,* edited by Matt. Taibbi, 156–172. New York: Spiegel & Grau.

Wisniewski, Mary. 2019. "Faster bus service: CTA says bus/bike lanes could be solution." *Chicago Tribune,* April 11, 2019: 4.

10 | *How Should We Deal with Climate Change?*

ANEIL TRIPATHY

The enormity of climate change and the many ways one might address it is overwhelming. This chapter examines two movements that have sought to do so. One, the green bond movement, seeks to explicitly create opportunities for market participants to prioritize labeled sustainable and climate investment. The other, the divestment movement, seeks to move investment away from fossil fuel companies via direct political action that pressures large entities like universities and nonprofits to take their money out of fossil fuel companies and emissions intensive industries. Tripathy's argument is twofold. First, he describes how the two movements, despite profound ideological and cultural differences, share an underlying assumption that climate change can be addressed by manipulating the workings of financial markets. Our increasing realization that neither of these movements, in isolation or in combination, has been even remotely successful in addressing the problem of climate change should remind us of a classical critique of market solutions: markets are inadequate when it comes to efficiently addressing problems with very distant and broad societal consequences. The chapter thus suggests that the failure of two market approaches with such diverse profiles should make us expand our political will and imagination to look beyond markets for future means to address climate change. Second, Tripathy suggests that in our necessary endeavor to develop alternative solutions, we may seek inspiration from the divestment movement. What is particularly interesting in this movement is its emphasis on democratic ideals of participation and inclusion in the political process itself, as well as its broad conception for a necessary agenda of societal change required to address climate change.

10.1 Introduction

If there is a problem that should make us realize that we need dramatic change to business as usual it is climate change. People around the world are increasingly aware of the ever-growing threat of climate change as well as the current impacts from climate change that we are already experiencing. Since 2015, the Paris Agreement has been the focal point of policymaking efforts to respond to climate change (UNFCCC, 2015). The Paris Agreement sets a framework for all countries to meet nationally determined contributions as quantified amounts of investment into infrastructure and technology deemed sustainable and climate-resilient by environmental and engineering experts. As this case book attests to, markets are increasingly purported to be the legitimate and primary sites of policy intervention to correct social and environmental problems (Frankel, Ossandón, and Pallesen 2019; Nik-Khah and Mirowski, 2019a, 2019b). The Paris Agreement defines climate finance and also explicitly emphasizes the use of finance to track global progress on climate. But should finance be the focus of climate interventions? And should financiers be the ones leading our response to climate change? Or are there other ways we can imagine collective action on climate change?

Many economists believe that the immediate time response of financial markets to economic activity makes them more efficient at managing resources and allocating goods than government planning, which is thought to take a longer time to respond (Nik-Khah and Mirowski, 2019b). However, the collective inaction of both governments and markets to respond to climate change effectively and limit the worst-case scenarios of warming challenges the assertion that markets are time efficient. This inaction shows that the response to the question of "How should we deal with climate change?" is far from just letting markets deal with it devoid of political and civil action. So, what then do we do, and who should do what?

In this chapter, I present two responses to the climate crisis. Both responses involve financial markets, but from different angles and led by very different groups of people. The first example is the movement of financiers in the green bond market, which has grown rapidly since its beginnings in 2007. The green bond market began when Sweden's pension fund managers wanted to invest their capital in sustainable debt. In response, the World Bank organized the first green bond issue in 2008. Since then, the market has grown rapidly, rising from $53.2 billion in 2014 to $723 billion total issuance at the start of 2020.[1]

---

[1] Climate Bonds Initiative.

However, there are concerns for whether projects funded by the market will live up to their environmental credentials. There has yet to be legal regulation for the market to assess the sustainability and climate resiliency of infrastructure projects financed by green bonds.

In contrast to the financiers that started the green bond market, the fossil fuel divestment movement began in 2012 with student and faculty climate activists at Swarthmore pressuring the college to ban any investment in fossil fuel extraction by its endowment. Since then, divestment movements have been active at both public and private institutions to sell all financial holdings in fossil fuels or greenhouse gas intensive industries. Movement organizers argue that the time to invest in fossil fuel use and extraction is over, and that the current financial value of these shares does not reflect our coming climate reality. So far, the divestment movement has pledged $39.88 trillion out of fossil fuel investment from the endowments of 1497 institutions.[2] Through this movement, organizers have also developed their own expertise in financial markets and instigated social change that increasingly interacts with and occasionally transforms financial expertise.

These two movements, one led by financial experts within financial markets and the other by activists and academics, demonstrate the need for political and public sector action to get markets to respond effectively to environmental and climate concerns. Their historical development and interaction show that markets do not exist in a vacuum. The divestment movement now includes Divest and Reinvest as a slogan, with sustainable financial products such as green bonds highlighted as good reinvestment choice. Many financiers in the green bond market also now call for government regulation. Both movements attempt to reorient the time focus of financial markets to mitigate the worst climate change scenarios.

The two movements represent different approaches for using financial markets to effect climate change; one is developed by investors, traditional market actors, and is therefore shaped by the values and assumptions of the culture within the financial sector. The other strategy is developed by activist and university climate organizers,

---

[2] Latest numbers on fossil fuel divestment from the Global Fossil Fuel Divestment Database in 2021: https://divestmentdatabase.org.

nontraditional market actors. The culture of the divestment movement is guided by a very different set of values than that of the financial sector. It is thus revealing that the divesment movement frames shareholders as moral actors and that they place their efforts for divestment within a more encompassing agenda for social justice. In contrast to the technocratic culture of green bonds, divestment also emphasizes the value of promoting democratic participation and increased awareness of environmental racism as an intrinsic part of their political efforts. At the same time, the two approaches fundamentally share an ambition to effect climate change primarily through a manipulation of the forces of a "free market."

Moreover, neither of the two movements, despite their ideological and cultural differences, have proven even remotely up to the task of effecting the necessary changes. There is, therefore, ample reason to question whether manipulating financial market forces is at all an effective way to combat climate change: If two so different traditions cannot find a way to use financial markets to solve the challenge, why should we think these markets are up to task at all? Taken together it seems that the two approaches confirm a classical critique of market solutions: Markets are ineffective in addressing distant future environmental and societal consequences. Working solely within markets to try to address environmental and climate impacts seems to not be an efficient solution for society and doesn't slow our current slide toward environmental catastrophy. Other solutions to meaningfully address climate change are called for, such as decisive government regulation, or more encompassing societal changes. Whereas inspiration for such broader changes is to be found in civic movements such as the divestment movement, it seems an impossible hope that the culture of financial markets and its focus on technocratic expertise can create the collective civic action that is presently called for.

I begin by analyzing how climate change is being interpreted and translated into market action in a manner that influences both the green bond market and the fossil fuel divestment movement. I then present the history of the green bond market and contextualize how this market has been evaluated by policymakers and financiers. I follow the green bond market with the history of the fossil fuel divestment movement and its philosophical underpinnings.

10.2 The Green Bond Market

The green bond market is a financial market that began in 2007 and 2008 with fund managers motivating development banks to put together a category of sustainable debt. A green bond is tradable debt that finances/refinances infrastructure evaluated by sustainability experts as environmentally beneficial. In 2014 the green bond market began to grow dramatically. From $53.2 billion outstanding in green bonds in 2014, the total issuance of green bonds has continued to rise to reach $1 trillion at the end of 2020 (Climate Bonds Initiative, 2020). Green bonds constitute the largest market in climate and sustainable finance more broadly (Clapp and Pillay, 2017). Climate finance is composed of financial instruments that fund projects marketed and evaluated as climate change solutions by financiers and environmental professionals. These markets are increasingly touted by public policymakers and financiers as a solution to climate change (Figueres et al., 2017).

The first time I was told about green bonds by an impact finance practitioner, I was told an origin story for the green bond market that centers on a banker at the Swedish bank Skandinaviska Enskilda Banken (SEB). The impact finance practitioner who told me this origin story described this banker as the first to come up with the concept of a green bond. He had been a banker his whole working life, and midway in his career he was diagnosed with a tumor and underwent a surgical procedure to remove it. While in recovery, the banker pondered the meaning of his life and became adamant that once fully healed he would leave banking and go try save the world, in order to give his life true meaning. However, once he fully recovered, he realized that it really was banking that he was good at! Thus, he sought to use his banking skills to do good in the world, rather than leave his profession entirely. He championed the cause of green bonds at SEB when the bank worked on the World Bank's first green bond in 2008.

While there is debate among market participants as to whether this banker really was the inventor of green bonds, this story highlights some key features of the green bond market. Working with green bonds and in climate finance is often described by market participants as a dramatic outcome of personal reflection and redemption for career bankers. The narrative of bankers being inspired by callings outside of banking itself, particularly one instigated by a major life event, is prevalent in the career biographies of other green bond practitioners. This outcome is also often described as an innovation in line with standard financial practice. Green bonds are an innovation that has developed among financial professionals.

The World Bank's green bond issuance in 2008 were the first bonds to be labeled explicitly as green bonds in response to Swedish pension funds asking for green financial products to invest in conversation with the sustainable finance team at SEB bank.[3] This desire for sustainable debt by Swedish pension funds and other institutional investors was instrumental to the start of the green bond market. Other development banks such as the International Finance Corporation (IFC) entered the market following the lead of the World Bank in 2011.

To evaluate the sustainability of the infrastructure projects that green bonds finance, SEB partnered with CICERO, a sustainability research institute at the University of Oslo. Reflecting on the need for environmental science in the green bond market, one climate finance practitioner told me that "decisions about what is green need to be based on the science – as per the World Bank's first green bond where climate scientists at CICERO in University of Oslo were asked to assess the green credentials of the World Bank's projects." Off of the World Bank's first green bond issuance, other branches of the World Bank such as the IFC also issued green bonds referencing the guidance of CICERO.

While highlighting the scientific analysis of infrastructure by organizations such as CICERO became a mainstay in the green bond market, the beginnings of this practice were not as robust as what would later be demanded by market participants. According to Michael Eckhart, former head of Sustainable Finance at Citi and the first author of the Green Bond Principles, this guidance began with a brief phone call from him with CICERO researchers to tangentially approve the scientific and environmental credibility for the World Bank and later the IFC's green bond projects. CICERO stands for the Center for International Climate and Energy Research-Oslo. During Climate Week 2018 in NYC, when I asked a longtime CICERO researcher what CICERO stood for, he told me that it was really a forced acronym to connect to the Roman orator Cicero. For the research center, Cicero invokes the orator's legacy of spreading truth to the

---

[3] An underwriter is a bank that works to sell an issuer's bonds to investors.

wider public and giving voice to scientific reason in financial markets and green building.

CICERO has become a gatekeeper for sustainable assessment in the green bond market. CICERO's climate finance team continued to be a relatively small group, even as their role grew dramatically in the green bond market. Ultimately, with a deluge of green bond second opinions, CICERO spun out as CICERO Shades of Green, a private company focused on providing second-party opinions to green bond issuers. By August 2020, CICERO would provide sustainability second-party opinions and verifications to 42 percent of the green bond market by cumulative volume. This translates to 82 percent of all green bonds with second-party opinions.[4] CICERO's evolution from a university research center to a private company highlights one concern from market-based solutions, that more public institutions gravitate toward commercial activity. However, this overlap has also established a nuanced ongoing conversation and critique around the green bond market (Clapp et al., 2015).

Alongside the growth of second-party opinions for green bonds, beginning in 2011, the Climate Bonds Initiative, an NGO in London, convened the Climate Bonds Standard for different project categories of green bonds to organize expertise around different sustainable infrastructure types. Through creating the standard, the Climate Bonds Initiative cemented itself as a standardizing agency in the green bond market, insuring the organization a place in both public and private green bond market development discussions around the world.

Meanwhile, the idea of green bonds continued to spread throughout the banking sector, particularly among bond underwriters. 2013 was a breakthrough year for green bonds, with municipalities issuing them both in Europe and the United States from the city of Gothenburg in Sweden to the state of Massachusetts in the United States. Private entities such as Credit Agricole, Toyota, and Unilever began to issue green bonds as well, learning about the concept from both the development banks and investment banks.

SEB's role started to be sidelined as larger banks entered into the market, driven by climate finance practitioners working as underwriters who did not want to be beholden to a regional Nordic bank. Suzanne Buchta at Bank of America Merrill Lynch, Michael Eckhart at

---

[4] Climate Bonds Initiative Communication August 2020.

Citigroup, and Marilyn Ceci at JP Morgan were particularly instrumental in bringing together those working in sustainable debt at investment banks around the world. Building on this momentum, in January 2014, the Green Bond Principles (GBP) were established by a consortium of investment banks, including Bank of America Merrill Lynch, Citi, and BNP Paribas. The principles began when Citi's Michael Eckhardt and Bank of America's Suzanne Buchta began talking at the Environmental Bonds conference in London in the winter of 2012–2013. In June 2013, on a flight to San Francisco, Michael Eckhardt took the time to hammer out the first draft of the principles, in a focused period of work over three hours. He told the flight attendant to make sure his wine glass was full.

While SEB's sustainable finance team initially resisted the formation of the GBP they soon joined its executive committee and collaborated with the other banks. After establishing the Green Bond Principles, the banks then searched for a third organization to be a secretariat for the principles, and coordinate communication and future work among the banks. They settled on the International Capital Markets Association (ICMA), an international association based in Switzerland focused on promoting robust debt capital markets.

With guidelines on how to issue a green bond now available to prospective green bond issuers and bond underwriters, 2014 and 2015 continued the upward momentum in the green bond market. The year 2014 ended with $36.6 billion issued by seventy-three institutions, bringing the market to a total of $53.2 billion outstanding green bonds (Olsen-Rong, 2015). By the end of 2015, the green bond market reached $100 billion (Climate Bonds Initiative, 2015a: 1). The growth of the green bond market during my fieldwork supported a number of narratives from different market actors. These narratives frame the interests of different stakeholders in the market, including underwriters, asset managers, civil society, public policy, central bankers, and pension funds.

The sustainability NGO Ceres's 2014 report, *Investing in the Clean Trillion* and discussions from the International Energy Agency (IEA) and the Intergovernmental Panel on Climate Change (IPCC) spearheaded the first financial milestone indicator for the green bond market (Fulton and Capalino, 2014). According to Mark Fulton and Reid Capalino in their report, to "have an 80 percent chance of maintaining [a] 2°C limit, the IEA estimates an additional $36 trillion in clean energy investment is needed through 2050 – or an average of $1 trillion more per year compared to a 'business as usual' scenario over the next 36 years" (Fulton and Capalino, 2014: 2). Fulton and Capalino were the first to highlight the need for $1 trillion in clean energy investment each year. They came to this number from the scientific and economic research of the International Energy Agency (IEA), where economists run cost–benefit analysis on top of climate change models to establish financial action in response to environmental risks. With the scientifically credible IEA behind the $1 trillion by 2020 campaign, Ceres and later on the Climate Bonds Initiative pushed this number into policy reports and private sector projections of green bond market growth. In December 2020, the green bond market met this $1 trillion in total issuance by 2020 goal.

As the green bond market continues to grow, evaluations of its climate and environmental effectiveness continue as well. Over the summer of 2018 a report came out from the climate finance NGO 2° Investing Initiative, arguing that the additionality of green bonds in financing sustainable infrastructure is negligible (Dupre et al., 2018). The basis of this claim came from 2 Degrees analysts looking at the entire carbon footprints of companies that had issued green bonds, and arguing that despite issuing green bonds these companies were still operating unsustainably to keep climate change within 2 degrees Celsius. The NGO's argument rested on critiquing the notion that green bonds were shifting company activity toward a low-carbon model, by saying that green bonds issued were only a fraction of the company's activity and did not transfer any cost of risk from issuers to investors. Thus, there was no additionality in the transaction; green bonds are only supporting infrastructure that could already be built in current market conditions.

Contrarians to the 2° Investing Initiative's green bond market narrative argued that green bonds open a pathway for companies with traditionally brown assets such as oil and gas production or standard combustion vehicles to green their balance sheet. This argument flips the critique by the 2° Investing Initiative that it is a bad thing that green bonds are still on the balance sheets of overall high carbon-dioxide emitting companies. In the transition argument, green bonds issued by brown companies can help shift more investment into sustainable infrastructure. By being part of a company's balance sheet, a green bond issuance is able to attract investors who have the assurance that the debt is backed not only by the green assets financed but by the entire company, including its preexisting operations.

The debate from the 2° Investing Initiative's white or position paper demonstrates the mixed perspectives in the green bond market, and how much of what green bonds are assumed to achieve is a result of how market actors look at the financial product. This debate rests on the scale of which one defines sustainability, and over what time horizon (Jaramillo, 2013; Limbert and Carr, 2016). On top of debate around the green bond market's impact, overall global emissions continue to climb, highlighting that the shift in capital toward climate resilient infrastructure is a drop in the bucket in comparison to the cumulative emission impact of our global economy. This present state leads climate finance practitioners in the green bond space to continually assess and doubt the value of their work in mitigating catastrophic climate change. The focus on the management of global emissions as the main criteria for the success of the green bond market can also serve to ignore and erase other unequal and exploitative social and environmental impacts of green bond financed infrastructure projects (Archer, 2020b).

The green bond market began as a response by financiers to personal crises and culpability for environmental degradation and climate change through their investments. The exponential growth of this market has now made it a focal point for interrogating the effectiveness of financial market responses to climate change. Green bonds have been leveraged for public policy intervention and have also created a space where participants argue markets can set the response to climate change beyond government action.

10.3 The Fossil Fuels Divestment Movement

I first heard about green bonds through my involvement and familiarity with the fossil fuel divestment movement. Fossil fuel divestment is a civic campaign that focuses on change in financial markets. However, this campaign and its composition is quite different from that of the green bond market. David Wood, the director of the Initiative for Responsible Investment at the Harvard Kennedy School, told me that green bonds were supported by student activists at Harvard campaigning for fossil fuel divestment realizing that they should also dress up in suits and make investment proposals to endowment fund managers.

Fossil fuel divestment is the selling of investments in fossil fuel extraction and use by institutional and individual investors. As a philosophy, divestment is tied to shareholder responsibility and the framing of shareholders as moral actors (Welker and Wood, 2011). Divestment focuses on the idea that avoiding morally repugnant companies can have a positive effect on society.

Two key reports catalyzed and established the philosophy behind fossil fuel divestment as a tactic for climate action. Similarly to the translation of climate scenarios into investment trajectories in the green bond market through the concept of *A Clean Trillion*, climate science is a grounding logic in the fossil fuel divestment movement (Tripathy, 2017). The first report was published in *Nature* in 2009 by Malte Meinshausen and colleagues at the Potsdam Institute for Climate Impact Research in Germany (Meinshausen et al., 2009). Meinshausen et al. calculated the quantity of greenhouse gases that could be emitted while remaining within a 2°C global average temperature increase. Meinshausen's research group estimated that no more than 565 gigatons of CO_2 could be released by 2050 to have a good statistical chance to stay within a 2°C limit (Ballantine et al., 2015).

Meinshausen et al. was followed by a similar study by analysts at the London-based climate finance NGO Carbon Tracker (Initiative, 2014). Carbon Tracker analysts added up all fossil fuel reserves claimed on publicly disclosed balance sheets of the 200 largest fossil fuel companies. This determined that companies hold enough coal, oil, and natural gas that they plan to exploit which would result in emissions of 2795 gigatons of CO_2, much above the 565 gigatons CO_2 that could be emitted while staying within an average of 2 degrees warming (Meinshausen et al., 2009; Initiative, 2014). Their report went the next step and named these companies directly, listing them in order by implicit emissions (Ballantine et al., 2015). While I conducted fieldwork on the green bond market in London, I worked at a desk just steps away from the Carbon Tracker team.

Middlebury College academic and climate activist Bill McKibben's NGO 350.org used Carbon Tracker's research to catalyze and underpin climate change activist campaigns. Founded at Middlebury College, 350.org has achieved a global presence. 350 refers to the parts per million (ppm) of carbon dioxide that many climate scientists argue is the safe upper limit for the concentration of CO_2 in the atmosphere

(Ballantine et al., 2015). In December 2020, the US National Oceanic and Atmospheric Administration recorded a monthly average of 414.02 ppm of CO_2 in the atmosphere from its observatory at Mauna Loa, Hawaii.

With website campaigns and an extensive mailing list of citizen and student activists, 350.org coordinates climate change teach-ins, marches, and rallies involving hundreds of groups around the world. 350.org is recognized as a leading climate activist group on the world stage today, aiming to both educate citizens and influence policy (Ballantine et al., 2015). I have interacted with 350.org activists both in the United States and in the United Kingdom. In 2015 the divestment campaign began to take off. There are now hundreds of campaigns, NGOs, and student groups working on climate change and divestment today. The divestment movement has marked approximately $39.88 trillion out of fossil fuel investment from the endowments of 1497 institutions.[5] Through its growth, the fossil fuel divestment movement has trained activists who have developed careers out of their activist work.

In 2012, students across a number of University of California schools organized the Divestment Student Network. They organized conference calls over FreeConferenceCall.com and trained each other in tactics to support campaigns to divest university endowments from fossil fuels. Alyssa Lee, a longtime fossil fuel divestment campaigner, started her climate activism and eventual career through being involved in the California Divestment Student Network as an undergraduate student at University of California Los Angeles (UCLA). Alyssa told me that the fossil fuel divestment movement "was the first space I experienced where a climate-focused group was very explicit about colonialism, racism, and like the impacts of like pollution and environmental racism as part of talking about climate change." The awareness of student divestment campaigns of environmental racism and a focus on justice as a guiding framework highlights a much more encompassing mission than the technocratic focus on green assets in the green bond market (Healy and Barry, 2017).

After her time organizing as a student in the Divestment Student Network and working and searching for jobs in California, Alyssa

---

[5] Updated numbers on fossil fuel divestment available in 2021 at: https://divestmentdatabase.org.

moved to Massachusetts to start a job at the Better Future Project
(BFP) as a fossil fuel divestment university campus organizer. BFP is
a grassroots climate action nonprofit organization that also runs 350
Massachusetts, along with other projects. She ended up working there
for four and a half years, during which BFP scaled up its fossil fuel
divestment work into a full-blown national campaign under Divest
Ed. Alyssa had just left BFP when I interviewed her in Cambridge,
Massachusetts.

Alyssa developed her expertise through the fossil fuel divestment
movement, and her initial learning in this space was directly from
other university students, which was very appealing to her. She told
me that "I got into it because I went to a workshop that was taught by
other students and I think that was always the hook that it was
something that students were teaching other students about and that
was in 2012 in California." It was also among fossil fuel divestment
activists that Alyssa felt there were the most explicit conversations
about the importance of linking social justice with any climate
change response.

Finding this space in fossil fuel divestment campaigning to be refresh-
ing, Alyssa continued to be involved with the movement after graduat-
ing from college as an organizer and sought to provide student
organizers she was mentoring with the support that she herself had
needed in coping with the difficulty of gaining traction for fossil fuel
divestment campaigns. Alyssa told me "I was motivated to apply for the
job [at Better Future Project] because I wanted to make sure students
didn't waste their energy and time and their motivation doing things
that were really not, effective and also not good for them." Alyssa had
experienced both the stagnation of and then rapid increase of fossil fuel
divestment activity. She told me that at UCLA, "divestment just doesn't
catch on . . ." Alyssa spent her undergraduate years organizing for quite
some time with little direct result, which had been discouraging. In her
role at BFP, she was able to share her experience and knowledge with
student activists by providing direct one-on-one coaching as well as
group trainings on concrete campaigning skills, such as negotiation,
recruitment, meeting facilitation, and how to plan rallies and marches,
as well as broader education on topics like climate justice, intersections
of climate change and racism, and self-care. She did this work with
students in Massachusetts and, later, across the country as the movement and the Better Future Project's work in it grew.

Similarly to Alyssa, my own career and research as an anthropologist was supported by my experience and work in fossil fuel divestment organizing. As an anthropology PhD student at Brandeis University, I joined the university's Exploratory Committee on Fossil Fuel Divestment in fall 2014. I had just started my research on the green bond market and was excited to be involved in work that clearly connected financial action to institutional sustainability efforts. Composed of a university administrator, business school lecturer, biologist/development practitioner, history doctoral student, development masters student, two undergraduates and myself, the Brandeis Divestment taskforce ultimately recommended that the university divest from fossil fuels (Ballantine et al., 2015).

We outlined a case for divestment and highlighted Brandeis University's particular responsibility to divest given the legacy of the institution's namesake. Supreme Court Justice Louis Brandeis is known for his regulatory stance on Wall Street and the financial industry. He stated that "there is no such thing as an innocent purchaser of stocks" (Welker and Wood, 2011: S59). Similarly, in the fall of 2014 at the beginning of the brainstorming of the name for the formal fossil fuels divestment undergraduate student activist group at Brandeis we settled on Brandeis Climate Justice, to invoke the legacy of Louis Brandeis and the social justice mission which has been attached to the university. The other two names brainstormed were Fossil Free Brandeis or Brandeis Climate Action. This focus on social justice on the part of the undergraduate climate change divestment organizers reflects Alyssa's experience in divestment organizing as an undergraduate in California.

While our committee report ultimately argued that Brandeis should divest its endowment from fossil fuels, the university did not respond to the report or take any steps for fossil fuel divestment until November 2018, when it was announced that there would be no direct investments in coal in the endowment and that any new partnerships in gas would be suspended for a review period of three years. This partial response highlighted the need for more sustained fossil fuel divestment campaigning. At that time, a new generation of motivated Brandeis undergraduates worked to step up pressure on the university's administration to act on divestment.

From my experience of the divestment movement, I observed the growth of multiple NGOs, student groups, and coalitions focused on divestment. I was also involved in the Multi-School Divestment Fund from January 2015 to the fund's payout in 2018. The divestment fund ultimately was paid out in the form of fellowships for student social justice activists at Salem State University, an institution that fully divested from fossil fuels in May 2018. This is another example of fossil fuel divestment campaigns supporting educational and knowledge sharing both through community and through financing.

My experience of divestment at Brandeis and in the Multi-School Divestment Fund emphasized to me that divestment is both a political, educational, and vocational movement that has influenced experts in the financial industry as well as also establishing its own form of expertise and community. A generation of student and faculty activists have driven the growth of the fossil fuel divestment movement, which has led to many of them establishing their own form of financial and activist expertise while also impacting the work of people with careers established in mainstream finance. This is a very different angle of change from the green bond market, that started with and has been driven by financial professionals. However, both fields of expertise increasingly intersect in calls for reinvestment strategies to go alongside with fossil fuel divestment.

The ten-year anniversary of the Carbon Tracker report on stranded assets in 2021 is a moment for reflection on fossil fuel divestment that also underlines how dramatic this change has entered into mainstream finance,[6] with a report from BlackRock, the world's largest asset manager, emphasizing this. BlackRock's sustainable investing team's report for the comptroller of the city of New York clearly documents and argues that owning fossil fuels is a failing investment.

Fossil fuel divestment campaigning was a training ground that has established forms of expertise and organizing, which has influenced mainstream finance. A number of NGOs and organizations have emerged from or been energized by the fossil fuel divestment campaign. The Intentional Endowments Network arose from divestment conversations as well, bridging into sustainable finance. The divestment movement continues to grow, with the climate activist and policy NGO C40 leading the mayors of Berlin, Bristol, Cape Town,

---

[6] www-newyorker-com.cdn.ampproject.org/c/s/www.newyorker.com/news/daily-comment/the-powerful-new-financial-argument-for-fossil-fuel-divestment/amp

Durban, London, Los Angeles, Milan, New Orleans, New York, Oslo, Pittsburgh, and Vancouver to pledge "to take all possible steps to divest city assets from fossil fuels" in September 2020 (C40, 2020).

The primary purpose of the divestment campaign remains focused on keeping fossil fuels in the ground and ending fossil fuel use and extraction, as the research that galvanized the movement stressed (Meinshausen, et al. 2009; McKibben, 2012; Initiative, 2014). The objective is to stigmatize fossil fuel companies and their industry associations, thereby making it increasingly difficult for them to continue to have a license to operate and influence public climate policy. These are the stated goals of the fossil fuel divestment movement by activists and organizations in this space. However, the campaign has also now increasingly focused on connecting plans to reinvest in a low carbon economy with divestment initiatives and many have developed hybrid careers between activist, policy, and financial organizations.

In parallel to my entry into climate finance through the fossil fuel divestment movement, a climate finance policy advisor told me at a climate finance conference in March 2019 that his days involved in Yale's campaign during the early days of fossil fuel divestment in 2012 was pivotal for his later work in climate finance and policy. His experience highlights the convergence of the fossil fuel divestment movement and climate finance initiatives.

10.4 Conclusion

The green bond market began among financial professionals and has been and continues to be evaluated by policymakers and scientists for its environmental and climate impact. In contrast, the divestment movement began among student activists and civil society protestors, with a targeted focus on high carbon intensive companies and holding private and public institutions accountable for the climate and environmental impact of endowment investments. The historical development and entanglement of the green bond market and the fossil fuel divestment movement highlight the embeddedness of financial markets in social and political movements.

Participants in both the green bond market and fossil fuel divestment are driven to act in response to climate change, faced with a lack of current necessary action that will lead to catastrophe within the next forty years. Debate continues on what the best strategies are to mobilize change, with the divestment of New York State pension funds from fossil fuels prompting a *MarketWatch* piece arguing that there was more leverage from holding oil and gas stocks, which also mentions buying green bonds from predominantly oil and dirtier utility companies as an advocacy strategy (Carlson, 2021). The convergence of both of these movements is also clear in a sponsored piece in *Financial Times* by wind company Iberdrola directly comparing the growth of the green bond market and the amount of capital divested from fossil fuels. The Climate Bonds Initiative and 350.org are cited for their data (Iberdrola, 2021).

Both the divestment movement and the green bond market address the problem of climate change by trying to manipulate the workings of the financial markets. It is therefore not surprising that the movements overlap and influence each other in practice. The divestment movement now includes Divest and Reinvest as a slogan, with sustainable financial products such as green bonds highlighted as good reinvestment choice. Pension funds and institutional investors are also increasingly directly using divestment from companies involved as fossil fuels as an engagement strategy, despite many finance professionals calls for share ownership and activism as a contrasting strategy (Verney, 2021). Neither the green bond market nor the divestment movement have been a solution to climate change. Global emissions continue to climb. However, through interrogating these two responses by different groups of people concerned with climate change, I highlight that the divestment movement is distinguished by its democratic demands to the civic process itself, as well as by its broader conception of the agenda of necessary change in order to address the problem of climate change. This is important, because civic and policy-based actions surround, support, and ultimately provide our ability to critique and shape market activity (Keucheyan, 2016). When we think about how to deal with wicked problems such as global climate change, we should challenge our preconceived models of who are the experts and which institutions should be in charge.

While many economists continue to argue that a carbon tax is the most elegant and simple solution to climate change, carbon taxes have not been politically feasible. As Nobel prize winning economist and debunker of the *Tragedy of the Commons* economic myth, Elinor Ostrom argues, there are numerous ways for humans to work together to collectively act and steward our environment (Ostrom, 2010). This stewardship rests on effective political organization where efforts on a broad array of societal issues are coordinated.

This does not rule out that financial expertise can be part of the response to climate change, but the privileging of financial expertise is one of the points of friction that prevents markets from changing in response to environmental and social needs (Dal Maso, 2020). Challenging this expertise creates possibilities beyond our current prospective policies and climate change action buzzwords that are yet to be acknowledge and supported. At the same time, acknowledging that the fossil fuel divestment movement remains a market solution, and recognizing that it hasn't been succesfull even when combined with the green bond movement, should make us take another serious look at degrowth policies, radical self-sufficiency, and the transformation of forms of work through Universal Basic Income programs as viable political agendas (Bregman, 2017; Archer, 2020a). Allowing market solutions to remain the primary horizon of our political imaginary leads to excessive degradation and damage to our planet from which there may be no turning back.[7]

References

Archer, Matthew. 2020a. "Navigating the sustainability landscape: Impact pathways and the sustainability ethic as moral compass." *Focaal* 1 (aop): 1–15.

2020b. "Stakes and stakeholders in the climate casino." *GeoHumanities*: 1–17.

Ballantine, John, Eric Olson, Aneil Tripathy, Elise J. Willer, Philip A. Wight, Michael Abrams, and Iona Feldman. 2015. *Final report and recommendations: Brandeis University Exploratory Committee on Fossil Fuel Divestment.*

Bregman, Rutger. 2017. *Utopia for Realists: How We Can Build the Ideal World.* London: Hachette UK.

C40. 2020. "C40: Mayors of 12 major cities commit to divest from fossil fuel companies, invest in green." C40. www.c40.org/press_releases/cities-commit-divest-invest.

Carlson, Debbie. 2021. "If you support green energy, you should buy utilities and oil stocks: here's why." www-marketwatch-com.cdn

[7] This project has received funding from the European Research Council (ERC) under the European Union's Horizon 2020 research and innovation programme (grant agreement No 772544 IMPACT HAU).

.ampproject.org/c/s/www.marketwatch.com/amp/story/if-you-sup
port-green-energy-you-should-buy-utilities-and-oil-stocks-heres-why-
11611235877.

Clapp, Christa, and Kamleshan Pillay. 2017. "Green bonds and climate
finance." In *Climate Finance: Theory and Practice*, 79–105. Singapore:
World Scientific.

Clapp, Christa S., Knut H. Alfsen, Asbjørn Torvanger, and Harald Francke
Lund. 2015. "Influence of climate science on financial decisions."
Nature Climate Change 5 (2): 84–85.

Dal Maso, Giulia. 2020. *Risky Expertise in Chinese Financialisation: Returned
Labour and the State–Finance Nexus*. New York: Springer Nature.

Dupre, Stan, Taylor Posey, Tina Wang, and Tricia Jamison. 2018. *Shooting
for the moon in a hot air balloon? Measuring how green bonds contribute to scaling up investments in green projects* (2° Investing Initiative).
https://2degrees-investing.org/wp-content/uploads/2018/10/Green-bonds-
updated-paper-Oct-2018.pdf.

Figueres, Christiana, Hans Joachim Schellnhuber, Gail Whiteman, Johan
Rockström, Anthony Hobley, and Stefan Rahmstorf. 2017. "Three
years to safeguard our climate." *Nature News* 546 (7660): 593.

Frankel, Christian, José Ossandón, and Trine Pallesen. 2019. "The organization of markets for collective concerns and their failures." *Economy and
Society* 48 (2): 153–174.

Fulton, Mark, and Reid Capalino. 2014. *Investing in the clean trillion:
closing the clean energy investment gap*. Ceres.

Healy, Noel, and John Barry. 2017. "Politicizing energy justice and energy
system transitions: Fossil fuel divestment and a 'just transition'." *Energy
Policy* 108: 451–459.

Iberdrola. 2021. "Plotting the progress of the Paris Agreement." *Financial
Times - Paid Post by Iberdrola*. https://iberdrola.ft.com/plotting-the-
progress-of-the-paris-agreement.

Initiative, Carbon Tracker. 2014. *Recognising Risk, Perpetuating
Uncertainty: A Baseline Survey of Climate Disclosures by Fossil Fuel
Companies*. London.

Jaramillo, Pablo. 2013. "Etnografías en transición: escalas, procesos y com-
posiciones." *Antípoda. Revista de Antropología y Arqueología* (16):
13–22.

Keucheyan, Razmig. 2016. *Nature is a Battlefield: Towards a Political
Ecology. Translated by David Broder*. Cambridge: Polity Press.

Limbert, Michael, and E. Summerson Carr, eds. 2016. *Scale: Discourse and
Dimensions of Social Life*. Berkely, CA: University of California Press.

McKibben, Bill. 2012. "Global warming's terrifying new math." *Rolling
Stone* 19 (7): 2012.

Meinshausen, Malte, Nicolai Meinshausen, William Hare, Sarah C. B. Raper, Katja Frieler, Reto Knutti, David J Frame, and Myles R Allen. 2009. "Greenhouse-gas emission targets for limiting global warming to 2 C." *Nature* 458 (7242): 1158–1162.

Nik-Khah, Edward, and Philip Mirowski. 2019a. "On going the market one better: economic market design and the contradictions of building markets for public purposes." *Economy and Society* 48 (2): 268–294.

2019b. "The ghosts of Hayek in orthodox microeconomics: markets as information processors." In Armin Beverungen, Philip Mirowski, and Edward Nik-Khah u.a. (Hg.): *Markets*. Lüneburg: meson press 2019, S. 31–70. DOI: https://doi.org/10.25969/mediarep/12241.

Ostrom, Elinor. 2010. "Polycentric systems for coping with collective action and global environmental change." *Global environmental change* 20 (4): 550–557.

Tripathy, Aneil. 2017. "Translating to risk: The legibility of climate change and nature in the green bond market." *Economic Anthropology* 4 (2): 239–250.

UNFCCC. 2015. The Paris Agreement. In *United Nations*. http://unfccc.int/ files/essential_background/convention/application/pdf/english_paris_ agreement.pdf: HeinOnline.

Verney, Paul. 2021. "Vacating their seat at the table: the rise of fossil fuel divestment." *Responsible Investor*. www.responsible-investor.com/art icles/vacating-their-seat-at-the-table-the-rise-of-fossil-fuel-divestment.

Welker, Marina, and David Wood. 2011. "Shareholder activism and alienation." *Current Anthropology* 52 (S3).

11 | *How Should We Make an Impact?*

MATTHEW ARCHER

Sustainability has become the privileged way businesses, NGOs, and governments think about actions they might take to remediate environmental problems and be good actors vis-à-vis natural resources and our shared climate. In turn, the way that sustainable actions are accounted for is in the language of "impacts" in which various accounting schemes seek to tabulate and communicate the degree to which some sustainable action has an effect in the world. The purpose of generating a quantifiable, representable impact is so that consumers might decide that it makes a company or product more worthwhile and more deserving of a consumer's money on a market. On a market, a consumer has the ability to decide that other qualities (price, brand, convenience, etc.) could potentially outweigh good environmental action. The purpose of explaining all this is to show just how limited a utilitarian approach (one in which goods are measured, weighed, and seen as interchangeable) to fixing environmental problems is. What Archer demonstrates is that by tracking environmental action in terms of comparable, fungible impacts, one allows corporate actors to count their pollution or bad action, and continue to do it anyway, both masking it behind impact measures and abdicating any final responsibility to consumers. At the close of the paper, Archer offers a different way of thinking about sustainable environmental action, one that draws on various strands of indigenous thinking to illustrate what it would look like and how much more effective things would be if we understood good environmental action in terms of nonnegotiable values (in philosophy language, a "deontological" approach).

In a contemporary corporate, financial, governmental, or NGO context, people often understand sustainability in terms of knowable effects or measurable "impacts." Whether reducing negative impacts (like eliminating greenhouse gas emissions), generating positive impacts (like the creation of well-paid, stable jobs), or figuring out ways to deal with the impacts of interconnected socioecological crises like climate change, pollution, sea level rise, droughts, and so on, the go-to language of understanding collective corporate action is in terms of causally explicable impacts. In a neoliberal context, one in which markets are the privileged mode of governance, policymakers feel that the extension of market-like activity should reach to any sort of social endeavor. When people or organizations make claims about how sustainable they are, or when they make claims about how unsustainable someone else is, these claims often turn on a particular notion of impact as a quantifiable, a measurable, and, most important for our purposes a *comparable, marketable phenomenon.*

Once sustainability becomes comparable and marketable, then "sustainability performance" quickly becomes a market-like competition, a sort of rat-race to see who can be the most impactful, a competition that is easy to correlate with financial performance. Consider the kinds of sustainable products that can be found in most supermarkets, where sustainability is often indicated with a label from an organization like the Rainforest Alliance or Fairtrade International. Here branding and labeling try to convey some product's environmental impact, inviting consumers to weigh such impacts against other things they might value such as quality or price. Sustainability, understood as social and environmental impacts, becomes just one more consumer preference weighed and considered, embraced or discounted at the moment of purchase. A complicated accounting infrastructure often supports impact branding. These labels generally promise consumers that the products they've purchased are more sustainable than similar products without those labels, a promise companies often support by presenting evidence in their annual "impacts reports" and on their sustainability web pages showing how many workers or how much of the environment was helped or protected as a result of these standards.

Corporate sustainability and sustainable finance follow a similar logic. Companies often allow impact claims to function as a stand-in for social responsibility and environmental sustainability, providing statistics on everything from waste water to women employees as evidence of their business ethics. Banks use these same kinds of quantitative data to make claims about the positive social and environmental impacts of their investments, often arguing that a portfolio is sustainable because it has invested in sustainable companies, creating a tenuous chain of claims about sustainability that are built on an even more tenuous chain of claims about social and environmental impacts, all with the goal of presenting some product, or company, or policy as relatively "impactful" in an environmental sense. In turn, a given product, company, or policy's "impactfulness" becomes one more relative attribute that some market participant can appreciate or discount according to their own consumer preferences.

Despite a veneer of quantitative objectivity, impact assessments are exceedingly political. From the data included in the analysis and the way those data are collected to the different ways the results of an assessment are disclosed and proliferated, every stage of an impact assessment involves decisions that are social, political, and highly subjective. In turn, these decisions are often masked by branding efforts at the point of consumption, or by abstract distancing that can come with aggregate numerical accounting. To this last point, for decades, critical social scientists have understood the political nature of numbers, leaving little doubt that they are pervasive and highly effective technologies of governance, both capable of extending the reach of governance (as in the case of a census or a tax registry), or reducing the complexity of that which is measured (as in the instance of turning a human being into a civil registration or social security number with an attendant data table).[1]

But what about the impact of impact assessments themselves? This chapter explores what happens when environmental and sustainability politics are reduced to fungible qualities attached to generic market objects. Put another way, this chapter asks what happens when people try to solve environmental problems according to market logics and via consumer choices instead of simply asserting and legislating certain environmental behaviors or collectively cultivating a moral ecology in which certain kinds of impacts are simply off-limits, rather than something left to the market to mediate.

Section 11.1 focuses on the neoliberal approach to impactfulness. As the Introduction to this volume describes it, neoliberalism is defined at least in part by the belief that markets can solve various problems, from parking shortages to water and food insecurity. The dominant approach to sustainability, as Section 11.1 will demonstrate, relies either implicitly or explicitly on the belief that the market, once provided with complete and reliable information about impacts, will efficiently – and thereby sustainably – allocate, among other things,

---

[1] See, for example, Porter (1995), Merry (2016), Desrosières (1998).

the environmental costs and benefits of production and consumption. This shifts power to determine what counts as sustainable to "the market" itself, obscuring the role corporate entities play in deciding for themselves what counts as sustainable. Indeed, large corporations and banks are playing an increasingly prominent role in debates about global sustainability, and over the past decade, it has gotten much harder to find examples of relatively large-scale sustainability initiatives that do not explicitly rely on market mechanisms to achieve their expected impacts (e.g., carbon markets, payments for ecosystem services, voluntary sustainability certifications, and so on).

This system relies on establishing a measurable, objective cause-and-effect relationship between something like a certified product or a sustainable investment, on one hand, and a positive social or environment effect, typically somewhere far away, on the other (Cashore, 2002). While quantification is not in itself a problem – after all any effective action on climate action would likely need to know the amount of and rate at which carbon is entering the atmosphere – market-based attempts to quantify and measure impact often elide important power relations in a way that helps companies hide real people and places behind the abstract distancing that corporate accounting tends to create. Standards often lie at the center of these relationships, especially when impacts intersect with consumption choices, leading not only to the standardization of different ways of talking about impactfulness, but the objectification of impact more generally, which obscures its fundamentally social and political nature, framing the discourse around sustainability in the depoliticized language of data-driven, market-based "solutions." A careful, critical analysis of these processes helps reveal the power dynamics that are not only embedded in this market-based approach to impact, but reinforced by it.

Section 11.2 of the chapter moves on to ways of thinking about impact that draw on work by indigenous scholars and activists who offer different possibilities for theorizing and enacting socioecological relationships. Whereas market-based approaches which commodify impact are ultimately utilitarian and see environmental values as fungible with other things that consumers might prefer, indigenous scholarship offers something closer to a "deontological" approach to climate and environmental issues. A deontological approach to values and ethics allows for essential, noninterchangeable values claims. From a deontological point of view something can just be important or an ethical responsibility in an absolute sense, and not subject to utilitarian interchangeability, comparison, or weighing. As such, some indigenous scholarship on the notion of sustainability will help illustrate the sorts of values we might embrace if we decided to use our governments to actively pursue good environmental stewardship instead of simply creating market-like contexts in which environmental justice is a hypothetical consumer possibility. Comparing these different modes of interacting with the world we inhabit attunes us to some of the more fundamental assumptions that the contemporary, dominant approach to sustainability relies on, assumptions that are neither necessary nor sufficient to imagine and realize better, more just presents and futures.

11.1 "Our Impact"

A Google search for the phrase "our impact" yields web pages for familiar organizations, a near-equal mix of governments, nonprofits, and multinational corporations. When I searched on September 12, 2020 in incognito mode on Google Chrome from my apartment in Copenhagen, Denmark, the first page of results were as follows (in order): Novartis, GlobalGiving, United Way Worldwide, Nestlé, CARE (two results for this one), ALIMA, Philips, the European Union, and the OECD. Notable here is that organizations as different as a pharmaceutical company, a supranational government, and a network of poverty alleviation organizations all use essentially the same language to describe their relationship with society and the environment, namely, as domains in which they make or have an *impact* that can be measured and evaluated and compared, where impacts become quantitative data that can be used to inform ostensibly objective, evidence-based sustainability strategies.

Consider Novartis, a global pharmaceutical company head-quartered in Basel, Switzerland (www.novartis.com/our-impact). According to their "Our Impact" page "At Novartis, we use science-based innovation to address some of society's most challenging healthcare issues. We discover and develop breakthrough treatments and find new ways to deliver them to as many people as possible." The top of the page features a photo of two dark-skinned women walking down a tree-lined dirt road. One is carrying a bucket on her head with another hanging from her arm, while the other pushes a wheelbarrow while gripping what looks like a jug for fuel or water. Below the photo, which is captioned "Our impact: building trust with society," four numbers in large, bold print advertise some of Novartis's biggest impacts. They have reached nearly 800 million patients in the 155 countries where their products are sold. They have valued their environmental impact at negative 5.3 billion US dollars, while their social impact approaches 70 billion US dollars. The negative value for environmental impact is derived from putting a price on different kinds of pollution and waste generated both directly and indirectly by their products, while the relatively large positive social impact is derived from the amount of living wages they pay, as well as their investment in worker training, health and safety improvements, etc.

These kinds of numbers help companies like Novartis legitimize their bad environmental actions as well as their sustainability claims by presenting their impacts as objective, neutral, scientifically valid, and ultimately interchangeable. In addition to rendering diffuse things comparable, this sort of accounting distances us from the politics that underlie their calculation. Quantification like this also begs the question of what exactly gets included in any sort of counting exercise. For example, it may be true that Novartis sold millions of doses of treatments for cardiovascular diseases, cancer, and depression to patients around the world, but it is also true that many other people around the world die because they do not have access to medicine that companies like Novartis produce, while many more go into debt paying the high drug prices Novartis's investors demand. Even in countries where medicines are free or heavily subsidized, Novartis's profitability relies on public money that might otherwise have been spent on things like art, education, and so on. But that sort of accounting would imply a critique of capitalist profit making and undermine Novartis's *raison d'être*, so these numbers remain conspicuously absent from the enumeration of Novartis's impacts.

When companies do present estimates of their negative impacts, as in the case of Novartis's resource-intense production and distribution process, it presupposes particular kinds of solutions and precludes others. For instance, by presenting its negative environmental impact as tons of carbon dioxide equivalent, Novartis makes carbon emissions comparable to other things it is doing, and then implicitly sets a goal of reducing that total cumulative bad number, which companies increasingly achieve through "carbon offset" schemes. The carbon is still in the atmosphere contributing to climate change, but some other activity that may have nothing to do with greenhouses gasses is now comparable and offsetting. Put differently, Novartis continues to pollute, and then presents a problem that it can improve on its own terms, making it harder for critics to get Novartis to do something specifically about carbon emissions. Writ large, the representations that these numbers conjure and the data infrastructures that are necessary to construct them are an important tools companies and other powerful actors use to govern global supply chains and the diverse cultures and natures they connect.

11.1.1 Standardizing Impact

Sustainability standards, that is, the aggregation of impact measures into a brandable label such as "fair trade", are one of the main tools companies use to make claims about and represent their sustainability and their impacts. Consider Unilever, a multinational corporation that owns popular brands like Dove soap, Lipton tea, Skippy peanut butter, AXE deodorant, and Magnum ice cream, among many, many others. In 2009, they committed to sourcing all of their Lipton tea from Rainforest Alliance-certified farms and factories. More recently, the company committed to procuring all of its teas – not only the Lipton tea sold in Europe and North America, but its wide range of both inexpensive black teas sold in other parts of the world and its more recently acquired specialty and loose-leaf teas – from "sustainable sources," as well. As Julie Guthman (2005) has argued, voluntary labeling schemes like the Rainforest Alliance Sustainable Agriculture Standard forms an integral part of "neoliberal governance," creating markets for previously nonmarketized values such as concerns about social and environmental justice. These schemes, in other words, create a market for social and environmental impacts that both depends on and reinforces an implicit conceptualization of impact as something that can be quantified, economically valued, and ultimately commodified.[2]

Since 2018, I myself have conducted research on the way these standards are developed and why they are adopted. Concerns about

---

[2] These processes are conceptually distinct, but in practice, they often go hand-in-hand. For a good overview, see Gómez-Baggethun and Ruiz-Pérez (2011).

the social, environmental, and economic impacts of standardization dominate conversations among standardizers. According to one interlocutor, the ability to demonstrate that a particular standard corresponds to a particular impact in a particular place is among the most challenging aspects of standards development. The problem, he told me, lies with the data, not only the validity of data, but the availability across the supply chain, in other words, its transparency.

Although this interlocutor is normally based in a nondescript office building in Washington, DC, his work often takes him abroad, where he visits farms and factories around the world who have adopted his organization's popular certification scheme. The reason for these visits is not to make sure that producers are complying with the standards – that's what independent, third-party auditors are for – but instead to make sure that both the local auditors and the local producers are invested in his (and his organization's) vision of impactfulness, which relies on the allegedly transparent collection, analysis, and dissemination of data on things ranging from employment and wages, to the number of bathrooms on a farm, to the types and amounts of pesticides used in the production process, to the area and location of land being cultivated for different crops. Not only do these data and their analyses have to be transparent, they have to facilitate traceability, so that a specific product (for example, the beans that go into a particular brand of coffee) can be traced to a specific farm, factory, or local ecology where a specific impact is claimed to have occurred. This kind of datafied traceability is central to corporate claims about their sustainability, since companies need to be able to point to the specific social and environmental impacts that (the production and subsequent consumption) of their products are having in the "real world." But this focus on traceability and transparency turns our attention away from the way impact is conceptualized in the first place, leaving the market-based and comparable neoliberal logic of impactfulness (and sustainability more generally) mostly unexamined.

An analysis of the impact evaluations these kinds of organizations conduct is instructive, because it reveals how many assumptions about socioecological relationships are embedded and hidden in the seemingly objective numbers and subsequent claims about impact and sustainability that these exercises produce. Take, for example, the Rainforest Alliance's 2018 Impacts Report, a nearly one hundred-page document replete with detailed methodological discussions, flow charts showing how broader social impacts connect to different parts of the standard, definitions of the many different indicators, and a detailed bibliography.[3] The reports are bogged down in the technical language of impact assessment methodologies, but typically rely on secondary research that has actually deployed the exceedingly technical methods of "life-cycle assessments," an important component of impact measurement and evaluation not only because it provides an apparently valid methodological foundation, but is also the source of important visual and ideological metaphors (such as the ubiquity of flow charts that make claims about causal relationships) that proliferate even in relatively informal discussions about impactfulness (Archer, 2020).

Again, just as important as what these reports include is what they exclude. Impact assessments are sterile and impersonal, atomizing producers and consumers alike, and then reconstituting them as data. It is easy to lose sight of what matters to different communities. For example, when you ask producers what matters to them in terms of the impact of a sustainability certification, they typically respond that they need more money, that is, higher wages or higher sale prices for their crops. But sustainability certifications have by and large failed to generate this impact, as costs for most crops continue to plummet and costs of living continues to rise. One might think that the single target identified by producers as the most important would be emphasized in an impact report about sustainability certifications, and yet income only appears as a small part of a broader, ambiguous indicator called "livelihood." Thus, the failure of certification schemes like the Rainforest Alliance's sustainable agriculture standard to achieve the one impact that producers themselves have identified as the most important impact, disappears behind a wall of quantified indicators of other impacts that they have achieved, a politics of opacity repackaged as apolitical transparency.

11.1.2 The Role of the Market

In these different contexts, sustainability professionals presume that the market will, as if by magic, digest all that data about impacts and

---

[3] www.rainforest-alliance.org/sites/default/files/2018-03/RA_Impacts_2018.pdf

generate the most sustainable outcomes. In the case of Novartis, this presumption is implicit in their impact reporting and disclosure methods. In a 2017 press release, for instance, they advertise the fact that their sustainability reports are consistently "structured in accordance with the Global Reporting Initiative's (GRI) G4 guidelines, with disclosure at 'comprehensive' level."[4] Although the GRI's description of its own impactfulness is couched in the ambiguous language of stakeholders and decision-makers, other outlets offer a more honest appraisal of the way standardized sustainability reporting leads to more sustainable outcomes. According to an article posted on the Harvard Law School Corporate Governance Forum, investors are one of the main drivers of standardization efforts in sustainability reporting (Clarkin, Sawyer, and Levin, 2020). Similarly, according to a report from PricewaterhouseCoopers (PwC), one of the primary benefits of standardized sustainability reporting is that it enables investors to "monitor the values and trends of non-financial indicators to get an overall picture of the company's future performance."[5] It is through these market actors that the impacts of impact reporting are supposed to be realized.

This is even more explicit in the context of sustainable agriculture standards. In the Rainforest Alliance's theory of change, conveniently represented as a color-coded flow chart, markets mediate the relationship between certification requirements, on one hand, and outcomes and impacts, on the other hand. Increased supply of sustainable productions, increased demand for sustainable products, increased prices for sustainable products, and improved market access for farmers who produce those sustainable products are some of the purported "direct outcomes" of certification that link the standard's various elements to longer-term outcomes and, ultimately, to a world where "people and nature thrive in harmony." One of the key elements of certification, as it were, is the collection, analysis, and dissemination of data about things like risk and performance, supply chain traceability, and marketing and outreach. The increasing datafication of these kinds of certification schemes is inextricably linked to the idea that more data

---

[4] www.novartis.com/news/media-releases/novartis-highlights-progress-towards-acce ss-and-environmental-goals-2016-corporate-responsibility-performance-report
[5] www.pwc.com/sk/en/assets/PDFs/Sustainability_Reporting_EN.pdf

leads to more sustainability, and, in turn, better market information and pricing.[6]

In both cases, the market plays the leading role in linking the measurement and reporting of impacts to managing and mitigating impacts. Investors use data about impacts to invest in companies that have better sustainability performance. Reliable data about the impacts of certification allows producers to charge higher prices for certified products and encourages consumers to pay higher prices for those products, which they prefer over noncertified products which they assume are less sustainable. This approach reinforces the idea that consumer demands, price mechanisms, and the dynamics of financial markets are the best ways to deliver positive impacts or mitigate negative impacts, all the while obscuring the way a reliance on markets benefits and empowers the actors who are already influential within those markets at the expense of those who aren't. Moreover, it reaffirms the notion of sustainability as the consideration of social, environmental, and economic impacts, which suggests that these domains are commensurable when in fact they are often fundamentally incommensurable. Drawing on indigenous and anticolonial theories of impact and sustainability, Section 11.2 of this chapter explores alternative ways of thinking about impacts and the relationship between impact measurement and impact management.

11.2 Impact Imaginaries: Decolonizing Impacts

How can we think differently about impacts? And just as important, how can we think differently about the relationship between measuring impacts and mitigating impacts, which neoliberal approaches to impact management contend are linked through investor-driven market mechanisms? Kyle Powys Whyte has written extensively about the way indigenous communities respond to the impacts of climate change and settler colonialism. "Many indigenous persons," he argues, "interpret climate change impacts as jeopardizing the values associated with the collective continuance of the communities in which they participate"; where "collective continuance" refers to "a community's aptitude for being adaptive in ways sufficient for the

---

[6] See, for example, Archer and Elliott, 2021.

livelihoods of its members to flourish into the future." The impacts of climate change affect "the quality of the relationships that constitute collective continuance," disrupting "webs of responsibilities" that "jeopardize some of what is valued intrinsically and extrinsically by certain indigenous peoples" (Whyte, 2014). If we follow Whyte in understanding impacts as the effects of climate change (or an investment, or a corporation, etc.) on the quality of the relationships that constitute collective continuance, it becomes immediately clear that treating these essential values as comparable and negotiable is impossible.

In discussions around indigeneity and sustainability, multispecies relations of responsibility across time and space emerge as a key theme and a start to illustrate what a value system built around community continuance might look like. Robin Wall Kimmerer (2013), for example, reminds us that individuals can take responsibility for their own impacts on the planet even as they recognize and accept that no individual is singularly responsible for various socioecological problems. Reflecting on Thomas Berry's claim that "we must say of the universe that it is a communion of subjects, not a collection of objects," she proposes a "grammar of animacy" that "could lead us to whole new ways of living in the world, other species a sovereign people, a world with a democracy of species, not a tyranny of one – with moral responsibility to water and wolves, and with a legal system that recognizes the standing of other species" (Kimmerer, 2013: 56–58). But later she makes a crucial point, one that strikes at the heart of this chapter and the way we conceptualize impact. A grammar of animacy doesn't exclude other grammars, but enfolds them, co-opts them. She explicates the notion of the Honorable Harvest, a set of "rules" meant to enshrine collective action and obligation around resource use that could help guide the way humans interact with the world around them, how much to take from the land, how much to give back, and so on. As soon as it starts to sound anachronistic, in a world where food is more regularly purchased than harvested, Kimmerer asks us to think about how the Honorable Harvest can be used to guide our consumption choices in places like craft stores, shopping malls, and supermarkets. She proposes money as a stand-in, a way to evaluate our decisions: "Dollars become a surrogate, a proxy for the harvester with hands in the earth, and they can be used in support of the Honorable Harvest – or not" (Kimmerer, 2013: 195).

Reflecting on the Menominee Nation's Sustainable Development Institute (SDI), Kyle Whyte, Chris Caldwell, and Marie Schaefer (2018) show how the SDI successfully prioritizes the "[consideration of] what processes support Indigenous peoples' sustainability in the face of the challenges of settler colonialism, starting from the Menominee experience and then branching out to others when mutual benefits are possible." This approach "is an active effort that expresses our gratitude to those before us and shows our responsibility to those who will come after us," one that "is maintained by sharing cultural values that have been passed down from generation to generation to show how we can act on the potential futurities of our peoples." They note how different this kind of sustainability is from nonindigenous communities' attempts to adopt and enact indigenous theories of planning, efforts that are typically motivated by a desire to "[save] themselves or humankind." In contrast, indigenous planning, which "refers to how … Indigenous peoples endeavor to sustain, revitalize, and continue [their] social, cultural, and ecological integrity under conditions of settler colonial oppression" (Whyte, Caldwell, and Schaefer, 2018: 154), "is about figuring out the planning processes arising from the contexts that we actually live in today, in which our societies are greatly limited and threatened by settler colonialism and other forms of oppression. Reflecting on sustainability in this way … keeps us aware of how oppression endures as one of the largest threats to Indigenous peoples and many other groups" (Whyte, Caldwell, and Schaefer, 2018: 174–175).

This is a crucial point: While indigenous theories and practices of sustainability may offer alternatives for well-intentioned social and environmental activists, and may involve quantitative approaches to measuring and evaluating impacts, they are distinct in that they privilege particular values such as community continuance, and insist that these values are nonnegotiable, nonfungible, and noncomparable.

11.2.1 Conclusion and Discussion: Indigenizing Impact Pathways

What if the goal of impact assessments was not to generate reports that rely on markets to be converted into the kinds of impacts that are commensurable with – and complementary to – profitability, but to determine what's needed to reach a specific, concrete goal? Processes of quantification may always be political, but their politics are not set in stone, and there is no reason the rigorous methods of lifecycle assessments, cost–benefit analyses, and other forms of calculating the impacts of products and processes should not become means to different ends. That kind of reappropriation is precisely the kind of political project that is at the heart of Kimmerer's work. It is also at the heart of recent interventions in organization studies to rethink the way corporations and other powerful organizations are studied. Abdelnour and Abu Moghli (2021), for instance, argue for more reflexivity in organizations research, especially in violent contexts, establishing a decoloniality continuum on which researchers might situate the politics of their research, from complicity on one side to liberation on the other. This applies to nonacademic research as well. Marketing, sustainability, and human resources consultants are increasingly tasked with doing research among people who are affected in various ways by the actions of corporations and other powerful organizations, to understand their impacts and how they might reduce or enhance them in a way that increases profits by creating new market opportunities. Although it is just one example of the kind of reframing our understanding of impactfulness might undergo, a decolonial approach offers an alternative way of both theorizing and enacting the relationship between measuring and managing impacts in the sense that it denies that impactfulness is (or more accurately, perhaps, *should be*) driven by markets, and in the sense that it establishes new goals that reject the prioritization of profits over people and planet.

Within the context of contemporary sustainability, highly technical impact measurement and evaluation methodologies reign supreme. Their dominance relies on the implicit assumption that markets can use the quantitative impact indicators these methodologies yield to generate sustainable outcomes, obscuring the politics inherent in both the creation of data and its analysis. Without being contextualized in the social and natural worlds in which they exist, these numbers allow different actors to hide their unsustainability behind a veil of objectivity, to obscure their role in perpetuating socioecological disasters behind a language of data-driven policies and evidence-based progress. In a broader sense, these techniques quickly morph into technologies of governance that enable corporations and corporate-adjacent organizations like banks and powerful NGOs to discipline both producers and consumers into specific modes of action, while at the same time limiting the possibilities of negotiation and contestation, effectively circumscribing other ways of organizing life.

And yet, as scholars like Kimmerer and Whyte remind us, these numbers and the methods used to generate them can and should be part of the solution, even if they can't be the only part. Impacts, according to Whyte, "include variations of the patterns of community relations of diverse entities. These patterns are the structures of organization, which include political, societal, cultural, religious, and familial institutions that tie together humans and multiple living, non-living, and spiritual beings, and natural interdependent collectives (forested areas, species habitats, water cycles, and so on)." Many of these patterns and variations *can* be measured, and some can even be assigned a price, especially when it comes to the market and in particular financial relations that, for better or worse, are an important aspect of most contemporary society. Whyte's conceptualization of disruptive impacts is particularly instructive: "impacts are disruptive," he argues, "when structures of organization can absorb the ecological changes only by changing key components of the structures themselves" (Whyte, 2014: 601).

In thinking about our impacts, then, it's a good idea to think about the kinds of values that need to be changed, one of which is surely the imperative to solve all of our problems via market-based competition and consumption. These values foster structures of power that place wealthy corporate executives and investors at the helm of global sustainability efforts and look almost exclusively at problems of unsustainability through the lens of market efficiency and diffuse consumer action. Thinking differently about impact, in other words, means situating these changes explicitly in the context of the oppressive structures neoliberalism relies on and imagining processes that can valorize other sorts of values. It means taking an active role not only in the way knowledge about impacts is produced, but in the way that knowledge is mobilized socially, economically, and politically.

References

Abdelnour, Samer, and Mai Abu Moghli. 2021. "Researching violent contexts: A call for political reflexivity." *Organization* 00 (0): 1–24, https://doi.org/10.1177/13505084211030646

Archer, Matthew, and Hannah Elliott. 2021. "'It's up to the market to decide': Revealing and concealing power in the sustainable tea supply chain." *Critique of Anthropology* 41 (3): 227–246.

Archer, Matthew. 2020. "Navigating the sustainability landscape: Impact pathways and the sustainability ethic as moral compass." *Focaal: The Journal of Global and Historical Anthropology.* https://doi.org/10.3167/fcl.2020.07200

Cashore, Benjamin. 2002. "Legitimacy and the privatization of environmental governance: How non-state market-driven (NSMD) governance systems gain rule-making authority." *Governance* 15 (4): 503–529.

Clarkin, Catherine M., Melissa Sawyer, and Joshua L. Levin. 2020. "The rise of standardized ESG disclosure frameworks in the United States." Harvard Law School Forum on Corporate Governance. Accessed October 5, 2021. https://corpgov.law.harvard.edu/2020/06/22/the-rise-of-standardized-esg-disclosure-frameworks-in-the-united-states

Davis, Heather, and Zoe Todd. 2017. "On the importance of a date, or, decolonizing the Anthropocene." *ACME: An International Journal for Critical Geographies* 16 (4): 761–780.

Desrosières, Alain. 1998. *The Politics of Large Numbers: A History of Statistical Reasoning.* Cambridge, MA: Harvard University Press.

Gómez-Baggethun, Erik, and Manuel Ruiz-Pérez. 2011. "Economic valuation and the commodification of ecosystem services." *Progress in Physical Geography* 35 (5): 613–628.

Guthman, Julie. 2007. "The Polanyian way? Voluntary food labels as neoliberal governance." *Antipode* 39 (3): 456–478.

Kimmerer, Robin Wall. 2013. *Braiding Sweetgrass: Indigenous Wisdom, Scientific Knowledge and the Teachings of Plants.* Minneapolis: Milkweed Editions.

Merry, Sally E. 2016. *The Seductions of Quantification: Measuring Human Rights, Gender Violence, and Sex Trafficking.* Chicago: University of Chicago Press.

Oswald, W. Wyatt, David R. Foster, Bryan N. Shuman, Elizabeth S. Chilton, Dianna L. Doucette, and Deena L. Duranleau. 2020. "Conservation implications of limited Native American impacts in pre-contact New England." *Nature Sustainability* 3 (3): 241–246.

Porter, Theodore M. 2020. *Trust in Numbers: The Pursuit of Objectivity in Science and Public Life.* Princeton: Princeton University Press.

Powell, Miles A. 2014. "'Pesteredwith inhabitants': Aldo Leopold, William Vogt, and more trouble with wilderness." *Pacific Historical Review* 84 (2): 195–226

Roos, Christopher I. 2020 "Scale in the study of Indigenous burning." *Nature Sustainability* 3: 898–899.

Sultana, Farhana. 2018. "The false equivalence of academic freedom and free speech." *ACME: An International Journal for Critical Geographies* 17 (2): 228–257.

Tuck, Eve, and K. Wayne Yang. 2012. "Decolonization is not a metaphor." *Decolonization: Indigeneity, Education & Society* 1 (1): 1–40.

Vaughn, Sarah E. 2017. "Disappearing mangroves: The epistemic politics of climate adaptation in Guyana." *Cultural Anthropology* 32 (2): 242–268.

Whyte, Kyle Powys, Chris Caldwell, and Marie Schaefer. 2018. "Indigenous lessons about sustainability are not just for 'all humanity'." In *Sustainability: Approaches to Environmental Justice and Social Power*, edited by Julie Sze. New York: NYU Press.

Whyte, Kyle Powys. 2014. "Indigenous women, climate change impacts, and collective action." *Hypatia* 29 (3): 599–616.

Yusoff, Kathryn. 2018. *A Billion Black Anthropocenes or None*. Minneapolis: University of Minnesota Press.

PART II

Our Lives

12 | Why Do Some People Want to Manage Human Fertility?

MICHELLE A. RENSEL AND
RACHEL A. VAUGHN

When life throws you a problem, the solution our contemporary market moment proffers tends to be some sort of phone-based computer program, that is, an app. In this chapter, the authors take a look at apps designed to manage menstrual cycles. In so doing, the authors show that apps tend to individualize a problem, prize forms of efficiency and normative ideas of gender, all with a mystifying veneer of utopian market optimization and self-help. What's interesting for us is the way that apps can individualize the problems they're trying to solve and in so doing often seek to assist people in enhancing their human capital. The authors close with a contrast to anticapitalist punks seeking not individual optimization but collective liberation. In turn these punks offer those who menstruate a liberatory relationship with their own bodies.

12.1 Introduction

Fitness trackers, calorie-counters, period trackers, pregnancy apps- Health and wellness apps are immensely popular and accessible to anyone with a smartphone. However, the demographics of health-based app usage reveal social and cultural differences in engagement. Indeed, users in the United States tend to be young (under 45 years of age), white, college-educated, and make more than $50,000 per year (Carroll et al., 2017). *Lifehack.org,* a site dedicated to all things self-improvement, summarizes what are arguably the most important goals of these technologies: "Apps can help you take charge of three of the most important aspects of your day-to-day life: your family, your health, and your time" (Bickov, 2016). While every application is different, the desire to optimize human time, health, relationships, and even fertility is perhaps best exemplified by the rise of period trackers, apps where users enter and track information on menstruation status, physical symptoms, emotions, dietary habits, and more.

If, as anthropologist David Harvey (2005) suggests, neoliberalism in its broadest sense is about generating the conditions and technologies best suited for capital accumulation, then the forging of new markets from historically ignored personal health data, or the management of otherwise "healthy" bodies, certainly applies. As we will explore in this chapter, the recent rise of these apps, a form of FemTech (female technology; Folkent, 2019) is not without precedence. Instead, the story of period tracking apps cannot be understood without unpacking longer histories of institutional reproductive management, scientific discoveries about the endocrine system and its role in behavior and physiology, and feminist activism that has resisted the influence of corporate medicalization of human health and bodily function.

Empowering people to control their reproductive (and nonreproductive) lives can transform and resist deeply entrenched societal norms and expectations surrounding the "biological imperatives" of feminized bodies. In addition, do-it-yourself health management tools like period tracking apps may teach menstruators about their bodies in a nonjudgemental, supportive space, promoting body positivity and resisting norms of shame, menstrual taboo, and bodily exploitation that have persisted in medical discourses around reproductive health. As such, period tracking apps have the potential to liberate menstruators and fertility trackers by putting the knowledge and resources to manage reproductive health in the hands of the end user. However, in this chapter, we question whether period tracking apps are truly empowering, asking who is in control and who benefits most from their usage. To answer these questions, we introduce the science of menstruation and menstrual/ovarian/uterine cycles, demonstrating how the reductionist approach to hormones and cycles marketed to individual consumers is at times scientifically inaccurate. Next, we briefly trace the origins of market-driven contemporary reproductive health management, demonstrating the entanglements of early endocrine science, eugenics, and neoliberalism in producing narratives about "correct" menstruation, individual optimization through consumerism, and reproductive management over the last one hundred years. In doing so, we identify the historical roots of contemporary "hormonal determinism," a form of biological determinism where hormones are thought to reductively control behavior and physiology; this idea prevails in popular narratives and scientific literature alike

(Daza, 2011). Hormonal determinism, along with the cycle science used in tracking technologies, points to the ways in which ideas about, "gender, ethnicity, class, race can be 'built into' technology at the design phase" (Boyer and Boswell-Penc, 2010: 120). Finally, we turn to period tracking apps to analyze how hormonal determinism and its pseudo scientific underpinnings are used to convince menstruators of the need to track, manage, and even "fix" their menstrual cycles via the consumption of personalized apps, aligning with what authors Sarah Fox and Franchesca Spektor pinpoint as manifestations of neoliberal feminism embedded in ideologies of self-care, optimization, and work-place productivity (2021: 5).

We focus our analysis on a popular period tracking app, MyFlo, which claims to help users "balance their hormones" by synchronizing the phases of the menstrual cycle with recommended foods, fitness regimens, social activities, sex lives, and work. As co-authors who are a behavioral endocrinologist and a food and waste specialist, the marketing strategies and dietary centrality of this particular app speak well to our scholarship strengths. Behavioral endocrinology is the study of the interactions between hormones, the brain, and behavior, often conveyed in popular discourse as simple deterministic relation-ships but in reality representing complex, intersecting social, environ-mental, and biological relationships. Ultimately, by framing an interdisciplinary analysis of science and scientific ideals as they present within popular culture (and vice versa), we argue that period tracking apps like MyFlo draw upon legacies of hormonal determinism to reinforce and uphold neoliberal ideals and social expectations about self-actualization, optimal health, and individual responsibility as tools for constructing efficient, economically productive citizens. In add-ition, and equally important, period tracking apps reify the medicaliza-tion of menstruation as a site of necessary intervention. Biomedical scholars Cecilia Roberts and Catherine Waldby have suggested such forms of monitoring "[transform] some women's fertility into a tan-gible asset, a material resource controlled and managed by the woman herself with the expectation of future value" (2021: 5). We argue that while many apps claim to put the "power" to control fertility and manage menstruation in the hands of the end user, instead they may represent a new iteration of reproductive management that is ultim-ately controlled by the forces of the market, big data, and corporate interests, rather than by ideals of user-health or education.

Ultimately, we conclude that period tracking apps, while likely beneficial for some users, fundamentally uphold societal expectations that our reproductive lives, including our fertility (or lack thereof), should be carefully tracked, managed, and understood as inseparable from our identities and social lives. To counter these deterministic ideas of gendered bodies as fixed, and to challenge the notion that our main purpose in life is to "optimize" our bodies and minds (and sometimes expressly for purposes of becoming efficient workers), we explore the "radical menstruation" movement, activism that "challenge[s] not only the menstrual status quo, skewering in particular the commercial industry they blame for disease and pollution, but also the dichotomous gender structure at the root of gender-based oppression" (Bobel, 2010: 99–100). We analyze the work of Klau Kinky and the GynePunks, feminist biohackers aiming to empower people with vaginas and uteri by creating resources for do-it-yourself reproductive health management, such as at-home STI tests for those who cannot afford medical visits or who face stigmatization (Bierend, 2015). By flipping the script on traditional bio- and life-hacking narratives around self-optimization and reclaiming biomedical knowledge in the pursuit of justice for historically and contemporarily marginalized menstruators, the GynePunks challenge us to think beyond the shiny veneer of capitalistic self-help apps to consider other ways of flourishing, caring for others, and living meaningful lives.

12.2 The Biological Basis of Menstruation and the Regularity of Irregularity

Period tracking apps commodify the complex biological and social experiences of people who menstruate, making what to some is a confusing and unpredictable process easily legible and manageable. However, this simplification runs the risk of obscuring the complexities and inherent variability of menstruation and fertility. In this section, we introduce the science of the menstrual, ovarian, and uterine cycles, demonstrating how hormones interact with these cycles and outlining the technical parameters used in cycle-predicting apps. We then complicate the use of cycle-predicting algorithms and "personalized" prescriptions for optimal cycle health by turning to the science of cycle *irregularity,* which points to complex socioenvironmental factors as enmeshed with endogenous biology in regulating cycles.

For those who menstruate, the routine shedding of the endometrial lining of the uterus is the result of an intricate coordination between the brain, ovaries, and uterus, regulated by the interplay of internal hormones and external socioenvironmental factors such as stress, diet, and environmental pollutants. While many users turn to period tracking apps in order to predict menstrual onset dates, menstruation is but one part of the ovarian/uterine cycle, which is typically broken into four phases: the follicular, ovulatory, luteal, and menstrual phases (Owen, 1975). As the site of menstrual sloughing, the endometrium responds to fluctuations in estrogen and progesterone, hormones produced by the ovaries in response to hormonal signals generated by the hypothalamus and pituitary gland.

During a typical follicular phase, when a developing ovarian follicle releases estrogen, the endometrium grows, developing a rich blood supply. A surge of luteinizing hormone as the follicle matures prompts ovulation, the release of an egg into the uterine tubes. During the subsequent luteal phase, estrogen and progesterone maintain the uterine lining, creating a space for an embryo (if fertilization occurs) to implant and initiate further development. Finally, if fertilization and implantation do not occur, ovarian hormone levels decline, prompting the sloughing of the lining and its rich blood supply. Sensitive to circulating levels of estrogen and progesterone, the brain detects this drop in ovarian hormones and responds by sending hormonal signals to stimulate the development of a new follicle, returning to the start of the follicular phase.

In the simplest terms, then, menstruation is a sign that an embryo has not embedded in the uterine lining, a prerequisite for pregnancy. However, anovulatory cycles may also occur (menstruation in the absence of ovulation), as well as planned routine endometrial shedding in the absence of ovulation, which occurs with some forms of hormonal contraception. Finally, and crucially, estrogen and progesterone, as well as testosterone (often problematically conceived of as the "male hormone") are produced by all bodies, regardless of sex, and regulate numerous physiological and behavioral functions outside of reproduction. For this reason, Anne Fausto-Sterling encourages us to resist the urge to reduce estrogen, progesterone, and testosterone to core signifiers of sex and gender, and instead to conceive of all as simply "growth hormones" (Fausto-Sterling, 2000: 28).

The cyclical process whereby the brain, ovaries, and uterus participate in ongoing cycles of egg development and uterine growth/sloughing occurs on a roughly 28-day cycle. A variety of techniques have emerged to predict fertile periods corresponding to ovulation (assumed to occur at the midpoint of the cycle) for the purposes of contraception, pregnancy enhancement, self-awareness, and communication with healthcare providers, most relying on a false assumption of cycle regularity (Epstein et al., 2017; Levy and Romo-Avilés, 2019). The oldest method, still used in contemporary period tracking apps, makes predictions about future cycle onset dates, fertile periods, and cycle duration based on past cycle information. MyFlo takes this a step further by predicting which of the four phases a user is currently in, using "the start and end dates, and average length of your period" to indicate when they are in the follicular, ovulatory, luteal, or menstrual phases (*Tracking Ovulation + Fertility*, n.d.). However, while menstrual (and uterine/ovarian) cycles are routinely described as strictly cyclical and "regular" (i.e., occurring on a 28-day cycle), in reality, they are immensely variable within and between individuals. Indeed, early investigations into the consistency of cycle lengths demonstrated that 70 percent of menstruating participants experienced irregular cycles, defined as cycle differences greater than eight days (Brayer et al., 1969). As noted by physician Eve C. Feinberg, the formulas used to predict future cycle timing, such as those employed in period tracking apps, still rely heavily on assumptions of cycle regularity, despite evidence to the contrary (Feinberg, 2019). Other measures, such as body temperature and cervical mucus assessments, can add additional information about the timing of ovulation, but are incomplete without assessment of hormones, which period tracking apps cannot currently measure (Feinberg, 2019).

The reasons for cycle variability among people with ovaries and uteri remain relatively obscure. While some regard variability as a normal process, others have correlated cycle irregularity with elevated risks of early death and disease, particularly heart disease (Solomon et al., 2002; Wang et al., 2020). Despite a seeming lack of clarity on the difference between "normal" cycle variability and pathological irregularity, a multitude of studies have documented variability induced by environmental factors. For example, a recent meta-analysis of published studies documented a higher incidence of "menstrual irregularity," cycles that were markedly shorter or longer than 28 days, among workers who rotated between day shifts, night shifts, and evening shifts, perhaps as a result of disturbance to the endogenous daily "clock" as well as alterations in cortisol, a hormone implicated in bodily homeostasis and stress responses (Chang and Chang, 2020). Stress, and its physiological sequelae, are well-known modulators of reproductive function, known in animal models to interact with the hormones of reproduction. Indeed, stress is increasingly implicated in infertility (Lynch et al., 2014; Santa-Cruz & Agudo, 2020). Other factors that appear to influence cycle regularity and the occurrence of anovulatory cycles include smoking (Kato et al., 1999; Rowland et al., 2002), exercise (Russell et al., 1984; Sternfeld et al., 2002), diet (Mumford et al., 2016), age (Chiazze, 1968; Kato et al., 1999), and exposure to endocrine disrupting chemicals (Ouyang, 2005; Gallo et al., 2016; Varnell et al., 2021). As we will demonstrate below, these external factors, which disproportionately affect people of low socioeconomic status and marginalized groups, can both complicate and reduce the accuracy of period tracking algorithms, but are also largely neglected in apps such as MyFlo that instead urge users to "take control" of their bodies with diet changes, exercise, and vitamin supplements.

12.3 A Brief History of the Science and Politics of Menstruation and Fertility Management

Much of what is known about the biological basis of menstruation and fertility can be traced to the rise of endocrinology in the twentieth century, a field that was both life-saving in many ways *and* immediately deployed toward reinforcing existing social norms and commodifying bodily processes. As described by Nelly Oudshoorn in *Beyond the Natural Body: An Archeology of Sex Hormones* (1994), this history not only illuminates the technoscientific developments that enabled the identification of hormones (for example, advancements in organic chemistry that led to the isolation and identification of steroid hormones such as estrogen and testosterone), but also how existing notions of male–female difference influenced scientific inquiry and public responses to the "new" hormonal science.

Hormonal "types" and genderings have existed since the birth of endocrinology in the early 1900s. First coined as "hormones" by physiologist Ernest Starling in 1905, the discovery of blood-borne chemical messengers opened up an entirely new way of thinking about bodily physiology that had for so long focused on the role of the nervous system (Starling, 1905; Oudshoorn, 1994: 16). Preexisting notions of the gonads as the site of masculinity or femininity enabled such practices as ovarian removal "for the treatment of menstrual irregularities and neuroses" (Oudshoorn, 1994: 8). These practices were now supplemented with advertisements for various potions and extracts that provided "male" and "female" hormones (e.g., Brown-Sequard's testicular extracts to promote male vitality [Borell, 1976]).

The notion of "hormonal balance," widely referenced in popular discourse and a key feature of the MyFlo app, can also be traced to this heyday of endocrinology in the early to mid-twentieth century. For example, physician and researcher Louis Berman directly linked behavior, both normal and abnormal, to the secretions of endocrine glands, in contributions such as *The Glands Regulating Personality* (Berman, 1921) and his own research into the endocrine basis of criminality among prisoners (Berman, 1931; Epstein, 2017). In keeping with contemporary eugenic thought and practice of the time, Berman proclaimed that people could be classified according to innate hormonal "types," stating that:

the life of every individual, normal or abnormal, his physical appearance, and his psychic traits, are dominated largely by his internal secretions. All normal as well as abnormal individuals are classifiable according to the internal secretions which rule their make-up. Individuals, families, nations and races show definite internal secretion traits, which stamp them with the quality of difference. The internal secretion formula of an individual may, in the future, constitute his measurement which will place him accurately in the social system. (Berman, 1921: 23)

This quote underscores the depth of belief, at least among some people, about the fundamental hormone-derived differences between humans, as well the inextricable links between biology and status.

With respect to gonadal hormones, Berman ascribed to the idea that femininity and masculinity were linked to hormonal balance, such that:

manliness and womanliness were now a question of hormone quantity. This quantity began to be measured to determine the correct balance. Since endocrinologists considered the balance between hormones easy to disturb, the sexual situation became uncertain. Thus, according to Berman, to ensure the survival of sexual attraction and to prevent sterility, it was necessary to exercise constant control and modification. Hormone therapy would thus be able to produce ideally male and ideally female individuals, as well as cure the infantile, the sterile, sexual deviants and generally perverse individuals, such as homosexuals. (Nordlund, 2007: 99)

Departing from other eugenicists of the time, Berman wanted to use hormones to elevate people of all races and social statuses: "every individual and thereby humanity as a whole would be refined for the good of all" (Nordlund, 2007: 101). As far back as the early 1900s, therefore, narratives about appropriate hormone balance and innate biological/hormonal differences between sexes and races were common, alongside an emerging desire to "regulate" hormones and thereby improve health. Such themes continue today through the mass marketing of hormones and technoscientific applications that rely on this knowledge, as we demonstrate below.

The logics of "hormonal balance" and hormonal determinism persisted beyond the early 1900s until today, taking the shape of research endeavors and medical interventions aimed at identifying and "correcting" perceived hormonal imbalances. While the scope of this chapter does not permit a full detailing of the many attempts to regulate hormones in the name of fertility management, as well as the roles of activists and health practitioners in shaping the current landscape of hormonal interventions, a few examples will help illuminate the ongoing legacies of this powerful belief (which often coincided with major opportunities for commercial profit at the expense of individual consumers' health and safety).

Though cultures around the world have long utilized a range of botanical birth control methods and abortofacients, development and introduction of the hormonal birth control pill highlights the conflicts between market forces, gender and racial essentialism, pursuit of bodily autonomy, and institutional control of reproduction and hormonal bodies, often targeted toward women of color. Originally funded and developed by Katherine McCormick, Margaret Sanger, and Gregory Pincus in the 1950s, and since modified to be less potent and reduce dangerous side effects, "the pill" consists of diverse versions of estrogen and/or progesterone taken on a daily basis. While debates about equitable access to and safety of hormonal contraception continue today, the history of the pill illuminates the eugenic aims to which this technical "fix" for managing fertility was employed. For example, early versions were tested on poor Puerto Rican women without clear conveyance of the fact that the drug was still experimental, and thus, carried potential health risks (Marks, 2001). In addition, the pill was heavily racialized in its marketing, where:

Magazines and newspapers of the day, salaciously covering the so-called sexual revolution, wrote about the birth control pill as a protective vehicle for the sex lives of (white) college girls. The media covered the so-called (black) welfare queen in exactly the same years, and just as salaciously. This female was directed to use the new pill as a social *duty,* to suppress her fertility. (Ross and Solinger, 2017: 46)

These strategies, combined with a long history of coercive repro-ductive racial projects ranging from medical experimentation on slave women to forced sterilizations of black women and other people of color (Roberts, 1997; Washington, 2008: Owens 2018; Theobald, 2019; Luna, 2020), highlight the systematic forces guiding access to and use of the pill, contradicting traditional narratives of bodily auton-omy and free choice. In the context of period tracking apps, which are used by some to track and manage fertility, these longer histories of institutional and commercial investment in regulating hormones, fer-tility, and menstruating bodies thus raise important questions about whether they might function contemporarily as a new opportunity for management couched in the language of personal empowerment.

12.4 The Rise of FemTech

The sloughed uterine linings (and hormonal shifts) that generate the process and experience of menstruation have long been socially com-plex, even stigmatized at various points in history (Vostral, 2008, 2010; Bobel, 2019; Hasson, 2020). Technologies such as menstrual pads and tampons (so-called FemCare [Bobel, 2010]) have served in the "erasure" and "management" of menstruation in order to hide evidence of a natural process often deemed shameful, as well as to enable the continuation of everyday activities without disruption (Vostral, 2008, 2010). The mass marketing of FemCare by corporate giants such as Proctor and Gamble and Kimberly-Clark also upheld gendered notions of menstruation through stereotypically "feminine" design, often while generating environmentally destructive and unnecessary product waste (Bobel, 2010; Fox and Epstein, 2020; Vaughn, 2020). Despite these critiques, the global market for FemCare is huge, with an estimated $21.6 billion (US dollars) market value in 2020 alone (*Feminine Hygiene Products Market Share, Trends & Forecast, 2026,* n.d.).

Amid the strength of the FemCare market, biotechnologies such as period tracking apps have likewise come to generate entirely new, extremely lucrative markets for period management. Dubbed *femtech* in 2016 by menstrual app Clue designer and CEO Ida Tin as the urban legend goes (Folkent, 2019), such technologies – ranging from period underwear to the period tracking apps we analyze in this essay – reflect a turn in market perspective, design initiative, and intended audience. Rather than managing menstrual discard, such tools often deal in the personalized data useful in managing the hormonal, reproductive, food, health, and comfort experiences of their menstruating users. Thus, information itself has become a new site for capital interest and investment. As science and technology scholars show, investment specifically in data reveals much about social beliefs in technology as global savior. Fox and Epstein argue, for instance, "Practitioners and 'tech evangelists' alike preach the almost limitless potential of data to tell us things about the world – with enough of it, we can cast away uncertainty and focus the fuzziness associated with forms of risk. [D]ata is seen as the answer to some of the world's most elusive concerns" (Fox and Epstein, 2020: 735). Likewise, sociologists and STS scholars Laura Mamo and Jennifer Ruth Foskett's analysis of birth control pills marketed for purposes of "regulating and minimizing menstruation" framed the concept of what they dubbed "lifestyle drugs, relatively new pharmaceutical therapies [promising] a refashioning of the material body with transformative, life-enhancing results" intended to streamline bodies for convenience and so-called life enhancement for nonmedical reasons (Mamo and Fosket, 2009: 925). Similarly, the app-based forms of technoscientific body management we analyze may offer the comfort and security of increased bodily knowledge or timing control, removing what, for some, proves an inconvenient "hassle" of guesswork and hormonal fluctuation in preparing for menstrual onset. In addition, period tracking apps provide for some users a sense of privacy amid social taboos about menstruation and menstrual knowledge (e.g. Epstein et al., 2017; Karlsson, 2019; Lutz and Sivakumar, 2020), despite ongoing concerns about app-based data collection and privacy (Fox and Spektor, 2021). But we prefer to ask: What are the stakes of such technoscientific maneuvers to access and make efficient the interior landscapes of the human body? Who, exactly, is doing the managing and to what ends?

12.5 Managing Periods as Empowerment?

In 2018, *Forbes Magazine* published an article titled "How Women Can Use Monthly Periods as a Productivity Tool," expounding on the virtues of taking control in the workplace through self-optimization to "finally shatter that elusive glass ceiling" (Mysoor, 2018). Using the language of movements for political enfranchisement (but with none of the collective obligations or rights-based goals), femtech companies are redefining women's health tools and products, as well as capital-intensive DIY biotech. To some, femtech is considered a social movement (Reenita Das qtd. in Health.com, n.p.), one that is perhaps finally putting tech in the hands of a broader range of users, even saving lives through data availability that might push back on the continued realities of exclusionary medical science. For instance, Clue suggests that their menstrual app has anonymized user data, which in turn aids in scientific discovery concerning user health and wellness experiences, especially for women where data is lacking (Tin, n.d.)

To others, such products reflect new capitalizations on erased or entirely ignored markets and users to construct "new" value from biological experiences or "reproductive emissions" (Kroløkke, 2018: 22). More critically, our analysis centers on conundrums of the persistence of the productivity narrative, including questions concerning the politics of data collection (who owns it, who uses it and how/when/to what ends); the stakes of intensified language of body optimization; increased focus on menstrual management; and the technoscientific reification of what we refer to throughout this article as *hormonal determinism*, i.e., capitalizing on the perception of hormones as predetermined, fixed, or defining of bodily experiences, rather than contextual and ever-respondent to environmental factors across the lifespan.

12.6 Analysis of MyFlo App

We begin our analysis with the popular app MyFlo Period Tracker, developed by functional nutritionist Alisa Vitti (*MyFlo App – Functional Medicine Period Tracker and Hormone Balancing App*, n.d.). While most period tracking apps, including MyFlo, offer standard data logging capabilities to track month-to-month menstrual cycles and associated bodily experiences, MyFlo also provides personalized suggestions to "sync" the phases of the menstrual cycle with appropriate foods, exercise regimens, romantic endeavors, work, and more. Recent scholarship has documented the ways in which period trackers reproduce stereotypes about femininity, exclude transgender and nonbinary menstruating individuals, reinforce gendered workforce narratives, and reinforce gender norms through design elements such as flowery imagery, exclusion of the ability to log cycle-relevant events such as abortion or taking hormonal replacement therapy, and more (Fox and Epstein 2020; Fox and Spektor 2021). In addition to our interest in these features, we selected MyFlo because it has ranked well as both a dietary and hormonal tracking technology in relation to the stock data about menstrual patterns. This particular app attempts to regulate both the hormonal dynamics of the human menstrual cycle experience, but also other interwoven components like diet and optimal wellness as well as symptom and/or pain management. The application marketing tactics claim statements such as: "reclaim your month [and] run your world"; "revolutionize your time management" through "hormonal clock" control, drawing upon body positive narratives of reclaiming the period from the culturally reviled to "your superpower" all through careful tracking and management.

MyFlo marketing recycles common gendered themes about hormonal determinism, but spins them as simply a matter of proper management to aid one's "natural cycles" and "working with" one's body for maximum productivity. Time and productivity are yoked together in hormonally deterministic ways by juxtaposing the presupposed binary ways in which "men's hormones operate on a 24-hour circuit, [whereas] yours operate on a 28-day cycle," despite the fact that recent reports document 24-hour rhythms in "female" hormones as well (Rahman et al., 2019). The broader MyFlo brand was invented by a lifestyle specialist (not a medical practitioner), who has become wildly popular with users looking to "cycle-sync," or in other words, to optimize their body and health by pairing dietary and lifestyle trends with personalized menstrual management of the four cycle phases, all in the name of tapping into one's "feminine energy" (Schiffer, 2019). Much of the optimization narrative generated by the app and its makers and advocates shows a clear definition of health as it is connected to skin (managing acne, for instance), size (weight management, cravings), and diminishing menstrual discomforts (painful periods, bloating, water retention). Yet, as food scholar Julie Guthman outlines concerning "healthism," ideas and idealizations about health are profoundly revealing of cultural norms and values about size, shape, and neoliberal norms of self-control, tending to emphasize or exaggerate certain bodily experiences while ignoring others (Guthman, 2011: 47).

App users are prompted to learn about the various phases of their menstrual experience by entering basic data from memory, and will receive regular information about "windows" of the menstrual cycle, for example, "Phase Three: 3–5 days." Users are then provided with dietary recommendations and sex advice complete with links to schedule "fun social nights out," and exercise suggestions: "You have energy to burn" [in this phase]. Choose high impact workouts." These messages read almost like daily horoscopes, encouraging users to blend pop culture understandings of hormonal changes with subjective emotional well-being: "connect with your community and enjoy being magnetic!" Dietary advice underscores the link between various hormonal surge or decline phases and the "correct" kinds of foods to consume, generating a lingo that reflects the dietary optimization "now" (though not necessarily accurate), such as consuming "ovulatory foods [for the] well-being of your ovaries"; or foods that help to "remineralize your body with iron and zinc," or that help to "stave off sugar cravings" and "flush out estrogen [from the] liver and large intestine." The standard MyFlo app user who pays $2.99 will receive broad dietary suggestions about "bright foods" for energy and "adding nutrients" lost during menstruation. For $297, users can subscribe to a three-month program to "get out of hormonal chaos and back into hormonal FLO. Learn how to use specific foods at specific times of your cycles to put an end to the symptoms that slow you down and start feeling good all month long." In addition to dietary advice, this subscription provides users with advice on "how to cycle sync your lifestyle – including exercise, work, and relationships" (MyFlo app).

Yet, there is a fine line here embedded in dietary, sexual, and acne advice. One approach represents wellness as multifaceted, a complex environmental dynamic affecting the body emplaced in specific contexts. But, in a context in which the broader cultural script concerning menstruation is increasingly something to manage for working menstruators, and ideas about optimal nutrition abound to perpetuate what feminist scholar Cecilia Hartley labeled a cultural "tyranny of slenderness" (Hartley, 2001), what role does this form of app-delivered hormonal determinism play in perpetuating confusing, nutritionally limiting messages about menstruation, food, and health? For instance, the idea that healthy, hormonally balanced periods are "symptom free" applies a troubling yardstick to a widely varying biological experience profoundly influenced by diverse environmental factors from stress, to chemical exposures, to synthetic food additives and preservatives. In fact, the company goes so far as to remind app users in an email, "When you're living in sync with your cycle, you won't dread your period every month because you won't experience acne, bloating, fatigue, irritability, PMS heavy or irregular periods, or severe cramps." We will return to the idea of syncing momentarily, but here first we must trouble the very conceptualization of optimal periods and nutrition as something universally definable, achievable, and feasibly broken down into digestible advice delivered via an app outside of any specific localized context.

Medical historian Lisa Haushofer has written about the turn toward "optimal nutrition" and "one-size-fits-all commercial nutritional products" as a concept rooted in biologically deterministic notions about fixed social categories: "The rise of modern nutrition science in the late eighteenth and nineteenth centuries was accompanied by a less individualistic thinking about the relationship between food and the body. [F]ood acted on the body through particular chemical constituents, which were believed to act the same in every body, regardless of age, sex, or race" (Haushofer, 2017). The very idea of a universal definition of "optimal" health and wellness should be questioned as not only subjectively interpreted, but as a questionable avenue for cultural hegemony via food. This concept appears through the MyFlo app not solely in terms of generalized nutritional advice, or so-called empowering reminders that "normal or healthy" periods should be regular, painless, and streamlined. It is likewise perpetuated in founder Alisa Vitti's own narratives about "becoming a hormone expert" concerning the ways in which hormones affect "our brains" (MyFlo app, "About," n.p.). Though this is framed within the language of menstruator's empowerment, gendered solidarity and "natural" remedies for period health, the push toward sync-centric language reiterates problematic ideals of biological determinism in which menstruators can take control of their body, harnessing their natural rhythms for increased work–life productivity. For instance, the app website especially highlights abstract things like "hormone flushing," "hormone healing," "alignment," "synchronicity," a sense of "community," "sustainability" of energy, and the need to honor one's menstrual experiences to better create life balance, all neatly delivered by way of biotechnological streamlining and cycle syncing, and all wellness factors that are supposedly and simply "chosen" by menstruators for bodily balance purposes (Supplement Guide n.p.; Flo 28: The CycleSyncing Membership, n.p.). On the one hand, users are framed as having unique, individual bodily needs, and on the other, these bodily codes are framed as universal to menstruators and able to be cracked, as one user attests in the membership video, through MyFlo optimization techniques. Whereas the experiences of so-called hormonal disalignment are affirmed through personalized testimonies on the app website and in app reviews, there is also a complicated reinforcement of common cultural scripts about menstruation as gross, problematic, or as a burden to be streamlined through diet, MyFlo supplements regimes named for the balance and restorative capacities they claim to deliver (Soothe, Boost, Sustain, Harmonize, Replenish), and cycle syncing.

12.7 An Obsession With Synchrony

The framing of well-being as a product of synchrony between endogenous hormones, diet, exercise, and work/home life carries strong echoes of menstrual synchrony. This idea, that women living and/or working in close contact synchronize their menstrual cycles, can be traced to the work of Martha McClintock, who in 1971 published a an article in *Nature* describing the "syncing up" of menstrual cycles among female dorm residents at Wellesley College (McClintock, 1971). This single paper spurred a decades-long flurry of attempts to replicate the phenomenon among female college student roommates, mothers and daughters, athletes, lesbian couples, Bedouin women living in multiple-female households, and "working women" (Weller and

Weller, 1992, 1993, 1995a, 1995b, 1997a; Weller et al., 1999). As metrics to establish the "closeness" of female relationships, authors such as Weller and Weller (1995b) collected data on how often participants went "shopping together" and "shared clothes," among other measures, assessments that were deeply gendered and reflected expectations about the nature of female–female social interactions. Throughout, researchers relied upon and were stymied by the requirement for participants to exhibit "regular" cycles in order to establish synchrony, attempting, for instance, to develop statistical methods for coping with said irregularity (Weller and Weller, 1997b).

After approximately three decades of menstrual synchrony research, much of which was contradictory and heavily debated in the scientific community, a general consensus was reached that menstrual synchrony does *not* exist. However, popular narratives about synchrony persist. Anecdotally, students in our research group several years ago were very familiar with the idea of menstrual synchrony, despite the fact that it had been long since "debunked." Other scholarship explores some of the reasons that menstrual synchrony retains power and meaning for people who menstruate (e.g., Fahs et al., 2014; Fahs, 2016). For our purposes here, we suggest that some of the power of menstrual synchrony lies in the ability of companies and popular figures to mobilize this "ideal" toward new ends, such as MyFlo's cycle-syncing function. By relying on long-held beliefs about the power of this mythical phenomenon to alter physiology while creating "gendered solidarity" (Fahs et al., 2014), prescriptions to sync cycles to our dietary environments, work choices, and even to our partners (e.g., MyFlo's option to "partner sync," where your partner receives information about cycle status) reinforce the idea that we are *out* of balance and in need of optimization.

12.8 Conclusion: Framing Alternative Methods of Empowerment

What might a different way of engaging with menstrual tools and biotechnologies even look like then, and/or how might we "articulate self-care otherwise" (Fox and Spektor, 2021)? In their analysis of design and aesthetics of menstrual tracking apps, Fox and Epstein argue for other ways of using this technology beyond biologically fixed imaginaries: "Rather than modeling an application on a particular understanding of the menstrual experience or set of attributes, we argue future technology should opt for design defaults which avoid such assumptions by, for instance, offering adaptability in the data presented" (2020: 246). While we certainly agree that design dynamics may perpetuate restrictive ideas about the body and/or build those ideas into the very design, aesthetics, and data outcomes of app technologies, our own analysis takes issue with the ways in which menstrual apps reflect neoliberal ideals of optimal health and intensified bodily adaptation to landscapes of capital worth. Yet ours is certainly not a false idealization of the so-called pure, the natural, or the antitechnological, taking to heart Donna Haraway's iconic reminder of our constant entanglement with technological and nonhuman worlds (Haraway, 1985, 2015) or Alexis Shotwell's reminder (vis-á-vis Anna Tsing) that living is never "pure" as we are all part of blasted regimes and disturbance landscapes (Shotwell, 2016: 9). We do, however, wonder after other imaginaries of DIY and menstrual biohack potential that attempt to sidestep the efficiency model narrative so embedded in MyFlo's technological veneer.

One alternative example is the work of Klau Klinky and the Spanish collective Gynepunks, which draws upon the long history of feminist DIY initiatives (such as the Women's Health Movement in the United States) for information sharing and medical health empowerment through the blending of anarchist, punk, and feminist knowledge-building with collectively shared biohacker spaces to explore, learn, share information, and tinker together. The Gynepunks are known for hacking common gynecological tools to give users the means to control their own health, with a focus on detecting cervical cancer, yeast infections, and sexually transmitted infections without the need to engage with the medical establishment. For example, the Gynepunks have pioneered instruction manuals for creating DIY microscopes and centrifuges, as well as 3D-printed speculums, with the aim of providing freely accessible health resources and product assembly instructions to all (Bierend, 2015). As a counterpoint to MyFlo, the work of the GynePunks stands out as an example of the pursuit of bodily autonomy and knowledge for those who have been historically harmed or erased by the medical establishment, including people of color, transgender, and nonbinary folks. Here we do not see any references to enhanced productivity or gendered hormonal balance, but instead the aim to make "safe spaces to practice and share the skills and knowledge of basic gynaecological healthcare, both online and in physical spaces" (Samms, 2019). Whereas "the subsumption of reproductive labor" has always historically been embedded in attempts to manage menstruation for capitalist accumulatory ends – from early gynecological experimentation on slave women, to pills, to apps that streamline menstruation – Gynepunk's goals, in contrast, are decidedly collectively oriented and anticapitalist in scope (Thorburn, 2017: 164). On this concept of more collective framings, Fox and Spektor suggest that whereas neoliberal feminist subjectivities tend to "lean in" to corporate management goals appealing to middle-class ideals of self-improvement and upward mobility through self-oriented optimization (2021: 5), more inclusive framings might flip the individualized tracking script to advocate for "collective data gathering meant to advocate for fairer working conditions across role or status"; or as a tool for workers to "[hold] companies accountable [for] improved compensation and liveable conditions" (2021: 15). Thus, tech that serves as a tool for repairing harmful medical histories used against marginalized populations; tech used for shared or collective knowledge building, accountability, or more just workplaces may prove distinct from tech that is motivated by data collection, middle-class ideals of self-optimization or capitalist biovalue goals. That said, in the post-overturning of Roe v. Wade America within which we as authors live and work, our hesitations about the data use component of these technologies remains strong. Such personalized menstrual and fertility information may now prove legally incriminating to app users living in states or nations with sanctions against those seeking abortions as basic healthcare. Thus, an exemplary political motivation for such data could include anti-abortion surveillance. Given such misogyny, we caution users to inform themselves of their legal contexts, of the data storage policies of the apps they use, and to carefully consider how, if and in what capacity they wish their menstrual or fertility data to be accessed and utilized beyond self-tracking (Elliott 2022; Torchinsky 2022). Mamo and Fosket have argued for reframing biomedicalization power dynamics, expressly asking "how and under what circumstances women are able to appropriate technologies to reshape their bodies, minds and practices as they see fit" (2009: 941). We might similarly apply this lens to other possibilities of menstrual app technologies that move away from attempts to interiorly fix or manage menstruating bodies, or to transform (ultimately unsick) bodies otherwise deemed hormonally "disturbed," "unbalanced", or just plain fat-shamed.

Acknowledgments

Many thanks to the members of the 2019 Society and Genetics Undergraduate Menstrual Synchrony Research Group: Kristienne Edrosolan, Isabelle Ick, Gabrielle Montalbano, and Jenny Tuell. Your careful research, enthusiastic collaboration, and curiosity laid the groundwork for this project.

References

Berman, L. 1921. *The Glands Regulating Personality: A Study of the Glands of Internal Secretion in Relation to the Types of Human Nature.* New Yotk: MacMillan and Co.

    1931. "Crime and the Endocrine Glands." *Journal of mental science* 79 (324): 217–217.

Bickov, A. 2016. "12 Free Apps to Improve Your Life." *Lifehack*, July 30, 2016. www.lifehack.org/433696/12-free-apps-to-improve-the-three-most-important-aspects-of-your-life

Bierend, D. 2015. "Meet the GynePunks Pushing the Boundaries of DIY Gynecology." *Vice*, August 21, 2015. www.vice.com/en/article/qkvyjw/meet-the-gynepunks-pushing-the-boundaries-of-diy-gynecology

Bobel, C. 2010. *New Blood: Third-wave Feminism and the Politics of Menstruation.* New Brunswick: Rutgers University Press. https://doi.org/10.36019/9780813549538

    2019. *The Managed Body: Developing Girls and Menstrual Health in the Global South.* London: Palgrave Macmillan. https://doi.org/10.1007/978-3-319-89414-0

Borell, M. 1976. "Organotherapy, British Physiology, and Discovery of the Internal Secretions." *Journal of the History of Biology* 9(2): 235–268.

Boyer, K., & Boswell-Penc, Maia. 2010. "Breast Pumps: A Feminist Technology, or (yet) "More Work for Mother"?" In *Feminist Technology,* edited by Linda L. Layne, Sharra L. Vostral, and Kate Boyer, 119–136. Champaign: University of Illinois Press.

Brayer, F. T., Chiazze, L., & Duffy, B. J. 1969. "Calendar Rhythm and Menstrual Cycle Range." *Fertility and Sterility* 20(2): 279–288. https://doi.org/10.1016/S0015–0282(16)36970-9

Carroll, J. K., Moorhead, A., Bond, R., LeBlanc, W. G., Petrella, R. J., & Fiscella, K. 2017. "Who Uses Mobile Phone Health Apps and Does Use Matter? A Secondary Data Analytics Approach." *Journal of Medical Internet Research* 19(4): 1–28. https://doi.org/10.2196/jmir.5604

Chang, W.-P., & Chang, Y.-P. 2020. "Meta-Analysis Comparing Menstrual Regularity and Dysmenorrhea of Women Working Rotating Shifts and

Fixed Day Shifts." *Journal of Women's Health* 30 (5): 722–730. https:// doi.org/10.1089/jwh.2020.8517

Chiazze, L. 1968. "The Length and Variability of the Human Menstrual Cycle." *JAMA* 203(6): 377–380. https://doi.org/10.1001/jama.1968 .03140060001001

Cowen, A. 2019. "14 Million People Have Taken This Personality Test That Shows If You're in the Best Relationship." *Women's Health*, July 2, 2019. www.womenshealthmag.com/uk/health/sexual-health/a28257629/per sonality-test/

Daza, D. O. 2011. "Ego sum Daniel: Oxytocin, ethnocentrism and "hormonal determinism." *Ego Sum Daniel,* January 24, 2011. http://egosumdaniel .blogspot.com/2011/01/oxytocin-ethnocentrism-and-hormonal.html

Elliott, Vittoria. "Fertility and Period Apps Can Be Weaponized in a Post-Roe World." *Wired.* June 7, 2022. Web.

Epstein, D. A., Lee, N. B., Kang, J. H., Agapie, E., Schroeder, J., Pina, L. R., Fogarty, J., Kientz, J. A., & Munson, S. A. 2017. "Examining Menstrual Tracking to Inform the Design of Personal Informatics Tools." *Proceedings of the SIGCHI Conference on Human Factors in Computing Systems. CHI Conference,* 6876–6888. https://doi.org/10 .1145/3025453.3025635

Epstein, R. 2019. *Aroused: The History of Hormones and How They Control Everything.* New York: WW Norton & Company.

Fahs, B. 2016. "Demystifying Menstrual Synchrony: Women's Subjective Beliefs about Bleeding in Tandem with Other Women." *Women's Reproductive Health* 3 (1): 1–15. https://doi.org/10.1080/23293691 .2016.1150132

Fahs, B., Gonzalez, J., Coursey, R., & Robinson-Cestaro, S. 2014. "Cycling Together: Menstrual Synchrony as a Projection of Gendered Solidarity." *Women's Reproductive Health* 1 (2): 90–105. https://doi .org/10.1080/23293691.2014.966029

Fausto-Sterling, A. 2000. *Sexing the Body: Gender Politics and the Construction of Sexuality.* New York: Basic Books.

Feinberg, E. C. 2019. Menstrual Cyclicity Is Predictably Unpredictable. *Fertility and Sterility 111* (3): 476. https://doi.org/10.1016/j.fertnstert .2018.11.040

Folkent, K. 2019. *"So what is FemTech, anyways?"* *FemTech Insider,* September 5, 2019. http://femtechinsider.com/what-is-femtech/

Fox, S. & Epstein, D. 2020. "Measuring Menses: Design Based Investigations of Menstrual Tracking Applications." In *The Palgrave Handbook of Critical Menstruation Studies.* edited by Chris Bobel, Inga T. Winkler, Breanne Fahs, Katie Ann Hasson, Elizabeth Arveda Kissling, Tomi-Ann Roberts, 733–750. Singapore: Palgrave Macmillan.

Fox, S. and Spektor, F. 2021. "Hormonal Advantage: Retracing Exploitative Histories of Workplace Menstrual Tracking." *Catalyst: Feminism, Theory, Technoscience 7* (1): 1–23.

Gallo, M. V., Ravenscroft, J., Carpenter, D. O., Frye, C., Akwesasne Task Force on the Environment, Cook, B., & Schell, L. M. 2016. "Endocrine disrupting chemicals and ovulation: Is there a relationship?" *Environmental Research 151*: 410–418. https://doi.org/10.1016/j.envres.2016.08.007

Guthman, J. 2011. *Weighing In: Obesity, Food Justice, and the Limits of Capitalism* (1st ed.). University of California Press. www.jstor.org/stable/10.1525/j.ctt1pp061

Haraway, D. 1985. "A Cyborg Manifesto: Science, Technology, and Socialist-Feminism in the 1980s" (Vol. 15). *Socialist Review 80*: 65–108.

Haraway, D. 2015. "Anthropocene, Capitalocene, Plantationocene, Chthulucene: Making Kin." *Environmental Humanities 6* (1): 159–165. doi: https://doi.org/10.1215/22011919-3615934

Hartley, C. 2001. "Letting Ourselves Go: Making Room for the Fat Body in Feminist Scholarship." In *Bodies Out of Bounds: Fatness and Transgression* edited by Jana Evans Braziel and Kathleen LeBesco. Berkeley: University of California Press.

Harvey, David. 2005. *A Brief History of Neoliberalism*. New York: Oxford University Press.

Hasson, K. A. 2020. "Not a "Real" Period?: Social and Material Constructions of Menstruation." In *The Palgrave Handbook of Critical Menstruation Studies* edited by C. Bobel, I. T. Winkler, B. Fahs, K. A. Hasson, E. A. Kissling, & T.-A. Roberts. London: Palgrave Macmillan. www.ncbi.nlm.nih.gov/books/NBK565603/

Haushofer, L. 2017. "Bachelorette Chow and the Contested Nature of Nutritional Knowledge." *Food, Fatness and Fitness*, November 1, 2017. https://foodfatnessfitness.com/2017/11/01/bachelorette-chow/

Imarcgroup. n.d. *Feminine Hygiene Products Market Share, Trends & Forecast, 2026*. Retrieved April 12, 2021. www.imarcgroup.com/feminine-hygiene-products-market

Karlsson, A. 2019. "A Room of One's Own?: Using period trackers to escape menstrual stigma." *Nordicom Review 40* (s1): 111–123. https://doi.org/10.2478/nor-2019-0017

Kato, I., Toniolo, P., Koenig, K. L., Shore, R. E., Zeleniuch-Jacquotte, A., Akhmedkhanov, A., & Riboli, E. 1999. "Epidemiologic correlates with menstrual cycle length in middle aged women." *European Journal of Epidemiology 15* (9): 809–814. https://doi.org/10.1023/a:1007669430686

Kroløkke, C. Global Fluids: *The Cultural Politics of Reproductive Waste and Value*. Berghahn Books: New York, 2018. pg. 22

Levy, J., & Romo-Avilés, N. 2019. "A good little tool to get to know yourself a bit better": A qualitative study on users' experiences of app-supported menstrual tracking in Europe." *BMC Public Health* 19 (1): 1213. https://doi.org/10.1186/s12889–019-7549-8

Luna, Z. 2020. *Reproductive Rights as Human Rights*. New York: New York University Press. www.degruyter.com/document/doi/10.18574/9781479894369/html

Lutz, S., & Sivakumar, G. 2020. "Leaking the secret: Women's attitudes toward menstruation and menstrual-tracker mobile apps." *Gender, Technology and Development* 24 (3): 362–377. https://doi.org/10.1080/09718524.2020.1786990

Lynch, C. D., Sundaram, R., Maisog, J. M., Sweeney, A. M., & Buck Louis, G. M. 2014. "Preconception Stress Increases the Risk of Infertility: Results from a Couple-based Prospective Cohort Study–the LIFE Study." *Human Reproduction (Oxford, England)* 29 (5): 1067–1075. https://doi.org/10.1093/humrep/deu032

Mamo, L., & Fosket, J. R. 2009. "Scripting the Body: Pharmaceuticals and the (Re)Making of Menstruation." *Signs: Journal of Women in Culture and Society* 34 (4): 925–949. https://doi.org/10.1086/597191

Marks, L. V. 2001. *Sexual Chemistry: A History of the Contraceptive Pill.* London: Yale University Press. www.jstor.org/stable/j.ctt1nqbnt

McClintock, M. K. 1971. "Menstrual Synchrony and Suppression." *Nature* 229 (5282): 244–245. https://doi.org/10.1038/229244a0

Mumford, S. L., Chavarro, J. E., Zhang, C., Perkins, N. J., Sjaarda, L. A., Pollack, A. Z., Schliep, K. C., Michels, et al., 2016. "Dietary Fat Intake and Reproductive Hormone Concentrations and Ovulation in Regularly Menstruating women12." *The American Journal of Clinical Nutrition 103* (3): 868–877. https://doi.org/10.3945/ajcn.115.119321

MyFlo. n.d. *MyFlo App – Functional Medicine Period Tracker and Hormone Balancing App*. Retrieved April 12, 2021. https://myflotracker.com/

n.d. "Tracking ovulation + fertility." Retrieved April 12, 2021. https://floliving.zendesk.com/hc/en-us/articles/360021577654-Tracking-ovulation-fertility

MyFlo app. n.d. "About Me," "Supplement Guide" and "Flo 28: The CycleSyncing Membership." FloLiving company website. n.p.

Mysoor, A. 2018. "How Women Can Use Monthly Periods As a Productivity Tool." *Forbes*, May 10, 2018. Retrieved April 12, 2021. www.forbes.com/sites/alexandramysoor/2018/05/10/how-women-can-use-monthly-periods-as-a-productivity-tool/

Nordlund, C. 2007. "Endocrinology and Expectations in 1930s America: Louis Berman's Ideas on New Creations in Human Beings." *The British Journal for the History of Science* 40 (1): 83–104.

Oudshoorn, N. 1994. *Beyond the Natural Body: An Archaeology of Sex Hormones.* London: Routledge. https://doi.org/10.4324/9780203421529

Ouyang, F. 2005. "Serum DDT, Age at Menarche, and Abnormal Menstrual Cycle Length." *Occupational and Environmental Medicine* 62 (12): 878–884. https://doi.org/10.1136/oem.2005.020248

Owen, J. A., Jr. 1975. "Physiology of the Menstrual Cycle." *The American Journal of Clinical Nutrition* 28 (4): 333–338. https://doi.org/10.1093/ajcn/28.4.333

Owens, D.C. 2018. *Medical Bondage: Race, Gender, and the Origins of American Gynecology.* Illustrated Edition. Athens, GA: University of Georgia Press.

Pallarito, K. ""Femtech" is busting taboos around women's health and wellness – but what is it exactly?" *Health,* November 12, 2020. Retrieved May 25, 2022. https://www.health.com/mind-body/femtech-womens-health

Rahman, S. A., Grant, L. K., Gooley, J. J., Rajaratnam, S. M. W., Czeisler, C. A., & Lockley, S. W. 2019. "Endogenous Circadian Regulation of Female Reproductive Hormones." *The Journal of Clinical Endocrinology & Metabolism* 104 (12): 6049–6059. https://doi.org/10.1210/jc.2019-00803

Roberts, D. E. 1997. *Killing the Black Body: Race, Reproduction, and the Meaning of Liberty.* New York: Pantheon Books.

Roberts, C. & Waldby, C. 2021. "Incipient infertility: tracking eggs and ovulation across the life course." Catalyst: feminism, theory, technoscience 7 (1). https://doi.org/10.28968/cftt.v7i1.34614

Ross, L. J., & Solinger, R. 2017. *Reproductive Justice: An Introduction* (1st ed.). Berkeley: University of California Press. www.jstor.org/stable/10.1525/j.ctv1wxsth

Rowland, A. S., Baird, D. D., Long, S., Wegienka, G., Harlow, S. D., Alavanja, M., & Sandler, D. P. 2002. "Influence of Medical Conditions and Lifestyle Factors on the Menstrual Cycle." *Epidemiology* 13 (6): 668–674.

Russell, J. B., Mitchell, D., Musey, P. I., & Collins, D. C. 1984. "The Relationship of Exercise to Anovulatory Cycles in Female Athletes: Hormonal and Physical Characteristics." *Obstetrics and Gynecology* 63 (4): 452–456.

Samms, A. 2019. "Weapons and Gynaecology: Making as Need and Desire." *V&A Blog,* December 19, 2019. www.vam.ac.uk/blog/design-and-society/weapons-and-gynaecology-making-as-need-and-desire

Santa-Cruz, D. C., & Agudo, D. 2020. "Impact of Underlying Stress in Infertility." *Current Opinion in Obstetrics and Gynecology 32* (3): 233–236. https://doi.org/10.1097/GCO.0000000000000628

Schiffer, J. 2019. "This Woman Wants to Help Regulate Your Period with Food." *The New York Times,* December 4, 2019. www.nytimes.com/2019/12/04/style/self-care/flo-living-pcos-periods.html

Shotwell, A. 2016. *Against Purity: Living Ethically in Compromised Times.* Minneapolis: University of Minnesota Press.

Solomon, C. G., Hu, F. B., Dunaif, A., Rich-Edwards, J. E., Stampfer, M. J., Willett, W. C., Speizer, F. E., & Manson, J. E. 2002. "Menstrual Cycle Irregularity and Risk for Future Cardiovascular Disease." *The Journal of Clinical Endocrinology & Metabolism 87* (5): 2013–2017. https://doi.org/10.1210/jcem.87.5.8471

Starling, E. H. 1905. "The Croonian Lectures ON THE CHEMICAL CORRELATION OF THE FUNCTIONS OF THE BODY." *The Lancet 166* (4275): 339–341. https://doi.org/10.1016/S0140-6736(01)11877-5

Sternfeld, B., Jacobs, M. K., Quesenberry, C. P., Jr., Gold, E. B., & Sowers, M. 2002. "Physical Activity and Menstrual Cycle Characteristics in Two Prospective Cohorts." *American Journal of Epidemiology 156* (5): 402–409. https://doi.org/10.1093/aje/kwf060

The Anatomy of Love. n.d. *Helen Fisher's Personality Test.* Retrieved April 12, 2021. https://theanatomyoflove.com/relationship-quizzes/helen-fishers-personality-test/

Theobald, B. 2019. *Reproduction on the Reservation: Pregnancy, Childbirth, and Colonialism in the Long Twentieth Century.* Chapel Hill: University of North Carolina Press. www.jstor.org/stable/10.5149/9781469653181_theobald

Thorburn, Elise D. 2017 "Cyborg Witches: Class Composition and Social Reproduction in the GynePunk Collective," *Feminist Media Studies* 17(2): 153–167, DOI:10.1080/14680777.2016.1218353

Tin, I. (n.d.). "Clue Archives." *WeAreTechWomen - Supporting Women in Technology.* Retrieved April 12, 2021. https://wearetechwomen.com/tag/clue/

Torchinsky, Rina. "How period tracking apps and data privacy fit into a post-Roe v. Wade climate." *National Public Radio.* June 24, 2022. Web.

Varnell, R. R., Arnold, T. J., Quandt, S. A., Talton, J. W., Chen, H., Miles, C. M., Daniel, S. S., Sandberg, J. C., Anderson, K. A., & Arcury, T. A. 2021. "Menstrual Cycle Patterns and Irregularities in Hired Latinx Child Farmworkers." *Journal of Occupational and Environmental*

Medicine 63 (1): 38–43. https://doi.org/10.1097/JOM
.0000000000002065

Vaughn, R. 2020. "Compost and Menstrual Blood" *Catalyst: Feminism, Theory, Technoscience* 6 (1): Article 1. https://doi.org/10.28968/cftt .v6i1.32379

Vostral, S. L. 2008. *Under Wraps: A History of Menstrual Hygiene Technology*. Lanham, MD: Lexington Books.

Vostral, S. 2010. "Tampons: Re-Scripting Technologies as Feminist." In *Feminist Technology* edited by Linda L. Layne, Sharra L. Vostral, and Kate Boyer. Champaign: University of Illinois Press.

Wang, Y.-X., Arvizu, M., Rich-Edwards, J. W., Stuart, J. J., Manson, J. E., Missmer, S. A., Pan, A., & Chavarro, J. E. 2020. "Menstrual Cycle Regularity and Length across the Reproductive Lifespan and Risk of Premature Mortality: Prospective Cohort Study." *BMJ 371*:3464. https://doi.org/10.1136/bmj.m3464

Washington, H. A. 2008. *Medical Apartheid: The Dark History of Medical Experimentation on Black Americans from Colonial Times to the Present*. New York: Knopf Doubleday Publishing Group.

Weller, A., & Weller, L. 1992. "Menstrual Synchrony in Female Couples." *Psychoneuroendocrinology 17* (2): 171–177. https://doi.org/10.1016/ 0306-4530(92)90055-C

1993. "Menstrual Synchrony between Mothers and Daughters and between Roommates." *Physiology & Behavior 53* (5): 943–949. https://doi.org/10.1016/0031-9384(93)90273-I

1995a. "Examination of Menstrual Synchrony among Women Basketball Players." *Psychoneuroendocrinology 20* (6): 613–622. https://doi.org/ 10.1016/0306-4530(95)00007-B

1995b. "The Impact of Social Interaction Factors on Menstrual Synchrony in the Workplace." *Psychoneuroendocrinology 20* (1): 21–31. https:// doi.org/10.1016/0306-4530(94)E0004-S

1997a. "Menstrual Synchrony under Optimal Conditions: Bedouin Families." *Journal of Comparative Psychology 111* (2): 143–151. https://doi.org/10.1037/0735-7036.111.2.143

Weller, L., & Weller, A. 1997b. "Menstrual Variability and the Measurement of Menstrual Synchrony." *Psychoneuroendocrinology* 22 (2): 115–128. https://doi.org/10.1016/S0306–4530(96)00037-6

Weller, L., Weller, A., Koresh-Kamin, H., & Ben-Shoshan, R. 1999. "Menstrual Synchrony in a Sample of Working Women." *Psychoneuroendocrinology 24* (4): 449–459. https://doi.org/10.1016/ S0306–4530(98)00092-4

13 | *How Should Childbirth Happen?*

AMANDA SHAPIRO

One feature of neoliberal market imperialism is the idea that no corner of life should be off limits from market-based competition and profit. Rather predictably, this sort of economic thinking has found its way into the provision of healthcare, even in the context of countries with socialized, nationalized healthcare such as the United Kingdom. Here, Shapiro examines what happens to care for mothers and children in the United Kingdom after the introduction of neoliberal reforms and compares it to Sweden, both ostensibly national systems, but differing in their degree of market creep. Shapiro makes use of a legal, human-rights-based frame of analysis to show that birth in Sweden is far better for human well-being than it is in the UK. In terms of the overarching theme of the book, the chapter is an example of the advantages of increased government planning against neoliberal orthodoxy. Her analysis also points to the alliance between neoliberal austerity policies and the defense of traditional conservative "family values."

13.1 Introduction

This chapter compares the laws, policies, and culture surrounding childbirth in two countries: the United Kingdom and Sweden. Based on a framework of human rights, it argues that Sweden is superior to the UK in its handling of childbirth in nearly every conceivable respect: pregnancy care, the birthing experience, postnatal care, maternity and parental leave, childcare, and gender equality. I came to think about the comparisons between these two countries' treatment of childbirth based on various coverage of two crude, but fundamental, statistics about birth: maternal and infant mortality. Why were the UK's maternal and infant mortality rates higher than they had been in recent memory, while Sweden's were steadily, and exceptionally, low? From what follows in this chapter, the adherence to austerity and neoliberal policies is the primary culprit of excess mortality among women and infants in the UK, as compared to its Nordic neighbor (Zylbersztejn et al., 2018: 2016).

At first blush, it's reasonable to feel that the UK's and Sweden's treatment of childbirth are not apt for comparison. Sweden is a much smaller country than the UK, has a more homogenous population, and comes from a distinct Nordic tradition that streamlines gender equality across Swedish law. Nonetheless, there are a few good reasons to pause and consider these two jurisdictions together. There is an outpouring of evidence in the UK that poverty for women and children is on the rise, indicating "a monumental shift" toward "a deteriorating quality of life" in Britain (Goodman, 2018). It didn't have to be this way. The UK used to have a welfare state, and while it was never of the same magnitude as that in Sweden, it was life-changing for children like Mark Blyth, a Scottish academic, who grew up with it:

I am a welfare kid . . .. Because of the British welfare state, threadbare though it is in comparison to its more affluent European cousins, I was never hungry . . .. The social mobility that societies such as the United Kingdom and the United States took for granted from the 1950s through the 1980s that made me, and others like me, possible, has effectively ground to a halt . . .. Frankly, the world can use a few more welfare kids that become professors. (Blyth, 2015: xi)

Childbirth, "the absolute centrality of human reproduction," is a fitting window into the effects of one country's choice to do away with the welfare state, and how another has sustained it (Williams, 1979: 146–147). In the 1980s, Prime Minister Margaret Thatcher made austerity – a cross-sector government policy of slashing benefits and public services in order to balance the budget and, theoretically, put more money into the hands of private companies and citizens – the hallmark of her rule. Thatcher's "trickle-down" economics held that "wealth generated by the giants would benefit the small" (Brown, 2015: 213). But in 2010 the government ruled by the Conservative Party took austerity policies a step further, praising budget cuts as a "virtue" and a "shared sacrifice" (Brown, 2015: 213; Mueller, 2019). No longer were austerity policies staked exclusively on a supposed scarcity of resources or in the name of efficiency (in the world's fifth largest economy, no less): austerity was an end unto itself. Nonprofit organizations, charities, and private companies, austerity proponents said, would fill in the gap of a leaner government bureaucracy, ultimately making government and society more efficient and – more importantly – more responsible (Mueller, 2019).

What have austerity policies and values meant for women giving birth in the UK? Maternity care and childcare operate based on market competition through a mix of private and public actors. Pregnant women and new parents are now "consumers" in this market, responsible for bargain hunting for everything from a maternity clinic to a childcare program (one they can't realistically afford in any event). Like the government services available to them, pregnant women's and mothers' legal rights are threadbare due to a lack of enforcement. Workplaces maintain "flexible" leave policies that effectively force women either back to work prematurely or into joblessness. One of the dominant implications in the neoliberal view of childbirth is that women are "natural" caregivers, who should rarely be working outside the home in the first place, and therefore should not be compensated for any subsequent childcare.

By contrast, Sweden supports women's overall childbirth experience through the twin values of social welfare/humanized care and gender equality. Pregnant women's and parents' legal rights to, and the availability of, continuous health care, maternity leave, and parental leave are so engrained in Swedish society that it is much more common for employers to celebrate workers' pregnancy and parental leave than to shame them for it. Paid parental leave is decidedly inflexible in Sweden – that is, new parents must take a certain minimum amount. And while these government programs are not cheap – Sweden has one of the highest effective marginal tax rates in the world – the benefits to women, children, and families are both concrete and incalculable. Sweden boasts some of the lowest maternal and infant mortality rates, as well as some of the lowest child poverty rates in the world, while the UK is exhibiting the abysmal outcomes (of maternal and infant mortality, and child poverty) usually only seen in one OECD country notorious for its family-unfriendly policies: the United States. This chapter highlights how Sweden has maintained these outcomes for women and newborns, while the UK has all but ignored "the dramatic decline in the fortunes of [its] least well off" (Office of the High Commissioner, 2018: 1).

13.2 A Tale of Two Births

The two stories of childbirth described below exemplify the experiences of low-income working women through: health care during their pregnancy and birth; time off from work during and after the birth of their child; and the support given for their newest family member by their respective governments, such as postnatal care and direct payments.

13.2.1 *The United Kingdom: Ava's Story*

Ava[1] and her partner, Caleb, are unmarried and live together with two children: Ava's daughter from a previous marriage; and Caleb's nephew, who was put in their care by a contested child arrangements order from family court. Ava and Caleb both identify as black. Ava had a cancer scare in 2016, a life-threatening experience that led her and Caleb to decide to have a child together. Before her pregnancy, Ava's and Caleb's combined income was around £30,000 per year. Ava worked part-time as an administrator. They also received a working tax credit and a child tax credit to supplement their income. According to Ava, she and Caleb are "just about managing financially – but it is tight."

Ava wanted to give birth in a birth center, but the one closest to her had closed down. She worried about having to travel more than fifty miles in order to give birth at another birth center, particularly since she still had to care for her other children. She therefore resolved to give birth at a hospital, where the midwives and doctor seemed particularly rushed and she found it difficult to get their attention. After Ava gave birth, she stopped working – a decision she came to reluctantly after weighing her options. Part of her reason to stop working was that she simply wanted more time with the new baby. But her

---

[1] "Ava" is a pseudonym. Her story is a compilation, but primarily is taken from the story of one of the Claimants (named in the case only by her initials, CC) in the case *SC & Ors* v. *Secretary of State for Work And Pensions & Ors*, Weekly Law Reports 5425, ¶ 17. 2018 (High Court Administrative Court, 2018), which challenged the UK's "two child cap," limiting the universal credit benefit to only two children in a given household (discussed later in this chapter). Other sources for Ava's story: Pregnant Then Screwed, 2016; Prochaska, 2020; Child Poverty Action Group, 2021.

manager also hinted that Ava wouldn't have a job after her maternity leave (new mothers, he said, weren't "teamplayers"). Caleb was only eligible to take two weeks of paternity leave, and because his pay was lowered considerably during that time, he wouldn't have taken more leave even if it were available to him. Despite carefully weighing these considerations after Ava gave birth, Ava and Caleb's financial situation tightened even more.

13.2.2 Sweden: Nadia's Story

Nadia[2] and Ahmed, her husband, originally immigrated to Sweden from Lebanon about ten years ago. They have two children, both of whom were born in Sweden, and were expecting a third child. At the time of her most recent pregnancy, Nadia was a permanent resident in Sweden and worked full time as a stylist in a beauty salon. Nadia decided to begin her leave a few weeks before her due date, and was due to take about a year of maternity and parental leave after the birth. Ahmed planned to take a few months of paternity and parental leave as well. In addition to both of their incomes, with the arrival of their third child, Nadia and Ahmed would qualify for a large-family supplement, as well as the child allowance they had been receiving for their first two children.

During her first birth here – when she had just arrived – Nadia had a doula with her, who spoke Arabic and translated what the midwives were saying and any requests Nadia had. At this point, her third birth in Sweden, the birth process was familiar to her. She and Ahmed would arrive in their room, and would stay until the baby was born, as well as rest thereafter (plus, Ahmed would have his own bed). After her and Ahmed's respective leaves, they were enrolling their newest addition to the family in the local childcare center.

13.3 A Human Rights Framework for Childbirth

A foundational principle of human rights law is to protect the dignity of both individual and collective persons. The Convention on the Elimination of All Forms of Discrimination Against Women

---

[2] "Nadia" is a pseudonym. Her story is a compilation from: Johnson, 2015; Robertson, 2015.

(CEDAW), a gender equality human rights treaty to which nearly every UN member state is a party (including the United Kingdom and Sweden), is based on "the dignity and worth of the human person" (CEDAW, 1981: Preamble). Both CEDAW and the European Convention on Human Rights (ECHR) (of which the UK and Sweden are also state parties) obligate parties to act affirmatively to ensure human rights are respected within their jurisdiction (ECHR, 1950: Art. 1; CEDAW, 1981: Art. 24). This means centering the experiences and needs of women first and foremost in childbirth, and ensuring that the state's treatment of childbirth does not discriminate against women or against particularly vulnerable groups of women (like immigrant women and women of color) by leaving them worse off than men. States cannot realize women's full dignity without gender equality with men, and childbirth continues to play a large role in perpetuating such inequalities. As the preamble to CEDAW states, "the role of women in procreation should not be a basis for discrimination" (CEDAW, 1981: Preamble).

The UK's austerity approach to childbirth is, at best, disinterested in issues of human rights and gender equality, and at worst, actively working against them. By contrast, under a legal and cultural framework that specifically focuses on women's human rights and children's well-being, Sweden actively works toward gender equality.

13.4 A Case Study in the Austerity Approach to Childbirth: The United Kingdom

13.4.1 Austerity Policies

Perhaps it's best to begin the story of austerity-based childbirth policies with one of the most (in)famous quotes from Margaret Thatcher, the UK's founding austerity advocate: "There is no such thing as society. There are only individual men and women ... and their families" (Brown, 2015: 100). This sentiment is a common thread woven through austerity and neoliberalism: that the private family unit should serve as the source of security and support, instead of a welfare state/ social democracy (Cooper, 2017: 9). But, knowing what we know about human birth, it is very difficult for an individual woman, and even her family, to deliver, let alone care for, a baby alone. Based on decades of research into primates' and humans' breeding and birthing patterns, anthropologists have concluded the following: human births are especially difficult and awkward among the animal kingdom. Compared to other species, humans produce "these very large off-spring that require a lot of long-term care" (Saini, 2017: 102). The "awkward style" of human delivery has created a physical and emotional need for support during childbirth, also known as cooperative breeding, where helpers assist before, during, and after childbirth (Saini, 2017: 102). What do these fundamental physical and emotional aspects of childbirth have to do with the UK's austerity policies? The need for both helpers in childbirth and long-term care of newborns thereafter is incompatible with policies that prize individualism and economic self-sufficiency.

Indeed, the austerity vision in the UK has made childbirth even more difficult than it is already. In one recent study, austerity measures had a more devastating impact on citizens' healthcare access across European states – where Europeans increasingly reported a medical problem for which they could not get treatment – than did the economic crisis of 2008 (Stuckler et al., 2017: 20). Women have been particularly affected by austerity because their "health and well-being are particularly sensitive ... to the spending priorities of governments" (Raphael and Bryant, 2004: 63; Stuckler et al., 2017). When the public provision of family and social services – like early childhood and afterschool programs, physical and mental health care, education, neighborhood parks and recreation centers – "are eliminated or privatized, the work and/or the cost of supplying them is returned to individuals, disproportionately to women" (Brown, 2015: 105). This disproportionate burden occurs for a host of reasons, but namely because women are much more likely to be a primary caregiver and/ or single parent, such as Ava, the primary caregiver to her and Caleb's two (soon three) children. As the United Nations Special Rapporteur on extreme poverty found, the disproportionate effects of these cuts and eliminations have deeply affected women in the UK (Office of the High Commissioner, 2018: 18). Black and minority ethnic women like Ava have been even more affected (Office of the High Commissioner, 2018: 18). These disproportionate harms on women and especially women of color implicate discrimination against women in their "economic and social life" (CEDAW, 1981: Art. 13).

A series of reports by the UK government between 2004 and 2015 confirmed the Special Rapporteur's bleak observations. The reports found striking links between women's overall welfare and birthing outcomes in the UK. In a shift since austerity cuts were implemented, "the major causes of maternal death ... were now social exclusion, social disadvantage or mental health problems" (McCourt, 2017: 194). Another study examining child mortality in England and Sweden found that women's vulnerable health before and during birth, as well as their socioeconomic position, accounted for England's higher child mortality rate (Zylbersztejn et al., 2018). In other words, austerity in the UK has unduly burdened childbearing women before they have even given birth. For Ava, whose income is well below that needed to support a family in the UK, going through pregnancy and childbirth is especially precarious. Ava is much more likely than women with comparably higher incomes to have either a stillbirth or a baby who dies within a year of birth (Squire, 2017: 43). Despite the evidence that social factors like poverty are enormously influential in maternal and infant health and survival, maternity care in the UK remains blinded to rectifying these needs (McCourt, 2017: 194).

13.4.2 Pregnancy Policies

Pregnancy policies in the UK remain similarly blinded by austerity and neoliberal policies. Under neoliberalism and austerity, pregnancy and work are largely incompatible, signaling to women that they should be mothers and nothing more. Viewing women-as-mothers also makes abortions more difficult to obtain. It may sound counterintuitive to include abortion policies in a discussion about childbirth but, on both a large-scale and individual level, it is impossible to discuss healthy childbirth without also acknowledging the role of abortion access. Laws supporting abortion access (and not merely legal abortion) create "the consequence that, for all practical purposes, all pregnancies are wanted pregnancies and all babies are wanted babies" (Jordan, 1983: 33; Zylbersztejn et al., 2018: 2016). Unwanted pregnancies are more likely to result in birth complications and dangerous outcomes for mother and child, including maternal and neonatal death (Bustan and Coker, 1994; Ralph et al., 2019: 8). The UK has legal abortion, but it also maintains a certification system for the procedure (unlike for other similarly simple medical procedures), which can stigmatize the procedure for women who do not want to be pregnant and/or do not want to have a child (Lee et al., 2018).

The stigmatization of abortion in the UK is nestled into larger austerity and neoliberal politics that prefer "traditional" family structures (such as a working father and stay-at-home mother), even though abortion legislation largely preceded the rise of austerity in the late twentieth century (Brown, 2015: 100–102; Brown, 2019: 12–13). As the political scientist Wendy Brown has observed, traditional values serve the cause of neoliberalism by staving off true equality in society (as opposed to formal, legal equality), be that between men and women, or among different races and ethnicities (Brown, 2019: 13–14). For example, by inhibiting women's access to abortion, and, as will be detailed below, by inhibiting pregnancy and maternity leave protections at work, the austerity government both forces women to become mothers and subsequently relies on their unpaid labor to raise children – a gendered phenomenon Brown deems "the invisible infrastructure" (Brown, 2015: 105; Cooper, 2017: 102). Gary Becker, the noted neoliberal economist, wrote about the biological differences between men and women that explain why women's labor is more "efficiently" confined to the home (Becker, 1991: 38).[3] The stubborn preservation of the invisible infrastructure of women is why CEDAW is one of the first human rights treaties to make reproductive choice and access a pivotal part of the treaty (CEDAW, 1981: Introduction).

In Ava's case, her first pregnancy was unplanned and happened right when she was trying to leave her husband. She considered getting an abortion, but the requirement to get two different doctors to authorize the procedure made her feel like it was unsafe (Abortion Act, 1967, c. 87, § 1). By the time Ava found reassurance from a local women's group that abortion was safe, she felt she was too far along to terminate the pregnancy (delay in abortion care becomes more commonplace when the procedure is stigmatized (Lee et al., 2018)). In the final

---

[3] "If women have a comparative advantage over men in the household sector when they make the same investments in human capital, an efficient household with both sexes would allocate the time of women mainly to the household sector and the time of men mainly to the market sector" (Becker, 1991: 38). Moreover, Milton Friedman, the father of neoliberal economics in the United States, advocated against publicly-funded childcare, child subsidies, and employer-mandated daycare for mothers, decrying – after an aside about his skiing trips with the editor of *National Review* – the "disturbingly large" number of families "in which both parents work" (the not-so-subtle implication here being those families in which the mother is working *in addition to* the father) (Friedman, 1988: 14).

months of her pregnancy, Ava agonized over being tied to her then-husband by a child, and worried about the kind of life she could give a new baby. When she finally gave birth, she had to go through a lengthy hospital stay at the end of her pregnancy, as well as her first child being born preterm. To be clear, Ava loves her daughter.[4] But she might have been able to avoid a traumatizing pregnancy and childbirth if the neoliberal opposition to abortion access had not pressured her into staying pregnant and becoming a parent.

For women who continue their pregnancies, it is a decidedly precarious time for their employment as well, in both getting hired at a new job, or keeping an old one. The precarity of pregnancy and work is one reason CEDAW features protections for pregnant people so prominently. Article 11 obligates states parties to take action to "prohibit, subject to the imposition of sanctions, dismissal on the grounds of pregnancy or of maternity leave" and to "provide special protection to women during pregnancy in types of work proved to be harmful to them." Despite the legal prohibition of pregnancy discrimination in the UK that technically aligns with CEDAW, retaliation against pregnant women in the UK is strikingly common. Ava, for example, was not fired outright for her pregnancy, but her manager's comments about pregnant women and mothers (including that they're not "team-players" and other comments demeaning pregnant women and mothers at the office) made it seem like she wouldn't be able to return to work anyway. She left her job, figuring that would look better for future employment prospects than being fired. Her manager's comments echo another tension between neoliberalism and gender equality: that women's bodies are not optimal or productive for the workforce. Recall, from Chapter 12, "Why Do Some People Want to Manage Human Fertility?" the neoliberal idea that women need period apps in order to increase their productivity at work. Employers, especially in a jurisdiction like the UK (where pregnancy and maternity

---

[4] Ava's experience is emblematic of the complicated emotions that women go through when they are denied an abortion. For more information about the effects on women who are denied an abortion, including worse health outcomes, and lowered socioeconomic status, but also positive feelings after bonding with their child (Rocca et al., 2021), see the Turnaway Study, a multiyear project in the United States and abroad conducted by the University of California San Francisco that followed the comparative life trajectories of women who were either denied or given an abortion: www.ansirh.org/abortion/denial.

leave can become an economic liability), view pregnancy and childbirth as antithetical to their bottom line and pregnant women as "less dependable" (Kitroeff and Silver-Greenberg, 2019; Collins, 2020).

The consequences for women whose employers have retaliated against them for their pregnancy can be devastating: lowering their financial security and independence, affecting their mental health, even putting them at risk of a miscarriage (Kitroeff and Silver-Greenberg, 2019; Oppenheim, 2020). Ava had a feeling that her manager's statements weren't right, but she wasn't sure they were illegal, exactly. The UK does have laws forbidding retaliation and discrimination against pregnant people at work (Equality Act, 2010, c. 15, § 18); but women have to file their claim within a brief time period, and only a miniscule proportion of women (0.6 percent) who believe they have been victims of such discrimination actually manage to file such a claim (Pregnant Then Screwed, 2020). By the time Ava had spoken to other new mothers about her experience (they indicated that her manager's conduct was unlawful), the three-month window to file her claim had passed, and she was, moreover, completely exhausted caring for the new baby. The UK's neoliberal policies of ignoring pregnant women's rights and dignities at work have effectively forced working women into motherhood, and maternal responsibilities, alone.

13.4.3 Midwives and Birth Centers

Under austerity, pregnant women are treated as consumers and given myriad "choices" for where they can give birth: a home birth, a birth center, or a hospital maternity unit (Department of Health, 2007). The idea of consumer choice is so pervasive that the Department of Health characterizes all the policies surrounding childbirth in the UK as the "national choice guarantees" as part of the NHS's surrounding "choice framework" for healthcare services: choice of where to access maternity care, choice of antenatal care, choice of place of birth, and choice of place of postnatal care (Department of Health, 2007: 5; Department of Health, 2016). It's not that giving pregnant women choices during their care is bad – in fact, many studies on this subject have found that women who are presented with meaningful options and control during childbirth, such as their physical position during labor, feel better overall about the experience (Odent, 1984; Lundgren, 2010; Cook and Loomis, 2012; Birthrights, 2013; National Maternity

Review, 2016; World Health Organization, 2018). (Article 8 of the ECHR, moreover, which protects the rights to private and family life, has been interpreted as providing women with the right to make decisions about childbirth [ECHR, 1950: Art. 8; Prochaska, 2020: 134].) And to be sure, the UK's focus on maternity care through midwifery makes childbirth safer than in countries like the United States which lack any institutionalized midwifery services, since midwives have some of the strongest evidence-based support for protecting women's dignity, autonomy, and health in childbirth (Cassidy, 2006: 49; Wrede et al., 2008; Cook and Loomis, 2012).

But the overarching focus on "choice" as an end unto itself, even amid the larger institutional support for midwifery, obscures the fact that many women, particularly low-income women, do not have access to the safest and most desirable places to give birth, namely birth centers. Women often have more positive childbirth experiences in the UK's birth centers than in a hospital, because there women feel they receive more respectful care and greater autonomy and control over the progress of the birth, and where they are less likely to receive intrusive medical interventions (like forceps or ventouse) (Birthrights, 2013). Yet the NHS recently shut down eight popular birth centers that were led by midwives because "too few women" were using them (Campbell, 2019). The reasoning for these shutdowns taps into two myths of austerity: the scarcity of state resources, and shutting down state institutions as responses to the lack of "market" demand for them (Brown, 2019: 18). The NHS shut down these birth centers based on the alleged failure of women to take advantage of them – even though it also increasingly restricts which women may use such centers because their pregnancies are considered "high risk" (Einion, 2017; Prochaska, 2020). For example, NHS policies often limit access to birth centers to women under a certain body mass index (BMI), effectively barring women with higher BMIs from the joys of a holistic childbirth (even though similarly "risky" pregnancies, like first-timers, are not so barred) (Prochaska, 2020: 137). As Ava's experience shows, it's not that "too few women" *want* to use a birth center, it's that too few women *can*.

13.4.4 Maternity, Paternity, and Parental Leave

After childbirth, new parents in the UK have a "flexible" parental leave policy, which emphasizes shared caregiving between parents as a "choice" for families. The idea of flexibility sounds promising, such as individualizing leave plans based on a family's unique circumstances. But like the flexible work model documented in Chapter 18 in this book ("What Should a Job Look Like?"), flexibility in parental leave here acts as a cover for a lack of meaningful access and choices (a "damned if you do, damned if you don't" scenario). In this case, the UK's flexible leave policies further entrench gender inequality and force parents of all genders to make impossible financial choices after the birth of a child. The provision of paid maternity leave is so fundamental to gender equality that CEDAW obligates states parties to ensure "maternity leave with pay or with comparable social benefits" (CEDAW, 1981: Art. 11[2]).

During maternity and parental leave in the UK, mothers receive, on average, 30 percent of the salary they would have been earning had they not given birth, for up to a total of nine months of leave (OECD Family Database, PF2.1: 2). Fathers, on the other hand, are only entitled to two weeks of paid leave, and they receive, on average, only 20 percent of their salary for that time (OECD Family Database, PF2.1: 7). These realities led Ava and Caleb to decide that it was in the best interest of their family for her to leave her job (even though she was subtly being pushed out of her job anyway), and for Caleb to increase his working hours to offset the loss of Ava's income. With the reality that women still earn less than men, families will continue to make similar choices to Ava's – because it's more financially prudent for the lesser-earning spouse (usually the woman, and more often low-income women) to leave work when childcare is unaffordable (Andersson, 2005; Krapf, 2014: 181). Policies like these, that entrench both lower pay for women and gendered caregiving, are antithetical to CEDAW's commitment that "the upbringing of children requires a sharing of responsibility between men and women" (CEDAW, 1981: Preamble).

13.4.5 Early Childcare

The Preamble of CEDAW not only commits that childrearing should be shared between men and women, but also that it should be shared with "society as a whole" (CEDAW, 1981: Preamble). This inevitably requires some sort of state provision of childcare (the "establishment and development of a network of childcare facilities") (CEDAW,

1981: Art. 11[2]). But the neoliberal idea running through the UK's approach to pregnancy policies, leave policies, and early childcare – that women have a "'natural' commitment to caregiving" (Brown, 2015: 102) – makes the state provision of childcare an afterthought. This recalls the fundamental tension between gender equality and neoliberal austerity: the neoliberal state fully relies on the individual family unit and the free labor of women for childbirth and childcare (Cooper, 2017: 9, 12; Brown, 2019: 13–14). One of the most praised neoliberal economists, Gary Becker, writing on the subject of maternal care labor "draws on the notion of 'psychic income' to explain the mother who sacrifices for her children and suffers economic privations for her 'natural' commitment to caregiving" (Brown, 2015: 102). Unfortunately for women like Ava, her local Tesco was not accepting "psychic income" as a form of payment for baby formula.

Childcare in the UK combines ideas of women as natural caregivers with ideas of markets and efficiency. Childcare is almost entirely left to private actors, a mix of for-profit and not-for-profit private childcare facilities (OECD, 2020: 3), and therefore also to the whims of the market. Injecting privatization and market competition into early childcare services is a hallmark of neoliberal austerity thinking: it saves the state money while at the same time making childcare more efficient and responsive to families' demands, so the belief goes. But it's also effectively inaccessible to many women (forcing them to fulfill their destiny as a caregiver) because the UK has one of the most expensive childcare systems in the world – more so than even the United States – eating up more than 50 percent of a woman's salary in a two-income household, and up to a quarter of the salary of a single mother (OECD, 2020: 2). Childcare only begins to become free for most UK residents when the child has reached three years old, and even then, the majority of eligibility for such childcare only covers fifteen hours per week (Gov. UK, 2020).

Like the elimination of birth centers, the reliance on market dynamics in the UK has led to scarce childcare coverage in poorer areas where children are not "profitable" to care for (OECD, 2020: 3). Given the overwhelming expense of childcare, it became clear to Ava that it was less expensive for her to stop working entirely than for her and Caleb to pay for childcare. Ava's decision is not unique: as one recent investigation found, "[a]lmost a fifth of parents have been forced into quitting their jobs due to the extortionate cost of childcare in the UK – with researchers saying it is predominantly women bearing this burden" (Oppenheim, 2019).

13.4.6 Child Benefits

The UK government does not make up for a childcare deficit with payments that might offset some of the financial insecurity from a parent doing caregiving full time. Instead, it has implemented Universal Credit, a consolidation of six benefits rolled into one (child supplements, housing supplements, and income support, for example) meant to offset poverty for vulnerable people and families (Office of the High Commissioner, 2018; Gov.UK, 2021a).[5] Most relevant for this chapter's focus on childbirth is Universal Credit's benefit cap for families with more than two children: families will receive benefits (the child tax credit) for their first two children, but if a woman gives birth to a third child, "[y]ou won't be paid an additional amount" (Gov.UK, 2021b). Again, the government's public justification for this limit was to "save a significant amount of money" (Mason, 2014). But the lurking neoliberal justification was to enforce "behavioural change" – that is, to "discourage people struggling with their finances from having more children" (Mason, 2014).[6] This justification is based on the assumption that people in poverty either refuse to work or are unable to (both of which are untenable to the neoliberal order) – and that they should be forced to make the same financial choices as those in working, higher-income households (Butler, 2020; Child Poverty Action Group et al., 2021: 2). As a testament to how engrained the

[5] As the Special Rapporteur noted in his report on poverty in the UK, the introduction of Universal Credit, which essentially slashed the value of what each individual benefit would have been otherwise was "'sold' as being part of an unavoidable program of fiscal 'austerity,' needed to save the country from bankruptcy" (Office of the High Commissioner, 2018: 3).

[6] As further evidence that the actual justification was making sure people in poverty acted with more "individual responsibility," the two-child benefit cap has an exception for a child conceived from rape – that is, a birth that occurred despite the responsible efforts of the woman herself (Gov.UK, 2021b). To add insult to injury, a woman giving birth to a third child as a result of rape has to fill out a form showing evidence of a criminal conviction or civil judgment from the assault, or evidence that she has spoken to a professional about the assault (in addition to other evidentiary demands) (Department for Work and Customs, 2019). This additional burden for women who have been raped also reinforces the neoliberal hostility toward gender equality.

neoliberal concept of individual responsibility for the poor is (McKinnon, 2005: 44; Brown, 2015: 105; Office of the High Commissioner, 2018; Cooper, 2020: 106–107), the child benefit cap enjoyed broad support across the political spectrum in the UK when it was introduced, including among Labour and Liberal Democrat voters (Mason, 2014).

But like many of the neoliberal concepts explored both in this chapter and other chapters in this book, the assumptions about people in poverty underlining this policy are simply not true. Government data have shown that a large majority of families receiving child benefits *are* working – their incomes are just not enough to support a family (Butler, 2020). Moreover, the remaining minority of parents receiving child benefits who are not working were largely forced out of the labor market by a crisis event – a sudden job loss, ill health, or a relationship breakdown – crises that have become much more familiar to a wider swath of society because of the COVID-19 pandemic (Child Poverty Action Group et al., 2021: 2). Ava and Caleb's situation is emblematic of these types of crises: they decided to have a baby together while both of them were still working. It was only after two crises collided – Ava being pushed out of her job, and the inordinate cost of childcare that made Ava's pursuit of another job irrelevant – that Ava and Caleb realized that their new baby would be ineligible for benefits, a loss of about £2900 per year.[7] As Ava put it, "the extras for the children and family outings have stopped" – but even the necessities have been stretched thin. It's gotten to the point where she and Caleb rely on their local food bank at least once a month to ensure the whole family has enough to eat.

For those learning about the cap for the first time, it still might sound relatively anodyne: people shouldn't have children that they can't provide for. But consider what the children's rights organization, Child Poverty Action Group, has said about the policy: even if you're sympathetic to the idea that parents with lower incomes should be acting more fiscally responsibly, why should the government treat a child as "less deserving ... because of the circumstances of their birth[?]" (*SC & Ors*

---

[7] To illustrate just how absurd the two-child rule is: Ava and Caleb would have qualified for an exception, and would have received three child benefits, if Caleb's nephew had joined their family *after* their new baby, since his nephew was put in their care under a nonparental caring arrangement, another exception to the two-child cap in addition to a child born as a result of rape (Gov.UK, 2021b).

v. *Secretary of State,* 2018: ¶ 47). From a human rights perspective, the two-child policy also disproportionately harms certain groups: women (who compose over 90 percent of single-parent households), families of color (who are much more likely to live in households with three or more children), and Muslim and Jewish families (who also are much more likely to have three or more children, and for whom childrearing is an integral part of their faith and culture) (Child Poverty Action Group et al., 2021: 3; *SC & Ors* v. *Secretary of State* 2018: ¶ 37).

This chapter has spilt a lot of ink on this one benefits cap policy. A big reason for this is that it encapsulates so many of the myths and assumptions of austerity and neoliberalism in general: demanding individual responsibility from poor people; imposing "traditional" values (like a four-person nuclear family) on families through threadbare welfare policy; justifying a reduced welfare state by cost savings and the deficit; making work participation the centrality of a (supposed) poverty-reduction initiative; and considerably hampering gender equality for low-income women. The perils of committing to this neoliberal philosophy have only begun to come to fruition: the two-child benefit cap has pushed children into poverty even before their birth. Antipoverty groups estimate that at least half a million children will have been pushed into poverty once the full rollout is in place (Child Poverty Action Group, 2021: 5). Statistics like these are compounded by the other cuts and eliminations described in this chapter: slashed healthcare services, weak pregnancy laws, inadequate parental leave, and unaffordable childcare. As they've been pushed into poverty, women and infants have an increased likelihood of death from childbirth. For the first time in decades, the gap in infant mortality rates between wealthy and poor communities in the UK has widened (Mellor, 2020). For some context about how the United Kingdom's figures could look, its maternal mortality rate is about twice as high as that in Sweden (Zylbersztejn et al., 2018).

13.5 A Case Study in How We Should Treat Childbirth: Sweden

13.5.1 *Social Democratic and Gender Equality Policies*

The two qualities of Sweden's policies supporting childbirth are its fully funded social welfare programs and its commitment to gender equality. Supportive social welfare policies, like publicly funded health care accessible to all regardless of ability to pay, are in the best position to support healthy childbirths (Raphael and Bryant, 2004: 75). Sweden's healthcare system enables "free, comprehensive and universal" prenatal care regardless of a woman's ability to pay, through which pregnant women have the legal right to attend prenatal appointments (Jordan, 1983: 40). As a testament to how engrained Sweden's universal health care system is, one eminent Swedish obstetrician called differential care depending on a woman's ability to pay "an obscenity" (Jordan, 1983: 69). National welfare systems like Sweden's that have invested in family policies – state support for parents' employment as well as generous benefits and social allowances for families with children – reduce families' poverty risk and are much less likely to conscript newborns into poverty, even though childbirth can be a "poverty-triggering event" (Barbieri and Bozzon, 2016: 100–101).

Sweden's surrounding social welfare policies help to ensure that immigrant women like Nadia are not worse off than women born and raised in Sweden. In a sign that Sweden is successfully working toward greater equality between immigrant women and women native to Sweden, immigrant and native Swedish women exhibit "remarkable similarity" in their fertility and childbearing practices (Andersson, 2005: 8). This is not to say that Sweden has solved existing discrimination against immigrant women and families – such disparities still exist, including in immigrant women's maternity care, where their experiences in the healthcare system are uneven (Robertson, 2015). But Sweden provides a baseline of care for immigrant and other minority women, regardless of their social and economic position, that the UK does not.

Where Thatcher-style austerity and neoliberalism focus on "only individual men and women and their families," Sweden is primarily focused on society, and equality among its citizens. To that end:

Sweden conceives of family support and the task of child-rearing not as private issues, but as collective responsibilities. As a result, the Swedish government socializes the cost of child-rearing across society. In these policies, Sweden has enmeshed the aims of gender equality, the combination of work and family, and high employment rates. (Collins, 2019: 29)

This doesn't mean that individual women's preferences in childbirth, for example, are sacrificed for the collective good of the Swedish state.

It means that the state recognizes the value and dignity of each woman as integral parts of society.

13.5.2 Pregnancy Policies

While Nadia very much wanted to have this child, there would have been few obstacles in her way if she had wanted or needed an abortion. Abortion is more readily accessible in Sweden than in the UK, and thus gives greater appreciation to women's reproductive autonomy (Zylbersztejn, 2018: 2016–2017). Subject to few revisions, abortion in Sweden has been available on demand until the eighteenth week of pregnancy since 1974 (*Abortlag, Svensk Författningssamling [SFS]* 1974: 595, § 1). The widespread availability of abortion in Sweden, free and without other cumbersome requirements, enables women to maintain wanted pregnancies and therefore healthy births. As a testament to Sweden's abortion and pregnancy protections, Sweden has maintained some of the lowest infant and maternal mortality rates in the world (Jordan, 1983: 7–8; World Bank, 2019).

Protections for pregnant women at work are similarly strong – preventing the devastating interruptions for pregnant women in the UK if they are fired, pushed out, or retaliated against for their pregnancy or birth. The sociologist Caitlyn Collins calls the Swedish policies supporting pregnancy and motherhood, like flexible schedules, reduced working hours, and ample leave time, a "culture of support" (Collins, 2019: 45). Nadia's experience of pregnancy at work was emblematic of this culture of support. The salon was supportive of Nadia's pregnancy, and, especially later in her pregnancy, made sure to schedule her only for appointments that she could perform while sitting down. Announcing one's pregnancy at work isn't a sensitive topic, and like the interviewees' in Collins' study of Swedish motherhood, Nadia's colleagues were simply happy for her (Collins, 2019: 41). Nadia also specifically took advantage of her legal right to use seven weeks of her maternity leave before she gave birth (she ended up taking five weeks of pregnancy leave) (Collins, 2019: 31) – which was especially useful for her when it became too tiring to see clients.

13.5.3 Midwives and Birth

Births in Sweden take place in hospitals and are managed by highly trained midwives (Jordan, 1983: 40; Akhavan and Lundgren, 2012).

Sweden's combination of highly trained midwives and the hospital setting also allow for more effective triaging of childbirths: midwives manage normal, routine deliveries, whereas doctors are summoned for more complicated cases (Jordan, 1983: 41). "What makes us successful is that we put women at the center of what we're doing[,]" notes the doctor who heads the maternal unit in Uppsala, "[w]e have everything technology can offer but, even more importantly, we treat mothers as individuals" (Moorhead, 2006).

Nadia developed a trusting relationship with her midwife. Whenever she was worried during her pregnancy, she went to her midwife's clinic, where she always felt taken care of, even if she had to wait for a while. However, for Nadia's first birth in Sweden, she took advantage of Sweden's "doula culture interpreters" (Akhavan and Edge, 2012; Anderson, 2019). Unlike midwives in the UK, who have viewed the participation of doulas in labor with some skepticism, midwives in Sweden welcome the presence of a doula, whom they believe can serve as a facilitator for immigrant women's wants and needs in childbirth (Akhavan and Lundgren, 2012; McLeish and Redshaw, 2017: 12–16). Doulas' continuous support provides translation help, understanding, and personalized attention to birthing women (McLeish and Redshaw, 2017: 12–16). In Sweden, doulas do act as continuous support for immigrant women, and lessen the likelihood of complications and interventions during childbirth (Anderson, 2019). (Since Nadia has now been in Sweden for a decade, and has since learned Swedish fluently, she didn't feel the need for a doula during her current pregnancy and birth.)

When it was time for delivery, Nadia went to the maternal health clinic, which, typical of hospitals in Sweden, also had an early labor lounge akin to a living room where Nadia could read, watch television, or chat with her husband (Jordan, 1983: 49). When Nadia felt like lying down, she was moved to a small (private) delivery room with her own bathroom with a tub where she would not be moved again until after the baby was born (Jordan, 1983: 49).

During labor, Nadia's midwife created a trustful, relaxed atmosphere: she played soft music and made sure Nadia had juice and water nearby, as well as pain medication at her request. Part of the midwife's treatment here stems from Sweden's patient safety act passed in 2011, *Patientsäkerhetslag (2010: 659)*, which, among other provisions, obligates that healthcare professionals consult the patient in all aspects of care, and show respect for the patient's wishes. Women and midwives in Sweden ultimately view childbirth as an "intensely personal, fulfilling achievement" for a woman, a cultural view in line with its larger commitment to gender equality (Jordan, 1983: 34).

13.5.4 Maternity, Paternity, and Parental Leave

Sweden's commitment to gender equality in childbirth has informed the structure of its maternity, paternity, and parental leave policies as well. Where the UK has its focus on flexibility and choice, Sweden focuses on gender equality and the best interests of children. Sweden's shift from an exclusive maternity-leave system to a shared, parental-leave one occurred in 1974. When parental leave became available to fathers, very few took advantage of it, and the few who did earned the nickname "velvet dads" (Bennhold, 2010). In the program's infancy, parental leave was entirely flexible between two parents, which had the unintended consequence of reinforcing gender norms around caregiving. This model, often called the "breadwinner" model, would effectively impose the burden of care on the lesser-earning spouse (usually the woman) – a dynamic that echoes Ava and Caleb's decision for Ava to stop working (Bennhold, 2010; Krapf, 2014: 177).

Based on a conscious decision by the Swedish government to root out gendered caregiving in 1995, Sweden introduced "daddy leave," a "use it or lose it" leave model (the "dual-earner" model), where fathers were eligible for leave that could not be transferred to the mother (Bennhold, 2010; Krapf, 2014: 177; Collins, 2019: 30). This "powerful symbolic shift" signaled to fathers that they "should share the responsibility for paid work and child-rearing" (Collins, 2019: 30). The Swedish state views the issue of shared parenting as a matter of gender equality, but also as one of child welfare (Collins, 2019: 30). For gender equality, parental leave policies that encourage fathers to care for new children are associated with "higher female employment, less gender stereotyping at home, and higher life satisfaction," while helping women stay in the labor market and maintain their financial independence (Saxonberg, 2013; Adema et al., 2015: 3). For child welfare, fathers spending more time at home during early infancy means they are more involved with their children, which benefits children's cognitive and emotional development (Adema et al., 2015: 3).

With some tweaks since the introduction of the dual-earner leave model, including greater time allocated, parental leave in Sweden effectively requires both the mother and father to take leave, and replaces between 80 percent and 90 percent of parents' salaries while on leave (depending on their income) for a total of 480 days between the two parents (Krapf, 2014: 17; Collins, 2019: 30–32).[8] In total, Nadia took a little over nine months of leave for their new baby, and Ahmed took eight. Now, fathers' leave patterns in Sweden are similar to Ahmed's: fathers often take more than ninety days of the allocated paternity and parental leave, which has normalized fathers' involvement in early childhood and increased their paternity leave participation (85 percent) to some of the highest in the world (Bennhold, 2010; Lee et al., 2016; Collins, 2019; Sweden.se, 2020).

13.5.5 Early Childcare

After their leave periods have ended, parents in Sweden can take advantage of some of the lowest childcare costs in the world, primarily because of the country's heavily subsidized public early childhood education and care from a very young age – between one and two years old (Collins, 2019: 33; OECD, 2020: 4). While the neoliberal policies of the UK rely largely on private actors for childcare and treat parents as childcare consumers, childcare in Sweden is publicly provided and any fees are based on parents' income. Ironically for austerity proponents, publicly provided childcare in Sweden actually performs what the private market in the UK was supposed to do: it keeps costs down, and very few households (only 2 percent) report that they would like to make use of childcare, but cannot afford to do so (Collins 2019: 33–34; OECD, 2020: 4).

Nadia and Ahmed were not put in the impossible position of having to decide between one of their livelihoods and childcare. Instead, when both of their parental leave periods ended, they sent their newest member of the family to their local childcare center, where they felt their child was in good hands because of the staff's expertise and training in child development (Collins, 2019: 33). Childbearing behavior is also similar among native Swedish women

---

[8] Notably, couples maintain the same combined amount of leave time regardless of their gender identity or sexual orientation (Collins, 2019: 31).

and immigrant women like Nadia (i.e., patterns in taking parental leave and taking advantage of subsidized childcare), indicating that Sweden's emphasis on comprehensive policies supporting childbirth have an impact on families regardless of cultural differences (Andersson, 2005: 8).

At one point, the Swedish state allowed for families to take a child homecare allowance as an alternative to early childcare (where the state pays a parent to care for their child at a reduced salary or a flat rate) (Collins, 2019: 34). The justification for the move to allow a homecare allowance was similar to that offered for privatizing and outsourcing childcare in the UK: it would provide parents with "more individual choice" in their childcare arrangements (Collins, 2019: 34). But it had the effect of what critics called the "housewife trap": mothers, and particularly low-income and immigrant mothers, were much more likely to use the homecare allowance than fathers were; again because mothers were usually the lesser-earning spouse (Collins, 2019: 34). This pattern has held across societies that offer homecare allowances, effectively creating an underclass of caregiving mothers, not least of which because the homecare payments were much less than for a professional childcare worker or a full-time worker in general (Krapf, 2014: 181–182). After less than a decade in effect, the Swedish state abolished homecare allowances, citing the program's tendency to reinforce gendered caregiving arrangements (Collins, 2019: 34).

There is a tension here between fostering a gender-equal society and respecting some parents' stated preferences – what neoliberal proponents often call the paternalism of the welfare state (Cooper, 2020: 106–107). Sweden's scrapping of the homecare allowance as well as its "use it or lose it" paternity leave policies certainly butt heads with how some parents want to arrange their lives after the birth of their child: mothers who would prefer to be paid to stay home with the new baby, and fathers who don't want to be involved in childcare. But the assumption for neoliberal proponents when they cry "Swedish paternalism" is that making parental leave "flexible" and inaccessible, and privatizing and outsourcing childcare are the nonpaternalizing alternative. As this chapter has alluded to, this supposedly neutral view of neoliberal policies is misleading. The austerity policies making it financially impossible and miserable for low-income people, people in poverty, and people in financial crisis to have children *are* telling people and compelling them[9] into what the neoliberal state views as in their best interest: to "behave as responsible free market actors" and not have children (Cooper, 2020: 106–107). Recall that the UK's two-child benefit policy was explicitly about changing "behaviour." As the United Nations Special Rapporteur on extreme poverty and human rights described in his observations about the UK's austerity policies:

In the area of poverty-related policy, the evidence points to the conclusion that the driving force has not been economic but rather a commitment to achieving radical social re-engineering …. The government has made no secret of its determination to change the value system to focus more on individual responsibility, to place major limits on government support, and to pursue a single-minded, and some have claimed simple-minded, focus on getting people into employment at all costs. (Office of the High Commissioner for Human Rights 2018: 2, 3)

It's difficult to imagine how policies that prize individual responsibility above all else aren't paternalizing, but Sweden's gender equality ones are.

Laws and policies "are powerful symbols: they delineate a social consensus about what is right and wrong, which shapes people's moral judgments and actions" (Collins, 2019: 8–9). Austerity and neoliberal laws around childbirth in the UK tell low-income families that having children is wrong. As one mother affected by the two-child benefit cap put it, "it feels as though my third child doesn't matter and his food, housing and basic living standards don't matter" (Child Poverty Action Group, 2021: 3). Considering that the Swedish state makes families less miserable and less poor, and achieves greater parity for women in terms of their financial independence, health, and well-being, it is worth reconsidering which supposedly paternalizing policies are worth maintaining when designing policies around birth.

13.5.6 Child Benefits

In contrast to the UK's view of child benefits as a vehicle to enact "behavioural change" on irresponsible parents in poverty, Sweden

---

[9] In one of the most extreme examples of how austerity in the UK has succeeded in making low-income people more "responsible" by limiting their birthing patterns, a reproductive rights group in the UK found that more women felt "forced" to get an abortion, despite wanting to have a child, because of at least one austerity policy. (Child Poverty Action Group et al., 2021: 6).

provides a child supplement (a child allowance, *barnbidrag*) to every child regardless of the circumstances of their birth (Collins, 2019: 34). In even starker contrast to the UK's two-child benefit cap, Sweden provides *extra* assistance to a third child or more children in a given household, called a large family supplement (Försäkringskassen, 2021). The justification is explicitly not about changing behavior (although arguably, one could view it as an encouragement to increase births), but about tackling the reality that raising more than two children is expensive for families: "The large-family supplement ... gives extra financial compensation to families with more than one child, as the costs are normally greater when you have more children" (Nordic Cooperation, 2021).

Nadia and Ahmed were one such family who benefited from the large-family supplement after the birth of their third child. In total, for all three of their minor children, they received about 2500 Swedish crowns (or about £238) per month in child allowances. When looking at all of the above figures around childbirth in the Swedish state together – a personal room in a maternity ward to give birth along with the individual attention of a midwife; Nadia and Ahmed's parental leave paid at 80–90 percent of their salaries; low-fee and no-fee public childcare; and child allowances of thousands of crowns (or hundreds of pounds) per month – it becomes almost unavoidable to ask: isn't all this *very expensive* for Sweden? It bears noting that concerns of ballooning costs and the need to lower the deficit are almost always at the forefront of austerity and neoliberal arguments for fewer and smaller state programs (in addition to the social reengineering central to more recent austerity measures). But one of the problems of a narrow focus on costs is that there are certain values and events in human life that are difficult to measure in crowns or pounds – birth and death are just two examples.[10] So, how do we design policies for monumental events like birth that are out of our control?

One of the goals of this chapter is to break out of the neoliberal cycle of cost comparisons for events as important as birth. As part of that goal, this chapter has also highlighted how women's labor, like the

---

[10] Although this hasn't stopped neoliberal economists from trying to put a monetary value on the birth of a child. Gary Becker, for instance, has written prolifically on the "demand" and "price of children" as well as a "child market" (Becker, 1991: 135, 140).

physical labor of childbirth and childrearing, rarely figure into neoliberal projections of cost savings, either because they are ignored, or are relied upon as naturally "free" (Brown, 2015: 105, 2019: 12–13). And, yes, of course Sweden's policies supporting childbirth are very "expensive" in the sense that the state has to spend much more money to support arrangements like Nadia and Ahmed's than the UK does for Ava and Caleb. That money comes from higher taxes spread across a broader swath of society, not just from the top earners (Collins, 2019: 42–43). But for events like childbirth, "[t]o put it simply, Swedes pay a lot in taxes, but they also get a lot for their money" (Collins, 2019: 43). And for the supposed cost savings and greater efficiency in the UK's childbirth policies:

the reforms have almost certainly cost the country far more than their proponents will admit. The many billions advertised as having been extracted from the benefits system since 2010 have been offset by the additional resources required to fund emergency services by families and the community, by local government, by doctors and hospital accident and emergency centers ... (Officer of the High Commissioner 2018: 3)

With lower income inequality, low child poverty, healthier births, and greater parity between men and women (Barbieri and Bozzon, 2016: 100–101; Zylbersztejn et al., 2018), some of the savings (like respect for human rights) from the Swedish approach to childbirth are simply incalculable under a strictly neoliberal set of values that prioritize monetary figures over human ones.

13.6 Conclusion

One of the curious aspects of the *market imperialism* described in the Introduction to this book is that many of the methods employed to such an end are antithetical to the goals of neoliberalism itself. In the context of childbirth, a purist (and cynical) neoliberal goal of childbirth is the (re)production of human capital, that is, the need for more and more workers in order to support the economy and care for an increasingly aging population (see Chapter 15, "How Should We Care for the Elderly?"). But many of the neoliberal policies here, like cutting the budgets of health and other services and limiting payments for families with more than two children, have the effect of *decreasing* human capital – either by increasing mortality rates for women and infants, or by making it more (usually financially) difficult for women to become pregnant and give birth in the first place. These strange bedfellows also belie a truth about Sweden's childcare policies: it too is not immune from neoliberal thinking in childbirth. Consider, for example, that the entire parental leave and childcare structure is focused on getting both mothers and fathers back to work and keeping them working, as well as ensuring the (re)production of human capital through policies that support more births in general. This isn't to say that this type of neoliberal thinking about work in Sweden is necessarily bad – it's to point out that even social democratic/socialist liberalism states like Sweden have a mix of welfare-based and neoliberal-based policies, even for issues as fundamental as childbirth.

Sweden is not immune from the neoliberal default to increase state savings either. In the rural area of Sweden's Sollefteå, the municipality decided that the only maternity unit would need to be closed down as a "cost-cutting" measure, forcing thousands of women to drive at least 100 km in order to access maternity care (BBC, 2017). The move sparked outrage after at least three women were forced to give birth in transit – in a car, a fire engine, and a taxi – while making their way to the nearest maternity ward (Branford, 2017). This may have saved the municipality a lot of money, but the human "costs" – to pregnant and birthing women and infants – were much more upsetting.

Hopefully, this chapter has shown that when it comes to childbirth – which, as a gentle and obvious reminder, is necessary for the continuation of the human race – we should strive for policies that are, on balance, based more on welfare than individual responsibility and competition. A welfare approach to childbirth recognizes fundamental principles of human rights: the respect for women's equality and dignity, and children's health and well-being.

References

Adema, W. et al. 2015. "Paid parental leave: Lessons from OECD countries and selected U.S. states." In *OECD Social Employment and Migration Working Papers* (Issue 172). Paris: OECD Publishing.

Akhavan, S. and D. Edge, 2012. "Foreign-born women's experiences of community-based doulas in Sweden: A qualitative study." *Healthcare for Women International* 33: 833–848.

Akhavan, S. and I. Lundgren, 2012. "Midwives' experiences of doula support for immigrant women in Sweden: A qualitative study." *Midwifery* 28: 80–85.

Anderson, C. 2019. "Where doulas calm nerves and bridge cultures during childbirth." *The New York Times,* January 2, 2019. https://nyti.ms/2RlVYF5

Andersson, G. 2005. *A Study on Policies and Practices in Selected Countries That Encourage Childbirth: The Case of Sweden."* Max Planck Institute for Demographic Research.

Barbieri, P. and R. Bozzon, 2016. "Welfare, labour market deregulation and households' poverty risks: An analysis of the risk of entering poverty at childbirth in different European welfare clusters." *Journal of European Social Policy* 26 (2): 99–123.

BBC. 2017. "Swedish midwives offer training for car births." *BBC News from Elsewhere,* January 16, 2017. www.bbc.com/news/blogs-news-from-elsewhere-38638416

Becker, G. S. 1991. *A Treatise on the Family.* Cambridge, MA: Harvard University Press.

Bennhold, K. 2010. "In Sweden, men can have it all." *The New York Times,* June 9, 2010. www.nytimes.com/2010/06/10/world/europe/10iht-sweden.html?_r=2&

Birthrights. 2013. *Dignity in Childbirth: The Dignity Survey 2013: Women's and Midwives' Experiences of Dignity in UK Maternity Care.* London: Birthrights.

Blyth, M. 2015. *Austerity: The History of a Dangerous Idea.* New York: Oxford University Press.

Branford, B. 2017. "Sweden reacts to anger at 'risky births' and maternity care shortages." *BBC,* March 28, 2017. www.bbc.com/news/world-europe-39418887

Brown, W. 2015. *Undoing the Demos: Neoliberalism's Stealth Revolution.* Brooklyn: Zone Books.

2019. *In the Ruins of Neoliberalism: The Rise of Antidemocratic Politics in the West.* New York: Columbia University Press.

Bustan, M. and L. Coker, 1994. "Maternal attitude towards pregnancy and the risk of neonatal death." *American Journal of Public Health* 84 (3): 411–414.

Campbell, D. 2019. "Concerns over birthing options as NHS shuts midwife-led centres." *Guardian,* February 11, 2019. www.theguardian.com/society/2019/feb/11/concerns-over-birthing-options-as-nhs-shuts-midwife-led-centres-england

Cassidy, T. 2006. *Birth: The Surprising History of How We Are Born.* New York, NY: Grove Press.

Child Poverty Action Group, Church of England and Nuffield Foundation. 2021. "'It feels as though my third child doesn't matter': The impact of the two-child limit after four years." https://cpag.org.uk/sites/default/files/files/policypost/It_feels_as_though_my_third_child_doesnt_matter.pdf.

Clark Callister, L. et al. 2003. "The pain of childbirth: Perceptions of culturally diverse women." *Pain Management Nursing* 4 (4): 145–154.

Collins, C. 2019. *Making Motherhood Work*. Princeton: Princeton University Press.

Collins, C. 2020. "Two new moms return to work: One in Seattle, one in Stockholm." *Harvard Business Review,* March 3, 2020. https://hbr.org/2020/03/two-new-moms-return-to-work-one-in-seattle-one-in-stockholm.

Committee on the Elimination of All Forms of Discrimination against Women (CEDAW). 1981. "Convention on the elimination of all forms of discrimination against women." www.un.org/womenwatch/daw/cedaw/text/econvention.htm

Cook, K. and C. Loomis, 2012. "The impact of choice and control on women's childbirth experiences." *The Journal of Perinatal Education* 21 (3): 158–168.

Cooper, M. 2017. *Family Values: Between Neoliberalism and the New Social Conservatism*. New York: Zone Books.

Cooper, M. 2020. "Neoliberalism's Family Values: Welfare, Human Capital, and Kinship." In *Nine Lives of Neoliberalism*, edited by D. Plehwe, Q. Slobodian, and P. Mirowski, 95–119. London, New York: Verso.

Department of Health, NHS. 2007. "Maternity matters." https://webarchive.nationalarchives.gov.uk/20130103035958/www.dh.gov.uk/prod_consum_dh/groups/dh_digitalassets/@dh/@en/documents/digitalasset/dh_074199.pdf

2016. "Your NHS care: Leaflet 5 - Having a baby." https://assets.publishing.service.gov.uk/government/uploads/system/uploads/attachment_data/file/520211/choice-Leaflet_5.pdf.

Department for Work and Customs. 2019. "Support for a child conceived without your consent." https://assets.publishing.service.gov.uk/government/uploads/system/uploads/attachment_data/file/810743/support-for-a-child-concieved-without-your-consent-0619.pdf.

Einion, Dr. A. 2017. "The medicalisation of childbirth." In *The Social Context of Birth*, edited by C. Squire, 169–180. New York: Routledge.

European Convention on Human Rights (ECHR). 1950. "Council of Europe." www.echr.coe.int/documents/convention_eng.pdf.

Försäkringskassen. n.d. "Child allowance (English)." Accessed June 2, 2021. www.forsakringskassan.se/english/parents/when-the-child-is-born/child-allowance.

Friedman, M. 1988. "Day care: The problem." *National Review* 40 (13): 14.

Goodman, P. 2018. "In Britain, austerity is changing everything." *The New York Times,* May 28, 2018. https://nyti.ms/2J8ApU5

Gov.UK. 2020. "Get childcare: step by step: 15 hours free childcare for 3 and 4-year-olds." www.gov.uk/help-with-childcare-costs/free-childcare-and-education-for-2-to-4-year-olds?step-by-step-nav=f237ec8e-e82c-4ffa-8fba-2a88a739783b

2021a. "Universal credit." Accessed June 2, 2021. www.gov.uk/universal-credit.

2021b. "Families with more than 2 children: Claiming benefits." Accessed June 2, 2021. www.gov.uk/guidance/claiming-benefits-for-2-or-more-children.

High Court Administrative Court. 2018. *SC & Ors v. Secretary of State for Work and Pensions & Ors,* Weekly Law Reports 5425.

Johnson, J. E. 2015. "Giving birth in different worlds." *The New Yorker,* September 23, 2015. www.newyorker.com/culture/photo-booth/giving-birth-in-different-worlds

Jordan, B. 1983. *Birth in Four Cultures.* Montreal and London: Eden Press.

Kitroeff, N. and J. Silver-Greenberg, 2019. "Pregnancy discrimination is rampant inside America's biggest companies.) *The New York Times,* February 8, 2019. www.nytimes.com/interactive/2018/06/15/business/pregnancy-discrimination.html

Krapf, S. 2014. *Public Childcare Provision and Fertility Behavior: A Comparison of Sweden and Germany.* Opladen, Berlin, Toronto: Budrich UniPress.

Lee, S., A. Duvander, and S. Zarit. 2016. "How can family policies reconcile fertility and women's employment? Comparisons between South Korea and Sweden." *Asian Journal of Women's Studies* 22 (3): 269–288.

Lee, E., J. Macvarish, and S. Sheldon. 2018. "The 1967 abortion act fifty years on: Abortion, medical authority and the law revisited." *Social Science and Medicine* 212: 26–32.

Mason, R. 2014. "Child benefit may be limited to two children, says Iain Duncan Smith." *Guardian,* December 14, 2014. www.theguardian.com/society/2014/dec/14/child-benefit-limited-two-children-iain-duncan-smith.

McCourt, C. 2017. "Social support and childbirth." In *The Social Context of Birth,* edited by C. Squire, 193–212. New York: Routledge.

McKinnon, S. 2005. *Neo-Liberal Genetics: The Myths and Moral Tales of Evolutionary Psychology.* Chicago: Prickly Paradigm Press.

McLeish, J. and M. Redshaw. 2017. "A qualitative study of volunteer doulas working alongside midwives at births in England: mothers' and doulas' experiences." *Midwifery* 56: 53–60.

Mellor, M. 2020. "How austerity ruined the UK's health, in numbers." *WIRED UK,* February 26, 2020. www.wired.co.uk/article/austerity-health-impacts-uk-life-expectancy

Moorhead, J. 2006. "Different planets." *Guardian,* October 3, 2006. www.theguardian.com/lifeandstyle/2006/oct/03/healthandwellbeing.health

Mueller, B. 2019. "What is austerity and how has it affected British Society?" *The New York Times,* February 25, 2019. www.nytimes.com/2019/02/24/world/europe/britain-austerity-may-budget.html

Nordic Cooperation. 2020. "Pregnancy and childbirth in Sweden." www.norden.org/en/info-norden/pregnancy-and-childbirth-sweden

Nordic Cooperation. n.d. "Child allowance in Sweden." Accessed June 2, 2021. www.norden.org/en/info-norden/child-allowance-sweden.

Odent, M. 1984. *Birth Reborn.* New York: Random House.

OECD. 2020. "Is childcare affordable?" *Policy Brief on Employment, Labour and Social Affairs,* 1–13.

OECD Family Database. n.d. "PF2.1 Parental leave systems." www.oecd.org/els/family/database.htm

Office of the High Commissioner for Human Rights. 2018. "Statement on visit to the United Kingdom, by Professor Philip Alston, United Nations Special Rapporteur on extreme poverty and human rights." www.ohchr.org/Documents/Issues/Poverty/EOM_GB_16Nov2018.pdf.

Oppenheim, M. 2019. "Women being plagued with debt due to gender pay gap, skyrocketing childcare costs and sexism, campaigners say." *The Independent,* December 3, 2019. www.independent.co.uk/news/uk/home-news/women-debt-stress-mental-health-credit-payday-loan-pay-gay-a9235621.html

2020. "There are hundreds more like me, says woman sacked for being pregnant." *The Independent,* January 10, 2020. www.independent.co.uk/news/uk/home-news/pregnant-woman-sacked-discrimination-work-baby-tribunal-employment-a9278736.html

Pregnant Then Screwed. 2016. "I started to regret having my baby and I am just now trying to come to terms with my financial situation and pull myself back together." *Pregnant Then Screwed,* May 3, 2016. https://pregnantthenscrewed.com/staging/4802/2016/05/03/3999-2/.

2020. "Extending the 3 month time limit." https://pregnantthenscrewed.com/extending-the-3-month-time-limit/.

Prochaska, E. 2020. "Human rights law and challenging dehumanisation in childbirth." In *Childbirth, Vulnerability and Law: Exploring Issues of Violence and Control,* edited by C. Pickles and J. Herring, 132–139. New York: Routledge

Ralph, L. et al. 2019. "Self-reported physical health of women who did and did not terminate pregnancy after seeking abortion services: A cohort study." *Annals of Internal Medicine* 171 (4): 238–247.

Raphael, D., and T. Bryant, 2004. "The welfare state as a determinant of women's health: support for women's quality of life in Canada and four comparison nations." *Health Policy* 68: 63–79.

Robertson, E. 2015. "'To be taken seriously': Women's reflections on how migration and resettlement experiences influence their healthcare needs during childbearing in Sweden." *Sexual & Reproductive Healthcare* 6 (2): 59–65.

Rocca, C. et al. 2021. "Emotions over five years after denial of abortion in the United States: Contextualizing the effects of abortion denial on women's health and lives." *Social Science and Medicine* 269 (January): 1–9.

Saini, A. 2017. *Inferior: How Science Got Women Wrong and the New Research That's Rewriting the Story*. Boston: Beacon Press.

Saxonberg, S. 2013. "From defamilialization to degenderization: Toward a new welfare typology." *Social Policy and Administration* 47(1): 26–49.

Squire, C. 2017. "Women, poverty and childbirth." In *The Social Context of Birth*, edited by C. Squire, 33–51. Routledge: New York.

Stuckler, D. et al. 2017. "Austerity and health: the impact in the UK and Europe." *European Journal of Public Health* 27 (4): 18–21.

Sweden.se. 2020. "Family-friendly life the Swedish way." https://sweden.se/society/family-friendly-life-the-swedish-way

Williams, R. 1979. *Politics and Letters: Interviews with New Left Review*. New York and London: New Left Books.

World Bank. 2019. "Maternal mortality ratio (modeled estimate, per 100,000 live births)." https://data.worldbank.org/indicator/SH.STA.MMRT

World Health Organization. 2018. "Intrapartum care for a positive childbirth experience." *WHO Recommendations*. Geneva: WHO.

Wrede, S. et al. 2008. "Equity and dignity in maternity care provision in Canada, Finland and Iceland." *Canadian Journal of Public Health* 99 (2): 16–S21.

Zylbersztejn, A. et al. 2018. "Child mortality in England compared with Sweden: a birth cohort study." *The Lancet (British Edition)* 391 (10134): 2008–2018.

14 Who Is Responsible for Children's Food?

JENNIFER PATICO

At school, what should kids eat for lunch? Mundane as this question seems, this chapter suggests that the answer we give can put us anywhere along a political and ideological spectrum. On the one hand, if we feel that people should choose their own meals and that parents, not schools, should police what their kids eat, we run the risk of bringing the larger society's inequalities into the lunchroom. If, on the other hand, we allow for state-sponsored meals, we run the risk of losing control over a basic aspect of our lives, and ceding it to the whims of outside political actors. What to do?. Patico argues that as things stand, in the United States enshrining individual choice and responsibility around student eating habits has led to a situation in which much school food is suspect and wealthy parents are able to separate their own children from eating it. In the context of a society shaped increasingly by market imperialism, this is the downside of privileging an ideal of consumer choice as well as the ideal of taking individual responsibility for optimizing your children's meals. One possible corrective to this is to consider what school lunches would look like under several different types of collective planning and alternative moral scrutiny which challenges structural inequalities and corresponding differences in the purchasing power of parents.

14.1 Introduction: Granola Parents, Cheese Puffs, and "Hamburgers with Real Hamburger"

When I first met Barbara, an administrator at an Atlanta, Georgia school that I call "Hometown Charter," she told me that parents there tended to fall into two distinct groups: they were either "green freaks" and "healthy food freaks" – also known as "granola parents" – or they were the type of parents who brought in cupcakes with blue frosting from a local grocery store chain for children's birthday celebrations and jugs of inexpensive, highly processed cheese puffs for classroom snacks. With this scheme of categories set out, Barbara made clear that the school's own nutritional priorities aligned more with those of the "healthy food freaks"; teachers encouraged parents to bring in items such as fruit, cheese, and crackers rather than highly processed or sugary snack foods. The job of school staff, as Barbara saw it, was to help educate people about what was best for their kids without offending them. She noted, too, that differences around food choices were connected with differences in "socioeconomics." Yet she believed some adults at Hometown who might otherwise object to the sugary and processed foods being brought in by other parents tried to "honor the cheese puffs for the children's sake" (Patico, 2020: 152–153).

When the school later made plans to hire a new chef – someone who would be an employee of the school itself, rather than a contractor similar to the one they currently used for their cafeteria lunches – another administrator explained to me that in her view, the best candidate for the job would be someone who had experience in food service at Whole Foods (a grocery store chain with a focus on organic products and generally considered to be expensive) or a similar establishment, yet also was aware that children preferred simple and familiar foods. In her view, children needed "hamburgers with real hamburger... [When] it's done in turkey, it looks different and so then the kids are a little skeptical of it." The foods offered children at school had to be "taster-friendly... Just really making it more like it's a destination restaurant down at the end of the hall [so that they would say,] 'Yeah, I'm going to lunch and I'm going to buy lunch today'." In this way, children might be enticed to choose school lunch rather than bringing lunches and snacks from home, and the school's lunch program would become more popular and sustainable.

Hometown Charter is part of the Atlanta public school system, but as a charter school, it also stands somewhat apart from that system. The school is free to attend but follows a distinctive, educationally progressive curriculum and has greater independence to make decisions on issues from course offerings to lunch menus, albeit within certain state and federal guidelines. While many public school districts, including Atlanta Public Schools, employ large contractors to provide school lunch service, Hometown was able to hire a separate, smaller contractor – and later its own in-house chef. As an anthropologist conducting immersive ethnographic research at Hometown, I spent countless hours in informal contexts of participant-observation: helping out in the elementary school cafeteria, helping to teach classes in the middle school, attending PTA meetings and parent discussion groups, and in some cases, sharing meals with families in their own homes, as well as conducting in-depth interviews. As I became more deeply familiar with Hometown's community, I tracked the ways in which adults (as well as children themselves) perceived and enacted social differences through food choices and food talk; and I returned often in my mind to Barbara's notion of "honoring the cheese puffs for the children's sake." What did this statement suggest about the things considered to be at stake in adults' conflicts around children's food? And what did deliberations about proper chefs and lunch programs reveal about the practical struggles and ideological assumptions underlying collective and institutional decisions about food for children?

To be sure, these discussions were about food quality: Barbara and like-minded parents considered "natural," less processed foods to be more wholesome and nutritionally desirable for children than with artificially dyed cupcakes and cheese puffs. Their concerns are best understood against the broader background of an industrial food economy in which many US adults worry about whether the content of foods will be harmful to their children – whether because of hidden toxins or hidden sugars – given a relatively poorly regulated food production system (MacKendrick, 2018; Patico, 2020). Middle-class parents devote resources of time, money, and knowledge to protecting their children from these potential harms. Those resources are, of course, inequitably available, and Barbara recognized as much by pointing to the role of "socioeconomics" at the school. Moreover, she seemed to suggest that middle-class, nutrition-conscious adults at Hometown often refrained from judging (or at least expressing judgment about) food choices they found suboptimal. These adults were not concerned only about their own children's well-being, then, and not only about food quality, but also about the maintenance of a larger community fabric and the preservation of positive relationships across social and economic difference.

Such dilemmas are entangled with parents' and consumers' experiences of living in a neoliberal economy, and as such are underlaid by specific kinds of assumptions that are interrogated in this volume. In the context of neoliberalism, not only do parents bear the burden of protecting their children from what they understand to be the dangers of a poorly regulated industrial food economy, but they also tend to accept implicitly that managing these burdens is rightly part of the task of parenthood: feeding children well is the responsibility of individual parents who make discerning consumer choices and resource-intensive investments for the benefit of their own families, rather than primarily a shared, societal project. Indeed, in neoliberal settings, individuals are expected "to make choices about lifestyles, their bodies, their education, and their health ... It is not simply 'consumer sovereignty' but rather a moralization and ... a regulated transfer of choice-making responsibility from the state to the individual in the social market" (Peters 2016, 301; see also Ganti 2014, 94–96). Even relatively collective endeavors such as school food programming tend to be guided by ideas about consumer taste and agency – not only adults', but also children's – as the story about Hometown's search for a new school chef illustrated.

This chapter does not offer any simple answers to what children actually should eat. It does interrogate, drawing from my Hometown study, how conversations about children's food in the US problematize individual parents' comportment and consumer choices and, in the process, end up sidelining some of the same interlocutors' ideals of social inclusion and equity. As we shall see, certain values and assumptions are easily smuggled into conversations about food, health, child socialization, and inequality, in ways that often go unnoticed so that even those who care deeply about both their own children's bodies and efforts toward broader social justice end up pitting one concern against the other. What role do neoliberal assumptions about personal responsibility for individual well-being play here, and how might reflecting on this invite us to think about alternative approaches to the well-being of children and of the social fabric – especially given that people like Hometown parents have priorities for their communities that seem ill-served by the individualist consumer approach to children's food?

Following discussion of these matters at Hometown, we shall turn to sociologist Janet Poppendieck for case study examples from another US setting (a universal free breakfast program in Rhode Island) as well a social democratic one (Sweden's free lunch program). Most recently, measures taken in the context of the COVID-19 pandemic in the United States have created new openings for school meal reform, though at this writing, the future of those programs is unclear. Universal school breakfast and lunch programs demonstrate how a state-led approach to children's food provisioning has been shown particularly, though not exclusively, beneficial to children of lower-income households – even if issues of food equity are far more complex to address than the simple provision of free meals can achieve.

The primary aim of this chapter, however, is not to outline specific policies to be implemented so much as it is to interrogate certain ideas about who is responsible for feeding children properly and why. To do so, we will consider broadly how responsibility for food quality at large – and for children's food in particular – has been framed differently in settings where neoliberal assumptions about the respective roles of the state and of individual parents are less hegemonic, or where they have been actively challenged. For although neoliberal political economy is powerful around the world, it remains true that such assumptions do not hold in every contemporary cultural and market context equally. Even as we think both critically and empathetically about the situations in which parents and administrators find themselves, recognition of such variability should open the way for thinking about alternative framings.

14.2 Neoliberal Framings of Food Responsibility in a Diverse Urban Community

The school I call Hometown is located close to downtown Atlanta, Georgia, in the United States, in an area once home primarily to lower-income, African Americans but increasingly also to relatively affluent, often white home owners. Hometown is a public charter school serving elementary through middle schoolers (kindergarten through 8th grade, ages approximately 5 to 14) and is free to attend, though admission is governed by a lottery due to high demand for spots. The school is known for its progressive educational approach, with significant attention given to socioemotional development and project-centered learning. Circa 2013 when I was in the thick of my research there, school statistics indicated that the elementary grades were about 57 percent Caucasian (the term used in their official records) and 30 percent African American, while middle schoolers were 50 percent African American and 33 perecnty Caucasian; across the board about 10–11% identified as multi-racial.

As one measure of the economic circumstances of the school's families, in 2014 about 20 percent of the school's families qualified for free or reduced lunch (FRL), meaning that the school's lunch program was supported partly through tax monies (which provided subsidies for meals for students from lower-income households) and partly by per-meal payments by self-paying students (and faculty). Under the Healthy, Hunger-Free Kids Act of 2010, schools where more than 40 percent of students come from households already enrolled in government assistance programs such as SNAP (Supplemental Nutrition Assistance Program) can supply free meals to all students (Blad 1 June 2021); Hometown had fallen significantly below that level at the time of my fieldwork, though just a few years before the FRL rate had been in the 40 percent range. The downward shift seems to reflect overall changes in the demographics of a gentrifying neighborhood as well as comparatively high demand for the spots by white and relatively affluent residents in the area.

Over the course of my research (2011–2015), I interviewed fifty-two adults (forty-two women and ten men), both parents and staff members, of whom thirty-eight self-identified as white, Caucasian, or European-American (including three who also identified as Chicano or Hispanic), nine as Black or African American, and five using other racial or ethnic categories (such as Filipino American or Mexican American). Their household incomes, when known, varied from $12,000 to $340,000 per year, with a median of $104,000. Thus while the interview group overall skewed more white and affluent than the school's population due to participant self-selection, some of Hometown's economic and racial diversity was reflected there. As a generalization, I refer to this parent group as "middle class" not only to reflect their median incomes, but also because of their high levels of education, irrespective of income. Most if not all were college-educated, and the group included professionals with graduate degrees (such as lawyers) as well as career teachers, stay-at-home parents, and others.

Many of my interlocutors at Hometown expressed attitudes and assumptions that, over the course of my fieldwork, I came to understand as exemplifying a certain kind of "neoliberal responsibilization." Often critical of the industrial food complex, they devoted a great deal of attention, information-gathering, and school volunteer hours to the attempt to ensure that what their children consumed was optimal for their ongoing physical health as well as their behavioral modulation. Further, a theme of shared concern among parents and teachers was that children had limited (though hopefully developing) capacities to "self-regulate" their behavior, including their eating: for example, to moderate their desires for sugary or junky snacks in favor of foods understood to be nutritionally beneficial. Though children's limited capacity for self-regulation (and the desirability of the same) may sound like truisms to many Americans, the concept has been thematized particularly in the fields of child psychology and development and increasingly popularized in the late twentieth and early twenty-first centuries, paralleling calls for workers' self-management, flexibility, and emotional intelligence in the neoliberal labor economies of the United States and beyond. At Hometown, parents and educators felt responsible for teaching skills of self-management and for regulating children and their consumption in the meantime, often not only through direct interaction with children but also through activities such as participating in school committees or complaining to school authorities about vending machine and cafeteria offerings (Patico, 2020). Yet as we shall see, Hometowners' efforts and the principles and priorities that drove them were sometimes mutually conflictual.

Many of these middle-class parents were indeed highly nutrition-conscious; they talked about favoring "real" and natural foods over highly industrialized and processed ones, and they worried about high levels of sugar and how this could negatively impact their children's weight, behavior, or mood. Some invested time in tasks such as growing their own vegetables; others preferred to buy such products from grocery stores or from local CSAs (community-supported agricultural enterprises, in which customers pay a set subscription rate to receive weekly or monthly boxes of produce from local farms). During the year of my most intensive fieldwork – and just after my conversation with the administrator about a new chef – the school indeed developed an exceptionally high-quality lunch program that focused on fresh foods, some of it locally acquired. It was orchestrated by a professional restaurant chef who managed to balance federal regulations and budget concerns with his own conceptions of healthful, appealing, and varied menus. Many parents seemed to applaud the new program, but there was still concern among them at times about less than ideal foods being served at classroom snacks, after-school groups, and extracurriculars.

In fact, despite Barbara's comment about "honoring the cheese puffs," items such as rice krispie treats being made in an after-school program or brightly colored, sugary breakfast cereal being brought for a school snack sometimes were cause for comment and consternation by parents and teachers. Although adults sometimes talked about training their children's tastes and how to do so effectively, there also was some general sense that children were naturally disposed toward sugary, mild-tasting, familiar foods and would always gravitate to these if available. It was on adults, then, to provide foods that were more nutritionally adequate and to socialize children into eating these foods habitually and ultimately voluntarily – though it was also accepted that sometimes sweet treats such as birthday cakes were a normal part of childhood and in that sense, to some extent desirable. Thus nutritional ideals and notions about "normal" childhood and necessary indulgences were sometimes in tension with one another, with caregivers seeking to moderate children's eating without eliminating what were often held to be natural childhood pleasures.

Similar tensions are evident in school lunch programs around the nation, exacerbated by the economic exigencies faced by school administrators. Sociologist Janet Poppendieck (2010) interviewed dozens of US school food service directors, managers, and workers, as well as speaking with legislators, local officials, and food activists, to document the struggles faced by cafeteria managers who are working to meet federal nutritional guidelines on limited school budgets.[1] Across the United States, discounted meals are made available to students who qualify based on their household incomes – about half of US students, according to recent statistics – and these programs are supported by tax-funded governmental programs.[2] To make ends meet and establish any kind of economy of scale, schools need students to participate in their lunch programs rather than opting out and bringing packed lunches from home, whether they are self-paying or drawing tax funds to the school by qualifying for FRL – hence the apparent necessity for cafeteria menu planners to appeal to children's consumer tastes. In some cases, "special" (not necessarily more healthful) items deemed more appealing are offered at an extra charge, in vending machines or

---

[1] For more information on the National School Lunch Program in the United States, see www.ers.usda.gov/topics/food-nutrition-assistance/child-nutrition-programs/national-school-lunch-program#:~:text=In%20fiscal%20year%20(FY)%202019,total%20cost%20of%20%2414.1%20billion.

[2] https://nces.ed.gov/programs/digest/d17/tables/dt17_204.10.asp. See also https://nces.ed.gov/fastfacts/display.asp?id=898.

in special lines, by lunchrooms to those students who can afford them. School-provided lunches often carry social stigma in the US, particularly when lower-income children who receive free and reduced-price lunches are separated out in lunchrooms from children who bring their lunches from home or opt to buy the more expensive lunch items many cafeterias offer (Poppendieck, 2010).

This separation and stigma dynamic was not particularly salient at Hometown, as far as I could tell. Perhaps about half the students took advantage of the school lunch program on any given day, few "extra" food items were available on campus, students of varying income levels participated in the school lunch program, their seating did not depend on what kind of lunch they had, and the charter school was able to use flexible hiring and ingenuity to create a relatively appealing lunch program for both paying and non-paying students. Nonetheless, administrators found themselves performing tenuous balancing acts to provide food that satisfied the requirements of legislators, parents, and students in an economically feasible way. As we have seen, the challenge was to provide what parents and staff thought to be high-quality nutrition and to cater to children's consumer tastes for the sake of children's pleasure and their perceived distinct natures – and ultimately in order to support the bottom line of the school lunch program by getting children to want to purchase the meals. The school's new chef, lauded by some parents for providing thoughtful menus of scratch-made food, emphasized his own mindfulness about students' consumerist leanings when he remarked that he used xanthum gum to thicken his teriyaki sauce because he knew it was important that it should feel familiar to children – especially those who were particularly skeptical of school lunches. Xanthum gum, he said, gave the same mouth feel as the teriyaki sauce these children might have tried at shopping mall food courts.

Not only did school administrators wish to please children in order to meet a bottom line, but adults at Hometown were more broadly concerned about what constituted adequate control versus over-control when it came to children's food. This balance had implications for the way people talked (or didn't talk) about social inequality in the context of children's food. On one hand, parents gave many examples that reflected the importance they attached to carefully managing their children's intake of food – as a matter of general health, sometimes for the sake of helping to regulating mood and behavior, and generally as a means of teaching children self-control and self-management. Parents' narratives often placed implicit emphasis on the importance of caring enough to pay attention to these things and to educate oneself about nutrition. These ideals are connected tightly with fundamental understandings about the importance of individual choice in the US context, where raising children is often considered a

> private arrangement that parents choose and thus are fully responsible for managing. This rhetoric of choice obscures larger social forces while instilling the idea that individuals have autonomy and freedom ... [leaving room for] very little analysis about how such choices are constrained by larger external factors such as social class, neoliberal economic pressures that emphasize individual responsibility and privatization, and the persistent wage gap between men and women. (Huisman and Joy, 2014: 100)

Parents and staff at Hometown also spoke about the high level of parental engagement that was both expected and carried out at the school, with parents not only bringing in snacks for the children's classes to share but also helping out with tasks during the school day, working to organize fundraisers, and spending money at them. Indeed, people at Hometown tended to feel that "engaged" parenting was an unquestionable good and part of what made Hometown a better school – or at least more desirable to them – than the local non-charter elementary school whose population was, overall, lower-income and less white than Hometown's. At the same time, somewhat contradictorily but in keeping with the importance attached in the US cultural context to autonomy and self-determination, adults – in their passingly critical comments about "helicopter parents" or their insistence that their efforts with their own children's nutrition were measured and not excessive or "crazy" – expressed the understanding that to excessively control or restrain another person's choices, even a child's, was distasteful, perhaps even morally suspect. The overall message was that one needed to be diligent and "engaged" but not overly controlling: a delicate and elusive balance.

Middle-class parents' concerns for their own children's well-being and for the foods that enter their bodies are reasonable in the context of industrial food production and poor regulation (MacKendrick, 2018), but looking at these problems through a moralized lens of parental approach – in which one must seemingly strike a perfect balance of careful regulation yet not bear a "controlling" persona; in which one must socialize children into autonomous self-regulation but must not excessively constrain their consumer choices in the meantime; and in which judgments about "care" can obscure the vital role of resources – does not much diminish (even more affluent) parents' worry and feelings of vulnerability around food and parenting, and it can undermine sincere efforts toward social inclusion. Many, though not all, parents prioritized maintenance of diversity in income levels when they debated updates to the school's lottery system (which neighborhoods would be given first priority to the school?); and they often expressed sensitivity to the financial and logistical constraints experienced by lower-income households within the school community. All of these implicitly conflicting judgments about food, care, and social equity were folded into their attempts to "honor the cheese puffs."

Tension between critiques of industrial food production and (sometimes occluded) matters of socioeconomic inequity is not uncommon in popular, even progressive discourse about food in the United States. For example, Julie Guthman (2007) has pointed out that Michael Pollan's highly popular book *The Omnivore's Dilemma* ultimately champions the making of informed individual choices about food rather than encouraging strategies such as writing to Congress about the harm wrought in the industrial food system by government corn subsidies, or to the FDA about food additives. This stance leads attention away from structural inequality and emphasizes the role of personal knowledge and choice, reinforcing the "highly privileged and apolitical" idea that some people are simply more enlightened than others (for example, those who eat "bad" industrial food or are obese) (2007: 78–79). In the realm of children's food in particular, this places the onus of responsibility for desirable outcomes primarily on the shoulders of individual parents working for their own children, each with highly variable resources and constraints, as opposed to the pooled resources of civic institutions or collectivities.

What are the alternatives to thinking about children's food in terms of the individual choice and prerogative to avoid harm to one's own individual child through great investment of time and resources? At the more socially coordinated level of the school lunch program, are there other options than feeling beholden to children as individual consumer choice-makers in order to make the bottom line of such programs work?

14.3 Other Approaches to Food Responsibility

The answers to these questions may lie in structural reforms as well as philosophical and moral reframings. If many middle-class parents are highly absorbed by the problem of seeking to ensure that the foods and other items their families consume do not contain harmful amounts of toxins, my intent here is not to question the wisdom of that goal but rather to imagine shifting the responsibility for those tasks away from individual parents and toward governmental and corporate bodies. This could take various forms, including greater investment of resources in, and transparency around, mechanisms for the assessment of health risks in food production (MacKendrick, 2018: 156–158). In the case of school lunch reform, as Allen and Guthman (2006: 412) have put it, "rather than concede the inevitable disparities of devolution, public funding and state support should be used to effect improvement across the board for all children, not just those who happen to be in 'progressive' or affluent schools" where privately funded Farm to School programs – or carefully planned menus such as those offered by Hometown's unusually innovative chef – present localized, partial solutions that are not easily scalable (see also Poppendieck, 2010: 243).

Instead, Poppendieck argues that all public school children in the United States should receive free lunches as a matter of course, and that this initiative could and should be funded by the federal tax structure. As noted above, US school cafeteria managers struggle to balance conflicting pressures and may cater to children's perceived consumer tastes in the interest of balancing their budgets. Poppendieck frames this strategy as an "abdication of adult authority and responsibility" and a failure to make schools "places where democratic ideals and beliefs are built into the fabric of the day," that is, where fair treatment is given to students regardless of class, race, or other forms of difference (Poppendieck, 2010: 264, 271).

To demonstrate what is possible, Poppendieck presents the success story of a dedicated group of activists who worked to bring free universal breakfast to a school in Rhode Island, and eventually to all schools in the state with a 40 percent or higher FRL rate. The Campaign to Eliminate Childhood Poverty in Rhode Island faced significant opposition in this effort, but it began by simply distributing muffins in the school yard with the help of a sympathetic school nurse.

Slowly, the activists were able to convince school districts to formalize and expand the universal free breakfast program, as it demonstrated clear success. Participation among students was high, which meant that reports of behavioral problems were down because the students were no longer hungry at school. High participation also meant that the food contractor was happy, as it was making more money.

Strikingly, participation numbers were up not only among families who previously had had to pay for their own meals, but even more so among families who previously had qualified for free or reduced-price meals. In schools with universal free breakfast in Rhode Island, 50 percent more children who qualified for FRL ate breakfast as compared to those at schools that provided free breakfast only for those who qualified by income. In other words, when meals were free for all, lower-income students ate more – a result Poppendieck attributes to the lifting of stigma that came with universalization (Poppendieck, 2010: 249). Now FRL and paying students were not separated, spatially or otherwise, in the context of the school meal; and no staff member caused embarrassment by drawing attention to students' unpaid bills, since no one was charged in the first place (ibid.: 253).

The implication of this is that relatively diverse urban districts stand to make the biggest gains in student participation with universalization, as opposed to either the wealthiest schools (where there is less need) or the ones with the highest rates of FRL (where the stigma attached to poverty may be a less salient factor, and which were granted eligibility for universal free meals by the 2010 legislation mentioned above) (Poppendieck, 2010: 254). Hometown is just this kind of urban district. The exclusionary, segregated cafeteria atmosphere Poppendieck describes as common in many public schools did not seem to exist there; yet, as we have seen, even in Hometown's relatively innovative and socially aware community, inequality manifested and was reinforced in talk about children's food. Poppendieck's proposal for universal school food may help to ameliorate child hunger and social tensions in such settings, not to mention in public school settings like those she observed elsewhere in the US, where the organization of lunch programs made for more obvious conflict and social harm.

Poppendieck offers Sweden's school lunch program, funded for grades 1–9 since at least the 1940s, as further proof of the soundness of universal school lunch (see also Osowski et al., 2015: 556).

Sweden's social democratic system provides universal welfare support, with public services largely distributed equally across the population; by contrast with more liberal democratic systems such as that of the United States (where "a minimal state is accentuated and social policies are directed only at the poor"), in Sweden it is understood that the school is an institution that carries out some "social and health-related political activities" also associated with the family (Osowski et al., 2015: 556–557). When Poppendieck traveled to Sweden and observed a cafeteria lunch in session, she concluded that "the program had no taint of poverty ... There was nothing for sale, so differences in purchasing power were not on display. No one was defined by whether or not they could afford to bypass the lunch, and as far as I could see, no one did" (Poppendieck, 2010: 264).

In the case of Rhode Island, where universal breakfast service ended up being so successful in its social impacts and its financial outcomes, initial opposition often was more philosophical than financial: critics asked whether ordering beds would be the next step after providing free breakfast, the implication being that the school system was being asked to fund what was properly the domain of the private home (Poppendieck, 2010: 245). Indeed, Poppendieck identifies Americans' deeply held belief that paying for children's food is a parental and not a societal responsibility as a key obstacle to innovation. To many Americans, inability to provide a child with adequate food is considered a failure, and further, it seems objectionable for taxpayers to pay for the food of affluent children (ibid.). Such attitudes are shaped by assumptions that tend to be prevalent in the United States concerning individual responsibility for personal health and well-being, and about consumerism as the primary path available for the exercise of agency and moral superiority – dynamics that have only intensified in the context of neoliberalism and the retrenchment of social welfare programs (Patico, 2020: 8–13).

Change may be underway in the context of the COVID-19 pandemic, as we shall see, and a cross-cultural perspective helps to highlight that such norms indeed are historically and culturally specific and that there indeed are other ways to frame food responsibility (see Patico, 2020: 104–108, 191–193). For example, Yuson Jung (2016) contrasts individualist thinking about private responsibility in food consumption with belief systems more popular in postsocialist Bulgaria, where citizens interact with capitalist markets against a longer-term background of familiarity with state socialism. In the state socialist economies of the USSR and Eastern Europe, not only were welfare supports provided relatively equitably by the government, but also the entire apparatus of production and distribution was organized by the state – albeit with variable effectiveness, as demonstrated by the well-known consumer shortages experienced in the socialist bloc – rather than by the mechanisms of a free market.

Given this experience, when faced with new questions about food quality in the postsocialist context, Bulgarian citizens were less likely to focus on the seemingly "intrinsic, superior" moral qualities of specific food commodities, as Americans might be more likely to do, but rather addressed concerns about "bad, fraudulent, or fake food" by asking pointed questions about governance and responsibility (Jung, 2014: 52–53).

Postsocialist citizens would ask: Who can I hold accountable for the additives, chemicals and other artificial or hazardous stuff in the food I purchased? How do I trust that what I buy is safe for my body and my health? To them, individual responsibility at the point of purchase is not a complete answer because they do not believe structural problems can be fixed only through individual consumption practices. From this postsocialist perspective, it appears deeply problematic that many proponents of ethical foods in advanced capitalist societies privilege individual consumption as the productive point for alternative food practices to overcome structural problems. (Jung 2016: 301).

My aim here is not to argue that Bulgaria or other postsocialist states provide the best models for thinking about consumer satisfaction, but rather to point out that many consumers in strongly neoliberal settings conceptualize questions of responsibility, morality, and food safety quite differently from those with alternative experiences of state support and governance. In a state socialist context, for example, the notion of providing food for all children during the school day would seem entirely natural and accustomed. We will do well to take a broad range of experiences into account in order to reimagine the mechanisms that may serve communities and their goals best.

14.4 Working toward New Normativities for Children's Food

Indeed, it is at the level of the reimagination of responsibilities that we must work to address more adequately contemporary anxieties about the safety, desirability, and accessibility of various foods – and to help ameliorate the social inequalities that inform and sometimes are exacerbated by these very debates. What would such a reimagination involve? Julie Guthman (2007: 79) has quipped that Pollan's individualized, consumer-choice model of food responsibility and its social politics are difficult to stomach and even "make me crave some corn-based Cheetos." Likewise, at Hometown, I wondered whether "honoring the cheese puffs" – thinking about children's food not just in terms of individualized consumer choices for individual bodies, but about the harmony of a larger social collective – might involve refocusing middle-class parents' concerns away from their own children's bodies and toward commensality and risk-sharing in broader communities … perhaps even by quite literally sharing more cheese puffs across households and social divisions (Patico, 2020: 195). This is not quite a serious proposal, but in raising it, I really mean to ask: are moralized consumer judgment and individualized conceptions of food purity – the notion that to protect one's own child's body from suboptimal foods is paramount – serving any parents' objectives (or their children's health) particularly well?

Poppendieck suggests that we might reconceptualize school lunch and meet Americans' skepticism about universal school meals by acknowledging that US society requires children to attend school each day. Since the school day falls during mealtimes and food is needed to sustain energy and attention for learning, food might simply be considered an integral part of the institution and the services it entails (2010: 266). Such a reconceptualization indeed could be transformative, but a different set of circumstances has made universal meal provision more imaginable in the United States: during the COVID-19 pandemic, the federal government provided waivers to all public schools that allowed them to offer federally funded, universal free meals – including offsite or "grab and go" meals for students studying remotely – without verification of financial eligibility (Blad April 20, 2021). These waivers were extended through summer 2022, despite the fact that many US schools returned to in-person learning for the 2021–2022 school year. I learned from Hometown's chef that the school provided universally free meals for both on-campus and remote students in 2020–2021, and that he welcomed the extension of the eligibility waivers into the next school year – as well as the prospect of a more permanent version of the policy.

The future is not yet clear, as President Biden has moved not to universalize school meals indefinitely but to expand the school lunch program by making it easier for elementary schools to qualify for universal meal funding (dropping the required threshold of students from households already enrolled in federal income-based support programs from 40 percent to 25 percent) (Blad June 1, 2021). Pushing further, Vermont Senator Bernie Sanders and Minnesota Senator Ilhan Omar introduced the Universal School Meals Program Act of 2021, which would allow schools to offer free breakfast, lunch, and dinner to all students on a more permanent basis. Further, the bill moved to prohibit schools "from (1) physically segregating or otherwise discriminating against any child participating in the free breakfast program, or (2) overtly identifying a child participating in the program with a special token or announcement" (Congress.gov). Meanwhile, conservative legislators and groups such as the Heritage Foundation have criticized such plans, as Poppendieck might have predicted, on the premise that it is wasteful to extend meal support to less needy students (Blad June 1, 2021). As of March 31, 2022, the pandemic waivers were still set to expire on June 30 of that year. Funding to extend them had been excluded from a major Congressional spending bill passed earlier in the month; meanwhile, a new bipartisan bill hoped to extend the waivers through September 2023 (Ortiz, 2022).

While permanent legislation such as Sanders's and Omar's could ameliorate social inequality and child hunger, it is important also to recognize that universal provision of food to children in school would not necessarily make children's food equitable – even in the realm of school cafeteria food. The goal of such a program would need to be not only to put "healthy" (as defined by whom?) foods in the mouths of all schoolchildren, regardless of their socioeconomic status, but also to create a more inclusive and equitable, if not to say uniform, culture of children's food in these shared, public institutional contexts. Universalizing school lunch may indeed increase the flow of resources into schools, put food into hungry children's bellies, and reduce the stigma of separate free lunches for poorer children; but for more complex cultural and institutional reasons, consuming the same foods at lunchtime is unlikely on its own to eliminate concerns about classism or racism in school food, or in community discourse around food and social difference.

A Danish case study provides one example of how this can be true. Karrebaek illustrated how institutionally defined, normative definitions of "healthy" food can carry strong associations with nationhood and, concomitantly, can be exclusionary toward children whose families identify with other national or ethnic food traditions. In the Danish case (where universal school lunch is not in place and children bring packed lunches from home), minority families' relative affinity for traditional Danish culture and their integration into mainstream Danish society is judged in part according to their consumption (or lack thereof) of rye bread, considered a normative Danish food (Karrebaek, 2012, 2016). Hence when teachers emphasize to their pupils the value of rye bread as a healthy food, they also, in effect, engage in practices of shaming and exclusion of children whose families do not share normative Danish foodways. One can easily imagine similar dynamics playing out across race, ethnicity, and national origin in the US (even if universal school lunch would reduce the possibility of home lunches being brought to school and criticized there), and such inequities certainly must be considered across class as well. As sociologist Annette Lareau and others have highlighted, middle-class and working-class adults often express similar ideas about parenting (and food), but their practices are shaped by divergent life conditions and resources, and middle-class kids benefit from the relative similarity of their home and institutional environments (Bourdieu, 1992; Lareau, 2003: 236–238). Nutritional recommendations and policies are embedded and work within social structures and cultural belief systems, even when guided by science that aspires to be objective. In short, having a shared and free menu at school will not guarantee that all children and families are positioned equitably toward the foods served there.

Nor does it guarantee that institutional food suddenly will be deemed as appealing to children as shopping mall foods or homemade foods. In fact, in a recent Swedish study, researchers investigating contemporary adults' memories of their own school lunches revealed that they thought of the meals as "second-class," not only in terms of the food itself but also in terms of the environment in which it was served. While research participants did not oppose the idea of free public school meals, they tended to cast school lunches as inferior to home-cooked meals, which were associated with familial love and care. Students in Swedish schools had limited interaction with school lunch staff, which was hypothesized to negatively impact their views of the food itself (Osowski et al., 2015: 563–564; see also Nestle as cited in Poppendieck 2010: 274). Further, the researchers suggested that institutional food was seen by Swedes as "eaten out of necessity and ... characterized by a lack of choice" (564). This reminds us that in many contemporary settings, ideals of personal consumer responsibility for food quality govern tastes and behavior in ways that contextualize and may constrain school lunch programs and other attempts at more collectivist and state-led solutions.

With all this in mind, how might we think creatively about ways to create shared, equitable access to what (some of us might deem reasonably) "healthier" food for children while also remaining aware of other, persistent and often implicit, practices that reinforce social inequality and could work paternalistically in institutional food programs to devalue some groups' tastes in comparison to others'? How could we envision some new kind of success in reconfiguring and redistributing responsibility for children's food? How can we find new ways to provide collectively for the well-being of children while being circumspect about forms of inequality that might flourish even, or perhaps especially, in contexts of "universal" provisioning?

Alexis Shotwell (2016) provides a useful concept in a distinct context. Shotwell explains that in queer and feminist theory, normativity is typically discussed as something to be resisted: a harmful kind of discipline and an exclusionary mechanism. Yet she notes that normativity also can be framed as an expression of something good and something to be pursued, in contrast to normalization, which entails the disciplining and shutting down of options. Shotwell thus uses the qualifier "open" to name "normativities that prioritize flourishing and tend toward proliferation, not merely replacing one norm with another" (2016: 155).

Spurred by this conceptualization, I ask: what might an open normativity for children's food and for school lunch programs entail? It would need to promote certain notions of health, perhaps some loose consensus ideas about basic nutritional priorities, while also not shutting down a broad array of possibilities for how those basic needs could be met. It would be based on a commitment not only to provide equity of access to "good" food, but also to pursue some kind of equity of opportunity to define what constitutes good food, albeit in the context of shared provisioning and collective funding, and with reference to nutritional science as well as diverse, historically and locally produced tastes. Structurally disadvantaged groups, particularly lower-income households with fewer resources to invest in time-consuming provisioning or to searching out nutritional information, would need to have their food concerns, strategies, tastes, and discourses incorporated into the local visioning of such programs so that they could meet the socionutritional needs of a broad spectrum of children (see Reese and Garth, 2020).

At Hometown, certain neoliberal understandings of individual and consumerist responsibility are influential and shape middle- and upper-class parents' strategies, but they do not fully encompass nor do justice to the same subjects' wishes for a more equitable society. Parents' anxiety to provide optimal nutrition for their own children, while reasonable under the circumstances in which they find themselves, can also work to reinforce class privilege and division, inasmuch as they depend upon individualist consumer responsibility as the primary lens for approaching the well-being of children. Programs such as universal school breakfast or lunch, on their own, constitute no panacea for ensuring higher quality food for all children – nor for the more complicated task of ensuring that food quality is perceived and defined collaboratively and equitably across socioeconomic groups. Even so, such state-led measures may begin the work of increasing equity and, more broadly, of challenging neoliberal assumptions about where the responsibility for children's food really lies. Though imperfect or limited on their own, they may present some of the best starting places for new conversations about what a public, civic culture of children's food could or should be – by shifting the emphasis away from individual adults' protection of their own children's bodies and toward a different kind of thinking about food production, regulation, and institutional provisioning as things we do for a more collective, if far from uniform, body.

References

Allen, Patricia, and Julie Guthman. 2006. "From old school to farm to school: Neoliberalization from the ground up." *Agriculture and Human Values* 23 (4): 401–415.

Blad, Evie. 2021. "Citing Pandemic, USDA Waives School Meal Regulations Through June 2022." *Education Week,* April 20, 2021. Accessed at

Citing Pandemic, USDA Waives School Meal Regulations through June 2022 (edweek.org).

2021. "The Pandemic Brought Universal Free School Meals. Will They Stay?" *Education Week*, June 1, 2021. Accessed at The Pandemic Brought Universal Free School Meals. Will They Stay? (edweek.org).

Bourdieu, Pierre. 1992. *The Logic of Practice*. Stanford, CA: Stanford University Press.

Congress.gov. 2021–2022. "H.R.3115 - Universal School Meals Program Act of 2021117th Congress (2021–2022)." Accessed at H.R.3115 - 117th Congress (2021-2022): Universal School Meals Program Act of 2021 | Congress.gov | Library of Congress.

Ganti, Tejaswini. 2014. "Neoliberalism." *Annual Review of Anthropology* 43: 89–104.

Guthman, Julie. 2007. "Can't stomach it: How Michael Pollan made me want to eat cheetos." *Gastronomica* 7 (2): 75–79.

Huisman, Kim, and Elizabeth Joy. 2014. "The cultural contradictions of motherhood revisited: Continuities and changes." In *Intensive Mothering: The Cultural Contradictions of Modern Motherhood*, edited by Linda Ennis, 86–103. Bradford, ON: Demeter Press.

Jung, Yuson. 2014. "(Re)establishing the normal." *Gastronomica* 14 (4): 52–59.

2016. "Food provisioning and foodways in postsocialist societies: Food as medium for social trust and global belonging." In *Handbook of Food and Anthropology*, edited by Jakob Klein and James Watson, 289–307. New York: Bloomsbury.

Karrebaek, Martha Sif. 2012. "'What's in your lunch box today?': Health, respectability, and ethnicity in the primary classroom." *Journal of Linguistic Anthropology* 22 (1): 1–22.

2016. "Rye bread for lunch, lasagne for breakfast: Enregisterment, classrooms, and national food norms in superdiversity." In *Engaging Superdiversity: Recombining Spaces, Times and Language Practices*, edited by K. Arnaut, M. Karrebaek, M. Spotti, and J. Blommaert. Bristol, UK: Multilingual Matters.

Lareau, Annette. 2003. *Unequal Childhoods: Race, Class, and Family Life*. Berkeley: University of California Press.

MacKendrick, Norah. 2018. *Better Safe Than Sorry: How Consumers Navigate Exposure to Everyday Toxics*. Berkeley: University of California Press.

Ortiz, Erik. 2022. "Free School Meal Program, Set to Expire, Would Be Restored Under Senate Bill." NBSnews.com, March 31, 2022. Accessed at Free school meals program set to expire would be restored under Senate bill (nbcnews.com).

Osowski, Christine Persson, Helen Göranzon, and Christina Fjellström. 2010. "Perceptions and memories of the free school meal in Sweden." *Food, Culture & Society* 13 (4): 555–572.

Patico, Jennifer. 2020. *The Trouble with Snack Time: Children's Food and the Politics of Parenting.* New York: NYU Press.

Poppendieck, Janet. 2010. *Free for All: Fixing School Food in America.* Berkeley: University of California Press.

Reese, Ashante, and Hanna Garth. 2020. "Black food matters: An introduction." In *Black Food Matters: Racial Justice in the Wake of Food Justice*, edited by H. Garth and Ashante Reese. Minneapolis: University of Minnesota Press.

Shotwell, Alexis. 2016. *Against Purity: Living Ethically in Compromised Times.* Minneapolis: University of Minnesota Press.

15 | *How Should We Care for the Elderly?*

AMY CLOTWORTHY

One remarkable feature of market imperialism as it has affected welfare provision is just how deep it has become entrenched in the act of caring for people. Here, Clotworthy describes how the provision of eldercare in Denmark has been taken over by a system that aims to create idealized, active, and independent older people. Eldercare is thus increasingly subject to a "competition state" focused on optimizing costs by "responsibilizing" both care providers and senior citizens as rational and independent decision-makers. What Clotworthy shows, though, is that creating a welfare system with this sort of ideal in place runs the risk of ignoring the actual person sitting in front of you. The system acts more as a gatekeeper than a care provider, and thus leaves people alienated in their old age. Clotworthy contrasts this with elder-care systems that make a direct provision of care in order to show another way of caring for older adults.

15.1 Introduction

Do you know someone age 65 or older? Well, they're a problem. OK, let me explain: For starters, the rapid development of new medical advances along with improved standards of living over the past century means that humans are living longer than ever before. And, in many places around the world, the population subset of "elderly" people (typically defined as age 65 or over) will grow significantly in the coming years – e.g., in Europe, this group will increase "from 90.5 million at the start of 2019 to reach 129.8 million by 2050" (European Commission, 2020). Such a demographic trend – combined with decades of low birth rates across the European Union – means that population ageing is accelerating while population growth is slowing down. If this current trend continues unabated, it is expected to lead to significant changes in the structure of many societies: An increased number of adults age 65+ combined with persistent low fertility rates could lead to a marked reduction in the labor force and transform the age composition of the overall European population. This would consequently alter "the economy, social security and healthcare systems, the labor market, and many other spheres of our lives" (European Commission, 2014: 5; European Commission, 2018). Hmm – yeah, that might be a pretty big problem.

Another problem is that biomedical research has found evidence that people over age 50 have an increased risk of developing chronic diseases related to, for example, obesity, late-onset diabetes, and cardiovascular disease, which are among the most common *and* the most costly health problems facing older adults. But with access to improved medical treatment (including pharmaceuticals) and technologies, these conditions are no longer an immediate death sentence for most people in high-income Western countries. Instead, many people are simply living more years with several comorbidities; i.e., multiple chronic illnesses (Crimmins and Beltrán-Sánchez, 2010). Due to the first problem of demographic change plus the second problem of increased longevity rates, which is entangled with a third problem of people living longer with costly chronic illnesses, population ageing has developed into a worldwide matter of concern – one that has been positioned as problematic since the issue of global ageing started to outpace more general worries about a "population bomb" that could destabilise financial and social institutions (Ehrlich, 1968; Johnson et al., 1989).

What this means, quite simply, is that the person you know who is age 65 or older is a *market problem* because providing years (perhaps decades) of care for someone who is sick, frail, disabled, and/or slowly dying is *expensive*. But please don't jump on the panic bandwagon just yet. This neoliberal economic concern is exactly what I want to address in this chapter. In particular, I want to examine how a certain phenomenon (in this case, providing care to a rapidly growing number of older people) has been positioned as a problem – and as a threat that is potentially devastating not only to economies but also to the basic structures of Western society. And then I'd like to consider how we might address this "problem" through other solutions. Of course, the way in which government officials and health experts provide older people with supportive services and determine what kind of care they might need can vary widely in different settings around the world – and can produce varying results. But in order to illuminate how we should (and should *not*) care for the elderly, I take a closer look at one particular European welfare society.

In many neoliberal systems, a political economy of healthcare services has developed over the past few decades, which frames the individual citizen (or patient) as a "freely choosing" consumer (Højlund, 2006: 43); this also means that community health workers have become positioned as sellers/providers of care services that should meet the consumer's demand. In this bureaucratic configuration, both municipal health professionals and citizens are expected to act as rational individuals who should work together to make the "correct" cost–benefit choices. And, as this chapter demonstrates, some older people consider any municipal offer to be yet another service option, wherein they as consumers can freely choose what they prefer.

In what follows, I'll illustrate two moments of care within the same, neoliberal Danish eldercare system. In the first moment, the state's investment of resources produces an outcome that benefits *the state*; while in the second, the investment benefits *the person*. Despite both moments of care happening within the same system, we can see in their contrast: (1) the bureaucratic limitations of a neoliberal welfare state as the process of rationing care and pushing for a specific type of citizen outcome unfolds; and (2) the potential advantages of putting people before markets when the unpredictability of direct, human-to-human care is allowed to happen. As I discuss, understanding each of these moments has larger societal implications – which is important for all of us to consider as we age and have an increased need for support from healthcare professionals and our local communities. So, without further ado, let's go to Denmark ...

15.1.1 The "Problem" of Caring for the Elderly in Denmark

The Nordic countries (i.e., the Scandinavian countries of Denmark, Norway, and Sweden plus Finland and Iceland) share a similar welfare model of social and economic development. The so-called Nordic model is generally characterized by "a strong emphasis on security, safety, equality, rationality, foresight, and regulation" (Gullestad, 1989: 73). This model has led to these countries consistently being ranked high on global measures of economic freedom (see Henriksen, 2006; Lidegaard, 2009; Heritage Foundation, 2017). According to annual rankings compiled by the Organization for Economic

Co-operation and Development (OECD), Denmark typically ranks among the richest global societies (OECD, 2019). This small Scandinavian welfare society is also considered to be one of the "best places in the world to grow old," primarily due to its supportive eldercare sector (Healthcare Denmark, 2019). Among other things, this sector includes government- (i.e., taxpayer-) subsidized senior housing and long-term care facilities (*plejeboliger* and *plejehjem*, respectively) as well as a range of in-home welfare services that help support activities of daily living (ADLs)[1].

However, due to a range of socioeconomic, political, and cultural developments that have occurred since the 1960s, Danish politicians have often struggled to regulate and maintain the universal and equal social benefits available to citizens, even as they have continued to expand the public sector. As a result, Denmark's social-welfare institutions have been undergoing a set of transformations since they were first established a century ago. In order to facilitate these transformations – and following socioeconomic trends in other high-income Western countries, such as the United States and the United Kingdom – Denmark began to emerge as a "competition state" (Pedersen, 2011) in the 1980s and 1990s. This meant that politicians began to focus on welfare reforms and developing a more "neoliberal" society; for my purposes, this refers to "the new political, economic, and social arrangements within society that emphasize market relations, re-tasking the role of the state, and individual responsibility" (Springer et al., 2016: 2). This neoliberal emphasis on "individual responsibility" positions the citizen as an infinitely productive worker and consumer who has a responsibility to actively contribute to industrial growth, development, and innovation; i.e., to ensure that Denmark would be able to compete in the global marketplace (Pedersen, 2011; also Knudsen, 2007). The political transformations also included comprehensive reforms to the Danish state's traditional social-protection systems in both 1970 and 2007, which had major implications for the provision of welfare services at the local level.

Due to the growing older population, Danish politicians have a vested economic interest in making this sector as efficient and

---

[1] *Activities of daily living* (ADLs) are "basic self-care tasks (...). They include walking, feeding, dressing and grooming, toileting, bathing, and transferring" from one body position to another (Better Health While Aging, 2021).

cost-effective as possible. As of 2017, approximately 25.3 percent of Denmark's total population of 5,750,000 inhabitants were age 60 and above, and 4.4 percent were age 80 and above (United Nations, 2017; Statistics Denmark, 2018). This 80+ group has been expanding, from 52,000 in 1950 to 228,000 in 2010, and it will continue to grow by 150,000 people over the next decade; this is equivalent to a rate of 58 percent (Statistics Denmark, 2018). Based on the current population-growth projections, by 2053, more than one in every ten Danes will be over age 80. By 2057, there will be 667,000 or 2.5 times more people age 80+ than there are today (ibid.). This means that, by 2060, one in four Danes will be over age 65. Furthermore, the median age of Danes is continuing to increase with an old-age dependency ratio that is expected to increase sharply in the coming years, "reaching 54.2 dependents per 100 persons of working age by 2100" (WHO, 2012). In 2018, approximately 2.2 million Danes received public welfare benefits, with elderly citizens receiving a majority of social services through state/disability pensions, senior housing, and long-term care (LTC) facilities, Home Care and Home Help services, etc. (Statistics Denmark, 2019). For the past several years, the Danish government has also been trying to promote an increase in the birth rate in order to ensure that its working population is large enough to continue to support the social-welfare system (Hansen, 2015).

By and large, the tax-paying citizenry in Scandinavian welfare societies like Denmark supports the equal and collective nature of the welfare system, believing that anyone who is not able to care for themselves should have access to benefits and assistance organized by the state (Petersen, 2008; Lidegaard, 2009). However, the societal structures that ensure that older people can continue to receive supportive services and care (either in their own homes or an LTC facility) are under increasingly intense pressure. And, because this stress is intertwined with finances, providing care for Denmark's elderly population has emerged as a market problem. To address this problem, the country's first Elderly Commission (1980–1982) resolved that concepts such as self-determination, continuity, and strengthening an older person's own resources should be central in the design of social-care policies for the elderly (Blom, 2014: 44). Although a number of in-home care services – e.g., nursing and specialized forms of assistance – have been available to citizens under the auspices of their local municipality since the "golden days" of the welfare state in the 1950s (ibid.), a neoliberal emphasis on "individual responsibility" and remaining independent (i.e., *not dependent* on costly welfare services) for as long as possible has become embedded in the political discourse regarding eldercare.

In the early 2000s, the Danish government began to focus on avoiding the "traditional top-down imposition of welfare" in relation to the provision of benefits and care services for all citizens (Rostgaard, 2006: 444). As a result, municipal health and welfare institutions began to transition from *providing help* to *enabling self-help* (Petersen, 2008; Blom, 2014); this means that municipal professionals should help the welfare recipient to do things for themselves. Due to an ongoing neoliberal drive to control expenditures and improve efficiency in the public sector, government officials introduced a "Free Choice" scheme in 2003, which primarily applies to citizens who are not healthy, fully active, and contributing members of the economic workforce (e.g., children, the disabled, the elderly; Petersen, 2008: 94). This policy document, "Free choice and quality – payment models for the municipal service areas" (*Frit valg og kvalitet – afregningsmodeller på de kommunale serviceområder*), was developed as part of the Ministry of Finance's modernization efforts to control the public sector and make it more efficient, as well as to improve quality and flexibility (Minstry of Finance, 2003). In addition, the government's "elderly package" (*ældrepakke*), which was first offered in 2002, outlined the municipal service options available to older citizens; being given a choice between municipal or private help thus created a market for welfare services, and constructed older people as "freely choosing elderly" consumers (Højlund, 2006).

The professionals who provide eldercare services in Denmark are generally not physicians or members of medicine's institutions; rather, they have specialized training in their discipline, which often includes a collectivity or service orientation (Freidson, 1988: 77). Traditionally, such community healthcare workers have held an important role within the political system; i.e., this type of professional "operates using powers delegated to it by society through government action" (Cruess and Cruess, 2008: 585). This means that their job function requires them to represent the municipality and promote its values when meeting the individual citizen. In Denmark, most of the work of the municipal health professional was politically formalized in the 1990s during the rise of neoliberalism and, since that time, their mandate has been to respond to a need – i.e., to evaluate, categorize, and stabilize "at-risk" citizens via the health and welfare services that the individual citizen is legally eligible to receive (cf. Højbjerg et al., 2015). In order to respond to a variety of complex needs, there are many different types of municipal health professional – this umbrella term encompasses both the (authoritative) visitator and the (non-authoritative) preventative home-visits visitor as well as health-promotion counsellors, exercise counsellors, dieticians, social and healthcare (*social- og sundhed, SOSU*) assistants or helpers, visiting nurses, physical/occupational therapists, and others – not to mention the specialized job functions associated with various municipal institutions such as activity centres, LTC facilities, hospitals, etc.

As a result of national public-sector reforms in 2007, local governmental authorities (i.e., the newly formed five regions and ninety-eight municipalities) were given more responsibility for instituting citizen-orientated initiatives in collaboration with professional experts and civic authorities. In practice, this means that there are often substantial variations in how each individual municipality has decided to organize its staff of specialized health professionals. But, in order to gain insight into how eldercare services are typically organized and provided in Denmark (as well as some of the differences between the particular problems/solutions that are involved), let's take a closer look at just one of these municipalities.

15.1.2 Tøftsby Municipality: A Microcosm of Care for the Elderly

The two cases I present in this chapter were generated from my PhD research (Clotworthy, 2017), which was conducted in association with the Center for Healthy Aging (CEHA) at the University of Copenhagen. A central objective of my project was to learn more about how the Danish state's political goals and individualized health policies influence the provision of in-home health services for older people. Over the course of fifteen months in 2014–2016, I conducted ethnographic fieldwork[2] together with health professionals from

---

[2] The two cases I present here are taken from my participant-observations and the semi-structured interviews I conducted with select health professionals and older people (who provided their informed consent to participate in my research project); all names are pseudonyms and any identifying details have been removed. Furthermore, I have translated all references and citations from Danish to English myself; although I may have asked a Danish friend or colleague for

various departments in the Danish municipality of Tøftsby (a pseudonym). There, I positioned myself within certain locations in order to trace the social correlates and connections between, e.g., politicians at the local City Hall, various health professionals in their municipal offices, and older citizens in their own homes. At the time of my research, nearly 75,000 people lived in the seven districts that comprise this quiet suburb of Denmark's capital city, Copenhagen; a defining feature of the municipality is its significant number of international and/or elderly residents.

Tøftsby has also long held a privileged position as one of Denmark's wealthiest municipalities and, although it is subjected to national budgetary equalizations, it has historically avoided much of the municipal consolidation that resulted from the comprehensive structural reforms in both 1970 and 2007. This means that government officials in Tøftsby have been able to operate with perhaps more autonomy than other political leaders who have struggled to ensure social equality and provide their citizens with access to a full range of welfare benefits and care services over the years. As a result, Tøftsby has been able to maintain a relatively consistent demographic profile, organizational culture, and socioeconomic stability for the past several decades. This made it an ideal setting to study the subtle effects of societal changes and transformations related to the provision of eldercare in Denmark.

15.2 Visitation: The Case of Sanne and Dyveke

The municipal health professionals who broker the "free choices" in relation to the government's *Free Choice* scheme are the authoritative visitation staff. This specially trained group of health professionals conducts in-home evaluations of the living conditions and functional needs of any citizen who wants to receive personal care or practical help from their local municipality. The visitator's primary function is to uphold laws and policies on behalf of the state, particularly the Social Services Act (*Lov om Social Service*). This national law (Ministry of Children, Equality, Integration, and Social Affairs, 2014) governs the provision of services related to personal assistance and care, assistance, or support for practical tasks at home, and meal

clarification of a specific word, phrase, or term, I accept full responsibility for any misunderstanding or mistranslation of the source material.

delivery – and the visitor alone has the power to make official, formal decisions (*afgørelser*) with regard to which care and supportive welfare services a citizen is eligible to receive. In other words, the visitor is the *only* professional who can refer a citizen to other municipal care and service providers. In fact, with the establishment of visitation as part of the municipal authorities in the 1990s, the political intention was specifically "to shift the assessment of older people's needs away from the care professions and put it into an administrative context with a broader overview. [This was done partly] to better manage the economy, and partly to ensure that the elderly received consistent help" (Lønstrup, 2008: n.p.).

During the 2000s and 2010s, many municipal health and welfare programmes continued to emphasize "free choice" and the citizen's individual responsibility to be more self-sufficient and *not dependent* on welfare services. Thus, the visitor's job became sedimented as a "management tool" that was used to regulate expenditures and control capacity, specifically with regards to "the municipality's decision on the allocation of specific offers and services to the individual citizen" (Ministry of Finance, 2003: 47). As part of the education to become a visitor, one is expected to be able to "analyse, critically evaluate, and manage transitions between functions, departments, and sectors to ensure consistency in healthcare services; this may involve both an interdisciplinary and an organizational perspective in the analysis of actual collaborative challenges" (University College UC Syddanmark, 2014). In general, the role of the visitor is to follow and enforce laws, policies, and rules; to offer citizens choices and opportunities; and to mobilize the appropriate actors within the framework set forth by national and local policymakers. Specifically, visitators are meant to manage the problems that "the client cannot solve, and only the professional can solve" (Goode, 1957: 196), and their work with citizens is regulated and controlled by national legislation, standards, and local policies that emphasize cost-savings and efficiency.

In practice, the work of visitation is activated by an individual citizen who needs assistance – i.e., a person who has been experiencing more difficulty in their everyday life, or who has undergone a sudden change in their health or social condition due to an illness or injury. After receiving a formal request from a citizen, the citizen's general practitioner (GP), or a close relative, the visitor is then deployed as a "risk assessor," traveling to the citizen's home to assess the "damage" that prevents the citizen from being fully self-sufficient; the visitator must then determine what can be done to solve the problem. When a visitator decides that a citizen requires supportive services, that individual is offered two choices under the *Free Choice* scheme: either municipal services (which are no-cost or subsidized) or private help (paid by the citizen) – and this private help must meet the same level of service quality that the municipality offers (Højlund, 2006). The visitator's main responsibility is then to coordinate services between specific professional departments and the citizen, and to uphold laws on behalf of the state – particularly anything related to the *Social Services Act*. But before any services can be offered, the visitator must first assess the citizen's living conditions (i.e., their home) and physical functionality (i.e., their body).

By way of example, I followed the visitator Sanne to reevaluate Dyveke (age 86), a widow who lives alone; according to the notes in her online medical journal, Dyveke was diagnosed with leukaemia twenty years ago, but has been in remission for many years. More recently, however, she had been diagnosed with depression and is having trouble managing daily tasks around her home. Dyveke had been evaluated by another visitator several months ago, who recommended that she start a programme of "everyday rehabilitation" (i.e., reablement) with the municipality's new cross-disciplinary training team. However, it appeared that Dyveke had not followed through with this after the first session; instead, she contacted visitation again to once more request help with housekeeping. In my field notes I wrote:

When we arrive, Dyveke invites us to sit on the sofa in her tastefully furnished living room; she has a lovely small apartment with large windows that look out onto a quiet residential street. Sanne begins the evaluation by asking how Dyveke has been doing lately.

DYVEKE: Well, I have a cancer on my back ... it's not too serious, but it
            needs to be removed. I also have it on my hand. [*She shows
            us her hand, with a small bandage covering the melanoma.*]
            Really, I'm just so tired at the moment – I feel a little heavier
            than usual. (...) I've always been able to manage for myself –
            cooking, cleaning. But I'm just so tired. I'd really like to get
            outside, but it's not so nice right now. (...) I really need help
            with vacuuming. (*There are several small rugs on top of the*

> *carpeting, which covers the entire apartment.*) I can do it myself, but I've had some falls.

SANNE: Do you tend to vacuum the whole apartment all at once, or break it up?

DYVEKE: Usually, I wait for a day when I feel good, and then I can manage [the whole apartment]. (. . .)

SANNE: I understand that you had a visit from the training team – how did that go?

DYVEKE: Well, it's different from how I usually vacuum – completely different.

SANNE: Do you feel like you have less energy now than when my colleague was here [in the summer]?

DYVEKE: Absolutely. I've had leukaemia and now skin cancer, so I've felt very low.

SANNE: So, what do you think about vacuuming with the training team? They were impressed by how mobile you are . . . I'm not sure the municipality can give you help with it.

DYVEKE: Oh, I understand. I'm sure there are others my age who need the help – others with less strength. It's just that I feel it in my back . . .

SANNE: Well, we could have the training team come out again . . .

DYVEKE: They'll just tell me to do it a certain way. It's difficult to take the vacuum out of the cabinet, and they won't move the furniture. I like to watch TV in the other room while I eat, so the furniture there in particular needs to be moved.

SANNE: But vacuuming is also exercise. You could see it as exercise . . .

Field notes; November 20, 2014

In this example, both Sanne and the training team (indirectly) consider Dyveke to be very "mobile" (i.e., active and functionally able) and thus physically capable of vacuuming her own apartment; as a result, Sanne determined that Dyveke was not eligible to receive help from the municipality, even though Dyveke was feeling exceedingly tired and depressed due to her various illnesses. When Sanne wrote her decision letter after the visit, she noted that Dyveke was able to set daily goals for herself – she walked regularly with her Nordic walking sticks, went out to buy groceries for herself, visited her sons' families, etc. – thus, Sanne concluded that Dyveke's functional ability was "not restricted." In other words, she believed that Dyveke's body, in the temporal framework of the evaluation, was mobile and capable *enough* to do the vacuuming herself. Sanne also made a special note in Dyveke's online medical journal: "The citizen can vacuum but chooses to do the whole apartment at once, rather than breaking it up (as recommended)." Even though Dyveke reported that she felt "heavier than usual" and "very low," Sanne did not address Dyveke's psychological or emotional state during the evaluation. To overcome feeling "low," Sanne instead suggested that Dyveke should join local exercise classes and take more walks outside – and that she should even think of vacuuming as exercise – because she is "not restricted" and thus able to do so.

This case demonstrates that, in contrast to the "golden days" of the Danish welfare state – wherein the provision of care and supportive services was guaranteed and framed as a universal right of citizenship – a neoliberal public sector means that older people can no longer expect to automatically receive long-term support and assistance from their local municipality, despite having contributed to the welfare system for their entire lives. This is because most welfare services in Denmark have been constructed as a commodity that the citizen can choose; specifically, since the early 2000s, help "no longer takes its starting point in everyday life, but instead in meticulous administrative pro-grammes" (Højlund, 2006: 47). The visitators in particular must act as the *Free Choice* scheme's "management tools," which means that these professionals have lost the universal responsibility to ensure that sup-portive care is available to all who need it (Fine, 2007: 4). Instead, the Danish state's neoliberal policies, laws, and regulations have defined the terms for which services the visitators are able to offer – and which services the citizen may actually choose – and this market is controlled and regulated by the municipal leadership with regard to both service providers and quality standards.

When it comes to older people in particular, the Danish state's goal is for them to retain and maintain a high quality of life with less need for (expensive) supportive services and hospitalization for as long as possible. Thus, the neoliberal perspective is that the visitator's main function as a "management tool" is to offer the individual citizen an opportunity to freely make the "correct" choices (Pedersen and Andersen, 2016: 37) – rational choices that should allow them to master their lives and take more responsibility for their own health and welfare, continuing to live productive, *not-dependent* lives until they die at a ripe old age. In this way, neoliberalism and its inherent market imperialism have moved beyond a certain political agenda – i.e., to support "healthy ageing" and to enable self-help – and have instead become "tacitly identified simply with the art of governing people" (Chapter 2, this volume).

However, as this case suggests, a neoliberal drive for self-sufficiency and *not-dependence* in order to create a healthy elderly population may be counter-productive if it ends up exhausting and over-exerting older individuals. From Dyveke's perspective as a freely choosing consumer, Sanne's suggestion to join local exercise classes and to take more walks outside was not an effective solution to her problem. Dyveke was able to walk outside because it gave her energy and lifted her "very low" mood. But she found it difficult to manage the household chore of vacuuming, and she did not consider it to be an enjoyable form of exercise. The only realistic choice Sanne provided to her, then, was to work with the training team (or hire private cleaning services). This resulted in a negotiation of power between Sanne and Dyveke – wherein "individuals try to conduct, to determine the behaviour of others" (Foucault, 1987: 18) – as Dyveke debated the first visitor's decision to send the training team and then pointed out to Sanne that she "feels it in [her] back" when she does try to vacuum. Such a negotiation also suggests that Dyveke had an expectation to receive the services to which she believed she was entitled – and that she as a "freely choosing" consumer *wanted* to receive. As such, this empirical example highlights how the neoliberal citizen-consumer feels they have the freedom to question and choose – and even reject – the services and opportunities they are being offered by the municipal authority (i.e., the visitor).

Like Dyveke, many older people question and resist the biopolitical forces that attempt to make them into a "good," docile subject of the state (Foucault, 1979). But, at the political level, it can be problematic if an older citizen decides to not participate in the health-promoting/-preserving activities and opportunities that the visitor suggests – the main consequence being that they will be left to fend for themselves, eventually reaching a point of decline where they *must* receive municipal services, be institutionalized (e.g., enter a long-term care facility), or be hospitalized; all of which would have a negative economic impact on the state. Thus, as the discursive move from providing help to enabling self-help becomes more embedded in municipal eldercare, the visitors are increasingly having to assess the older person's body in terms of its potential to retain its functionality and remain *not dependent* for as long as possible. As another visitor, Brynja, explained to me, "[When] the municipality gets the first referral from a citizen regarding assistive devices or something – you already begin to think, 'Could there be a need for physical activity or training that could maintain or prevent a decrease in function?'" (interview; February 25, 2016).

And this is where the training team comes in. As I mentioned earlier, when a visitor determines that an older citizen needs "helping services," they have traditionally been presented with two choices: either no-cost/subsidized municipal services or citizen-paid private help. But with the Danish state's need to manage its looming "elder burden" and to reduce municipal eldercare costs, older people who ask for help are now being given a third choice: a programme of "everyday rehabilitation" (i.e., reablement) services. During the time I spent following the visitors on home visits, I noticed that they were frequently beginning to refer older citizens to the municipality's new cross-disciplinary training team. This is because, in January 2015, the national government activated §83-A of the *Social Services Act*; this addendum states all Danish municipalities must offer a short, time-limited reablement programme to any citizen who has been evaluated as having decreased functional abilities but who could benefit from supportive training at home. Brynja told me that she considered the reablement offer to be another "opportunity" for the citizen "to manage as many things as possible at home for the longest possible time" (ibid.). But, as I suggested earlier, the training team's approach to caring for older people – and the outcome of this form of "help to self-help" – is quite different.

15.3 Reablement: The Case of Sofie and Norah

The concept of "restorative care" emerged in the late 1990s when practitioners in the United States developed a new model for restorative care versus the "usual care" for older adults who were receiving an acute episode of home care (Tinetti et al., 2002). In their evaluation, the researchers suggest that "a primary goal of health care for older, particularly multiply and chronically ill, persons should be to optimize function and comfort rather than solely to treat individual diseases" (ibid.: 2098). This innovative model was based on principles adapted from geriatric medicine, nursing, rehabilitation, and goal attainment, which refers to the belief that people "are more likely to adhere to treatment plans if they are involved in setting goals and in determining the process for meeting these goals" (ibid.: 2100). This foundational model transitioned to being called "reablement" in the late-2000s as interventions with similar service models became more widely implemented in Western countries around the world. These interventions were most often called *reablement* or *re-ablement* (United Kingdom) or the *active service model* or *restorative home support* (Australia, New Zealand, and USA). In Scandinavia, the Swedish version is known as *hemrehabilitering* (home rehabilitation), while the term *hverdagsrehabilitering* (everyday rehabilitation) is used in both Norway and Denmark.

In Scandinavia, reablement programmes started to be offered in the 2000s; the first was piloted in Sweden's Östersund Municipality in 1999, and positive evaluations of the so-called Östersund model inspired local governments throughout the Nordic region to implement similar programmes. The pilot programme "As long as possible in one's own life" (*Længst muligt i eget liv*) was the first in Denmark; it was launched in Fredericia Municipality in 2008. This initiative aimed to focus on the rehabilitative efforts of in-home eldercare and to strengthen older citizens' ability to "master their own lives" (Kjellberg et al., 2011; Blom 2014: 45). Based on positive evaluations of the Fredericia model – and a savings of 15 million Danish kroner (over 2 million Euro) in the programme's first year (Kjellberg et al., 2011) – the Danish government decided to activate §83-A of the *Social Services Act* in 2015.

Although reablement programmes worldwide have had different characteristics, components, aims, and target groups over the years (Clotworthy et al., 2021), experts attending the International Federation on Ageing (IFA) Global Think Tank and Copenhagen Summit 2015/2016 defined reablement as "an active process of (re) gaining skills and confidence in maintaining or improving function, or adapting to the consequences of declining function. It also supports the individual to remain socially engaged within the community context in a safe, culturally sensitive and adaptable way" (Mishra and Barratt, 2016: 7). More recently, an international Delphi study defined "reablement" in part as "a person-centred, holistic approach that aims to enhance an individual' s physical and/or other functioning, to increase or maintain their independence in meaningful activities of daily living at their place of residence, and to reduce their need for long-term services" (Metzelthin et al., 2020: 11). In many Western countries, reablement services are offered to anyone who may benefit from this form of time-limited support, regardless of age.

Just prior to the national enactment of *§83-A* in 2015, Tøftsby established a cross-disciplinary training team consisting of occupational therapists, physical therapists, and SOSU assistants. In general, the aim was for this professional group to improve older citizens' functional ability, prevent hospital admissions, and reduce (or at least maintain) their need for municipal help. The reablement offer is specialized training that aims to reskill a citizen's functional ability related to ADLs, which will thereby enable them to remain self-sufficient within their own homes for as long as possible. Part of the text inside the municipality's promotional pamphlet says, "For [Tøftsby], it is valuable that you have a long and active life with a high quality of life. (...) We see [reablement] as an investment in you. If you become more active, you will preserve and increase your resources, so you can master your life as long as possible and avoid being dependent on others" (municipal pamphlet).

I followed the physical therapist Sofie through a reablement programme with Norah (age 79), a widow who lives by herself in a small apartment. To prepare for their first meeting, Sofie learned that Norah had been in the municipal system since 2009, when she suffered a stroke. In addition, she fell and severely broke her leg in 2001, which has caused her problems ever since; she also has partial sight in her left eye (caused by a work accident) as well as osteoporosis. She had recently been hospitalized for several days – according to the notes in Norah's online journal, it was because she had had another small stroke ("admitted after a blackout at home – blood clot in the cerebellum"). After a visitator evaluated her situation, the official referral said that Norah chose to participate in reablement so that she could "regain her former skills" and be "freely mobile and self-reliant" again, and it recommended that she receive "training in everyday activities in the home and on the street/stairs" (field notes; October 26, 2015).

During the initial assessment, Sofie asked if Norah had any particular wishes for the training sessions; Sofie emphasized that she takes her point of departure in Norah's everyday life and what she specifically wants to accomplish. Norah said that, primarily, she would like to be better at walking: "My greatest wish is to be more confident" (ibid.). Sofie and Norah therefore agreed that a training goal would be to walk down to Drikkelund (a pseudonym) – this is a municipal facility located less than one kilometre from Norah's apartment, and where she had previously attended exercise classes twice a week. Since her latest hospitalization, Norah said she was not "back on my feet yet" (ibid.), and she generally struggled with balance due to her poor eyesight and damaged leg, so they also agreed to train with Norah's new outdoors rollator. When we arrived for a subsequent training session, Norah was looking out of her first-floor kitchen window, waiting for us to arrive. I wrote in my field notes:

We come upstairs to the apartment, and Norah opens the door before we knock. She shakes our hands, and immediately asks if we were going to go out for a walk. Sofie answers that we're going to go down to Drikkelund (as agreed). But Norah says that she wants to go to the corner store: "I need to get some cash and buy avocadoes." She seems very definite and determined to go out. (...) After reluctantly agreeing to try walking with her large outdoors rollator, which Sofie tells her is "more supportive and stable," we walk down to the main street. Norah and I chat while Sofie walks behind us and to the side to observe Norah's gait and balance. When we get to the intersection, Sofie suggests we go over to Drikkelund.

NORAH: No! We're going to the corner store.
SOFIE: Sure, we can go there afterwards.
NORAH: No, not today. Next time!
SOFIE   (*pause*): Yes, the next time we go out, we'll go to Drikkelund. (...)

Field notes; November 13, 2015

In this example, Norah assumed the identity of a "freely choosing elderly" consumer (Højlund, 2006); i.e., she wanted to choose from among the options presented to her, and then to decide exactly when and how to participate in the reablement training. And, in alignment with the neoliberal political discourse about the citizen's "free choice," Sofie acknowledged Norah's ability to make these choices and decisions for herself – and they walked to the corner store, not to Drikkelund as they had originally planned. However, this case doesn't simply reflect a last-minute change of plans based on Norah's whims and demands – umm, I mean, her *choices* – or Sofie's need to be flexible as a provider of supportive services. Such changes are actually quite typical: reablement training takes its point of departure in whatever type of activity the citizen decides is important to them – e.g., going up and down stairs or bathing, lifting a laundry basket or vacuuming floors, putting on support stockings, cooking food, etc. – and the therapists then emplot (Mattingly, 1994) the training programme to build these specific actions.

In Norah's case, it was the act of walking outside that was more important than the actual destination. Moreover, any kind of physical rehabilitation is a process that must be continually adjusted and modified based on the person's physical, emotional, and ontological limitations, which are always in flux (ibid.). But a central feature of reablement programmes is also that they frame the older person as "an expert in their own life" (Aspinal et al., 2016: 2). Based on the older person's individual values, needs, and priorities, the therapists should then focus on guiding them toward discovering resources and determining activities that are meaningful to them. In many countries, the reablement offer is also framed as a partnership; in Tøftsby, the programme is described as "a health-orientated effort to maintain the citizen's functional abilities in a partnership between the citizen and [the team member] (...), where the focus is on the citizen's everyday life and resources" (municipal pamphlet).

This focus on the older person's goals, limitations, and priorities makes a difference. Specifically, it requires the reablement therapists to acknowledge a vast array of emotional and psychological factors that are necessary for the training to be "successful"; i.e., for the older citizen to attain the personal goals they choose. In an interview, Sofie described her approach:

In the beginning, it's really clear that, deep down, you're sitting across from another person with full respect and the humble task of trying to know another person. So you try to ask about them – who they are, what does this mean to them right now? (...) I think that being able to clean [the house] yourself is a very small part of the whole picture, if one looks at the whole person. You have to think about the baggage they have, what about their relatives, what they've been through in their lives, how they're doing right NOW – what's their condition now, are they sick? How are they doing? So I think that's primary in describing [reablement]. (*Interview; December 21, 2015*)

In this quote, Sofie explained how she tries to relate to the older citizen on a *personal* level, not merely on an abstract individual level.

Specifically, she emphasized that she needs to determine whether or not training certain ADLs could be meaningful and valuable to that particular *person*. To achieve this with Norah, it was essential that Norah express her "true" self – both positive and negative – so that Sofie could personalize the training programme for her. By acknowledging Norah as a complex person, Sofie was able to locate and transform Norah's willingness to act in relation to the goals that Norah articulated for herself. This meant that Sofie could make the training meaningful for Norah by basing it on her everyday life and the future-orientated activities that she wanted to accomplish (i.e., being "better at walking," going to Drikkelund, being more self-reliant). In this way, reablement programmes offer a somewhat subversive internal contrast to the larger neoliberal goals of the Danish competition state, wherein municipal health professionals (like the visitators) are simply expected to find ways for citizens to remain self-helping for as long as possible.

Fundamentally, reablement therapists do much more than simply work with an older person's corporeal body, training them to maintain their functional ability in order to remain *not dependent* on welfare services. As I mentioned, reablement programmes are based on a partnership between the therapist and the older person – this partnership requires a form of "shared decision-making" wherein both parties make an investment in the outcome; the citizen because their health is at stake, and the professional because they are concerned for the citizen's welfare (Charles et al., 1999: 656). This means that, during the training sessions, both the therapist and the older citizen exchange a social acknowledgment (Liveng, 2011), which confirms their identities as professionals and persons. In a long-term perspective, this form of recognition may ultimately lead to an improved quality of life for both parties. But, in the context of reablement, such mutual recognition also generates a form of care. As a concept, "care" is a slippery term that can be defined in many different ways; the meaning of "care" is subjective, always contextual, and thereby nonessentialist (Tronto, 2017: 29, 33). I understand it as a way that others may help us "to maintain, continue, and repair our 'world' so that we can live in it as well as possible" (Fisher and Tronto, 1990: 40). As this case suggests, an important component of reablement is that the therapists engage in caring action (cf. Åström et al., 1993); in my conceptualization, this refers to the decisions that the therapists make that reflect their concern for the older person's welfare, and which consequently help the older person make choices that will "repair" their world.

In an interview after her reablement programme was over, Norah told me: "[Sofie] directed me just so I could get started. That's what she directed me in – just to get started. (...) What she showed me was common-sense. And she showed me that I could do more than I thought I could" (interview; December 15, 2015). Norah's assessment points to a simple yet significant result of the reablement training: By directing her just so she "could get started" in a "common-sense" way, Sofie ultimately helped Norah to remain an active and valuable member of the social collective. Thus, the outcome of this form of eldercare is profound and far-reaching. In particular, health programmes like reablement are grounded in a need for social acknowledgment and care – not just of the welfare recipient, but also care for and about others in their shared social environment. The form of social recognition and interaction that occurs during reablement training may also produce a form of "relational citizenship" (Pols, 2016: 177); i.e., by creating particular relationships and social spaces together, people become constituted as citizens through their interactions.

15.4 Conclusion

In 2015, then Danish Prime Minister Lars Løkke Rasmussen described the Nordic model as "an expanded welfare state which provides a high level of security to its citizens, but it is also a successful market economy with much freedom [*sic*] to pursue your dreams and live your life as you wish" (Yglesias, 2015). This description echoes a central tenet of liberalism: i.e., "there is a fundamental value in the freedom of individuals to choose their own trajectory through life" (Chapter 2 this volume). Having the freedom to make such life choices is considered significant to cultivating well-being in the Nordic states (Martela et al., 2020). But, as I've suggested elsewhere (Clotworthy, 2020), "freedom" is conceptualized differently in Denmark. The Danish form of freedom of choice – "to pursue your dreams and live your life as you wish," as former Prime Minister Rasmussen said – contains a number of reciprocal exchanges and obligations between the citizen and the state. Such exchanges are seen as necessary because they are fundamental to preserving Denmark's wealth and thereby its status as an "exceptional" Nordic welfare society. In this type of market-based system, "individuals exert their 'free choice' but are at the same time guided by those who designed the incentives to induce more or less of a certain behavior" (Larsen, 2015; Larsen and Stone, 2015: 5).

This can be seen in the first case with the authoritative visitor – a job function that was specifically defined and sedimented during the rise of neoliberalism in the 1990s. This municipal health professional's epistemology and approach reflects one of the hallmarks of capitalist forms of production; e.g., they are often "near-sighted," focusing on short-term profit first and long-term outcome/impact second. By expecting and encouraging older people to make certain choices – i.e., to "take over," to "take responsibility ... as long as they can," and to not "get worse and worse," in the words of the visitors I followed – the neoliberal approach to elderly citizens implies that they are inherently passive, incomplete, and not doing *enough*. As such, this logic of choice (Mol, 2008) frames self-care and individual responsibility not only as a moral obligation to benefit the state, but also assigns blame to citizens who may make the "wrong" choices and fail to "properly" manage themselves in accordance with the municipal guidelines (Otto, 2013). Ultimately, a political and economic emphasis on older people achieving better physical functionality so they can continue to take care of themselves for as long as possible may work to marginalize those who cannot achieve the neoliberal goals. *Some just can't* – and this should not be seen as a personal failure.

In the second case, the political framework for the reablement programme also contains neoliberalist terms and expectations for what the training team as a professional group should be able to achieve; i.e., their work is meant to contribute to the national and municipal ambition to reduce costs in the public sector, enhance citizens' productivity, and improve longevity rates. In other words, reablement training in Denmark has been implemented to address the market problem of providing supportive welfare services to an increasing – and increasingly dependent – elderly population. However (however!) in contrast to the authoritative and bureaucratic evaluations conducted by the visitors, reablement programmes are specifically allowed to focus on meaningful goals and activities in order to achieve each older person's "hopes and dreams" for the future (Guldager, 2011). In fact, the interpersonal work of reablement *requires* the training team therapists to acknowledge the heterogeneity and "messy subjectivity" of an older person; my conceptualization of this term refers to the complexity of the human agent as a person (Clotworthy, 2017: 29). This means that, in order to achieve a "successful" outcome, the therapists must consider not only a person's "needy" body and limited abilities but also their unique identity and history of lived experience; their intrinsic motivations, personal hopes, dreams, values, and priorities – and especially their irrationalities, paradoxes, and contradictions. In other words, their agency and essential personhood.

As I've suggested in this chapter, a neoliberal emphasis on self-governance, wherein a citizen is obligated to take individual responsibility for their own care in order to benefit society (Halse, 2009: 51; Mik-Meyer, 2014) – combined with a focus on retaining the functionality of a citizen's physical body as a resource to benefit the state – becomes strongly tied to morality (Taussig et al., 2013: S6). This means that, instead of being dependent on others for help, the individual citizen is strongly encouraged to make the choices that the "experts" want them to make; specifically, to take control of their own health (Powers, 2003: 232), to help themselves, and to remain *not dependent*. But, I would argue that – "by leaving aside the issue of emotion and preferring that of rational maximization" (Ballet et al., 2018: 189) – neoliberalism and mainstream economics have missed the point with regards to caring for the elderly. If we consider the work of moral philosophers like Adam Smith (1759), economic behavior has long been entangled with emotional self-interest – but it has also reflected a concern for the welfare of others; in this way, "the excesses of an unregulated market can be curbed by an appeal to our moral sentiments" (ibid. in Terjesen, 2011: 70).

So, if we think about what it means to be moral and to live well together in a society, then perhaps we should stop monetizing the individual citizen's ability to remain productive and independent. If a citizen is only valued for their individual productivity – i.e., their ability to work and contribute to society as a consumer – then they may lose a sense of their identity as a social being, and may ultimately feel oppressed and experience a lack of personal freedom. And, if we remove the neoliberal drive to capitalize on the capacities and abilities that certain individuals (e.g., elderly people) can contribute to the state and society-at-large, then perhaps we can begin to establish "institutions and social arrangements that not only respect rights, but also provide for meeting adequately the care needs of all citizens" (Lanoix, 2020).

One initiative that seems to be "doing it right" is a Dutch home-care provider called *Buurtzorg* ("neighborhood care"). First developed in 2006, this nurse-led form of holistic care has revolutionized community care in the Netherlands and is now expanding into many other countries worldwide (it is currently being piloted in Denmark). The *Buurtzorg* model is grounded in "the client perspective and then works outward to assemble solutions that bring independence and improved quality of life" (Buurtzorg, 2021); in particular, this direct-care approach focuses on the client's "living environment, the people around the client, a partner or relative at home, and on into the client's informal network; their friends, family, neighbors and clubs as well as professionals already known to the client in their formal network" (ibid.). A key element of the model is that employees must have "a sustained focus on the opportunities (in care as well as the local community) that exist to support the citizen's autonomy and self-help" (Gray et al., 2015); as such, the *Buurtzorg* approach is meant to provide the greatest possible continuity in care as well a starting point for an ongoing and holistic approach to the citizen's need for help (Buch, 2020: 20).

Although experiences in other countries have raised questions regarding "the applicability and relevance of the model within different cultural contexts and the potential of the model to produce both local and global impact" (Kreitzer et al., 2015: 44), the significance of the *Buurtzorg* concept may ultimately lie "not just in the wholesale spread of this model but in the recognition of the value of its key components" (Gray et al., 2015). Specifically, founder Jos de Blok said, *Buurtzorg* is "a company that is driven by a belief in 'humanity over bureaucracy,' and that belief deeply impacts the patients and those who care for them" (Kreitzer et al., 2015: 40). As the title of this book suggests, putting markets before people can be problematic. So, similar to the *Buurtzorg* model, the two cases I've presented here demonstrate that most industrialized Western societies would benefit from developing solutions and reinforcing discourses that promote older people's social value as essential, productive, and still-contributing members of society. That means that government officials and health experts should focus less on trying to improve older people's functional ability in order to train these individuals to be "free" from the need for health and welfare services, and should instead put more effort into building stronger, more inclusive communities of care. Because each of us has social value – not just as a productive consumer, but as a complex person.

Such an approach is likely the best way to care for all people, not just the elderly.

References

Aspinal F., J. Glasby, T. Rostgaard, H. Tuntland, and R. Westendorp. 2016. "Reablement: supporting older people towards independence" *Age and Ageing* 45: 574–578.

Åström, G., A. Norberg, I. R. Hallberg, and L. Jansson. 1993. "Experienced and skilled nurses' narratives of situations where caring action made a difference to the patient." *Scholarly Inquiry for Nursing Practice* 7 (3): 183–193.

Ballet, J., E. Petit, and D. Pouchain. 2018. "What mainstream economics should learn from the ethics of care." *Œconomia* 8 (2): 187–208.

Better Health While Aging. 2021. "What are activities of daily living (ADLs) & instrumental activities of daily living (IADLs)?" Last accessed April 19, 2021. https://betterhealthwhileaging.net/what-are-adls-and-iadls.

Blom, A. 2014. "Det kommunale sundhedsområde i et historisk perspektiv." (The municipal health area in a historical perspective.) In *Det kommunale sundhedsvæsenet (The Municipal Healthcare Sector.)*, edited by B. M. Pedersen and S. R. Petersen. Copenhagen: Hans Reitzels Forlag.

Buch, M. S. 2020. *Buurtzorgs model for hjemmesygepleje og hjemmepleje: Introduktion til modellen, oversigt over litteraturen og perspektiver for afprøvninger i en dansk kontekst (Buurtzorg's Model for Home Nursing and Home Care: Introduction to the Model, Overview of the Literature, and Perspectives on Trials in a Danish Context)*. Copenhagen: VIVE, Det Nationale Forsknings- og Analysecenter for Velfærd. https://pure .vive.dk/ws/files/4552337/301713_Buurtzorgs_model_for_hjemmesyge pleje_og_hjemmepleje_PDU_UA.pdf. Last accessed September 24, 2021.

Buurtzorg. 2021. "Buurtzorg's model of care." Last accessed September 24, 2021. www.buurtzorg.com/about-us/buurtzorgmodel.

Charles, C., A. Gafni, and T. Whelan. 1999. "Decision-making in the physician–patient encounter: revisiting the shared treatment decision-making model." *Social Science & Medicine* 49: 651–661.

Clotworthy A. 2017. *Empowering the Elderly? A Qualitative Study of Municipal Home-Health Visits and Everyday Rehabilitation."* PhD diss., University of Copenhagen, Faculty of Humanities.

2020. "'Train yourself free': How elderly citizens exercise freedom of choice in the Danish state." In *The Cultural Context of Aging: Worldwide Perspectives 4th edition*, edited by J. Sokolovsky, 608–630. Santa Barbara, CA : Praeger Publishers.

Clotworthy, A., S. Kusumastuti, and R. G. J. Westendorp. 2021. "Reablement through time and space: A scoping review of how the concept of 'reablement' for older people has been defined and operationalized." *BMC Geriatrics* 21 (61): 1–16.

Crimmins, E. M. and H. Beltrán-Sánchez. 2010. "Mortality and morbidity trends: is there compression of morbidity?" *Journal of Gerontology: Social Sciences* 66B (1): 75–86.

Cruess, R. L. and S. R. Cruess. 2008. "Expectations and obligations: professionalism and medicine's social contract with society." *Perspectives in Biology and Medicine* 51 (4): 579–598.

Erlich, P. R. 1968. *The Population Bomb*. New York: Buccaneer Books.

European Commission. 2014. "Population ageing in Europe: facts, implications and policies." Last accessed February 6, 2017. Luxembourg: Publications Office of the European Union. https://ec.europa.eu/research/social-sciences/pdf/policy_reviews/kina26426enc.pdf

2018. "2018 ageing report: Policy challenges for ageing societies." Last accessed April 19, 2021. Luxembourg: Publications Office of the European Union. https://ec.europa.eu/info/news/economy-finance/policy-implications-ageing-examined-new-report-2018-may-25_en.

2020. "Ageing Europe: statistics on population developments." Last accessed April 19, 2021. Luxembourg: Publications Office of the European Union. https://ec.europa.eu/eurostat/statistics-explained/index.php/Ageing_Europe__statistics_on_population_developments#Older_people_.E2.80.94_population_overview.

Fine, M. D. 2007. *A Caring Society? Care and the Dilemmas of Human Service in the Twenty-First Century*. Basingstoke, UK: Palgrave Macmillan.

Fisher, B. and J. C. Tronto. 1990. "Toward a feminist theory of caring." In *Circles of Care*, edited by E. K. Abel and M. Nelson. Albany: SUNY Press.

Foucault, M. 1979. *Discipline and Punish*. Harmondsworth, UK: Penguin.

1987. "The ethic of care for the self as a practice of freedom: an interview with Michel Foucault on January 20, 1984." *Philosophy and Social Criticism* 12 (2–3): 112–131.

Freidson, E. 1988. *Profession of Medicine: A Study of the Sociology of Applied Knowledge*. Chicago: University of Chicago Press.

Goode, W. J. 1957. "Community within a community: the professions." *American Sociological Review* 22 (2): 194–200.

Gray, B. H., D. O. Sarnak, and J. S. Burgers. 2015. "Home care by self-governing nursing teams: The Netherlands' Buurtzorg model." Last accessed September 24, 2021. www.commonwealthfund.org/publica tions/case-study/2015/may/home-care-self-governing-nursing-teams-netherlands-buurtzorg-model.

Guldager, A. 2011. "Drømmen er gået i opfyldelse" (The dream has come true). *Fysioterapeuten 5.* Last accessed May 24, 2021. https://fysio.dk/ fysioterapeuten/arkiv/nr.-5-2011/Drommen-er-gaet-i-opfyldelse.

Gullestad, M. 1989. "Small facts and large issues: the anthropology of contemporary Scandinavian society." *Annual Review of Anthropology* 18: 71–93.

Halse, C. 2009. "Bio-citizenship: virtue discourses and the birth of the bio-citizen." In *Biopolitics and the "Obesity Epidemic": Governing Bodies,* edited by J. Wright and V. Harwood, 45–59. London: Routledge.

Hansen, R. 2015. "The politics of Denmark and Germany's low birth rates." *Brown Political Review,* October 23, 2015. Last accessed February 6, 2017. www.brownpoliticalreview.org/2015/10/the-politics-of-denmark-and-germanys-low-birth-rates.

Healthcare Denmark. 2019. "Assisted living: A dignified elderly care in Denmark." Last accessed April 19, 2021. www.healthcaredenmark.dk/ media/plvbj4yz/elderly-care-v10919.pdf.

Henriksen, I. 2006. "An economic history of Denmark." In *Encyclopedia of Economic and Business History,* edited by R. Whaples. Last accessed February 6, 2017. https://eh.net/encyclopedia/an-economic-his tory-of-denmark.

Heritage Foundation. 2017. "Index of economic freedom." Last accessed March 28, 2017. www.heritage.org/index/country/denmark.

Højbjerg, K., N. Sandholm, and K. Larsen. 2015. "Grænser for professionel autoritet i mødet mellem sundhedsprofessionelle og patienter/klienter" (Limits for professional authority in the meeting between health professionals and patients/clients). *Praktiske Grunde* 1–2: 43–60.

Højlund, H. 2006. "Den frit vælgende ældre" (The freely choosing elderly). *Dansk Sociologi* 1(17): 42–65.

Johnson, P., C. Conrad, and D. Thomson. 1989. *Workers Versus Pensioners: Intergenerational Justice in an Ageing World.* Manchester: Manchester University Press.

Kjellberg, P. K., R. Ibsen, and J. Kjellberg. 2011."Fra pleje og omsorg til rehabilitering: viden og anbefalinger" (From care and compassion to rehabilitation: knowledge and recommendations). Copenhagen: KORA, Det Nationale Institut for Kommuners og Regioners Analyse og Forskning. Last accessed April 6, 2017. www.kora.dk/media/1039625/ fra-pleje-og-omsorg-til-rehabilitering-viden-og-anbefalinger.pdf.

Knudsen, T. 2007. *Fra folkestyre til markedsdemokrati (From government to market democracy)*. Copenhagen: Akademisk Forlag.

Kreitzer, M. J., K. A. Monsen, S. Nandram, and J. de Blok. 2015. "Buurtzorg Nederland: A global model of social innovation, change, and whole-systems healing." *Global Advances in Health and Medicine* 4 (1): 40–44.

Lanoix, M. 2020. "Re-conceptualising the political subject: the importance of age for care theory." *International Journal of Care and Caring* 4 (1): 43–58.

Larsen, L. T. 2015. "Fra ventelister til frit valg: neoliberal guvernementalitet i sundhedsvæsenet" (From waiting lists to free choice: neoliberal governmentality in the healthcare sector). *Gjallerhorn* 20: 17–24.

Larsen, L. T. and D. Stone. 2015. "Governing health care through free choice: neoliberal reforms in Denmark and the United States." *Journal of Health Politics, Policy and Law* 40 (5): 941–970.

Lidegaard, B. 2009. *A Short History of Denmark in the 20th Century.* Copenhagen: Gyldendal.

Liveng, A. 2011. "The vulnerable elderly's need for recognizing relationships: a challenge to Danish home-based care." *Journal of Social Work Practice* 25 (3): 271–283.

Lønstrup, L. 2008. "Samarbejdsproblemer i ældreplejen: forskerinterview med Tine Rostgaard" (Cooperation problems in eldercare: researcher interview with Tine Rostgaard). *Djøfbladet* 32 (9): 42–45.

Martela, F., B. Greve, B. Rothstein, and J. Saari. 2020. "The Nordic exceptionalism: What explains why the Nordic countries are constantly among the happiest in the world?" In *World Happiness Report 2020*, chapter 7. Last accessed April 19, 2021. https://happiness-report.s3 .amazonaws.com/2020/WHR20_Ch7.pdf.

Mattingly, C. 1994. "The concept of therapeutic 'emplotment'." *Social Science & Medicine* 38 (6): 811–822.

Metzelthin, S., T. Rostgaard, M. Parsons, and E. Burton. 2020. "Development of an internationally accepted definition of reablement: A Delphi study." *Ageing and Society*: 1–16.

Mik-Meyer, N. 2014. "Health promotion viewed in a critical perspective." *Scandinavian Journal of Public Health* 42 (S15): 31–35.

Ministry of Finance (*Finansministeriet*). 2003. "Frit valg og kvalitet: afregningsmodeller på de kommunale serviceområder" (Free choice and quality: payment models for the municipal service areas). Copenhagen: Ministry of Finance Working Group. Last accessed February 27, 2020. www.fm.dk/publikationer/2003/frit-valg-og-kvalitet.

Ministry of Children, Equality, Integration and Social Affairs (*Ministeriet for Børn, Ligestilling, Integration og Sociale Forhold*). 2014.

"Bekendtgørelse af lov om social service" (Announcement of the Social Services Act). Last accessed February 7, 2017. www.retsinformation.dk/Forms/r0710.aspx?id=161883.

Mishra, V. and J. Barratt. 2016. *"Final report: reablement and older people."* Last accessed April 19, 2021. www.ifa-copenhagen-summit.com/wp-content/uploads/2016/04/Copenhagen-Summit-Final-Report.pdf.

Mol, A. 2008. *The Logic of Care: Health and the Problem of Patient Choice.* Milton Park: Routledge.

OECD 2019. *Economic Surveys: Denmark 2019.* Paris, France: OECD Publishing. Last accessed April 19, 2021. www.oecd.org/economy/surveys/Denmark-2019-OECD-economic-survey-overview.pdf.

Otto, L. 2013. "Negotiating a healthy body in old age: preventive home visits and biopolitics." *International Journal of Ageing and Later Life* 8 (1): 111–135.

Pedersen, L. H., and L. B. Andersen, 2016. "Ved NPM's dødsleje: tre ting vi har lært" (At NPM's deathbed: three things we have learned). *KORA Publications.* Last accessed February 7, 2017. https://www.altinget.dk/kommunal/artikel/ved-npms-doedsleje-hvad-har-vi-laert.

Pedersen, O. K. 2011. *Konkurrencestaten (The Competition State).* Copenhagen: Hans Reitzels Forlag.

Petersen, J. H. 2008. *Velfærd for ældre: holdning og handling (Welfare for the Elderly: Attitude and Action).* Odense, Denmark: Syddansk Universitetsforlag.

Pols, J. 2016. "Analyzing social spaces: relational citizenship for patients leaving mental health care institutions." *Medical Anthropology: Cross-Cultural Studies in Health and Illness* 35 (2): 177–192.

Powers, P. 2003. "Empowerment as treatment and the role of health professionals." *Advances in Nursing Science* 26 (3): 227–237.

Rostgaard, T. 2006. "Constructing the care consumer: free choice of home care for the elderly in Denmark." *European Societies* 8 (3): 443–463.

Smith, A. 1976 [1759]. *The Theory of Moral Sentiments.* Oxford: Clarendon Press.

Springer, S., K. Birch, and J. MacLeavy, eds. 2016. *The Handbook of Neoliberalism.* London and New York: Routledge.

Statistics Denmark. 2018. "Markant Flere Ældre i Fremtiden" (Significantly more elderly in the future). Copenhagen, Denmark. Last accessed November 12, 2018. www.dst.dk/da/Statistik/nyt/NytHtml?cid=26827.

2019. "Denmark in Figures 2019." Copenhagen, Denmark. Last accessed February 28, 2021. www.dst.dk/Site/Dst/Udgivelser/GetPubFile.aspx?id=28924&sid=dkinfigures2019

Taussig, K.-S., K. Høyer, and S. Helmreich. 2013. "The anthropology of potentiality: an introduction to Supplement 7." *Current Anthropology* 54 (S7): 3–14.

Terjesen, A. 2011."Adam Smith cared, so why can't modern economics? The foundations for care ethics in early economic theory." In *Applying Care Ethics to Business, Issues in Business Ethics, no. 34*, edited by M. Hamington and M. Sander-Staudt, 55–72. New York: Springer.

Tinetti, M. E., D. Baker, W. T. Gallo, A. Nanda, P. Charpentier, and J. O"Leary. 2002. "Evaluation of restorative care vs usual care for older adults receiving an acute episode of home care." *JAMA* 287: 2098–2105.

Tronto, J. 2017. "There is an alternative: *homines curans* and the limits of neoliberalism." *International Journal of Care and Caring* 1 (1): 27–43.

United Nations. 2017. *World Population Ageing 2017: Highlights* (ST/ESA/SER.A/397). New York: United Nations, Department of Economic and Social Affairs, Population Division.

University College UC Syddanmark. 2014. "Visitator Uddannelse" (Visitator education). Last accessed April 11, 2017. https://evu.ucsyd.dk/download.php?id=279.

World Health Organization (WHO). 2012. *Healthy Ageing in Denmark*. Copenhagen; Regional Office for Europe. Last accessed February 6, 2017. www.euro.who.int/__data/assets/pdf_file/0004/161797/Denmark-Healthy-Aging-Strategy-Final-July-2012.pdf.

Yglesias, M. 2015. "Denmark's prime minister says Bernie Sanders is wrong to call his country socialist." *Vox*, October 31, 2015. Last accessed April 19, 2021. www.vox.com/2015/10/31/9650030/denmark-prime-minister-bernie-sanders.

16 How Are People Who Take Drugs Treated?

JOHANNES LENHARD AND EANA MENG

The war on drug users developed in tandem with neoliberalism. By examining the way that society polices and treat people who use drugs, Lenhard and Meng offer a perspective on how neoliberal governance individualizes responsibility and abstains from any kind of collective support. Lenhard and Meng make use of narratives drawn from their fieldwork to illustrate both what criminalized drug use looks like, and how people's lives change when criminalization goes away. The chapter shows that it's not necessarily the drugs that make people's lives difficult and painful but rather the approach that is taken to their behavior. In one model of treatment – exemplified by the war on drugs and the use of methadone programs – a responsibility to change lies solely with the individual, and drug users are criminalized, surveilled, and disciplined primarily by law enforcement. Lenhard and Meng contrast this model with one where society is conceived as collectively responsible to provide support for whomever requires it (e.g., in the form of safe injection facilities) and addiction is understood as something to be managed both medically and holistically. What is interesting in the first model is the way that individual autonomy and responsibility is taken for granted as a preexisting, self-standing capacity that needs only to surveilled, incentivized, and disciplined from the side of the authorities. In the second model, on the contrary, autonomy and responsibility are conceived as capacities that needs to be nourished and cultivated within collective structures of trust and support.

16.1 Sirens: The Sound of War

The sirens are loud and frequent in Brooklyn, downtown San Francisco, and just north of the University of Chicago campus. The *BWEEP bip bip BWEEP* of police cars speeding through traffic or the *Eee-Aww-Eee-Aww*s of ambulances rushing to locate an overdosing person might very well be related to drugs; US law enforcement and emergency medical services are very often called out to overdoses, shootings, and drug-related crimes these days. The sirens are the most audible and most obvious incarnation of the ongoing "war on drugs" launched by President Nixon in the United States over fifty years ago at his press conference speech on June 18, 1971 (Vulliamy, 2011). Drugs of all kinds – in general substances which physically and psychologically alter the body and mind – have been defined as legal or illegal in different places at different times; condemned here, celebrated there (Goodman, Lovejoy, and Sherratt, 1995; Singer, 2012). But how are the people that consume them treated?

In the 1970s, drug use and its prosecution under the guise of the war on drugs was mostly confined to include illegal substances such as heroin, cocaine and crack, and prescription medication (e.g., Oxycontin). New substances such as fentanyl have since extended the repertoire of people who use drugs. By casting drug use as the "public enemy number one," the American war on drugs solidified the illegality of drugs, and by direct extension, the criminalization of people who use drugs. Under the 1973 Rockefeller laws, for instance, people can be sentenced to prison for a minimum of fifteen years for possession of small amounts of heroin; similar convictions are still in place for marijuana and crack/cocaine in many states. For the last fifty years, poor communities, mostly of color, have borne the brunt of this criminalized approach in the US – legacies of which have lasted well into the twenty-first century (Hansen and Netherland, 2016; Hart, 2017).

Currently, almost one in six arrests in the US is directly related to drugs with around 85 percent related to possession (Real Reporting Foundation). This results in 47 percent of all inmates in federal prisons being incarcerated for drug-related offenses, versus 5 percent for burglary and just over 10 percent for weapons according to 2018 data (Flores et al., 2018). On the other hand, over 1.1 million of emergency department visits were generally due to drug-related incidents, according to data collected between 2008 and 2011 (Albert, McCaig, and Uddin, 2015). Overdose-related visits have gone up dramatically in recent years, increasing the absolute number further – by over 100 percent in Wisconsin and 66 percent in Illinois (Centers for Disease Control and Prevention, 2018). The number of overdose-related deaths has surged during the last decade and over the course of the COVID-19 pandemic. In May 2020, the CDC registered 81.230

drug overdose deaths in the US in the past year, the highest annual rate ever recorded (Centers for Disease Control and Prevention, 2020). Partly, this development is driven by the arrival of new highly potent substances such as fentanyl and its derivatives, but many of these deaths, incarcerations, and the never-ending sirens of ambulances have been a result of the ongoing war on drugs.

The criminalized treatment of people who use drugs is not without its alternatives. While many countries – from the UK to the Philippines – still have an approach that is loosely based on law enforcement and an understanding of people who use drugs as "deviants," other countries have completely changed their policies. Portugal and Denmark have followed early adopters such as the Netherlands or Vancouver, Canada, and Geneva, Switzerland, in their focus on harm reduction (EMCDDA, 2018). Harm reduction is an approach that acknowledges the inevitable presence of drugs and substances in society. Instead of criminalizing users of drugs, it aims to "reduce adverse health, social and economic consequences of the use of legal and illegal psychoactive drugs without necessarily reducing drug consumption" and recognizes that abstinence is often unrealistic or undesirable (International Harm Reduction Association, 2010). What has kept countries such as the US "stuck" in the war of drugs modus for the last fifty years? How *have* policies changed and where are we now?

Methadone maintenance treatment came to be the predominant detoxification treatment in the United States starting in the 1970s, particularly in New York City, and the regulatory framework for methadone maintenance was established from 1970 to 1975 (Institute of Medicine, 1995). The approach was pushed by policy-makers, drug companies, and doctors as medical treatment for addiction and aimed to wean people who use drugs off of heroin by replacing it with another pharmaceutical with similar (biomedical) effects: methadone. There have been a number of reported benefits of methadone such as the lower risk of death or infection, as well as, for some patients, the sense that they are moving along their recovery journey. Many people, especially communities of color facing the most amount of criminalization that was ongoing with methadone maintenance, pushed back strongly against it. For example, in the South Bronx, the Young Lords and the Black Panther Party – two revolutionary parties which advocated for the self-determination of poor and oppressed peoples – took radical action to protest against systemic medical neglect, discrimination, and healthcare failure to address the heroin epidemic. They took over a local medical facility, the Lincoln Hospital, and implemented their own Lincoln Detox clinic. Methadone was quickly abandoned there even as a treatment option and instead replaced with acupuncture (Melendez, 2003; Reverby, 2020; Meng, 2021). Methadone was seen as the replacement of one drug with another and patients were weary of the dangers of methadone, from "brainwave changes" to "crib deaths" (White Lightning, 1974). Patients distrusted highly regulated pills that "white doctors, in white coats, in white hospitals" prescribed. Similar to the war on drugs, methadone was seen by one Lincoln Detox organizer as an attack on the Black community, by means of "chemical warfare," a government-manufactured way of "controlling the community." He recalls in an interview:

the Methadone Maintenance came into the community as a requirement for aid to dependent children, a requirement if you wanted to get on welfare, a requirement for parole and requirement for probation. It was called the Rockefeller Program in New York ... They brought methadone into the community. In New York City, 60 percent of the illegal drugs on the street during the early 1970s was methadone. So we could not blame drug addiction at that time on Turkey or Afghanistan or the rest of that triangle ... It was coming in through Eli Lily and the Brinks trucks that was delivering the drugs to the various methadone clinics around the country. And instead of people being detoxified off of methadone, they were being increased in dosages. (Shakur, 2017)

In contrast, another part of the world was beginning to experiment with a different approach to drugs in the 1970s. In the Netherlands, the first legally staffed safe injection sites (SIS) were being established; in addition to offering a space for people to use drugs, they also offered a needle exchange program as well as provided for basic healthcare, food, and laundry services. Since then, a number of countries have established SISs, including Switzerland, Denmark, France, and Portugal (EMCDDA, 2018), but no legal site has been sanctioned in the United States or in the United Kingdom. While much evidence points toward SIS's lowering fatal overdoses as well as more general healthcare costs (Boyd, 2013; Kinnard et al., 2014; Bowers, 2019; Kral et al., 2020), there still remains little consensus on whether or not to pursue SISs for a number of reasons, not least of which is stigma.

In this chapter, we are contrasting methadone maintenance with safe injection facilities along a number of dimensions and parameters.

Overall, we are contrasting two different models of how drugs are regulated and treated through these concrete examples; on the one hand people who use drugs are treated as deviants who need to be punished, controlled, disciplined, and regulated. In this model – exemplified by the war on drugs – a responsibility to change lies with the individual, a pressure which is often collectively enforced (e.g., by police). On the other hand, people who use drugs can be treated as autonomous individuals who can choose to engage in "managing the harm" which the substances might have on them. On this approach society is conceived as collectively responsibly for providing support for whomever requires it (e.g., in the form of safe injection facilities) and addiction can be conceptualized as something to be managed both medically and holistically.

While the two cases we present in this chapter map loosely onto the two contrasting models, they are not the most extreme examples; in fact, we deliberately chose specific settings and practices which clarify the nuance that the above schema-of-contrast requires. Focusing on the same parameters as points of comparison – core beneficiaries and actors, form of responsibility, mode of surveillance, discipline, time horizons – will allow us to show the continuum of "treatments" between a criminalized war on drugs to collectivized measures of support for autonomous people who use drugs.

Case 16.1 Supervised, Daily Methadone Distribution in a Criminalized System[1]

A queue of people waited for the arrival of the converted white van. Every day, the same men and women lined up at a specific spot just east of the train station for the vehicle to open its doors. Victor was first that day. He was there with his long-term girlfriend, Masha, who was not feeling good that day. It was hard for her to stand, look people in the eye, and talk.

---

[1] The two field notes forming the basis for our cases are loosely based on our own participant observation, but fictionalized and turned into two composite case studies of research from the US, France, and the UK. We are also relying on contextual sources (medical papers, legal documents, government policies) and other accounts (ethnographic, sociological, and journalistic) illuminating similar settings. We chose this path to protect the different groups of collaborators and informants as much as possible (e.g., Hammersley, 2006) but also to make the case study independent of locations and relatable beyond geography.

Victor and Masha were both Polish and in their late twenties; the streets of London had been their home for over a year now and they hadn't made much progress with finding longer-term housing. Stuffed backpacks were their constant companions.

While Victor was waiting inside the first room collecting clean needles and syringes from Sara, Masha was talking to the driver. John, the pharmacologist, and Mary, the nurse, finally called Victor into the second, main room. Victor closed the door behind him and Mary asked him to show his registration card. She quickly typed the long number into her computer to confirm the exact dosage of Victor's methadone. Changes to this dosage could only be administered by the doctor in the organization's head office; Victor would have to go and see his doctor there if he felt like changing anything. He was on 60ml at the moment and a tablet of Lexapro (anti-depressant) every Wednesday too (to help with his neurosis).

While Mary filled single-use plastic cups from a 5-liter methadone bottle and placed them on the counter for the people coming in, John checked in with Victor. *Was everything okay? How was Masha?* Word had already made it into the van about her state. John and Victor had gotten to know each other because of their nearly daily interactions at the van; a relationship was slowly developing but the short intervals in the van were not quite enough for it to become fully established. Could John take Victor's explanations for granted; did he say the truth? Victor took the cup with the syrupy liquid from Mary and emptied it on the spot. He filled a larger cup with water from a fountain behind him himself to swallow the pill Mary handed him right after. Both cups were disposed of in a recycled bin on his side of the counter; with a wave and the hint of a smile, Victor left the van through the back door. "See you tomorrow – or soon." Mary made a note in the computer system that Victor had taken his medication and reported no specific irregularities.

Masha had in the meantime just about climbed up the one step into the "reception" room in the middle of the van; she was barely able to stand up but did not want to miss her methadone dose for the day. John called her in and his voice immediately gave away his concern. Masha was holding onto the counter to stand up, could barely look into Mary's eyes; she didn't have her card but Mary was able to find her easily. John, on the other hand, was struggling with what to do with Masha. It was ultimately up to him to decide about the methadone distribution at the point as the *"responsable"* (manager). He ended up going down the more inconvenient path and confronted Masha; he explained that he could not give her the methadone that day because he assumed that she had already consumed other substances. The likelihood of a "dangerous cocktail" leading to an overdose was simply too high. Masha was not happy with this decision and it was hard to help her maneuver out of the back door of the van while she was yelling at John.

***

John and Mary are (medical) operators in a typical methadone distribution system as it is employed in many countries, from the US and the UK and to most other European countries. In fact, methadone was one of the first measures applied under the guise of the war on drugs in America that can also be seen as a means of harm reduction (Campbell, 2020). Methadone has been shown to have positive outcomes – from a lowered risk of death and reduction of drug use to increased engagement with recovery services and a sense of improvement (Neale, 1998 ; Zanis and Woody, 1998; Bell and Zador, 2000; Brinkley-Rubinstein et al., 2018; Moore et al., 2018). While we do not want to dispute this positive effect that methadone distribution can have for some, we want to focus here on how the principles of the kind of supervised daily methadone distribution[2] go hand in hand with the principles that have been driving the war on drugs for the last fifty years: both are built on ideas of individual responsibility, (time) discipline, surveillance and control, and distract from who should really benefit from drug treatment: the people who take drugs themselves.[3]

The pharma industry producing the different prescription medications are an important financial benefactor from methadone distribution. The business of methadone has seen huge surges in activity in the past five years, more so than the previous decades combined (Vestal, 2018). Pushed by pharmaceutical companies such as Eli Lilly back in the 1970s in the United States, methadone has also seen an increase in production by rival companies, including Purdue Pharma who have long been dominating the alternative painkiller market. Overall it is a

---

[2] Supervised daily methadone distribution is in contrast to alternative regimes, such as an unsupervised weekly pickup. As we will explain below, the two parameters of supervision and pickup schedule (time horizon) make a difference on the continuum of treatment options.

[3] There are other ways of administering methadone maintenance that instead of having a daily supervised consumption allow people to take the methadone home and pick it up for instance once a week or once every two weeks, however the majority of programs administer methadone daily, and switching to a less-frequent dosage takes quite a bit of time before a provider agrees to it (Vestal, 2018; UMASS; Riley, 2020).

60-million dollar international market expected to grow by at least 5 percent every year going forward (The Express Wire, 2020).

The people administering the prescriptions play a core role, as we have seen above, with the important role that John and Mary take as gatekeepers, disciplinarians, and operators. Methadone distribution brings addiction into the purview of medical professionals based on a view of addiction as a brain disease to be treated by biomedical means. While the development of the brain disease model of addiction has had some benefits in removing moral failure from the (deviant and criminal) individual as the cause of their substance use (Heather et al., 2018), placing addiction firmly into the hands of medicine has led to a number of unfortunate consequences: it obscures the inextricable social and economic conditions that contribute to and underlay addiction, promotes social injustices, and reduces the notion of "cure" to the Western cultural obsession with the fallible "magic bullet" idea (Mendoza, Rivera-Cabrero, and Hansen, 2016; Hart, 2017; Heather, 2017). This model puts power into medical professionals' hands – in particular to enforce discipline and surveillance. One way of how this can occur is very obvious above: through imposing a schedule and consumption pattern onto the people who use drugs. John – and his counterparts and the institutions behind them – set up a specific schedule, a routined timescape of supervised, daily consumption. While many operators, including John and Mary, are highly conscious that building relationships is key for recovery, their freedom to maneuver is small. The network of permissions and conditions – with the doctor in the headquarter being the only one able to change the prescription (to one of weekly distribution, for instance) – as well as the short amount of time spent together in the van directly makes building trust complicated. While empathy is core for many of the professionals we observed, there is very little room for it in the system of almost mechanical methadone distribution. As a result, many of the people who use drugs and who are involved in this scheme feel what Hatcher, Mendoza, and Hansen (2018) call clinical abandonment – whereby the singular focus on prescribing medication leads to a lack of attention to the multiple oppressions and survival needs of patients. Receiving a daily dosage, usually at the same time, at the same spot, is a perpetual regime with often no endpoint in sight. This routine in itself creates a disruption to people's usual (drug) practices, but instead of empowering the individual it inserts an institutionally imposed rhythm.

As American anthropologist Phillipe Bourgois has stated for a similar case during his observations in San Francisco: this kind of strict regime can lead to – instead of release and support – "metadeath."

The political economic constraints limiting one's life chances (i.e., unemployment, felony record, medical bills, housing market, etc.) are already overwhelming, and methadone's rigid institutional regulations further curtail one's options for autonomous change. The ethnographic literature on methadone confirms widespread resentment as well as a passive self-deprecating obedience on the part of structurally vulnerable methadone addicts (cf. Rosenbaum and Murphy, 1984). One study quotes addicts as referring to their relationship with methadone as "a ball and chain" (Johnson and Friedman, 1993: 37); other researchers cite methadone addicts as complaining of "feeling like automatons," and of "becoming robotic" (Uchtenhagen, 1997; Koester et al., 1999). In Denver street addicts had nicknamed methadone "methadeath" (Koester et al., 1999) (Bourgois, 2000).

On top of this, paradoxically, the imposed discipline is projected onto the individual's responsibility. The move toward the biomedical conception of addiction corrected the once well-accepted notion that addiction was purely caused by moral failure, laziness, and lack of will. The shift in ideology and policy was however only really one from broken morals to "broken brains" (Wiers and Verschure, 2020). Responsibility for the *management and treatment* of addiction remains located within the individual: instead of "getting a grip of themselves," people who use drugs are now expected to structure their schedules around the methadone distribution. This expectation has been highly criticized for its unrealistic demand on people who use drugs and also for singularizing responsibilization (Heather, 2017). In fact, progress is "measured" (and constantly surveilled, see Mary taking notes above) based on whether people can keep to appointments and how they are moving along their projected "dosage timeline." The titration of doses is a direct link to the perception of how far along the recovery process people have progressed (Bourgois, 2000). Oftentimes, if a person misses too many appointments, they are penalized through this instrument: the people might be made to start over their "methadone course," or regress a few stages (i.e., take a higher dosage again). No change to the rigid treatment course is possible apart from renewed plans following check-ins with doctors – putting the medical professional *again* in the role of a disciplinary and overseer. Not only does this approach present a false linear conception of recovery, it also puts blame squarely and singularly on the individual. If a person doesn't progress on the path of their recovery, usually with the ultimate goal of abstinence, then it is their fault. Bourgois notes that this shift created and reinforced the perception that a person who remained addicted to heroin was seen as "self-destructive and irresponsible," while someone nearly permanently maintained on methadone was praised as a "worthy, well-disciplined citizen/patient who is dutifully on the road to recovery from substance abuse" (Bourgois, 2000: 169). The social and communal responsibility of stakeholders other than the people who use drugs is not defined as essential; as it is, methadone maintenance is only conceived of as a collective effort insofar as some programs are free as part of public health interventions.

Where does that all leave the people who use drugs? How do they benefit from methadone programs? While we undeniably recognize positive lived experiences with methadone, many people who use drugs either categorically or based on their own experiences with the disciplinary regime (of daily, supervised pickups) laid out above keep away from the programs. A number of interlocutors we have spoken to over time have described the inefficacy of methadone at best, and addiction to methadone and as a result a lowered sense of self at worst. One man in the UK, James, who had struggled with addiction since his teens, explained to us that methadone still felt like the drugs he wanted to get away from:

I tried the methadone; I didn't find it helped. Since I finished the course, I started using again anyway, so it wasn't nearly, well, it keeps you in the loop, do you know what I mean? Someone wants to move off heroin and you give them a heroin substitute ... it doesn't really help, I don't think. You're still, you know, you're still taking something, do you know what I mean?

Naturally, interlocutors also expressed frustration with the medical professionals – doctors, nurses, pharmacists – who worked to facilitate the prescription, administration, and any possible change in scripts. The frustration stemmed not only from the nature of the inevitable entwinement of care and coercion, but also from a lack of empathy. James relayed, "I've been offered help by the government before with getting off drugs and it just seemed to be sitting around chatting or getting methadone and I don't know, people who didn't have that sort of life experience, I didn't really see how they could understand or help me." Many of the current healthcare workers who monitor methadone programs are not people who used to use drugs and as a result, lack the kind of understanding and relatability that many interlocutors mention is important to them. Trust relationships – found to be so crucial for the development of meaningful therapeutic relationships and recovery (Collins et al., 2019; Petterson et al., 2019) – can develop less easily.

We also want to shine a light on a last actor we have so far not mentioned as a crucial participant: law enforcement. As we explained above, methadone is often part of what we describe as a criminalized system of drug treatment where drugs (usually involving the production, possession, consumption, and commercial activity around them) are illegal. Hence, law enforcement plays a crucial role as a further disciplinarian. Continuing Victor's story briefly will help us further understand law enforcement's role.

The street right around the corner from where the distribution van parked close to a major underground station was widely known as one of the main trading spots for drugs. One street corner housed mostly the opioid dealers stocked with both prescription and illegal substances, as well as – if need be – the necessary prescriptions to legally carry the former through the city. At the other end of the short street, crack could be purchased at any time of the day. The police knew about the trading – and also about the methadone distribution in the middle of it. Officially, only the trading was the excuse for their almost daily checks; conveniently, the van made it easy for the officers to find but also to identify people who use drugs. The fact that many of the registered methadone users were also taking "on top," i.e., regularly consumed opioids and other illegal substances, made them an easy target for stop-and-search controls by law enforcement. Chances were that they not only came outside to drink their daily dosage of methadone but also to stock up on other substances at the same time.

Viktor – despite being white – was stopped regularly by the police. He was widely known as a heavy poly-drug user and many of the searches he was subjected to were often successful. "They look through all your belongings – searching for drugs. That's it." The likelihood was high that Viktor had some methadone he had bought on the streets with him (that he had bought on the street on top of his free daily ration from the van), or another subscription opioid, or used syringes, or crack left in the glass pipe he always carried with him (and that was also handed out by the methadone van as a means of harm reduction).

If Viktor didn't have the right prescription with him for either the methadone or any other prescription drug, the law enforcement would take him in. The same was true for other obvious paraphernalia, and while the tools themselves wouldn't be enough for a sentence, they led to a drug test which in turn could lead to a prison sentence.

The methadone distribution, particularly in systems where overall principles of the war on drugs (e.g., the illegality of drugs) are still in place, in fact not only presented a disciplinary regime enforced by the medical professionals; it also created a convenient time and place for police officers to locate and stop persons they suspect of taking part in illegal activity (Lupick, 2018). Worse, the responsibility of law enforcement is framed as justifiably continuing to criminalize drug use – proven to not only disproportionately affect marginalized communities but also making it nearly impossible for people who use drugs to recover, trapping them in endless cycles through the penal system and addiction (Rodgers, 2020).

Case 16.2 Sanctioned Safe Injection Facility within a Decriminalized Zone

It was a long time in the making: years of campaigning and several illegal makeshift predecessors and approximations preempted the eventual opening of this site in Paris. People who use drugs-turned-activists, healthcare workers and health administrators, some politicians, and even the police were ultimately in favor of opening the site in the middle of what was known as the downtown drug circuit. For many decades this area of the city has been known to house, hide, and facilitate the lives of people who use drugs and drug dealers, their support institutions, and the underlying infrastructures from cheap hotels and shops to hidden alcoves and "drug dens."

The entrance to the safe injection site (SIS) wasn't hard to find despite the lack of signage. Word of mouth travelled quickly and the involvement of the major drug user support organizations which had been on the ground for years facilitated the fast spread of the information. While the initial opening hours weren't exactly sufficient – the equivalent of a 9-to-5 doesn't work when it comes to drug consumption – people agreed: it was a crucial start to get the site open at all. And once they found their way into the space, they couldn't have been happier.

Similar to the mobile needle exchange that was in operation (first illegally and eventually funded by several public sources of money) and serving as the proto-SIS for years, the site allowed people to enter on a nickname basis. Familiar faces welcomed the visitors from an inviting large reception desk, and the same social workers, nurses, pharmacists, and doctors who had operated the previous services ran the SIS. At the SIS, the trust and continuation of these relationships was a central principle. The receptionist would register people and hand out paraphernalia whenever required and requested. People could access a plethora of different types of needles, syringes, cups, clean water, and acids. Staff handed out material for usage on site or take-away. The key imperative aimed to enable safer and cleaner habits – and to allow the people themselves to make choices as much as possible.

There was no limit to the number of times people could come to the SIS a day; only the opening hours limited usage. Later, increased funding allowed staff to run the site for longer. Similarly, there were no restrictions on the amount of time people could spend inside the SIS and consuming drugs was only one of the options provided at the site. A social worker – in addition to the healthcare professionals – was on site at any one point, and pointed people to the right service providers (such as for housing or benefit applications). Similarly, a simple "chill-out room" provided space to stay warm (in the winter) and protected after consuming drugs.

Just behind the reception desk, the main room opened up widely. It was split into two parts: the smaller part was cut off completely and essentially consisted of a glass cube with a full air-conditioning system inside. This enabled safer consumption of crack. A large bin right next to the entrance to the cube filled up every day with glass crack pipes. The bigger area on the right was in itself cut into a row of small cubicles facing the greyed-out windows. The opening in the back allowed healthcare professionals on duty to see everyone consuming at any one point while also affording relative privacy to people who use drugs. Once sitting down, people had around twenty minutes to prepare and consume their substances, just to allow as many people as possible to profit from the site on any given day. This "deadline," however, was usually sufficient for most people, and for those who needed more time it was never enforced. Most people naturally went to the chill-out room, separated through a big wooden door at the back, after their injection. This is where the relationships and the community were built through long conversations, spending time together, and learning from and about each other.

* * *

Safe injection sites like the one we describe above have only been adopted very slowly over the last twenty years; the first one in North America, Insite, opened in Canada in 2003 (Boyd, 2013; Kerr et al., 2017). While Canada now has 39 SISs, still none exist in the United

States (Government of Canada; Kerr et al., 2017). Parts of Europe have taken the lead in rolling them out; the Netherlands, Germany, Switzerland, Denmark, Norway, parts of Spain, and most recently France (on a trial basis) have been engaged in this policy. In 2018 ninety official sites were open in Europe in eight countries (including Switzerland) (EMCDDA, 2018). Portugal, Ireland, and Belgium have opened sites, as well. SISs represent a fundamentally different approach to addiction from the "war on drugs" and also from methadone distribution; they not only stand for comprehensive harm reduction instead of criminalization, but also emphasize the importance of collective solidarity and care instead of individualized control and responsibility.

One reason for this different ethos in place in most SISs might be the kind of core actors involved; many of the early SISs sprang out of activist efforts, often driven by people with lived experience of drug use and addiction themselves. They knew from the start what, for instance, the problems with the war on drugs were – from violence and coercion to discipline and control – and what kind of a space was really lacking. As a manager in a Vancouver SIS, whom the journalist Lupick encountered, described:

"A lot of other things that we'd done in psychiatry had felt off-base, overly controlling or coercive, robbing people of their individual rights and freedoms," relays a manager of a SIS in Vancouver, "We saw the addiction not as characterizing the person, but as a coping mechanism." (Lupick, 2018: 162)

Unlike methadone programs, SISs are designed to not only provide a "medicine" for people using drugs but also a safe, accessible, and open space; they embody a safety net that does not coerce individual behavior while offering guidance and support whenever desired and chosen by the people who use drugs. Here, the SIS's staff are more easily structurally filling in the role not of a surveilling enforcer but a supportive hand to catch people in case they overdose, or to push them with a gentle nudge toward seeking help with various specialized services when they are ready (such as a rehab facility). Drugs are not fundamentally seen as deviant and as in need of replacement; individual people's choices to consume are respected, and support provided to mitigate harm. Lupick reflects with the same sentiment on his observations of the role of staff in Vancouver; he concludes that their "job was

to meet the patients where they were at, and then to help them there"
and to ask people, "how can we support you?" (Lupick, 2018: 165).

This attitude of staff also shines through very strongly in the treatment of time; while for many people methadone program's time was a
disciplining factor as we describe above, in most SISs it is a buffer. The
people who use drugs can form, use, and shape the intervention and
space in the way they want both in the short and long term. They were
welcome as many different times and in whatever interval they chose
(in contrast to the rigid pickup system in the case of a daily-supervised
methadone distribution). At the SIS "they can prepare their injection
with a clean needle, taking their own time … cutting down on the
chance of mistake," and a nurse is close by – but not hovering – to
make sure to mitigate any negative reactions such as an overdose (Patel
Shepelavy, 2018). This practice of "taking one's time" is usually
correlated with decreased risky behavior (e.g., injecting more calmly,
no syringe sharing, disposing of syringes more securely, at times even
injecting less frequently) (Boyd, 2013; Kinnard et al., 2014). On the
other hand, in a more long-term timescale, the SIS was not built around
the assumption of a linear and enforceable process of recovery (punished for instance by the means of decreasing titration and "throwing
you back" on your recovery path as a means of disciplining).
Interestingly, as a result, SISs have been shown to be spaces where
people who use drugs are "more likely to take steps into sobriety" –
but on their own timeline (Lupick, 2018: 344; see also Wood et al.,
2016; Drug Policy Alliance; AMA, 2017).

SISs foster the empowerment of one's own sense of self and time,
allowing people who use drugs to set their own timelines, rhythms, and
agendas as autonomous individuals. People are more likely to
"engage" with services on offer (therapy and rehab for instance) and
a radically reduced number of overdose deaths (Bowers, 2019). For
example, a legally unsanctioned experiment site opened by a social
service agency in the US saw 10,514 injections and thirty-three opioid-
involved overdoses over five years; not a single death occurred as all
thirty-three overdoses were reversed by naloxone (Kral and Davidson,
2017; Kral et al., 2020). SISs have also been shown to drastically
decrease the number of HIV/AIDS and hepatitis C infections
(Highleyman, 2018). These numbers demonstrate that not only do
people who use drugs benefit but so does the healthcare system more
broadly. The healthcare system overall, even by the most conservative

estimates, saves money and life-years. In Vancouver, a SIS observed more than $18 million in incremental net savings per year and the number of life-years gained amounted to 1175 (Bayoumi and Zaric, 2008). In Sydney, Australia, the burden on ambulance services on opioid-related deaths decreased drastically in the surrounding vicinity of a SIS (Salmon et al., 2010). Tentatively, overall crime rates are going down over time in cities where SISs are operational, reducing the pressure on law enforcement (and the penal system) (Myer and Belisle, 2017).

This benefit was made even more stable and secure when embedded in a reform of the criminal justice system. Let us go back briefly to the situation from our second case below with the continuation of the description:

Stepping outside back into the city, people were able to continue to feel safe; the facility was not installed as an isolated, unreflected push but as part of a much wider rethink of how people who use drugs were supposed to be treated. The two most important accompanying changes were about legislation and law enforcement. On the one hand, a decriminalized zone of about ten blocks was created around the SIS overseen by the police. This did not mean that police stayed *away* from the SIS or the zone as a whole, but that they fulfilled a fundamentally different task: instead of enforcing rules around illegal possession and consumption of drugs (both of which were legal within the zone, for personal use), police oversaw dealing activities (which remained illegal) and breakouts of violence. For this to happen, the legal structure had to be changed to allow possession of certain (illegal) substances for personal use (Fortson, 2006).

The distinct groups that had previously worked toward fulfilling different goals and different agendas – from people who use drugs, healthcare workers, social workers, law enforcement officers, politicians, and legislators – were united. A shift in attitude, even including the neighbors who had most adamantly opposed SIS, was occurring quickly.

Establishing a zone of decriminalization around the SIS – as happened for instance in Denmark (Kinnock, 2019) – and ideally changing the drug laws (especially around possession and consumption of drugs) more generally expands the possible impact of the intervention even further. What results is not just healthier pursuits for people who use drugs, but a fundamental shift in how our society thinks and acts on drugs. It more directly signals a rethinking in terms of responsibility: instead of placing the locus of responsibility purely with the individual (as with the methadone distribution), SIS offers people who use drugs a community that ideally extends beyond the simple facility site. The SIS can act as a central point for learning about access and connection with other services and other users, whether it is for basic needs or specific support for addiction. The zone of decriminalization around the site reinforces this sense of trust into the wider geography, thus establishing a space of security and stability so crucial for working toward any eventual recovery and abstinence (Treloar et al., 2016).

16.2 Conclusion

Though it may seem a thing of the past, the war on drugs persists. Several countries including the US, the Philippines, Mexico and to a certain extent the UK still explicitly follow the principles of violence, surveillance, and criminalization in their policies toward addiction. What is holding us back if there are alternatives such as harm reduction approaches out there that are proven to be beneficial on multiple axes? There is no clear answer, but we believe one significant factor is ideology.

One of us was at a panel in late 2019 in the UK to discuss this exact question: what keeps us back from changing? The panel included a person with lived experience of addiction and homelessness, one support worker, the editor of an international medical journal, and the author. We heard a lot about local efforts to support homeless people struggling with addiction, about the role of voluntary organizations, and spoke for almost an hour circling the question of inadequate drug treatment generally. Given that the data points in a clear direction – harm reduction and specifically SISs are more cost-effective, safer, empowering – we concluded that the decision not to shift toward such approaches and away from "war on drug" practices was a political decision influenced by ideology. This ideology is rooted in a kind of artificial morality that has long been used to divide people – one that took hold especially in the lead up to and beginnings of the era of the war on drugs, where policies were enacted to demonize minority populations such as African Americans. This is an ideology of individualized responsibility and a total lack of collective support; an ideology that sees the police and also healthcare providers as a means of surveillance and control rather than helping hands for citizens. Its insidious legacies remain, and we must be critical in examining the consequences of modern policies. Addiction has to move away from being seen as an issue of deviance that requires law enforcement to step in (and put people who take drugs in prison). While the next step is conceptualizing drugs primarily as a public health concern that demands care and solidarity, the underlying shift is an even bigger one. We have to begin seeing people who use drugs – like all people – as autonomous individuals and respect their decisions to determine the extent of which drugs play a role in their lives; we have to see all people as part of our collective society which encourages agency, mutual support, and empathy.

References

Albert M., L. F. McCaig, and S. Uddin. 2015. *Emergency Department Visits for Drug Poisoning: United States, 2008–2011. NCHS Data Brief, no 196.* Hyattsville, MD: National Center for Health Statistics.

American Medical Association. 2017. "AMA wants new approaches to combat synthetic and injectable drugs." www.ama-assn.org/press-center/press-releases/ama-wants-new-approaches-combat-synthetic-and-injectable-drugs

Bayoumi, A. M., and G. S. Zaric. 2008. "The cost-effectiveness of Vancouver's supervised injection facility." *CMAJ* 179 (11): 1143–1151.

Bell, J., and D. Zador. 2000. "A risk–benefit analysis of methadone maintenance treatment." *Drug Safety* 22 (3): 179–190.

Bourgois, P. 2000. "Disciplining addictions: The bio-politics of methadone and heroin in the United States." *Culture, Medicine and Psychiatry* 24 (2): 165–195.

Bowers, L. 2019. "Safe injection sites and drug injection overdose: A literature review." *SSRN Electronic Journal.*

Boyd, N. 2013. "Lessons from INSITE, Vancouver's supervised injection facility: 2003–2012." *Drugs: Education, Prevention and Policy* 20 (3): 234–240.

Brinkley-Rubinstein, L., M. McKenzie, A.. Macmadu, S. Larney, N. Zaller, E. Dauria, and J. Rich. 2018. "A randomized, open label trial of methadone continuation versus forced withdrawal in a combined US prison and jail: Findings at 12 months post-release." *Drug and Alcohol Dependence* 184: 57–63.

Campbell, Nancy D. 2019. *OD: Naloxone and the Politics of Overdose.* Cambridge, MA: MIT Press.

Centers for Disease Control and Prevention. 2018. "Emergency department data show rapid increases in opioid overdoses." *Centers for Disease Control and Prevention*, March 6, 2018. www.cdc.gov/media/releases/2018/p0306-vs-opioids-overdoses.html.

2020. *Increase in Fatal Drug Overdoses across the United States Driven by Synthetic Opioids Before and During the COVID-19 Pandemic.* Atlanta, GA: US Department of Health and Human Services. https://emergency.cdc.gov/han/2020/han00438.asp

Collins, D., J. Alla, C. Nicolaidis, J. Gregg, D. J. Gullickson, A.Patten, and H. Englander. 2019. "'If it wasn't for him, I wouldn't have talked to them': Qualitative study of addiction peer mentorship in the hospital." *Journal of General Internal Medicine.*

Drug Policy Alliance. n.d. "Supervised consumption services." Retrieved January 21, 2021. https://drugpolicy.org/issues/supervised-consumption-services

EMCCDA. n.d."Drug consumption rooms: an overview of provision and evidence." Retrieved January 21, 2021. www.sallesdeconsommation.com

Flores, P., J. Lopez, G. Pemble-Flood, H. Riegel, and M. Segura, 2018. *An Analysis of Drug Treatment Courts in New York State.* New York: Rockefeller Institute of Government

Government of Canada. n.d.. "Canadian supervised consumption sites statistics – 2017 to 2019." Retrieved January 21, 2021. https://health-infobase.canada.ca/datalab/supervised-consumption-sites-blog.html

Hammersley, M. 2006. "Ethnography: Problems and prospects." *Ethnography and Education* 1 (1): 3–14.

Hatcher, A. E., S. Mendoza, and H. Hansen, 2018. "At the expense of a life: Race, class, and the meaning of buprenorphine in pharmaceuticalized 'care'." *Substance Use and Misuse* 53 (2): 301–310.

Highleyman, Liz. 2018. "Supervised injection sites reduce drug-related harm." *MedpageToday*, October 23, 2018. www.medpagetoday.com/hivaids/hivaids/75871.

International Harm Reduction Association. 2010. *What Is Harm Reduction?* (Vol. 44). London: International Harm Reduction Association.

Kerr, T., S. Mitra, M. C. Kennedy, and R. McNeil. 2017. "Supervised injection facilities in Canada: Past, present, and future." *Harm Reduction Journal* 14 (1): 28.

Kinnard, E. N., C. J. Howe, T. Kerr, V. S. Hass, and B. D. L. Marshall. 2014. "Self-reported changes in drug use behaviors and syringe disposal methods following the opening of a supervised injecting facility in Copenhagen, Denmark." *Harm Reduction Journal*, 11 (1): 29.

Kinnock, J. 2019. *"The glass box": accommodating addicted bodies in a café in Copenhagen*. [BA dissertation from Queen's College Cambridge]

Kral, A. H., and P. J. Davidson. 2017. "Addressing the nation's opioid epidemic: Lessons from an unsanctioned supervised injection site in the U.S." *American Journal of Preventive Medicine* 53 (6): 919–922.

Kral, A. H., B. H. Lambdin, L. D. Wenger, and P. J. Davidson. 2020. "Evaluation of an unsanctioned safe consumption site in the United States." *New England Journal of Medicine*, 383 (6): 589–590.

Lupick, Travis. 2017. *Fighting for Space: How a Group of Drug Users Transformed One City's Struggle with Addiction*. Vancouver, BC: Arsenal Pulp Press.

Melendez, Miguel. 2003. *We Took the Streets: Fighting for Latino Rights with the YoungLords*. New York: St. Martin's Press.

Mendoza, S., A. S. Rivera-Cabrero, and H. Hansen. 2016. "Shifting blame: Buprenorphine prescribers, addiction treatment, and prescription monitoring in middle-class America." *Transcultural Psychiatry* 53 (4): 465–487.

Meng, E. 2021. "Use of acupuncture by 1970s revolutionaries of color: The South Bronx "toolkit care" concept." *American Journal of Public Health* 111 (5): 896–906.

Moore, K. E., L. Oberleitner, K. M. Z. Smith, K. Maurer, and S. A. McKee. 2018. "Feasibility and effectiveness of continuing methadone maintenance treatment during incarceration compared with forced withdrawal." *Journal of Addiction Medicine* 12 (2): 156–162.

Myer, A. J., and L. Belisle. 2018. "Highs and lows: An interrupted time-series evaluation of the impact of North America's only supervised injection facility on crime." *Journal of Drug Issues* 48 (1): 36–49.

Neale, J. 1998. "Drug users' views of prescribed methadone." *Drugs: Education, Prevention and Policy* 5 (1): 33–45.

Patel Shepelavy, R. (2018). "Everything you need to know about safe injection sites." *The Philadelphia Citizen*, February 5, 2018. https://thephiladelphiacitizen.org/everything-you-need-to-know-about-safe-injection-sites

Pettersen, H., A. Landheim, I. Skeie, S. Biong, M. Brodahl, J. Oute, and L. Davidson. 2019. "How social relationships influence substance use disorder recovery: A collaborative narrative study." *Substance Abuse: Research and Treatment* 13: 1–8.

lReal Reporting Foundation. 2021 "Arrests and criminal law enforcement." Drug Policy Facts. Real Reporting Foundation, February 27, 2021. www.drugpolicyfacts.org/chapter/crime_arrests

Rettig, R. A., and A. Yarmolinsky. 1995. *Federal Regulation of Methadone Treatment*. Washington: National Academies Press (US). Accessed January 21, 2021. www.ncbi.nlm.nih.gov/books/NBK232105/

Reverby, Susan M. 2020. *Co-Conspirator for Justice: The Revolutionary Life of Dr. Alan Berkman*. Chapel Hill: University of North Carolina Press.

Riley, A. 2020. "My working week: 'I worry about giving a drug user a week's worth of methadone'." *Guardian*, April 27, 2020. www.theguardian.com/society/2020/apr/27/working-week-drug-alcohol-services-coronavirus

Rodgers, D. 2020. "The drugs consensus: The spatial policing of dealing and consumption in Geneva, Switzerland." *City & Society* 33 (1).

Salmon, A. M., I. Van Beek, J. Amin, J. Kaldor, and L. Maher. 2010. "The impact of a supervised injecting facility on ambulance call-outs in Sydney, Australia." *Addiction* 105 (4): 676–683.

Shakur, Mutulu. 2018. "2018 interview about acupuncture & the opioid crisis." Accessed January 3, 2019. http://mutulushakur.com/site/2018/11/acupuncture-interview

Stoicescu, Claudia, and Catherine Cook. 2011. *Harm Reduction in Europe: Mapping Coverage and Civil Society Advocacy*. London: European Harm Reduction Network. Retrieved January 21, 2021. www.eurohrn.eu

The Express Wire. 2020. "Methadone hydrochloride market size 2020 global industry leading players update, gross margin analysis, development history, business research report 2026." www.theexpresswire.com/pressrelease/Methadone-Hydrochloride-Market-Size-2020-Global-Industry-Leading-Players-Update-Gross-Margin-Analysis-Development-History-Business-Research-Report-2026_11506517

Treloar, C., J. Rance, K. Yates, and L. Mao, 2016. "Trust and people who inject drugs: The perspectives of clients and staff of Needle Syringe Programs." *International Journal of Drug Policy* 27: 138–145.

University of Massachusetts Medical School. n.d. "Fact sheet: Methadone – common questions about methadone." Accessed January 21, 2021. www.umassmed.edu/globalassets/center-for-integrated-primary-care/amber/final-fact-sheet-on-methadone.pdf

Vestal, C. 2018a. "Long stigmatized methadone clinics multiply in some states." *The Pew Charitable Trusts*, October 31, 2018. www.pewtrusts.org/en/research-and-analysis/blogs/stateline/2018/10/31/long-stigmatized-methadone-clinics-multiply-in-some-states

    2018b. "In opioid crisis, methadone clinics see revival." *The Washington Post*, November 12, 2018. Accessed January 21, 2021. www.washingtonpost.com/national/health-science/some-states-add-more-methadone-clinics-to-fight-opioid-epidemic/2018/11/09/8cace992-e133-11e8-b759-3d88a5ce9e19_story.html.

Vulliamy, Ed. 2011. "Nixon's 'war on drugs' began 40 years ago, and the battle Is still raging." *Guardian*, July 23, 2011. www.theguardian.com/society/2011/jul/24/war-on-drugs-40-years.

White Lightning. 1975. *In Memory of Richard Taft.* New York: Come! Unity Press. www.freedomarchives.org/Documents/Finder/DOC58_scans/58.White.Lightening.RichardTaft.pdf.

Wiers, Reinout W., and Paul Verschure. 2021. "Curing the broken brain model of addiction: Neurorehabilitation from a systems perspective." *Addictive Behaviors* 122: 1–10.

Wood, E., M. W. Tyndall, J. S. Montaner, and T. Kerr. 2006. "Summary of findings from the evaluation of a pilot medically supervised safer injecting facility." *CMAJ* 175 (11): 1399–1404.

Zanis, D. A., and G. E. Woody. 1998. "One-year mortality rates following methadone treatment discharge." *Drug and Alcohol Dependence* 52 (3): 257–260.

Zhang, L., X. Zou, Y. Xu, N. Medland, L. Deng, Y. Liu, S. Su, and L. Ling. 2019. "The decade-long Chinese methadone maintenance therapy yields large population and economic benefits for drug users in reducing harm, HIV and HCV disease burden." *Frontiers in Public Health* 7: 594–602.

17 | How Should We Design Access to a Healthcare System?

JOHAN GERSEL, DANIEL SOULELES,
AND MORTEN SØRENSEN THANING

Healthcare is a wonderful, tragic case of the limits of individual capacity in making consumer choices. Often health and medical decisions are so complicated, so expensive, and have consequences so far in the future that it is practically impossible for ordinary individuals to make informed choices about their medical priorities. Given this, it is a natural reach for expert help (i.e., doctors), and the hand of government regulation (in the form of national insurance schemes). Here, Gersel, Souleles, and Thaning look at two national healthcare systems (Switzerland and the United States) that make use of market-based and for-profit mechanisms to provide healthcare. The crucial difference between them is that the United States remains wedded to the idea that individuals can and should make their own informed choices about their care (see pp. 32–36). In contrast, Switzerland has put a hard limit on what can reasonably be expected of individual choice in healthcare provision and has enacted a number of mandatory regulatory guardrails. It should come as no surprise, at this point in the case book, that citizens are taken better care off in the system that actually recognizes limits to individual consumptive behavior in healthcare, rather than sticking to the presumption of the hyper-intelligent *Homo-economicus*. It turns out we can in this case predict what people need, better than they themselves can through their purchases in an open market (see pp. 38–44).

17.1 Introduction

Switzerland and the United States both rely heavily on private health insurance companies to expand access to coverage. Despite this seemingly common starting principle, decisions about how to design and implement healthcare access have resulted in the creation of two vastly different health systems.

The differences between the two systems are the product of a century of policy choices driven by different views on the right of citizens to access care and the role of government in the administration and regulation of the industry. Over the past few decades, the United States and Switzerland have both reached critical junctures motivated by similar challenges – the need to expand access to coverage. Both countries faced similar barriers: rising uninsured rates, rising per capita health expenditures, and insurance companies that were denying high-risk patients' coverage. The reforms offered in both countries were designed to address these challenges and did so with some degree of success. But critical differences in approach have yielded hugely different outcomes today.

The World Health Organization considers healthcare one of the fundamental rights of every human being. Whether healthcare is a right is a question of morality. But among the wealthiest countries in the world, this appears to be a settled question. The United States is the only country out of the top twenty-five that does not provide universal health coverage, and is a striking outlier given that 54 percent of Americans believe the government has a responsibility to ensure Americans have healthcare coverage (Jones, 2019).

Over the last twenty-five years, both countries passed historic reforms with the aim of dramatically expanding access to coverage. Given that both these systems have historically relied on for-profit private insurers, it's important to understand that health insurance is most profitable when it is providing services to the fewest sick people. If the goal is profit, health insurance for a person who is both healthy and wealthy isn't hard to manage, but making money selling insurance to a person who is both sick and poor is impossible. Group health insurance solves this problem by pooling the risk of many individuals together, but it's tricky. Charge too much and healthy people don't sign-up, leaving you with just expensive sick people. Charge too little and sick people cost more than your revenue. As across-the-board costs increase, the problem gets even more complicated – even middle-income people can't afford coverage. But for a for-profit company, covering the sick hurts the bottom line, which some might consider a contradiction for an industry whose purpose is to help people when they are sick. For this reason, government regulation and subsidization of this sector has been vital to the expansion of access to care around the world for nearly a century.

An informed consumer that knows their own preferences is also a vital part of a functional market process. Do they know how to obtain insurance? Will it have the benefits they need? Is it optimal for their budget? What does it cost if they break a leg? Develop diabetes? Get Cancer? Or a rare disease? The more choices the consumer faces, the more complex the system, the more hypotheticals they are expected to evaluate, the harder it is for them to assess comparative values of choices and make informed decisions.

In America and Switzerland, both countries that celebrate capitalism, there is an understandable desire to use market processes to drive efficiency and innovation. But recognizing the inherent limitations in the market's ability to deliver efficiency in this space is vital to the design of an efficient health system. Government regulation and assistance are critical to the goal of universal coverage – the private sector alone cannot be the solution. If the goal is universal coverage, the idea that we just need one more guardrail to keep a bad actor in check or one more incentive to motivate good behavior is like trying to build a Rube Goldberg machine to make breakfast. Even if you could do it, why would you if there was a better way?

We'll take a look at the history of healthcare access in the United States and Switzerland, how each country approached major health reform initiatives, the result of that reform, and whether there is a better way.

17.2 Unfolding of the Setting

17.2.1 United States

The United States is a federal republic composed of fifty states, a federal territory, and five self-governing territories. It has a population of approximately 328 million. It covers an area of 3,796,742 km^2 and shares borders with Mexico and Canada. The United States had $3.6 trillion dollars in healthcare expenditures in 2018.

It wasn't until the early twentieth century that discussions about a national health system began. At the time, Americans relied on industrial sickness funds for primarily nonagricultural wage workers that were organized by companies or unions providing "workingman's insurance" or "sickness insurance." By World War I, these funds covered 8–9 million Americans (about 10 percent of the total population) (Murray, n.d.). Despite the rise of progressivism in Europe, it's likely that these funds, along with a strong national ethos that prized a small and decentralized government, played an important role in limiting public calls for a national health system. Even state-based efforts to provide health assistance were unsuccessful at this time (Murray, n.d.).

During World War II, a combination of wage and price controls created incentives for employers to offer employment benefits to augment wages. In 1943, the Internal Revenue Service determined that health insurance should be tax exempt for employees (Bartlett, 2013). This accelerated the creation of a more standardized form of employer-sponsored insurance growing those covered from 1.3 million people in 1940 to 32 million people in 1945 and 40 million people in 1951 (Berkowitz, 2005). It was around this same time that President Harry Truman unsuccessfully submitted the first comprehensive federal insurance bill to Congress, and the VA, the veterans-only single-payer health system, started to take shape (Petersen, 2015). In 1954, the US Congress would further entrench employer-sponsored insurance coverage by exempting employers from payroll and income taxes. By 1960, 122 million Americans were covered (Bartlett, 2013). The tax exclusion is still in place today and effectively subsidizes private health insurance. In 2019, this subsidy totaled $273 billion per year – disproportionately benefiting high-wage workers (Tax Policy Center, n.d.).

Despite this progress, one in four Americans was uninsured. Nearly half of people over the age of 65 did not have any type of hospital insurance – even fewer had insurance covering surgical or out- of-hospital physician costs (Social Security, n.d.). Many insurance companies were terminating the policies of high-risk patients. Programs that did exist to aid the elderly were falling short of needs and the problem was getting worse. The situation was more dire for low-income and disabled Americans who relied on charity care and public hospitals for healthcare (Dickson 2015).

In 1965, President Lyndon B. Johnson signed into law the legislation that enacted Medicare and Medicaid. Medicare was a single-payer system that covered hospital and supplemental medical expenses for people over 65. Over 19 million people enrolled in its first year (De Lew, 2000). Medicaid allowed the federal government to fund a program for low-income people that was cofinanced and managed by the states. Over 4 million people enrolled in its first year (Klemm, 2000). In the decades that followed both Medicare and Medicaid enrollment would grow, boosted in part by changes that expanded coverage to more people. By 1975, the uninsured rate had dropped significantly with just over 10 percent of Americans uninsured.

For those people who could not get coverage through an employer, were not over 65, disabled, or low-income, the nongroup health insurance market was an option if you were healthy and wealthy. These plans typically excluded high-risk patients from coverage or charged exorbitant premiums for coverage. They also questionably terminated the policies of individuals who developed high-cost illnesses (Goin and Long, n.d.).

By 1990, rising costs were directly and indirectly causing a growing number of people to go uninsured. These trends led to new calls for comprehensive health reform. Early attempts at reform were met with fierce opposition and failed. Costs continued to rise in the 2000s. By 2010, 46 percent of Americans said they were "very worried" or "somewhat worried" about their ability to pay for medical costs for normal healthcare – the highest recorded percentage since Gallup began asking the question in 2000 (Gallup, n.d.). The uninsured rate hit 16.3 percent in 2010 – the highest it had been since the passage of Medicare and Medicaid (Department of Health and Human Services, 2011). National health expenditures as a percent of GDP were rising quickly from 13.4 percent in 2000 to 17.4 percent in 2010 (Kamal, McDermott, Ramirez, and Cox, 2020). The path the United States was on was unsustainable.

17.2.2 Switzerland

Switzerland, officially the Swiss federation, is a federal republic composed of twenty-six cantons. It has a population of approximately 8.5 million people. It covers an area of 41,287 km^2 and shares borders with Italy, France, Germany, Austria, and Liechtenstein. Switzerland had $84.4 billion dollars in healthcare expenditures in 2018.

In 1848, when the Swiss Federal Constitution was adopted, the cantons and municipalities were entirely responsible for administering health systems in Switzerland. The first types of health insurance in Switzerland, called help funds (Hilfskassen) were the product of trade unions, religious organizations, and entrepreneurs. By 1880, these

Hilfskassen insured over 200,000 people or roughly 7.5 percent of the Swiss population (De Pietro 2015).

The first attempt at introducing a national health system was made in 1899 inspired in part by the German health system, but it wasn't until 1911 that the first health insurance law was passed. The law provided subsidies to health insurance companies based on how many people they insured but required companies that hoped to benefit from these subsidies to register with the Federal Office for Social Insurance. The law prohibited subsidized insurance companies from making a profit and set a limit on how much more women could be charged for coverage than men (10 percent). The law also required subsidized insurance companies to provide a specific set of benefits which included ambulatory care, drugs, and limited-duration hospital stays. The law provided basic consumer protections like the ability to change health insurance provider if people moved or changed jobs (World Health Organization, 2000).

Insurance coverage was not federally mandated, but even so demand for coverage was far higher than projected. In 1915 about 11 percent of the Swiss population had health insurance, growing to roughly 40 percent in 1930 and 60 percent in 1947. The system struggled financially, and multiple attempts were made to reform the system. It wasn't until 1958 that major reform began. The federal government restructured how the insurance companies were subsidized. They factored in the age and gender of the covered population and man-dated direct charges to consumers by the health insurance funds including a deductible and coinsurance. When it was completed in 1964, these reforms stabilized the health insurance funds (World Health Organization, 2000). By 1959 about 80 percent of the Swiss population had coverage.

In the decades that followed, Swiss health spending rose dramatic-ally. Swiss healthcare costs as a percentage of GDP grew from just over 5 percent in 1960 to over 8 percent in the 1990s. Switzerland faced shortages of hospital-based doctors and dentists and struggled to provide adequate rural healthcare. Government attempts at reform in 1974 and 1987 failed in referendums because they were viewed as incremental solutions that could not resolve the fundamental structural problems.

Inequality in the system was becoming more acute. Since most people bought private coverage through an employer-based plan, nearly all employed people had health coverage. People without employer-based coverage initially relied on nonprofit insurance companies for coverage, but the number of uninsured started to grow as for-profit companies purchased the nonprofit insurance providers, raised premiums, and denied people with preexisting conditions coverage. This made the cost of coverage unaffordable for a growing number of people. About 5 percent of the Swiss population, 400,000 people, did not have health coverage (Thacher 2015). These growing costs and the inequality that resulted was unacceptable to most Swiss people, who viewed "solidarity" as a core Swiss principle.

17.3 How the Solution or Action Came to Be

17.3.1 United States

During the 2008 presidential election, rising costs and roughly 46 million uninsured people made health reform a top issue for the Democrats. Democratic candidate Barack Obama proposed a healthcare plan inspired by legislation introduced by Republican Governor Mitt Romney in 2005. Obama's proposed plan would cover an estimated 33 million more people. At the time, 65 percent of Democrats thought "providing insurance to the uninsured" was a top priority, while just 27 percent of Republicans shared the same belief (Pew Research Center 2008).

After an overwhelming victory, Barack Obama introduced The Patient Protection and Affordable Care Act (commonly known as the ACA). The legislation immediately faced fierce partisan opposition. Early versions of the ACA included a "public option" – a government-administered insurance plan that could compete directly with private plans. During an almost year and half long legislative battle, conservative opponents warned of "socialized medicine" and a "government takeover of healthcare" despite the legislation's globally unique reliance on the for-profit private insurance industry. Stuart Butler, a distinguished fellow at the ultra-conservative Heritage Foundation proposed the idea for the "individual mandate" in 1989 – a clause requiring people to have health coverage or pay a fine. This conservative solution designed to achieve universal coverage was the most hotly contested element of the legislation.

The ACA increased access by dramatically expanding eligibility for Medicaid and creating regulated state marketplaces where the uninsured could shop for coverage and secure subsidies based on their income. These marketplaces offered community-rated premiums – a policy that requires all people in a region to be offered a premium at the same price regardless of health status – and offered standardization of coverage options for consumers based on actuarial value. The ACA introduced revolutionary across-the-board consumer protections including the prohibition of: discrimination based on preexisting conditions (guaranteed issue); price discrimination based on gender; annual or lifetime caps on coverage; and coverage cancelation (for reasons other than nonpayment). It included a requirement that people aged 26 and under could stay on a parent's plan, and also limited profits for private insurance companies. It included provisions designed to slow the rising costs of healthcare including: more competition between insurance companies; additional taxes on high-priced health plans; and a review board that could limit Medicare cost increases and provide incentives to increase efficiency.

The ACA passed in 2010 with a vote of 219 : 212 on March 21, 2010. It represented the greatest expansion of coverage and the most significant regulatory change since the passage of Medicare and Medicaid.

17.3.2 Switzerland

In 1987, Swiss lawmakers set out to find a proposal that would address the underlying structural problems of inequality and cost. Politically, there was little disagreement about the need for reform, but there existed different views on how to achieve it. Capitalism and solidarity, two ideas celebrated by the Swiss, were at odds during the debate over the legislation. It centered around two core questions: the continued role of private insurance and whether, and to what degree, should the unequal distribution of costs be regulated.

Loi de l'Assurance Maladie (LAMal) was opposed by the for-profit insurance industry, the drug industry, and the business community on the grounds that it would harm the quality of care currently experienced by those with insurance. It was supported by unions, farmers, and liberal parties on the grounds that it expanded access. The Christian Democratic Party, typically the voice of business, remained neutral on the legislation – not wanting to be on the wrong side of solidarity (Reid 2010).

LAMal passed in 1994, was accepted in a close public referendum the same year, and went into effect in 1996, changing how the provision of healthcare worked for every person living in Switzerland. The Swiss would continue to rely on the private insurance industry, but would heavily regulate it to ensure universal access and manage the unequal distribution of costs.

LAMal would rely on premiums from individuals to finance the bulk of the system. Private insurers would be forbidden from making a profit on basic health services. The government would stop subsidizing private insurance companies based on the number of enrollees they covered, instead shifting to a means-based subsidy. The law banned discriminatory pricing based on gender and preexisting condition, exempting age alone for price differences. It introduced a significant expansion of the standardized basic services that had to be offered by every insurance carrier. The new law introduced community rated premiums and also allowed for the introduction of health maintenance organizations. Health coverage would stop being voluntary and become compulsory with a requirement that coverage could not be denied to any applicant.

For a fairly broad set of basic health needs, Switzerland transitioned from a voluntary market-driven health system to a compulsory system with a regulated private industry not allowed to profit off of the compulsory system. It retained core elements of its voluntary free market system for supplementary insurance – insurance and amenities beyond those provided in the compulsory package. Private insurance companies can profit from the supplementary insurance that 70 percent of the Swiss purchase.

17.4 Explanation of What the Solution Looked Like in Practice: What Were the Anticipated and Unanticipated Consequences?

17.4.1 United States

The passage of the Patient Protection and Affordable Care Act (ACA) resulted in the largest expansion of coverage since the passage of Medicare and Medicaid in 1965. Key provisions of the law went into effect in 2013. Over 20 million people (Center on Budget and Policy Priorities, 2019) gained coverage and the uninsured rate dropped to

8.6 percent in 2016 (Greenstein, Sherman, and Broaddus, 2020) – the lowest in American history. The expansion of Medicaid eligibility resulted in 12.7 million people gaining coverage, and 11.4 million people were covered in the health insurance marketplaces.

The consumer protections offered by the ACA are the most popular aspects of the law – for the first time Americans cannot be denied coverage due to a preexisting condition like diabetes, pregnancy, or acne. Every American with coverage also has a limit on out-of-pocket costs and plans are prohibited from having annual or lifetime limits. Small business, the individual market, Medicaid, and the marketplaces need to cover the ten essential health benefits (EHB). These EHBs are specific categories of services plans are required to offer, but insurance companies choose which services within each category they cover. Taken together these protections create the first-ever national guardrails to protect against the worst practices of insurers and make consumer decision-making easier.

Early evidence suggests the ACA may have slowed the growth of healthcare spending, but not stopped it. Current health expenditure as a percentage of GDP has risen from 17.3 percent in 2010 to 17.7 percent in 2018 (Centers for Medicare & Medicaid Services, n.d). The average annual national health spending grew by 4.3 percent between 2010 and 2018, less than the 6.9 percent growth rate between 2000 and 2009. Given the simultaneous coverage expansion, it's important to note that spending on a per capita basis grew even less – 3.6 percent between 2010 and 2018 (Buntin and Graves, 2020). But the United States still spends significantly more as a percentage of GDP each year on healthcare than any other country in the world.

The ACA provided means-based federal subsidies for people purchasing coverage through the health insurance marketplaces which are estimated to be responsible for 37 percent of the coverage gains (Frean, Gruber, and Sommers, 2016). People who have a household income just high enough to make them ineligible for the threshold for qualification or who don't receive enough subsidies, can still face unaffordable healthcare costs. Additional subsidies or price controls are still needed to provide affordable coverage options.

Even after passage of the ACA, opposition to the legislation continued. Numerous provisions were undermined, obstructed, or delayed. Three elements critical to expanding access to coverage were particularly hard hit: Medicaid expansion, the individual mandate, and consumer assistance.

- *State Rejection of Medicaid Expansion:* Medicaid, a health program that offers coverage to the poor, is administered by states. The ACA included a provision that expanded Medicaid access to the same baseline income level in every state. The federal government would pay 100 percent of the costs for three years, then states would be responsible for 10 percent of the costs. Initially, twenty-four states refused Medicaid expansion funding. This left 4.8 million of their residents in a "coverage gap" – ineligible for the subsidies available to other people in their state with higher incomes. Since 2013, twelve of the states that had refused, expanded Medicaid, often against the wishes of state legislators, through state referendums. Key holdouts include Texas and Florida which alone represent roughly 15 percent of the US population.
- *Severing the Individual Mandate*: The individual mandate required people without health coverage to pay $695 per adult or 2.5 percent of yearly household income at tax time. Due to gradual implementation starting in 2013, it was in full effect for just three years (2016–2018) before it was effectively eliminated. Starting in 2019, Congress lowered the penalty an uninsured consumer would need to pay to $0. Six states have reinstated the mandate at the state level. The importance of the individual mandate will take additional time to assess, but early research suggests it wasn't a primary reason people enrolled.
- *Consumer Protections and Assistance:* Through executive action President Trump has taken other actions to weaken the implementation of the law including changing the definition of Short Term Limited Duration plans, previously a form of coverage allowed for three months, to allow them to last a full year. These plans are exempt from consumer protections which means they can deny coverage based on preexisting conditions, not cover emergency care, and are often misrepresented when they are sold (Levey, 2019; Young and Hannick, 2020). The budget for consumer assistance for the health insurance marketplaces was also cut by 88 percent – this includes advertising the deadline to enroll in coverage and a program that offers enrollment assistance.

The uninsured rate rose each of the first three years of the Trump administration to 9.2 percent in 2019 (Greenstein, Sherman, and

Broaddus, 2020). The number of people who are underinsured – pay high out-of-pocket (OOP) costs relative to their household income – is also growing from 12 percent in 2003 to 29 percent in 2018 (Collins, Gunja, and MichDoty, 2017; The Commonwealth Fund, 2019). This growth is occurring in Employer Sponsored Insurance as OOP costs continue to increase faster than wages. Healthcare continues to be a top political issue in America. One of the hottest issues in the 2020 Democratic presidential primary was whether to build on the ACA or create a single-payer health system.

17.4.2 Switzerland

Passage of Loi de l'Assurance Maladie (LAMal) was widely viewed as a success, but it did not achieve all of its intended goals.

After having an uninsured rate of 5 percent, Switzerland quickly achieved something close to universal coverage. The law requires people to have coverage within three months of arriving in a Canton. Cantons are responsible for enforcement of the mandate – and each has its own approach. Cantons compare the list of people who've registered as residents in a canton with the list of people who've enrolled in coverage and track down people who aren't on both lists. If people don't enroll after three months, they are automatically enrolled in a plan of the Canton's choosing. Some cantons assess a penalty of 30 percent to 50 percent above the premium for those who do not enroll.

As the law was implemented, it became clear that some Swiss citizens were not paying premiums after being enrolled. In 2006, the government allowed insurance companies to disenroll people who hadn't paid for coverage in six months with the intent of increasing payment rates. But the reverse happened. The uninsured rate grew to 2 percent as a result of the legislation. The Swiss discovered that most of the people who weren't paying were experiencing financial hardship and weren't receiving the intended subsidies to cover care costs. This led to another revision in 2012, when the Swiss government once again banned insurance companies from disenrolling people and began paying 85 percent of the premiums of defaulters with serious financial problems directly to the insurance companies. Swiss insurance companies were permitted to sue defaulters for nonpayment and the Canton would be responsible for mediation (Ginneken, Swartz, and Van der

Wees, 2013). This lowered the uninsured rate to less than 1 percent. Undocumented immigrants can purchase health coverage and are eligible for subsidies through charitable nonprofits. Roughly 30,000 people (0.35 percent of the population) in Switzerland are ineligible for "basic package" services due to nonpayment and have been added to a "blacklist" – though they do have access to emergency services. Temporary foreign visitors in the country also do not have access to basic health coverage.

The system also preserved quality. Maternal mortality, infant mortality, and life expectancy have all improved since its passage (Thacher, 2015). The Swiss have relatively short wait times for care (De Pietro et al., 2015). Switzerland now has the highest number of doctors per capita (Knoema, 2021), physicians are among the highest paid (Biller-Andorno and Zeltner, 2015), and customer satisfaction remains high (De Pietro et al., 2015). The amenable mortality rate in Switzerland, a key measure of quality, is lower than in any other OECD country (De Pietro et al., 2015).

The Swiss continue to have a lot of choice in their care. Switzerland has over fifty insurance companies offering the basic package of services – premiums are published in newspapers in the fall every year. Every Swiss citizen is guaranteed coverage through the expansive "basic" package of services offered by these companies. Despite its name, the basic package is a comprehensive set of services that includes outpatient care, hospital care, mental health, pharmaceuticals, rehabilitative services, acupuncture, and some dental and herbal medicine. Once a person selects an insurance company, they choose from a list of covered doctors and hospitals in their canton. Insurance is not tied to employment. People can change plans up to twice per year. Beyond the basic package, about 70 percent of the population voluntarily choose to pay for some kind of supplemental insurance that covers additional services or benefits (Cheng 2010). The European Health Consumer Index found that Switzerland was tied for first with Belgium in health system accessibility (De Pietro et al., 2015).

The legislation failed to control costs which pose a challenge for a growing state budget and for individuals. Healthcare costs as a percentage of GDP have risen from 8.9 percent in 1995 to 10.3 percent in 2005 and 11.4 percent in 2015 (Auskunft: Bundesamt für Statistik (BFS), 2020). While the individual share of costs has actually decreased from 31.8 percent to 25.5 percent in 2015 – out-of-pocket costs remain very high compared to other OECD countries. "In 2016, 22% of the Swiss population reported going without needed care because of costs, with this rate being particularly high among people with low-income (31%)" (OECD, 2017).

17.5 Analysis of What Happened

17.5.1 United States

The Affordable Care Act relied on neoliberal solutions to expand access to the 46 million uninsured in America. The Affordable Care Act was successful in its historic expansion of coverage to over 20 million people, but through a combination of intended limitations to its design and deliberate efforts to obstruct its implementation, it fell far short of universal coverage. In 2019, 9.2 percent or 29.6 million people in America still did not have health coverage. (Keisler-Starkey and Bunch, 2020).

The Affordable Care Act didn't attempt to completely overhaul the US healthcare system. It built on the existing health insurance system and focused on addressing the system's greatest inadequacies. The Affordable Care Act was transformative for America but compared to the policymaking implemented in Switzerland almost fifteen years earlier it relied too heavily on flawed notions of market efficiency. Between the history of the US health system and politics of passage, this was a near certain outcome, but not one that future lawmakers need to replicate.

Even with full implementation it's design wouldn't have achieved universal coverage. Between 3.2 percent and 3.6 percent (10.5–12 million people) of the US population is undocumented – roughly 25 percent of the remaining uninsured (Kamarck and Stenglein, 2019). These undocumented immigrants are ineligible for coverage through the ACA – even if they pay all the costs themselves. Nearly half of the remaining uninsured in America are eligible for subsidies or Medicaid but have not enrolled. An additional 14 percent would be eligible for subsidies or Medicaid if their state expanded Medicaid.

The state of Massachusetts has the lowest uninsured rate (3 percent) in the country, which was achieved with their own implementation of the ACA starting in 2006. Of the remaining uninsured in Massachusetts, 20 percent are ineligible because of their immigration status and 64.4 percent are not enrolled but eligible for some form of subsidized health insurance, giving us some insight into what a best-case scenario might look for the ACA. Enrollment itself, even for free or subsidized coverage, remains a significant obstacle for many Americans. In contrast, people turning 65 are automatically enrolled in Medicare Parts A and B – and people over 65 have the lowest uninsured rate (1 percent) for any age group in the US.

The US is unlikely to nationally replicate the incredible coverage gains seen in Massachusetts in the near future. The uninsured rate in Texas is the highest in America at 18.4 percent (down from 23.7 percent before the ACA). Over 60 percent of Texans report that they or a family member in their household have postponed or skipped any type of healthcare in the past twelve months due to cost (Hamel et al., 2018). Yet 46 percent of Texans (76 percent of Republicans) prefer the current system to a universal health insurance system in 2020 (The Texas Politics Project, n.d.). The will for universal coverage in the United States is not universal.

The individual mandate is a solution that likely incentivized coverage for some, but wasn't the primary driver of coverage gains for the ACA (Frean, Gruber, and Sommers, 2016). Americans paid the penalty along with their taxes, nearly a year and a half after the sign-up period for the relevant coverage year ended. It was viewed by some as an alternative to getting coverage. It's possible that with a longer period of implementation or a more severe penalty, it would have been more effective, but other factors were far more important. Data shows that the availability of subsidies to lower the cost of coverage and expanded eligibility for Medicaid were responsible for the biggest gains in coverage. This is consistent with research that shows the cost of coverage as the primary obstacle to coverage in America. Access to information about the availability of affordable coverage may be an even bigger obstacle. In 2019, over 4.7 million uninsured Americans could enroll in a plan with a $0 monthly premium as a result of federal premium subsidies – up 4.2 million in 2018 (Fehr, Cox, and Rae, 2019).

The ACA's consumer protections made shopping for health coverage less treacherous – especially for those in the individual market. Guaranteed issue, annual and lifetime limits, community rated plans, and essential health benefits have all contributed to ending the horror stories that had in some respects defined the industry. But for those outside the individual market, shopping for coverage isn't any easier. For the relatively small group in the individual market, shopping for coverage is much easier – though still far from easy. The application process has been streamlined; all health plans are available in one place with integrated out-of-pocket cost calculators. For the first time there are requirements for searchable provider directories and formularies. But aside from actuarial tiers (the percentage of costs covered by the consumer vs. the issuer), plan benefits are not standardized, so they remain extremely difficult to compare unless you're an insurance expert.

The ACA introduced a cap on insurer profits and overheads. Depending on the market, it limits profits and administrative overheads to between 15 percent and 20 percent based on a three-year rolling average. If the insurance companies make more than that, they must rebate the excess to consumers. Between 2012 and 2019 more than $5.3 billion dollars have been rebated to consumers.

The ideological divide between conservatives and liberals on healthcare access in the United States is vast. But the currently rising uninsured rate and growing healthcare costs mean the legislative debate about how to provide access is certain to continue.

17.5.2 Switzerland

The Swiss values of capitalism and solidarity were at odds when they determined how to design access to their current health system. Their existing, private but subsidized system was failing to cover every Swiss citizen which was viewed by the public as a violation of the principle of solidarity. LAMal balanced these two values by retaining the role of private insurance companies in the system, while also providing access and affordable premiums by regulating toxic inefficiencies out of the system. Achieving this balance required reorganization of the health system, extensive regulation of the private insurance industry, and compulsory coverage.

The Swiss overhauled the health experience of every Swiss citizen with the goal of achieving universal coverage. Every Swiss citizen would be required to purchase the same "basic package" of health services – creating a nationwide standard of "basic" care. Private insurance companies would be required to accept every applicant and offer the exact same benefits, not merely a standardized plan. While the price between insurance companies would vary, they were also required to charge all their customers the same amount regardless of health status. Finally, the private insurance companies would be prohibited from profiting from the "basic package."

With these choices, the Swiss eliminated inherent inefficiencies in healthcare markets: Private insurers could no longer avoid sick customers. Nor would they be incentivized to skimp or cut benefits to maximize profit. For consumers, decision-making is dramatically simpler for the basic package of benefits – the only difference between companies is the premium and deductible. While LAMal was a complete overhaul, it built on principles that were established as early as 1911 – when the law limited price discrimination based on gender, included consumer protections and mandated specific benefits in subsidized health plans.

When Switzerland made coverage compulsory, they instituted an individual mandate as a disincentive. But the mandate doesn't operate in isolation or even serve as the primary mechanism for promoting coverage in Switzerland. The Swiss made the law compulsory because they believed the existing inequity was wrong. The actual implementation is designed to motivate coverage, not penalize people for failing to do so. Before assessing a mandate, cantons track down and auto-enroll a person. Auto-enrollment in Switzerland is just as important as the penalty in facilitating coverage expansion. The mandate isn't the alternative to having coverage in Switzerland, it's designed to build urgency into an onboarding process. Most importantly, the mandate isn't the primary incentive to get covered in Switzerland. Once again going back to 1911, the Swiss government subsidizes coverage to keep it affordable. People want health coverage if they can afford it.

While the cost of care is far less expensive to individuals in Switzerland than it is in the United States, it is still the second most expensive in the world. Compulsory coverage that requires individuals to pay a share of costs must be affordable. LAMal attempts to protect consumers from these costs through subsidies, community rated plans, maximum OOP costs, protections from having coverage canceled, so the health system, not the consumer, bears the burden. Rising costs continue to be a problem, and the Swiss will need to identify a way to reign them in or they will once again find solidarity and capitalism at odds.

17.6 Conclusion

17.6.1 United States

Switzerland and the United States have long celebrated the importance of capitalism. Before reform, both relied heavily on for-profit private health insurance companies and post-reform they continue to share a unique reliance on the private sector for the delivery of health coverage compared to other wealthy countries. It is because of this that an evaluation of the choices each country made during health reform is valuable.

Given the small size of the Swiss population, it was far easier to overhaul the health system in a single piece of legislation than it would be in the United States. It was also easier to build on principles that had been ingrained in the delivery of care in Switzerland for over eighty-five years. But LAMal also reflected a recognition that the existing system was delivering an unequal standard of care and that it was the only way to achieve the goal of solidarity while preserving the role of private companies. In contrast, the ACA built on an existing system heavily reliant on for-profit companies. While a huge advance for America, this reliance on the private sector and market incentives didn't come close to universal coverage.

In 2009, 1 percent of US patients were responsible for 21.8 percent of expenditures, the top 5 percent were responsible for nearly half of the country's spending and the top 20 percent were responsible for 80 percent of health costs (Harbage, 2009; Weissmann, 2012). While this distribution might somewhat mirror income inequality in America, health expenditures are highest for people who are sick. As a result, there is a free-market incentive to limit access to coverage. For-profit insurance companies are heavily incentivized to exclude the most expensive patients from their balance sheets. In the US and Switzerland, prior to passage of the ACA, there is clear evidence that private insurers cherry-picked enrollees and routinely canceled the plans of high-expenditure patients. These types of practices were a core function of the business strategy of private insurers in the individual market prior to the ACA (Girion, 2009).

Requiring private insurance companies to cover these expensive enrollees as both the US and Switzerland did, with guaranteed issue, has significant consequences. It upends the existing business model.

The cost of these patients is so significant that companies cannot remain financially solvent if they get a disproportionate share of these enrollees. As a result, consumer protections that prohibit discrimination based on preexisting conditions, age, or gender, and prevent annual or lifetime limits on coverage, are paired with regulations that require community-rated plans and offer risk adjustment further maligning free-market healthcare.

At the same time, many of the uninsured are often younger and healthier and choose not to enroll because they can't afford it or don't believe they need it. When these freeriders don't contribute to the health system, they increase the costs of other participants. These healthy uninsured people, of course, can and do get sick or injured – and can face financial ruin if they are lucky enough to survive. The risk they take on is small, but potentially catastrophic. But in yet another affront to the free market, they pass that risk on to other health system users in the form of uncompensated care. In 2013, uncompensated care to uninsured individuals in the US was $84.9 billion with the vast majority of these costs ultimately picked up by state and federal budgets (Coughlin, Holahan, Caswell, and McGrath, 2014). Unsurprisingly, we've seen uncompensated care costs decrease as the uninsured rate decreased (Schuble and Broaddus, 2018).

Designing healthcare access that addresses freeriders is a critical policy challenge in addressing universal coverage. The individual mandate offers a financial disincentive to remain a freerider. In the US, the enrollment impact of this disincentive has been modest, which could be the result of its specific implementation. But even when the cost of coverage is less than the penalty, freeriders remain without coverage. In 2017, the fourth plan year of the ACA, the majority of uninsured people were eligible for coverage for less than the cost of individual mandate and 42 percent could find a plan that didn't require any contribution at all (Rae, Levitt, and Semanskee, 2017). Most of the uninsured aren't making a financial calculation in their decision to remain uncovered or, if they are, their decision-making is impaired by other factors that undermine the intended efficacy of the mandate. The mandate alone is not achieving universal coverage.

This is dramatically different in both purpose and practice in Switzerland. Switzerland's pre-LAMal mandate uninsured rate was lower than the US's post-ACA uninsured low – likely further evidence that adequate subsidies for coverage are far more effective than a disincentive to remain uncovered. Importantly, the auto-enrollment and subsidies offered through LAMal actually address the underlying market inefficiency. A person who doesn't know their preferences, how to enroll, choose an insurance company, or a plan, has those choices made for them. Subsidies make coverage affordable to people who wouldn't be able to afford it otherwise.

Navigating the US healthcare system is enormously complex. Market incentives require informed actors with adequate knowledge to make favorable decisions for themselves and their families. But the majority of the uninsured in America have no more than a high school education. In fact, 26.9 percent of the uninsured did not graduate high school vs. the 11.8 percent of the total population (Berchick, 2018). Health literacy is critical for navigating the health system. But the health literacy of nearly half of people without a high school diploma in the United States is assessed as "below basic" – for example they cannot read and understand information in simple documents. The health literacy of people with a high school diploma, the majority of uninsured, is only slightly better. The study found that 44 percent had either "basic" or "below basic" literacy – for example they could not correctly use a body mass index chart to determine a healthy weight range for a person of a given height. But health literacy is a challenge for people with the highest levels of educational attainment in America. Just 33 percent of people with a graduate level degree were assessed "proficient" – which includes being able to "calculate an employee's share of health insurance costs for a year, using a table that shows how the employee's monthly cost varies depending on income and family size" (Kutner, Greenberg, Jin, and Paulsen, 2006). Without adequate health literacy, there is little reason to believe that individuals can serve as informed market participants able to act on their preferences

For most Americans, the ACA added protections that eliminated some of the worst practices of insurance – either denying coverage or offering inadequate coverage – offering a giant leap forward in healthcare. For the small group of Americans buying coverage on the individual market, these same protections combined with a significantly improved shopping experience provided a revolution. But as incredible as these ACA provisions were, the Swiss LAMal reforms were far more significant because they established a basic standard of care for every Swiss person. The United States added guardrails around historically bad actors, while Switzerland eliminated the devil whispering in their ear completely. In the process, they effectively made it easier for consumers to make informed decisions about their own healthcare.

The ACA capped the amount of administrative overhead and profits an insurance company can make to no more than 20 percent. Meanwhile the Swiss banned private insurers from making any profit on basic coverage – a legislative articulation that basic healthcare is a right, not a for-profit enterprise. Once again in order to protect consumers and control rising costs the ACA limited a practice a for-profit company is directly incentivized to carry out. In the US context, this was a huge step forward, but not nearly the type of accomplishment that Switzerland achieved.

The United States and Switzerland have the highest health expenditures per capita in the world. While the ACA appears to have been more successful than LAMal at controlling costs, both the United States and Switzerland spend more on health expenditures per capita than any other countries in the world. The efficiency of the private sector doesn't appear to be terribly efficient at controlling costs either.

The WHO Director-General, Dr. Tedros Adhanom Ghebreyesus, said "No one should get sick and die just because they are poor, or because they cannot access the health services they need" (Gorman, 2015). But in America today, this is sadly still the case. People living in high-poverty areas have an amenable mortality rate that is lower than those living in low-poverty areas. Much like Switzerland did in 1994, the United States must answer the fundamental question: "Is healthcare a right?"

References

Auskunft: Bundesamt für Statistik (BFS). 2020. "Kosten und Finanzierung des Gesundheitswesens seit 1960." Auskunft: Bundesamt für Statistik (BFS). www.bfs.admin.ch/bfs/de/home/aktuell/neue-veroeffentlichungen .assetdetail.12567514.html

Bartlett, Bruce. 2013."The question of taxing employer-provided health insurance." *The New York Times*, July 30, 2013. https://economix .blogs.nytimes.com/2013/07/30/the-question-of-taxing-employer-provided- health-insurance/?_php=true&_type=blogs&_r=0

Berchick, Edward. 2018."Most uninsured were working-age adults." United States Census Bureau. www.census.gov/library/stories/2018/09/who- are-the-uninsured.html

Berkowitz, Edward. 2005."Medicare and Medicaid: The past as prologue." *Healthcare Finance Review* 27 (2): 11-23. www.ncbi.nlm.nih.gov/pmc/articles/PMC4194925/

Biller-Andorno, Nikola, and Thomas Zeltner. 2015. "Individual responsibility and community solidarity: The Swiss health care system." *The New England Journal of Medicine* 373: 2193–2197. www.nejm.org/doi/full/10.1056/NEJMp1508256

Buntin, Melinda Beeuwkes, and John A. Graves. 2020."How the ACA dented the cost curve." *Health Affairs*, 39 (3): 403–412. https://www.healthaffairs.org/doi/abs/10.1377/hlthaff.2019.01478

Center on Budget and Policy Priorities. 2019."Chart book: Accomplishments of affordable care act." *Center on Budget and Policy Priorities*, March 19, 2019. www.cbpp.org/research/health/chart-book-accomplishments-of-affordable-care-act#:~:text=Thanks%20to%20the%20Affordable%20Care,people%20have%20gained%20health%20coverage.

Centers for Medicare & Medicaid Services. n.d. "Historical." www.cms.gov/Research-Statistics-Data-and-Systems/Statistics-Trends-and-Reports/NationalHealthExpendData/NationalHealthAccountsHistorical

Cheng, Tsung-Mei. 2010. "Understanding the 'Swiss watch' function of Switzerland's health system." *Health Affairs* 29 (8): 1442–1451. www.healthaffairs.org/doi/full/10.1377/hlthaff.2010.0698

Collins, Sara R., Munira Z. Gunja, and Michelle M. Doty. 2017. "How well does insurance coverage protect consumers from health care costs?: Findings from the Commonwealth Fund Biennial Health Insurance Survey, 2016." *Issue Brief*, October 18, 2017. www.commonwealthfund.org/sites/default/files/documents/___media_files_publications_issue_brief_2017_oct_collins_underinsured_biennial_ib.pdf

Coughlin, Teresa A., John Holahan, Kyle Caswell, and Megan McGrath. 2014. "Uncompensated care for the uninsured in 2013: A detailed examination." *KFF*, May 30, 2014. www.kff.org/uninsured/report/uncompensated-care-for-the-uninsured-in-2013-a-detailed-examination/

De Lew, Nancy. 2000."Medicare: 35 years of service." *Health Care Financing Review* 22 (1): 75–103. www.cms.gov/Research-Statistics-Data-and-Systems/Research/HealthCareFinancingReview/downloads/00fallpg75.pdf

De Pietro, Carlo, Paul Camenzind, Isabelle Sturny, Luca Crivelli, Suzanne Edwards-Garavoglia, Anne Spranger, Friedrich Wittenbecher, and Wilm Quentin. 2015. "Switzerland: Health system review." *Health Systems in Transition* 17: 4. www.euro.who.int/__data/assets/pdf_file/0010/293689/Switzerland-HiT.pdf

Department of Health and Human Services: Office of the Assistant Secretary for Planning and Evaluation. 2011."Overview of the uninsured in the United States: A summary of the 2011 current population survey."

Department of Health and Human Services: Office of the Assistant Secretary for Planning and Evaluation. 2011. https://aspe.hhs.gov/ basic-report/overview-uninsured-united-states-summary-2011-current-population-survey#:~:text=According%20to%20the%20Census%20 Bureaus,16.3%25%20of%20the%20total%20population.

Dickson, Virgil. 2015."Medicaid a lifeline for the poor and disabled." *Modern Healthcare*, May 23, 2015. www.modernhealthcare.com/article/20150523/ MAGAZINE/305239941/medicaid-a-lifeline-for-the-poor-and-disabled

Fehr, Rachel, Cynthia Cox, and Matthew Rae. 2019. "How many of the uninsured can purchase a marketplace plan for free in 2020?" *KFF*, December 10, 2019. www.kff.org/private-insurance/issue-brief/how-many-of-the-uninsured-can-purchase-a-marketplace-plan-for-free-in-2020/?utm_campaign=KFF-2019-Uninsured&utm_source=hs_email& utm_medium=email&utm_content=2&_hsenc=p2ANqtz-9HA_1wbFa FSDV2lfXwSav4mBHnGEd_vdBoCtqUVT5gchTq3zYHtVSjlGsm741 4Kox_spd53yfhCo4HYKMKK0qvra3Z4g&_hsmi=2

Frean, Molly, Jonathan Gruber, and Benjamin D. Sommers. 2016. "Disentangling the ACA's coverage effects: Lessons for policymakers." *The New England Journal of Medicine* 375: 1605–1608. www.nejm .org/doi/full/10.1056/NEJMp1609016

Gallup. n.d. "Healthcare System." Gallup. https://news.gallup.com/poll/ 4708/healthcare-system.aspx

Ginneken, Ewout van, Katherine Swartz, and Philip Van der Wees. 2013. "Health insurance exchanges in Switzerland and the Netherlands offer five key lessons for the operations of US exchanges." *Health Affairs* 32 (4): 744–52. www.healthaffairs.org/doi/full/10.1377/hlthaff.2012.0948

Girion, Lisa. 2009. "Blue Cross praised employees who dropped sick policy-holders, lawmaker says." *Los Angeles Times*, June 17, 2009. www .latimes.com/archives/la-xpm-2009-jun-17-fi-rescind17-story.html

Goin, Dana and Sharon K. Long. n.d."Prior experience with the nongroup health insurance market: Implications for enrollment under the Affordable Care Act." Health Reform Monitoring Survey. http://hrms .urban.org/briefs/nongroup_health_insurance_market.html

Gorman, Sean. 2015."Dan Gecker says U.S. only wealthy nation without universal health care." *Politifacts*, September 1, 2015. www.politifact .com/factchecks/2015/sep/01/dan-gecker/dan-gecker-says-us-only-wealth-nation-without-univ/

Greenstein, Robert, Arloc Sherman, and Matt Broaddus. 2020."Uninsured rate rose in 2019: Income and poverty data overtaken by pandemic recession." *Center on Budget and Policy Priorities*, September 15, 2020. www.cbpp.org/research/poverty-and-inequality/uninsured-rate-rose-in-2019-income-and-poverty-data-overtaken-by

Hamel, Liz, Bryan Wu, Mollyann Brodie, Shao-Chee Sim, and Elena Marks. 2018. "Texans' experiences with health care affordability and access." *KFF*, July 10, 2018. www.kff.org/report-section/texans-experiences-with-health-care-affordability-and-access-findings/

Harbage, Peter. 2009. "Too sick for health care: How insurers limit and deny care in the individual health insurance market." *Center for American Progress*, July 20, 2009. www.americanprogress.org/issues/healthcare/reports/2009/07/20/6453/too-sick-for-health-care/

Jones, Jeffrey M. 2019."Americans still favor private healthcare system." *Gallup*, December 4, 2019. https://news.gallup.com/poll/268985/americans-favor-private-healthcare-system.aspx

Kamal, Rabah, Daniel McDermott, Giorlando Ramirez, and Cynthia Cox. 2020."How has U.S. spending on healthcare changed over time?" *KFF*, December 23, 2020. www.healthsystemtracker.org/chart-collection/u-s-spending-healthcare-changed-time/#item-nhe-trends_total-national-health-expenditures-as-a-%-of-gross-domestic-product-1970-2018

Kamarck, Elaine, and Christine Stenglein. 2019. "How many undocumented immigrants are in the United States and who are they?" *Brookings*, November 12, 2019. www.brookings.edu/policy2020/votervital/how-many-undocumented-immigrants-are-in-the-united-states-and-who-are-they/

Keisler-Starkey, Katherine and Lisa N. Bunch. 2020."Health insurance coverage in the United States: 2019." KFF, September 15, 2020. www.census.gov/library/publications/2020/demo/p60-271.html

Klemm, John D. 2000."Medicaid spending: A brief history." *Healthcare Finance Review* 22 (1): 105–112. www.ncbi.nlm.nih.gov/pmc/articles/PMC4194698/#:~:text=During%20the%20same%20period%2C%20enrollment,%24750%20per%20resident%20this%20year.

Knoema. 2021. "World development indicators (WDI)." Knoema. https://knoema.com/WBWDI2019Jan/world-development-indicators-wdi

Kutner, Mark, Elizabeth Greenberg, Ying Jin, and Christine Paulsen. 2006. *The Health Literacy of America's Adults: Results From the 2003 National Assessment of Adult Literacy.* Washington, DC: US Department of Education. https://nces.ed.gov/pubs2006/2006483.pdf

Levey. Noam N. 2019."Skimpy health plans touted by Trump bring back familiar woes for consumers." *Los Angeles Times*, April 2, 2019. www.latimes.com/politics/la-na-pol-trump-shortterm-health-insurance-consumer-problems-20190402-story.html

Murray, John E. n.d."Industrial sickness funds." Economic History Association. https://eh.net/encyclopedia/industrial-sickness-funds/

OECD. 2017. *Health Policy in Switzerland.* Paris: OECD. www.oecd.org/els/health-systems/Health-Policy-in-Switzerland-July-2017.pdf

Petersen, Hans. 2015."Roots of VA healthcare started 150 years ago." Veterans Health Administration. www.va.gov/HEALTH/News Features/2015/March/Roots-of-VA-Health-Care-Started-150-Years-Ago.asp

Pew Research Center. 2008."An even more partisan agenda for 2008: Election-year economic ratings lowest since '92." *Pew Research Center*, January 24, 2008. www.pewresearch.org/politics/2008/01/24/an-even-more-partisan-agenda-for-2008/

Rae, Matthew, Larry Levitt, and Ashley Semanskee. 2017. "How many of the uninsured can purchase a marketplace plan for less than their shared responsibility penalty?" *KFF*, November 9, 2017. www.kff.org/health-reform/issue-brief/how-many-of-the-uninsured-can-purchase-a-market place-plan-for-less-than-their-shared-responsibility-penalty/

Reid. T. R. 2010. *The Healing of America: A Global Quest for Better, Cheaper, and Fairer Health Care.* London: Penguin Books https://books .google.com/books?id=OLqLDgAAQBAJ&lpg=PA181&ots=CxX7Mszi 7V&dq=switzerland%20christian%20democratic%20party%20leader %20lamal%20solidarity&pg=PA181#v=onepage&q=switzerland%20 christian%20democratic%20party%20leader%20lamal%20solidarity &f=false

Schuble, Jessica, and Matt Broaddus. 2018. "Uncompensated care costs fell in nearly every state as ACA's major coverage provisions took effect: Medicaid waivers that Create Barriers to Coverage Jeopardize Gains" *Center on Budget and Policy Priorities*, May 23, 2018. www.cbpp.org/research/health/uncompensated-care-costs-fell-in-nearly-every-state-as-acas-major-coverage

Social Security. n.d."History of SSA during the Johnson administration 1963–1968." Social Security. www.ssa.gov/history/ssa/lbjmedicare1.html

Tax Policy Center. n.d."How does the tax exclusion for employer-sponsored health insurance work?" Tax Policy Center. www.taxpolicycenter .org/briefing-book/how-does-tax-exclusion-employer-sponsored-health-insurance-work#:~:text=Employer%2Dpaid%20premiums%20for%20 health,after%2Dtax%20cost%20of%20coverage.

Thacher, Emily. 2015. "Switzerland: Regarding health system reform." *Yale Global Health Review* 3 (spring). https://yaleglobalhealthreview.com/ 2015/10/03/switzerland-regarding-health-system-reform

The Commonwealth Fund. 2019."Underinsured rate rose from 2014–2018, with greatest growth among people in employer health plans." *The Commonwealth Fund*, February 7, 2019. www.commonwealthfund.org/press-release/2019/underinsured-rate-rose-2014-2018-greatest-growth-among-people-employer-health

The Texas Politics Project. n.d. "Current health insurance system vs. universal health insurance system." The University of Texas at Austin. https:// texaspolitics.utexas.edu/set/current-health-insurance-system-vs-universal-health-insurance-system-february-2020#party-id

Weissmann, Jordan. 2012. "5% of Americans made up 50% of U.S. health-care spending." *The Atlantic*, January 13, 2012. www.theatlantic .com/business/archive/2012/01/5-of-americans-made-up-50-of-us-health-care-spending/251402/#:~:text=And%20the%20top%201%25%3F,one %20fifth%20of%20medical%20expenditures.&text=When%20it%20 comes%20to%20America's,of%20the%20country's%20medical%20 spending.

World Health Organization. Regional Office for Europe & European Observatory on Health Systems and Policies. 2000. "Health care systems in transition: Switzerland." World Health Organization. Regional Office for Europe. www.hpi.sk/cdata/Documents/HIT/ Switzerland_2000.pdf

Young, Christen Linke, and Kathleen Hannick. 2020. "Misleading marketing of short-term health plans amid COVID-19." *Brookings*, March 24, 2020. www.brookings.edu/blog/usc-brookings-schaeffer-on-health-policy/2020 /03/24/misleading-marketing-of-short-term-health-plans-amid-covid-19

PART III

Our Work

18 | What Should a Job Look Like?

HANNAH ELLIOTT

Increasingly jobs are impermanent, insecure, and gig-based. From a neoliberal perspective gig work is imagined as granting more freedom than traditional forms of employment and gig workers are portrayed as entrepreneurs who work for themselves, maximizing their human capital in a flexible manner. In this chapter Elliott writes about what its like to be a tea plantation worker in Kenya, particularly given the rise of gig work in that sector. What Elliott found in the course of her field work is that many tea plantation worker are nostalgic for the permanent job and its attendant benefits, legacies of latecolonial welfare paternalism. In fact, what remaining permanent plantation jobs there are often seem like a good deal compared to gig work, since it may offer benefits absent in the gig economy, such as housing, water, and some kind of pension scheme and health insurance. Elliot does not argue in favor of a return to the "security" and "benefits" of traditional plantation labor, a highly hierarchized, exploitative, and often oppressive system with limited possibilities for social mobility. Rather, she suggests that something is fundamentally wrong with the way work happens and is conceived under neoliberal conditions when traditional plantation offers preferable options to gig work. Human flourishing requires options beyond colonial tyrany and the neoliberal conception of freedom. She thus suggests that we may need to imagine ways of making a living that don't involve a job.

18.1 Introduction

Kenya is the world's leading producer of black crush-tear-curl (CTC) tea, roughly one third of which is produced on large tea plantations established during British colonialism. Tea is a labor-intensive crop, and Kenya's tea plantation sector employs tens of thousands of workers across the country, mainly in low-level jobs in fields and factories. Within expansive plantations lie company villages or "camps" to accommodate these workers, replete with kitchen gardens, dispensaries, daycare centers, primary and secondary schools, and recreational facilities. A legacy of the welfare paternalism that burgeoned under late colonialism, this infrastructure for labor has endured through to the present. Over the years, roofs have been repaired, windows replaced, and houses wired with electricity. One rarely hears of a tea worker who became rich from a plantation job, yet in the context of chronic unemployment in Kenya, a job on a tea plantation – with its trade union-negotiated wage, free housing and water, pension, contribution to health and social security insurance schemes, and possibility for taking loans against the guarantee of wages – is valued for the security it provides. However, tea plantation companies lament the heavy costs of tea labor, calling union demands for biannual increments and the costs of maintaining worker infrastructure unsustainable in the context of stagnant, and at times declining, prices of tea on the global market.

In efforts to cut costs and improve efficiency, companies have gradually been replacing the hand plucking of plantation tea with mechanized harvesting. Even after mechanization, however, maintaining vast plantations requires a good deal of labor. In a further effort to reduce resident labor forces and their associated costs, companies have been experimenting with outsourcing "noncore" activities. The outsourced job comes with none of the benefits of the company job. Gradually, as mechanization and outsourcing become the norm, companies are dismantling their infrastructure for labor. Some worker housing stands empty and marked for demolition.

Drawing primarily on fieldwork on a large multinational-owned tea plantation in Kericho in Kenya's Rift Valley,[1] this chapter takes the outsourcing of low-level work formerly carried out by company-employed staff as a case through which to reflect on the changing nature of the tea plantation job. Here, the tea plantation company, following an industry-wide trend, delegates out noncore areas of work

---

[1] This research was conducted in spring 2020. The chapter also draws on fieldwork carried out during the same period with other tea producers in Kericho, including small-scale farmers, and on fieldwork on tea plantations in Limuru in central Kenya in autumn 2018. It also draws on archival research conducted in 2018 and 2020. The research was conducted as part of the SUSTEIN project (PI Martin Skrydstrup), funded by the Independent Research Fund Denmark, Cross-council committee, Sapere Aude: DFF Starting Grant # 7023-00115AB.

to private contractors, who in turn hire labor by which to complete contracted tasks. While the company oversees the work of the contractor, it does not provide him or her with the benefits enjoyed by people employed by the company. Furthermore, the company does not employ the workers a contractor hires. This means that the company can forgo the responsibilities and costs of providing large numbers of manual laborers on the plantation with housing and welfare. In addition to this cost saving, companies claim that outsourcing improves efficiency. Contracts are assigned to discrete tasks, such as the pruning of a prescribed number of tea bushes. Contractors are paid per task rather than per number of days to complete the task, which motivates their quick completion. Since there are numerous contractors offering the same services to a company, competition for contracts is high, further pushing contractors to complete tasks as quickly and cheaply as possible.

The outsourcing of noncore activities on tea plantations resembles post-Fordist global employment trends across diverse industries in which secure company jobs are being replaced by insecure terms of employment. A recent instantiation of these trends has been dubbed the " gig economy." "Gig" work is often marketed as flexible and as granting more freedom than traditional forms of employment; gig workers are portrayed as entrepreneurs who work for themselves. Yet gig work comes with no guarantees: workers are only paid when they perform, so that absences on grounds of sickness, maternity or paternity, bereavement, or vacation are not accounted for. In some cases, workers can even be fined by a company for absences, or compelled to source replacement labor. Gig work typically does not provide future security in the form of pension contributions or health insurance.

Although insecure work is a global phenomenon, there are important distinctions to be made between insecure work in, for example, the United States and in so-called developing countries like Kenya. First, post-Fordism better describes conditions in Global North economies, where formal employment was, once upon a time, the norm (at least for certain segments of the population, notably white males). In countries like Kenya, formal, secure employment opportunities have always been limited. As a result, formal unemployment is high and the majority of Kenyans make a living in the informal economy without the guarantee of contracts, paid leave, and other benefits associated with formal jobs. The tea plantation sector has historically been one of the few industries in Kenya that has provided low-level workers with formal employment. Second, and as anthropologist of work Kathleen Millar (2017: 2) has noted, analyses of insecure work can inadvertently "smuggle in a conservative politics" that valorizes a Fordist past of secure wage labor. This is particularly problematic in a context like Kenya's tea plantations, where formal, low-level wage labor has roots in an exploitative colonial economy. While low-level company jobs have offered workers a degree of security, this has been within a highly hierarchized and often oppressive system with limited possibilities for social mobility.

In this context, the recent outsourcing of low-level plantation work and gradual decline of the company job makes for a complex comparative case. Outsourcing opens up opportunities for middle-class entrepreneurs known as "contractors," who are able to create lucrative incomes and better themselves and their families. They value outsourcing, especially given the shortage of formal employment opportunities in Kenya. But their contract work depends on the cheap, insecure labor of poor youth, in particular men, who have little choice but to take these jobs. Outsourcing thus further adds to the problem of inequality in Kenya. For outsourced low-level workers employed by contractors, company jobs are often favorable due to the security they offer, in spite of the oppressive restrictions that are associated with permanent tea plantation employment.

In what follows, I describe the outsourced job and its precarity, and then compare it to the coexisting company job where people continue to be employed directly by the company in the undertaking of "core" tasks, and the relative security of this work. While some management personnel talk of company employment as archaic and point to the risk workers face of falling into a "cycle" of dependency and intergenerational plantation employment, current and former workers talk nostalgically about the security of the dependencies that the company job facilitates. In contrast, work for contractors is akin to the "hustle" of the informal economy where the majority of Kenyans must struggle to survive while a few are able to thrive. In this context, the company job, in spite of its exploitative roots, is venerated as a vestige of security in an increasingly precarious labor market. I conclude by reflecting on how the securities associated with the company job might be created outside of the conditions of economically productive work.

18.2 "Creative Destruction"

Kericho, located in the highlands west of the Rift Valley, is the heart of Kenya's tea production. Year-round rain and sunshine and a cool, highland climate makes for ideal growing conditions for the perennial tea bush. Tea can be harvested all year round and continuously generates income, a major part of its appeal for large- and small-scale producers alike. Vast plantations of lush green tea bushes extend around Kericho town, today the Kericho County headquarters and former colonial administrative center. Originally founded in the 1920s by two British companies now owned by multinational giants, these plantations together cover almost 20,000 hectares. Travel a few kilometers out of the town and you meet smaller tea holdings founded by European settlers during the colonial era and today run by Kenyan-owned companies. Kericho's rural areas that were, under the colonial system, designated "reserves" for local African populations, are today a patchwork of smallholder farms dominated by tea interspersed with maize, leafy green vegetables, and a little grass for grazing dairy cows. Tea monoculture dominates just about all of Kericho. Tourists who stop off here do so to witness its lush green undulating landscape, participate in a tour of a plantation, and indulge in a spot of colonial nostalgia.

But, picturesque as it is, Kericho's tea monoculture is troubling. It commemorates a history of land appropriation, displacement of local populations, and deforestation. Barrack-like, company villages testify to decades of low-paid manual labor. Tea is also troubling because of its uncertain future. Companies and smallholder farmers alike talk about a crisis in the tea industry due to low and stagnant prices at the Mombasa tea auction where most of the region's tea is sold. Part of the problem is over-production: tea is such a popular crop in Kenya that it has reached the point where simply too much tea is being produced. Over-supply depresses prices. At the time of my most recent fieldwork in early 2020, an unexpectedly long rainy season had seen production at an all-time high. Tea factories were working on overtime and warehouses in Mombasa were flooded with processed tea. I lost count of the number of times that people in Kericho talked about the need for diversification and mused over what they could possibly plant instead.

While smallholder farmers toy with the idea of planting alternative cash crops such as avocados or French beans, for companies owning large tea plantations, uprooting and planting thousands of hectares of something else is unthinkable. Rather, companies are focusing on how to make tea more profitable. Ironically, given the problem of over-supply for price, their strategy is to generate higher volumes while cutting labor costs.

Companies have long lamented the burden of high labor costs in the tea industry. Tea is a labor intensive crop, requiring year-round har-vesting and factory processing as well as the work of maintaining the crop through pruning, weeding, and replanting. Companies provide the large resident labor force needed for plantation production with free housing and water and a package of employment benefits: contributions paid into pension, health insurance and social security schemes, and access to subsidized healthcare via company dispensaries and hospitals. Workers are free to join the Kenya Agricultural and Plantation Workers Union, and all pay an obligatory agency fee out of their salaries that entitles them to a union-negotiated wage. Over the decades, this negotiation has been increasingly fraught: the union has fought for wage increments in line with the rising cost of living in Kenya while companies have claimed that this is unsustainable for business. Salaries of general workers currently stand at a minimum of 612 Kenyan shillings (under 6 USD) per day, which is above the national minimum wage for this kind of work. Workers engaged in tea harvesting have the possibility of earning more since this is "piece-work" that pays per kilogram harvested. According to the managing director of one tea plantation company, this salary, when combined with the costs of housing, water, and employment benefits, means that an unskilled worker on a tea plantation actually earns the equivalent of about 25,000 KES (approx. 230 USD) a month, which is compar-able with a low-grade nurse or teacher's salary in Kenya. Employing thousands of people on such a salary is not, he claimed, sustainable in terms of what the company makes from selling the tea it produces. His comment attests to the fact that plantation production of tea is only viable when labor is cheap.

The discrepancy between labor costs and income from tea sales has led to a growing trend on large, multinational-owned tea plantations toward mechanized harvesting, significantly reducing the numbers of people the company needs to employ. One of the largest tea plantation companies in Kericho now does entirely mechanized harvesting, while other plantations in the area and Kenya's other major tea producing regions expect to follow suit. While hand-plucked tea under union-negotiated rates pays workers 13 KES per kilogram of green leaf, machine-harvested tea is paid at just 2 KES per kilogram. Those people who are hired to do mechanized tea harvesting will earn similar amounts, if not more, than they would earn doing hand plucking, since the volumes they are able to harvest are much higher. Yet while hand plucking necessitated a large work force, machine plucking requires far fewer people. One manager estimated that the most widely used MTH (mechanized tea harvester) machine that requires the labor of three people replaced fifteen to twenty hand pluckers. Tea plantation managers I interviewed all talked about mechanization as the future of Kenya's tea industry and key to making tea production sustainable.

In conversations with senior personnel working for tea plantation companies, a diminishing labor force was often framed positively, not only in terms of the sustainability of the business but also as good for the workers themselves. "It's not something every parent would want his kid to get into," noted a manager at one Kenyan-owned plantation when we talked about plantation work.[2] When I asked the general manager of a tea factory in central Kenya if, as in other tea-producing former British colonies such as India and Sri Lanka, there were families living on the plantations which supplied his factory who had plucked tea for generations (see Besky, 2014; Jegathesan, 2019), he explained that, in his opinion, it was the role of management to discourage people from getting locked in such a "cycle":

It depends on the leadership. What we advise them is to make sure that they educate their children. The factory has a cooperative, a SACCO [Savings and Credit Cooperative], where now they contribute money on a monthly basis and they can pick loans to further the education of their children. To make sure that they don't fall into that cycling system of working in the estates.

Drawing on Joseph Schumpeter's notion of "creative destruction," the same manager went on to discuss the merits of mechanization in terms of modernization and improvement, breaking the need for a large labor force:

I believe in what we call continuous improvement. Even plucking should be mechanized. You know the labor cost in the tea sector goes up every year,

---

[2] Interviewed in Kiambu County, November 2018.

but the auction prices are relatively static. So there must be a cost-effective way that should be able to address plucking as a cost. So personally I believe in a theory developed by somebody called Joseph Schumpeter, 1942. It's called creative destruction theory... For you to develop better systems, you must destroy the existing systems. For you to come up with a better technology, you must study what is existing now, improve it. So that the systems are able to work better. So if hand plucking was introduced before Independence, there should be a system that should be able to harvest the tea at a cheaper cost. [More c]ost effective and sustainable than hand pluckers.[3]

In such accounts, technological innovations in the sector were celebrated as progress, while the low-level company job, and that of a tea plucker in particular, was portrayed as something outdated and belonging in the colonial past. Workers, it was hoped, would move out of plantations themselves through the social mobility that their children's education promised, or find alternative livelihoods. The sustainability report of one multinational tea company in Kericho cites its Entrepreneurship Programme in collaboration with Starbucks that seeks to support budding entrepreneurs among its ranks to become financially literate, develop a "business mindset" and become "economically independent," implicitly pointing to the future workers are expected to pursue outside the plantation gates (Finlays, 2020: 36). Meanwhile, in efforts to curtail the numbers of people on permanent contracts, the tea plantation company that was the focus of my fieldwork in 2020 was offering voluntary early retirement to permanent workers replete with a payment package. The company's plucking operations were almost entirely mechanized, and permanent general workers were no longer being recruited. In the context of a prolonged rainy season and a high crop of tea that needed harvesting, the company was managing the need for MTH machine labor by hiring seasonal workers on contracts of six months or less.

Mechanization, as a solution to high labor costs, was a celebrated form of "creative destruction" across many of my interviews, even among some low-level workers who argued that such technological developments were an inevitable part of Kenya's quest for economic development. Yet another, more furtive, tool of "creative destruction" is outsourcing. While mechanized harvesting resolves high labor costs

---

[3] Interviewed in Kiambu County, November 2018.

for the core task of green leaf harvesting, vast plantations continue to have high labor needs in the form of noncore activities, which have traditionally been carried out by company-employed staff. In the pursuit of a reduced labor force, plantations have begun to outsource this work, the basis for a new kind of plantation job.

18.3 The Outsourced Job

Tea plantation companies continue to employ directly those employees carrying out the company's "core" activities such as tea harvesting and factory processing, but the numerous additional jobs, known by employees as "side" (*kando*) jobs and that were formerly done "in house," are increasingly being delegated out to service providers external to the company. "Side" jobs include weeding, tea bush planting, tea bush pruning, splitting felled trees into firewood to fuel the company's tea factory, security provision (manning entrances to the plantations, managers' compounds, etc.) and what is known as "camp maintenance," which includes cutting grass, sorting waste, and trimming hedges in worker villages. Company employees used to welcome the availability of side jobs, since they could earn them additional income on top of their core activities. Outsourcing this work is justified by companies as cost-effective, as it further enables the reduction of company-employed general labor.

Aspiring entrepreneurs compete to become contractors with the company in the completion of particular tasks. These individuals are typically relatively well off to the extent that they have access to a vehicle and equipment with which to carry out the service that they are offering – such as power saws with which to do firewood splitting or pruning machines with which to do tea bush pruning. Upon agreeing rates of service with the company during a prequalification round, the successful applicants are approved to provide services with the company for a fixed period; at the Kericho tea plantation where I did fieldwork, this was two years. During this time, contractors apply for contracts with the company to carry out discrete tasks. The contractor hires a team of laborers to do these jobs while he or she oversees the work.

It is the job of the worker hired by the contractor that is the focus of this case study. Although contractors lack the security and benefits enjoyed by company employees, contract work can be very lucrative.

This is largely because the labor that contractors employ is cheap. Because contracted work is piecemeal, contractors often hire workers for very short periods, sometimes as short as a few days. While the company obliges contractors to pay their employees the national minimum wage, it is difficult for the company to oversee the actual practices of the numerous contractors they hire. In my interviews with company personnel in supervisory and managerial roles, some informants flagged the challenges of internal auditing and ensuring contractors' compliance with company policies. Even when contractors do pay the minimum wage, this works out as less than half the daily salary of a worker employed directly by the company. As casual workers hired on short-term contracts, employees of contractors are not eligible to be members of the Kenya Agricultural and Plantation Workers Union and therefore are not eligible for the union-negotiated wage. Companies are also obliged to ensure that their contractors cut contributions from their workers' wages toward Kenya's national health insurance scheme (the National Health Insurance Fund or NHIF) and social security fund (the National Social Security Fund or NSFF). Once again, however, the high numbers of contractors working with the company makes this policy difficult to enforce. Some contractors are said to find ways to avoid paying contributions to NHIF and NSFF by hiring workers for even shorter periods of time so that their salaries don't reach the minimum 1000 KES (less than 10 USD) required to make a contribution. Employees of contractors themselves may even favor these terms as their salaries are so low that they would rather take everything now and avoid contributing to insurance schemes that could, in the future, buffer them in case of sickness or other misfortune. Although most workers for contractors are local to the area, they often choose to stay in company housing to avoid the costs of public transport and the time it takes to travel across the vast plantations. Unlike workers employed directly by the company who are provided with free housing, outsourced workers must pay rent for the privilege. Their short periods of work and tendency to shift to different locations across the plantation means they are unable to save on food costs through cultivating kitchen gardens like company employees. Workers hired by contractors do not receive sick or holiday pay or parental leave. If they sustain an injury while at work they may seek superficial treatment at one of the plantations' dispensaries, after which the cost of treatment in a government or private hospital must be covered by their health insurance scheme, to the extent that they have actually been able to contribute to it.

Given these working conditions, why do people choose to work for contractors? The short answer is that people are desperate. Youth unemployment rates are high in Kenya. High hopes for national development at Independence in 1963 were dashed by a series of economic crises during the 1970s that undermined the state's capacity to invest in developing the country's economy. Neoliberal reforms during the 1980s and 1990s in the name of "structural adjustment" further dismantled the economy through cuts in government spending. Population growth and rural–urban migration meant that there were many more people looking for work than there were jobs. In smallholder farming areas in former "native reserves," land access became increasingly limited. Plots have been subdivided between children to the extent that for many, farming is not an economically viable activity. This post-agrarian economy pushes ever-growing numbers of young people into provincial centers and cities in search of jobs. Increasingly, many young job seekers are highly educated, their parents having worked hard to pay secondary and higher education fees with the hope that this will improve their chances of a good job and, ultimately, social mobility. Yet university graduates, too, are confronted with a lack of job opportunities and are often prepared to take on jobs for which they are over-qualified or to enter the "hustle" of the informal economy. Surplus continues to characterize Kenya's labor market, even in a time when Africa is supposedly "rising."[4] It is in this context of labor surplus that outsourcing on tea plantations thrives.

Meet Sarah. Sarah is in her mid-thirties and a single mum of two. She hails from the Kericho area but studied in Nairobi at a good, public university from which she graduated with a bachelor's degree in biochemistry. On completing her degree she struggled to find a relevant job for her qualifications: "You know this Kenya," she said, resignedly, by way of explanation. After trying with little success to break into Kenya's NGO sector, she accepted a job with a telecommunications company, but it didn't pay much. She decided to move back to her home area of Kericho to raise her first-born child who had been residing there with relatives, but failed again to find a job. It was then that she sought work as a contractor with one of Kericho's large tea

---

[4] The notion of "Africa rising" can be traced back to a 2011 article in *The Economist*.

companies. She started out by offering tea bush pruning services, initially buying four tea pruning machines, a huge investment at 92,000 KES each (around 850 USD). As she accumulated savings from the contract work, she gradually built up her stock of pruning machines to fifteen. Today, Sarah offers services to three tea plantation companies in Kericho in tea bush pruning, firewood splitting, camp maintenance, and road grading. Business is good, she told me, and the profits she makes go beyond feeding and educating her children. Since embarking on contract work six years ago, Sarah has bought a car, invested in a two-acre plot of land in a nearby rural area where she plans to plant her own tea bushes, and begun building a two-storey house. She constantly keeps an eye out for new opportunities for contracts with tea plantation companies.

Sarah's is a happy story that tells of the fortunes that can be made for those who are able to offer services as contractors. Notably, Sarah was in a position to source the start-up capital for the initial four pruning machines that she needed in order to be able to offer services as a contractor for pruning jobs. She didn't disclose any connections she may have had with managerial staff at the company, but rumors circulate in Kericho that companies find ways of giving "their people" contracts, including former senior staff who have retired from the company, so that contracting has become an avenue for patronage. This has certainly been seen elsewhere in Kenya, in particular in relation to the contracting-out of work such as road building by the national and county governments (see, for example, Klopp, 2011). Outsourcing enables and consolidates an entrepreneurial class with access to capital and, probably, a few connections in the right places.

Importantly, the profits to be made in this line of work depend on the availability of willing and cheap labor. Meet Benjamin, 29, who also holds a degree from a good, public Kenyan university, this time in political science. Benjamin is also from the Kericho area and is the son of small-scale tea farmers. In the 1980s, 1990s, and 2000s, Benjamin's father worked for a large tea plantation company in Kericho as a driver before retiring and focusing on his own tea farm. Now Benjamin works on the same plantation as his father did but, unlike his father, is not employed by the company. Rather, he works for four different contractors doing pruning, weeding, firewood splitting, and "slashing" in the tea company's blue gum forest plantation (the source of firewood for its factories). Benjamin explains his situation as resulting from the unemployment crisis in Kenya, that in spite of being highly educated he has little choice but to take on casual work for a contractor: "No educated person takes on manual jobs unless [the situation] is extreme." Benjamin describes working for contractors as his only means of survival.

Sarah's and Benjamin's stories illustrate the ways in which Kenya's labor surplus enables outsourcing as a viable cost-saving mechanism for tea plantation companies. It also shows that, beyond increasing companies' profit margins, outsourcing generates new inequalities through the creation of middle-class entrepreneurs like Sarah whose success hinges on the labor of people like Benjamin who are prepared to work under exploitative conditions. Let us now, by way of comparison, turn to the company job, under which conditions Benjamin's father was employed a couple of decades earlier and which today coexists alongside the outsourced job.

18.4 The Company Job

Just as outsourcing has come about in the particular historical context of widespread unemployment and labor surplus in Kenya, the company job with its associated benefits of free housing, health insurance, and pension also came about in particular historical circumstances during the late 1950s. This was the heyday of British colonial welfare paternalism, a time when there was heightened awareness that older trends of employment in colonial enterprises such as the tea industry were essentially exploitative and unsustainable for business. Reforms that transformed conditions of employment in the tea plantation sector in the 1950s sought to remedy an enduring problem that had long troubled tea companies: labor shortage. Creating decent working conditions was a way that employers tried to transform an irregular, short-term labor supply into a permanent resident labor force. This, it was hoped, would allow for the consolidation and expansion of tea plantation production in Kenya while projecting a positive image of the industry overseas where colonial enterprise was under increasing scrutiny (McWilliam, 2020).

From the 1920s, while establishing Kericho's extensive tea plantations, companies were faced with the major challenge of sourcing labor. Initially this was for the clearing of bush to prepare the land for the plantations. Later, once tea plants were established, a large labor force was required for harvesting leaf, operating tea factories and the kinds of "side" jobs described above through which plantation and factory operations could be maintained.

Recruiting labor for colonial enterprise was a problem throughout Kenya during the early decades of British rule. While today Kenya faces an excess of young people struggling to find work, back in the early twentieth century employers struggled to find enough people to hire, and there was much competition over those who did avail themselves to the colony's farms and industries. Most "natives" were self-sufficient in livestock or agriculture and had little need to engage in wage labor. The British applied various strategies to coerce people out of "native reserves" into European-owned farms and industries, including through imposing taxation per individual and per hut (Hut and Poll Tax) and conscripting labor (Anderson, 2000). Nevertheless, the labor supply to tea plantations continued to be unreliable. It became clear that people were not interested in becoming permanent wage laborers but rather engaged in such work sporadically, such as when taxes needed to be paid. Wage labor had become a means through which colonized Kenyans could supplement economies in their rural homes. As one commentator in the tea industry lamented in an article in 1954: "[Labor] merely works for us as a secondary interest to maintain the family in the reserve, and consequently there is no continuity of interest on the tea estate."[5] Competition for labor between tea plantation companies meant that workers had a degree of agency within an exploitative system of plantation work. If conditions were bad on one plantation, a worker could shift to a neighboring farm and find employment there.

Upon realizing this trend, tea companies, in partnership with the British administration, began seeking ways in which to stabilize labor in the tea industry and address the problem of a 100 percent annual labor turnover. Some employers sought to replicate employment models on plantations in British India and Ceylon, where work was carried out by a permanent resident labor force who had been imported from elsewhere, a process which had severed ties to their previous homes and promoted permanent settlement in company

---

[5] Excerpt from "New Commonwealth" of July 22, 1954: "Tea in Africa" by T. D. Rutter, Deputy Chairman, Brooke Bond & Co. Ltd. (KNA ABK/12/2 Labour for Tea Industry).

villages. During the 1940s and 1950s, one company imported labor from the Belgian protectorate of Ruanda, to the extent that imported labor came to constitute 10 per cent of the company's labor force. Government restrictions on immigration brought this scheme to an end, however, and the company, like others, continued to face the problem of high turnover from the local labor force.

By the early 1950s, the British administration and the tea industry were cognizant that a major part of the problem of unstable labor was attributable to low wages and inadequate working conditions. Plantations had been able to get away with paying workers low wages because workers maintained their livelihoods in their rural homes. In order to "break the pull of the reserve," as the commentator cited above put it,[6] plantations would need to pay a living wage and provide living conditions to facilitate permanent settlement, as well as forms of social security such as pensions that would mean that workers could risk breaking relations in rural homes. Improving conditions on plantations was also a response to greater scrutiny from Britain, where developments were underway regarding labor organization and social security (McWilliam, 2020: 34). To continue employing people on exploitative terms in the colonies would be hypocritical.

In this context, companies began to invest in building married housing quarters to promote the settlement of families rather than bachelors. Along with a house, each household was provided with a plot of land to grow food that could supplement the salary of their employed member. Additional facilities were added to company villages: social halls where employees could assemble, recreational areas such as playgrounds and football pitches, crèches, primary schools and dispensaries. Pension schemes were introduced so that workers would have some income in their old age. In 1961, the first trade union for tea workers was registered (McWilliam, 2020).

It must be noted that, although the welfare paternalism that flourished during this period generated clear improvements in the working conditions that characterized the early days of Kenya's tea industry, the very foundations of tea plantations are exploitative. Plantations occupy vast tracts of land that were once occupied and used by local

---

[6] Excerpt from "New Commonwealth" of July 22, 1954: "Tea in Africa" by T. D. Rutter, Deputy Chairman, Brooke Bond & Co. Ltd. (KNA ABK/12/2 Labour for Tea Industry).

communities. The descendants of those who were displaced by plantations today suffer from land shortages in the former "native reserves"
to which they had been relocated. Land shortages and the resulting
unsustainability of rural agricultural livelihoods are major culprits of
the unemployment crisis that pervades Kenya and that has continued
to push people into work on tea plantations. While companies sought
to create "village life" on plantations, employees have never been able
to own the houses they live in, nor have they ever been given tenure for
the plots they cultivate. In seeking to create a stable workforce that
would render Kenya's tea industry sustainable, the colonial administration destabilized rural economies and created a class of landless
people who would be forced, for generations, to seek wage labor.

Yet Kenya's tea industry never did manage to produce the kind of
permanent resident labor force that was found on tea plantations in
India and Ceylon. It is hard to find families who have lived and worked
on tea plantations for generations. Generally, plantation work is not
something that people aspire to. The highly hierarchical structure of
plantation life mirrors a colonial strategy of indirect rule, with worker
villages or "camps" under the watch of village elders and a "camp
supervisor" who reports issues – from roof leakages to conflicts
between neighbors – to management. Any relatives or friends visiting
workers must register with the village elders and state the reason and
duration of their stay. One former general worker for a multinational
in the Kericho area commented in an interview that such restrictions
and a pervasive sense of one's behavior being monitored can push
people to give up permanent jobs on plantations in favor of lesser-
paid casual work, for example as pluckers for smallholder tea farmers.
Nevertheless, since the implementation of welfare measures in the late
1950s, an overall trend has been that workers have gradually committed to longer-term employment on plantations, often bringing their
families with them to reside and school there (McWilliam, 2020). As
Kenya's economy was battered by the neoliberal reforms of the 1980s
and 1990s and the cost of living increased, plantation jobs became
more attractive for the security they offered in the context of declining
rural economies and a labor market increasingly characterized by
informality. Workers have, however, largely continued to approach
the company job as a springboard to greener pastures as opposed to an
end in itself. During my interviews with workers at a multinational-
owned plantation in Kericho in the spring of 2020, workers talked

about the value of a predictable salary for long-term planning, in particular with regard to the education of children, which is seen as a key vehicle for social mobility in Kenya. Borrowing money through the worker's Savings and Credit Cooperative was frequently cited as a means through which to make future investments, channeled toward the aforementioned school fees, plots of land in rural homes (since many people don't inherit enough land to cultivate), and starting small businesses to turn to on retirement. Workers also cited retirement packages and pension payments as important future sources of income.

18.5 Precarious Dependencies

In spite of the formal framework through which the benefits of the company job reach workers, many of my informants talked about the advantages of their work in terms of being "helped" and of their gratitude to the company and its management. I found myself feeling uneasy about these seemingly submissive attitudes and wondered if I wasn't digging deep enough. I had read and heard about the strikes that had, on numerous occasions, brought tea plantation operations in the area to a standstill following failed negotiations between tea plantation companies and the union over wage increments, mechanization, and job losses, the most recent of which was in 2017. I had expected to get at least some sense of workers' critique of the company. I wondered if workers had been prepped to paint a rosy picture of plantation life to the foreign researcher. Media coverage and NGO reports have, in recent years, sought to expose poor working conditions on Kenyan tea plantations, in particular those owned by multinationals, and question the validity of their claims to "sustainable" production, including through adherence to certified sustainability standards (e.g., van der Wal, 2011; Chepkoech, 2019; ICFI, 2019). As a result, gaining access to multinational-owned tea plantations isn't easy. Having been denied access by the managing director of one major multinational in Kericho, I was, happily, granted access by another, but only through the close facilitation of management. An estate was identified where I could meet workers, and the estate manager, via a team of supervisors, selected the workers with whom I would meet. Each afternoon, when I arrived at the plantation gates, a security guard would write down the name and phone number of the estate manager whom I had arranged to meet, sometimes asking me to call the manager in question so that security could confirm that the meeting was to take place. On reaching the estate where I had arranged to meet with workers after they had completed their work for the day, I would report to the estate manager at his office. Insisting that it was too far to walk, the manager would then drive me down to the village crèche building where I would conduct interviews, picking me up a few hours later when I was finished. I feared that such close mediation by management prohibited me from building trusting relationships with workers and restricted what they felt able to share in our discussions. During interviews, I felt exasperated as workers faithfully recounted how great the company was: how it had "helped" them, how they were "one family," and how grateful they were for the kindness of the particular manager who was driving me around the estate. Most likely, workers *were* being careful about what they told me and concerned that any negative criticism of the company and the nature of their work and living conditions could get back to management. Nevertheless, as my fieldwork continued, and I started to situate these kinds of statements within the particular context in which the company job was being phased out, they began to resonate.

In a 2013 essay on labor, welfare, and personhood in southern Africa, the anthropologist James Ferguson reflects on struggles among unemployed youth and their seeming aspirations to enter into paternalistic, unequal relations which can seem regressive and reactionary to what he calls "the emancipatory liberal mind." Ferguson argues that this is, however, an entirely contemporary response to a situation in which people and their labor power are surplus. Across the region, ordinary people have historically sought to position themselves as dependents in hierarchical polities, a trend that continued during the colonial era as people voluntarily offered their labor to colonial enterprises and industries. Although exploitative and hierarchical, colonial and Apartheid-era employment of black southern Africans (in particular young men) created conditions for belonging and dependency that ordinary people actively sought out, not only for basic survival but also as a means through which to become respected persons in society. These relations of dependency were the means through which people could, in turn, sustain rural dependents and raise the funds to pay bride price and get married. Rather than something passive and disabling, Ferguson argues, dependence here can be seen as a "mode of action."

Ferguson charts a shift from a situation of labor shortage during the colonial period to a contemporary situation of labor surplus. As in Kenya, labor was highly sought after during colonialism in southern Africa, and enterprises often had to compete to recruit and retain labor, giving workers some degree of agency and leverage. Population growth, the decline of rural economies, and the reduction of formal sector job opportunities following neoliberal reforms has led to chronic unemployment of young people across the region. This shift, Ferguson argues, has created a crisis of belonging among the young male population in particular who struggle to forge the relations of dependency so necessary for personhood. One outcome has been the significant rise in female-headed households as many men lack the resources to marry and support families.

A similar broad trend to that which Ferguson describes for southern Africa – a shift from labor shortage during the colonial period to a contemporary situation of labor surplus and a related struggle for work and belonging – can be seen in Kenya. When tea plantation company employees in Kericho talked about their relationship with the company and its managers in terms of "help," gratitude, and even kinship, they were highlighting the value of the relations of dependency that the company job facilitates. Notably, these relations were often described in personal, paternalistic terms even as they unfolded within the formal framework of the company job. In one interview with Bett, a general worker in his mid-thirties who operates an MTH machine, he compared work at the multinational-owned plantation he worked for with things he had heard about employment at the neighboring multinational-owned plantation. There the money is a bit better, he reflected, but "you can't talk to a manager."[7] His comment hinted to the informal opportunities that could arise for general workers through relationships with senior staff. Low-level employees and managers alike told me stories of bright young people whose parents had been general workers on plantations and had "made it" due to the kindness of the company. Here's one among many examples of such a story, told by a former manager at a multinational plantation in Kericho whom I'll call Sam. Sam told me about a boy who was the son of a general worker. The boy was bright but his father didn't value education. Sam, who was working for the company at the time, decided to support him. It was

---

[7] Interviewed Kericho, February 2020.

during the 1980s, Sam explained, when plantations were allowed to employ child labor. Sam gave him jobs in the tea nursery during the school holidays so that he could save some money for his schooling.[8] The boy did well in his primary school exams and got into a good secondary school, but his father didn't want to pay the fees. Sam rallied around fellow employees at the company to raise money to pay for his schooling. Sam told me proudly that the boy went on to study medicine at university and today is one of fewer than ten internal radiologists in the country.[9] Others told me of company managers today who had grown up on the plantation as the children of general workers. Here's a current manager at the same company, whom I'll call Colin: "[I]f a child is good in school he or she will get a scholarship from [the company] and [the company] can favor them for employment later. [The company] has been very kind. It sees people rising."[10]

Beyond the guarantee of the salary, housing, pension, and other forms of security offered by the company job, company workers also value their jobs for the more informal relations that they can open up with senior staff and the opportunities that can arise from such relations. To be sure, these relations are undergirded by asymmetrical power relations, and have been shown by media and NGO reports not only to be exploitative but also at times abusive, such as where senior employees solicit sexual favors from general workers. Notably, such incidents have reportedly been on the increase in the context of a reduction in company job opportunities on plantations and growing numbers of applicants for those jobs (mainly temporary, seasonal positions) that are available. An influential report (van der Wal, 2011) documented the accounts of general workers, in particular those employed on seasonal contracts, who reported seniors demanding bribes and/or sexual favors in return for jobs and the renewal of contracts. Nevertheless, people have continued to seek out the company job for the securities it guarantees and the potentiality of cultivating more informal paternalistic relations with management, even as these relations risk becoming abusive.

Similar relations of dependency are sought out by those employed in outsourced jobs, only on even more precarious terms. Benjamin, whom

---

[8] Up until 2003, government primary education in Kenya was fee paying.
[9] Interviewed Kericho, February 2020.
[10] Interviewed Kericho, February 2020.

we met earlier, talked optimistically about his work in a way that surprised me. When I asked if he wouldn't apply for a seasonal job for six months with the company given the significantly better rates of pay and the other benefits of the company job noted above, he insisted that he preferred outsourced work:

Those [company] workers are salaried. They have that security. But for ours, the more you do it the more you earn [while] they are in fixed salary. For myself, I go home if I have other engagements. Weekends are free. I'm not restricted. I'll have more freedom, that's why I opted for this job.[11]

Here, Benjamin emanates the spirit of the neoliberal individual who welcomes the flexibility of outsourced work for its opportunities to self-maximize. But Benjamin, too, talked about the importance of his relationships with others for this self-maximization. The first contractor Benjamin worked for was a friend who gave him the job because they knew each other. Benjamin works hard to cultivate relationships of mutual dependency with the contractors he works for, even spending unpaid time trying to procure new contracts for them in the hope that this will get him more work. Such efforts have earned him the trust of some contractors who have elevated him to the role of supervisor, so that he now oversees the work of his fellow employees and earns a slightly higher daily rate of 350 KES per day (about 3 USD). Benjamin hopes that, through his hard work, he can ultimately become a contractor himself. He describes the typical contractor as a "big breadwinner" and "someone in society," underlining that becoming a contractor doesn't only mean becoming wealthy but also implies having the capacity to redistribute wealth through the provision of work to youth like himself. In the meantime, Benjamin hopes that the relations he has nurtured with his employers will provide him with some security such as an advance on his salary if, for example, he became unwell and needed money for hospital fees. Benjamin calls this "a local arrangement." He reminds me that, in contrast to the conditions of employment in the company job, such arrangements are informal: "Remember, this is contract, not company."

In spite of Benjamin's optimism, the informality of outsourced work puts workers in a vulnerable position with regard to their employers.

---

[11] Interviewed Kericho, February 2020.

The short duration of contracts means that workers are frequently –
sometimes as often as weekly – in a position where they need to
renegotiate employment, and this gives employers plenty of opportunities to negotiate reduced pay or to solicit bribes or favors in return for
a job. As Benjamin notes, there are opportunities for forms of assistance if a contractor is kind and well-meaning, but this depends entirely
on the individual contractor and is not backed up by any formal
framework. Benjamin is a fit and healthy young man, unmarried, and
without dependents, which may in part explain his hopes that he can
"make it" through outsourced work. But his hopes rest on being in a
position, most of the time, to work optimally and be employed by an
individual who is able to help him out should misfortune strike.
Otherwise, if he becomes ill and unable to work, or has an accident
at work and is hospitalized, he could face a period without salary and a
hefty hospital bill that his national health insurance may not be able to
cover. Benjamin's dream of becoming a contractor is, in this sense, a
fragile one.

18.6 Conclusion

This chapter has examined a growing trend on Kenya's tea plantations
toward outsourcing noncore activities, and compared the outsourced
job with the longer-standing, and currently still existing, company job.
I have recounted the particular historical conditions which led to the
relative securities of the company job – i.e., labor shortage and colonial
welfare paternalism – as well as those which have enabled outsourcing
and its precarities – i.e., labor surplus and low tea prices relative to
labor costs. The company job, its hierarchies, inequalities, and dependencies are unsettling to the outside observer and reminiscent of the
exploitative colonial capitalism under which it was first established.
Yet workers insist on their gratitude to the company and its senior staff
in terms of "help." These utterances, although undoubtedly attributable in part to workers' trepidation that negative comments about the
company could get back to management, must be contextualized in the
current climate whereby tea plantation companies are reducing their
labor forces via mechanized harvesting and outsourcing. Tea plantations have been important sites through which ordinary people have
sought to cultivate relations of dependency with senior staff. The
formal conditions of the company job have created a relatively secure

basis for this cultivation, while the guarantee of a union-negotiated salary, free housing, pension, health coverage, and access to credit has allowed employees to make future investments which can support them on leaving plantation work. While the outsourced job might appear to offer flexibility and freedom, workers also try to cultivate relations of dependency with contractors, only on much more precarious terms.

While the outsourced job is a relatively new phenomenon on Kenya's tea plantations, its insecure conditions resemble those of Kenya's informal economy in which the majority of Kenyans find work. In this respect, the company job and its formal privileges are seen as a vestige of security in a labor market characterized by insecurity. This was clearly expressed by Benjamin's father when I interviewed him at his rural home. He talked about the benefits that he was entitled to between the 1980s and 2000s as an employee of the company that owns the plantation Benjamin today works on in an outsourced job:

We got a free house. But they [outsourced workers] have to pay rent. We were being supplied electricity, water, houses, pension. *Zamani* [back then] you could be sent to the [company] hospital. These days, no. You run to the district [public hospital]. *Unakuwa raiya tu* [You just become a citizen].

Benjamin's father's description of outsourced workers as reduced to "citizens" points to the relatively privileged position of company employees. In an economy characterized by informality and lack of formal job opportunities, outsourced workers find themselves, like most Kenyans, running to the district hospital when they're sick and hoping that the national health insurance scheme to which they may or may not have contributed some of their scant salaries might cover the costs.

Outsourcing on tea plantations also has an impact on company operations. Companies tend to defend their decision to outsource by arguing that contractors are required to operate according to company standards. Yet it is very difficult to monitor large numbers of contractors and their short-term employees. Under the scrutiny of the media, workers' union and audits by certification bodies on behalf of sustainability standards providers like the Rainforest Alliance and Fairtrade, the pressure to have an oversight of the real conditions under which operations are taking place has led to an unprecedented amount of time, energy, and expertise being channeled into internal auditing. Thus, although companies may save on labor costs, auditing and oversight costs increase. Outsourcing has also had an impact on plantation security. Company employees complain of growing instances of insecurity and theft in workers' villages due to the presence of outsourced workers who come and go on short contracts and are unknown to the company. Given the low wages and precarious employment of outsourced labor, this isn't particularly surprising.

More generally, outsourcing contributes to Kenya's major problem of inequality, as contractors' wealth and middle-class lifestyles are effectively enabled by the enduring poverty of their employees. Kenya, like South Africa, struggles with high rates of violent crime as an effect of deep inequality. The casualization of low-level labor in the tea plantation sector thus has worrying implications for social cohesion writ large. Although outsourcing has emerged as a way of addressing what companies see as an outdated plantation labor system, what this "creative destruction" leaves in its wake seems even more problematic.

What is the solution? In a working paper entitled "Beyond the 'Proper Job'," James Ferguson and Tania Murray Li (2018) challenge the ways in which the figure of the wage laborer and formal sector or "proper" job has endured as a norm or telos of "development." Rather than continuing to insist upon "jobs for all," we need to think more creatively about how the forms of social security and belonging that have traditionally been linked to formal sector jobs can be created outside of the conditions of economically productive labor. This need becomes even more striking through the case of Kenyan tea plantation jobs described in this chapter, where the "benefits" of the company job, while easily romanticized in the present context of outsourcing, are nevertheless rooted in highly exploitative sets of economic relations. Rather than arguing for a return to the company job, we need to imagine alternatives. Campaigns for a Universal Basic Income (UBI), for example, argue for the provision of a flat income for all, regardless of their employment status. Recipients could top this up with paid work, but their most basic living costs would be covered. Another alternative is Universal Basic Services (UBS), a policy which has been proposed for the UK (Institute for Global Prosperity, 2017). Here, services such as housing, travel, food, and phone and internet access are freely available, alongside services that are, in the UK, already entirely or partially free, such as healthcare and education. While the neoliberal solution to the decline of formal employment is typically "entrepreneurship," alternatives such as UBS and UBI establish solutions to poverty and inequality that do not hinge on individuals' economic productivity. Such alternatives can allow people to live meaningful, purposeful lives even on the lowest of wages in the most insecure of jobs, with important implications for wider social cohesion.

References

Anderson, David M. 2000. "Master and servant in colonial Kenya." *Journal of African History* 41: 459–485.

Besky, Sarah. 2014. *The Darjeeling Distinction: Labour and Justice on Fair-Trade Tea Plantations in India.* Berkeley: University of California Press.

Chepkoech, Anita. 2019. "Tea farms brew sexual abuse and misery for poor workers." *Daily Nation,* December 8, 2019. Accessed January 29 2021. https://nation.africa/kenya/news/tea-farms-brew-sexual-abuse-and-misery-for-poor-workers-230376

Ferguson, James. 2013. "Declarations of dependence: Labour, personhood, and welfare in southern Africa." *Journal of the Royal Anthropological Institute* 19: 223–242.

Ferguson, James, and Tania Murray Li. 2018. "Beyond the 'proper job': Political-economic analysis after the century of labouring man." *Institute for Poverty, Land and Agrarian Studies,* Working Paper 51, April 13 2018. Belville: University of the Western Cape.

Finlays. 2020. "Sustainability report 2019". Accessed January 29 2021. www.finlays.net/wp-content/uploads/2020/07/Finlays-Annual-Report-2019-Singles.pdf

ICFI. 2019. "A visit to the workers' quarters at a Unilever tea plantation in Kenya." *World Socialist Website,* October 1, 2019. Accessed January 29 2021. www.wsws.org/en/articles/2019/10/01/kein-o01.html

Institute for Global Prosperity. 2017. *Social Prosperity for the Future: A Proposal for Universal Basic Services.* London: IGP Social Prosperity Network, University College London.

Jegathesan, Mythri. 2019. *Tea and Solidarity: Tamil Women and Work in Postwar Sri Lanka.* Seattle: University of Washington Press.

Klopp, Jacqueline. 2011. "Towards a political economy of transportation policy and practice in Nairobi." *Urban Forum* 23 (1): 1–21.

McWilliam, Michael. 2020. *Simba Chai: The Kenya Tea Industry.* Charlbury: Prepare to Publish Ltd.

Van der Wal, Sanne. 2011. *Certified Unilever tea: Small cup, big difference?* Amsterdam: Somo. Accessed January 29, 2021: www.somo.nl/certified-unilever-tea/

19 | How Should Innovation Work?

MICHAEL SCROGGINS

When we think about how innovation happens, we're at a bit of a loss to understand it because our common-sense notions of innovation owe so much to Silicon Valley hype and propaganda. When we imagine innovation, we often think about strong personalities, aggressive and spectacular disruption, and ruthless profit-seeking. Scroggins suggests that much meaningful innovation actually happens beyond attempts at disruptive innovation and attraction of venture capital where innovation is narrowly seen as a driver of economic activity. Instead, innovation tends to emerge from stable, rather boring groups of people working outside of job markets and for-profit corporations, on projects that are of personal or group interest, valuable to the people working on them for intrinsic, seemingly self-evident reasons. To show this, Scroggins describes two paths both taken in the same Silicon Valley do-it-yourself biotechnology laboratory. A neoliberal approach tried to use the democratization of a technology, in this case synthetic biology, as a lever to implement the classic disruptive strategy of entering low-end and opening new markets. The alternative approach proceeded on a slower and more deliberate path, without market forces and the promise of funding. What separated the alternative from the neoliberal approach is, according to Scroggins, its constant focus on community over commodity, and process over product.

In 2011 a cohort of individuals opened a Do-It-Yourself biology (DIYbio) laboratory in a Sunnyvale, California office park (Scroggins, 2017, 2019). They named the laboratory Biocurious and began referring to themselves as Biocurians. The individuals hailed from a range of backgrounds: experienced nonprofit volunteers, veteran entrepreneurs, aspiring entrepreneurs, startup consultants, retired engineers, undergraduate students from San Jose St and Santa Clara, postdoctoral researchers from Stanford and Berkeley, a computer scientist from Lawrence Livermore National Laboratory, independent researchers without institutional affiliation, science teachers, faculty from Singularity University, and the recently unemployed looking to improve their skills (see Gershon, 2017). Among this cohort, a simmering conflict took hold between those who believed Biocurious should act as a Silicon Valley startup and move to disrupt industries and institutions through innovation and those who believed that Biocurious should become "a laboratory for the community" where people could "experiment with friends" in the relaxed environment of a "garage lab." The crux of this conflict were the tenets of two competing visions of how innovation should work and who it might work for. Is innovation the province of a special social class, "makers" in Silicon Valley parlance, who are fluent in taking technology to market? Or is innovation something that bubbles up from the ordinary business of tinkering and playing with technology?

Propelling the dream of a public DIYbio lab was one of the first successful crowdfunding campaigns. The Biocurious organizers raised more than 30,000 dollars on Kickstarter.com, enough to put down a deposit and pay several months' rent. This success was due in no small part to the well-placed pitch on Biocurious' Kickstarter website. The organizers not only promised to revolutionize biotechnology, they also promised that the revolution would offer something for everyone. Entrepreneurs would find cofounders while pioneering new markets, hackers would find a do-acracy where democratic norms reigned, and job seekers would be able to gain laboratory experience and network with company-hiring managers (see Souleles and Scroggins, 2017). While you might think that a single institution could not possibly hold so many contradictory norms and aspirations, the organizers believed the heat and hype of their new approach to biotech could fuse these contradictory ideas into a unitary institution.

This chapter examines the early years of Biocurious, between 2011 and 2013, when the direction and purpose of Biocurious was an unavoidable topic of deliberation, debate, and conflict among Biocurians. One case probes the neoliberal Biocurious, predicated on disruptive innovation and attracting venture capital, that came and went; the other case examines what I will call the do-ocratic (Zacchiroli, 2011) Biocurious of more modest aim and scope, predicated on volunteer labor, community education, and mutual aid, that still exists in Sunnyvale.

As might be surmised, one answer to the question on how innovation should work lies in the nature of social ties at the two Biocuriouses. The neoliberal Biocurious directed its activities from the top down through a board of directors in consultation with corporate sponsors, and mediated relationships between the laboratory and members and volunteer staff through the norms of human resources. This Biocurious had a brief but spectacular existence, beginning with a barrage of friendly media coverage, seeing an infamous startup launched from within its laboratory, and ending with the departure of the original board members and the election of new board members drawn from the ranks of Biocurious' members and volunteers. Another answer to the question of how innovation should work lies in the purpose of the two Biocuriouses. Should innovators aim to disrupt industries by using the democratization of a technology, in this case synthetic biology, as a lever to implement the classic disruptive strategy of entering low-end and opening new markets, such as direct-to-consumer genetically modified organisms? Or should innovation proceed on a slower and more deliberate path, without market forces and the promise of funding (and the fame that comes with it) pulling innovation into the same predictable shapes?

19.1 The Neoliberal Biocurious

Early in my fieldwork at Biocurious I received a lesson in how innovation happens in Silicon Valley. A Biocurious member, who had turned down a seat on the board because of Biocurious' non-profit status (he thought Biocurious should have been a for-profit), explained to me the current state of play in Silicon Valley. Talking about the numerous synthetic biology startups then attracting venture capital, he opined that early in the life of a new company the main product is always is heat and hype. Attracting attention, he said, is the entire game. If you have to make outrageous claims, make them. If you have to stretch the truth about a product into a white lie, stretch it. The companies that survive their early days are those that attract attention because attention can be turned to dollars and dollars into survival. And being one of the two or three companies to survive the early days of a new industry leads to pivoting, and pivoting, he explained, is where profitability lies. This, in a nutshell, is the neoliberal model of innovation.

I am going to suggest a metaphor drawn from American professional wrestling to describe neoliberal innovation. American pro-wrestling has a complex and subtle vocabulary for describing the interplay between staged events (works), real events (shoots), and staged events presented as real events (a worked shoot). Wrestling also has a complex and subtle vocabulary for discussing the audience's relationship to fact and narrative. There are viewers who mistake the staged for the real (marks), those who discern the difference between staged and real (smarts), and those who enjoy searching for the boundary between the staged and the real (smarks).

The lesson I urge you to take from my informant's story of heat and hype in the life of innovation is that some of what passes for innovation in Silicon Valley and elsewhere is a staged event, a shoot, but more often what is called innovation is a staged event presented as a real event, a worked shoot. Success in this world depends on more than being a smart; you must be a smark and have a keen eye for the line between the real and the staged.

19.1.1 The Setting

The place was Silicon Valley. The year 2011. This was the year the United States officially (if you follow official metrics) recovered from the Great Recession of 2008. Silicon Valley led the recovery, with Google, Apple, Facebook, and newcomer Netflix all posting banner profits. It was a time of renewed optimism in Silicon Valley, with new faces, new technology, new business models and, most importantly, new money flowing into the valley.

Biocurious opened that year in what, by most measurements, is the geographical heart of Silicon Valley. A stone's throw from 843 Stewart was the original Intel chip factory and the other hardware companies that emerged in the postwar silicon boom that gave the valley its moniker. A generation prior it had been the economic heart as well, though by 2011 the action had largely moved north to Palo Alto, home to a steady pipeline of software engineers and entrepreneurs pumped out by Stanford and near to the powerful venture capital firms affronting the south side of campus. It had become common by then for would-be tech titans to follow Mark Zuckerberg's path of using Stanford to scout potential cofounders and collaborators, coding and taking meetings with venture capitalists at the many coffeeshops near campus.

By contrast, the organizers of Biocurious belonged to an older style of Silicon Valley entrepreneurship. They were heir to the hardware and software entrepreneurs of previous generations who made fortunes by democratizing access to tools and techniques. They aimed to do for biology what the integrated circuit had done for electronics and the personal computer for the software industry – make available democratic design tools and techniques that anyone could use to decode DNA and create novel organisms.

Physically, the two Biocuriouses shared the same location; socially they were worlds apart. Biocurious was populated by the following classes of people, each with attendant rights and responsibilities: six board members, a couple dozen paying members, a few professional scientists (graduate and postdocs from Stanford and Berkeley), and several dozen volunteers. The neoliberal Biocurious was populated by the six board members and about half of the paying members: that half with entrepreneurial experience in the software and hardware industries. The board and entrepreneurial members were bound together by a set of overlapping and interlinking elective affinities. Half the board members were young with Ivy League degrees, half older with experience in the entrepreneurial trenches. With the members, they shared focus on startup companies, venture capital, and shared networks of funding and startup infrastructure.

19.1.2 The Solution in Theory

The theory of the case I present in the next section was elucidated by the Biocurious board members during their Kickstarter campaign. During my fieldwork several board members told me this part of the Kickstarter appeal was intended to attract entrepreneurs looking for new industries to disrupt, and angel investors and venture capitalists looking for new companies to invest in. In a section explaining what they expected Biocurious to become, they opined:

Entrepreneurship Incubation, Mentoring, Angel Investment.

The Bay Area is home to many networks that help entrepreneurs launch web businesses with a shoestring budget and a dream. Similar support infrastructure does not yet exist for biotech ventures. Until recently, biotech has required large startup costs. An ecosystem of mentor ship and a network of investors who understand the possibilities for lean-biotech-startups to

leverage shared resources and amplify their creative efforts to have disproportionate commercial impact, is urgently needed. BioCurious will catalyze
the formation of this system.

The call to action above is couched rhetoric that was at once new to
Silicon Valley, in conceptualizing biology as a technology, and traditional in Silicon Valley, in claiming that like the hardware and
software industries before it a new era of democratized access to tools
and equipment was at hand. Rhetorically, this was entirely normal
for a Silicon Valley startup. Innovation demands claiming the mantle
of both revolution and tradition, e.g., claiming the means of revolution is low-cost access to high-powered tools is a traditional strategy.
More telling were the lines about the ecosystem of mentors and
investors Biocurious would bring into existence. At the neoliberal
Biocurious this ecosystem worked by using corporate sponsors to
raise money and pay expenses, thus avoiding the problem of sharing
management decisions with do-ocratically enabled members. Like the
warmth of the sun, the constant flow of corporate money made life
easy at Biocurious. Corporate sponsors also allowed the Biocurious
board to shape the space in subtle ways by forcing out those who do
not fit the image the board wished to circulate through media
accounts of the lab. As well, "the right" fit became a de facto argument for exclusion of members or volunteers based on the needs and
desires of the corporate sponsors.

19.1.3 The Solution in Practice

While the theory put forth by Biocurious seemed workable, albeit with
a few open questions, such as whether of not Biocurious was the
startup of interest or, like Y Combinator, a highly publicized incubator. In practice, a story as old as Fairchild's Traitorous Eight unfolded
at Biocurious, For those unfamiliar with the story of the Traitorous
Eight, it refers to the eight original employees of Shockley
Semicondutor (many of Shockley's former Stanford graduate students
who found his management style oppressive) who left Shockley
Semiconductor, thus putting it out of business, to form Fairchild
Semiconductor. From Fairchild Semiconductor and the Traitorous
Eight sprung the dozens of startup companies – including Intel and
AMD – leading to the moniker Silicon Valley.

Like the semiconductor industry when Fairchild Semiconductor was formed, it was believed that the first direct-to-consumer genetically modified organism would inaugurate a new industry and create new fortunes. For the Biocurious board, who were managing Biocurious like a startup company/business incubator, this was a great thing until they ran across an entrepreneur who saw the game of creating new markets for what is was – a staged event presented as real, i.e., a worked shoot.

Like Biocurious, the Glowing Plant startup used crowdfunding as a strategy to build a customer base, a media profile, and raise money that otherwise would have come from angel investors. Also, like Biocurious, the Glowing Plant kickstarter campaign was sponsored and supported by a number of startup companies associated with Singularity University and maintained close ties to its startup ecosystem. The core team consisted of a technical founder, a Stanford-trained laboratory scientist, one Stanford postdoc, a software engineer with a background in biological applications, and a former Bain & Company consultant. Prior to their crowdfunding campaign Glowing Plant hired a digital marketing firm to manage the Kickstarter and advise on a public relations campaign. Though crowdfunding is often portrayed as the product of the wisdom of the crowd, the pump was primed well before the Kickstarter campaign was underway.

What happened at Biocurious was this: Glowing Plant poached the most active teach at Biocurious, elevating him from mentor to former tech entrepreneurs, and de facto leader of a popular community project at Biocurious to the technical founder of a heavily hyped startup company. And though the founders of Glowing Plant met at Biocurious, they left without giving anything back to the laboratory. There was no contractural reason (read neoliberal rationale) to do so, but it would have been a gesture of good faith. Most disconcertingly, though, the existence of the Glowing Plant startup left the broader DIYbio community in a no-win situation. If Glowing Plant was an utter failure (which it ultimately was) then DIYbio would be seen as largely ineffective. On the other hand, if Glowing Plant was successful then DIYbio might be subject to heavy regulation and negative scrutiny from the media.

From Glowing Plants perspective, however, the situation was a win-win. If they were an utter failure (which they were) they would still be lionized as visionaries who pioneered a new market strategy and would find ready employment in the startup world (in fact, this is what happened). On the other hand, if they succeeded any regulation they faced would be as a for-profit corporation and could easily be handled using strategies pioneered by Monsanto and Dupont in previous decades. And here we come to another truism of neoliberal innovation: the benefits of success can adhere to only one party, here Glowing Plant, while the risks of failure are spread widely.

To give a brief technical overview, Glowing Plant intended to take a luciferin system from the marine bacteria Vibrio Fischeri, found in squid, and place it into an Arabidopsis plant, thus causing the plant to bioluminescence, or light up, at night. You might think that such a company would surely be illegal, and in Europe or Asia where the rule of thumb is that if something is not explicitly allowed it is illegal, and you would be right. But in the United States, the rule is the opposite – that which is not explicitly banned is legal. For example, in the United States, effecting a bacterial transformation via bacteria is regulated as a potential plant pest but using a gene gun (yes, a literal gun used to shoot plant callus cells) to effect the transformation is unregulated. Glowing Plant planned to drive their product through this regulatory loophole straight to market and ship their genetically modified organism (GMO) to consumers without regulatory oversight. In doing so, Glowing Plant was just following a strategy pioneered by Monsanto years before to market genetically modified Bluegrass.

Glowing Plant had a brief, but spectacular existence. Once they left Biocurious, they were accepted into Y Combinator as the first non-software startup in their history. Though, as you can probably guess from the lack of bioluminescent lighting in your house, Glowing Plant came to an inglorious end. As the years went by, and failed attempt followed failed attempt, the technical founder left followed by the software engineer. At the end, the man from Bain was vainly trying to pivot from manufacturing a Glowing Plant to creating a software platform for genetic analysis called TAXA. TAXA raised just over USD750,000 from fifty-three investors in a crowdfunding investment scheme. But even in Silicon Valley there is a finite number of marks willing to put cash on the table based on a dramatic story of heat and hype. Eventually TAXA, too, failed and the audience left for greener pastures.

19.1.4 *Analysis*

At a time when Biocurious' Kickstarter honeymoon was over and they needed cash and peer support in the laboratory, their own neoliberal rhetoric came to haunt them. Instead of support, the founders of Glowing Plant tried to run the weakened Biocurious into the ground in order to purchase the intellectual property built into the Biocurious brand. I participated in several conference calls in the months following Glowing Plant's departure from Biocurious in which Biocurious members, volunteers, and the Glowing Plant founders schemed ways to lower Biocurious' membership and revenue in a bid to take over the laboratory and, therefore extract what was valuable from Biocurious, its brand.

Then there was the broader question of Glowing Plant itself. Despite the huge Kickstarter – nearly USD 500,000 – and the promise made to 2000 supporters that they could make a common model organism, the plant Arapadopisis, glow after dark like a household lamp – was this actually possible? Of course not. Did their Kickstarter backers believe it was possible? For many of these marks the answer was yes. Was this fraud? Not exactly. Many knew it was impossible but were invested in the effort, or, more accurately, the performance of effort. It was a shoot for some and a worked shoot for others. But most disconcertingly, Glowing Plant was a gamble with the good reputation of DIYbio which, to that point, had carefully avoided negative publicity.

19.2 The Do-ocratic Biocurious

Despite the neoliberal overlay, much of the spirit of the Bay Area counterculture lives on in Silicon Valley. By this I mean the clichéd version of the counterculture. The one in which people pursue self-study despite the lack of immediate material gain, and the one in which people work together in the spirit of mutual aid toward a common goal that none alone can reach. In the ordinary business of creating, maintaining, and repairing the laboratory at Biocurious, this happened.

The do-ocratic Biocurious emerged slowly, animated from the bottom up by the work of laboratory volunteers and members who cared for and repaired Biocurious' mishmash of new and old, purchased and homemade equipment, taught classes, and took out the biotrash. This Biocurious was built on durable social ties that hold it together to this day. This Biocurious had more modest aims, seeking to "experiment with friends" in the informal atmosphere of a garage lab by connecting the earliest Biocurians to the newest Biocurians in an unbroken chain of curiosity and scientific education directed by the interests of laboratory members and volunteers.

If neoliberal innovation is comparable to professional wrestling in its uncertain relationship with reality and complex plot lines, then do-ocratic innovation is comparable to the rambling, improvised, and carnivalesque business practices of the Grateful Dead (Drobnik, 2000). And the power of do-ocratic innovation lies in the flexibility and durability of weak ties and the, well fun, of jamming with friends and fellow travelers.

Like the Grateful Dead, the project I will describe toward the end of this section, the Bioprinter Community Project (BCP), received little media attention in its early years; ignored industry trends; avoided singular authorship and middlemen (or investors); exhibited a tinker-er's, not a businessman's, interest in technology. But most of all, like the Grateful Dead, the BCP played the long game by maintaining relationships with and networks of like-minded tinkerers.

Before continuing, dear reader, I need you to understand something important about the do-ocratic Biocurious: it was boring. One advantage of neoliberal reason is the constant invention of crisis and interventions. It lends a ready-made dramatic element to any story about innovation you wish to tell. The do-ocratic Biocurious lacked all drama. There will not be the hubris and flameout of Glowing Plant in what follows. Here is the impossible-to-dramatize story of slow and steady progress made possible by slow and steady democratic deliberation. So I must warn you before we go further, do not expect to be entertained with tales of ambitions run amok. Innovation, the kind that brings real and lasting change into the world, takes time, focus, and a lot of help and coordination from friends and like-minded fellow travelers.

19.2.1 The Setting

Physically the setting was the same. Both Biocuriouses occupied 843 Stewart in Sunnyvale, California. The two Biocuriouses used the same laboratory equipment, shared the same storage racks, and used the same reagents. If a visitor were to walk into the laboratory, they would have a difficult, if not impossible time telling the two Biocuriouses apart. Many policy researchers, innovation specialists from government agencies, visitors, and media audiences visited and only saw the neoliberal Biocurious. When you fly in for a visit of no more than a few days, it is easy to focus on hype and heat and ignore the slow and mundane. To see the do-ocratic Biocurious, you had to look more closely. In fact, you have to start on the inside and look outward.

If the physical setting was the same, socially the settings diverged. The do-cratic Biocurious consisted of part of the membership – a handful of independent scientists working on personal projects, some engineers who enjoyed tinkering with technology of all kinds, volunteers who had membership privileges because they volunteered more than twenty hours per month, and volunteers who were at Biocurious to augment graduate training or to change careers – in short and ironically, those at Biocurious for reasons other than innovation.

19.2.2 *The Solution in Theory*

During the Kickstarter campaign, Biocurious also announced itself as a hackerspace for biology with member input in governance. Rhetorically, this was smart. Biocurious promised something to everyone interested in biotech: entrepreneurs had an incubator and networking, hackers had free reign to hack, anarchists had a new space to engage in do-ocratic organizing, and those curious about biology had a selection of curated class experiences to try. From a governance angle, however, promising something to everyone caused predictable problems.

"Curious about Biology? Find out more at the new biology collaborative lab space where citizen science moves out of the classroom and into the community. Following the successful example of hackerspaces such as Noisebridge, Langton Labs, Hacker Dojo, and co-working spaces such as the Hub, we're pleased to offer the first Bay Area space dedicated to NonInstitutional Biology. Got an idea for a startup? Join the DIY, 'garage biology' movement and found a new breed of biotech. Meet cofounders and friends, and make things you'd never dreamed possible."

In practice Biocurious was managed by the board more as a place to meet cofounders than as a place to make friends, i.e., nothing like the hackerspace Noisebridge. This manifest itself in two techniques deployed by the Biocurious board: a) a surveillance technology deployed, called an "incident report" designed to police the space to ensure that volunteers were adhering to board set policy, rather than improvising, and b) a design language designed to ensure, as one board member artfully put it, "a consistent look and feel" to the interior spaces at Biocurious. As you may have guessed, these twinned techniques were in service to promoting the Biocurious brand. Per the board's actions, the first step for a "a new breed of biotech" was building a recognizable and durable brand name. And building a brand does not include the kind of deliberation and debate found at hackerspaces like Noisebridge.

19.2.3 The Solution in Practice

Though set up along an organizational model pioneered in a corporate environment, the *in situ* organization of the lab followed a path described more by the doctrine of mutual aid than corporate governance. The idea of meeting and "experimenting with friends" was persuasive at Biocurious. Many members told me over the course of my fieldwork that if it wasn't for the people at Biocurious they would have left to set up private labs in kitchens, basements, spare rooms, or actual garages. One member, who was very active in the lab, moved out of state and established a laboratory in his basement on the east coast, yet continued to participate in meetings and classes at Biocurious. He went so far as to create a video conferencing system at Biocurious so he could coordinate his own lab work with groups working at Biocurious. Which is to say that personal relationships among members and volunteer generally followed the impulse to make friends rather than meet cofounders. And making friends encouraged a do-cratic organization based on reciprocity and shared resources.

Beneath the corporate gloss designed to paint Biocurious as an innovation space amenable to cofounders and investors, the work of democratizing biotech was undertaken by volunteers and members in the form of self-organization and self-education. Solutions to common problems were often and openly discussed in informal conversations around the lab, and following a discussion solution were often improvised and implemented without notifying or involving the board.

A notable example of self-organization involved maintaining and repairing the laboratory equipment.

From the start and despite the board's desires, Biocurious maintained a junk pile of uncertain paternity hidden away in a storage room. Additionally, the working equipment in the lab always threatened to stop working and move to the junk pile. Some of the equipment was donated, other was sourced from the numerous laboratory liquidations happening in the Bay Area. Sometimes the equipment was repaired and put in service, other times it served as the basis for a class, and more often it served as a repository of hard-to-find spare parts. Which is to say, a working DIYbio laboratory requires a fix-it person who can repair and maintain equipment. This skill is difficult to acquire, unappreciated, and often unrecognized (Scroggins and Pasquetto, 2020). Incidentally, lack of working equipment was one reason Glowing Plant left Biocurious for a professional laboratory set up inside a shipping container in San Francisco.

More quotidian was the discipline to regularly clean and calibrate the laboratory equipment. Cleaning and calibrating were even more vital at Biocurious than a professional laboratory due to the number of amateur biologists taking classes at the lab, many of whom were encountering scientific instruments for the first time and lacked the dexterity and knowledge required to handle precision instruments. Most of what could charitably be called the scientific program was about making Biocurious's old equipment, along with an organically growing library.

As few of the volunteers and members had laboratory experience, they were often in the same position as the would-be biotech innovators at Biocurious in that they knew little, or nothing, about laboratory norms, techniques, and equipment. While bringing in graduate students and postdocs from nearby Stanford and UC Berkeley went some way to rectify the educational gap, it did not go far enough. This gap became consequential when Biocurious' only autoclave, their lifeline to preparing media for experiments and sterilizing biotrash, broke. A new autoclave was purchased by a helpful member, but it needed to be cleaned and calibrated for a biological laboratory with its agar preparation and plastic petri dishes, rather than the dentist's office with its stainless-steel tools where it was previously used.

Luckily, the self-organized library provided an answer in the form of a donated book titled *At The Bench* which had directions for calibrating and cleaning common laboratory equipment, including autoclaves. Through close consultation of the book, a group of volunteers was able to work up operating protocols for the new autoclave, test those protocols, and teach them to everyone working in the laboratory. Unfortunately, and despite the utility of the library, it became a controversy at Biocurious when its disorderliness clashed with the board of director's design language and branding efforts. The controversy came to a crisis when a board member deemed the library an eyesore and threw it in the trash. The incident throws the difference between the neoliberal and do-ocratic Biocurius into sharp focus.

Trashing the library led to a sharp exchange of emails between board members and volunteers. The crux of the conflict was whether or not old scientific journals and textbooks should be classified as periodicals and removed every three months, as per board-dictated policy, or whether they were essential scientific resources for a group of hobbyists with no formal background in biology. The board argued, with words and the concrete deed of emptying the trash, that old scientific journals and textbooks detract from the appearance of the laboratory and offered no value, as scientific journals are available online. After a volunteer fished his copy of *At the Bench* out if the trash, he offered the counterargument that not everyone at Biocurious had journal access (with my university access, I was the main source of journal access to those working in the lab), the textbooks were both useful and relevant and, more to the point, many of the materials were loaned by members and volunteers, not donated. This last argument exposes the difference between the neoliberal and the do-ocratic approaches to innovation. In the former, ownership of the innovation is centralized in the hands of a few. Innovation, both the intellectual and physical property, belong to the corporate person. In the do-ocratic, innovation, both physically and intellectually, is a collective achievement.

And collective innovation, though slow and, at times, tedious, is durable. For example, in contrast to Glowing Plant, through self-organization, self-education, and a do-ocratic approach the BCP is approaching a decade of uninterrupted work. As of this writing (January 2021) the Bioprinter project, started in January 2012, is still meeting twice a week (virtually through the pandemic) and its long-term goal of printing human organs for medical use is unchanged. Yet, the heat and hype of its ultimate goal has not prevented the BCP from adopting a series of practical intermediate steps to slowly advance their end goal of printing human organs. Often, these intermediate steps are both simple and practical; evolving their original printing chassis, a primitive desktop inkjet printer, to a sophisticated 3D printer and switching from printing bacterial cultures to printing plant callus cells, a rough approximation of the animal or human stem cells required to print an organ. Along the way, they have used plant callus cells to show genetic variations useful for plant breeding programs (callus cells have many uses including developing therapeutics). Supporting these efforts is a public wiki where instructional materials for building a 3D bio-printer and beginning experiments with plant tissue culture can be found, along with video links to join in the weekly Biocurious meetings.

Members have come and gone over the years and the long-term goal is still in the distant future, yet, the collateral effects of this community project have included the unemployed finding work in biotech, Science Faire projects being launched, admissions to graduate schools, and hundreds if not thousands learning the basics of software program-ming and electronics as they attempt to create their own bioprinters at home from the template published by Biocurious.

Perhaps a more telling development for those primarily interested in the products, rather than the process of innovation is the fate of Glowing Plant's technical founder. He left the excitement and hype of Glowing Plant to work for a smaller, slower, but more substantive startup. Endura Bio has been a so-called stealth startup throughout its life, quietly pursuing the work of engineering crops to grow in the saline conditions found where freshwater aquifers become inundated with saltwater. Endura Bio benefits from and contributes to the Bioprinter Community Project is subtle but telling ways – sharing protocols developed in their work with the BCP and benefitting from the community of potential investors and researchers created by the BCP. And here we come to a truism of do-ocratic innovation: the risks of failure are trivial and local, but the benefits of success are global and important.

19.2.4 Analysis

Where Glowing Plant was focused on producing a product – a glowing plant and laboratory/innovation space respectively – the do-ocratic

Biocurious focused on the process of innovation. It might seem commonsensical and obvious that making a product is innovation. However, the history of the biotech industry belies this assumption.

The durable pattern of innovation in the biotech industry is this: small companies or groups of university researchers do the speculative work of research and development while larger companies move those ideas into production. Biotech is notorious for its long development cycles and investment rounds that occur only in the early and last stages of research, leaving long stretches with seemingly little development. The do-ocratic Biocurious and the BCP fit this model. Both are a place where ideas are tested, preliminary research carried out, and proof of concept established; in short, the unfunded and forgotten middle of the biotech business cycle where most of the work is actually done. And it is not only Biocurious where do-ocratic innovation is being carried out. The last few years have seen projects to develop an open-source supply of insulin, Open Insulin, and work toward making fully vegan cheese, the Real Vegan Cheese project. Currently, there are no fewer than three DIYbio led efforts to develop a COVID-19 vaccine.

During my fieldwork at Biocurious, I joined the Bioluminescence Community Project rather than the Bioprinter Project. Why? Because I, like the technical founder of the Glowing Plant and like so many others, was caught up in the glow of possibility around hacking novel organisms. I now pass this lesson onto you: beware the heat and hype and keep your eyes open for the slow, serious, tedious, and boring work of preparing the ground for durable change. That is where your efforts can be most effective.

19.3 Conclusion

The neoliberal view of innovation views innovation narrowly as a driver of economic activity. Accompanying this view is an assumption that what is vital and important about innovation is the essential qualities of the innovation itself. In contrast, a do-ocratic approach emphasizes that the process of innovation and the innovation itself exists as a set of relations. In this view, the innovation itself is less important than the relations it engenders and the economic activity it generates in the short-term than the potential it carries over the long-term.

Indirectly, I have contrasted these two approaches in terms of attention and outcome. The neoliberal model flits from innovation to innovation in an endless, and often fruitless, search for the what was described at Biocurious as "the next big thing." The do-ocratic model patiently pursues a line of work over years or decades. The outcomes of the two approaches are often radically different. The neoliberal approach is predicated on extraction; Glowing Plant extracted resources from Biocurious then, with Biocurious in a weakened state, tried to take over what branding and intellectual property was left. The do-ocratic approach, on the other hand, largely saved Biocurious from this fate. It is an additive and constructive approach to innovation, strengthening relationships and networks and mobilizing the capacity for self-organization and self-education.

I have also described neoliberal innovation in terms of professional wrestling, insisting that it is always a mixture of the real and the staged. More often than we might care to consider, neoliberal innovation is a staged event, a work. Consider the lean startups, where a...well let's politely call it a business model, is tested by offering a prospective product for sale then forming a company around that product on the hopes it can produce the product while there is still interest. Or consider the lean startup's cousin, vaporware. Vaporware is a concept or idea floated as a finished product. Astute readers will notice that this leap requires one more act of faith than the lean startup. The smarts on the inside of Silicon Valley and other startup hubs know the difference between startups with solid business models and working products and act accordingly. But beware, hopeful business student, many businesspeople who think they are smarts are actually marks. Woe be to the balance sheets of those investors who mistake a work for a real event, a shoot. Rarer, but still too common, is innovation as a worked shoot. That is, as a fake event that appears, and is presented as, real. The poster child for this kind of innovation is Theranos, whose fake blood test managed to raise billions in venture capital while fooling its own board of directors, its advisors, and medical regulators in a couple of states into believing the blood test was real.

In contrast, I have compared the do-ocratic approach to innovation to the business practices of the Grateful Dead. As counter-intuitive as this exercise might seem, I am proceeded by a general reevaluation of the Grateful Dead's legacy by recent work in business and entrepreneurship (Gazel and Schwer, 1997; Drobnik, 2000; Barnes,

2011). The main difference I have drawn is that the Grateful Dead and the BCP were relentlessly process-, not product-focused. Again, like the BCP, the Grateful Dead produced no hit records, encouraged recording at their concerts, constantly increased their circle of collaborators, and were open to improvisation (as opposed to pivoting). The thread running through these practices, and separating them from the neoliberal approach to innovation, is the constant focus on community over commodity and process over product.

In closing, I exhort you to judge innovations not only for what they do (their bare functionality) but for the kinds of people, social relations, and futures they make. Self-education and tinkering, and most importantly the ability to experiment with friends in an environment free of commercial pressure; that is, to be critical, experimental, artistic, and to explore new and perhaps controversial ideas remain the condition of possibility necessary for the slow, deliberative work of innovation.

References

Barnes, Barry. 2011. *Everything I Know About Business I Learned from the Grateful Dead: The Ten Most Innovative Lessons from a Long, Strange Trip*. New York: Grand Central Publishing.

Drobnik, Brian C. 2000. "Truckin' in style along the avenue: How the Grateful Dead turned alternative business and legal strategies into a great American success story." *Vanderbilt Journal of Entertainment Law & Practice* 2 (2): 242–266.

Gazel, Ricardo C., and R. Keith Schwer. 1997. "Beyond rock and roll: The economic impact of the Grateful Dead on a local economy." *Journal of Cultural Economics* 21 (1): 41–55. https://doi.org/10.1023/A:1007372721259.

Gershon, Ilana. 2017. *Down and Out in the New Economy: How People Find (or Don't Find) Work Today*. Chicago: University of Chicago Press.

Scroggins, Michael. 2017. "'This is a new thing in the world': Design and discontent in the making of a 'garage lab'." Thesis, Columbia University. Teachers College. https://doi.org/10.7916/D8GM8CZQ.

2019. "Designing, animating, and repairing a suitable do-it-yourself biology lab." In *Educating in Life: Educational Theory and the Emergence of New Normals*, edited by Hervé Varenne, 49–63. New York: Routledge.

Scroggins, Michael J., and Irene V. Pasquetto. 2020. "Labor out of place: On the varieties and valences of (in)visible labor in data-intensive science." *Engaging Science, Technology, and Society* 6 (0): 111–132. https://doi .org/10.17351/ests2020.341.

Souleles, Daniel, and Michael Scroggins. 2017. "The meanings of production(s): Showbiz and deep plays in finance and DIYbiology." *Economy and Society* 46 (1): 82–102. https://doi.org/10.1080/03085147.2017 .1311134.

Zacchiroli, Stefano. 2011. "Debian: 18 years of free software, do-ocracy, and democracy." In *Proceedings of the 2011 Workshop on Open Source and Design of Communication - OSDOC'11*, 87. Lisbon, Portugal: ACM Press. https://doi.org/10.1145/2016716.2016740.

20 | *Who Should Get Investment Capital?*

MELISSA BERESFORD

Often when we think about investors we think about a singular heroic individual. This lends itself well to neoliberal ways of imagining people as individual economic agents. In this way of thinking, an entrepreneur with some amount of capital is able to heroically create a business due largely to their own drive, creativity, and hustle. What this accounting misses though, are the historical contexts and social resources that entrepreneurs draw on to make their businesses work. This is a problem too, if we imagine that individual entrepreneurial action will be adequate to pull people out of poverty or to right historical wrongs. In this chapter, Beresford takes us to South Africa to show the different resources that black and white entrepreneurs have when they start their businesses. Due to the legacy of apartheid, white entrepreneurs have access to more capital and deeper support networks that allow them to navigate the earlier, vulnerable stages of a business's life. By contrast, many black entrepreneurs face a relatively resource poor environment for starting their businesses. Altogether, Beresford shows the limits of individualized thinking when it comes to entrepreneurs, and for using entrepreneurship to lift people out of poverty. The chapter also questions the theoretical assurance of neoliberalism that government should not intervene, but rather wait for the superior knowledge embedded in the market mechanisms to weed out the bad, and adequately increase the chances that good solutions flourish.

20.1 Introduction

Lufefe Nomjana started with $3 and "a big idea." At 28 years old, Lufefe was like many young Black South African men: unemployed and desperately seeking not only employment, but also a path to upward socioeconomic mobility. Living in a shack in Cape Town's Khayelitsha township with his girlfriend, he had few resources to start

427

a business, but he wanted to help address the growing diabetes epidemic in South Africa's Black population by making healthy food more available in his community. His plan was to sell bread he made from spinach. In 2011 he used his neighbor's oven to bake twenty-four loaves of spinach bread and sold them door-to-door. Through word of mouth, he soon earned a reputation for baking some of the best bread in the community. The manager of a big-name local retailer approached him and offered him the use of the store's industrial kitchen in exchange for selling his bread in the store. Increasing his production to over 200 loaves a day, Lufefe had the money to employ a small team to sell and deliver his bread to offices around Cape Town. His business, Espinica Innovations, was born. In 2014 he opened the first Espinica Innovations bakery: a bright-green converted shipping container in the heart of Khayelitsha. He now runs multiple locations of his bakery and employs a sizeable team of people to help run the business. Now known as "The Spinach King," he is widely hailed as one of the most successful young Black entrepreneurs in Khayelitsha.

Lufefe's story has been featured by CNN, the BBC, and dozens of local and regional African news agencies (Clark, 2016; BBC, 2017). *Forbes Africa* named him one of the "30 Most Promising Young Entrepreneurs in Africa" (Forbes Africa, 2014). The narrative of Lufefe's success, told by the myriad of press organizations that have reported his story, emphasizes the modern entrepreneurial "hero narrative" of economic self-reliance and individual determination – pulling one's self up by the bootstraps, mobilizing the few resources at one's disposal, and using the market for not only one's own advantage but also to benefit society as a whole. This narrative – told not just about entrepreneurs from poor and marginalized communities like Lufefe, but also about entrepreneurs from wealthy Western nations like Steve Jobs, Bill Gates, Elon Musk, and Richard Branson – undergirds an increasing veneration of entrepreneurship that is being promoted around the world as policymakers and economic development officials endorse entrepreneurship as a panacea to solve the problems of unemployment, poverty, and inequality.

This intense focus and celebration of entrepreneurship has become a hallmark of neoliberal logic and thinking around the world. As an economic philosophy, neoliberalism highlights the importance of productive labor. By productive labor, I mean labor through which people make, grow, build, or overall *produce* things and resources to sell via markets. Entrepreneurs are often highlighted as ideal "productive" citizens. By identifying and executing new market-based opportunities, entrepreneurs are praised because they *produce* their own income, they create new businesses, they expand the market, and they produce more jobs. According to neoliberal thinking, if people can just produce *more* things to sell, then more jobs, more money, and more wealth for everyone will follow. Following this logic, significant social and economic policies around the world have been predicated on an assumption that *everyone* has the potential to be a productive entrepreneur and to produce something that can be sold on the market (Elyachar, 2002; Hickel, 2019).

But is this really the case? Can *anyone* become a successful entrepreneur by just coming up with an idea to produce something? But more importantly, can entrepreneurship enacted on a mass scale rectify socioeconomic inequality within a given country or economy? Or are there other facets of entrepreneurship and productive labor that neoliberal thinking has overlooked?

This chapter examines these questions through a look at the economic transformation strategy of South Africa in the wake of its post-apartheid democratic transition. Focusing on two different groups of entrepreneurs across the racialized socioeconomic divides of Cape Town, South Africa – White South African entrepreneurs in the city's central business district and Black South African entrepreneurs in the city's largest township of Khayelitsha – this chapter compares the ways that these two groups of entrepreneurs launch and maintain their businesses. My goal is to investigate the practices that best enable the productive labor of entrepreneurship. In doing so, I show that the ability of entrepreneurs to *produce* profits heavily depends upon the resources that are *given* to them by other people. I conclude by discussing the implications that this has for the way that scholars and policymakers understand the economic potential of entrepreneurship to rectify inequality and build wealth for marginalized populations. But first, some background.

20.2 Background: Entrepreneurship as Economic Development Policy in "The New South Africa"

On May 10, 1994, Nelson Mandela was inaugurated as South Africa's first democratically elected president and the nation began its journey to rectify the atrocities of its colonial and apartheid past. But more than two decades later, the deracialization of public policy has failed to close the nation's racial wealth gaps or alter the nation's racialized geography. South Africa currently ranks among the countries in the world with the highest rates of income inequality (Roser and Ortiz-Ospina, 2016). And the government has increasingly turned to market-centered policies like the promotion of entrepreneurship to address these problems (Bond, 2000).

There are many factors that have contributed to the extreme levels of income inequality in South Africa but one of them is the country's legacy of apartheid which ended in 1994 (Seekings and Natrass, 2005). Under apartheid policy, White South Africans controlled the nation's government and economy and benefited from a world-class government-subsidized public sector, including publicly funded elementary and higher education, healthcare, and retirement. Black South Africans and other South Africans of color, however, had no voting rights or political representation. They were for forbidden from living, working, or recreating in any areas of the country deemed "White" without legally codified permission. They could not own land, received very little compensation for their labor, and were excluded from all aspects of the government-subsidized public sector.

The White-owned and controlled South African economy, however, relied Black South African labor. "Townships" were built on the outskirts of towns and cities to serve as government-delineated dormitories for Black South African migrant workers. Black South African men and women, both voluntarily and by coercion, migrated from their rural home communities to these townships in order to work as cooks, gardeners, janitors, maids, childcare workers, and other menial labor positions for very low pay. Despite the idea – frequently promulgated by the apartheid government – that Black South Africans merely supplemented their rural "traditional" livelihoods with money they earned from these jobs, South African families heavily depended on the wages they earned through oscillating labor migration to secure agricultural inputs, purchase daily subsistence needs, and support their families (Murray, 1980).

Although the end of apartheid in 1994 and the election of South Africa's first democratic government meant that Black South Africans were finally considered full citizens with legal rights to vote and partake in all aspects of South Africa's public sector, Black South Africans today – over two decades later – continue to disproportionally suffer extreme rates of unemployment and poverty (Seekings and Natrass, 2005; Makhulu, 2016). The majority of Black South Africans continue to live in peri-urban or rural areas with limited access to basic public services like plumbing or sanitation (Makhulu, 2015). While the country's official national unemployment rate is 27 percent, scholars estimate that the unemployment rate among poor Black South Africans is upward of 60–70 percent (Seekings and Natrass, 2005; Makhulu, 2016).

Although South Africa's current ruling party was previously committed to socialist policies during the struggle against apartheid (calling for the redistribution of wealth and resources to provide basic necessities to the nation's poor), since the democratic transition, they have yielded to the structural adjustment requirements of Western gatekeepers and favored a neoliberal, market-based approach to solving these problems. The South African government has thus relied on deregulating markets and attracting investors in the "New South Africa," claiming that such business-friendly measures will produce jobs and therefore improve living conditions for millions of poor South Africans (Bond, 2000; Marais, 2011).

Part of the South African government's strategy for bolstering the economy and reducing the unemployment rate has been to heavily embrace entrepreneurship and entrepreneurial training. For example, in 2015, South Africa's Minister of Small Business Development, Lindiwe Zulu stated that, "We must strive to be a nation of entrepreneurs and not a nation of job seekers" (Dirk, 2015). Mmusi Maimane, the former head of South Africa's Democratic Alliance party asserted later that year, "If we can have an efficient small business culture in South Africa and a growing economy, we can ensure that we address our challenges of poverty, inequality, and ultimately unemployment...we need to stop speaking about 5 million jobs; we need to speak about 1 million entrepreneurs" (Democratic Alliance, 2015).

But can *anyone* become an entrepreneur? Does entrepreneurship provide a pathway for historically marginalized populations to build wealth and achieve upward social mobility?

20.2.1 The Cases

To investigate these questions, I conducted in-depth ethnographic research in two communities within Cape Town: the high-income area of downtown Cape Town, and the lower-income area of Cape Town's largest township, Khayelitsha. My participant observation and semi-structured ethnographic interviews stretched over thirteen months between 2015 and 2016, involving sixty entrepreneurs, community leaders, NGO officials, and entrepreneurship teachers/trainers. For this research, I worked daily at entrepreneurial "hubs" (coworking spaces) and attended entrepreneurial networking events, pitching competitions, workshops, and training events.

The two entrepreneurial hubs in the higher-income downtown site, Co-share and IdeaLab, were established in in 2014 and 2000. White South Africans make up 90 percent of the entrepreneurs at each of them. The entrepreneurial hub in the lower-income township site, The Station, was established in 2015.[1] All members of the township hub are Black South Africans.[2] While entrepreneurs in the downtown-based hubs pay membership fees, the township hub does not charge its members.

Before I introduce the cases, I want to begin with the stories of two different entrepreneurs: Jack, a 34-year-old White entrepreneur based in downtown Cape Town, and Mbulelo, a 34-year-old Black entrepreneur based in Khayelitsha.

20.2.2 Jack's Story

Jack was born in the early 1980s to an upper middle-class family in Cape Town. Jack's mother is South African and works in public relations. His father is the son of a tobacco farmer from Zimbabwe, and is now an entrepreneur. Jack's father began his career fresh out of university in the 1970s as a chartered accountant working for a company in Hong Kong. However, he soon left his position to start a business manufacturing and importing plastics from China into the United Kingdom. Jack's father used his profits from that venture for other entrepreneurial pursuits back in South Africa during the 1970s and 1980s. Jack's parents had upper middle-class family backgrounds and university educations funded by their own parents. They raised him with the expectation that he would also go to university and

---

[1] To protect identity, names of the entrepreneurial hubs and individual entrepreneurs are pseudonyms.

[2] At the time of my research, The Station was the only entrepreneurial hub in Cape Town's township communities.

launch his own career. They paid for his private boarding-school fees and for his university degree in the United Kingdom. Jack briefly worked in London after finishing university, in early 2004, before returning to Cape Town to work for a major South African export brand.

In 2007, Jack and a friend (his current business partner) recognized what they perceived to be a gap in the South African market for honey production. They decided to start a business manufacturing honey for both domestic and international sales. However, Jack had no collateral, so he did not qualify for a business loan or a personal line of credit. Jack therefore approached his father for the funding required to start his honey business and his father agreed, being an entrepreneur himself. This initial round of financing was needed to lease warehouse space and purchase 400 bee hives, bottling equipment, a delivery truck, and cover other miscellaneous startup costs. Six years later, Jack's company had several major domestic and international contracts, and he employed over a dozen people. Jack still considers his business to be in the early stages of growth and therefore is cautious about how much salary he pays himself. He takes home about R500,000/year (approx. $38,000) from his business.[3] Jack is not married and has no children at this point in his life, and he has no obligation to support his parents or siblings. His salary only supports himself, so he reinvests his profits back into the business. He focuses on expanding to more international markets and increasing its production capacity.

20.2.3 Mbulelo's Story

Mbulelo grew up in the small city of De Aar in the Northern Cape province. Born in the early 1980s under the apartheid regime, Mbulelo, his parents, and his two sisters lived in a township on the outskirts of De Aar. Mbulelo's father moved to DeAar in the 1970s to find wage work that could support his family's subsistence farm in the Eastern Cape province. As his parents' only son, Mbulelo was raised with the expectation that one day he would also financially support his parents in their retirement. His father worked at a bakery in town and his mother was a domestic worker; they used their wages to pay for his local government (public) school fees. As a strong student, he earned a

---

[3] At the time of my research, the exchange rate was, on average, 1 USD to 13 ZAR.

bursary (scholarship) for a degree in accounting at the Cape Peninsula University of Technology in Cape Town. Mbulelo's parents encouraged him to earn a university degree that would position him for a middle-class job that could better support their whole family.

In the early 2000s, Mbulelo started university in Cape Town, living with extended family in an informal shack in the Gugulethu township. He quickly became bored with accounting and dropped out of that program. However, he had always had a keen interest in computers and regularly fixed computers and mobile phones for his friends and family. In 2010, he began to think about turning this hobby into a business, wanting to start his own IT company. Seeing that many new businesses in Cape Town's townships needed IT and web design services, Mbulelo envisioned a business that provided IT services within township communities in multiple locations throughout South Africa. He went back to university to earn an IT certificate, taking night courses part-time while working at a furniture warehouse, where he earned enough to cover his living expenses and send money home to support his parents. After completing his certificate in 2012, Mbulelo quit his job and formally registered his business.

While Mbulelo's initial startup costs were low, he realized that he needed money to expand his business so it could provide him with a consistent income. For example, since he was living in an informal shack home with no hardwired internet, Mbulelo regularly ran out of cell phone data allowance. He would have to run to the nearby internet café in order to complete work for his clients. He needed office space with good internet access, where he could meet with clients and be seen as a legitimate business. But he could not afford to rent space and did not qualify for a loan.

In 2013, Mbulelo met a client who worked out of a newly established entrepreneurship coworking space in Khayelitsha. He was intrigued by the space, but he could not afford the monthly membership fee they charged. So he arranged a meeting with the site manager and offered his IT services in return for office space on the premises. The manager agreed and Mbulelo worked out of this entrepreneurial hub until it closed in 2015. At that point he moved his business to The Station, which had just opened and was not charging for membership. While Mbulelo's business has been very successful, he still does not have enough money to expand further. He is able to pay himself approximately R60,000 a year (approx. $5000). While he remains unmarried and without children to support, he sends money each month to his parents to supplement their state-funded pension.

The stories of Jack and Mbulelo exemplify the major differences in the ways that entrepreneurs across South Africa's racialized class launch and maintain their businesses. While the goal of entrepreneurship is to produce something – a product, or a service – to sell for profit, Jack's and Mbulelo's stories illustrate that in order to start a productive business, entrepreneurs need resources to start that enable them to produce. To start their businesses, Jack and Mbulelo both relied heavily on recourse given directly to them through social networks. But the social networks that they are able to turn to, and the resources within those social networks differ quite drastically depending upon an entrepreneur's position within South African society. Wealthier White entrepreneurs in downtown Cape Town (like Jack) frequently acquire the resources they need to start a business by turning to *intergenerational wealth* – financial or material resources acquired from parents or grandparents. Black entrepreneurs in Khayelitsha and other townships, however, not only have fewer intergenerational resources to draw on, but are also responsible for providing financial support to their own kin networks. For these reasons, Black entrepreneurs in Khayelitsha typically acquire the resources they need to start a business through *lateral modes of social support* – resources acquired from friends, colleagues, neighbors, siblings, community organizations, and so on. The differences have massive implications for who is able to more easily build a successful business.

Case 20.1 Funding and Support Among White South African Entrepreneurs via Intergenerational Wealth

In the higher-income downtown entrepreneurial hubs, White South African entrepreneurs frequently spoke about keeping startup costs "lean" and "bootstrapping" expenses as much as possible. This entrepreneurial jargon referred to the process of keeping overhead expenses low and acquiring capital without formally borrowing from banks or venture capitalists (who charge interest or take equity). These colloquialisms were a way of discussing the importance of resources given directly to them for their businesses. In downtown Cape Town, the vast majority of entrepreneurs I spent time with turned to their parents (and sometimes grandparents) for those resources. They "bootstrapped" their businesses by tapping into the pools of intergenerational wealth at their disposal.

Not all White entrepreneurs within the downtown Cape Town hubs came from wealthy backgrounds, but almost all were able to rely on some significant form of intergenerational resources to start their businesses or to keep them going through the tenuous early years. For example, Jackie, a 31-year-old White female entrepreneur based in town, grew-up in a middle-class family in Cape Town. After attending university and working for a few years, she decided to start a business selling her homemade almond milk. Starting a business like this required many upfront costs – equipment, storage space, and transportation. She also needed money to cover her living costs until her business earned enough profit. Jackie approached her family with some success. Her mother gave Jackie an old car for transport, and Jackie's father gave her R9000 to purchase equipment. Jackie's fiancé gave her R40,000 to rent space for manufacturing. As Jackie was living with her fiancé, he also covered her living expenses. Her almond milk is now sold in several major grocery store chains around Cape Town, and she intends to expand sales into other cities in the next few years.

Intergenerational resources, however, are not always financial. Celestine, a 30-year old White female entrepreneur based in town, is working with her husband to develop a web app that connects and facilitates the hiring of service workers in South Africa. As a web-based business, their startup costs have been relatively low; Celestine's husband is a software engineer, and therefore they have very few software development costs (usually the largest expense for web-based businesses). They sold their house and car (both purchased while they were working in corporate salaried jobs) to invest that capital in their business. Knowing that monthly rent would quickly drain their savings, they moved in with Celestine's grandmother-in-law, where they pay no rent or utilities. Her husband's grandmother also covers many of their everyday costs, such as food and household items, allowing them to devote most of their financial resources to their business.

White entrepreneurs turned to intergenerational resources not only for initiating a business, but also for the ongoing maintenance of their businesses. For example, Greg, a 31-year-old White male entrepreneur based in town, started his data visualization business with his own savings from working a corporate job. His business had been going for two years and was doing well, but he occasionally ran into problems with cash flow – generally when a client took too long to pay him. One month he had two such contracts overdue, while he still had expenses to pay, including his membership fees at IdeaLab and costs for a new project that required upfront spending. This situation is common for Greg, and when it occurs, he approaches his father for "bridge financing." His father loans him the money that he needs to settle his accounts, and Greg then pays his father back several weeks later when his payments come through (interest free). Greg considers himself fortunate to be able to rely on his own money for most of his needs, but he depended heavily on these small, quick, informal loans from his father, who is happy to support Greg's business. This was a common practice among entrepreneurs in town. Many reported turning to family to borrow money during times of slow business, especially during the Christmas holidays, when it becomes difficult to line up new business.

Among entrepreneurs in town, support from family also served as a safety net in the wake of costly business mistakes. David, a 38-year-old White entrepreneur in town, started a software development company in 2013, generating much excitement for his unique business model in the Cape Town tech community. He pitched his business idea to several venture capitalists, seeking funding to pay for software developers and equipment. A venture capital firm offered funding, but, as with most such investments, it was given in exchange for equity in his company. As David's business grew, he regretted not having full financial control of his company. He began using his profits to buy back equity, but regaining majority control of the company proved to be too costly. He, therefore, approached his parents and asked them if they could purchase shares in his company. Now, David has regained majority control of his business, with his parents informally agreeing to be silent partners. Eventually, he says, their shares in his business will be part of his inheritance from them. Looking back, he wishes that he had found other ways to acquire startup funding. Like David, many other entrepreneurs in the two downtown-based hubs turned to their parents in the wake of costly business mistakes. Some borrowed money directly from them, while others had parents put up collateral or cosign on business loans.

Among Black entrepreneurs in Khayelitsha, however, intergenerational resources were not as readily available. This is not to say that entrepreneurs in Khayelitsha did not rely on parents and grandparents; for example, they often paid (or contributed to) educational expenses. Families of Khayelitsha-based entrepreneurs often gave what they could, which generally manifested in the form of housing assistance. For example, Kabelo, a 28-year-old Black entrepreneur in Khayelitsha, did not receive any financial assistance from his parents, but his father gifted Kabelo his RDP (government issued) house when Kabelo turned 18. This enabled Kabelo and his housemate to live rent free while his father moved back to his home village in the Eastern Cape. Some entrepreneurs like Mbulelo lived in informal shack homes built in the yards of extended family members. Others continued to live in multigenerational family homes to keep living expenses to a minimum. Only one entrepreneur I spoke to in

Khayelitsha was able to turn to his parents for financial assistance. John, a 30-year-old Black entrepreneur, started a music production business. His parents were financially secure and had savings set aside, so they gave John R4000 to purchase sound equipment. John recognized this as an uncommon privilege among entrepreneurs in township communities.

While John and Kabelo both spoke readily about the financial and material support their parents provided, White entrepreneurs in town often failed to recall the intergenerational resources they had relied upon. In discussing the labor of "bootstrapping," White entrepreneurs in town talked about their need to acquire funds via pitching competitions, finding informal "angel investors" (investors that gave smaller amounts of money at smaller costs to the business), or relying on personal savings from previous jobs. It was only upon deeper probing (which often required me to specifically ask whether they received resources from family), that White entrepreneurs in town reflected and recalled just how often they turned to their families for help. In my estimation, White downtown-based entrepreneurs did not immediately recall these intergenerational forms of support because they were so ubiquitous. All entrepreneurs I met in the downtown hubs assumed that families gave different forms of assistance that enabled entrepreneurs to "bootstrap." Upon my probing and their recall of the specific resources that their families gave them, however, many entrepreneurs recognized their situation as privileged and acknowledged that entrepreneurs in poor communities rarely had the same avenues for support. As Jack reflected upon telling me about the financial support he received from his father, "I come from a privileged background so, especially in the context of South Africa, I recognize the advantages I have."

Case 20.2 Funding and Support Among Black South African Entrepreneurs Via Lateral Modes of Social Support

Among Black entrepreneurs in the lower-income township site, conversations about how to "bootstrap" and obtain resources for their businesses were also common. But rather than emphasizing the need to avoid the costs of banks and venture capital arrangements, Khayelitsha entrepreneurs more often stressed the importance of *lateral modes of social support* within the community. While the intergenerational resources available to township entrepreneurs were fewer and farther between, every township-based entrepreneur I encountered relied heavily on diverse social ties to acquire what they needed.

Among the social connections of township entrepreneurs, one of the most important was someone – a friend, a mentor, a neighbor – who could help navigate access to government or community-based resources. Corporate Social Investment (CSI) programs and government agencies, like the Small Enterprise Development Agency (SEDA), provide material resources for Black entrepreneurs as a part of the government's broader Black Economic Empowerment agenda, which requires companies over a certain size to make investments and contributions to economic development in South Africa's Black communities. But accessing these resources is arduous. Government agencies that provide such services are located in town (an expensive and time-consuming journey for many Khayelitsha residents), generally require extensive application processes, and take several months from time of request to delivery of requested resources. Given the bureaucratic structures around these programs, many entrepreneurs in Khayelitsha remain unaware of them. Those entrepreneurs who do acquire resources through these programs generally hear about them through their social networks. For example, when Nselo (a 29-year-old entrepreneur who runs a recycling business) came up with his business idea, a friend told him that he could request funding for resources from SEDA and gave him insight on how to navigate the process. After a six-month application process, SEDA provided Nselo with a laptop computer that enabled him to develop a business proposal and pitch in competitions. Through these competitions, he received small amounts of seed funding (approx. R5000) from companies like Red Bull and South African Breweries, who host events with CSI funds to support Black entrepreneurship.

Of course, the Khayelitsha entrepreneurial hub itself is an important resource. The hub does not charge membership fees for office space, printing, or wireless internet. Like those accessing resources from SEDA, every entrepreneur at the Khayelitsha hub had heard about the opportunity to obtain free membership via word of mouth from friends, neighbors, clients, and colleagues. Thus, while these distributive resources come from the government and/or community organizations, access to them is intricately bound up with, and often dependent upon, the social ties within township communities.

Although the small funds and assets available via government and community organizations are vital, they are often insufficient to cover all startup costs. Township entrepreneurs, therefore, often form partnerships with other individuals who maintained wage labor or salaried positions. For example, Christine, a 32-year-old entrepreneur at The Station who started a SharePoint consulting firm, has two other business partners. Christine left her position working in human resources for a company in Cape Town in order to focus her efforts full time on their business, but her two partners have each maintained their jobs working for IT companies.

These partners use portions of their salaries to cover the initial costs of their business. They plan to leave their jobs when the company can provide salaries for all three partners.

While strategic partnerships provided long-term and predictable resources, the impromptu trading of resources and services among themselves enabled township entrepreneurs to quickly acquire many things they needed without tapping into their cash reserves. These trades were viewed as the lifeblood of the township entrepreneurial hub. Tandiwe, a 28-year old entrepreneur who runs a computer education business, explained, "You need to have connections amongst yourselves as entrepreneurs…if there's a certain service that you need, instead of going to town and being charged expensively you can just ask someone who's around the community." Lwazi, for example, who runs a financial consulting business, was looking for ways to do marketing and attract new clients. Rather than paying for a stall at the local market, he approached Matt, another entrepreneur at The Station who already had a stall at the Khayelitsha mall. He asked Matt if he could put out some of his flyers at his stall and hang around the stall for a few days to talk to people about his business. In exchange, Lwazi offered to look over Matt's yearly finances and give him advice for next year's financial planning. Other exchanges included trading web design services for tax preparation services, fixing a computer for borrowing a digital camera, editing a business proposal for borrowing a car and graphic design work for loaning sound equipment. As Tandiwe explained, "we'd rather focus more on partnerships than to wait for funding…that's how we are able to actually survive as Black people."

While these strategies allowed entrepreneurs to access the resources they knew they needed, township entrepreneurs often lamented the more difficult problems posed by unforeseen expenses, costly mistakes, nonpaying clients, or slow business. During these times, township entrepreneurs turned to neighbors, friends, siblings, and community members for favors – an extremely common practice within South African township communities (Habib and Maharaj, 2008). As Christine told me one afternoon, "You know, I grew up with far less than what I have now, so I'm not gonna have sleepless nights because I'm running out or I can't afford to pay that. It's just money at the end of the day. As long as you can still live another day to come up with a different plan, if Plan A didn't work, Plan B can work in your favor." While Christine had drawn a salary from her business for the past three months, her contracts had slowed down. She wasn't sure if she could draw a salary for herself in the upcoming months. She continued, "the township gives you certain ways of handling situations that would freak a lot of people out when it comes to finances. I often have to ask for favors." These favors – a meal here, a bus fare there – are part of the lived reality of township life in South Africa, and the only way that township entrepreneurs could keep going at certain times. As Lwazi explained when recounting the forms of support he depends on for his business, "I depended on people assisting me. If I go to your house and you're cooking, lucky for me you will dish out for me; then I can go and sleep."

Lateral modes of social support were by no means unique to the township entrepreneurial community. In town, White entrepreneurs also turned to their social networks for resources, but often these activities were explained as a way to "save cash" rather than an absolute necessity. For example, Zach, a 38-year-old White entrepreneur in town who started a consulting firm that assists startup businesses, often receives legal advice from a friend of his father. Zach explained that calling him up to look over a contract or ask a legal question enables him to save money by not paying for such services. Similarly, Ashely, a 29-year-old White entrepreneur in town relies on her brother – a chartered accountant – to file her business taxes, look over her books, and provide financial advice. As these cases demonstrate, the favors that White, town-based entrepreneurs relied upon were generally gifts, given from close social relations with no expected return.

None of the town-based entrepreneurs I interviewed reported trading resources or services among each other, though several did express that they wished such exchanges would occur. "I wish people were more collaborative here, but I feel that everyone is kind of working on their own thing and has their own hours," one town entrepreneur told me over coffee. Among township entrepreneurs, however, maintaining the social relations that are integral to lateral modes of social support was a key concern. While they did not view this form of social labor as arduous, they nonetheless continually spoke about the maintenance of social relations within the entrepreneurial hub as a key business strategy. As Tandiwe said, "We see each other every day. I don't spend a lot of time in the office, but whenever I do, I make sure I check in with whoever is here, you know...That's how we maintain those partnerships... you have to prove yourself to be someone who is reliable, otherwise, you will lose a lot of opportunities."

20.3 Lessons Learned: The Role of Distribution

The major strategic differences in how White and Black entrepreneurs start their businesses in Cape town illustrate two major points about the potential of entrepreneurship to lift people out of poverty or rectify socioeconomic inequality.

First, for entrepreneurs to produce things to sell, they need resources that enable them to produce. Economic theorists have long argued that productive labor (i.e., producing goods or services) inevitably relies upon resources that people need in order to produce in the first place (Gudeman, 1978; Robinson, 1983; Gibson-Graham, 2008; Fraser, 2014; Ferguson, 2015; Marable, 2015). At the most basic level, these resources include water, food, and shelter. But in industrialized economic contexts, these "resources" also include the ability to acquire education and training and the necessary capital to establish a business and support that business through the early years during which very few businesses make any profits. For all entrepreneurs in this research, the resources provided by kin and community were key to their business's success. Those resources enable entrepreneurs to cover startup costs, buffer their businesses in times of lagging cashflow, and serve as safety nets to rectify unexpected and costly business mistakes – all common factors in the early stages of entrepreneurship. Although neoliberal thinking purports that production is the primary activity through which people can and should secure resources, the actions of these entrepreneurs remind us that people depend upon care work, gifts, trades, and other acts of *direct distribution* to get what they need. In other words, while neoliberal thinking idolizes production as the primary activity that drives an economy, we can see how acts of distribution form the base of productive activities.

Second, these cases illustrate that the distributive resources that South African entrepreneurs rely upon to start their businesses are not equitable due to the exploitation of Black labor enacted through colonial and apartheid-era policies. While White South African families benefited from publicly funded state resources throughout the twentieth century – including education, healthcare, and pension systems – to build private wealth within their families, Black families received virtually no state support and received only minimal wages to work in the service of an economy designed to benefit and enrich White South Africans exclusively. Although the South African government has now instituted programs that provide small amounts of resources to Black entrepreneurs (both directly from the state and via private sector incentives), these cases show how and why these resources are rarely sufficient to make up the gaps in the resources that are more often available to White South Africans through family resources.

Today, while many White entrepreneurs are able to draw on pools of intergenerational wealth, most Black entrepreneurs simply do not have such resources within their families and thus rely on smaller pools of resources acquired from lateral modes of social support. But beyond this, the resources that Black entrepreneurs derive laterally from their networks also put them in a double bind: they have fewer resources to draw upon in the first place, *and* they have more obligations to give resources back to people within their networks (like retired parents or siblings who depend upon them). White entrepreneurs in town, on the other hand, typically draw from their networks in times of need and are rarely obligated to give back at once. The intergenerational wealth at the disposal of higher-resourced White entrepreneurs in town thus serves as both a safety net and a springboard, enabling them to reinvest profits back into growing and expanding their businesses (and profits).

These cases demonstrate why it is very unlikely that entrepreneurship alone will address inequality and enable socioeconomic mobility. Contrary to neoliberal thinking, entrepreneurs do not rise and fall solely by virtue of their individual action and productive labor. Rather, hidden forms of assistance provided by family, social networks, and state institutions – all acts of distribution – are necessary for entrepreneurial success. But the uneven development and distribution of these hidden forms of assistance also establish structural advantages for White populations who have historically benefited from capitalism, while exacerbating structural disadvantages for peoples of color for who capitalism has been designed to exploit (Robinson, 1983; Trouillot, 1995; Fanon, 2007; Marable, 2015). Entrepreneurship under these conditions reproduces racialized class inequalities that have been centuries in the making. Thus, if we truly want a world in which anyone can become a successful entrepreneur, we must remember that resource flows are not only the product of entrepreneurship, but also as a vital precondition for it.

Acknowledgments

This chapter is based on my article, "Rethinking entrepreneurship through distribution: distributive relations and the reproduction of racialized inequality among South African entrepreneurs" previously published in the *Journal of the Royal Anthropological Institute* 27(1),

108–127. This research was supported by the National Science Foundation (award No. 1459004), the Social Science Research Council with funds from the Andrew W. Mellon Foundation, and both the School of Human Evolution and Social Change and the Graduate College at Arizona State University. I would like to thank the South African entrepreneurs who participated in my research, generously giving me their time, attention, and friendship.

References

BBC. 2017. "It's miraculous, says South Africa's spinach king." *BBC*, March 26, 2017. www.bbc.com/news/av/business-39378919/it-s-miraculous-says-south-africa-s-spinach-king

Bond, P. 2000. *Elite Transition: From Apartheid to Neoliberalism in South Africa*. London: Pluto Press.

Clark, C. 2016. "Cape flats: New hope in 'apartheid's dumping ground.'" *CNN*, January 25, 2016. www.cnn.com/travel/article/cape-town-town ships/index.html

Democratic Alliance. 2015. "The state can't create millions of jobs, but entrepreneurs can: Bokamoso by Mmusi Maimane." Uploaded by Democratic Alliance, June 22, 2015. www.youtube.com/watch?v= Xp8E0iOWf5g

Dirk, N. 2015. "Stop looking for jobs: start your own business." *IOL News*, March 3, 2015. www.iol.co.za/capetimes/news/stop-looking-for-jobs-start-your-own-business-1827032

Elyachar, J. 2002. "Empowerment money: The World Bank, non-governmental organizations, and the value of culture in Egypt." *Public culture* 14 (3): 493–513.

Fanon, F. 2007. *The Wretched of the Earth*. New York: Grove/Atlantic, Inc.

Ferguson, J. 2015. *Give a Man a Fish: Reflections on the New Politics of Distribution*. Durham: Duke University Press.

Fraser, N. 2014. "Behind Marx's hidden abode: For an expanded conception of capitalism." *New Left Review* 86: 55–72.

Gibson-Graham, J. K. 2008. "Diverse economies: performative practices for other worlds'." *Progress in Human Geography* 32 (5): 613–632.

Gudeman, S. 2012. "Community and economy: Economy's base." In *A Handbook of Economic Anthropology*, edited by J. Carrier, 95–110. Cheltenham: Edward Elgar Publishing.

Hickel, J. 2019. "The contradiction of the sustainable development goals: Growth versus ecology on a finite planet." *Sustainable Development* 27 (5): 873–884.

Makhulu, A. M. 2015. *Making Freedom: Apartheid, Squatter Politics, and the Struggle for Home*. Durham: Duke University Press.

 2016. "A brief history of the social wage: Welfare before and after racial fordism." *South Atlantic Quarterly* 115 (1): 113–124.

Marable, M. 2015. *How Capitalism Underdeveloped Black America: Problems in Race, Political Economy, and Society*. Chicago: Haymarket Books.

Marais, H. 2011. *South Africa Pushed to the Limit: The Political Economy of Change*. London: Zed Books Ltd.

Murray, C. 1980. "Migrant labour and changing family structure in the rural periphery of Southern Africa." *Journal of Southern African Studies* 6 (2): 139–156.

Robinson, C. J. (1983) 2000. *Black Marxism: The Making of the Black Radical Tradition*. Chapel Hill: University of North Carolina Press.

Roser, Max, and Esteban Ortiz-Ospina. 2016. "Income inequality". Published online at OurWorldInData.org.'https://ourworldindata.org/income-inequality

Seekings, J., and N. Nattrass. 2005. *Class, Race, and Inequality in South Africa*. London: Yale University Press.

Trouillot, M. R. 1995. *Silencing the Past: Power and the Production of History*. Boston: Beacon Press.

21 | *Who Should Own a Business?*

DAVID WOOD AND LENORE PALLADINO

It's easy to assume that all businesses (of any scale at least) are corporations, and that all corporations are run the same. They have executive leadership, boards of directors, and their overriding aim is to make profit for their investors. This is how most large corporations are organized and operate; and you could be forgiven for assuming that this is just the way things work. That said, close readers of this volume have likely intuited that this way of running a business is in fact historically specific, and owes a lot to neoliberal ideas about how a business and how society should work (hierarchically, with a minimum of democracy, and all organized to generate profits and reward shareholder owners). Here, Wood and Palladino take these assumptions apart by illustrating all the different way that other people (even workers!) can in fact own and control companies. One simple thing this chapter shows is that in designing a business or organizing a company, it doesn't need to be top-down and oriented toward maximizing shareholder value; but can be oriented toward other values, and these values can be reflected in its organization.

21.1 Introduction

Corporations are fictive persons, able to produce, buy and sell things, sue and be sued in court, pay or avoid taxes, speak out in the public square. All this, and they can live forever too. Corporations are owned and governed by people in real life, who try to use the corporate form to produce stuff, make profits, reward themselves and their investors, and, perhaps most importantly, indemnify themselves from the consequences of actions that the fictive person takes. Corporations are powerful and lucrative fictions. It's important to ask who owns corporations and who controls them, because ownership and control significantly determines which people have wealth and power in society.

For the last fifty years or so, the neoliberal answer has been that corporations exist to serve their shareholders, and management should control them accordingly, for both ethical and instrumental reasons. In this vision, shareholders are the rightful claimants to corporate profits because they bear the risks and responsibilities of ownership. And pressure to meet shareholder return expectations will make corporations more efficient, so this theory goes, making the world a better place by driving money to its most profitable use. Linking executive compensation to investor returns aligns incentives to tie ownership and control together, and ensures that corporations are vehicles for growth rather than sinecures for unaccountable management.

It hasn't really turned out as planned, or at least argued. Which isn't much of a surprise: why should maximizing profits for shareholders make the world a better place – especially when, as in the United States, the top 10 percent of wealthiest households owns 80 percent of the shares? Shareholder value maximization has led to accounting fraud and other corporate malfeasance, unproductive activities such as share buybacks that inhibit economic flourishing, and growing inequality resulting from extractive practices that channel money away from workers and communities up toward those at the very top who own and control – even in companies where funding for innovation is coming from the government. Even everyday shareholders haven't done all that well – it's the executives with stock options and the asset managers who handle lots of other people's money who've really made out.

What might alternatives to this rather unimpressive neoliberal model look like? On the one hand, we can change who owns corporations. Rather than abstracted investors at several removes (most of whom have no idea that they own the equity of a specific company), corporations can be owned by their own workers, or by the public, and managed to optimize the good they do for workers and the public rather than the amount they can channel to investors. We can also look at models that rethink control, with boards integrating workers and communities into corporate governance to ensure that the interests of more than the already wealthy are represented, and governing documents that ensure that the corporation attends to this broad set of interests for as long as it exists. The result would be a better alignment of corporate activity with the public good, more productive innovation, a more equal distribution of the resources that corporations generate, and fewer legal and illegal efforts to extract wealth by shunting costs onto workers, communities, and the environment.

21.2 Shareholder Value Maximization: The Neoliberal Unification of Ownership and Control

To understand the neoliberal model of shareholder primacy, we have to understand a bit about what came before.

Early corporations – in the early modern era, before the industrial revolution – were created in order to diversify risk through collective ownership: the conventional example is diversifying the risk of a single oversea voyage – those ships sank, or fell victims to pirates, etc. – so that one owner wasn't on the hook if things went bad. These corporations formed under government charters: the conventional example here is the East India Company, a single entity owned jointly by many (well-heeled) individuals who received a state-sanctioned monopoly on trade with certain parts of the British Empire, and who shared the spoils of that horrifically exploitative monopoly among themselves as company stockholders.

Joint ownership diversified risk and generated profit for the stockholders. At the same time, diversified ownership gave rise to an independent institution that existed apart from its particular owners. Corporations, drawing on earlier definitions of the body politic, were fictive persons. They had their own legal rights and obligations and could speak with a single voice. The tension between collective ownership and unified management implied in this structure has become central to modern analyses of ownership and control.

The publicly traded (that is, owned by shareholders trading on public markets) corporation of today grew out of this legacy. Modern corporations – the big ones, especially those in countries operating in an Anglo-Saxon legal tradition – tend to have their stock owned by many many people these days. Some own individual shares, but most participate in retirement funds or other pools of money that own shares for their benefit. Most shareholders own these stocks at a complete remove from the actual functioning of the business – stock ownership grants the right to residual profits after obligations are paid off, not the right to order people around. Corporate management, the C suite, makes the day-to-day decisions. The shareholders have their voice delegated to boards of directors who in theory represent their interests, though in practice are often closely aligned with existing management.

The business economists Adolf Berle and Gardiner Means, in their book *The Modern Corporation and Private Property* from 1932, highlighted the division of ownership and control as an, if not the, essential element of the modern corporation: shareholders could own the corporation but there were too many, too far from business operations, to control it. (Berle and Means, 1932). In the postwar United States, theories of corporations were developed, and business school education curricula devoted to, the modern techniques of management that the C Suite needed to run these large, complex institutions. Not coincidentally, many of these theories – as seen in, say, John Kenneth Galbraith's 1967 book *The New Industrial State* – focused on the broader role that corporations play in society, and the obligations they have toward workers and communities as well as shareholders (Galbraith, 2007). The "institutionalist" tradition, as these business theories came to be called, treated corporations as agents in the world. General Motors, for instance: a behemoth auto manufacturer that required immense bureaucratic control, was able to shape consumer desires, whose agreements with organized labor set wage standards across industries, a corporation understood to be so embedded in the US political economy that a phrase like "what's good for GM is good for America" resonated.

What for the institutionalists was the nature of the modern corporation, was for neoliberal critics an optimization problem to solve. Neoliberal economists and business theorists argued that corporate managers, if free from significant shareholder influence, could manage corporations for their own benefit, or for the benefit of others (like the workforce), at the expense of the corporation's real owners. With full control, managers could divert corporate activities to their own reward – think big expense accounts, corporate jets jetting off to fancy golf tournaments – rather than that of their notional owners. Or they might turn corporate activity toward political or social goals rather than the company's core purpose. The prototype of the managerial corporation – a large conglomerate whose management negotiated competing obligations with workers (sometimes represented by the neoliberal's nemesis, organized labor), communities, shareholders, and the state – loomed in the neoliberal imagination as an unwieldy, bloated bureaucracy untethered from efficiency and focus.

How to solve this problem? For the neoliberals, it was to stitch rightful ownership back with control; in publicly traded corporations, to make profits for shareholders the organizing principle of management. Corporate activity would best be ordered around primary obligations to shareholders.

Shareholder primacy grew out of a normative vision of what corporations should do in society and the primacy of the free market. Milton Friedman boiled this down in the doctrine famously announced in 1970 in the *New York Times*:

the social responsibility of business is to increase its profits...A corporate executive is an employee of the owners of the business. He had direct responsibility to his employers. That responsibility is to conduct the business in accordance with their desires, which generally will be to make as much money as possible while conforming to the basic rules of the society. (Friedman, 1970)

Friedman frames the relationship between managers and shareholders as one of obligation: these are duties in the moral sense. Of course, there's another normative claim associated with shareholder primacy: the world will be a better place if corporations focus on what they do best, which is making profits for their owners. The wonders of market competition will optimize for efficiency, and businesses (constrained by the big asterisk of "the basic rules of society") are rewarded with profit by meeting the needs of their customers, who in the whole represent society itself. And so market efficiency unites the interests of owners with the optimal performance of business with the well-being of everybody.

To get from here, the modern managerial corporation, to there, the primacy of shareholders to management and everybody else, neoliberal theorists neglected the role of the corporation as an institution with its own character and goals. Instead, the corporation was just a bunch of connected contracts negotiated in a competitive market. That meant reform to ensure market discipline. One such reform, popularized by Henry Manne in 1965, was "the market for corporate control" (Manne, 1965). This was the owners' stick. If a company's purchase price – the value of its stock on the market – was lower than its potential value in the world, savvy investors could swoop in, buy the business, improve its performance, and reward shareholders with a higher stock price as a result. So owners, newly minted in the case of takeovers, disciplined managers through actual or threatened take-overs into focusing on share price. Legal and financial reforms, sup-ported by the ideology of shareholder primacy, helped usher in a golden age of takeovers in the 1980s. The complement to the market for corporate control was the carrot of executive compensation. For instance, Michael Jensen, a pivotal figure in the swing to shareholder primacy, proposed that executives should be paid with company stock, so that their own pay tracked company performance as measured by share price (Jensen and Meckling, 1976). Too many executives, Jensen argued, were paid handsomely whether the businesses they managed did well or not. Better to pay for (share price) performance. If manage-ment became owners, their interests aligned. With stick and carrot, the problem of managerial capitalism is solved: managers who control companies benefit when share price goes up, and they are punished when share price underperforms.

Shareholder primacy had become the conventional way to talk about ownership and control as we rolled into the twenty-first century, in business schools, economics departments, and the business press among other places. This ideological triumph corresponded to prac-tical victories: takeovers enabled, executive compensation tied to stock options, strategic decisions regularly justified by the goal of maximiz-ing shareholder value.

But the actual results of the shareholder revolution did not match its projections. In the United States, executive compensation – buoyed by stock options – shot up, but it wasn't tied to corporate productivity. Indeed, management seems to have become adept at managing short-term stock price volatility to increase compensation rather than benefit their notional ownership: as economist Dean Baker insists, average real returns to stockholders were no better in the age of purported share-holder value maximization (Baker, 2019). Economic growth on the whole did not skyrocket thanks to the wonders of market competition. The benefits from the growth that did occur concentrated at the top, increasing economic fragility and social incohesion. The Global Financial Crisis decisively undermined belief in market discipline. Even we can't lay all these ills at the feet of shareholder primacy alone, but surely the widespread belief that organizing corporations to serve their shareholders alone played its role.

A recent example from the COVID-19 pandemic helps make the point. Research by Bill Lazonick and Matt Hopkins has demonstrated how public investments into private companies that were tasked with producing affordable and high-quality ventilators fell victim to shareholder primacy: "the financialized business corporation undermined development and delivery of ventilators to the Strategic National Stockpile" (Lazonick and Hopkins, 2020). Why did this happen? According to Lazonick and Hopkins, federal contracts were made with companies with a demonstrated history of product innovation, including in ventilators, and a commitment to reinvest their profits into their firms. But corporate takeovers led to shareholder payments taking priority: in one firm executives allocated 75 percent of profits to stock buybacks and dividends from 2010–2014; in another the firm spent a whopping 127 percent of profits on shareholder payments and dividends in the 2010s (in both cases, executives benefitted handsomely from their own stockholdings). Shareholder value maximization had not optimized for social utility; it had worked against it.

21.3 Alternatives to Shareholder Primacy

So, what would different kinds of ownership and control look like?

Corporate governance reformers and critics of shareholder primacy sometimes begin where the institutionalists left off. Corporations are better understood, these critics think, as a complex web of relationships among and obligations to different stakeholders both within and with those who are affected by the institution – their shareholders, sure, but also their workers, their management, their suppliers, their customers, the communities in which they operate, and so on. Stakeholders don't even have to be human; corporations take resources from and have positive and negative impacts on the environment as well as people. If the neoliberal model of shareholder primacy became the dominant answer to ownership and control in business school curriculums from the 1970s, stakeholder capitalism emerged as its most prominent rejoinder.

Advocates argued that a proper understanding of stakeholder capitalism required corporations to reorient away from a singular focus on maximizing shareholder wealth. On an instrumental level, advocates argued that stakeholder capitalism could help corporations resist the counterproductive emphasis on short-term stock price fluctuations which came at the expense of long-term value in order to refocus on innovation and improving productivity. Stakeholder capitalism insists that corporations cannot assume that what is good for shareholders is good for the world, and indeed that corporations should be understood as agents in the world.

What does this sound like? In the 2010s, political and business leaders started to openly question shareholder primacy. In 2019, the Business Roundtable – America's premier trade association for the largest businesses; when people bring it up, the statement is often prefaced with "even the Business Roundtable" – issued a new "Statement on the Purpose of the Corporation," claiming to "modernize" its conception of corporate purpose by stating that corporations "share a fundamental commitment to all our stakeholders" including customers, employees, suppliers, communities, and a focus on long-term value for shareholders: "we commit to deliver value to all of them, for the future success of our companies, our communities and our country." In other words, corporations are better thought of as social beings, with obligations to all their stakeholders. Moving from shareholders to stakeholders will make for better and more productive businesses and a better world. (Business Roundtable, 2019). This statement superseded previous Roundtable declarations that corporations existed to create shareholder value.

But rhetorical acknowledgment of stakeholders alone doesn't challenge the current model much. That requires institutional change. Naturally, concern for a broader range of stakeholders underpins alternative answers to the questions "Who should control a corporation? Who should own it?" If stakeholders are implicated in and affected by corporate activity, why shouldn't they have a seat at the table or a piece of the pie? In theory, if stakeholders gain voice and power, corporate activity would more closely align with social utility, because they would be responding to a broader range of interests, moving closer to the whole of society rather than its most entitled. There are a variety of structures that can implement a new approach – below we describe changing the composition on the corporate board by including the workforce, referred to as "codetermination" in Europe; reforming who the board of directors is responsible to through the "benefit corporation" charter; and ownership alternatives like worker cooperatives and public ownership.

21.3.1 Who Should Control a Corporation?

Shareholder primacy is built on the idea that those who manage and oversee a corporation should subordinate stakeholder considerations in the service of shareholder value. But what if the perspectives of stakeholders were embedded in management and oversight? Changing who controls corporations can recenter the social value that corporate activity generates or mitigate the harm it creates.

21.3.1.1 Co-Determination

What if a company's board of directors wasn't seen as the mechanism to assert shareholder primacy, but rather a vehicle for stakeholder deliberation on corporate strategy? In some places – Germany has become the conventional example – corporate governance includes workers (as opposed to management or shareholder representatives) who participate in strategic planning and decision-making through seats on boards of directors or advisory boards with oversight authority. This practice, which goes by the name of "codetermination," projects an understanding of corporate activity understood as the interdependence of union of labor and capital. Workers in codetermination systems of governance hold their board seats both because they bring important insights into corporate operations, and their interests and contributions as stakeholders deserve explicit representation in service of balanced decision-making.

Codetermination tends to single out labor's role in corporate governance, highlighting the immediacy of workers' connection to and knowledge of their places of employment. Workers' role in governance emerged, as in Germany, as a projection of trade union power; but also as a reflection of social dialogue, a term that describes the interchange of ideas and mutual strategic discussion among business, labor, and government in civil society. Codetermination is meant to work against shareholder value maximization by giving workers a seat at the table: proponents point to German companies' resistance to short-termism as one outcome; better worker productivity another (Saxena, 2020).

There is no need, at least conceptually, to limit codetermination to representatives from labor. Communities affected by corporate activity could also push for a seat on the board to represent their interests, as might environmental activists. Activists have even used shareholder power under the current regime to propose stakeholder representation on boards, for instance calling for board members with competence on climate change in order for corporations to better manage the transition to a low-carbon economy. The long-term value of company shares, they argue, will suffer if only the immediate interests of shareholders are represented on the board.

While codetermination is sometimes invoked as a response to the negative impacts of shareholder primacy on workers and others, in practice it has had limited if important impact on corporate behavior (Holmberg, 2017). Codetermination does not necessarily prevent corporate scandal or rent-seeking. Marketplace pressures such as short-termism can be hard to resist even with workers on the board – relative short-term performance benchmarks and ideological capture may constrain the kinds of long-term thinking that codetermination is meant to promote. The case of worker representation on pension-fund boards is instructive. Even on pension-fund boards with equal representation between labor and management, or indeed majority labor representation, labor representatives find themselves beholden to return expectations and legal and cultural norms that limit their ability to put on their "worker's hat" even when their role on the board is explicitly created for worker representation.

21.3.1.2 Benefit Corporations
Advocates for stakeholder capitalism may argue that shareholder primacy destroys long-term value and creates negative social effects, but, as those same advocates lament, legal norms and business conventions drive corporations to manage against the ups and downs of their share price. Publicly traded corporations are, in a sense, controlled by those norms and conventions, compelled to subordinate stakeholders to the goal of returning profits to shareowners.

An alternative is to rewrite the fiduciary duties of the board of directors in corporate charters so that the interests of stakeholders was explicitly built into corporate purpose and directors are responsible to a wide variety of stakeholders, not just shareholders. The idea of the Benefit Corporation, the name given to this idea, is designed to build a defense against shareholder pressure (Marquis, 2020). With stakeholder capitalism written into a corporate charter, managers can resist short-term market pressures that impose costs on labor, communities, and the environment – because the corporation they manage would have legal obligations to those stakeholders.

The Benefit Corporation emerged in the wake of the social enterprise craze to answer the question: How can we avoid shareholders who destroy social value in their chase of profit? The story in caricature: social entrepreneurs with bright ideas and big hearts create businesses that balanced the profits they needed to sustain operations with their social goals. Say, a bakery whose business is designed to employ returning citizens who make sweets to sell to supermarkets. To grow to scale, to have major social impact, that entrepreneur has to go to capital markets; to really get to scale, this business ought to go public. But investor pressure in public markets, under the conventions of shareholder primacy, may force the business to turn away from its social goals in the service of delivering profits to shareowners – if recruitment, training, and support for returning citizens eats into those profits, shareholders will demand change. Enter the Benefit Corporation, a legal commitment to stakeholders that defines the business itself as delivering on its social goals. Shareholders won't be able to demand change, because the legal commitment ensures that they know what they are getting into when the company goes public.

As the Benefit Corporation – and the B Corp certification, a closely related concept – has gained traction, the immediate focus on going public has given way to a more general commitment to an accountable, enforceable mechanism to guarantee a business' devotion to stakeholder capitalism. B Corps, for instance, must demonstrate positive social and environmental practices in order to use the label. Commitment to stakeholders can't just be public relations, because the obligations are binding. The fundamental structure of the corporation isn't necessarily changed – there are still managers, who may be managing on behalf of absent owners. But those managers cannot dedicate themselves to serving shareholders at the expense of stakeholders. By explicitly writing stakeholders in the corporate charter, the Benefit Corporation creates implicit stakeholder control.

A useful example of a successful Benefit Corporation is Patagonia, recently voted the top brand in America, according to the Axios Harris survey (above Pfizer and Moderna, in 2021!). Patagonia, an outdoor apparel retailer, became a benefit corporation in 2012, as soon as the option was legally available in California, committing to specific public benefits in its supply chain and to its workforce. The company provides onsite childcare, and sued the Trump administration to protect public land (as well as adding "Vote the Assholes Out" tags to its clothing in 2020). As stated by Patagonia founder Yvon Chouinard, "benefit corporation legislation creates the legal framework to enable mission-driven companies like Patagonia to stay mission-driven through succession, capital raises, and even changes in ownership, by institutionalizing the values, culture, processes, and high standards put in place by founding entrepreneurs."

Though the Benefit Corporation meaningfully changes the place of stakeholders in corporate purpose, it doesn't remove the corporation from shareholder pressure entirely. The idea depends on owners who are willing to commit to stakeholder obligations at the expense of their own primacy. In practice, there haven't been a lot of Benefit Corporations going public, maybe because there aren't yet enough potential owners willing to give up on their notional control, and the notional profits it promises to bring them. Instead, B Corporations have become a recognized brand, a way to signal to the limited set of socially minded investors that a business really takes environmental and social issues into account.

21.3.2 Who Should Own a Corporation?

Codetermination and Benefit Corporations work within conventional corporate design to resist shareholder primacy. But you can also change the owners, taking the absent shareholders out entirely. These alternative ownership structures call into question the essential relationship between corporations and society, at least so far as neoliberal convention would have it. Businesses' efficiency and utility can no longer be measured by the profits returned to shareholders if those shareholders do not hold title to those profits.

21.3.2.1 Worker-Owned Businesses

One answer to the question "who should own a corporation?" is that the people who do the corporation's work should own it. Arguments for worker ownership put forth a seamless unification of labor and capital within an institution, a flipside image of the neoliberal unification of ownership of corporate stock and control by corporate management. Rather than management subordinating concern about workers (and other stakeholders) for the benefit of absent owners, workers themselves are owners and managers both. These can be moral arguments: workers deserve to own the fruits of their labor, and society is better when cooperatives reduce rather than exacerbate economic inequality. But they can also be instrumental arguments: worker-owned cooperatives are not subject to shareholder pressures, giving them the freedom to prioritize long-term sustainability over short term profits. As a matter of fact, employee ownership of corporate equity is more common than many realize – many large companies grant employees equity as part of their retirement plans, and a smaller set of companies are employee-owned or collectively governed such as cooperatives.

Employee ownership has been shown to have positive, stabilizing effects of firm business, as well as reducing turnover and increasing employee satisfaction. Broad-based employee ownership could increase worker input into the production process and reduce economic inequality by lowering the extractive practices of shareholders and top executives. Workers, when they are owners, have more reason to commit to the success of the enterprise. And workers who own their place of work have more opportunities to bring their experiential learning into strategic decision-making, improving innovation. Worker-owned businesses don't have to maximize profits; they instead should optimize for long-term sustainability to meet the needs of their members.

A useful example of the success of the cooperative business model is the region of Emilia-Romagna, Italy. In the largest city in the region, Bologna, eight out of the ten largest businesses are cooperatives (and roughly two out of three people in Emilia-Romagna is a cooperative member), which Italian cooperative expert Vera Zamagni defines as "profit-making companies that distribute benefits to the members of the cooperative in a solidaristic way" (Zamagni, 2012). The success of the cooperative model is not new, but is deeply rooted in the networks between small industrial enterprises that have developed over the last hundred years. Highly specialized SMEs (small and medium-sized enterprises) meant that workers had deeply rooted skills in their craft, while the left political and religious movements in the region contributed to the promotion of cooperative businesses. The Italian Constitution of 1948 gave its blessing to the cooperative model: "recogniz(ing) the interest of the nation in the promotion of cooperation as a way of keeping together economic activity and solidaristic motivations."

Scale is a challenge for cooperatives, though perhaps not always necessary. The exception that proves the rule is the Mondragón

Cooperative Corporation, a large manufacturing cooperative born out of very particular circumstances in the Basque Country in Francoist Spain, an enterprise whose unique size and success has made it the object of much attention as an alternative to publicly traded multinational corporations in the neoliberal model. Alternately, the cooperatives in Emilia-Romagna are spread across goods-and-services sectors in a networked ecosystem, rather than centered around one or two large enterprises. This, according to Zamagni, gives the cooperatives a resilience that has been key to their longevity. Social coops are a main provider of social services, delivering roughly 80 percent of social care, including childcare and eldercare. However, some economies of scale do make sense: the grocery-store chain "Coop" is Italy's retailer, and is a consumer coop that has been funded by its members over decades.

In practice, while everyone in a cooperative mutually owns the enterprise, some are more equal than others through managing it, though there are a wide variety of management structures in worker-owned cooperatives. The corporate governance entailed by collective ownership typically makes it hard to grow very large, because the bigger a cooperative gets, the more distance between those who direct it and those who work in it. It also can be harder for cooperatives to raise capital for expansion – freedom from the pressure of absent owners is another way of saying no access to external equity for growth. So for the most part, cooperatives tend to be small- and medium-sized enterprises, reducing the need for outside investment and facilitating capacity for democratic control.

21.3.2.2 Public Ownership
Public ownership is a direct challenge to the neoliberal model of the corporation. The latter rests on assumptions of competition and private market efficiency which, at their core, have public ownership as their negative. But if corporations are chartered to achieve some public purpose, perhaps it's best if the public itself owns them? It seems pretty straightforward: ownership aligns with the collective of stakeholders, and tensions between profit for owners and benefits for society at large is definitionally erased.

There are any number of ways for the public to have ownership stakes in corporations. We'll stick here with those cases where the public owns them entirely. Take, for instance, broadband provision in a city. The way that the fiber runs to buildings supports a natural monopoly for broadband provision – experience with cable companies in the United States reinforces the point. The result of monopoly power is poorer service and higher prices for those who receive broadband service, and lack of service in poor and hard-to-reach communities. If broadband connections are a fundamental need for citizens, and they are best provided by a single provider, why shouldn't the public own the corporation that provides the service?(Hanna and Mitchell, 2020). In Chattanooga, Tennessee, the municipally owned utility provides fast high-quality internet in part as an economic development program in response to deindustrialization. The success of public broadband provision by the Electric Power Board of Chattanooga has led to articles with titles like "Chattanooga has its own broadband: Why doesn't every city?" (Taplin, 2017).

Public ownership is common practice for utilities of all sorts, and evidence suggests there are significant benefits that come from public ownership, not least public (ideally democratic) control over the terms of service and the quality of jobs that deliver it. That incumbent private providers lobby for laws blocking public ownership only adds to arguments in favor. Public ownership, especially in cases of natural monopolies providing essential goods, can allow for the effective delivery of service without the excess costs – what economists would call rents – that private operators can capture.

The case for public ownership has to answer to important challenges. Control of public provision offers opportunities for management to enrich themselves – just as it does with private corporations. And the imperatives of political expediency similarly create incentives for those who control publicly owned corporations to reward their friends at the expense of long-term public value.

These dangers must be dealt with through democratic and accountable governance over publicly owned corporations. It's not enough to just change the ownership structure of corporations, because ownership and control must be aligned. There is no need to cede that insight to advocates of shareholder primacy. Different forms of ownership enable different forms of control, but do not guarantee them.

21.4 Conclusion

Alternatives to the neoliberal model of ownership and control emphasize different aspects of governance; they variously work within and against the system. We should see alternative ways to think about purpose of corporations – who should own? who should control? – as addressing both the fundamental purpose of corporate activity and the ways that corporations can be most successful over the long term.

The alternatives we have briefly reviewed here are structural approaches to remaking corporate ownership and control. They do not depend on the enlightenment of capitalists to do their intended work. But it is worth noting again, in conclusion, that the work they do at the level of the corporation can only go so far in pushing against shareholder value maximization, because, if they remain concentrated on the institution of the corporation, these new models will have to exist in the same networks of corporate power and financing systems that have been built over the past fifty years. They are subject to the vicissitudes of market conventions where shareholder primacy is the norm – as political theorist Max Krahe puts it, if corporations are islands, finance is the sea (Krahe, n.d.). Shareholder value-maximization focuses on the corporation as an object of finance. Successful alternative answers to ownership and control will have to take on both.

References

Baker, Dean. 2019. "CEOs say they will stop maximizing shareholder value. Would be better if they stopped maximizing CEO compensation." *Commondreams*, August 19, 2019. www.commondreams.org/views/2019/08/19/ceos-say-they-will-stop-maximizing-shareholder-value-would-be-better-if-they

Berle, Adolf and Gardiner Means. 1932. *The Modern Corporation and Private Property*. New York: Routledge

Business Roundtable. 2019. "Statement on the purpose of a corporation." www.businessroundtable.org/business-roundtable-redefines-the-purpose-of-a-corporation-to-promote-an-economy-that-serves-all-americans

Friedman, Milton. 1970. "A Friedman doctrine: The social responsibility of business is to increase its orofits." *New York Times Magazine*, September 13, 1970. www.nytimes.com/1970/09/13/archives/a-fried man-doctrine-the-social-responsibility-of-business-is-to.html

Galbraith, J. K. 2007. *The New Industrial State*. Princeton: Princeton University Press.

Hanna, Thomas and Christopher Mitchell. 2020. "United States: Communities providing affordable, fast broadband Internet." In *The Future is Public: Towards Democratic Ownership of Public Services*, edited by Satoko Kishimoto, Lavinia Steinfort, and Olivier Petitjean, 138–152. Amsterdam: Transnational Institute.

Holmberg, Susan. 2017. *Fighting Short-Termism with Worker Power: Can Germany's Co-Determination System Fix American Corporate Governance?*. New York: Roosevelt Institute.

Jensen, M. C. and W. H. Meckling. 1976. "Theory of the firm: Managerial behavior, agency costs, and ownership structure." *Journal of Financial Economics* 3: 305–360.

Lazonick, William, and Matt Hopkins. 2020. "How 'maximizing shareholder value' minimized the strategic national stockpile: The $5.3 trillion question for pandemic preparedness raised by the ventilator fiasco." *Institute for New Economic Thinking Working Paper Series No. 127.* https://doi.org/10.36687/inetwp127

Manne, Henry G. 1965. "Mergers and the market for corporate control." *Journal of Political Economy* 73 (2): 110–120.

Marquis, Christopher. 2020. *Better Business: How the B Corp Movement Is Remaking Capitalism.* London: Yale University Press.

Max Krahe. n.d. "Islands and the seas: making firm-level democracy durable." Working Paper.

Saxena, Akhil. 2020. "The case for codetermination: Advantages of worker representation." *Brown Political Review*, December 24, 2020. https://brownpoliticalreview.org/2020/12/the-case-for-codetermination-advantages-of-worker-representation/

The Daily Beast, July 24, 2017. www.thedailybeast.com/chattanooga-has-its-own-broadbandwhy-doesnt-every-city

Taplin, Jonathan. 2017. "Chattanooga has its own broadband: Why doesn't every city?" *The Daily Beast* (website) July 24. www.thedailybeast.com/chattanooga-has-its-own-broadbandwhy-doesnt-every-city. Accessed 13 April 2022.

Zamagni, Vera Negri. 2012. "Interpreting the roles and economic importance of cooperative enterprises in a historical perspective." *Journal of Entrepreneurial and Organizational Diversity* 1 (1): 21–36. doi:10.5947/jeod.2012.002

22 | *How Should the Government Decide from Whom to Buy Stuff?*

JEPPE GROOT

As we noted in our Introduction, one thing that distinguishes neoliberalism from plain old liberalism was the recognition that the state was necessary to allow market-based activities to occur. There needed to be regulatory and judicial guardrails that allowed for and even encouraged market activity. That said, this conception of the state was meant to indicate that the state creates an arena for market life to happen, not that the state should become a consumer. However, an unfortunate reality of life for neoliberal thinkers is that the state is often an outsized participants in markets. Moreover, the state often attempts to exercise its values (say, reducing greenhouse emissions) in the consumption choices that it makes. Consuming with values in mind is particularly complicated when you have a state and international organizations set up to allow neoliberal market arenas. This chapter attempts to capture just how complicated and confusing this situation can be by hearing about Groot's experience managing government procurement in an EU nation. What quickly becomes apparent is how vertigo-inducing the whole exercise is, and how easy it is to get carried away by various institutional constraints and priorities that often don't make much sense. Rather than presenting a viable contrast case, this chapter provides a view from the inside of one our eras biggest market actors, the state.

What is the state? When I ask you this question, what is the first thing that comes to your mind? Perhaps you think about nations, flags, lines on a map. Maybe it is parliaments, politicians, sovereignty, and separation of powers that pop into your head. If you think yourself the cynic, you might say that it is the monopoly on violence. But, actually, I did not mean the question in the abstract. Rather, I was asking quite literally, though I shall not fault you if any of the above came up in your mind. When thinking about or discussing our state, we usually do so in terms of politics, or, if we are at our most specific, policies.

We generally tend not to give much consideration to the literal, material constitution of our state. What the state *is* to us, is what it *does*.

Yet, one of the most universally applicable answers to the question of what the state is ought to be: Lots and lots of *stuff*. What I mean, of course, are all those things that the many people in the many organizations that make up the institutional structure of the state use in their daily work producing those political outcomes that we associate with the state: from lowly office supplies and furnishings to service personnel cleaning, cooking food, watering plants, and taking down the trash. Then there are other external staff such as consultants, lawyers, and engineers. And in most contemporary states there is a vast digital infrastructure; from the hardware of thousands of computers, smartphones, and servers to the whole software-based virtual grid holding it all together through millions of lines of code.

Unless the state decides to produce the stuff itself, everything mentioned above and much more is something that it buys. In the European Union, member states spend on average 14 percent of their GDP on goods and services excluding utilities annually. That is roughly 2 *trillion* euro flowing from public authorities into the private sector every single year. In addition to the fact that this is in itself a staggering amount of money spent on something other than what most people think their taxes go into, it is also a market-moving consumption. As such, public procurement is in fact more than simply purchasing things. Although commonly overlooked in the grander schemes of policymaking, procurement is one of the key ways in which governments *materialize* their ambitions in the most concrete sense. Because of this, one of the most proficient agents of societal change available to the state is its own procurement behavior, potentially more so than the otherwise vaunted fiat. Imagine, for example, what would happen if your state decided to only do business with companies with a gender balanced C-suite.

As far as objects of analysis within the realm of politics are concerned, however, public procurement doesn't exactly communicate the level of gravitas that usually draws people toward the public sector. You would be hard pressed to think of anyone who ever went into politics under the banner of smooth supply chains in public institutions. What draws many ambitious people to work in the backroom of the public sector, i.e., the public bureaucracies, is more often than not the fantasy of influencing world affairs; the idea of getting called into the prime minister's office, high wooden panels and all, late at night to decide whether to push the button or not. And there sure isn't a lot of high wooden panels in public procurement.

To paraphrase a rather tacky and most often misattributed inspirational quote, to most people working in the public sector, procurement is what happens while they are busy doing what they're *actually* hired to do. If you're a biologist working on biodiversity policy, you need an office space, a desk with assorted trimmings, a computer, lunch and coffee, possibly specialist equipment for research activities, and so on. And to you the most important thing about all of that is not who made it or what it costs, but that it *works* (or, in the case of coffee, that it tastes sufficiently good to prevent you from spending too many working hours dashing off to the local roaster to ensure sufficient and satisfactory caffeination).

A consequence of this is that, despite the potential for engendering societal change afforded by the sheer amount of money that goes into public procurement, systemic shifts in procurement behavior are slow. Yet, it currently seems like the tide is turning. Although the European Union and other national and international actors have been trying to encourage the use of public procurement to support so-called sociopolitical goals for decades, it appears that something substantial is happening now. There might be several things contributing to this, but there are two events standing out. One is that the devastation brought on by global climate change has entered mainstream politics in a manner that means it is often a decisive electoral factor. There is resultantly a consistent and forceful demand from the public that climate sustainability is integrated into public policy, and accordingly a robust demand from elected officials for opportunities to showcase political action. Public procurement is an attractive representation of one such opportunity, because it is at once fairly relatable and rather occult. Relatable because most everyone can understand choosing, say, a reusable cup rather than a disposable, single-use one, and because everyone can understand that two trillion euros is a lot of money. Occult because scarcely any member of the public has a detailed grasp, or even just a rudimentary one, really, of what is actually being bought in the public sector and how (disclosure: cups aren't at the top of the list). This combination makes it a fine vessel for political messaging; it offers a horizon of possibility, but the outlook is conveniently opaque on how to, navigationally speaking, get there.

The other event is COVID-19. The pandemic has, among a host of other things, displayed two realities. The first is that supply chains matter greatly to the functioning of public sectors and that they cannot be taken for granted. Globalization of supply chains may have delivered extraordinary advantages, but it has turned out to be fragile, perhaps rather a lot more than we imagined. Advances in supply chain management may have produced staggering optimizations enabling governments to shift funds into policies and public services, but now it seems to be dawning on us that we might just have paid for that by mortgaging the resilience of the chains. With this, considerations of various interests that are not immediately commercial, whether it's the nationalist underpinnings of "Made in X" or the ecological considerations of "going green," have entered mainstream political discourse in relation to public procurement decisions in a manner previously largely reserved for fringe opinions. The second reality is that governments, in case anyone should have forgotten and written them off as cumbersome behemoths tripping in red tape spun by themselves, can enact sweeping changes at spectacular speed, even if it goes against previously fairly well-established political orthodoxies, such as ones of economic policy, so long as they have the trust of a substantial majority of the electorate. To some this is a hopeful realization, a demonstration of the raw power of the state, which, now that it has unveiled itself, can be summoned in other instances where the need seems dire. To others of a more pessimistic proclivity, it is a reminder that it takes the threat of imminent death to maybe galvanize governments into action. Regardless, discoursing on direct government intervention in all kinds of areas seems legitimized in a way that it wasn't before the onset of the pandemic.

All of this is to say that now is a very good time to give thought to how the government should decide from whom to by stuff. Nevertheless, you might well ask what place this has in a casebook on alternatives to neoliberalism. After all, I'm talking about dynamics of consumption, of buying and selling, and I've already used terms such as "collective consumer" and "market moving," so aren't we already firmly within a marketized domain? It is certainly true that the formal structures governing public procurement, in a European context at least, are predominantly based on a logic of marketization in the sense of the belief that having private actors competing for public funds constitutes the best way of maximizing the value generated by the expenditure of those funds. In fact, the EU directives regulating the procurement activities of member states could very well be viewed as a clear example of the attempt to translate certain neoliberal principles directly and explicitly into legislation. And yet, the activities stemming from the legislation frequently end up with public institutions buying something other than what they want and/or the supplier delivering something other than what they would like to. This results in outcomes ranging from mildly frustrating, say, a type of coffee beans that no one at the office really likes, to spectacularly catastrophic, often related to public infrastructure; think the Berlin Brandenburg airport debacle. If marketization was indeed the best way of delivering value, how can this be? The answer to this question is not necessarily incompatible with neoliberalist principles. However, the manifest fact that public procurement procedures frequently render outcomes that are perceived as suboptimal, despite being structured according to apparently strict marketization, should prompt us to consider that, perhaps, the concepts championed in neoliberalist thought are more mercurial and less uniform in their blessings than they are made out to be. Or, at the very least, that they encounter a good deal of friction when transformed into a practical reality. And that, as such, the effortlessness with which they are frequently deployed as so commonsensical as to require no justification in the tackling of societal issues, is largely without merit. So think of this chapter not as a comparative case study, but rather as an exploration of some of the problems we encounter if we actually try to be neoliberal when deciding from whom the government should buy stuff.

I imagine that it is productive to begin with a brief explanation of how procurement is governed in a public institution. It bears noting that I'm writing from the point of view of the EU, where public procurement is regulated at the highest level by a series of directives transposed into the national legislation of member states. At its core this means that public institutions must follow certain procedures when buying stuff, the comprehensiveness of which depends of the estimated value of the purchase. In any case, regardless of value, a purchase should be carried out under "market conditions," meaning that it should be subject to competition among suppliers, which at its most basic entails that you should always solicit offers from more than one supplier. If the value of the purchase exceeds €139.000 for most basic goods and services (thresholds for contracts within defense, utilities, and public works are different), the procuring institution must put the contract in question up for *tender*. Once you enter this realm there are a host of different procedures to be deployed depending on the specific circumstances of the purchase. The unifying goal of these, according to the EU directive (2014/24/EU), is that "public procurement is opened up to competition" in order to facilitate that the principles of equal treatment, transparency, and proportionality, which are understood as deriving from the Treaty of Rome, are given "practical effect." It is added that public procurement "plays a key role [in the policy strategies of the union] as one of the market-based instruments to be used to achieve smart, sustainable and inclusive growth while ensuring the most efficient use of public funds." This is the foundation of public procurement in Europe, and it is not hard to spot the neoliberal influence. Across the different procedures, the goal above results in some unifying characteristics, which I will now explore further.

For competition to function properly, the preferences that constitute the demand bringing about any procurement activity in a public institution must be made *known*, and they must to the fullest extent possible be free of discretionary judgment. To be legitimate, desired qualities in a product must be commodifiable and communicable. What this means practically is that the procurer must describe the characteristics of their preferences, and declare how these characteristics will be assessed. This must be made public, in writing, and everything, the characteristics and the way they are assessed, must refer to *objective* standards. This objectivity has two sides: One says that the demands you make of a product must be generally verifiable by others. At first glance, this is a principle with which it is hard to disagree in the abstract. It only seems fair that companies wanting to supply the public sector should know what's wanted. However, it turns out that expressing one's preferences in writing in a manner that is generally understandable is not as easy as it sounds. It is not uncommon for demand specifications to run to fifty pages or more. And even so, you *will* eventually discover that you disagree with the supplier on the interpretation of some of the demands. I have experienced legal disputes over what constitutes a plate. Is a disc a plate? No? Well, did you specify that it should have angled edges? At another time, a supplier of hotel accomodation tried the argument that seeing as it wasn't specified that the bathroom should come furnished with toilet paper that was to be considered an extra feature for which a surcharge was applicable (they did not get away with it). These are eccentric examples to be sure, but they serve to illustrate an important feature of the European public procurement system, and, by its negative, of markets in general: While public procurement systems in Europe are fundamentally based on principles of marketization, the regulatory framework creating them also formalizes those principles and the resulting market structure is an *artificial* one, in some senses more pure than the, for lack of a better term, *real* market. In fact, the private markets that we're usually thinking about when referring to the Market, the places where things are exchanged for money, are subject to all kinds of phenomena that would not pass muster under the scrutiny of principle of objectivity as laid out in the public procurement directives. Personal relationships, previous experience, habit, hopes and desires for the future, fashions, or other herd behavior, and the list goes on. It is unnecessary to go into a full critique of the concept of stable preferences. Even if preferences are taken as relatively stable, their objective mediation is enormously difficult. Well, says the neoliberal economist, this is precisely the magic of markets. By making a choice you express your preferences, whether you can articulate them or not. But this is anathema to marketized public procurement, because the whole point was to limit the discretionary choice of individual public officials, since such discretion is perceived as a risk of hampering competition. So already here we have a tension within the concept of competition in the context of public policy: It is supposed to deliver on its promise of utility maximization because it is a low-friction, or in blunter terms the least corrupt, mode of facilitating the interplay of preferences. But the behavior of actors in actual markets, buyers and sellers both, are shaped by all kinds of factors that are incompatible with the principles laid out in the EU public procurement legislation, and in broader terms in most people's conception of a just society.

The other side of the objectification of preferences in public procurement says that you can only make demands of the object itself, which is to say the *product* and not of the *producer*. What this latter point means is that the example of the gender balanced C-suite that I put to you in the beginning of this chapter would actually be illegal. Why is that, you may ask, especially if you're in favor for gender balance in top management? On the other hand, if you accept that such demands could and should be made, try to extend your imagination to the possibility that they could be used for more nefarious purposes. Would you think it was a good idea if your government refused to do business with companies based on, say, their country of origin or on the religion, sexuality, or skin color of the owners? As soon as you open yourself to the possibility of making specifically political demands of suppliers to the public sector, you get to the problem of which ones, who should decide them, and how to prevent nefarious abuse and perpetuation of inequities. Now, you should refuse to take this here bait of mine. There's no slippery slope here, you ought to say. We'll decide it the same as how we decide all kinds of other extremely difficult things in our society, namely through the messy process of parlimentary deliberation, institutional checks and balances, and the tempering of public discourse. The result might not be perfect, there might be missteps, but you won't have me accepting that making demands of companies who supply the public sector on generally accepted issues, such as combatting climate change, is stepping on to the road to facism. To which I would reply that you're right, although current events in many so-called developed nations has my confidence wavering. However, in any case, this much should be clear: An abso-lutely key part of the intoxicating allure of neoliberalism is that we can circumvent the difficulty of politics and its associated risks; that the dynamic of preference-based transactions really does constitute an invisible hand that can allieviate us from getting our own hands dirty. As I think is amply demonstrated throughout this book, this is of course an illusion. And it's a curious one at that: markets are rife with risk. They are premised on advantages generated by the more or less accidental destruction of certain practices and perpetuation of others. One must marvel that we've convinced ourselves that intentional pol-itical action is somehow more risky.

The formal reason why you cannot make general demands of the supplier is that it is not a *proportional* demand for a public buyer to make of a private company. The intention is to safeguard private companies against governments deploying their special position to impose on them behavior that is not conforming to the market. Because, of course, the state is not just any odd consumer. Recalling the example of royal warrants, allowing suppliers to festoon them-selves with the epithet of being *purveyor to the court of* this or that monarch, supplying government institutions, even in markets where government consumption is not a dominant factor, signals trustworthiness, reliability, and stability. Conversely, being disavowed for trading with government institutions on account of yours not living up to their standards can be a serious blemish to the reputation of any company. And, naturally, failure to meet the requirements of government institutions in markets where their consumption is dominant will be devastating for your business. For neoliberalism, such behavior is ominous and should be avoided. Government institutions, in so far as they are consumers, should *follow* the market. They should not attempt to *shape* it. In discussions of the US judiciary, what is usually termed "legal activism" is a cardinal point of contention, and critics of legal practice deemed to be of an activist proclivity will often be heard saying that you shouldn't legislate from the bench. This discussion is a fairly apt analogy for an enduring discussion in public procurement as to whether you should *actively* try to further sociopolitical goals through government consumption. Let's call it activist public procurement. And its critics will say, following a line of thought similar to critics of legal activism, that you shouldn't legislate with your wallet. The core of this argument is that it is somehow a democratically deficient mode of governing for the public administration to further political goals through its behavior, even if at the behest of the government. This is, however, a simplistic view of democratic government that conveniently sidesteps the political outcomes of administrative *in*action: You say that the government shouldn't legislate with its wallet. Well, considering the staggering size of the flow of cash out of said wallet, it's going to have a normative effect whether you like it or not. So even if you're pretending not to drive policies with government spending, you still are, just differently, by way of choosing to abstain from intentionally influencing matters.

Despite the theoretical nature of the previous paragraphs, this is not just an academic question entertained by procurement nerds by the coffee machine (cost effective, naturally, with milk powder). It has quite a substantial bearing on public procurement policy and, in turn, on the policy areas affected by public procurement decisions, which is, frankly, a lot of them. Let's take a timely example: combatting climate change. As mentioned in the beginning of this chapter, environmental and climate related sustainability has long been seen as an important secondary goal for European public procurement policy, but currently there is, for good reason, a great deal of pressure for making it a primary one. The Danish government has recently, as one of the first in the world, calculated the greenhouse gas emissions resulting from Danish public procurement. The result is 12 million tonnes of carbon dioxide equivalents, 4 of which are emitted in Denmark. That's a lot. Policies trying to counter climate change usually do so on the side of production, for example by investing in renewable, zero-emission energy or by imposing taxes or fees on polluting means of production. And so, with public procurement, the logic would go that if you make production cleaner, emissions from consumption would be reduced too. What we're seeing now is that there's growing political momentum behind addressing emissions from the consumption side of things. Now, the logic goes that if you structure consumption in particular ways, favoring emission-reducing factors, you'll encourage a cleaner production. There are some clear merits to this thinking. For example, it is generally an issue for production-aimed policy that production is mobile and globally so. Accordingly, if you put too many constraints on production, it'll be moved somewhere else. Consumption, however, is not mobile. You can't outsurce it. However, it is also a fickle approach and one that is less studied than taxation or infrastructure. Let's say the public sector in Denmark reduces it's consumption of beef in public kitchens significantly. Will that mean that the carbon footprint of the public sector gets smaller? Undoubtedly. Will it also mean that less greenhouse gasses are emitted from meat production globally? Not necessarily, because that will only occur if the drop in public consumption results in a corresponding drop in global production. And that might not happen. The supply might be absorbed by others. So there's a not insignificant risk that it might not be as effective as agricultural policy work aimed at reducing emissions from Danish meat production. Another example would be public works, specifically construction. This is, unsurprisingly, the largest single category measured by emissions. Construction materials is a major contributor to this, and concrete is a big part of this. This is not because concrete is particularly foul compared to other materials, but rather because it is used so much. There are already a lot of companies developing lower-emission concrete, however it is still more expensive than conventional concrete. Should the government absorb that extra expense at the nascent state of product development as an investment to move the market in a more climate friendly direction by guaranteeing demand? This would, in effect, constitute state subsidized production which is not inherently a bad thing. However, what if it later turned out that recycled concrete, or another material altogether, was much more effective at reducing emissions and that the subsidies for "green concrete" had delayed the maturation of the production of these alternatives significantly? Of course, that might be a risk you're willing to take. But public and private risk management operates differently. Governments can't fall back on the promise of profits, so they have to deal in other currencies. Private money can, to a certain extent, afford to make the wrong bet in the long run so long as they deliver profits while doing so. Governments, by and large, can't. This is part of the reason why the public sector is usually risk-averse. On the other hand, governments have a particular ace up their sleeve, which is that, for all the talk of balanced budgets, if the political momentum is sufficient, money matters little. In the end, you can just create some more. After all, while private companies come and go, a state can be around for thousands of years.

Being philosophically inclined, as a way to end this, I'm turning to Plato's *Republic*. In the beginning of that dialogue, Socrates has everything pretty much figured out: To get a just society everyone merely needs to be self-supplying in terms of their basic needs; produce simple crops for their sustenance, simple clothes to ward off the elements, simple housing for shelter. His interlocutors object that you cannot expect people to desire such primitive conditions. Oh well, says Socrates, and I'm paraphrasing here, then it will be difficult.

Society is an enormous endeavor and has been so for millennia. Today, politics is often framed in a binary of government vs. market, the valence of each depending on your point of observation. Debates tend to get ideological, in the sense that they become about ideas of societal dynamics. All the while, the gears of society continue to grind. Public procurement is part of those gears, a part of shaping our society that most of us give little thought to. We should, though. It shows us, in all its messiness, that in building a common good there are no binaries. And that governments should take their role as market makers, or at least influencers, very seriously.

Index